Religion in America

THE WRITINGS

OF

JOHN LELAND

Edited by

L. F. Greene

ARNO PRESS & THE NEW YORK TIMES

New York 1969

Reprint edition 1969 by Arno Press, Inc.

*

Library of Congress Catalog Card No. 73-83420

*

Reprinted from a copy in
The State Historical Society of Wisconsin Library

*

Manufactured in the United States of America

Reprinted 2010 by Local Church Bible Publishers

www.LocalChurchBiblePublishers.com

THE

WRITINGS

OF THE LATE

ELDER JOHN LELAND

REV. JOHN LELAND.

John Leland

THE
WRITINGS
OF THE LATE
ELDER JOHN LELAND,

INCLUDING

SOME EVENTS IN HIS LIFE,

WRITTEN BY HIMSELF,

WITH ADDITIONAL SKETCHES, &c.

BY

MISS L. F. GREENE,

LANESBORO, MASS.

NEW YORK:

PRINTED BY G. W. WOOD, 29 GOLD-STREET.

1845.

PREFACE.

The candid reader is earnestly requested, before entering upon the perusal of the following pages, to follow the compiler through a short preface. It was at the suggestion of one of Mr. Leland's family that I first thought of attempting this work; and after her removal by death, it was with the subsequent encouragement and approbation of others, that I continued to pursue it. When first proposed to me, I viewed it as an impossibility, both on account of my inadequacy, and of the little leisure afforded me by a vocation which involved arduous labors and anxious cares; but an ardent desire to see the work accomplished, and the uncertainty that it would be attempted by an abler hand, together with the consideration that time was continually thinning the number of those who could furnish accurate information, or correct unavoidable mistakes, at length determined me to make the trial. Had I then foreseen, that, by the death of some, and the removal of others, I should be deprived of the aid on which I mainly depended, and left to complete the task alone, I should have yielded entirely to the sense of incompetency which, even *with* the prospect of such assistance, scarcely permitted me to hope for success. It is not, therefore, as a mere matter of form, but with a painful consciousness of the imperfect manner in which the work has been executed, and of the disappointment which many will probably feel on seeing it, that I mention the circumstances under which it was commenced, and *some* of the embarrassments that have attended its progress and completion. Viewed as a literary performance, I am happy to feel assured, that, so far as my own share in it is concerned, it is beneath the notice of criticism; on that point, therefore, I am free from solicitude.

Circumstances have rendered the task a much more arduous one than I at first anticipated. These circumstances were so unexpected to me, that I should have supposed their occurrence, in this instance, singular, had I not met with the following passage, in a book of similar kind, published many years ago, which describes so nearly my own difficulties, that I cannot forbear transcribing it. "Various causes have contributed to create the delay which has attended the publication of the book. It was with considerable difficulty that I collected the materials necessary for my purpose. I had imagined, from the general impression which prevailed, at least, among" (Mr. L.'s) "friends, of the propriety of such a publication, that information would have been spontaneously offered, from every quarter whence it might be furnished. But in this I was disappointed; and it was some considerable time from the annunciation of my design, before I was sufficiently supplied to commence, with any degree of prudence, the composition of the volume. In addition to this, the laborious duties of my charge, conspired often to suspend the prosecution of the work, for the appearance of which, I knew many to be anxious, but none more so than myself." Several important works it has been impossible to obtain, and I have, therefore, though with deep regret, been compelled to omit them. Whether they are entirely out of print, or whether the notices calling for them, have not been seen by those who possess them, or from some cause they were not disposed to furnish them for publication, it is in vain to inquire. Such, however, is the fact. And here I would present my sincere and heartfelt thanks to those kind friends, in various parts of the Union, who have interested themselves in procuring such materials as I have needed, and would assure them, that their efforts, though many of them may have been unsuccessful, shall ever be remembered with gratitude. In one or two instances, writings have been forwarded, supposed by the friends who sent them to be those of Leland, which proved to have been from some other pen; but my thanks are equally due to those friends for their promptness in offering the aid I needed, though their kindness was, by that mistake, rendered unavailing.

The object proposed in this work, is a full and correct exhibition of the character and sentiments of John Leland. Every thing, therefore, that seemed calculated to throw additional light on these, or without which the exhibition of them would have been imperfect, has been inserted. Some pieces have been omitted wholly, and others in part, to prevent the unnecessary repetition of the same ideas; and this has been done, in most cases, except where those ideas are so connected with others, or so brought to bear upon different subjects, that they could not be disconnected without doing violence to the author's evident meaning.

In some of his poetical efforts, Mr. Leland evidently falls below himself. While some of his hymns are equal in poetical merit, as well as in spirituality and devotion, to most of those in general use, there are other pieces which are manifestly deficient in the former of these qualities. In such cases, they are inserted, not *because* of their poetical merit, but for other reasons which their deficiency, in this respect, could not set aside.

It is well known that his sentiments, on some subjects, differed from those entertained by many of his brethren at the present day. Individuals have, therefore, sometimes attempted to explain his ideas in such a way as to make them harmonize with their own views; in some instances, entirely destroying, by their exposition, the force of his own words. This I have had opportunity of knowing, was extremely annoying to him. He has frequently been heard to express the wish that his own language might be permitted to speak for itself, and to express, as he intended it to do, the honest convictions of his own mind. This being known to be his feeling on the subject, it is hoped that if ever any of his writings are republished, his wishes may be regarded as sacred. His opinions can be by no one better expressed than by himself, and his *life* is their best *comment.*

The order followed in the arrangement of most of the works is that of the time (as nearly as can be ascertained) when they were written or published. This will enable the reader to trace the workings of his mind, and to discover whatever changes took place in his views from time to time.

A number of pieces will, perhaps, appear to those acquainted with them, somewhat changed. It may be proper to mention, in regard to such, that there being several copies differing from erch other, I have taken the liberty, in some cases, to put the parts together, and in others to select the one that appeared to me the best.

I will only add that the delay in the appearance of the work, since its preparation for the press has been completed, (a period of more than a year,) has been occasioned entirely by the want of a sufficient number of subscriptions to defray the expenses of publication.

NOTE.

It having been thought advisable, by those who executed the following work, to throw it into smaller type than was at first contemplated, the number of pages falls considerably short of the original estimate, though the same amount of matter is contained. It was deemed most expedient, under the circumstances, to include the whole in one volume; but it is presumed the consequent reduction in the price, together with the superior style of binding in which it now appears, will render it equally satisfactory and acceptable to subscribers.

With great reluctance the compiler was obliged to forego the personal examination of the proof-sheets, which could not be done without occasioning great delay in the issuing of the work. A number of errors of considerable importance remain uncorrected except in the errata, which the reader is desired to consult. Other inaccuracies in orthography, punctuation, etc., may be observed; but those which it was supposed the reader would easily understand and correct for himself, are not noticed in the errata.

CONTENTS.

CONTENTS

EVENTS

IN THE

LIFE OF JOHN LELAND:

WRITTEN BY HIMSELF.

And thou shalt remember all the way which the Lord thy God led thee.——MOSES.
Now the things which I write unto you, behold, before God, I lie not.——PAUL.

I WAS born in Grafton, about 40 miles west of Boston, in the year of our Lord 1754, on the 14th of May.

The earliest public events which I can remember, are the death of George the Second, and the coronation of George the Third, together with some melancholy accounts of the French and Indian war. But a number of juvenile incidents are fresh in memory, which took place when I was two, three, and four years old; some of which I will here relate.

When my father was a young man, he was convinced, (as he has told me,) by reading the Bible, that believers were the only proper subjects of baptism, and immersion the only gospel mode; but when he broke his mind to his mother, she gave him an alarming warning against heresy; and as there was no preachers thereabout but pedobaptists, he sunk from his conviction, and concluded that his mother and the ministers were right. Accordingly, after he was married, and had a son born unto him, he presented his child for baptism: but after the rite was performed, his mind was solemnly arrested with the text, "Who hath required this at your hands?" that it was with difficulty he held his son from falling out of his arms; nor did he get over the shock until he had six more children born. He then got his scruples so far removed, that he invited the minister of the town to come to his house on a certain Sunday, after public service was over, and baptize all of them. At this time I was something more than three years old. When I found out what the object of the meeting was, I was greatly terrified, and betook myself to flight. As I was running fast down a little hill, I fell upon my nose, which made the blood flow freely.

My flight was in vain; I was pursued, overtaken, picked up and had the blood scrubbed off my face, and so was prepared for the baptismal water.

All the merit of this transaction, I must give to the maid who caught me, my father and the minister; for I was not a voluntary candidate, but a reluctant subject, forced against my will.

In early life I had a thirst for learning. At five years old, by the instruction of a school dame, I could read the Bible currently, and afterwards, in the branches of learning, taught in common schools, I made as good proficiency as common. But what proficiency soever I made in learning (owing to a stiffness of nature and rusticity of manners) I could never gain the good will of my masters, nor was I a favorite among the scholars.

The character which one of my masters gave me, seems to have been the opinion that all of them formed of me. Said he, "John has more knowledge than good manners."

The minister of the town was importunate with my father to give me a collegiate education for the ministry. The doctor of the place was equally solicitous to make me a physician. My father designed me to live with him, to support his declining years. My own intention was to be a lawyer, if possible; but in our designs and wishes, we have all been disappointed.

As my father had no library, and I was fond of reading, the Bible was my best companion.

Deism and Universalism I never heard of, and of course was what is called a believer in revelation.

I had no thought that I myself was right, but believed that some great thing must be done for me (I did not know what) or I could not be saved.

At times I had awful horrors of conscience, when death, judgment and the world to come arrested my attention; but these horrors did not reform me from vice nor turn me to the Lord.

I was almost in all evil, full of vanity, exceedingly attached to frolicking and foolish wickedness. When I reflect on the follies of my youth, the question of Paul involuntarily rises in my heart; "What fruits had you then in those things whereof ye are now ashamed?" In this course I continued until I was eighteen years old.

In the summer of 1772, I met with one thing singular. When I was returning from my frolicks or evening diversions, the following words would sound from the skies, "You are not about the work which you have got to do." The last time I heard those sounds, I stood amazed; and turning my eyes up to the heavens, it seemed that there was a work of more weight than a mountain, which I had yet to perform.

Soon after this, I cannot tell how or why, a conviction took place in my mind, that all below the sun could not satisfy or tranquilize the mind.

The world and all that was in it appeared of small consequence. And without any unusual horror of mind or dread of damnation, the charms of those youthful diversions, which had been sweeter to me than the honeycomb, lost all their sweetness, nor could I conceive how there could be any pleasure in them.

About this time, there was an evening frolic in the neighborhood, and I concluded to go to see whether there was delight in it or not; and if not, to find out the cause of its death in my mind. Accordingly I went, but found nothing to please, but everything to disgust. After I had tried the experiment, I asked a young man if he would return home with me, which he agreed to do. On our return, I introduced the subject of religion for conversation on the road. The next day he reported, that he believed John would soon be a preacher, for he would talk on no subject but religion.

At this time, a young preacher (Elhanan Winchester) came into Grafton, and preached and prayed to the astonishment of the people; and a young woman, it was said, was converted. When I heard the report, it greatly effected me, for I had been at many dances with her. The result with me was, now the waters are troubled, and it is time for me to step in.

Reading the Bible and meditating on the shortness of time, and the importance of being prepared for death and judgment, occupied the chiefest of my time.

After a few weeks, in the month of September, Mr. Winchester came to Grafton again. I heard of it on Saturday evening, and concluded that I would read the Bible that evening, and attend meeting the following Sunday, and be converted like Priscilla, (for that was the name of the young woman.) When I went to meeting, I heard the man preach, and while he was preaching, something kept answering in my breast, yes, yes, yes, it is so. After he had done, I question whether all the men in the world could have convinced me that it was not the truth. After public service was over, the people retired to the water, where Priscilla was baptized. What I saw and heard at the water, greatly effected me. There I stood upon a rock, and made my vows to God to forsake all sinful courses and seek the Lord, if he would direct me how.

From this, I began to pray, but was hard put to it to find a place secret enough. I was afraid some one would hear me, and was confounded to hear my own voice. How often did the words of Jesus sound like thunder in my ears: "He that is ashamed to own me before men, I will be ashamed to own him before my Father and before his angels."

From this time down, fifteen months, a volume might be written on the views, exercises and conflicts of my mind.

As the work of God broke out in Grafton, Northbridge and Upton, I heard much preaching and conversation about the *change* which is essential to salvation; on which I formed the following conclusions:

1st. That I must be deeply convicted of sin, greatly borne down under the weight of it, and heartily repent of it. This led me to pray much for conviction, read the threatenings of God to alarm myself, and study to make sin look horrid.

2dly. That if ever I was converted, I should know it as distinctly as if a surgeon should cut open my breast with his knife, take out my heart and wash it, put it back again and close up the flesh. This caused me to think light of any pleasing views, which sometimes would break into my mind, how God could pardon sinners for the sake of the Mediator. All was nothing to me, without I could be converted in the way which I laid out, and know for certain that I was born of God.

3dly. That whenever I should be enabled to believe in Jesus, I should see him as plainly as I could see an object of sense. While waiting and hoping for these things, (some of which I have never yet seen or felt,) my mind was led to the following views and exercises :

First. To see the extent and purity of the holy law: That it was the perfect rule of eternal right, which arose from the relations that exist between God and man, and between man and man ; that it will remain unalterable while the perfections of God and the faculties of men exist, and that the least deviation from this rule is sin.

Secondly. By looking into the law, as a clear glass, to see my own weakness and wickedness. Here, I found myself as incompetent to repent and believe in Jesus, as I was to keep the whole law. Never was a poor creature more perplexed with a hard, unyielding heart, and a corrupt nature, than I was. I often compared my heart to a spring of water, rising up against God and godliness.

Thirdly. To view the justice of God in my condemnation. Never did the benevolence of God appear more pleasant to me than justice did. I was not willing to be damned ; but thought, if damnation must be my lot, it would be some relief to my mind that God would be just.

Fourthly. To discover the sufficiency of a Mediator. For a number of months before I had a settled hope of my interest in Christ, the plan of atonement, by the blood of the Lamb, appeared to me as plain as ever it has since. Once, I remember to have broke out thus, when walking in the road: "O what a complete Saviour is Jesus, every way suited to my needs: I can be saved no other way—I do not wish to be saved any other way—but fear I shall never be saved in that way."

There were a number of young people converted in the place, who assembled together for religious worship, with whom my heart was greatly united. While thinking of them, at a certain time, the words of John came into my mind: "We know we have passed from death unto life, because we love the brethren ;" which gave me a small hope, for a few minutes, that *perhaps* I was born of God.

One morning, about day-break, as I was musing on my bed, upon this text, "After ye believed, ye were sealed with the Holy Spirit of promise," it struck my mind that souls first believed before they were sealed; on which conclusion, the following words rushed into my mind, as if they had been spoken by some other, "Ye are already sealed unto the day of redemption." If so, said I to myself, then surely I am converted. But as I had never passed through stages of distress equal to some others, nor equal to what I supposed an essential pre-requisite to conversion, I could not believe for myself. And yet the words continued to run in my mind, "Ye are already sealed unto the day of redemption."

One morning, my father was reading a chapter, when the following text arrested my attention with irresistible force: "If ye will not believe, ye shall not be established." At another time my thoughts ran thus: "If it is possible that I am a Christian, it is certain that I am the least of all." On which the words of the Prophet came into my mind with great force: "Peace, peace to him that is near, and to him that is far off, saith the Lord, and I will heal him."

Though very far from being satisfied with myself, yet with a very feeble hope which I began to have, on the solicitation of others, I did sometimes attempt to pray in small circles. And here I will relate a strange event, which I know to be true, but can never account for it. In the month of February, 1774, in the time of great snow, a very respectable preacher, Rev. Samuel Dennis, came into Grafton and preached one afternoon at a Mr. Wheeler's. I attended; and notwithstanding his talents, he appeared muddy in his mind about salvation freely by grace. After he had done, the people all took their seats, and strange to tell, that I, naturally bashful, with hardly any hope that I was converted, should rise and state my objections against the discourse, and give another interpretation to the texts which the preacher had quoted to support his doctrine: after which I retired into another room; but very soon a messenger came and told me I must return and dispute the point with Mr. Dennis. I returned, but who can describe what I felt? I said thus to myself: "I am not converted myself, and it must be the Devil that has instigated me to harrass the people of God." Mr. Dennis addressed me like a gentleman and Christian. Said he, "Mr. Leland, you have lodged your objections against my doctrine; I wish to discourse with you on the subject, for the cause is not mine but God's." Upon which the battle began between a venerable preacher, clothed in black, with a large white wig on his head, and a beardless boy, not twenty years old, coarsely clad, and wearing a leather apron. The people all stuck to see and hear. After about three-quarters of an hour, there was a cessation of arms. At any rate, as I was the querist, and he the defendant, such questions were flung in his way that he could not well solve; and concluded by saying, "The Lord have mercy on us, for we are poor ignorant creatures."

On this, there sprang up immediately in my heart a strong desire to pray. Indeed, I felt as if I must pray or burst; but the preacher, the whole congregation, and my father among the rest, were all present, and I had never attempted the like before. At this crisis, one of the young converts came to me, and said, "John, won't you pray?" I durst not refuse, lest I should quench the Spirit. I proposed it, and the congregation united by rising. I had not spoken many words, before the preacher, my father, and all others were out of the way. I felt strong in the grace that is in Christ Jesus. Prayer being closed, I felt impelled to give the people a word of èxhortation, which was the first address of the kind that ever I made. After this a psalm was sung; when the line came forward, "We tremble and rejoice," I felt confident in myself that I did tremble before the greatness, and rejoice in the goodness of God; and spake within myself thus: "I am converted, and will not believe Satan any more when he tells me otherwise." This frame of mind continued a few minutes, and then the vision closed, and I returned home full of heaviness, reproaching myself for my forwardness and presumption. The next day, I went around and told some who heard me the day before, that they need not mind any thing that I had said, for I was a poor unconverted sinner.

My desire was to be searched and not deceived. I spent nearly a whole day, as I was going a little journey, praying in David's words, "Search me, O God, and try me, and know if there be any evil in me, and lead me in the way everlasting. The night following, I dreamed that I must read Psalm xxxii. 8, which I did as soon as I awoke. The words are, "I will instruct thee and teach thee in the way which thou shalt go. I will guide thee with mine eye."

My heart was greatly attached to the Holy Scripture. I have not yet forgot the burning desire—the soul-longings that I had to know what was the mind of God, contained in his word. I would read—then pray—then read and pray again, &c. that I might know the truth as it is in Jesus.

One evening, as I was walking the road alone, I was greatly cast down, and expressed myself thus: "I am not a Christian; I have never been convicted and converted like others, who are true saints. The Devil shall deceive me with false hopes no longer. I will never pretend to religion, until *I know* that I am born of God!" These words I spoke aloud; but immediately the words of Peter rushed into my mind, with great energy, "I know not the man." These words dashed my conclusion and resolution to atoms in a moment. It was a shock to the centre of my heart. From that day to this minute, which is a term of forty-six years, amidst all the doubts, darkness, troubles and temptations that I have had, I have never said that I knew not Christ, or that I was unconverted.

Soon after this, I received great comfort from Proverbs xxx. 5. Every word of God, both precept and promise, seemed pure. I felt my soul yield up to Christ and trust in him, and believed he would be my shield and defence.

A young man, about my age, in the neighborhood, professed to be converted. The work was short with him, and he came out strong and bold. He and myself set up evening meetings, to sing, pray, and speak according to our proportion of faith, as the Spirit gave us utterance. A number of men opened their houses, and many came in to hear the boys. It was common for each of us in turn to preach two or three of our sort of sermons at each meeting. When I was going to these meetings, I often had such fears that I was not converted, but only deceived—that I had learned these things of men and not of Christ; and viewing the greatness of the work of manifesting truth to the consciences of men in the sight of God; all together would nearly take away my strength, so that I could not walk. At such times, I would resolve to appoint no more meetings. But when I got to the meeting, the gloom and horror of my mind would subside, which emboldened me to appoint another; but when I had left the meeting and was returning home, the same load would fall upon me. In this course I continued from February to June.

The work of ingathering, which prevailed the year before, seemed to be over; and I know not that any new cases of conversion took place at these little meetings.

Within the time that I have been treating of, I visited one of the young converts, who told me his dream. Said he, "I dreamed I was down by the burying-ground in Grafton, and saw a large company of people coming from the north-east, and you were in the midst of them, riding in a horse-cart. The procession came to the place where a gallows was erected. The hangman drove his cart under the gallows, and fastened the halter which was around your neck to the transverse of the gallows. You then arose, and, with hands and eyes towards heaven, said, 'Lord Jesus, for thy cause I am brought to this end.' The hangman then led off the horse and cart—you swung, and I awoke. Soon I slept and dreamed again, that I was in Worcester, where was a vast concourse of people, and Captain G. among the rest: said the Captain to me 'Do you know John Leland?' I answered, 'yes.' 'Well,' said he, 'John is to be hanged to-day, for preaching heresy.' The procession then moved into the burying-ground, in Worcester, with you in the cart, where the same tragedy was repeated that was done in Grafton."

This dream, told to me with great solemnity, when I was so weak and fearful, made me more ready to halt than I was before.

Two things greatly perplexed me at this time. One was, that I felt more moral evil in myself, than I could see or believe there was in the young converts. When I saw them with their lamb-like faces and dove-like eyes, and heard them pray and praise, they appeared to me seraphical; and I had formed the conclusion, that if I should ever be converted, I should be so too; but now, (notwithstanding the little hope which I entertained for myself, and durst not deny it,) I found more corruption in me than can be described. The other was, the want of will. At times, I would feel as if my whole soul was absorbed in the fountain of love, and devout prayer was the breath of my heart; at other times, I would feel such amazing languor and want of will, that if I might have had all the glories of heaven for asking, I could not have sincerely done it. This gave me a very poor opinion of myself. Indeed, from that time to the present, I have had a constant falling out with myself; which leads me to cry out, O, wretched man that I am!

To these two perplexities, I may add another, which was a constant worry in my mind about preaching. No sooner was my mind exercised about the salvation of my soul, than it was agitated about preaching. The number of sermons (such as they were) that I preached, when alone by myself, was very great. Both saints and sinners said, "John will be a preacher." My mother professed that she had the same impressions about me when I was a sucking child; but my fears were, that the Devil was at the bottom of it, seeking to deceive me, and cheat me out of my soul.* Text after text would crowd into my mind to urge me on; but I could not tell whether they were the voice of God or the voice of Eli—whether the Devil suggested them to me—whether they were accidental, or whether they came from the good spirit of God.

Strange to relate, one hour I would entertain a comfortable hope that my sins were pardoned; the next hour, nearly give up all hope; fearing that all my exercises were self-learned, and that I had not been taught of God; the third hour, be impelled that I must preach or perish. This conflict wore off my flesh, and made me irresolved about anything.

My faith was firm in this: that no man should undertake to preach until he was born of God: that no man born of God was, by that change, prepared to preach; that Christ called unto him *whom he would*, for the work of preaching, either fishermen, herdsmen, or men of science; and when he called and ordained them, if they neglected the work, and conferred with flesh and blood, they would be disobedient to the heavenly vision.

The first of June, 1774, Elder Noah Alden, of Bellingham, came to Northbridge, and baptized seven others and myself. Four of them were men, and the others women. I was extremely dark in my mind; but when I gave a relation of my exercises, I had this hope, that if I was deceived, the preacher would discern it and reject me: and that if he rejected me, it would strike such conviction into my heart that would lead me on to a sure conversion. The preacher, however, only asked me if I believed in the Calvinistical doctrine? I replied, I did not know what it was, but I believed in free grace.

As he received me, dark as my mind was, I would not give back. The

* To quote and transcribe all the texts, with the peculiar bearings each had on my mind, would swell the narrative to large.

preacher was a short man, and, therefore, requested me to go into the water with him, to assist him in raising and leading the women, which I consented to. After it was over, the people said, "John has begun and he will keep on." The day afterwards, on reflection of what was past, I felt strengthened, and could say, "Thus it is written, and thus it behooved me."

On Sunday, the 20th of June, I went to meeting at Grafton, where there was no preacher. My mind was greatly embarrassed about preaching, and my prayer was, that I might know my duty. The words of the Prophet occurred to my mind, "There is none to guide her of all the sons she has brought forth." Having the Bible in my pocket, I drew it out, and, without design, opened to Mal. ix. chap. "—— this commandment is for you. If ye will not hear, and if ye will not lay it to heart, to give glory unto my name, saith the Lord of Hosts, I will even send a curse upon you ——." Whatever the original design of the text was, at that time it arrested my conscience thus: *Thou art the man.* Attempts to evade the force of it were all in vain. I must either lay it to heart, open my mouth and give glory to the name of God, or his curse would fall upon me. Fearing the hot displeasure of the Lord, I rose in great distress, and, having read Mal. iii. 16, 17, I told the people, if there was no objection, I would attempt to speak a little from the text. Being answered with silence, as custom led the way, I divided my text into several heads of doctrine. At the beginning, my mind was somewhat bewildered, and my words sounded very disagreeable to myself; so much so, that I partly resolved to quit; but continuing, my ideas brightened, and after a while I enjoyed such freedom of thought and utterance of words as I had never before. I spake about half an hour and then closed. One of the old Christians made a prayer, and thanked God for what he had discovered in the young man. At noontime, I was all delight; my burden of soul, which had borne me down so long and so low, was all gone, and I concluded I should never have it any more. But when the people collected for afternoon worship, my spirits sunk within me. I retired into a lot, and fell down upon my face, by a fence, full of dismay; but suddenly the words which God spake to Joshua, "Why liest thou upon thy face?—up," gave me to understand that there was no peace for me in indolence. I therefore went to the meeting-house, and tried to preach again, but made miserable work of it. I continued, however, to try to preach, as doors opened; but I tried it more than ten times before I equalled the first, in my own feeling. A question rose in my mind, whether I should be received if I gave myself wholly to the work; which was answered by Solomon thus: "A man's gift maketh room for him, and bringeth him before great men." From a sense of my insufficiency, I trembled at the attempt; but what was said to a king in another case, was now spoken to a feeble youth: "Be ye strong, therefore, and let not your hands be weak, for your work shall be rewarded."

I finally surrendered, and devoted my time and talents to the work of the ministry, without any condition, evasion or mental reservation. In myself, I have seen a rustic youth—unacquainted with men, manners and books; without the smallest prospects, or even the thought of gain or applause, turn out a volunteer for Christ, to contest with all the powers of darkness. It is possible, however, that I have been deceived in the affair, (for thousands are,) but if I have been deceived, it was an error in my judgment. A hypocrite, I was not; for, at that time, nothing could have tempted me to engage in the work, until I was moved by the Holy Ghost. The greatest obstruction that I had, when undertaking the work, was this: I did not believe that I had the longing desire and holy zeal for the salvation of sinners, that some preachers had; indeed, this was my heaviest trial for the first five years of my ministry. I had, however, a love for the gospel and the gospel worship, and was pleased when I saw people turning to the Lord.*

From this beginning, I preached in the towns around where I was requested.

The first preaching tour that I made, was a small one, about forty miles in length; preaching to little congregations on the way. My mind was dark when first setting out, but grew darker and darker all the way, till, at length, I concluded that I had run before I was sent, and, therefore, returned home with precipitance, resolving to attempt the work no more.

Before I went on this journey, I had appointed a meeting to attend after my return; had it not been for this circumstance, I know not what would have brought me into action. But attending that appointment, I obtained great comfort, and resolution to persevere.

At one of these little meetings, a young woman received a gracious change, and gave good evidence of it. This encouraged me, that my labor was not in vain. About thirty years afterwards I saw her. She had joined with the Presbyterians, and blamed me for being a close communi-

---

* From a manuscript, written mostly in 1800, the following extract is taken:—

"Volumes might be written upon the wanderings, darkness and errors of my life, which would afford no pleasure to others in hearing thereof, and which would be of no advantage to myself to relate; and, therefore, I shall pass them by, and attend onlv to a few of God's gracious and notable dealings with me, a great sinner, in my ministerial labors. Under all the trials and temptations that I have passed through for twenty-six years, I have never felt guilty for undertaking to preach at the time when I began. I cannot reproach myself with undertaking the work from any other motive than a real belief that it was my indispensable duty. I might have been deceived; but a hypocrite I was not, so far as I have ever yet seen. Yet, from the 20th June, 1774, until November, 1779, I had one general trial in my mind. It was this: I did not possess that strong desire for the conversion of sinners, that many others evidently had. This made me fear that all was not right with me."

cant. I asked her, if her ministers and church would let me preach in their meeting-house; she said, she believed not. Why then, said I, should I be blamed for not communing with those who have no fellowship with me?

The autumn of this year, I joined Bellingham church, (for till then, I belonged to no church,) and after about six months, that church gave me a license to do that which I had been doing for a year before.

In October, 1775, I took a journey to Virginia, and was gone eight months. One person in New Jersey, one in Connecticut, and two in Virginia, professed to receive some impression, under my improvement, which turned them to the Lord.

September 30, 1776, I was married to Sally Devine, of Hopkinton; and immediately started with her to Virginia. As we made a stay of six weeks at Philadelphia, and a longer stay in Fairfax, Virginia, we did not reach Culpepper until March. At Mount Poney, in Culpepper, I joined the church, and undertook to preach among them half the Sundays. In August, I was ordained by the choice of the church, without the imposition of the hands of a Presbytery. As this was a departure from the usage of the churches in Virginia, I was not generally fellowshipped by them. I spent all my time travelling and preaching, and had large congregations. The first person that I baptized, was Betsey Tillery. I saw her in 1814. She had then supported a Christian character for thirty-eight years. In the close of the year 1777, I travelled as far south as Pee Dee river, in South Carolina, and returned to Culpepper early in 1778. Soon after this, I removed into Orange county, where I acquired me a residence, and where I continued all the time of my stay in Virginia. My stay in Culpepper was not a blessing to the people. I was too young and roving to be looked up to as a pastor. Difficulties arose, the church split, and I just obtained a dismission and recommendation. God had another man for Mount Poney church. William Mason became their pastor, and he has done wonders in the name of Jesus. Having moved to Orange, I commenced my labors with ardor. Twelve and fourteen times a week I frequently preached. But, notwithstanding the constancy of my preaching, and the multitudes that attended, there was but small appearance of the work of God's spirit. I said before, I knew my heart did not burn with the holy fire as it ought to.

In the spring of 1779, I appointed a string of meetings, about one hundred and twenty miles, as far down as York county. As I had sold my horse to pay for my house and lot, I concluded to go on foot: accordingly I started; but, as I had a pair of new shoes that pinched my feet, I found I must either desist—go barefoot, like the old Apostles, or purchase a horse. I chose the last, and promised the Lord if he would aid me to pay for the horse, I would spend it in his service. I gave my note for the beast, and pursued my journey. It so happened, in the event, that when I returned home, I had more than money enough to pay for my mare; and many thonsands of miles she carried me about to preach. But though she was good, she was not invulnerable; for, on the 8th of June, as I was returning from Bedford county, I called at a friend's house, and found, by the badness of the saddle, her back was so swelled that I could not ride her. A man, twenty miles distant, had fallen from a fence and broken his neck, and this day I had appointed to preach his funeral sermon commemorative. My friend could not help me, and, therefore, I arose at daybreak and travelled twenty miles, preached to the people, and then returned on foot to my friend's, where my beast was.*

In September, this year, I was likewise returning from Bedford, and had an evening meeting at a place called the North Garden. After preaching was over, a Mrs. Baily informed me that she had a desire to be baptized, but her husband had told her, if she was ever baptized he would whip her within an inch of her life, and kill the man that should baptize her. That he had once seen me, and liked me so well, that he said if Leland should come that way he might baptize her; and now she wished to embrace the opportunity. I asked her if she was willing to suffer, on supposition her husband should revolt to his first resolution. "Yes," said she, "if I am whipped, my Saviour had long furrows ploughed upon his back." "Well," said I, "if you will venture your back, I will venture my head." Accordingly, the candles were lighted—we went to the water, and she was baptized. My engagements called me to start very early next morning. I heard afterwards that he whipped her, but the head of John the Baptist is not taken off yet.

I now come to a period, which was very interesting to me, and, possibly, on account of the incidents of this period, may be profitable to others.

In the month of October, my mind was graciously impressed with eternal realities. Souls appeared very precious to me, and my heart was drawn out in prayer for their salvation. Now, for the first time, I knew what it was to travail in birth for the conversion of sinners. The words of Rachel to Jacob were the words of my heart to God: "Give me children or else I die." One night, as I lay on my bed weeping and praying, I thought if it was spring instead of autumn, I would spend all my time at the feet of Jesus in prayer, and at the feet of sinners, praying them to be reconciled to God; but winter was coming on, the summer was ended, and the opportunity past. On which reflection, the following words burst into my mind with surprising effect: "The shepherds rejoiced on a win-

* In June, this year, the first *Camp Meeting* was attended in Caroline county, that I ever heard of. By arrangement, eight or ten Baptist preachers held the meeting three days and nights; but, as nothing extraordinary followed, it was not repeated; and it was a number of years before those meetings arose in the West, and have spread all over the United States.

ter's day." These words awakened all the latent energies of my soul. I resolved to double my vigor, and had faith to believe that I should see souls return to the Lord, and that I should rejoice at it that winter. For eight months after this, I had the spirit of prayer to a degree beyond what I ever had it in my life; and, if I mistake not, my preaching savored a little of the same spirit. My field of preaching was from Orange down to York, about one hundred and twenty miles. From November, 1779, to July, 1780, I baptized one hundred and thirty, the chiefest of whom professed to be the seals of my ministry. As this was the first time that ever such a work attended my ministry, it was refreshing indeed; nor can I think of it now, without soft emotions of heart. The chiefest of my success was in York, where Lord Cornwallis and the British army were made prisoners, in October, 1781. Matthew Wood, Robert Stacy and Thomas Cheesman, (all preachers afterwards,) were the children of this revival.

In the first of my preaching in York, I had a meeting in the edge of Warwick. Just as I had read my text, Col. Harwood, with six others, entered the house. "Sir," said the Colonel, "I am come to stop you from preaching here to-day." Without any time to think, I gave a heavy stamp on the floor, and told him in the name of God to forbear. He replied, "I did not come to fight, but to stop you from preaching." A Mr. Cole Diggs, son of a counsellor, was there, and said, "Col. Harwood, you are a representative in the General Assembly, and the Assembly has just made a law to secure the religious rights of all, and now you come to prevent them. What does that look like?" Said the Colonel, "Mr. Diggs, I only came to prevent an unlawful conventicle, for this meeting draws away the people from the church!" Mrs. Russell, the mistress of the house, replied, "Hah! Colonel, I think it is a pity that people cannot do as they please, in their own house." "Madam," said the Colonel, "I did not come to dispute with ladies." And here the fracas ended. The Colonel and Co. went off, and the meeting was continued. When he returned home, his mother said unto him, "Well, Neddy, what did the man say unto you?" "What?" said the Colonel, "He stamped at me, and made no more of me than if I had been a dog. I shall trouble them no more." Some of his servants I baptized afterwards.

Captain Robert Howard, of York, had a beautiful and pious wife whom he adored. She wished to be baptized, but as he was a vestryman in the church, he opposed it. At a time, however, she came forward and was baptized. When he heard of it, he called for his carriage, and took his cow-skin, and said he would lash me out of the county. His sister replied, "Brother Bobby, Mr. Leland is a large man, and will be too much for you." "I know it," said the Captain, "but he will not fight." His wife made answer, "Perhaps he may—he goes well armed; and if he should wound you in the heart, you would fall before him." "Ah!" said the

Captain, "I know nothing about this heart-work.' "I wish you may, my dear," said his wife. He finally declined the contest, and afterwards became serious, penitent, believing, and was baptized. After his reform, as he was riding in company with me to meeting, one of his uncles met him in the road, and accosted him thus: "Nephew Bobby, I pity you in my heart, to see you following that deluded people, and wasting your time so much, that you will raise no corn this year." "My uncle," said the Captain, "I wish you had pitied me as much two years ago, when you cheated me out of my mill."

About the same time, a gentlewoman, in James City, was convinced that it was her duty to be baptized, but neglected it until she could evade it no longer. She came to my quarters on Saturday, and made known her desire; accordingly the neighbors were collected, and she was baptized: when she returned and told her husband of it, he would not sleep with her that night, nor eat breakfast with her in the morning. She came to meeting on Sunday and informed me of what had taken place, and asked my advice in the affair. I knew the lady to be an excellent cook, and her husband was fond of good dinners. My answer was, "My sister, give yourself no uneasiness; his appetite will bring him to his reason by dinner time;" which accordingly came to pass.

At the close of the eight months, which I am now treating of, as I was taking leave of the young disciples in York, to return home to Orange, and was preaching to them, from "Little children, keep yourselves from idols," I was taken with a pain in my head, and an ague, followed by a bilious fever, and preached not again for eighteen weeks. Reports reached my home that I was dead, and a kind of funeral sermon was preached on the occasion. Notwithstanding this, I was carried home in a carriage, after six weeks sickness, but did not preach until twelve weeks more had elapsed. In this sickness, my mind was greatly depressed. The spirit of prayer left me. My hope for heaven was shaken to the centre. The truth of what I had been preaching was doubted. The fear that I had been governed by an ambitious spirit, like Jehu, was great. In short, I was a poor, forlorn, sick worm of the dust.

One thing, however, stuck by me, because I felt it, viz: "That a death unto sin, and a new birth unto righteousness, was absolutely necessary to constitute a man either safe or happy.". When my sickness abated, my spirit was so peevish that I was out of all esteem of myself.

When my health was so far recovered that I could preach, I resumed the work again, but ah! my hair was shaven, my strength was gone. Through the mercy of God, however, I was holpen with a little help; and after I was tried I saw brighter days.

From this time to the year 1785, by the siege of Lord Cornwallis, the refunding of paper money, and removals to Kentucky, religion ran low in

Virginia. A few events that took place in those four years, connected with the narative which I am here giving, I shall nevertheless notice.

One day, I went from home about eight miles. On my return, there arose a heavy thunder storm. Being in summer dress, I stopped under the large branches of a lofty oak, to shelter me from the rain. The rain, however, continuing, I started for home. I had gone but a little distance before the lightning struck. The next time I passed the road, I found the lightning had struck the oak, and split off one of the huge limbs, which had fallen on the very spot where I had stood about three minutes before.

In the bend of Pamunky river, a little below New Castle, there is an Indian town. By the circle of the river, and a cross creek, a gate, with two lengths of fence, enclose it around. There was at that time about seventy-five proprietors. The name of their king was John Tohon. His royal majesty gave me an invitation to visit the town, and preach among them. Accordingly I went, and preached at the royal pavilion. After preaching, I baptized two persons, and then heard the king preach; for, like Melchizedeck, he was priest as well as king. His majesty did not seem to be possessed with much regal power, and by the text which he preached from, one would think that he did not seek after hierarchal authority. His text was, "Be ye not called Rabbi, for one is your master, even Christ, and all ye are brethren." I ate a good dinner with the king, slept in his apartment the following night, and left the town in the morning. Soon after this he died.

Funeral sermons in Virginia are seldom preached at the time of the interment, but sometime afterwards. I was invited to preach a sermon, on the death of a small child, long after it was dead. This was in the county of Louisa, about eighteen miles from home. The text was Isaiah lvii. 2. At this meeting, three persons were first awakened, who became and lived shining Christians. This was the first fruits of my labor in Louisa, where, afterwards, the Lord gave me a rich harvest.

An inn-holder in Pagestown strongly importuned me to preach at his house. When I went there, he did not open his own doors for worship, but provided another place. There was some appearance that he wished the people to collect, more to purchase his drink and dinner, than to have their souls converted. After some time, he pressed me again to come and preach; when I went, he would not open his house, nor could he get any other; we, therefore, repaired to a tobacco house for worship. In this instance, I felt as if my master was mocked; and if I had felt gracious enough, I should have shaken off the dust of my feet against him; but as I was a poor imperfect creature myself, I peaceably pursued my course, after the meeting was over. Some weeks afterwards, as I was travelling the road a little distance from the place, I saw the landlord's chimney standing, but the house was consumed by fire. When I saw it, my heart burst out in sacred language, "Righteous art thou, Lord God Almighty, because thou hast judged thus."

In the year 1784, I travelled northward as far as Philadelphia, where I tarried six weeks. As I went in company with Mr. Winchester, the Baptists in Philadelphia were so fearful that I was a Universalist, that I was not invited by them to preach in their meeting-house. I therefore preached Sundays and almost every night in the Hall of the University, and in private houses. But when I saw the many thousands of people in the city, and those who attended at the Hall did not exceed 200, I was resolved to try the street. Accordingly, I appointed a meeting to preach one afternoon at five o'clock, at the sign of the Blue Bell. When I went, but few appeared. I stepped upon a stick of ship timber and began by singing: on which the people came running from every lane, and continued to increase until preaching was over, when I judged there was about three hundred people. I then appointed to preach there again, when there were about twice as many. During my stay in the city, I baptized four persons in Schuylkill river, and returned home to Virginia by water. Six years afterwards I was in Philadelphia, and having preached one evening in the Baptist meeting-house, a man took me by the hand and invited me to take lodgings with him that night, which I accepted of. As we were walking to his house, he gave the following account of himself: "Sir, formerly I attended meeting nowhere, but when you was here six years ago, as I was at work in my shop, I heard the voice of singing as if it came down from heaven. I left my shop and ran out to see what was coming, and beheld you, sir, upon a stick of ship-timber at prayer. After prayer, I attended to your preaching, which sunk so deeply into my heart, that I have never lost it; and am now a member in the Baptist church."

Late in the year 1784, I travelled to the south-east about one hundred and fifty miles, near the Dismal Swamp, and returned in six weeks.

In the spring of 1785, I went to the same district, and ranged and preached much more than I did in my first visit.

I now come to a period when religious appearance began to assume a more pleasing face than it had done for many years. In Powhattan county the work first broke out, and many became the subjects of victorious grace. Some old professors, on the other side of James River, about Chickahominy, went to see what was going on, who caught the spirit, and returning home, were instrumental of a similar work in their neighborhood, and round about in Goochland.

The last of this year I took a preaching tour into the lower part of North Carolina. Preached eighteen times in that state, in a circular course, then came into Virginia and steered home.

There was a place for preaching on the line between Louisa and Goochland, called Hodger's Seats, where I sometimes preached. In the spring of 1786, I appointed a long and circular string of meetings. And as I had a strong impression that God would work at that place, I reserved five days in my tour to spend among that people. After the Association at Boar Swamp was over, I travelled through Goochland, where many people seemed to be on the alert for heaven, and came to Mr. Hodger's, where a large number of people were waiting for me. I introduced worship by repeating a hymn,

"O that my load of sin were gone," &c.

All of a sudden, it seemed as if something fell from heaven upon the people. I could not speak for weeping, for some time. I am but a poor preacher, at best, and the sermon which I then preached was hardly middling, but the effect on the people was amazing. Some were crying out, some on their knees, and others prostrate on the floor. In the course of a few weeks about forty were baptized; and I believe that a majority of them dated their first awakenings at the meeting at Mr. Hodger's.

In August, the same year, I attended a meeting of the General Committee, at Buckingham; after which I travelled southward to Pittsylvania, to visit that great man of God, Rev. Samuel Harris; and on my return, preached on a Sunday in Prince Edward. In the midst of the meeting, a Mr. Owen Smith was brought out, and by his shouting, and praising, and exhorting, he set the whole assembly in motion. I have never seen him since, but have received a number of letters from him. His last letter was in 1816. He was then well, and reminded me of the meeting in Prince Edward, and wrote that nine of his family belong to the church.

I had met Mr. Harris on the banks of James river, and accompanied him at his meetings through Goochland, Fluvanna and Louisa to Orange. At a meeting in Goochland, after preaching was over, Mr. Harris went into the yard, and sat down in the shade, while the people were weeping in the meeting-house, and telling what God had done for them, in order to be baptized. A gentlewoman addressed Mr. Harris as follows: "Mr. Harris, what do you think all this weeping is for? Are not all those tears like the tears of a crocodile? I believe I could cry as well as any of them, if I chose to act the hypocrite." On this address, Mr. Harris drew a dollar out of his pocket and replied, "Good woman, I will give you this dollar for a tear, and repeat it ten times;" but the woman shed no tears.

Among the seven that were baptized at that time, was a Mrs. Johnson, daughter of Col. James Dabney, of whom take the following account: Col. Johnson's son Christopher paid attention to the young lady, and gained her good will, but could not obtain the consent of her father; on which Miss Betsey agreed to elope with young Johnson; and from her chamber window, on a ladder, she descended in the night, and was conducted by her lover to the house of his father. In the morning Col. Dabney missed his daughter, and suspecting where she was gone, he armed himself with sword and pistol, and steered his course to Col. Johnson's. When he got within call, he demanded if his daughter Betsey was there? Being answered in the affirmative, he gave orders for her to meet him on the risk of her life. Betsey's affections no ways accorded with the demand of her father, and seeing him thus armed, she was greatly distressed. Col. Anderson being at the house, seeing what was passing, said, "Come Betsey, don't be discouraged, I'll effect a reconciliation." With that, he armed himself with sword and pistol, and marched into the field to meet Dabney, with his arm stretched out, holding his glittering sword, and Betsey walking under it. When he got near Dabney, he exclaimed, "Col. Dabney, here is your daughter, Betsey, who wishes for a reconciliation; I have undertaken to protect her, and shall defend her with the last drop of my blood." Betsey fell upon her knees—Dabney softened—a reconciliation was effected—the young couple were married; and, at the meeting just spoken of, she was baptized: nor was it long before her husband followed her example.

This event has often led my mind to reflect on an incident, infinitely more important. The guilty runaway sinner is pursued by the holy, fiery law, and threatened with eternal death; but the Mediator appears to interpose, and when the sinner is humbled by grace, a reconciliation is obtained.

In June, 1787, I was ordained by laying on of hands. The ministers that officiated, were Nathaniel Saunders, John Waller and John Price. By this, not only a union took place between myself and others, but it was a small link in the chain of events, which produced a union among all the Baptists in Virginia, not long afterwards.

In 1787, old Col. Harris made me a visit, whose coming called out a vast crowd of ministers and people. His eyes—his every motion was preaching; but after he had read his text, his mind was so dark that he could not preach; and of course the lot fell on me.

From my house, Col. Harris went down to Spottsylvania, where the work of the Lord, like a mighty torrent, broke out under his ministry. A few weeks afterwards, I went down through Spottsylvania and Caroline, and was glad to see the grace of God, but was extremely mortified to find myself so far behind the work of God. In this visit, however, I caught the spirit of prayer, which lasted me home.* Indeed, before I got home, I gained an evidence that God would work in Orange. Having such confidence, I addressed myself to the work of the ministry with fresh courage.

* "On my return through Caroline county, after I had been preaching, I sat in the door-yard of a friend's house conversing as usual; but here a strange solemnity seized my mind, and a strong drawing of soul to God inspired my breast, such as I had not enjoyed for some years. I soon lost sight of my company, and was conversant at the throne of grace. This frame of mind continued, with some abatements, until I reached home, which was two days afterwards. About three miles before I reached home, I obtained great comfort in believing that God would work among the people in Orange.—*MS.*

There was a dancing school set up in the vicinity, which was much in my way. On Sunday, after service, I told the people that I had opened a dancing school, which I would attend one quarter gratis: that I would fiddle the tune which the angels sung, if they would dance repentance on their knees. The project succeeded; the dancing school gave way, and my meetings were thronged. Solemnity, sobs, sighs and tears soon appeared. The last Sunday in October I began to baptize those that were brought out, and the work prevailed greatly. The tract of land which I occupied in this revival was more than twenty miles square, including the corners of Orange, Culpepper, Spottsylvania and Louisa.

When the work seemed to languish in one neighborhood, it would break out in another, and consequently, there was a continual fall of heavenly rain from October, 1787, until March, 1789, during which time I baptized about 400. Precisely 300 of them were baptized in 1788—more than I have ever baptized in any other year. During the ingathering, the following events took place. In the south part of Orange, a man took his gun, with the professed intention of killing me. He had given his consent for his wife to be baptized, and the meeting was appointed for that purpose; but when we got to the water, and I had taken her by the hand to lead her into the water, there was an alarm that the man was coming with his gun. While a detachment of the congregation went to meet the man and pacify him, I thought, "now or never," and baptised her. No mischief ensued.

In another part of Orange, a woman, who was in the habit of intimacy with myself and wife, invited me to preach at her house on a certain evening. When we got at the gate, her son, who was a Captain, (having been reproved by his mother, and taken offence at it,) met us, and said I should not preach there. I asked him if he thought he was right. "No," said he, "I know I am wrong, and I expect to be damned for it; but I have said it and shall abide by my word." The man of the house came also to the gate, and desired us to go into the house, and said the house was his own and not his son's. The woman was at a loss what was best. I hesitated, but finally went in. As the people began to collect, the Captain withdrew with threatenings. After I arose to open the meeting by singing, he came rushing into the house, like a bear bereaved of her whelps—sprang upon the bed—took his sword and drew it out of the scabbard—and stepping off the bed with his arm extended and sword glittering, exclaimed, "let me kill the damned rascal!" As he made a stroke towards me, the point of the sword hit the joists, and he behaved like an awkward soldier. The case was this: my wife, who was seated near the head of the bed, when she saw the Captain step from the bed with his sword drawn, and draw back his arm to give the thrust, like a female angel, sprang like the lightning of heaven, clasped her arms within his elbow, around his body, locked her hands together, and held him like a vice, till the men took away his sword. We then took a lantern and went into the road and carried on our meeting. As God would have it, a young man and a young woman dated their change of heart at this meeting.

As I was returning from Fredericksburg, in the lower part of Orange, a young man had married and brought his bride to his father's, where there was music and dancing. I stopped in the road, and the groom came out and wished me to drink sling with him. I asked him what noise it was that I heard in the house? He answered it was a fiddle. As he was going to the house, I requested him to bring the fiddle to me. But as this was not done, I lighted off my horse and went into the house. By the time I got in, the fiddle was hidden, and all was still. I told them, if fiddling and dancing was serving God, to proceed on, and if I could gain conviction of it, I would join them. As they did not proceed, I told them I would attempt to serve God in my way. I then prayed among them and took my leave. The next week I was sent for to come and preach at the same house. The power of the Lord was present to heal. In the course of a few weeks, numbers were converted and turned to the Lord, whom I baptized in a stream of water near the house.

At another time, I had a meeting at John Lea's, in Louisa, when something seemed to descend on the people, like that which took place at Mr. Hodgers's, (mentioned before,) but the effects were not so great. The next day there were five to be baptized. The day was very cold.

While Mr. Bowles was preaching to the people, I composed the hymn:

Christians, if your hearts be warm,
Ice and snow can do no harm;
If by Jesus you are priz'd,
Rise, believe, and be baptiz'd.

Jesus drank the gall for you,
Bore the Cross for sinners due;
Children, prove your love to him,
Never fear the frozen stream.

Never shun the Saviour's Cross,
All on earth is worthless dross;
If the Saviour's love you feel,
Let the world behold your zeal.

At an Association in Caroline, two others with myself were chosen to preach on Sunday. When my turn came, I felt every way unprepared. I was hoarse with a cold, and exceedingly barren in spirit. I therefore declined, and one of the others preached. While he was preaching, I doubted whether I was right in declining, and resolved that as soon as he had finished, I would do what I could. Accordingly I did. My voice improved; my ideas brightened so much that I preached about forty minutes. The people were greatly affected. On account of a similitude used, together with the shortness of the discourse, it was called the GINGER-CAKE sermon. Mr. Waller, who was the stated minister at that place, told me afterwards, that in the relations which the people gave before baptism, not less than fifteen persons had reference to the GINGER-BREAD sermon.

In the year 1789, nothing of importance turned up.

In 1790, I travelled into New England, to see my father and relations. I preached on the way, going and coming. The term of my absence from home was four months. The number baptized thirty-two.

The winter following, I made my arrangements to move into New England. Having baptized precisely seven hundred while I lived there, and leaving two churches, one in Orange, and the other in Louisa; the first containing three hundred and the other two hundred members. On the last of March, I started, with my family of a wife and eight children, and a small quantum of effects, and travelled by land to Fredericksburg, where I took ship for New England. We fell down the Rappahannock river, crossed the Chesapeake, and entered the sea between the Capes of Henry and Charles. The day after we entered the Atlantic, we were attacked by a thunder gust and heavy gale of wind, which lasted fifteen hours. The boat was crippled, the oars swept off, the quadrant injured, and some of my goods were swept from the quarter-deck. That passengers should be affrighted, is not to be wondered at; but here, the sailors all turned pale. In the midst of the gale, the wind shifted, and flung the vessel into the trough of the sea; on which the Captain stepped to the cabin door and said, "We shall not weather it many minutes." This he said, (as I judged,) not to terrify the sailors, but for my sake. The sense of it, to me, was this: "Leland, if you have got a God, now call upon him." But there was no need of this admonition, for I had begun the work before; and can now say, that that night is the only one of my life that I spent wholly in prayer. That I prayed in faith, is more than I can say; but that I prayed in distress, is certain. About day-light, April 15th, the wind abated, but we knew not where we were for five days; for the quadrant was injured. The distress which I had at that time, so affected my nervous system, that I did not entirely recover from it for more than ten years. In time, however, we gained the port of New London, on a certain Saturday night. I did not intend to make any stay at that place, save only to get some refreshments, but the Captain had written from Fredericksburgh, to his friends in New London, that he had turned his vessel into a meeting-house, and was bringing a preacher and his family with him. On Sunday morning early it was known that the vessel lay by the wharf, and before I was up the brethren in New London came down to the vessel, to see what, for a cargo, the Captain had brought into port. The Captain told them that he intended to go to the insurance office, and demand the sum that was insured on the vessel; for if it had not been for my prayers he was sure the vessel would have been lost. The brethren invited me to go ashore, and preach to them in the state-house, which I acceded to. Finding myself courteously received, I tarried there about two months. Here I met with some success in winning souls; and here my wife was sick nigh unto death; but she had more faith in prayer than she had in physic. The godly old Elder, Z. Darrow, came to visit us, whose prayer for my wife seemed to be answered, and she recovered. The people were very kind and liberal to me; but the expenses of my family, and the sickness of my wife, cost me about twenty dollars more than I received. But this thought came to my mind: "Jesus gave his life and blood for sinners, and shall I begrudge a few dollars for their salvation!" After preaching around in the towns about New London, on the 1st of July we left the place, and, in boats and scows, went up Connecticut river to Sunderland, and then by land to Conway, where my father and old acquaintance were living. In Conway, I purchased a house and small lot, for a temporary residence until I gained more acquaintance in the country. At this place, my family abode eight months. My travels in the meantime in the country were considerable—my success some.

The last day of February, 1792, I moved into Cheshire, which has been my home the chiefest of the time since. For two or three years there was a sprinkling of blessings on the people in Cheshire, Lanesborough and Adams, so that about seventy were baptized. And in Philip's town, Canaan and the Gore, I had good success. In the year 1795, the work of God appeared in Conway. A messenger came and desired me to visit them; I went and preached twelve times among them, and baptized twelve persons at that time, and more afterwards. Here my heart caught a little heavenly fire, and I returned home to Cheshire, longing and praying that God would pour out his spirit on the people in Cheshire. I set up evening meetings, and preach about as often as once a day, for seventy days running. I have never known a time like this, when I had so much of the spirit of praying and preaching, and met with so small success. No more than seven came forward as the reward of my painful labor. In the compass of these seventy days, I had a night meeting at Deacon Wood's, in Cheshire. Going to the meeting, my mind was so solemnly impressed, that I could hardly walk. When I arose to speak, I could scarcely stand. Of the many thousands of sermons that I have preached in my life, (for solemnity of mind, discovery of heavenly things, and flow of words,) I give that the preference, and yet but small effects followed. An individual young woman only was divinely wrought upon. Christ's time was not yet come to work miraculously in Cheshire.

I continued my travels in the New England states, and state of New-

York, until 1797. In August, that year, I made a tour to Virginia, and was gone six months. I preached all the way there, and travelled and preached among my old friends three months, and then returned home, having travelled more than two thousand miles, and preached more than one hundred and seventy times. My friends through the whole received me kindly; but I saw no great revivals of religion anywhere, save only at Scotch Plains, among Mr. Vanhorn's people. After my return, I was busily employed in domestic concerns for about eighteen months, preparing to go to Virginia again, in August, 1799. To this end, I had sent on appointments for meetings, about one hundred miles on my way, as far as Carmel meeting-house. Having finished my domestic affairs a fortnight before my appointments began, I told the people in Cheshire, that I would preach for them every day or night until I started. At this time, a heavenly visitant came to my house—my heart, with the salutation of "Peace be to you—peace on earth and good will to men."* When I sat in my house, it would seem as if the room was white-washed with love. When I went into the field, a circle of heavenly mildness would seem to surround me, and the following words would be injected into my heart again, again, and again: "The Lord will work." My meetings, during this feast of tabernacles, (as I called the fortnight,) were crowded. At the meeting-house, such silence reigned as I had never seen before. My struggle of mind was great, whether I should go to Virginia and leave these hopeful appearances, or stay at home and strive to fan the sparks. And as the time drew on, my struggles increased. I prepared for my journey, and preached my last sermon a few miles on the way. The people followed in droves, and, in time of meeting, wept bitterly. I finally went on my journey, and attended my appointments, which I before had made, the distance of one hundred miles, and then returned back. I was gone about twenty days, and preached about the same number of sermons, and baptized thirteen persons. On my return, I found the work had broken out like the mighty rushing waters. This induced me to preach every day or night until the March following, in which time more than two hundred were baptized.

Before the work made a visible appearance, and for three months afterwards, there was not a day but what I had the spirit of prayer, and a travail for souls; and often felt as if I should sink under the weight of my burden if souls were no delivered. Sometimes, individuals would lay in my heart; at other times, the longing desire would be more general. After three months I felt that spirit of prayer abate, but the spirit of

* In August, 1799, my soul was again visited with the same peace and holy longings after God and the salvation of men as at former times. My preaching then, through grace, was not coasting around the shallow shores of doubt and uncertainty, but launching out into the deep for a draught. Attention and solemnity followed."—*MS.*

preaching continued for three months afterwards, until the ingathering was over, and then the peculiar impression which I had, subsided.*

In 1800, I made a tour of four months, travelling southward as far as Bedford, N. Y. Then eastward through Connecticut to New-London. Then pursued my course through Rhode Island, (visiting Providence and Newport,) into Bristol county. Then returning through Worcester and Hampshire counties, reached home the last of October. I was somewhat debilitated when I left home, and the summer was unusually hot, but I was preserved and enabled to preach about as many times as there were days. In this journey, I saw eight old preachers, whose ages in average, exceeded eighty years. The venerable Backus was one of them. There was a revival in his congregation, and on his request I baptized a few in the place. I have never seen him since, nor either of the eight; nor shall I ever see them in mortal bodies, for they are all dead. My journey was not altogether lost. By letters and verbal accounts, I was afterwards informed that in several places a divine blessing attended the preaching, which proved effectual unto salvation.

In November, 1801, I journeyed to the south, as far as Washington, in charge of a cheese, sent to President Jefferson. Notwithstanding my trust, I preached all the way there and on my return. I had large congregations; led in part by curiosity to hear the Mammoth Priest, as I was called.

After this, I lived several years in great barrenness of soul, and had but little, if any success.

In March, 1804, I removed into Dutchess County, N. Y., where I continued two years, which, (as it respects my ministry,) was a gap of lost time. Just before I left the place, a revival took place about ten miles off, where brother Luman Birch, an unordained preacher, improved, which called me there to baptize a few.

In 1806, I removed back to Cheshire. The day before the total eclipse, brother Birch was ordained. It was my lot to preach the sermon, which seemed to be blessed among the people. The substnace of that sermon was offered to the public, in a pamphlet, afterwards entitled "*The Flying Seraphim.*" The following winter, I sunk into great distress of mind. It has always been a question with me of great importance, to know how

---

* At the close of the original MS., before referred to, he writes, "I have experienced seven instances in my life in praying for the sick and maimed, when there appeared to be such an immediate relief granted, that I should be unbelieving and ungrateful not to mention them among the signal favors of God to me. I have passed through many fatigues in travel, several perils occasioned by mobs and furious men, many wants and pinches in life, and many tokens of providential relief; but after all, remain an unholy, helpless creature, and if the Lord does not keep me, I shall fall, disgrace myself, bring the ministry under blame, and be ashamed to read what I have now written. Amen."

to address a congregation of sinners, as such, in gospel style. And this winter it attacked my mind with great force. Neither Gill, Hopkins, Fuller nor Wesley, could remove my difficulties. My fears were, that I did not preach right, which was the cause why I was so barren in myself and useless to others. This burden lay heavy upon me a long time. At length, at an evening meeting at a school house in Cheshire, my heart waxed a little warm with holy zeal, and I gave my spirit vent to the youth and school children, regardless of all authors and systems, which had a good effect. Four of the school children and a young man besides, came forward for baptism in a few weeks, who dated the beginning of their religious impressions at that meeting. This little success, obtained at that trying time, gave me both relief and courage.*

The year 1808 was a memorable year in Pownal. Religion had a great triumph in that place at that time. A man by the name of John Williams was their preacher; but he was not ordained; of course I preached and baptized,through the cold winter. The number baptized was more than sixty. Williams did not behave like a wolf, seeking to destroy, but like a goat, as if he was ignorant of what was going on. He finally turned out an abandoned character. In this revival some little boys set up a conference meeting; and as they were poor, they would meet in cow-sheds and on the mountains. This was in the winter, and some of them had no shoes. When it was known, the neighbors gladly opened their houses for their accommodation.

In the year 1811, while I was in the General Court at Boston, a time of refreshing came in Cheshire. After my return I baptized forty. There

* "At the close of the year 1806, I got amazingly distressed on account of my preaching, fearing that my barrenness in the ministry was owing to improper addresses. The Methodists were amazing successful and zealous, and the addresses of their ministers were general and undaunted. I visited them—I conversed with them; they were all for heaven, and assured they were in the way; but their zeal and confidence appeared to me like the mighty wind and fire in Elija's vision, and I could not discover that any with whom I conversed had any knowledge of themselves, of the law of God, or of the way of pardon.

The Gillite mode of addressing sinners, seemed a little different from the New Testament mode. The Hopkinsian method appeared as if it took all the wisdom of God to devise a way for an honorable pretence to damn men. Dr. Fuller only cast another bundle of straw on the fire. So that the great query which has agitated my mind for more than thirty years, 'How is a congregation of sinners to be addressed?' at the time I am speaking of, fell with such distress upon my mind, that I could hardly contain myself. But in the midst of my difficulties, I had a meeting at a school house; in the time of service my soul got into the *trade winds*, and without consulting Gill, Hopkins, Fuller, or Wesley, without comparing our translation with the Septuagint, Chaldee, or the King of Spain's Bible, I addressed the scholars and young people in a way I never can without God helps me. The spirit of the Lord fell upon them. Very soon after this, five of them came forward and confessed Christ." Continuation of MS. 1807.

was a division among the people. Other ministers baptized about ten. In the height of this revival, I was taken sick of the typhus fever. What I passed through in that sickness has been published in a pamphlet.*

In December, 1813, I started again for Virginia; and preaching on the way to Washington, I crossed the Potomac into Virginia the last day of January, 1814. I was in the state eighty days, in which time I travelled seven hundred miles, and preached more than seventy times. I never had before—I never have since—nor do I ever expect to preach to as many people in so short a time. The kindness of the people to their old friend, whom they had not seen for sixteen years, was unbounded. I shall never forget it while my memory remains. I reached Richmond on Saturday, March 5th. The Sunday before that, Elder Courtney had baptized seventy-five persons in the basin on the canal. He descended into the water and took his stand, from which he did not remove until all were baptized. He had assistants who led the candidates to and from him; and he performed the whole in seventeen minutes, notwithstanding he was seventy years old. The chiefest of the candidates were people of color. As I returned home, I preached in Dr. Staughton's meeting-house in Philadelphia, on the evening preceding the meeting of the great Convention which formed the plan of the missionary society. I arrived at home in June, after an absence of six months; having travelled in that time eighteen hundred miles, and preached about one hundred and fifty times.

After my return home, I went into the Genessee country to see my children, and late in the fall I sold my residence in Cheshire, with a view to move westward; but before I had made any purchase, as I was travelling for that purpose, about eighty miles from home, the beast on which I rode, like Balaam's ass, not only crushed my feet, but threw me to the ground and fell upon me, which broke my leg. After nearly a fortnight, I was carried home in a sleigh. The old bone was a long while growing and strengthening, and I was reduced very low. As this disaster happened, I was entirely defeated in my object of moving to the westward. My family advised me to purchase the place where I now live, which, with great reluctance I consented to, and was drawn in a sleigh, on bare ground, to my new home. After my leg got well enough, and my strength sufficient, I began to preach again, *leaning on my staff.*

Late in the fall of 1817, there was a precious, though not a very extensive revival in Hancock, where I attended as preacher, and baptized thirty-one, who (excepting three others) were the first that I baptized after my leg was broken.

In March, 1819, a like work began in the north part of Adams, which progressed several months. The people in that place had no settled min-

* Five Hours Conflict.

ister, but were visited by ministers who lived around them; of the seventy who united with the church, I baptized twenty-seven.

Since I began to preach in 1774, I have travelled distances, which, together, would form a girdle nearly sufficient to go round the terraqueous globe three times. The number of sermons which I have preached, is not far from eight thousand. The number of persons that I have baptised is one thousand two hundred and seventy-eight. The number of Baptist ministers whom I have personally known is nine hundred and sixty-two. Those of them whom I have heard preach, in number, make three hundred and three. Those who have died, (whose deaths I have heard of,) amount to three hundred. The number that have visited me at my house is two hundred and seven. The pamphlets which I have written, that have been published, are about thirty.

I am now in the decline of life, having lived nearly two-thirds of a century. When Jacob had lived twice as long, his days had been few and evil. I have spent my years like a tale that is told. Looking over the foregoing narrative, there is proof enough of imperfection; and yet what I have written is the best part of my life. A history seven times as large might be written of my error in judgment, incorrectness of behaviour, and baseness of heart. My only hope of acceptance with God, is in the blood and righteousness of Jesus Christ. And when I come to Christ for pardon, I come as an old grey-headed sinner; in the language of the publican, "God be merciful to me a sinner."

How long I have to stay on earth I know not. What labors or sufferings I have yet to sustain below, I cannot tell. O, that the God of all grace would keep me in his holy care, and never suffer me to make shipwreck of faith and a good conscience, but make me faithful unto death, that I might finish my course with joy and receive a crown at last.

June 15, 1824.—It is now more than four years since I closed the foregoing narrative of events. My life and health have been preserved until the present time. In several places within the district of my ministration, there have been times of refreshing, so that I have baptized seventy-four persons in the four years.

The 14th of May past was my birth-day: I preached on the occasion a *septennarian* sermon.

January 14, 1825.—I have preached in four hundred and thirty-six meeting-houses, thirty-seven court-houses, several capitols, many academies and school-houses; barns, tobacco-houses and dwelling-houses: and many hundreds of times on stages in the open air. Not the place, but the presence of Christ, and a right temper of mind, makes preaching solemnly easy and profitable. My congregations have consisted of from five hearers to ten thousand.

December 12, 1826.—Faint yet pursuing. The summer past I have spent chiefly in travelling and preaching. I have attended three Associations—the jubilee and funeral of three Presidents—as also a general meeting which lasted four days—preached eighty-one times, and seen eighty-six Baptist preachers since the first of June.

Two remarkable events have taken place the present year. Two old patriots, both of them Ex-Presidents, died on the 4th of July; just fifty years after they signed the Declaration of Independence—John Adams and Thomas Jefferson. The first aged ninety-one, the other eighty-three. Mr. Jefferson drew the Declaration of Independence; and by his writings and administration, he has justly acquired the title of the Apostle of Liberty.

In the state of Vermont, the Governor and Lieutenant-Governor are both Baptist preachers—Ezra Butler and Aaron Leland. This is a new thing in the world.

March 25, 1827.—Baptized ten candidates, which makes my baptismal number one thousand three hundred and sixty-two. It is not probable that I ever shall baptize many (if any) more.

From pretty correct information, I find I have now living eighty-two descendants, including children, grand-children, and great-grand-children. A few of my posterity have died at their respective homes; but I have never had a coffin or a death at my house.

If a conscious sinner may apply words to himself which were spoken of Abraham, they are as follows: "For I called him alone, and blessed him, and increased him."

May 6.—Beyond my expectation, this day I baptized fifteen, making up the number 1,377

May 27.—Wondering still: preached this day to a large concourse, and baptized eleven, making 1,388

Baptized 4

July 4.—Preached to nearly 1,000 people, and baptized six, two of whom were my grand-children, making 1,398

July 15.—Baptized another of my grand-children and four others, 5

Baptized 3

July 29.—Baptized 6

Aug. 12.—Baptized five in Cheshire and three in Lanesborough, 8

Making 1,420

I have a great-grand-child, (Helen Maria Brown,) who has now living ten direct, and great grand-fathers and grand-mothers.

Aug. 26.—Baptized	5	Oct. 21.—Baptized	4
Baptized	1	Nov. 4.—Baptized	2
Sept. 9.—Baptized	5	Nov. 5.—Baptized	2
Oct. 7.—Baptized	10		

One of these last was Eunice Baxter, whose grand and great grand-mothers I baptized more than thirty years past.

Nov. 11,—Baptized....................2.

One of these was seventy-seven years old, which added to the age of the administrator, (seventy-three,) would make one hundred and fifty years.

Nov. 30.—Baptized	1	Dec. 30.—Baptized	2
Dec. 9.—Baptized	2	Feb. 1, 1838.—Baptized	1
Dec. 17.—Baptized	1		

The father and mother of this candidate have fourteen children now living; ELEVEN of whom I have baptized.

Baptized five more, making............1,465.

May 14, 1828.—I am this day seventy-four years old, able to travel and preach as doors open; and labor with my hands as duty calls.

The sins of childhood—the vices of youth—the improprieties, pride and arrogance of riper years; with the presumptuous and blasphemous suggestions of my mind, up till the present time, lie heavy on my mind, and sink my spirits very low. It is true, I have had a hope for more than fifty years, that my sins were attoned for by the blood of Christ, and forgiven for his name's sake; but still I find them attached to my character, and must forever, for truth cannot decease.

When the saints in heaven look on the blessed Jesus, and remember the doleful sorrow and pain which their sins cost him, what kind of feeling must they have? To call their feeling sorrow, tears or mourning, would be unscriptural; but a remembrance of their sins, a view of their Redeemer, and a sense of his bloody agony, must give them a surprizing ——— ———, fill them with an exquisite hatred to sin, and raise their songs of praise to him who has redeemed them.

December 7, 1828.—This day, for the first time, I baptized a man in a font, near the pulpit, in Albany. During my stay in Albany, which was four days, I was introduced to three governors. My rusticity of manners, and the humble rank I fill, make such interviews more painful than flattering.

May 14, 1829.—This day I am seventy-five years old. Nothing singular with respect to myself has occurred in the course of the last year.

My greatest afflictions in life have been of that character that I have had to bear them *all alone*; a communication of them to others, (if indeed I could have done it,) would only have added to their weight.

I noticed, in a former page, that in the year 1795, I had the most solemn meeting at Deacon Nathan Wood's, that I had ever experienced, which was attended with but small success. I have now to add, that in the lapse of something more than thirty years, I have baptized fifty-seven grand and great-grand-children of the said Deacon Wood; all of whom, except *one*, are now living, as is believed.

May 14, 1830.—Another year of my unprofitable life is gone. Nothing worth recording has taken place with me in the year. Of the fourteen hundred and seventy-one that I have baptized, but very few of them had *the seal of the covenant* put upon them in infancy, and but one or two ever attended *Sunday Schools.*

May 14, 1831.—I am yet living and enjoying good health. The year past I have had a large epistolary correspondence with distant friends ; and have been advertised in the newspapers, through the states, as an infidel and an outcast. May the Lord increase my faith and make me more holy, which will be the best refutation of the libel. From the uttermost parts of the earth have we heard songs ; even glory to the righteous : but I said, my leanness, my leanness. It is now said that there is a great ingathering into the fold of Christ in all the country around ; but according to appearances, I am left behind. Well, let me, like John the Baptist, be full of joy, that others increase while I decrease. I have had my day, and must now give way to the young. The unchangeable God has one class of servants after another to work in his vineyard.

July 11.—Why art thou cast down, O my soul ! The morning cometh as well as the night. Since writing the above note, God has graciously poured out his spirit in Hancock.

Yesterday I baptized ten, which, together with three scattering ones, raises my baptismal list to fourteen hundred and eighty-four.

Baptism does not put away the filth of the flesh ; it is the answer of a good conscience towards God, and only figures out the salvation of the soul ; which is by the resurrection of Jesus Christ from the dead : who died for our sins and rose again for our justification.

July 17.—Baptized....................4
" 24.—Baptized....................2
" 31.—Baptized....................4

One of these four was eighty-two years old. In the winter of 1800, I baptized one who was ninety years of age. The youngest that I ever baptized was nine years old, in 1788. I have ever found water a harmless element, and baptism a pleasing work.

Aug. 22.—Baptized	1	Oct. 16.—Baptized	3
Sept. 4.—Baptized	1	" 23.—Baptized	7
" 18.—Baptized	2	" 30.—Baptized	3
Oct. 2.—Baptized	4	" Making	1,515

Nov. 10.—After living in New-Ashford more than sixteen years, this day I removed into Cheshire again. My age and decays admonish me that the time of my departure is not far distant. When I die, I neither deserve nor desire any funeral pomp. If my friends think best to rear a little monument over my body, "Here lies the body of JOHN LELAND, who labored ——* to promote piety, and vindicate the civil and religious rights of all men," is the sentence which I wish to be engraved upon it.

* It is now (1831) 57 years.

May 14, 1834.—I am this day fourscore years old; have just returned from Chatham, (30 miles off,) where I preached three times, at the opening of a new meeting-house, and this day at Cheshire, to 600 people by estimation. I have now several little preaching tours appointed; but my Maker only knows whether life and strength will be given me to fill them.

It is now sixty years since I began to preach. But ah! how little I have done! and how imperfect that little!

May 15.—Last night fell the largest snow that I ever knew so late in the season.

Many changes in the mechanical, political and religious world have taken place in the course of my life. Most of the changes among us in factories and machines are trans-Atlantic. The steam machines are original Americans. The plea for *religious liberty* has been long and powerful; but it has been left for the United States to acknowledge it a right inherent, and not a favor granted: to exclude religious opinions from the list of objects of legislation. Sunday schools and missionary societies are of long standing; but camp-meetings and protracted meetings (in their present mode of operation) are novel. What changes may hereafter take place, to me is uncertain. None, however, that will change the character of God, destroy the kingdom of Christ, or assure any of heaven without repentance towards God, and faith towards the Lord Jesus.

I have never labored hard to support the CREED of any religious society; but have felt greatly interested that all of them should have their RIGHTS secured to them beyond the reach of tyrants.

Brevity is the soul of wit, the nerve of argument and the bone of good sense, but loquacity palsies attention, massacres time, and darkens counsel.

August 17, 1834.—This day I baptized five, which are the first that I have baptized since I was eighty years old. My baptismal list is now fifteen hundred and twenty-four.

January 28, 1835.—I have been preaching sixty years to convince men that human powers were too degenerate to effect a change of heart by self-exertion; and all the revivals of religion that I have seen have substantially accorded with that sentiment. But now a host of preachers and people have risen up, who ground salvation on the foundation that I have sought to demolish. The world is gone after them, and their converts increase abundantly. How much error there has been in the doctrine and measures that I have advocated, I cannot say; no doubt some, for I claim not infallible inspiration. But I have not yet been convinced of any mistake so radical as to justify a renunciation of what I have believed, and adopt the new measures. I am waiting to see what the event will be; praying for light; open to conviction; willing to retract, and ready to confess when convicted.

July 4, 1835.—It is now fifty-nine years since the independence of the

United States was declared. In this length of time the inhabitants have increased from three to fourteen millions. The changes that have taken place are innumerable. Sixty-five years ago I was old enough to observe the face of things, and see what was going on: had I been in a dead sleep the sixty-five years, and were now to awake, such a change has taken place in the face of the earth, in architecture, in all the arts, in costume and regimen, and in the forms of religion, that I should doubt whether I had awakened in the same world. The love of money, sexual correspondence, diseases and death, however, remain stationary.

FURTHER SKETCHES

OF THE

LIFE OF JOHN LELAND.

It is much to be regretted that Mr. Leland has not left us a more full and minute history of his eventful life. Rich as it was in interesting and instructive incidents, he has compressed the whole in the space of a few pages, remarking, with his characteristic modesty and humility, that "this was all that was worth preserving;" while, had he registered them all with as much minuteness as is usually found in biographies, the narrative must have extended to volumes.

The difficulty of authenticating incidents, as well as the narrow limits to which the further notices must be confined, render it impossible to add more than a brief continuation of his history to the time of his death, together with slight sketches of some important circumstances, which he has deemed proper entirely to omit, or slightly to mention.

The intervening period, between the year 1835, (at which time his narrative closes) and the death of his wife, October 5th, 1837, was spent in Cheshire, Massachusetts, to which place he had removed in 1831. Here he occupied the leisure left him by his ministerial labors, in the care of the little spot of ground he had chosen, where he probably expected to end his days; while Mrs. Leland, who had been emphatically a "helpmate" for him through many years, attended, alone, to the management of his domestic affairs, and gave considerable attention to the cultivation of a small garden. Here they exercised that cordial hospitality for which they were always remarkable, in the entertainment of the many friends who visited them from time to time, setting examples of piety and of the Christian virtues which will not soon be forgotten by those whose good fortune it was to be their neighbors.

The afflictive stroke which at length deprived him of the companion who had trodden with him so great a share of the rough path of life, was rendered doubly painful by the nature of the disease, which left to her friends not even the sad consolation of alleviating the distress they could not remove. A difficulty in her throat, which had been a long time increasing, at length reached such a height, that some months before her death, she could swallow nothing but liquids. The ability to do even this, continued to decrease from day to day, her strength wasting for want of nourishment, till life could no longer retain its feeble hold, and she literally *starved to death.*

A more than passing notice is due to the character of this extraordinary woman. She was not less remarkable in her sphere, than her husband in his. Her eulogy has been written by the pen of inspiration. No one who knew her and was acquainted with her history, can fail to observe that in the whole of the admirable discription of the virtuous woman, (Prov. 31.,) there is scarcely a circumstance named, that did not meet in her, a *literal* fulfilment.

Liberality, and kindness to the needy, formed a prominent feature in her character; none that appealed to her for aid that it was in her power to bestow, were ever sent empty away. This liberalality, joined with that love of independence, which was always a predominant and cherished peculiarity of both Mr. and Mrs. Leland, forbade her ever forgetting an act of kindness shown to herself, or failing to cancel the obligation by bestowing a much greater in return. In strength of mind, firmness of purpose, courage and self possession in danger, fortitude in circumstances of trial and suffering, indeed, in all those qualities that combine to produce energy of character, she has probably had few superiors, in any age; yet, in the exercise of these *manly* virtues, as they are sometimes called, she never acquired that masculine bearing that is too apt to accompany the possession of these qualities in the female sex. Though far removed from the softness and weakness which unfits a woman for enduring hardship, privation, and suffering, she was equally so from the opposite extreme; sustaining as well the delicacy as the dignity of the female sex.

An example of that habitual presence of mind as well as courage, which never failed her in any emergency, is found in the instance in which, like a guardian angel, she saved her husband from the murderer's sword. A similar illustration of these, and other strongly marked traits, is presented in the fact, that when one of her children, a little girl of four years old, had her head crushed under the wheels of a loaded cart which passed directly over it, she sat through the long hours of night with the child in her arms, pressing with her fingers a divided artery, to prevent the effusion of blood which would have caused immediate death. The child, almost miraculously saved, "rose up to call her blessed," and still lives to receive the same tribute of gratitude from a numerous posterity.

Constant, active industry was a distinguishing characteristic of Mrs.

Leland. From its beginning to its close, her life was one of unceasing toil. Even in age, when necessity no longer required such exertion, the habit of active employment had become so much a part of her being, and her natural independence of feeling was so strong, that she could not be prevailed upon to desist from her accustomed round of domestic labors, till her exhausted strength compelled her to relinquish them into other hands. Neither was her industry of that noisy, bustling kind, whose results are usually in inverse proportion to the amount of effort employed. To her might be applied, with peculiar propriety, the encomium bestowed upon another. "She was *always busy*, and *always quiet*."

The guiding hand of Providence was never perhaps more evident, than in directing Elder Leland's choice to so suitable a companion for the stormy times of the revolution. Her training had been emphatically in the school of adversity; and her history is a striking exemplification of the sentiment which one of her own sex has no less truly than beautifully expressed.

> —— Strength is born
> In the deep silence of long suffering hearts;
> Not amidst joy."

At the age of two years she lost a fond and somewhat affluent father, and was driven from a good home by a brutal step-father, when a little more than four years old. Her feet were partly frozen off by exposure; soon after the canker attacked her throat, eat out her palate,* and for a long time her life was despaired of. At length, he, who in the midst of wrath even remembereth mercy, bound up her broken constitution, and gave her grace to see how great things she must suffer for his name's sake. When she recovered her health, she found that others had taken possession of all the property, and nothing lay before her but a life of dependence and servitude. But the God in whom she trusted fortified her heart and strengthened her hands, and when he, to whom her faith was plighted, said, "I go to proclaim a Savour's love in a land overrun with Brittish soldiers and American tories, and trodden down by a dominant established clergy, she replied like Rebecca, "*I will go*." Her faith was firm in him who had said, "I will never leave thee nor forsake thee."

The "poor man's blessings" were his. She had a numerous family, but scanty means, and through the revolution which had begun when she married, her trials were many and severe. Often was she left alone with her little ones, far from neighbors, her husband gone, with very little prospect of pecuniary reward, while runaway blacks who had neither courage to join the British army, nor patriotism to join the American, were horded together around her for plunder and sometimes murder. Many a

* In consequence of this misfortune, her speech was so much impaired, that through life it was difficult for persons not well acquainted with her, to understand her.

long hour she plied her needle by moonlight, to prepare clothing for her little ones, fearful lest the ray of a lamp from her window might attract a bloody foe. Often, too, the famished soldier came to her for food and shelter through the stormy night. Her God had said, "feed the hungry," and she obeyed; but when she had given till naught was left, the sleepless hours were spent in watchfulness and prayer—for oh! if the assassin's knife should be concealed beneath the soldier's garb, she could not fly and leave her little ones behind. How often she prayed that God would preserve the children he had graciously given, and all were preserved to lament the best of mothers.

This sketch, given by one of her family, who had often heard from her own lips, the story of those "troublous times," may serve to give some idea of the strength of character and depth of piety which sustained her in the midst of trials such as few women are called to endure.

The following circumstance is introduced as illustrating her capability of endurance, not only of physical, but of mental suffering. Incredible as it may seem, and inexplicable as it certainly is, the *fact* itself is unquestionable, as it rests on the testimony of Elder Leland himself.

One afternoon, they were startled by a sound somewhat similar to that made by a large fly when suddenly confined, apparently proceeding from within the wall of the house. After an unsuccessful effort to discover the cause, he left home and was absent six weeks without thinking again of the circumstance. On the evening of his return, however, he was reminded of it by a groan so sudden and piercing as to make him start up in amazement; his surprise was not lessened, when, upon inquiry he learned that the same had been heard every night of his absence, recurring each night a few minutes later than the preceding, and continuing about ten minutes at a time. It continued to be heard in the same manner, eight months, becoming at every return louder and more terrible. As this was at the period (spoken of in the autobiography) of an extensive revival in York and the adjacent counties, he was, consequently, absent a considerable part of the time, and Mrs. Leland was left alone with two little children, the eldest less than three years old, who, when the sound began to be heard, would cling around her in terror, exclaiming "the groaner has come." As often as any examination was made of the spot whence the noise seemed to issue, with the view of discovering whether it proceeded from some animal confined within the wall, it removed to another place, and thus defied all attempts at investigation. Wearied at length by unsuccessful efforts to discover a natural cause, Elder Leland resolved to try the effect of prayer; accordingly, when in the darkness of midnight, the dreadful moanings again commenced, he betook himself to the all-conquering weapon. Said he, in relating it to a friend, "if ever I prayed in my life, it was then." He prayed, that if it was a messenger of good, he might be emboldened to speak to it, and learn its errand, but if it was a spirit of evil, that it might be commanded to depart, and suffered to trouble them no more. During the prayer, the sound grew louder and more terrific, till at the conclusion, in a piercing shriek it departed, and never returned again. Those who have heard Elder Leland relate the incident, describe the sound he made in imitation of it, as unearthly and frightful to the last degree. It may be left to the imagination of the reader to picture to itself the amount and intensity of mental suffering which this event alone must have produced.

It has been remarked of Mrs. Leland, that her faith was strong. Indeed, on some occasions, it seemed to rest on grounds that partook of the character of revelations. An instance of this kind occurred in the storm by which they were overtaken on their passage from Virginia to New England, in 1791. After twelve hours of incessant watching and agonizing prayer, expecting momentarily to go to the bottom, she appeared to sink into a slumber; but presently turning to her husband, she exclaimed, "*We shall not be lost.*" She had received this assurance from a figure in white which seemed to stand before her, measuring off piece after piece of a long white cord, and which said to her, "*The vessel cannot sink, I have undergirded it.*"

In her last illness, she exhibited the utmost patience and resignation under all her sufferings. She spoke with great warmth and animation of the Divine goodness to her, and especially found cause of thankfulness in the circumstance, that for many weeks before her death, she did not feel the sensation of hunger. She had very humiliating views of herself; and desires proportionably great to exalt and magnify the riches of that grace which had proved sufficient in every scene of trial hitherto, and which she trusted would not fail her in the last; and truly it did not; for when the hour of release arrived, so gently did the hand of death loosen the bonds of her captivity, that not a groan was heard by those who stood around her bed, and a long life of eminent usefulness was crownd by a death of "perfect peace."

On the 12th October, 1837, a few days after the death of his wife, Elder Leland removed to the house of his son-in-law, Mr. James Greene, in Lanesborough, where he resided most of the time until his death. Thence he made frequent preaching excursions to the neighboring towns, and sometimes took journeys of considerable length. In the summer of 1838, he visited Utica and its vicinity, (the residence of his eldest son,) and was absent several weeks. The following letter, to his daughter, was written during his absence.

August 8, 1838.

* * I am now at Deerfield, and have made it a call-by home for about ten days past. The crops of the earth, and the heat of the air, are

great in all places where I have been. I have calls enough to preach, and have hitherto had strength to answer those calls, though in a poor, imperfect manner. My health and appetite are as good as common. All is uncertain when, or whether ever I shall return to Berkshire again. My life is not in my own hands, but I commit it, and all that I have, to the care of that Gracious Being who has fed and preserved me through an unprofitable life. I hope you will indulge no unnecessary anxiety about me; for I deserve but small favors from men, and less from the Creator. Farewell, my Fanny. Shun all the errors you have seen in me: be faithful unto death, and you will receive a crown of life.

JOHN LELAND.

His health, after his return, was such as for some days seriously to alarm his friends. He, however, soon recovered.

In the fall of 1839, his daughter, with whom he resided, was attacked by an illness, which, after two years and a half of intense suffering, released her from the world and its cares; not, however, till she had seen her father, whose anxious solicitude in her behalf she fully reciprocated, removed to a better world. During the winter of 1840–41, he thought best, in consideration of her health, and some other circumstances, to remove, for a few weeks, to the house of Mr. Chapman, in Cheshire. He continued to "do the work of an evangelist;" and at the time of his last call at his daughter's, was on his way to North Adams, where he was soon to end his days.

On the evening of the 8th January, he preached, for the last time, to the people of that village. It is matter of regret, that this discourse, interesting not only in itself, but especially so from the circumstances of its delivery, cannot be presented entire to the public. But, as it is well known that he never wrote even the heads of his sermons, the memories of his hearers are the only source from which we can draw, for even these. A friend has kindly furnished a sketch from recollection, which is here subjoined.

"The text was from the 20th and 27th verses of the 2d chapter of the First Epistle of John.—'But ye have an unction from the Holy One, and ye know all things. But the annointing which ye have received of him, abideth in you; and you need not that any man teach you; but as the same anointing teacheth you of all things, and is truth, and is no lie, and even as it hath taught you, ye shall abide in him.'

"He first spoke of the nature and character of the Holy Spirit, the unction referred to, from whence it came, &c., and remarked that the same that is sometimes compared to fire and water, is here likened to oil. He spoke of the properties of oil; its being used to lubricate the wheels of machinery; and when ignited, to give light and heat; and when applied to an abraded surface, or painful limb, to mitigate pain and suffering, and to heal the injury or wound; in all which uses it resembled the unction spoken of in the text. True Christians are anointed ones; anointed with gifts and spiritual endowments by the Spirit of Grace which comes from the Holy One, enlightening and strengthening the eyes of the understanding, and enabling those who receive it, to '*know all things*' concerning Christ and his religion. Those who know the truth, are by it prepared to discern what is contrary thereto. It will preserve those in whom it abides, and teaches them to abide in Christ. He spoke of the resurection—of the new birth—said no one could experience it while believing in the doctrine of universal salvation.* He could extend hope and charity to those who believed that sentiment, after a change of heart, but not before.

"It is pleasant and mournful to my soul, at this moment, to recollect with what benignity of countenance he pronounced his last benediction."

After the services were closed, he went to the house of Mr. Darling. A number of friends calling, he conversed freely and cheerfully, and attended prayers before retiring to bed, which he did at a rather late hour. An unusual noise being soon after heard in his chamber, Mr. D. went immediately to the room, where he found him prostrate on the floor. Feeling unwell, and a disposition to vomit, he had attempted to rise, and, as he said, "his limbs would not obey him." He was placed in bed, and means used to restore warmth to his stiffened limbs. They were partially successful, and he obtained a little rest. He had chills, however, through the night, followed by heat and thirst. He arose and dressed himself in the morning; but, being very feeble, a medical friend in the village was called in. He was pronounced very ill; and, when asked whether he thought he should recover, said "*he had not the token.*" In his former illnesses, though he had been, to human appearance, on the very verge of the grave, he had received some token which impressed him with the conviction that he should recover. But as, in this instance, he gained no such evidence, he seemed to think it useless to make much effort for his recovery. "In this," says the physician who attended him, "I was not much disappointed, having known before that he had little confidence in medicine, unless well mixed with prayer. He freely consented, however, to use whatever remedies I thought best to administer. Not wishing to burthen his mind with even the small quantity of medicine I thought proper to give him, I directed the watchers, during the night, to mingle it with his drinks. This plan succeeded only until the next morning, when he said, 'take it away, and give me some *clean water*.' On the morning of the 10th, he was ap-

* He has been heard to express the same opinion on other occasions, drawing his conclusions from the fact, that persons, in being made partakers of the grace of life, are brought to view themselves utterly lost without that grace—a conviction which they cannot feel, while they imagine themselves in no danger of receiving the "wages of sin, which is death."

parently better—rather talkative—related a story, or drew a comparison at every change in the conversation. At evening he was worse. He complained that he could neither stop thinking, nor direct his thoughts. His cough was becoming harder, and his breathing more laborious. He spoke with difficulty—said his tongue would not obey him. He had now most of the distinguishing symptoms of *peripneumonia notha.*

"11th. In the morning, easier—at evening, worse than the preceding. He had so little command of his tongue, that it was difficult to understand him. I continued the use of some medicine, though I now despaired of his recovery. On the morning of the 12th, we thought him somewhat better. He conversed pleasantly, and his eyes sparkled with much of that brilliancy of intellect which they were accustomed to exhibit when in health. In the evening, he was again worse; and while I was sitting by his bed, supposing him asleep, he said, (addressing himself,) 'well, I have nothing more to do, but die.'

"13th. Failing. He suffered apparently little, exeept his laborious breathing. Indeed, during his sickness, there was but a solitary instance in which he mentioned having any pain—it was in his left side, and continued but a few minutes. His dissolution was now almost hourly expected.

"On the 14th, Mr. and Mrs. Chapman, with whom he had been boarding in Cheshire, visited him. He seemed much gratified, and, to our surprise, immediately began to make arrangements to return with them. In this, a little aberration of mind was apparent. With some assistance he clothed himself, called for his satchel, into which he put his Bible, then for his bills for board and medical attendance, all which being adjusted, he expressed a desire to set out for home. He was, however, prevailed on to lie down and rest a while after the fatigue he had undergone, and was assisted to the bed, from which I do not recollect that he ever again rose."

To those members of his family who could not be with him, it was a consoling reflection, even in the midst of their grief, that the hand of Providence had cast him into a family of kind friends, where nothing conducive to his comfort or recovery, would be left untried. One daughter alone was permitted the privilege of watching his pillow of sickness, and standing by his dying couch. Speaking of some of his exercises, and of the closing scene, she thus remarks:—"In the beginning of his sickness he seemed conscious of his approaching dissolution—said he was ready when called, and calmly gave orders respecting his funeral. The day on which he died, he said to his physician—'Yesterday, doctor, a dark cloud came over—I did not know but I should fail in my expectations above.' Choked with the bitter remembrance, he paused, but soon added—'*It's not so to-day.*'

"His thoughts would frequently run back to her who had so often bent over his wasting form in previous sicknesses, and he would speak of the good things she used to do for him.

"Early in the evening, a young preacher (Rev. Mr. Alden) came in, and said to him—'Well, Father Leland, we are going to hold a prayer-meeting this evening. Have you any advice to give?' 'If you feel it in your *hearts*, I am glad. *Forms are nothing.*' These were nearly his last words; but his arm was not paralyzed, neither was his heart chilled. With his own hand he gave his own tobacco to his friends present, and indicated by signs that they should smoke. About 11 o'clock, he beckoned me to him, and tried to say 'go to bed.' I found his limbs were stiffening, and his senses lulling, and anxious to be near him till all was over, I hesitated, but finally, at the the solicitation of one of the watchers, left the room. The man soon followed, and said, 'you had better come back.' I came. Not a finger had moved. His spirit had taken rest in the bosom of its God."

Thus died John Leland—a man eminent above many for piety and usefulness, whose name is connected with all that is pure in patriotism, lovely in the social and domestic virtues, philanthropic in feeling and action, arduous, disinterested, and self-denying in the labors of the ministerial calling; one whose place in society, in the church, and in the ranks of the ministry, will not soon be filled—in the hearts of those who knew him—never.

He died, as he had lived, a witness for the truth, testifying, with his last breath, the value of that religion, and that only, which has its seat in the *heart*. His life had been unostentatious; his aspirations after worldly honors, ever low and feeble; his humility and sense of dependence on God, deep-felt and abiding—and thus he died. "Being with him in his last illness," (Mr. Alden remarks in his funeral sermon,) "more or less every day, I think I may say, I never saw a Christian feel more deeply his own unworthiness. 'Bury me,' said he, 'in an humble manner. I want no encomiums; I deserve none. I feel myself a poor, miserable sinner, and Christ is my only hope.' Being asked, very near his end, what were his views of the future, he exclaimed, with both hands extended upward, and a smile I can never forget, 'My prospects of heaven are clear.' He seemed already to feel the everlasting rest laying its sweet influences over his soul, and bearing it up, taking away the sting of death."

His remains were conveyed to Cheshire for interment, where, on the 17th, a funeral discourse was pronounced over them by Rev. John Alden, from Rev. 14th and 13th.* The weather was extremely unpropitious, yet

* This discourse is already before the public, which circumstance, together with our limited space, will sufficiently account for the omission of any further extracts.

the concourse, assembled from that and the adjacent towns, was large, and many a tearful eye testified that no common occasion had called them together. Though but one child, "according to the flesh," was permitted to follow his relics to the grave, yet many, from the youth to the gray-haired man, who mingled their tears over his coffin, felt that they were gazing for the last time upon the countenance of a beloved "father in the Lord."

He was laid beside his wife, and a simple obelisk of blue marble, commemorative of both, marks their common resting-place. On its west side is inscribed the epitaph prepared by himself some years before his death: "Here lies the body of the Rev. JOHN LELAND, of Cheshire, who labored 67 years to promote piety and vindicate the civil and religious rights of all men. He died January, 14, 1841, aged 86 years and 8 months." On the north side is the following: "Sarah, consort of Rev. John Leland. She died October 5, 1837, aged 84 years." On the south: "This monument was erected by the children of the deceased, to point out the resting-place of their revered parents."

Having followed him to the end of his course, it remains for us to glance, in a brief retrospect, at some circumstances which he has omitted. It is doubtless the case that many of these, could they be collected, and their authenticity proved, would add greatly to the interest of the narrative; but the fact, that it has been found impossible to obtain them, will sufficiently account for the omission of any that may be deemed important.

To understand and appreciate the character of Elder Leland, it is only necessary to read his writings, and to trace the operation of the principles and sentiments they contain, in the actions of his life. That his writings were a transcript of his mind and heart, none will deny, who knew him. The candor and openness with which he ever avowed his sentiments, even when they subjected him to reproach and censure, are well known. Conversing with a friend on one occasion, he remarked—"Though I have secrets which I would not reveal to you, or any one else, I have not a *religious* secret in the world." The same frankness marked the expression of his political opinions. That his independence of mind aided materially in supporting this character, will be evident when we consider how many individuals there are who *dare not* be honest—who have not the moral courage to sustain them in a course which they feel to be right, and in the expression of sentiments which they inwardly approve. A remark of Elder Leland, on this subject, is suggested by these reflections. "Though in a religious point of view," said he, "self-dependence (by which he meant the opposite of the Christian's trust in God) is most pernicious and fatal in its tendency, yet, in worldly matters, it is one of the best qualities a man can possess."

Through a long life, Elder Leland sustained, with uniform consistency, the two-fold character of the *Patriot* and the *Christian*. For his religious creed he acknowledged no directory but the Bible. He loved the pure, unadulterated word of truth; and, as a minister of that word, zealous and faithful, he preached it, as far as he was able, unmixed with the doctrines and commandments of men, "not for filthy lucre, but of a ready mind." He was clear in exposition, happy in illustration, often powerful and eloquent in appeals to the conscience and heart. He insisted, in absolute and unqualified terms, on the great fundamental truths of the gospel, the necessity of regeneration, faith and repentance; but, on points not essential to salvation, though his opinions were no less firmly established, and he never shrunk from advocating them on proper occasions, yet he did not censure or denounce those who differed from him, nor exclude from fellowship, as Christians, any who gave evidencc of a gracious change, whatever might be their peculiar doctrinal views. He never engaged in controversy; and when any of his published opinions were disputed, or commented upon, as was sometimes the case, with severity, he preferred to "let the matter rest a little, and then give another thrust," as he expressed it, to the waste of time, repetitions, and tediousness of reviews and replies.

His political creed was based upon those "sufficient truths" of equality, and of inherent and inalienable rights, recognised by the master spirits of the revolution as the principles for the support of which they pledged "their lives, their fortunes, and their sacred honor." As a politician, he was above the influence of any but sincere and patriotic motives. He was a statesman, rather than a politician. He studied the fundamental principles of government, and drew his conclusions directly from them, without any intervening medium of self or party interest. He judged men by their measures, and measures by their adaptedness to secure that result which he deemed the legitimate object of government—the *greatest good* of the *greatest number*. In his attachment to the administrations of Jefferson, Madison, Jackson and Van Buren, he felt that he was contending for the same principles of democracy that nerved the arms and strengthened the hearts of the whigs of '76. His sentiments, on particular measures, it is unnecessary to comment upon, as they are clearly expressed in his writings. His feelings on the subject of slavery may be gathered from the fact that, during his fourteen years' residence in Virginia he never owned a slave, as well as from his remarks in in the Virginia Chronicle, and from the resolution offered by him, when a member of the Baptist General Committee, and passed by them, in 1789, in the following words:—

"RESOLVED—That slavery is a violent deprivation of the rights of nature, and inconstent with a republican government; and we, therefore, recommend it to our brethren, to make use of every *legal* measure to extirpate this horrid evil from the land, and pray Almighty God that our honorable legislature may have it in their power to proclaim the great Jubilee, consistent with the principles of good policy."

His late writings on this subject, though expressing disapprobation of the measures of abolitionists, we apprehend, will not be found, upon examination, materially different in sentiment. In all, while he recognizes the supremacy of law, he pleads for individual right.

The great object, (next in importance to his mission as a preacher of Christ,) for which he seems to have been raised up by a special Providence, was to promote the establishment of religious liberty in the United States. His efforts, perhaps, contributed as much as those of any other man, to the overthrow of ecclesiastical tyranny in Virginia, the state of his adoption, and exerted a beneficial influence, though less successful, towards the promotion of the same end in that of his nativity. In the former, in the years 1786–7–8, we find his name in the doings of the Baptist General Committee, with which he stood connected, as messenger to the General Assembly, appointed to draft and present memorials respecting the *Incorporating* act, the application of the *glebe lands* to public use, etc. Though the cause of religious freedom was the common cause of all dissenters, yet the Baptists, as a sect, took the lead in those active, energetic, and persevering measures, which at length pervailed in its establishment. Many individuals of other denominations took an active part, and aided materially in bringing about the glorious result;* nay, that even many of the more conscientious and patriotic among the members of the established church, made praiseworthy exertions in its favor, is a fact too honorable to themselves, and to the state that produced them, to be passed unnoticed. Enrolled among the ardent champions of religious liberty, are the names of Virginia's most illustrious sons—of Washington, Henry, Jefferson, Madison. To particularize, in regard to the efforts made, and the good accomplished by each, is unnecessary in this place; the following Address† and Reply, which are inserted entire, will serve to exhibit the enlarged views and the unselfish spirit of the patriots of that day, as well as the harmony, one might almost say identity, of sentiment that prevailed among them.

Address of the Committee of the United Baptist Churches of Virginia, assembled in the city of Richmond, 8th August, 1789, to the President of the United States of America.

SIR:—Among the many shouts of congratulation that you receive from cities, societies, states, and the whole world, we wish to take an active part in the universal chorus, in expressing our great satisfaction in your appointment to the first office in the nation. When America, on a former occasion, was reduced to the necessity of appealing to arms, to defend her natural and civil rights, a Washington was found fully adequate to the ex-

* See quotation from the speech of a Presbyterian, Vol. —, page —.

† Drafted by Elder Leland.

igencies of the dangerous attempt; who, by the philanthropy of his heart, and the prudence of his head, led forth her untutored troops into the field of battle, and by the skilfulness of his hands, baffled the projects of the insulting foe, and pointed out the road to independence, even at a time when the energy of the cabinet was not sufficient to bring into action the natural aid of the confederation, from its respective sources.

The grand object being obtained, the independence of the States acknowledged; free from ambititon, devoid of sanguine thirst of blood, our hero returned, with those he commanded, and laid down the sword at the feet of those who gave it him. Such an example to the world is new.' Like other nations, we experience that it requires as great valor and wisdom to make an advantage of a conquest, as to gain one.

The want of efficacy in the confederation, the redundancy of laws, and their partial administration in the States, called aloud for a new arrangement of our systems. The wisdom of the States, for that purpose, was collected in a grand convention—over which, you, sir, had the honor to preside. A national government, in all its parts, was recommended, as the only preservation of the Union, which plan of government is now in actual operation.

When the Constitution first made its appearance in Virginia, we, as a society, had unusual strugglings of mind, fearing that the liberty of conscience, dearer to us than property or life, was not sufficiently secured. Perhaps our jealousies were heightened, by the usage we received in Virginia, under the regal government, when mobs, fines, bonds and prisons were our frequent repast.

Convinced, on the one hand, that without an effective National Government, the States would fall into disunion and all the consequent evils; and, on the other hand, fearing that we should be accessary to some religious oppression, should any one society in the Union preponderate over the rest; yet, amidst all these inquietudes of mind, our consolation arose from this consideration,—the plan must be good, for it has the signature of a tried, trusty friend, and if religious liberty is rather insecure in the Constitution, 'the Administration will certainly prevent all oppression, for a WASHINGTON will preside.' According to our wishes, the unanimous voice of the Union has called you, sir, from your beloved retreat, to launch forth again into the faithless seas of human affairs, to guide the helm of the States. May that Divine munificence, which covered your head in battle, make you a yet greater blessing to your admiring country in time of peace. Should the horrid evils that have been so pestiferous in Asia and Europe, faction, ambition, war, perfidy, fraud, and persecution for conscience sake, ever approach the borders of our happy nation, may the name and administration of our beloved President, like the radiant source of day, scatter all those dark clouds from the American hemisphere.

And while we speak freely the language of our hearts, we are satisfied that we express the sentiments of our brethren, whom we represent. The very name of Washington is music in our ears; and although the great evil in the States is the want of mutual confidence between rulers and people, yet we have all the utmost confidence in the President of the States; and it is our fervent prayer to Almighty God, that the federal government, and the governments of the respective States, without rivalship, may so co-operate together, as to make the numerous people over whom you preside, the happiest nation on earth, and you, sir, the happiest man, in seeing the people, whom, by the smiles of Providence, you saved from vassalage by your valor, and made wise by your maxims, sitting securely under their vines and fig-trees, enjoying the perfection of human felicity. May God long preserve your life and health for a blessing to the world in general, and the United States in particular; and, when, like the sun, you have finished your course of great and unparalleled services, and go the way of all the earth, may the Divine Being who will reward every man according to his works, grant unto you a glorious admission into his everlasting kingdom, through Jesus Christ. This, sir, is the prayer of your happy admirers.

By order of the Committee,

SAMUEL HARRISS, Chairman.

Reuben Ford, Clerk.

To the General Committee, representing the United Baptist Churches in Virginia.

Gentlemen,—I request that you will accept my best acknowledgments for your congratulation on my appointment to the first office in the nation. The kind manner in which you mention my past conduct, equally claims theexpression of my gratitude.

After we had, by the smiles of Divine Providence on our exertions, obtained the object for which we contended, I retired, at the conclusion of the war, with an idea, that my country could have no farther occasion for my services, and with the intention of never entering again into public life. But when the exigencies of my country seemed to require me once more to engage in public affairs, an honest conviction of duty superseded my former resolution, and became my apology for deviating from the happy plan which I had adopted.

If I could have entertained the slightest apprehension that the Constitution framed by the Convention where I had the honor to preside, might possibly endanger the religious rights of any ecclesiastical society, certainly I would never have placed my signature to it; and if I could now conceive that the general government might even be so administered, as to render the liberty of conscience insecure, I beg you will be persuaded, that no one would be more zealous than myself, to establish effectual barriers against the horrors of spiritual tyranny, and every species of religious persecution. For you, doubtless, remember, I have often expressed my sentiments, that any man, conducting himself as a good citizen, and being accountable to God alone for his religious opinions, ought to be protected in worshiping the Deity according to the dictates of his own conscience.

While I recollect with satisfaction, that the religious society of which you are members, have been, throughout America, uniformly, and almost unanimously the firm friends to civil liberty, and the persevering promoters of our glorious revolution ; I cannot hesitate to believe, that they will be the faithful supporters of a free, yet efficient general government. Under this pleasing expectation, I rejoice to assure them, that they may rely upon my best wishes and endeavors to advance their prosperity.

In the meantime, be assured, gentlemen, that I entertain a proper sense of your fervent supplications to God for my temporal and eternal happiness. I am, gentlemen, your most obedient servant,

GEORGE WASHINGTON.

Elder Leland's removal to New-England took place in 1791.* As soon as he landed again on its shores, he commenced anew the warfare against religious intolerance, and the defence of the cause that had so signally triumphed in Virginia. During his stay in New London, he published his "Rights of Conscience Inalienable," and afterwards, from time to time, other works of the same character; some of which will be found in these volumes, and others it has been impossible to obtain.

Our limits do not allow us to enter upon the history and progress of religious liberty in Massachusetts. This may be found elsewhere. It had struggled for existence, and found some advocates from the first settlement of the state, but was kept constantly shackled by certificate laws, and other expedients of ecclesiastical tyranny. At length, in the beginning of 1811, a decision by Judge Parsons, that no society, not incorporated by law, could claim even the pitiful privilege of drawing back money, awakened the fears of the dissenters, and a circular Address, accompanied by a petition to the legislature, praying for a revision of the laws respecting public worship, was circulated through the state. At the solicitation of the people of Cheshire, Mr. Leland accepted a seat in the legislature, for the special purpose of aiding the measures petitioned for. His speech, delivered during the debate on the subject, may be found in another part of this work.

* It may be proper to mention, in this place, that while a member of the General Committee, he was appointed one of a committee to collect materials for a history of the Baptists in Virginia; and had made considerable progress towards it, when his removal caused him to relinquish the trust into other hands.

A law was finally passed that gave some relief, but not complete satisfaction. The "stump" of the tree of ecclesiastical oppression, so carefully preserved "with a band of iron and brass," continued, therefore, to furnish a subject for his animadversion, in various essays, addresses, etc., and he improved such opportunities as were offered him, as a matter of duty, and in fulfilment of the public pledge he had given, that "as long as he could speak with his tongue, wield a pen, or heave a cry to heaven, whenever the rights of men, the liberty of conscience, or the good of his country were invaded by fraud or force, his feeble efforts should not lie dormant." His letters, etc., on the Sunday Mail question, have the same bearing, and breathe the same spirit. To neutralize the effect of these, and to destroy the confidence reposed in him, reports were industriously circulated in some newspapers, that "he had renounced the Christian faith, and the sacrament of the Lord's Supper, and been excommunicated from the church." The reader is requested to turn to his reply to a letter from Rev. O. B. Brown, on this subject, where he will find a sufficient refutation of this calumny. To show its probable foundation, however, it will be necessary to return to the period of his removal to Cheshire, and give a connected narrative of a series of events, which misrepresentation and falsehood have so distorted to his prejudice, as to render a true statement of them an act of indispensable justice to his memory. As the professed object of this work is to exhibit fully his character and sentiments, facts which have so important a bearing upon that object, cannot, with propriety, be withheld.

Soon after Elder Leland came to reside in Berkshire, the town of Cheshire was organized. There was, at that time, within its bounds, a large and flourishing church, called New Providence Grant, whose pastor was Elder Werden. There was also, another, called the Six Principle Church, making the laying on of hands a pre-requisite to communion. The church, with which Elder Leland united, and of which he continued a member until his death, had dissented from the Six Principle Church, and contained about seventy members. This was usually called the Second Baptist Church.

Considerable additions were soon made, and in 1793, it was determined to build a meeting-house. Elder Leland drafted a Constitution which was unanimously adopted, and the house was built during the succeeding year. The Constitution reserved the control of the pulpit to the Baptist church, giving any proprietor, not a member, the liberty of inviting any man, "in character," to occupy it his pastorial part of the time, and if, at any time, the church should fall away, or be unable to support a meeting, or a minister, it secured the property to the original proprietors, and their heirs at law.

The inhabitants of Cheshire, were, at that time, principally thriving farmers, who had removed there when the country was yet a wilderness, and by untiring industry had cleared their lands, built comfortable houses, school-houses, etc., and were training up large families of very intelligent children. The wealthier portion of the church seemed ever ready to help the poor, and encourage the weak. Their records furnish numerous instances of their watchfulness and promptness in providing for the wants of their needy members.

This church, with all others in Berkshire, belonged to the Shaftsbury Association; a very respectable body, but containing a number of talented men, who were every way aristocratic, in their views of the powers of Associations over churches, and of churches over their respective members. As Elder Leland, and his brethren in Virginia, had just thrown off the yoke of the established clergy, and built up their institutions upon the most liberal plan, it will not be thought strange if his feelings and views were not relished by the more narrow-minded, and his increasing popularity looked upon with other than friendly feelings.

Revivals of religion in Cheshire, and the adjacent towns, for some time kept up large congregations in their new meeting-houses, and scarcely a covenant-day passed, without the addition of one or more to their number. Under date of December, 1795, the following entry is found upon the records: "Elder Leland appears to stand in the power and demonstration of the spirit of God, in the administration of the word and ordinances of the gospel." But when religion began to decline, and a worldly spirit crept in, he was exceedingly pained to see leading members of the church, (of which he then had the care,) indulging in harsh language towards each other; yet ever ready to give a word of exhortation, to draw the reins of discipline closely with their neighbors, and virtually to say, by coming to the communion, "we are *one*." This became very trying to his feelings, and as he had never enjoyed the Lord's supper, as he had preaching and baptizing, he felt no little embarrassment in constantly administering it under such circumstances. But as these members were respectable, stood high in church and society, were warm friends to him, and not complained of by others, he thought it more prudent to smother his feelings, and seeing his own imperfections to be great, to exercise forbearance towards the faults of others.

At length, however, he manifested his feelings to the church, who, being unable to remove them, consented, according to his request, to "have patience to wait on him a little longer." It is not certain at what time he left the pastoral charge, but it is probable he had not filled that office for some time previous to 1799, when he was requested to resume it, but declined. He spent considerable portions of every year in travelling and preaching from place to place, but when at home, (as may be seen by reference to the auto-biography,) he was never idle.

In August, 1799, the peaceful work of grace, called, by way of eminence, "the great Reformation," commenced in Cheshire, and its vicinity.

His labors and successes during that interesting season, are recorded by his own hand. One of the members of the church, who had, during the ingathering, not only absented himself from public worship, and church-meetings, but "spoken lightly of the work of God among the people," professed to be aggrieved that Elder Leland should not break bread to the church, "let the embarrassments be what they might in his own mind," and also found fault with the church "for not forbidding him to pray and preach, inasmuch as he had neglected a known precept." The church sustained Elder Leland in his course, and contended that they had no right to forbid him to pray and preach, "inasmuch as he had been guilty of no immoral conduct." After a series of unsuccessful efforts to convince the refractory member of his errors, and to bring him back to duty, the church withdrew from him the hand of fellowship.

Thus it appears, that the church both knew and respected his feelings, and did not feel disposed to urge him forward in the performance of that which he could not look upon as duty, nor to impute to him the omission, as a crime; and it is believed, that, when he removed to Dutchess county, he left no enemies in Cheshire.

Not long after his removal, Elder Lemuel Covell, a young, talented, and highly esteemed minister, passing through Cheshire, preached so much to the edification of the church, that they immediately appointed a committee to visit him, with a view to obtain his services as pastor. They found him rather disposed to come; but as he had been unfortunate in his outward concerns, had become involved, and the church at Pittstown had paid the demands against him, (amounting to nearly seven hundred dollars,) on the condition, "that he should never leave them to become the pastor of any other people, unless that people would refund the money to them; an obstacle was presented apparently difficult to be overcome. The trial which followed, would, but for its consequences, have found no place in these pages.

The committee, who waited on Mr. Covell, were disposed to engage him, but on submitting it to the church, a number of the members in good standing, and somewhat wealthy, objected, and by their arguments, nearly dissuaded others. The committee took the alarm—insisted strongly upon the *powers of the church*—and, though their reasoning did not convince, their perseverance conquered—and perhaps it will not be uncharitable to say, that Elder Covell's debts were paid, and his family removed to Cheshire, rather in a spirit of defiance. The terms of settlement were the same as at Pittstown, with the additional promise, that if the church failed in affording him a decent maintenance, the seven hundred dollars were not to be refunded, though he should leave the place.

About this time, a mortgage being closed on the farm where Elder Lelad resided, his friends in Cheshire gave him a pressing invitation to come and reside with them; to preach whenever he felt disposed, and duty seemed to call him. Having children residing there, and being still a member of the church, he complied with the solicitation. He and Mr. Covell had always been warm friends, and their intimacy continued uninterrupted till the lamented death of the latter, while on a mission to Canada, October 19, 1806, less than six months from the time of his removal to Cheshire.

Mr. Covell viewed the proceedings of the church in the same light with the majority of the people of Cheshire. In a conversation with Elder Leland, he said, "had I foreseen the troubles that would ensue in consequence of my coming here, I would sooner have begged my bread from door to door."

The shock produced by Mr. Covell's death, was succeeded by a calmness, which lasted a considerable time, and gave the friends of peace, reason to hope that the breach in the church would soon be healed. Both church and society seemed seriously to regret the hurrying spirit that had set them at variance. Not so with a few leaders of the opposite party. "Recantation or excommunication," were their terms, and strange as it may seem, acquainted as they were with Elder Leland, they applied to him for help to carry out their plans. Owing no ill will to either party, his answer was such as might have been anticipated. He thought a little forbearance, on their part, might have saved all the trouble, and hinted, that by some recantation from them, the church might still be kept together.

Disappointed in their favorite plans, smarting under the loss of property, their fond hopes in the grave, they were not a little chagrined at receiving a slight rebuke where they had expected much assistance. They did not however proceed immediately to extremities, but, after conversing with members of the Shaftsbury Association, unfriendly in their views to Elder Leland, (of whom mention has already been made,) they determined to apply to him as friends, and pretending ignorance on the subject, to draw from him an expression of his views respecting church discipline, communion, etc.* He freely made a statement, and at their request committed it to writing. This paper has long been before the religious world, but as there may be many, who have never seen it, and who have but vague and indefinite, if not incorrect ideas of what Elder Leland's views were, a copy of it is here subjoined, taken from the original on file:

1. I have no doubt about the necessity of internal religion, nor of the great advantage of social worship, to preach, pray, and praise.

2. Some doubts have ever been in my mind, whether the advantage of what is called *church order*, more than compensates for the disadvantages. It is uppermost in my mind, however, that good church order is scriptural.

3. I lodge no complaint against communing with bread and wine, but

* For the sake of brevity, details are omitted, and only a sketch of the important facts given.

for myself, for more than thirty years experiment, I have had no evidence that the bread and wine ever assisted my faith to discern the Lord's body. I have never felt guilty for not communing, but often for doing it. I have known no instance that God evidently blessed the ordinance for the conversion of sinners, which often attends preaching, praying, singing and baptizing.

4. Putting all together, the best conclusion that I can form, is, that church labor and breaking bread is what the Lord does not place on me, any more than he did baptizing on Paul.

5. If the church can bear with me, while I possess these feelings, and let me do what I have faith and confidence in, (which will be but a little while, for there is nothing left but a stump,) I shall be glad. Whenever I think I can do good, or get good, I will attend church-meeting. and whenever the doubts of my mind are removed, I will commune.

6. If the church cannot bear thus with me, I wish them to give me a letter of dismission—such a letter as they can.

7. If such a letter cannot be given, consistently with the order and dignity of the church, I suppose excommunication must follow of course.

JOHN LELAND.

Cheshire, August 22, 1811.

This is a compendium of what I stated last church-meeting, and is here written on your request. Let no man follow me where I do not follow Christ. J. L.

It will probably appear evident to all, that more of the cunning of the serpent than of the harmlessness of the dove was displayed in this manœuvre of false friends. Most of the church agreed to forbear according to his request. A motion (made at the same meeting) to call a council, was negatived. A similar attempt at a subsequent meeting also failed.

They therefore called an *ex parte* council; but being defeated in this attempt, by the refusal of the church to attend, etc., they applied to the Association for aid. A committe of fifteen were appointed, who came and made an effort to convince the people of their error, in holding in fellowship a man who entertained sentiments so heretical. The committee met with no better success than the council.

Previous to the sitting of the committee, Elder Hull, of Berlin, had endeavored to mediate a peace between the parties, and a vote had been passed mutually "to bury all passed difficulties, never again to call them up." As subsequent events showed this to be a false peace, and it became evident to all, that real and permanent harmony could not now be restored, the ten dissenting members at length consented to accept letters of dismission, of which the following is a copy: "Whereas, there has been a difficulty subsisting among the members of this church, and a general agreement cannot as yet be obtained, we have thought it advisable to part.

Accordingly, the ten dissenting members are dismissed from us, and we will not now fellowship any church that may receive them into their communion."*

The result of another council, convened about a year after, to which the church deputed a committee, and submitted a written statement of facts, may be sufficiently gathered from the following allegory, written by Elder Leland:

NAVAL ENGAGEMENT.

In the year 1811, a small, diminutive vessel, with American colors, was seen sailing on the coast near the place, supposed to have on board contraband goods. A number of gun-boats called "*Aggrieved Brethren,*" formed a line and bore down upon the little vessel to sink her; but as the wind shifted they could not succeed. Their failure only fired them with resolution.

Some of the inhabitants provided a number of armed schooners called a Party Council, commanded by Captain H——, and made a second attack upon the little vessel, in March, 1812, but could not bring her to action. They next obtained two brigs, M—— and T——, to join the squadron, and in May, following, attacked the little vessel with all their force; but when they had spent all their powder in raking her, they retreated without sinking the worthless vessel. They then applied to my Lord Shaftsbury for a squadron of armed brigs called a Committee, with Admiral W—— the commander; but before this squadron arrived, there came a Hull of a vessel from Berlin, with a white flag, and the captain, in behalf of his government, tendered his services to mediate a peace between the enraged inhabitants and the little vessel: but did not effect his wish. The July following, the line of armed brigs arrived; but with all their manœuvring they could not bring the little vessel to action, nor get near enough to cut down the rigging. The inhabitants again applied to Lord Shaftsbury for a squadron of frigates to blow the little vessel from the ocean. His Lordship granted them five more frigates, to be commanded by the bold Admiral W——, which formidable force hove in sight August 25th, 1813. The little vessel came up to the fleet, and showed her papers, colors, and cargo, at sight of which the squadron divided. Two of the frigates veered off, and said the little vessel was not a picaroon, but was pursuing lawful commerce, and there were not contraband goods on board sufficient to condemn her according to the law of nations. The other frigates said they had no orders from Lord Shaftsbury as yet to sink her to the bottom; but unless the inhabitants would join and destroy the little vessel, they would inform his Lordship of it next June, who would send a force that would distroy every individual that gave aid to the little vessel, or allowed her to sail on the face of the deep.

* This was done at the July meeting, 1812.

Early in 1814, a vote was passed that the dismissed members should have the use of the meeting-house so much of the time as they were entitled to it, by the share they held in the property, and they were requested to appoint their days of worship.*

At the meeting of the Shaftsbury Association in June, 1817, at the request of the messengers of the church, they were dropped from their connection with the Association. In the afternoon of the same day on which this was done, "A certain schedule of articles of belief, dated at Cheshire, August 22, 1811, signed John Leland, being presented by the messengers of the Leyden Association, who desired to know if we held in our fellowship a public character or church that embraced such sentiments:

Voted, unanimously, that this Association hold fellowship with no man or church, embracing, or countenancing such sentiments as contained in the paper then presented."†

Possessed of that charity which "hopeth and endureth all things," and neither wishes nor works ill to its neighbor, Elder Leland was employed, during this long period of persecution, in the pursuit of his domestic concerns, and the duties of his calling. His friends, surprised at the extraordinory and unconstitutional proceedings of the "aggrieved party,"‡ sought, by every means, for many years, to set the party and the public right. On the other hand, the wicked, seeing themselves backed by so many zealous professors, and ever ready to take advantage of such dissensions, spared no pains to invent and circulate the most unblushing falsehoods respecting his opinions and practices. No good ever resulted from the whole course of proceeding; nothing was gained by any one; but a bad impression was left upon the minds of the people generally, who seemed to doubt the purity of purpose that actuated to such a course of conduct as had been pursued, nor could ever be brought to see how any blame could justly fall upon Elder Leland.

Years passed on, the particular circumstances of which it is unnecessary to detail. At length, in 1824, a new church was formed, consisting, in part, of the surviving members of the aggrieved party, and partly of such as withdrew at that time from the Second Church, or had never united with any. Each church occupied the meeting-house half the time.

A revival in 1827, produced some accessions to both, and also to a Methodist society which had been constituted in 1823.

As many of the dissenting members had, in years previous to church

---

* Soon after this, Elder Leland removed to New Ashford. See autobiography for circumstances. He continued to preach from time to time in Cheshire.

† See minutes for that year.

‡ Though only a small minority, they had at one time assumed to be the church, and as such, had sent a letter and messengers to the Association, in addition to that sent regularly by the church.

difficulties, been warmly attached to Elder Leland, none but his God and nearest friends knew how trying to his heart was the loss of their society and friendship. At the darkest hour of the contest, no uncharitable expression escaped his lips, nor could he ever be induced to occupy the desk, when he thought it belonged, of right to them.

In 1831, another revival occurred. Numbers were baptized, and united with the churches to which their friends respectively belonged. Others were deterred from uniting with either, by the consideration that the existence of two churches of the same faith and order, in one place, necessarily involved the certainty that a wrong existed somewhere; and, as they could not determine satisfactorily to themselves *where* it existed, they judged it better to remain neutral. Indeed, for the most part, the younger portion of the community knew not why they should stand aloof from their neighbors in religious concerns, when they were all of one faith, and friendly in every other respect. The lapse of years had thinned the number of those whose grievances had first occasioned the division, and those living, seemed to feel deeply their estrangement from their brethren, and manifested, by suitable acknowledgments to Elder Leland and others, or by their friendly conduct, that they retained no longer any hostile feeling. Time had smothered the disputes that had once risen like mountains between them and their brethren, and the Holy Spirit's influence, which, as has justly been remarked, "can accomplish more in one hour, in bringing Christians together, than years spent in disputes and discipline," was doing its perfect work, and fostering a growing spirit of charity in all hearts.

In the winter and spring of 1833–4, Elder Leland and his wife had some rather unusual exercises of mind respecting the churches, which left upon them the impression that a union might be effected. Prompt in executing what his feelings of duty led him to undertake, he immediately visited several members of his own church, told his feelings and wishes, and proposed, if possible, to bring about a reconciliation, by meeting their brethren of the other church, on the broad basis of universal forgiveness, and mutual oblivion of the past. Some did not readily concur: but he presented to their minds the powerful motives on which their common Master had urged the duty of forgiveness, and reminded them that every Christian must have a forgiving spirit. At length their scruples gave way to the reflection, that if he, who had suffered most, could heartily forgive, they ought to throw no obstacle in the way of the accomplishment of his wishes.

A meeting was accordingly appointed, and the churches came together. Many spectators were also present; some, no doubt, drawn by curiosity, and expecting to hear the grounds of the long trouble laid open and discussed; and others, truly rejoicing at the prospect of a speedy end of those troubles. The plan proposed by Elder Leland was characteristically liberal. The following is a copy of it, as written by him on the first page of the "new church-book."

Cheshire, March 6, 1834.

This day the Second and Third Baptist Churches in Cheshire united together, to be called hereafter the Second Church, upon the following plan of agreement, viz. :—

All former differences shall be buried in the sea of universal forgiveness ; and all the members of both churches, whether present or absent, shall be considered in the union, under the following provisions :—

Any member here present, who, from local situation, or any other cause, may decline the union, shall be subject to no censure therefor. Those members who are not present, shall have the same indulgence, when they make their requests known. In both cases, the non-unionists shall be under no obligation to tell their reasons why.

A clerk shall be chosen, in whose office the books and papers of both the former churches shall be deposited, merely for imformation, but shall not be appealed to for rules of proceeding.

A new book shall be procured, in which the proceedings of the church hereafter shall be registered.

As soon as the plan was laid before the meeting, a spirit of union seemed to run from heart to heart ; and, to the great joy of all present, not an opposing voice was raised. The union was effected without a discussion of difficulties, without a surrender of private judgment—upon the only ground on which it is believed it could ever have taken place. It was a source of great consolation to Elder Leland, to have his early friends take him so cordially by the hand ; and from this time until his death, it is believed no member of either church bore him any ill will ; such, at least, was the appearance. The approving smile of Heaven seemed to ratify the act; for though but few additions to their number have since taken place, a spirit of harmony has prevailed in all their deliberations, and brotherly love has continued uninterrupted among the members of the united church.

In this brief sketch of events, we have endeavored to perform with candor the task which duty imposed. Its object has been, not to call up painful remembrances from the oblivion where they were buried, but to do justice to the memory of the man to whose prejudice those events have been perverted, and to exhibit his character, course, and principles in their true light. No apology is, therefore, deemed necessary for an act so clearly and imperatively demanded by truth and justice. That which goes down to later generations as matter of history, should be sober fact, divested of all the false coloring which prejudice, ignorance, or party spirit may have thrown around it. Such, it is hoped, this narrative may be found. Great care has been taken to ascertain truth, and few assertions have been made that are not sustained by documentary evidence of undoubted authenticity. A few observations of a miscellaneous character, will close these sketches.

The following extract, from Semple's Virginia Baptists, published in 1810, will serve to show the estimation in which Mr. Leland was held in that state.

"Mr. Leland, as a preacher, was probably the most popular of any that ever resided in this state. He is, unquestionably, a man of fertile genius. His opportunities for school learning were not great; but the enegetic vigor of his mind quickly surmounted this deficiency. His memory was so retentive, that by a single reading he stored up more of the contents of a book, than many would by a dozen careful perusals. It is probable that his knowledge, derived from books, at this day, taken in the aggregate, is surpassed by few. His preaching, though immethodical and eccentric, is generally wise, warm and evangelical. There are not many preachers, who have so great command of the attention and of the feelings of their auditory. In effecting this, his manner has been thought, by some, to approach too near to the theatrical. Cowper, the poet, says:

'He that negotiates between God and man,
As God's ambassador, the grand concerns
Of judgment and of mercy, must beware
Of lightness in his speech.'

"Here Mr. Leland and the poet are at variance; he does, sometimes, and, indeed, not unfrequently,

'Court the skittish fancy with facetious tales.'

"If Cowper says, 'So did not Paul,' Leland can say, So did George Whitfield, Rowland Hill, etc., and they have been the most successful of modern preachers. Mr. Leland's free and jocund manners have excited the suspicions of some, that he wanted serious piety. His intimate friends are confident that these are groundless suspicions. They believe that, among his other singularities, he is singularly pious."

It is true, there was nothing of superstitious austerity in the tone of his piety; it corresponded with his own description of the feelings of the heaven-born soul—"lively as angels, yet solemn as the grave." Deep solemnity characterized his public ministrations. In prayer, he seemed to have an overwhelming sense of the perfections of the Being he addressed; and his manner, his words, and the tones of his voice, were expressive of the most reverential awe, the deepest self-abasement, and the humblest adoration. He was in the habit of confessing the immense distance of men, as creatures, below the infinite Jehovah, and the immeasurable increase of that distance by reason of sin. "Supremely great, infinitely glorious, highly exalted, everywhere present, all-wise and eternal God," was often, either wholly, or in part, the introduction of his prayer. His audience felt themselves carried directly into the presence of Him who is "fearful in praises," and it was impossible to listen with an irreverent or trifling spirit. In the administration of the sacrament, few, if any, were ever more deeply solemn and impressive. In his preaching, he sometimes, by a single sentence, presented before the mind a view of eternal things, which left an indelible impression on the memory. Such was the manner in which he was accustomed to speak of death. "It is," he would say, "a solemn thing to die; to go—we know not where; to be—we know not what." His manner, however, was far from being affected or theatrical; and he did not deem it inconsistent, either with real solemnity, or with the spirit of true piety, to mingle, not only in his writings and conversation, but in his preaching, occasional strokes of humor or of satire. But the "facetious tales" had always a higher object in view than to excite a smile, or "court the skittish fancy." They were brought in illustration of some important truth, which he wished to exhibit in the clearest light, and to impress forcibly upon the mind; effects which their aptness was well calculated to produce. The shafts of satire, too, pointed though they might be, were not dipped in the gall of malice or ill will, nor aimed at anything which he esteemed valuable or sacred. Instances illustrative of this part of his character may be found among his writings, and will be recollected by all who ever heard him preach or converse. The following is one example, and will serve to show his manner of treating those circumstances, which, to many persons of different temperament, or of less elevated views and aims, would seem to afford sufficient ground for resentment, and which not unfrequently result in irreconcilable animosity.

THE CHESHIRE RACES.*

As the annual races of Cheshire drew nigh, about the first of April, 1823, the hippodrome was prepared for the contest. As the speed, wind, and bottom of the horses were to be tested, the hippodrome included hills, levels, lanes and hedges, reaching from Savoy to Hancock. The prize to be run for, was

* To those acquainted with the circumstances, any attempt at an explanation of this allegory would be superfluous; to others, perhaps, impossible, as well as unprofitable. It will be sufficient to remind the reader that a revival occurred in 1823—that the same year a Reformed Methodist Society was formed in Cheshire, and early in 1824, the Third Baptist Church was constituted. Among the ministers represented by three horses, no one, it is presumed, can fail to recognize the features of "Old Dray."

MEETING-HOUSE AND MAJORITY.

The horses brought on the ground were, first, the Duke of Marlborough; a fine, high-bred horse, in fine style; supposed by some, who judge of horses, to be the best racer ever seen on Cheshire race ground. The second, was Little Jolly, sired by the imported Jolly Rogers, the famous courser. Little Jolly had never run but a few races; but his make, nimbleness and wind, raised the confidence of many. The third horse, was Old Dray, the sight of whom made some laugh, and others sneer. Old Dray had often been on the ground; but was never formed for speed, and rarely won the prize; had now grown old, and unfit to contend with young steeds in high perfection; in short, he had nothing to commend him, except his being of the *fear-not* blood. On this condition alone could he be admitted, that he should carry an extra burden of a plough and pitchfork on his back, during the race.

The distance stake was stuck forty feet short of the goal, and all things were made ready for the start. At the beat of the drum, the halters were slipped, and, by some unknown cause, Old Dray got four feet in front; but this advance was very short, for the Marlborough came up, and went by him, with great facility; and, had it not been for two causes, there was every reason to believe that the Marlborough would have distanced all the rest. The first cause was, he made a violent kick and bite at Old Dray, and some affirm that he spake, (like the beast that Balaam rode,) and said, "If Old Dray can be kicked out of the path, it will be the most glorious race that ever was run," which rather crippled him in the stifle joint. His friends, however, say that there was neither kick nor bite; that although he is all activity to run the race, yet he has no venom in him. The second cause was, that when he came to Savoy Heights, far ahead, there was a certain berry on the hills, called Woodberry, which had so strong a scent, that it rather paralyzed his limbs.

Little Jolly started with great alertness, and the bets in his favor were greater than for any of the horses on the ground; but, making a bite at Old Dray, he incautiously stepped over the line, and crossed the path, in doing which he received a wound; but his friends produced a medicine, made of fabrication, and administered by offset, which proved a catholicon. They said that Old Dray had done as bad as Jolly, and one must be offset against the other. This medicine they had tried on a former occasion, and knew its efficacy. This treaty, made with their consciences, healed the wound of Jolly, and they declared him to be the soundest and swiftest horse in the race. And truly, in that part of the race ground called lanes and hedges, he performed wonders. Being acquainted with such kind of ground, he jumped with all the agility of a rabbit. In going over the flat ground of Hancock, Old Dray made considerable advances on Marlborough, but could not come up with him. In coming out at the goal, the Marlborough was seventeen feet in advance of Old Dray, and Old Dray seventeen feet before the Jolly. The judges seemed somewhat divided; but the decision was, that the Marlborough should have the *majority*, the Little Jolly have the *meeting-house*, and that Old Dray should carry the plough and pitchfork upon his back as long as he lived, and never be allowed to enter the race ground again.

It will be admitted, perhaps, by all whose freedom from educational bias, and habits of close and independent thought, prepared them fully to appreciate the preaching of Elder Leland, that he was more than usually successful in reconciling those apparently conflicting portions of the system of gospel truth, which have been the theme of so much controversy in all ages of the Church. This was mainly owing to the care he took, never to "mix *law* and *grace* together;" or, in other words, never to confound the "system of God's moral government," with the "scheme of grace through a Mediator." He viewed the line of distinction, as commencing at the "covenant of peace," formed in the counsels of eternity, and continuing for ever. He did not, therefore, apply to the unregenerate, the promises and precepts addressed to the penitent and believer, nor hold forth the terrors of the law to "them who are in Chirst Jesus." Yet that he did not pretend to understand the whole mystery of the gospel, may be distinctly seen in the following detached paragraphs, from which, with other of his writings, may be gathered the fundamental points of his belief.

"The gospel is so internally profound, and the minds of men so limited, the obstructions to science so many and great, that it is but a little of the gospel that men understand; and yet, no scheme, fraught with fewer incomprehensibles, could have brought relief to fallen man. The *unsearchable* riches of Christ, which pass knowledge, will be continually unfolding themselves to the saints in light."

"To reconcile the *eternal designs* of *God* with the *freedom* of the *human will*, is a question that puzzles all men. That both are true, admits of no reasonable doubt; but there is a great doubt whether the mind of man is large enough to reconcile the question: if it is, why is not the matter settled long ago? It appears to be one of the deep things of God, which we are to believe without comprehension. Should the Lord use ever so many words to elucidate the subject, still, the mind of man is so limited, that the matter would remain in the profound. That God is good, and that men are rebellious; that salvation is of the Lord, and damnation of ourselves, are truths revealed as plain as a sunbeam."

"The *preceptive* part of the gospel addresses men as *able to do*, and *commands* them to *do;* but the *gracious* part considers men as *weak* and *polluted*, and reveals what *God* does *for* them. The former shows *holy authority*, the latter *gracious benevolence*."

"Repentance for bad works, and the practice of good works, I strive to preach; but, as repentance will not expiate crimes, and the deeds of the law will not justify, redemption by Christ is essential. The salvation of God includes three things: first, something done *for* us, *without* us; second, something done *for* us, *within* us; third, something done *by* us."

"The moral insolvency of man, has not destroyed the equity of God's law, nor cancelled the demand."

"The sinner, until he is changed by grace, never feels guilty because he has not the holy unction, but for the sins he has committed. The prayer of his heart is not for internal holiness, but for deliverance from punishment."

"Adam, in innocency, with his life of natural purity, was happy on earth, but not fit for heaven. Had he never sinned, he must, nevertheless, have been born of the Spirit, (received the holy unction,) to have prepared him for heaven."

"*Grace* and *effort*. Some preachers fix their eyes so steadfastly upon the unchangeable nature of God, his immutable decrees, his personal and unconditional election of some unto eternal life, that they leave themselves but little liberty to preach, 'Repent, for the kingdom of heaven is at hand'—'Repent, and believe the gospel'—'Repent, and be converted, that your sins may be blotted out'—'Labor not for the meat that perisheth, but for that which endureth unto eternal life'—'While ye have light, believe in the light, that ye may be children of the light,' etc. Others place their minds on the rebellion of man, the necessity of repentance, and the willingness of Christ to save sinners, so strongly, that they overlook such passages as these: 'As many as were ordained to eternal life, believed'—'The election hath obtained it, and the rest were blinded'—'No man can come unto me, except the Father draw him'—'Thou hast hidden these things from the wise and prudent, and revealed them unto babes'—'Then shall ye seek me and shall not find me'—'Not according to our own righteousness, but according to his own mercy he saved us,' etc."

Though his sermons, conversation and writings, were characterized by perspicuity and simplicity, it must be supposed that he was sometimes misunderstood; for he was claimed, by some sectarians, as the advocate of doctrines which he considered fundamentally opposed to the truth. He incurred, also, the censure of many, by carrying farther than they thought necessary the Protestant sentiment, of the sufficiency of the Scriptures as a guide to Christian faith and practice, and by questioning the propriety of measures for which Scripture authority could not be adduced. Some of this class of individuals, however, while they could not but acknowledge the sincerity of his desires to be "*made right*," and of his fervent prayers to be enabled to discern the truth, sought for other motives than love of truth, to which they might attribute his dissent from their own views.

This was entirely uncalled for; for if ever there was a man, who, in his search after truth, was honest, unbiassed by sectarian partialities, unshackled by previously formed opinions, uninfluenced by any selfish considerations, none who knew him well, will hesitate to aver, that John Leland was that man. There is evidently a wide difference between searching the Scriptures to *find* a system of truth, and searching them for evidence to support one already adopted. That the latter was not the course pursued by him, the candor evinced in all his researches fully proves. His object being not so much to convince others, as to discover truth for himself, he avoided those sophistical methods of reasoning which too many employ to bring the unwary and unreflecting to their own views, nor did he resort to denunciation and fiery zeal, or to quibbling and evasion, to cover the weak part of an argument. He did not undervalue the importance of the objections that might be urged against his opinions; but giving them their full weight, he advanced his own arguments to meet them; following, in this respect, the example of Madison, whom he often quoted as a model of candor and fairness in debate.

With regard to his writings, it may be well to remark, that he never rewrote his pieces; whatever they are, they were in the original draught. This consideration, while it accounts for many inaccuracies in language, both historical and grammatical, shows, at the same time, the systematic order in which his thoughts naturally arranged themselves, following one upon another with such method, that it would be difficult, if not impossible, to find an instance where any important proposition was assumed without proof, or a succeeding one in a series taken as proof of a preceding.

His views, in relation to the office and work of the ministry, are contained in various parts of his writings. It was never either his principle or practice to set a price upon his labors, nor to demand or receive a fixed salary. But though he never solicited, or made money a *condition* of preaching, he never refused what any chose to give him; and he received it, not as alms, but as a gospel debt. It was his counsel to one who was about to engage in the work of the ministry, never to make any dependence upon what he expected to receive for preaching; "if you get anything," said he, "you can work it in afterwards." Such was his own practice. His own hands, and those of his family, who were all trained to habits of active industry, supplied their wants, and he had the pleasure of knowing that whatever he did receive, was given, "not grudgingly, but with free will, and of a ready mind."

His practice with regard to baptism was in accordance with the views expressed in the letter found on page —— of volume ——. He considered baptism a duty plainly enjoined on all the followers of Christ, by an express command; but connection with a church to be a matter of choice and expediency. Accordingly he always baptized such as gave evidence of piety, if they desired it, and left them to connect themselves with whatever church they pleased, or with none, if such was their preference. He thought the First Epistle of Peter, to the "*strangers scattered*" through various places, was, probably, addressed to such as, from local situation, or other causes, were not numbered with any of the churches.

His preaching, in latter years of his life, was almost entirely of the expository kind. He would frequently, after naming his text, go back a number of verses, or to the beginning of the chapter, and comment upon each clause in succession, and sometimes the close of the sermon would come without his having reached his text at all. But "it is no matter," he would say, "so long as I keep within the lids of the Bible. Indeed, it makes but little difference what text I take, I must come to the *third of John* before I close. If I take an Old Testament text, I must preach a New Testament sermon.

It was equally true of him as of Mr. Haynes, that "though he seldom held a congregation long without exciting a smile, yet the predominant influence of his preaching was to produce solemnity of feeling, and deep conviction of truth. His eccentricities would have been faults in any other man, but in him they were so inherent and essential to his character, and his wit was so spontaneous, and came, as it were, without his bidding, that they neither interrupted the current of his own piety, nor often weakened the religious influence of his discourses upon others."*

Many anecdotes and amusing incidents have been related of him, some, probably, without foundation in truth. Want of space forbids the introduction of more than two or three in this place. The following, cut from a newspaper, is judged to be authentic, from the fact that it is characteristic of him. Riding one day in company with Elder Hull, they were overtaken by a slight shower. Elder Leland was for seeking a shelter, but the other remarked, "Brother, I am ashamed of you—a Baptist minister, and afraid of a little water!" "Ah! Brother Hull," replied he, "I never like these *sprinklings*."

Calling one day on a Baptist minister, to whom he was not personally known, said the latter, after the first salutations, "by what name shall I call you?" He replied, "Why askest thou thus after my name, seeing it is secret?" "Well," said the other, "is this all the answer I am to have?" "It is the answer of an angel, what better can you wish for?" "If you are an angel, doubtless you are a fallen one."

On another and similar occasion, being asked the same question, he replied, "call me Leland." "Ah!" replied the minister, "there are many who come along, wishing to be called by that name. I have been tricked in that way several times." But after looking steadily at him a few moments, his doubts seemed to yield to the conviction that he was indeed no

* Reminiscences of Rev. Samuel Haynes.

other than he pretended, and he exclaimed, "Is it possible that the Almighty has placed such a soul as Leland's in such an insignificant body!"

Should this expression convey the idea that he was small of stature, the impression will be incorrect. His height was not far from six feet, though as he advanced in years, his form became more stooping, and his stature, consequently, somewhat less. In flesh, he was rather thin and spare. Of his personal appearance, generally, the accompanying portrait will furnish a more correct and definite idea than any language can convey.

Perhaps these sketches cannot be more appropriately closed, than by the following brief extracts from the concluding part of the funeral sermon: "Great and good man, he is gone! The tender and effectionate father, the kind husband—the wise counsellor—emphatically the peace-maker—the social, warm-hearted friend—the sage—patriot—the lover of sound doctrine—the eloquent and unusually successful minister of Christ, is no more! Is no more? He still lives, we doubt not, where his intellect has found congenial spirits, and a wider range in the upper empire of Jehovah. He lives below in the affections of thousands, and 'his works do follow him.'" "To live live like him, is to mourn over the sins of earth, and hold up God's everlasting truth to a dying world. To die like him, is to stand on the confines of earth, looking off into eternity, and depart with the 'prospect of heaven clear.' To rest, at last, like him, is, we doubt not, to rest forever in the Paradise of God."

THE HISTORY OF JACK NIPS.

I CANNOT say that my father was a Hittite, and my mother an Amorite, but my father was a Presbyterian, and my mother a high-flying, separate new-light. I was as far from being a new-light myself, as men's hearts are from their mouths, or as *old darkness* is from *new light;* but when my school-fellows got mad at me, they would call me a new-light, and if I asked them what a new-light was, they would be as confused in their answers as if they did not know B from a bull's foot. Sometimes, when I was reading, they would laugh at me for my new-light tone; once, in particular, as I was reciting a lesson, to a Latin master, he told me "not to preach like a new-light, but to speak like a scholar." This put me upon a search into the nature of tones, and I was soon convinced that a holy tone did not make a holy man, for some who had the tone, would be as hypocritical as Lucifer himself; but the same persons who laughed at me for my tone, had a disagreeable tone of lying, swearing, and sneering at all good sense and religion, yet there was no harm in that tone, because it was polite.

Like other boys, I wished to be in fashion, and as the Presbyterians were the most fashionable, I applied myself to the study of their books, but was not a little puzzled to reconcile their writings with my boyish thoughts. I could not, for my gizzard, understand their *orthography,* until I was more than sixteen. They would spell thus: c-i-r, cir, c-u-m, cum, c-i, ci, s-e-d, *baptism.* This, I say, puzzled me greatly: and if I asked any body how they reconciled it, they would tell me that "great, learned, and good men said it was right, and it would be presumption in me to call it in question." I further observed that sometimes those authors would put the cart before the horse; as for instance, where it said, "he that believeth and is baptized shall be saved," they would have it, "he that is *baptized* and *believeth,* shall be saved." Surely, said I, this is a Presbyterian tone; for I did not then know that there was a Papist, a Russian, or an Episcopalian in the world.

Another thing also confounded my youthful thoughts. Men and women would bring their childen to the minister to be baptized, if but one of them was a believer, and it was supposed that the faith of one parent was sufficient to initiate the child; but my thoughts would be running thus: "is the soul of that child made by God, and infused into the body while in the womb, or it is begotten by the parents? If it is made and infused by God, then the children of wicked parents bring as good souls into the world as the children of good parents do. But if souls are begotten in ordinary generation, then regenerate men will beget regenerate souls, and wicked men will beget wicked souls; and if Adam was regenerate before he begat any of his children, by succession down to this day, we are all regenerate." But as this was to me uncertain, I was casting my eyes and thoughts on my neighbors. Uncle Benson had married aunt Nancy, by whom he had a son whose name was Peter. Uncle was a believer, but aunt was not. Here I had a great query in my mind, to find from which parent the soul proceeded. Aristotle informed me, that the child, in animalcula, came originally from the mother. Surely, then, said I to myself, cousin Peter has no right to baptism, for his mother is an infidel. But the European philosophers said that the animalcula that formed the fœtus, came from the father. If so, said I, again, then Peter is a Christian. But here I was perplexed again: if Peter came into the world a Christian, how can he be made a Christian by water? Can a priest and water make him what he was before he was born? Uncle Sam said, Peter came into the world a Christian, and *therefore* had a right to baptism; but uncle Ned insisted upon it, that it was his baptism that *made* him a Christian, and confirmed his sentiment by observing, that the name given him in baptism, was his Christian name; that is, a name given him when he was made a Christian; but others declared that the child came half from each parent; then, said I, Peter ought to have but half his face sprinkled, for half of it came from his heathen mother.

While I was thus as full of thought as Don Quixote was of projects, I went to meeting: and how was I surprised to see a man and his wife stand in the broad aisle, owning the baptismal covenant, as they called it. I had read of baptism being a command—a fulfilling of righteousness—the answer of a good conscience; but never heard it called a covenant before. What wind next? said I within myself. But here I soon found that neither the man nor his wife were believers; that they had never given *themselves* to God, and yet were offering their *child* to him. This made me think of uncle Tim, who would never give any of his own interest to any body, but when he was at another man's house, he would be as liberal as a prince, in giving to every one that came in. If these people, said I, loved their child as well as they do themselves, they'd never trust it where they durst not trust themselves. But after the priest had read what he had written for them, and they had consented by a bow and courtesy, he declared that they had a right to all the privileges of the church except the Lord's supper.

The thought that arose in my mind was this: they may have a right to the privileges of *that* church, but have they a right to all, or any, of the privileges of *Christ's* church? If, from the innocency of the children—

the confession of the parents, or the faith of one or both of them, they have a right to baptism, why not to the eucharist? Here I remembered to have read an account of Cyprian, the African bishop, who, in the middle of the third century, first introduced infant baptism, and, to be consistent with himself, introduced infant communion at the same time.

I could not but observe what force and violence were used on the occasion. The little candidate, who never proposed himself, nor, indeed, had sense enough to know anything that was going on, was taken by force, and, notwithstanding all his struggles and screams, had the name of the Trinity called over him, and was, somehow or other, shut up in the pales of the church. Is this Christian liberty? thought I, more than a hundred times.

About this time, my father, schoolmaster, and minister, took much pains to teach me the catechism, where it is observed that baptism is not to be administered to any who are out of the visible church, till they profess their faith in Christ, and obedience to his revealed will. What, in the world of wonders, thought I, do these people mean? The man and his wife, now in the broad aisle, do not profess to be believers, and yet they claim baptism for their child, contrary to that oracular catechism, composed by so many D. D.'s, and M. A.'s. Here my zeal broke over all bounds, and turning to old neighbor Turnpie, said I, "do these people hold to the Westminister catechism?" "Yes," said he, "but, they are constantly gaining more light, and, therefore, altering their modes; but still they are the same people." This made me think of the Irishman's knife which he kept for antiquity's sake, which had been his grand-father's, his father's, and his own; and, although it had worn out two or three blades, and three or four handles, yet it was the very knife that his grandfather first bought.

After pausing awhile, I remembered that the article concluded thus: "but the *infants* of those who are enemies of the visible church, are to be baptized." You lie, reverend sirs, said I. What! first tell us that baptism is not to be administered to any out of the church, and then tell us it is, and think boys and men too will believe your contradictions? Here I should have proceeded, but a man in the seats not only began to knock his black staff, but really came and took me by the hand. "What now?" said I. He replied, "I am a tything-man to keep order." Here a thousand thoughts rushed into my mind, some of which were as follows: did Jesus, or his apostles, ever appoint tything-men to keep boys or men in order? Did they ever give orders to civil rulers to make laws to force people to go to meeting once a month, or pay a fine? Did they ever institute black staves and stocks to prevent disorder in religious worship? Have those people New Testament authority to establish creeds for others, and go contrary to them, themselves, and punish others if they cannot receive their glaring inconsistencies and absurdities? Some say that the laws of men are the sinews of the gospel: but are they not rather the sinner's gospel? Is not every kind of cruelty and oppression executed under the pretext of civil law? Have not the majority in every part of the world christened all their madness and self-will by the names of civil law and good order? These things are so, said I, in my heart, but durst not speak, for the tything-man held me by the hand. After meeting was over, and I had escaped from the black staff, I returned home, resolving to read for myself.

Carefully reading the New Testament, I found that the word *baptize*, with its various declensions, occurred about one hundred times; but in none of these places did it countenance baby baptism, and as I had made some proficiency in Greek, I searched the Greek Testament and lexicon, where I found that *baptism* came from the word *baptizo*, and that the word *sprinkle*, came from the Greek *rantis*, so that sprinkling could not be baptizing.

The Greek *baptizo*, in a few places, is translated *wash*; but as bodies, cups, and platters cannot be washed well, by sprinkling a few drops of water upon them, I concluded that all who undertook to baptize, by sprinkling, were religious sluts.

About this time, my father was often telling me that he designed me for the gown; that I was of a weakly constitution, not able to get a living out of the ground, and if I could furnish my mind with letter and theological knowledge, I might be inducted into a parish where I might receive a good benefice. But here my foolish heart kept running thus: my father intends me for a minister, but does God? Those who are sent by men to preach, must look to men for their pay; but those that are sent by God, must depend on him.

If I have but a weakly constitution, why should a runt, of a family, be imposed on a parish to eat more than he can work? If a benefice tempts me to preach, I shall preach for filthy lucre, and not out of love to God and souls. If I learn to preach by rule, I shall fall upon the plan of others, of long prayers and short sermons, to save the trouble of writing much. And when I have my sermons all penned down, I shall have to pray, not for God's assistance, but for good eye-sight.

Upon the whole, I concluded that the religion I had been acquainted with, was little more than a state trick of court intrigue, and was therefore resolved to study politics. By this time, I had gained my twenty-second year; and being fired with ambition to know what other men did, I first purchased a book containing the several constitutions of government adopted in the different states. Now, thought I, I shall be a wise man. I had such profound reverence for the men who framed these constitutions, that I concluded that it would be presumption, and almost blasphemy, to call in question a single word: but, attending to their strictures, I found there were not two of them agreed. What, said I, do *great* men differ? boys, women, and little souls do; but can learned, wise patriots disagree so much in judgment? If so, they cannot all be right, but they may all be wrong, and therefore, *Jack Nips for himself.* What encouraged me to search and judge for myself, was this: when I was a small boy, I fancied that I stood in the middle of the world, and that the earth extended no further than my eye-sight explored: but people told me that I was wrong in my judgment; but after a few years study, I found I was half right. That the earth exceeded my eye-sight, I soon found by experience; herein I was wrong. But that I am always on the centre spot of the surface of the globe, is an undeniable truth. And as mature experience convinced me that my boyish thoughts were some of them right, I concluded it might be so with my study in politics.

* * * * * * * *

The above is the only portion of this piece that could be obtained; as every effort to find an unmutulated copy of it has proved unsuccessful.

THE BIBLE BAPTIST.*

Discordant sentiments agree
To make the sons of Adam free.

EXTRACT FROM THE PREFACE.

TRUTH *needs* no apology, and error *deserves* none. Prefatory lies have often atoned for ignorance and ill-will in the Eastern and European worlds; but let the sons of America be free. It is more essential to learn *how* to believe, than to learn *what* to believe.

The doctrine and spirit of the following remarks, are left for the reader to judge of for himself. Truth is in the least danger of being lost, when free examination is allowed. * * * * *

BIBLE BAPTIST.

Christian writers generally agree to reproach the Jews, for treating the Rabbies with as much respect as they did the Prophets; giving as great credit to their traditions as they did to the sacred volume. But many Christian writers are guilty of the same absurdity. It is not more insignificant for Jews to quote the Talmud or the Targum, to prove a Mosaic rite, than it is for Christians to depend on Tertullian, Cyprian, Origen, and the other fathers of the church, for a gospel ordinance. In the following remarks, no attempts will be made to mend our translation of the Bible, and equal credit will not be given to any other writings.

The word *baptism*, is not to be found in the Old Testament; and if it were a thousand times, would be no precept for a New Testament sacrament. Nor is there but one place in the New Testament,† where the word refers to a transaction recorded in the Old Testament: 1st Cor. x., 2, "and were all baptized unto Moses in the cloud and in the sea," refer-

---

* Published in Virginia before the year 1790; the precise year is not known.

† No notice is taken of Heb. vi., 2, because, it is doubtful whether the word refers to the Levitical customs of washings, or to the practice of Christians. The same Greek word is found elsewhere, but differently translated in our version.

ring to Ex. xiv., 19. "When Israel passed through the sea, the waters were a wall to them on the right hand and on the left," see verse 22. The cloud returned and stood behind them, covering them over in an arched form, 1st Cor. x., 1. Now as the waters were a wall to them on the right and left, and the cloud over them, they were covered or buried in the cloud or in the sea; which is what Paul, in the above quoted text, calls baptism.

Some have feigned that the cloud at this time sprinkled down a shower of rain upon the Israelites, and a very vain fancy it is, for it is certain they all passed over dry-shod, which they could not have done had there been a shower of rain; Ex. xiv., 21, 29. Others have quoted this passage to prove household baptism; but it would be more natural to apply it to national baptism; for all the nation of Israel, and a mixed multitude besides, were there baptized to Moses: but if this is a proof for household or national baptism, in gospel times, it must be an equal proof for the baptism of quadrupeds. It is certain that their flocks and herds, even very much cattle went with them, not a hoof was left behind, and were all baptized: Ex. x., 26—xii., 38. If this wondrous miracle is a precedent for New Testament baptism, it requires us all to have our cattle baptized as well as our children.

The New Testament is introduced with the history of a famous Baptist preacher and his order of baptizing. John, the forerunner of Jesus, is called a Baptist fifteen times in the four Evangelists. Is it ignorance or ill will, that so often reproaches the Baptists with novelty? Is it not certain that the first preacher spoken of in the New Testament was a Baptist? Why should they be called a new sect, when they can name their founders antecedent to the founders of any other society? Did not Jesus submit to John's baptism, to fulfil all righteousness? Was not Jesus, therefore, a Baptist? These things are so. Baptism is no strange word in the New Testament. The noun, with its relative verb and participle, occurs one hundred times; which may be found in the following places: Mat. iii., 6, 7, 11, 13, 14, 16.—xx., 22, 23.—xxi., 25.—xxviii., 19. Mark i., 4, 5, 8, 9, 10.—x., 38, 39.—xi., 30.—xvi., 16. Luke iii., 3, 7, 12, 16, 21.—vii., 29, 30.—xii., 50.—xx., 4. John i., 25, 26, 28, 31, 33.—iii., 22, 23, 26, 4, 1, 2. Acts i., 5, 22.—ii., 38, 41.—viii., 12, 13, 16, 39, 38. ix., 18.—x., 37, 40, 47, 48.—xi., 16.—xiii., 24.—xvi., 15, 33.—xviii., 8, 25.—xix., 3, 4, 5.—xxii., 16. Rom. vi., 3, 4. 1st Cor. i., 13, 14, 15, 16, 17.—x., 2.—xii., 13.—xv., 29. Gal. iii., 27. Eph. iv., 5. Col. ii., 12. Heb. vi., 2. 1st Pet., iii. 21.

As John the Baptist was the first who baptized with water by divine authority, it appears necessary to make a few strictures on his baptism. The place of his preaching was the wilderness of Judea, Matt. iii., 1. His doctrine was repentance for sin, faith in the Messiah among them, and good works. See Mat. iii., 2, 11, 12. John i., 26, 34. Luke iii. 7, 15.

The places where he baptized, were the rivers Jordan and Enon, where there was much water: Mat. iii., 6, 16—John iii., 23. What he required of his subjects was confession of sins, and good fruits, Mat. iii., 7, 10. Mark i., 5., and he would not admit the multitude of the Pharisees and Saducees to his baptism, without confession and reformation, although they were the children of Abraham: Mat. iii., 7, 10. Luke iii., 7, 8. What words soever John used when he baptized, whether the same that the apostles were taught to use at the ascension of our Lord, or a set of words telling his subjects to believe in him who should come after him, or any other words, is to me unknown; but he certainly received his commission from heaven, and Jesus, the head of the church, submitted to his baptism.

Whoever carefully considers the texts quoted under the above head, together with corresponding texts respecting the ministry of John, will find that John baptized none but those who are old enough and good enough to make confession of sin, which babies cannot do; that parental virtue was not a sufficient recommendation, without "fruits meet for repentance," and that he baptized in the river Jordan and the waters of Enon. Not a word about infant sprinkling in the whole history of John, nor anything that looks like it.

In John iii., 22, and 4, 1, it looks as if Jesus himself baptized; which he did in the same mannner that Solomon built the temple; that is, it was done by his orders, as John iv., 2, explains it. "Though Jesus himself baptized not, but his disciples." As Jesus never baptized any with water, consequently the children brought to him were not brought for baptism. The passages referred to are Mat. xix., 13, 16. Mark x., 13, 17. Luke xviii., 15, 18. These children were brought to Jesus, that he should put his hands upon them and pray; and the disciples forbade them. Had it been a usual thing for them to be brought to Jesus, for baptism or any thing else, it is not likely that the disciples would have forbidden them. Parents are generally too negligent about bringing their offspring to Jesus; but these, like the mother of James and John, seemed anxious for the good of their infants, and brought them to Jesus that he might bless them, which in great mercy he did, and said "Of such is the kingdom of heaven." From this, it is certain that some, if not all children are meet for the kingdom of God; and indeed, whoever is thus blessed by Jesus, whether young or old, is graciously prepared for that holy place. There is no account that he ever did this but once, and not the least hint that he ever enjoined it upon his disciples; and with what propriety could he enjoin a work upon them, which none but God could do; that is, bless children.

From the passage under consideration, I have heard the following argument drawn, viz., "that if Jesus received children, ministers should; and that if he declared them meet for heaven, they have a right to all the ordinances of the church below." If this argument has any weight in it, it equally pleads for the Lord's supper; and truly, if a child has a right to baptism, he has the same claim to the communion. As the face of the child can bear a few drops of water, while in the arms of the pereacher or father, so the mouth of the child can receive a crumb of bread and a drop of wine while in the arms of the nurse or mother. But what man in his senses will quote these passages to prove infant sprinkling, when there is not a syllable in them about water sprinkling or dipping? If there is, let it be named, and I will take conviction.

Infant sprinkling can be no proof of obedience in a child, who is ignorant of the meaning, and passive in the action. If any virtue, therefore, attend it, it must be either in the parents, gossips, or priest. A virtue in the parents it is not, unless they can prove from scripture that God has commanded it. This proof I have not yet seen, and am inclined to believe I never shall, while the Bible remains as it is.

A virtue in the gossips it cannot be, without religious lying is a virtue. They promise, before God and the congregation, to renounce the world, the flesh, and the devil, for the child, and keep God's holy law as long as life lasts; which an angel could not do, and which *they* take no pains to do. This, they promise, not only for the children of their neighbors, but for many that they never see afterwards; and priest, clerk, parents and gossips, all thank God that he has blessed the water to the mystical washing away of sin.

How inconsistently men talk! First, they say that children come into the world innocent, free from sin, fit for heaven; and next inform us that water, in baptism, washes away sin. If they are clear of guilt and corruption, how can water wash them away? If they are unclean, what can cleanse them but the blood of the Lamb? In one breath, we are informed that none have a right to baptism until they repent, believe, and are in the visible church; in the next, we are told that baptism is an initiating ordinance. While men speak so inconsistantly, who can believe them? Can we think that they believe their own testimonies?

A virtue in the priest it is not, because he has no New Testament commission for it; and what is not virtuous must be vicious, and everything vicious should be abandoned.

After the resurrection of our Lord, just as he was going to heaven, to leave his apostles, he renewed their commission, made some enlargements and additions thereto, and more fully described their work; which Mat. xxviii., 19, expresses thus: "Go ye, therefore, and teach all nations, baptizing them in the name of the Father, and of the Son, and of the Holy Ghost." Mark, in xvi., 15 16, has it—"Go ye into all the world, and preach the gospel to every creature. He that believeth, and is baptized, shall be saved; but he that believeth not, shall be damned." Matthew seems to speak most on the work of the preacher, and Mark on the character of the disciple. This enlargement of the commission authorized them to go and preach among the Gentiles, as well as the scattered Jews. Wherever they went, they were to preach, and those who were taught and believed, were to be baptized; and those who were taught, believed, and were baptized, had the promise of salvation.

Those who practise infant sprinkling, often have recourse to this commission of the apostles, as a foundation for their practice. It is altogether likely that the apostles understood their own commission, and acted accordingly. The surest way, therefore, to get a true understanding of the nature of the commission, is carefully to consider their conduct. Let Peter take the lead. In Acts xi., 14, 37, Peter lifted up his voice, and preached a very pointed sermon; and when the people heard his doctrine, "they were pricked in their hearts, and said to Peter and to the rest of the apostles, men and brethren, what shall we do? Then Peter said unto them, repent and be baptized, every one of you, in the name of Jesus Christ for the remission of sins, and ye shall receive the gift of the Holy Ghost; for the promise is uuto you and to your children, and to all that are afar off, even as many as the Lord our God shall call. Then they who gladly received his word, were baptized; and the same day there were added unto them about three thousand souls. And they continued steadfast in the apostles' doctrine and fellowship, and in breaking of bread, and in prayers."—37, 42. From this passage, we find that Peter preached according to his orders; the people heard, which was their duty; the Holy Ghost applied the truth to their hearts. Filled with godly sorrow for sin, they cried out, "what shall we do?" which is the language of grace in its first operation; Peter had an answer ready, and said, "repent," (this little word is always a prerequisite to baptism,) "and be baptized, every one of you." He does not say, be baptized if you feel the weight of it upon you, but enjoins it upon every one of them, that they might receive remission of sins; and, to encourage them in their godly sorrow for their sins, in general, and crucifying the Lord, in particular, he adds: "For the promise (of the remission of sins and the gift of the Holy Ghost) is to you, (fathers,) and unto your children, and to all that are afar off, (both scattered Jews and Gentiles,) even as many as the Lord our God shall call."

The promise here does not intend baptism, which is never viewed in the light of a promise, but always as a command. Here, observe, none were baptized, but such as asked what they should do? who did repent, gladly receive the word, continue steadfast in the apostles' doctrine and fellowship, in breaking of bread, and in prayers; all of which things infants can not do.

The objection raised here, that three thousand could not be baptized by immersion in one day, equally militates against sprinkling, which takes as long a time. The twelve apostles, and seventy disciples, could soon do it.

Three thousand, divided among eighty-two, would be about thirty-six or thirty-seven for each, who could easily be baptized in less time than an hour. It is no novelty in Virginia, for a Baptist minister to baptize more than thirty-seven in a small part of a day.

The next account of Peter's baptizing, is in Acts x. Cornelius was warned of God by a holy angel, and Peter was called by a vision to go to Cornelius. When he came to his house, and preached to him and his neighbors, the Holy Ghost fell on all those who heard. "Then answered Peter, can any man forbid water, that these should not be baptized, who have received the Holy Ghost as well as we? And he commanded them to be baptized in the name of the Lord." No account that he went to baptizing before they were converted, but as soon as they received the Holy Ghost, he commanded them, in the name of the Lord, to be baptized. And these were persons who heard Peter, spake with tongues, and magnified God.

What Peter thought baptism figured out, appears from his First Epistle, iii., 21. "The like figure whereunto even baptism doth also now save us, (not the putting away the filth of the flesh, but the answer of a good conscience towards God,) by the resurrection of Jesus Christ." Here observe, that baptism does not remove the filth of the flesh, but figures out the way in which we are saved: viz., by the death and resurrection of Jesus Christ. When we are plunged beneath the wave, we figure out the death and burial of Jesus; and when we rise from beneath the wave, we figure out the resurrection of the Saviour; in doing which, we have a good conscience.

From the history of Peter, then, we have every reason to believe that he understood his commmission in such a manner as did not entitle him to baptize any but penitent believers.

The next baptizer to be taken notice of, is Philip. Whether this was Philip of Bethsaida, one of the twelve, or Philip the deacon, who was an evangelist, or another man of the same name, is not certain; but Philip went down to Samaria, and preached Christ unto them. Acts viii., 5. "And when they believed Philip, preaching concerning the kingdom of God, and the name of Jesus Christ, they were baptized, both men and women." See verse 12. They were not baptized until they believed, and yet were baptized before they received the Holy Ghost in its great effusion; which proves that faith should be antecedent to baptism, and that the receiving of the Holy Ghost in this sort, is something distinct from that grace which makes men saints.

In this same chapter, from verse 26, to the end, we have another account of baptism bv Philip. A certain eunuch of Ethiopia had been up to Jerusalem, to worship the God of Israel; and, as he was returning homeward in his chariot, was reading the 53d of Isaiah; from which it appears that he was a Jewish proselyte, and, no doubt to me, a real saint, who had not yet been taught a risen Saviour. Philip was commanded by the Spirit to go and join himself to the chariot, which he did, and began at the same scripture which the eunuch was reading, and preached unto him Jesus. And as they came to a certain water, the eunuch said, "See, here is water, what doth hinder me to be baptized?"

How the eunuch came to the knowledge of his duty, in this ordinance, is not certain. Whether he had learned at Jerusalem, or some other place, that such was the practice of the Christians; or had some impressions of the Spirit upon him, teaching him his duty; or whether Philip taught it to him, I cannot say; but he certainly requested baptism of Philip. "And Philip said unto him, if thou believest with all thine heart, thou mayest. And he said, I believe that Jesus Christ is the Son of God. And they went down both into the water, both Philip and the eunuch, and he baptized him. And when they came up out of the water," &c. What can be plainer? Philip preached Jesus; the eunuch believed in him; they came to a certain water; they went down both into it, both the administrator and the subject; baptism was administered; and then they came up out of the water.

The next baptizer in course, is Ananias. When Saul was struck to the earth by the power of God, and led blind to Damascus, the Lord sent Ananias unto him, who went and laid his hands on him, and he received his sight. Then said Ananias unto him, why tarriest thou? Arise, and be baptized, and wash away thy sins, calling on the name of the Lord. And he arose, and was baptized. Acts ix., 1, 19—xxii., 16.

Paul, the chief apostle of the Gentiles, comes next before us. The first place where he baptized any, that we have an account of, was in Macedonia. (Acts xvi., 14.) He was called by a vision to go to Macedonia; and when he came to that part of it called Philippi, "Upon the Sabbath day went out of the city by a river's side, where prayer was wont to be made; and he sat down, and spake unto the women who resorted thither; and a certain woman, named Lydia, a seller of purple, of the city of Thyatira, who worshipped God, heard him, whose heart the Lord opened, that she attended unto the things that were spoken of Paul. And when she was baptized, and her household, she besought Paul, and his companions, saying: If ye have judged me to be faithful to the Lord, come into my house."

This woman came from Thyatira to Philippi, trading in purple: she was a female merchant, and, perhaps, a manufacturer, who first made her purple, and then sold it. She employed either her own children or journeymen to assist her in her trade. She was a worshipper of God, heard the gospel, had her heart opened, attended to the things spoken by Paul, and was judged to be faithful to the Lord, and, therefore, a proper subject for baptism.

The character of her household is not given in this place; but, in the last verse of the chapter, they are called brethren, and were comforted by Paul; which could with no propriety be said of children or unbelievers.

In the 33d verse of the same chapter, an account is given of the baptism of a certain man, and his household. The jailer being alarmed by the earthquake, and the open doors of the prison, drew out his sword, and would have killed himself, supposing that the prisoners had made their escape; rather, therefore, than be tried, condemned, and executed for his neglect, he would have been his own judge, jury, and executioner. "Which Paul perceiving, cried out: do thyself no harm, for we are all here. Then he called for a light, and sprang in, and came trembling, and fell down before Paul and Silas, and brought them out, and said, sirs, *what* must I do to be saved? And they said: believe on the Lord Jesus Christ, and thou shalt be saved, and thy house. And he took them, the same hour of the night, and washed their stripes, and was baptized, he and all his, straightway. And when he had brought them into his house, he sat meat before them, and rejoiced, believing in God, with all his house."

Here note, the word *all* is mentioned three times. The jailer and *all* his household heard the word of the Lord; he and *all* his house believed and rejoiced in God; he and *all* his house were baptized. Let his household be young or old, they all heard, believed, rejoiced in God, and were baptized. Now it is well known that infants can neither hear, (so as to understand,) believe, nor rejoice in God, and, therefore, are not fit subjects for baptism. Next, observe, the jailer brought them out of prison into his house; and as he brought them again into the house to eat, after he was baptized, it is altogether likely that they were baptized out of any house.

The next instance of Paul's baptizing, is, Acts, xviii., 8: "And Crispus, the chief ruler of the synagogue, believed on the Lord with all his house; and many of the Corinthians, hearing, believed, and were baptized." Crispus, Gaius, and the household of Stephanas, were baptized by Paul: Cor. i., 14, 16. The rest of them, to complete the *many*, very likely, were baptized by Silas and Timotheus, who were Paul's companions at Corinth, verse 5. Paul was a wise master-builder, among the Corinthians, who laid the foundation, and left Silas and Timotheus to build thereon: 1 Cor. iii., 10. It is not certain that the household of Crispus were baptized, but it is certain that they all believed, and very likely that they, with the other Corinthians, that heard and believed, were baptized. The character of Stephanas andhis household is given, 1 Cor., xvi. 15, where they are said to be the first fruits of Achaia, and they addicted themselves to the ministry of the saints, which is a work too masculine for infants.

The family and neighbors of Cornelius, were baptized, even those who heard and received the Holy Ghost, and magnified God. The household of Lydia, were baptized, who are called brethren, and were comforted by Paul. The household of the jailer, were baptized; such as heard, believed, and rejoiced in God. The household of Stephanas were baptized, who were the first fruits of Achaia, and ministered to the saints. And, if the household of Crispus were baptized, they believed in God, as well as Crispus himself.

Now, if there is any account of any one household beside, that were baptized upon the faith of their father, or promises of their gossips, I should be glad to see it. I confess I have not yet found it in the New Testament.

Some have quoted 1 Cor. vii., 14, to prove the right of household baptism—"For the unbelieving husband is sanctified by the wife, and the unbelieving wife is sanctified by the husband; else were your children unclean, but now are they holy." If this sanctity, or holiness, is truly gracious, we are all in a safe state. Noah, the father of the new world, was a strong believer, if his wife was not; before he married her, she was sactified on the wedding day; their children, consequently, were holy, Ham among the rest; and so, by succession, down to this day, all are sanctified; which is a doctrine that good Pedobaptists do not believe, any more than we do. The word, therefore, must have a qualified signification, and if we attend to the context, we shall easily find their quality. Read the first part of the chapter. So many of the Corinthian church were connected with unbelievers, (who were idolaters,) in marriage, that they wrote a letter to Paul, to know whether they had not better part believers and unbelievers, that were joined together in wedlock; which Paul did not consent to. The text under consideration, is a part of his answer to their letter, and which, according to our common dialect reads thus: "For the unbelieving husband is legally bound to his wife, and the unbelieving wife is legally bound to her husband; else were your children bastards, but now are they a lawful offspring." This text has no more relation to baptism, than the first verse of Genesis.

But one place more remains to be considered concerning Paul's baptizing: Acts, xix., 1, 8. These twelve men believed, and were baptized unto John's baptism, I suppose by apostles, who had not been taught a risen Saviour, nor received the Holy Ghost in its great effusion. Whether Paul baptized them again, or only explained John's baptism to them, is not so certain. When John taught his disciples, he charged them to believe in one who stood among them, and when they heard it, they were baptized in the name of Jesus. But if it is true, that John's baptism is done away, and that the baptism instituted by Jesus, and practiced by the apostles, is radically different from that of John, and so these twelve men were baptized again by Paul, it is no proof at all for the baptism of infants or unbelievers. If these men were baptized by Paul, they believed first, as the text is plain; and although they had been baptized by John, or more likely by apostles, (one of John's order,) they were not baptized until they brought forth the fruits of repentance.

The opinion of Paul concerning baptism, may be seen in Rom. vi., 3, 4— 1 Cor. xii., 13, Col. ii., 12, where baptism is called a burial; that it represents the death of Christ, and a putting on of Christ. Now, I appeal to common reason, whether believers, baptism, by immersion, upon confession of sin, and an annunciation of a life of obedience to Christ, or infant sprinkling, comes nearest to the sense of these expressions.

I have proved, and can prove, that persons were forbidden baptism on the claim of parental holiness, because they did not bring the fruits of repentance with them; that others were not suffered, until they gave satisfaction of faith in Christ; that when they were baptized, they went down into the water; that they were baptized before they came out of the water; that baptism is a burial of the body; and that, after baptism, they came up out of the water. And, now, if any man can prove from scripture, that infants were ever baptized upon the faith of their parents. or promises of their gossips, in private houses, or meeting-houses, by sprinkling water in the face, I will own that they have an equal authority with us for what they do: otherwise, we shall triumph and say, that we act according to the scripture, and they according to human tradition.

Some have run into a gross error respecting the *baptism of the Holy Ghost;* thinking that nothing more is meant thereby than regeneration. The phrase occurs six times in the New Testament, and is implied in other places, but always intends something extraordinary. Zachariah and Elizabeth were filled with the Holy Ghost, and prophesied, but not in such a manner as to be called a baptism, and to speak with tongues. The disciples never received this blessing, while Jesus was with them on earth; he always spoke of it as something to come; and after his resurrection, he told his disciples plainly, that they should be baptized with the Holy Ghost and fire in a few days; which was fulfilled, first at the day of Penticost, and afterwards at particular times, in a wonderful manner. Some were not baptized until they had thus received the Holy Ghost, and others were before; but though many were baptized before they were thus overwhelmed with the spirit, yet none were until they had repentance and faith, or at least made profession of them.

It is said by some, that baptism, by immersion, before a large congregation, especially of the female sex, is very indecent. This objection may have weight with those who are too delicate to obey God rather than man; but will have no effect with those who simply regard the Bible. Circumcision was performed, not only on children, but on old Abraham, and upon more than six hundred thousand men at Gilgal; and the reader may judge for himself, which of the two is more indecent. If circumcision, therefore, was an institution of heaven, no man can object to baptism upon the principle of modesty.

Others observe, that, although the scripture says that Jesus was baptized by John *in* Jordan, and that Philip, and the eunuch, went down *into* the water, and came up *out* of the water; that nothing more is meant than that they went down *to* the water. Although this objection is void of good sense, yet I wish to make a few remarks upon it. If the observation be true, it is not complied with by any but the Baptists; other societies never go nigh the water to baptize. I have never known of an instance of a man, whose faith, in this sense, carried him to the water-side, but it also led him into the watery tomb.

The law of nature, is one criterion to explain scripture by. When it is said that Jesus went up *into* the mountain, nature says, that he went into, or among the trees, or whatever grew upon the mountain; for into the earth he could not go, without miraculous power, which we have no reason to think he exercised at that time: that he went further than the foot of the mountain, is certain, for he went *up*. Where it is said that Philip and the eunuch went down into the water, by the law of nature, the argument turns. A man can no more walk upon the water without sinking, than he can walk into the earth. This objection is no good criticism, it is mean pedantry: a desperate subterfuge, to shelter in, for want of plain truth. Can any man believe it, who is not blinded by tradition, prejudice, or systematical mists? If he can, he will then believe, that when the hogs ran down *into* the sea, and were choked, they only ran *to* the sea-side, and were choked in the sand.

A like observation is made on Mark xvi., 16. "He that believeth and is baptized, shall be saved." The argument is formed thus: that the auxiliary, *is*, and the participle, *baptized*, determine the sentence in the past tense. Why not then written, "He that believeth, and *has been baptized*, shall be saved?"

It is not certain that the Jews ever baptized their children; and if they did, it was one of their vain traditions, for they had no divine command to do so; and I wish to know who had been in the Gentile world to baptize before the apostles went thither? Matthew records the same commission: "Go teach all nations, baptizing them," &c.; and I am inclined to believe that it would puzzle the greatest scholar in Virginia, to prove that the verb, *teach*, and participle, *baptizing*, place the sentence in the past time.

I confess I am presumptuous enough to say that, let other Christians have ever so many promises made to them, yet the promise in Mark xvi., 16, is made to none but Baptists; and the same is true of Acts ii., 38.

But the most serious and weighty objection against believers' baptism, that I have seen or heard of, is this: "That many great reformers, and very successful preachers, in past ages, have believed in, and practised infant sprinkling; and if this was an error, would not God have convinced them of it, when he was with them, in so great a degree?" As this objection appears judicious, I shall endeavor to give it a candid answer.

If our inquiries extend as far back as the first ages of Christianity, immediately after the close of inspiration, we shall find ourselves upon disputed ground. Some say that infants were never sprinkled, upon the faith of their parents, until the *third* century; others say they were, in the *first*; and, if we consider the carelessness of transcribers, and the partiality of translators, it will not be wondered at. My argument is, that if they were sprinkled the first day after John finished his Revelations, they had no order from Jesus, or his apostles, to do so; and, therefore, it was no way valid or exemplary. The mystery of iniquity began to work, and the man of sin to show his power, before the apostles were dead; and, by little and little, prevailed over all Christendom, and sunk the church into the greatest labyrinth of darkness, as all Protestants confess, which lasted a number of centuries. But in these last ages of the world, God has raised up men of renown, to reform his people, who have been successful in their work; and these have, for the most part, believed in, and practised infant sprinkling.

If we consider the principles of the great reformers, from Luther to the present day, we shall find no entire uniformity in sentiments; which proves them fallible, uninspired men. A number of the real, or supposed errors of one reformation, have been always opposed in the next. That Luther, Calvin, Truinglius, Knox, and the English reformers, did much for God, we do not deny; but what enlightened American would make any of them his complete pattern? If God never blessed a man, while holding some error, he could never have blessed but one of them, for no two of them agreed in all things. If the men of one reformation improve upon the doctrine and forms of a prior reformation, we cannot think it a piece of arrogance to say that, in point of baptism, all the Pedobaptist reformers were in an error.

The feast of tabernacles was instituted in the days of Moses. Lev. xxiii., 38–43. Deut. xvi., 13. At this feast, the children of Israel were to dwell in booths; but from the days of Joshua, the son of Nun, to the days of Nehemiah, this rite was never observed, (Neh. viii., 13–18,) which was more than a thousand years; in which time, all the good kings of Israel, and many prophets of high rank, lived. It is, then, not sophistry, but honest reasoning, to say, that if there had not been a Baptist in the world, since John the Divine, it would be no sufficient objection against believers' baptism by immersion now.

I have human testimony to prove that a number of the reformers were Baptists, and, particularly, John Wickliff, the great reformer in England, called, by way of eminence, the Morning Star; but if there never had been one, from the days of Constantine to the present day, the Scripture is full of proof, that all were of that order, in the days of Christ and the apostles; at least, no account is given of any other way of baptizing, save only by immersion, upon profession of repentance and faith.

The argument, to prove infant sprinkling from circumcision, I have said nothing about. Consequences upon consequences, drawn from false premises, are used so much in the argument, that it appears foolish to an accurate mind, and inconclusive to the vulgar. If its advocates can produce a single text, where the last is a substitute for the first, it will be worth regarding; otherwise, infant sprinkling may as well be proved from the Hebrew servant's ear, that was bored through with an awl.

THE VIRGINIA CHRONICLE.

PREFACE.

I have neither his Lordship, his Grace, nor his Highness, to dedicate this little Chronicle unto, for patronage; but, like its author, it must stand upon its own merits, and like him, it has many imperfections.

The piece will in no wise answer its title, save only in giving an account of the different religious sects in the state: and, even in this particular, the account is general, without descending to minute circumstances. To make the pamphlet small, where I have quoted the words of others, or taken passages out of histories, I have given the authors no credit. If I have bourne too hard upon the Episcopalians, it is because they only have been established by law, and I am no great admirer of *legal religion.* And even in this point, I hope the note, under the twelfth head, will sufficiently palliate. In the description of the Baptist principles, I have sometimes used the plural pronoun, *we, us,* etc., but if I have inadvertently misrepresented the general opinion, and only written my own, I I should be glad to be corrected. A particular narration how the Baptist religion broke out and spread, and by what means, and marvellous ways God wrought, is likely to be offered to the world, in a History now preparing by the General Committee. Although I have presumed to appear in public, yet I will by no means recall a former observation:

Some books are written in ambition,
Others to change a low condition;
Some are th' effect of pride and spite,
And some, perhaps, are written right;
But should the gospel clearly shine,
How many books, now call'd divine,
Would be committed to the flames,
And authors lose their mighty names.

THE VIRGINIA CHRONICLE.*

Truth is as essential to history as the soul is to the body.—FREDERICK.
In omnibus rebus magis offendit nimium quam fiarum.

A DESCRIPTION OF VIRGINIA.

THIS state, from the Virgin Queen, (Elizabeth,) is called VIRGINIA. Bounded on the north, by Maryland, Pennsylvania, etc.; on the west, by the Ohio and the Mississippi; on the south, by Carolina, and on the east, by the Atlantic. From east to west, the state is about seven hundred and fifty-eight miles; but from north to south, it is very unequal, being much wider at the west than at the east. According to the best calculation of the boundary lines, it includes one hundred and twenty-one thousand, five hundred and twenty-five square miles, or, seventy-seven million, seven hundred and seventy-six thousand acres. The state is divided by several ridges of mountains: the Blue Ridge, the North Mountain, and the Alleghany, are the most notable. Though some mountains are of a greater altitude from their bases in the two first ridges mentioned, yet the Alleghany is the ridge-pole of the state. All the waters, east of that mountain, fall into the Atlantic; and all west of it, fall into the Mississippi, and empty themselves into the Gulf of Mexico. The state, at present, is divided into ninety counties, each of which, is entitled to send two delegates to the General Assembly. There are also, in the state, about one hundred parishes.

In England, there are nine thousand three hundred and forty-eight parishes; in Scotland, nine hundred and thirty-eight; in Ireland, fifteen hundred and eighty-six; in all, eleven thousand eight hundred and seventy-two. In some counties, there are not more than one parish; in others, there are as many as four; in rare instances, parishes include parts of two counties. Those counties that have been established since the revolution, have no parishes in them. Under the regal government, parish-officers provided for the poor, as well as the preachers; but now, the poor are otherwise provided for, and preachers are not supported by legal force; and was it not for the preservation of parish property, viz., glebes, churches, etc., there would be no need of parish bounds in the state.

* Published in Virginia, 1790.

NUMBER OF INHABITANTS.

In the year, 1584, Queen Elizabeth, by her letters patent, licensed Sir Walter Raleigh, to search for remote heathen lands, not inhabited by Christian people, and sent out two ships, which visited Wococon Island, in North-Carolina; and the next year he sent one hundred and seven men, who settled Roanoke Island. And, in the year, 1586, he sent fifty men more, and in 1587, one hundred and fifty more, with a governor and twelve assistants, who landed at Hatteras. Sir Walter being attainted at home, could take no more care of his new colonists; and what became of them, whether they were devoured by hunger, or wild beasts—destroyed by savages, or incorporated among them, no mortal man can tell.

But, in 1607, King James executed a new grant of Virginia, to Sir Thomas Gates, and others, which was superseded, 1609, to the Earl of Salisbury, and others.

The first settlement they made, was at Jamestown, few in number, and surrounded almost by savage nations; but, by the blessing of God, the little one is become a strong nation. Mr. Jefferson says, that in 1782, there were in this state, five hundred and sixty-seven thousand six hundred and fourteen inhabitants, of every age, sex, and condition. Of which, two hundred and ninety-six thousand eight hundred and fifty-two, were free, and two hundred and seventy thousand seven hundred and sixty-two, were slaves; which makes the proportion of slaves to the free, nearly as ten to eleven. Mr. Randolph, in 1788, stated the round numbers, thus: three hundred and fifty-two thousand whites, and two hundred and thirty-six thousand blacks; in all, five hundred and eighty-eight thousand. According to Mr. Randolph's statement, from 1782, to 1788, the whites had increased above fifty-five thousand, but the blacks had decreased about thirty-four thousand. These gentlemen had both official accounts, being both governors of Virginia, but the returns from the counties are imperfect, and from some counties, no returns at all are made to the Executive. According to Mr. Randolph's account, the proportion of blacks to the whites, is nearly as two is to three. To do honor to both these great characters, and to make allowance for population, and emigration in the west part of the state, since 1788, I conclude that the number of six hundred thousand inhabitants, is not far from truth. And to form a compromise between their proportions, ten to eleven, and two to three, we may suppose that the number of blacks, compared to that of whites, is like six to seven. By this rule, there are in Virginia, three hundred and twenty-three thousand and seventy-seven whites, and two hundred and seventy-six thousand nine hundred and twenty-three blacks. It has been observed, that the number of acres in Virginia, is seventy-seven million seven hundred and seventy-six thousand, which, equally divided among the inhabitants, would be more than one hundred and eleven acres for each soul; which is above thirty times as much as the nation of Israel had, when they took possession of the promised land, according to Richard Tyron, Esq.

OF THE QUAKERS.

THE first settlers in this state, were emigrants from England, of the English church, just at a point of time when the Episcopalians were flushed with complete victory over all other religious persuasions; and having power in their hands, they soon discovered a degree of intolerance towards others. The oppressed Quakers, flying from persecution in England, cast their eyes on these colonies, as asylums of civil and religious liberty, but found them free for none but the reigning sects. Several acts of the Virginia Assembly, of 1659, 1662, 1693, made it penal in parents, to refuse to baptize their children; prohibited the unlawful assembling of Quakers, and made it penal for any master of a vessel to bring a Quaker into the colony; ordered those already here, and those who should come thereafter, to be imprisoned till they should abjure the country; provided a milder punishment for their first and second return, but death for the third; forbid all persons from suffering Quaker meetings in, or near their houses, entertaining them individually, or disposing of books that supported their tenets. It is a satirical saying, that every sect will oppress, when they have the power in possession, and the saying is too serious as well as satirical.

When we read of the sufferings of the Quakers, or any other society, we can hardly believe that those oppressed innocents, would ever retaliate, if it was in their power; much less, that they would ever oppress those who had not oppressed them; but stubborn fact declares the contrary. I have pretty good authority, that the Penn Quakers, in Pennsylvania, imprisoned and fined the Keitbian Quakers, in 1692, on account of some religious disputes. What contributes greatly towards this kind of oppression, is the erroneous scheme of receiving all the natural offspring into the pales of the church: by this method, in general, a great majority of the church will be ignorant of the *new birth*, and consequently of the nature of the gospel; and therefore, of course, appeal to the civil law, for protection, which naturally brings on oppression upon all nonconformists.

Notwithstanding the laws of Virginia were so severe against the Quakers, yet there is no account that any of them were put to death; and a remnant of them have continued in Virginia, down to this day, holding the same principles, and pursuing the same manners, of their brethren in the northern states, and those in Europe.

OF THE SLAVES.

THE horrid work of bartering spirituous liquor for human souls, plundering the African coast, and kidnapping the people, brought the poor slaves into this state; and, notwithstanding their usage is much better here than in the West Indies, yet human nature, unbiased by education, shudders at the sight. They populate as fast as the whites do, and are rather more healthy.

The first republican assembly ever holden in Virginia, passed an act, utterly prohibiting the importation of any of them into the state. In some things, they are viewed as human creatures, and in others, only as property; their true state then, is that of *human property*. The laws of Virginia, protect their lives and limbs, but do not protect their skin and flesh. The marriage of slaves, is a subject, not known in our code of laws. What promises soever they make, their masters may and do part them at pleasure. If their marriages are as sacred as the marriages of freemen, the slaves are guilty of adultery, when they part voluntarily, and the masters are guilty of a sin as great, when they part them involuntarily; and yet, while they are property, it is not in the power of the masters to prevent their being forced apart, in numberless instances.

The marriage of a Hebrew servant, with a Canaanitish slave, could be dispensed with, at the servant's option, without sin. From this, we should imagine, that there was little or no validity in the marriage of two slaves; but, if it is maintained that their marriages are equally binding with the marriages of the free-born, the inevitable parting of married slaves, holds forth the idea of slavery in a still more aggravated point of view.

Liberty of conscience, in matters of religion, is the right of slaves, beyond contradiction; and yet, many masters and overseers will whip and torture the poor creatures for going to meeting, even at night, when the labor of the day is over. No longer ago than November, 1788, Mr. ——— made a motion in the assembly, for leave to bring in a bill, not only to prevent the assembling of slaves together, but to fine the masters for allowing it; but, to his great mortification, it was rejected with contempt.

No change is yet discernible among the negroes in Virginia, in point of color; but the children of the third and fourth generations retain as much of the jet, as their ancestors did, who were imported from Africa. The difference of climate, therefore, cannot be the cause of the difference of colors; and, as they live upon the same kind of food that the whites do, their diet cannot be the cause of a diversity of color, hair or shape.

Letters were not much used, if any at all, before the days of Moses; consequently, 2,500 years elapsed without registers, which answers for our ignorance of the cause of the many colors, different shapes, and diversity of hues among the sons of grandfather Adam, and father Noah; and also apologizes for our uncertainty, how the many islands and continents were peopled, at first, with those animals that the ark unladed upon the mountains of Ararat.

From the blacks, in Virginia, there have been few Albinos born. These Albinos proceed from black parents, but are in color like the tawny plastering of a wall, without any seams in their flesh, or much Cornelian. Their hair, in length and curl, is like that of blacks, but of a white color; their shape like blacks. Their eyes are sharp and tremulous, and cannot endure the light of the sun as well as others, but see better in the night. Some of their children are black, and others are Albino. I have seen a few of them, and heard of others.

Romulus, the first king of Rome, placed the patricians in the senate, and divided the plebians into tribes, but as for the slaves, they were not considered at all, which is true of the slaves in Virginia, as far as it respects incorporation, but not in every respect. Among us, they are tried before magistrates and courts, and their evidences are as valid, one against another, as the testimonies of the free-born are; but the concurring testimony of a thousand blacks against a white man, is but a cypher in law. If a slave is ever so much abused by his master, or overseer, with unmerciful tasks, barbarous chastisement, etc., if his life and limbs are secure, nothing is done to the abuser. The slave has none to apply to for redress.

In our federal government, the slaves are treated with some more respect than they are in the state government. Although they have no vote in the choice of representatives to Congress, yet, according to the census established in the federal constitution, five of them number equal to three whites, which amounts to this, that a slave is possessed of three-fifths of a man, and two-fifths of a brute.

The state of slaves is truly pitiable, and that of the master, in some things, more so. Slaves drudge and toil for others, and but seldom please them. Men seldom please themselves, and others are almost sure to displease. When the mind is out of humor, it always seeks an object to accuse with the cause of its trouble: so Adam blamed Eve, and Eve the devil. Overseers commonly scold at slaves, let them do ill or well, from the generally received opinion, that negroes will not bear good usage; the slave grows heartless, and sinks in despair, and, knowing that he labors for another, has nothing to stimulate him. The master finds that, without force, nothing will be done; and, therefore, without rage and lightning in his eyes, and a lash in his hand, can make him happy, he is sure to be miserable. If a hard hand and a meek heart, are preferable to a soft hand and a turbulent, fretted, disappointed heart, the master would be better without them than with them.

The whole scene of slavery is pregnant with enormous evils. On the master's side, pride, haughtiness, domination, cruelty, deceit and indolence;

and on the side of the slave, ignorance, servility, fraud, perfidy and despair. If these, and many other evils, attend it, why not liberate them at once? Would to Heaven this were done! The sweets of rural and social life will never be well enjoyed, until it is the case. But the voice of reason, (or perhaps the voice of covetousness,) says, it is not the work of a day; time is necessary to accomplish the important work: a political evil requires political measures to reform. Insurmountable difficulties arise to prevent their freedom. Can government free them? The laws have declared them property; as such, men have bought and enjoyed them. Is it not unconstitutional for government to take away the property of individuals? Can government ransom them? Their number is 276,923; if they should be valued at £30 in average, the sum would be £8,307,690, infinitely beyond what the commonwealth could pay to the holders of slaves, for their ransom, unless they should be made to ransom themselves in discount; which would cast an intolerable burthen upon those who, through conscience or poverty, have none of them in possession.

Some men have almost all their estates in slaves, while the estates of others are in lands; should the legislature, therefore, force one part of the community to give up their property, and leave the other part in full possession of all, would they not be justly accused of injustice?

Others, there are, who owe great sums of money; they were credited upon the value of their slaves; should their slaves be now emancipated by law, the creditors would lose their just dues.

The custom of the country is such, that, without slaves, a man's children stand but a poor chance to marry in reputation. As futile as this may appear to a foreigner, I am well convinced, that *now* it is one of the great difficulties that prevent liberation of slaves among the common sort. To this I would add, that bad custom has so far prevailed, that it is looked upon rather mean for a free man to be employed in drudgery. Were they freed from their masters, without being eligible to any post of honor and profit, it would only be another name for slavery; and, if they were eligible, it is not easy to say what governors, legislatures, and judges we should have. If they were walking at liberty, in every respect, I know not what past injuries might prompt them to do. And how much mixing of colors in marriage, and how many forcible debauches there might be, no mortal man can foretell.* But one thing is pretty certain, that fancy can hardly point out, how they could serve the whites worse than the whites now serve them. Something must be done! May Heaven point

* If we were slaves in Africa, how should we reprobate such reasoning as would rob us of our liberty. It is a question, whether men had not better lose all their property, than deprive an individual of his birth-right blessing—*freedom.* If a political system is such, that common justice cannot be administered without innovation, the sooner such a system is destroyed, the better for the people.

out that something, and may the people be obedient. If they are not brought out of bondage, in mercy, with the consent of their masters, I think that they will be, by judgment, against their consent.

It is the peculiarity of God, to bring light out of darkness, good out of evil, order out of confusion, and make the wrath of man praise him. The poor slaves, under all their hardships, discover as great inclination for religion as the free-born do. When they engage in the service of God, they spare no pains. It is nothing strange for them to walk twenty miles on Sunday morning to meeting, and back again at night. They are remarkable for learning a tune soon, and have very melodious voices.

They cannot read, and therefore, are more exposed to delusion than the whites are; but many of them give clear, rational accounts of a work of grace in their hearts, and evidence the same by their lives. When religion is lively, they are remarkably fond of meeting together, to sing, pray, and exhort, and sometimes preach, and seem to be unwearied in the exercises. They seem, in general, to put more confidence in their own color, than they do in the whites. When they attempt to preach, they seldom fail of being very zealous; their language is broken, but they understand each other, and the whites may gain their ideas. A few of them have undertaken to administer baptism, but it generally ends in confusion. They commonly are more noisy, in time of preaching, than the whites, and are more subject to bodily exercise, and if they meet with any encouragement in these things, they often grow extravagant.

THE UNIFORMITY OF RELIGION FOR ONE HUNDRED AND THIRTY YEARS.

Under the regal government, the Episcopal form of worship was established by law in Virginia. The ministers of that order, solemnly affirmed, that they gave their unfeigned assent and consent to the thirty-nine articles, and book of common prayer, and declared that they were inwardly moved, by the Holy-Ghost, to enter upon the work of the ministry; this they avowed at their ordination, and being consecrated by a spiritual lord in England, they were proper subjects to fill the vacant, or new created parishes in Virginia. If it could be supposed, that they were avaricious salary-hunters, they surely had a tempting bait before them; like the people of old, who said, "put me, I pray thee, into the priest's office, that I may have bread to eat." But, as it is not my wish to inculcate slander, or raise a mean jealousy in the minds of any, I shall attend to matter of fact. When an incumbent was inducted into a parish, he was entitled to a wealthy glebe, having all necessary houses built upon it, at the expense of the parish, which he held during good behaviour. His fixed salary was sixteen thousand pounds of tobacco, which was stated at 16*s* and 8*d* per hundred, which made the sum of £133 6*s* 8*d*, Virginia currency. He was also entitled to

20*s*, for every marriage that he solemnized in the mode of a license, and 5*s* for every one by publication. He had a further perquisite of 40*s* for every funeral sermon that he preached. His parishioners, were under no legal bonds to have a funeral sermon preached for their deceased friends, but custom led all persons of reputation, to request it. Whether it was owing to their superabundant virtue, or the indolence of the people, or any other cause, it seldom so happened that they were dismissed from their parishes, after they were once inducted into them.

The king of Britain was the head of that church; every child that was baptized was a member of it, and no discipline was executed among them but the civil law. The Quakers were few and peaceable, and, as there were none to oppose Episcopacy, it may be said, that they enjoyed the full possession of the state, until about 1740, without having any to call in question their doctrine and forms of worship.

OF THE PRESBYTERIANS.

THAT part of Virginia, between the Blue Ridge and the Alleghany, is peopled in part by emigrants from Pennsylvania, of Irish extraction, and Presbyterian profession, who, before the middle of this century, set up their form of worship; but, being in the then frontiers of the state, were not troubled by government; but the rise and treatment of the Presbyterians, below the Blue-Ridge, was as follows: A number of persons in the county of Hanover, grew very uneasy in the state they were in; could not find that satisfaction, under the preaching of Episcopal ministers, which they desired, and had no opportunity of hearing any others; but, in the year 1743, a young gentleman from Scotland, got a book of Mr. Whitfield's sermons, and one Mr. Samuel Morris read it, and received great benefit therefrom. He next invited his neighbours to come and hear the book read, and as the truth had great effect upon them, Mr. Morris was invited to meet the people at various places, and read to them, which was much owned and blessed of God; but, for absenting from the church, they were cited to appear before the court, to assign their reasons, and declare what denomination they were of. As they were not acquainted with any dissenters but the Quakers; and as they had heard and read of Luther, the Reformer, they declared themselves, Lutherans. About this time, Mr. William Robinson, from a northern Presbytery, travelled through the back parts of Pennsylvania, Maryland, Virginia, and North Carolina. On his return, he founded a Presbyterian congregation in the county of Lunenburg, Virginia, and preached, with great success, in Amelia. The people in Hanover, hearing of him, sent a messenger, desiring him to come into their Macedonia, and help them. Accordingly, on July 6th, 1743, he came and preached among them four days, with remarkable success, and directed them to pray and sing, at their meetings, as well as read. After him, came Mr. Roan, from the Presbytery of Newcastle, who was instrumental in spreading the work further around; but, for speaking a little freely of the degeneracy of the Episcopal clergy in Virginia, he was accused of speaking blasphemy. A vile wretch, (like Jezebel's witnesses,) deposed that he blasphemed God and the clergy, whereupon an indictment was drawn up; but he was returning to the northward, when the trial came on, no witnesses appeared against him, so that the indictment fell through. The people in Hanover, then sent to the Synod of New York, in 1745; the Synod drew an address to Sir William Gooch, governor of Virginia, and sent it by the Rev. Messrs. Tennant and Finley. The governor received them very politely, and gave them license to preach. After they left Virginia, Mr. Morris was several times presented to the court, and fined, for neglecting the church. Soon after, came Messrs. William Tennant, and Samuel Blair, and after them, Mr. Whitfield, and preached among them four or five days. In the spring of the year, 1747, came Mr. Samuel Davies, in a time of great need. A proclamation was set up at their meeting-house, obliging all the magistrates to suppress all itinerant preachers; but, Mr. Davies went to the governor and obtained a license to preach at four meeting-houses. He moved into Virginia, in 1748, and preached there eleven years; he had seven meeting-houses, three of them were in Hanover, and four in the counties of Henrico, Caroline, Goochland, and Louisa.

In 1759, he removed from Virginia to New Jersey, to be President over Nassau Hall College, at Princeton; but the great and good man, did not live long there, for he departed this life, February, 1761.

About the time of the revival, in Hanover, there was a great awakening in Augusta, under the ministry of Messrs. Dean and Byram, and something of a like work in Frederick. The Presbyterians are pretty numerous in Virginia; they have several academies in the state, and one college in Prince Edward, presided over by Mr. Smith, under whose ministry there has been a sweet revival of religion of late. Their doctrine and discipline, are too well known to be repeated. They were all obliged to pay the Episcopal clergymen, as much as if they had been Episcopalians, until the late Revolution; and, if their preachers solemnized the rites of matrimony, in the mode of license, the parish preachers claimed and recovered the fees, as though they had solemnized the rites themselves. The Presbyterians indulge, perhaps, in too much mirth at their houses, yet, it may be said in truth, that they have the best art of training up children, in good manners, of any society in the state.

OF THE METHODISTS.

The Methodists took their rise in England, fifty or sixty years ago; but what concerns us at present, is to consider their rise and spread in America, and particularly in Virginia, which was as follows:

About 1764, Philip Embury, a local preacher, from Ireland, came to New York, and formed a society, of his own countrymen, and others. About the same time, Robert Strawbridge, another local preacher, from Ireland, settled in Frederick county, in Maryland, and formed a few societies. In 1769, Richard Boardman, and Joseph Pilmoor, came to New York, who were the first regular Methodist preachers on the continent. In 1771, Francis Asbury, and Richard Wright, came over, and many classes were formed, and many ministers were raised up among them. From their first rise in America, until 1784, they called themselves the members of the church of England, and went to the Episcopal ministers for baptism and the eucharist.

They never spread much in Virginia, till about 1775. Since that time, they have spread so much, that they have a sprinkling all over the state, and, in some counties, are numerous. In 1784, Rev. Thomas Coke came over from England, having authority from Mr. John Wesley, (the first founder of the society,) to organize the Methodists into a distinct church. Pursuant thereto, Mr. Francis Asbury was ordained superintendant, and a number of elders and deacons were consecrated for inferior services. Their number, on the continent, is above forty-three thousand, and they have been the most fortunate, in increasing their number of preachers, of any society in Virginia. They deny the doctrine of predestination, according to the Calvanistic explanation; hold that Christ died for all Adam's progeny; believe that, after men are converted and sanctified, they may fall away, and be finally damned; their doctrine, in fine, is Arminian, their magazine bears the name.

Their ministers are very constant preachers, and they exceed all societies in the state, in spreading their books and written tenets among the people. They generally baptize by sprinkling, but their rules allow of pouring or immersion.*

---

* Baptism, by some, is made *everything;* by some, *anything;* and, by others, *nothing*. The Episcopalians make it *everything;* they say that the water is blest to the mystical washing away of sin; that, by it, children are regenerated, and engrafted into the body of Christ, which is *everything* we need. The Methodists make it *anything;* either sprinkling, pouring or immersion. No matter how it is done, if it is done. Can it be supposed, that Jesus, who was faithful in all his house, in the character of a son, should be less definite in his orders than Moses was, who was only a servant? See (says the Hebrew prophet) that thou makest the tabernacle, in all things, according to the pattern shown to thee in the Mount; and is the pattern of Jesus of no more use than to be made *anything* of? That which is to be done but once in a man's life, should be well done. Are the words of St. Paul inapplicable here? "One baptism."

The Quakers make it *nothing;* but when they regard the word of God more, and the

OF THE TUNKERS.

THERE are a few Tunkers and Mennonists in Virginia, and, as it is the design of this chronicle to treat of all the religious sects in the state, I shall give an account of their first rise and peculiarities. First of the Tunkers.

The Germans sound the letter *t* like *d*, for which reason they are called Dunkers, which name signifies Sops or Dippers. They first arose in Schwardznau, in the year 1708. Seven religious neighbors, chiefly Presbyterians, consorted together, to read the Bible, and edify each other in the way that they had been brought up, having never heard that there was a Baptist in the world. However, being convinced of believers' baptism, and congregational government, they desired Alexander Mack to baptize them, which he objected to, considering himself unbaptized; upon which they cast lots for an administrator.† Upon whom the lot fell, has been cautiously concealed; but baptized they were, in the river Eder, by Schwardzenau, and then formed themselves into a church, choosing Alexander Mack for their minister. As God prospered their labors, and made them increase, both in members and preachers, so Satan raised persecution against them. Some fled to Holland, and some to Creyfelt; and the mother church voluntarily removed to Frizland, and thence to America. In 1719, and in 1729, those of Holland and Creyfelt followed them. In Pennsylvania, Maryland, etc., there is a considerable number of them; and a few from those states have found their way into Virginia. They hold that Christ not only died for all Adam's race, but that he will finally restore all to glory. They practise trine-immersion in baptism; leading the candidate into the water, he kneels down, and the minister dips him, face downward, first in the name of the Father, then in the name of the Son, and then in the name of the Holy Ghost; which being done, while he

---

word of Barclay less, they will then find baptism, not only to be a command, but the first commad, after repentance and faith.

If baptism is *everything*, Simon, the witch, is gone to heaven, and the thief dropt from the cross to hell. If it is *anything*, we may say of it, as Mr. Wesley does of praying time, "any time is no time." And if it is *nothing*, why is the noun, with its verb and participle, recorded almost one hundred times in the New Testament? If men can be perfect, or obedient in all things, without it, what means this bleating of the Scriptures which I hear?

† This mode was used in the ordination of Matthias to the apostleship; and, like every other account in the New Testament, is a precedent without a second. As no *two* instances of ordination are uniform, can it be a piece of licentiousness to treat the subject, as to its mode, with a degree of indifference? In Virginia, Episcopal, Presbyterial, and Congregational ordinations are all contended for. Imposition and non-imposition of hands are equally pleaded for; but, after all, a commission from Heaven, to preach and baptize, is the great quintessence.

continues on his knees, the minister imposes hands upon his head, prays, and then leads them out. They also practise washing of feet, anointing the sick with oil, and the holy kiss. They will neither swear, fight, nor keep slaves. They make little or no use of the civil law, and take no use for money. As Christians, they live mortified, self-denying lives; and, as citizens, they are patterns of peace; well deserving their common title—*harmless Tunkers.*

OF THE MENNONISTS.

The Mennonists derive their name from Menno Simon. He was born in the year 1505—got into orders in 1528—continued a famous preacher and disputer till 1531. He then began to question the validity of many things in the church of Rome, and among the rest, infant baptism; but neither the doctors of his order, nor those of the Protestant faith, gave him the satisfaction he wished for. He finally embraced believers' baptism, and continued preaching and planting churches in the low countries for thirty years, and died in peace, January 31, 1561. Menno was dipped himself, and dipped others, and so did his successors, except when they were in prison, or were hindered from going to the water, and then pouring was practised. What they used in Europe, only of necessity, is become the only mode practised by them in America. They hold a profession of faith a prerequisite to baptism, which, in Virginia, is made by learning to answer a number of questions. The candidate being received, kneels down before the minister, and water is poured on his head; after which, follow imposition of hands and prayer. They believe the doctrine of universal provision, but not the doctrine of universal restitution; they are equally conscientious of swearing and bearing arms, with the Quakers and Tunkers. The only Virginia Baptist church that I know of in the state, that refuse to bear arms, or take an oath before a magistrate, is one in Shenandoah; the chiefest of whom, are the natural descendants of the Mennonists. In worship and discipline, they are like other Baptists in the state; but some peculiarities of the Mennonists, keep them from uniting.

The Tunkers and Mennonists seem to be more consistent with themselves than the Quakers, in disusing the law as well as arms. Perhaps the reason is, because the two first have been small, persecuted societies, and have learned to bear affliction patiently, and have but little to do with mankind; but should they undertake to settle a colony themselves, as the Quakers did Pennsylvania, it is probable that they would see the necessity of civil law. Civil government is certainly a curse to mankind; but it is a necessary curse, in this fallen state, to prevent greater evils. It is yet a question, whether the good Quakers have a sufficient reason for using the law, and not appealing to arms. If an internal foe arises, and kills a man, they execute the law, and hang the murderer; but if external foes invade, and kill and burn all before them, no means must be used to bring them to punishment. Is it bad reasoning to say, that when innocency is injured, it appeals first to *law* for redress; but if it finds no redress at law, it finally appeals to *arms*? The law of a state, is the compact of citizens in the state, and the law of nations in confederation, is the compact of bodies of men; and why the violators of one should be punished, and the breakers of the other pass with impunity, is not so easily answered. If all nations were true to their engagements, there would be no war in the world; so, if all the citizens in a state, lived agreeable to the laws of it, there would be no punishment. If there was no sin in the world, there would be no laws needed. The more virtuous people are, the more liberal their laws should be; but the more vicious the people are, the more severe the laws must be, to restrain their unruly passions. Where rulers are more virtuous than the people, the more independent and important the rulers are, the better for the people; but where the people are more virtuous than the magistrates, magistrates should be dependant on, and responsible to the people. As it is generally seen that the people are more virtuous than those in power; consequently, a republican, responsible government is best. Great salaries given to officers, are as dangerous to the good of the community, as no salaries are. Great salaries stimulate avaricious men, to make use of undue means to acquire those offices, while men of real merit feel a disgust to prey so much upon the industrious. Incompetent salaries, disable men of small forturnes from filling those offices their real merit entitles them to, and consequently fix government in the hands of the rich, who generally feel more for themselves, than they do for the poor. To fix salaries high enough, and not too high, is the work of the wise; and to give power enough to men to do good, and yet have it so counterpoised, that they can do no harm, is a line so difficult to be drawn, that it has never yet been done.

OF THE BAPTISTS.

THE Baptists took their rise in Virginia, before the Methodists; but, as I purpose to treat more largely on the doctrine and forms of the Baptists, than I have done on other societies, I have reserved them for the last.

There were a few Baptists in Virginia, before the year, 1760, but they did not spread, so as to be taken notice of by the people, much less by the rulers, till after that date. About the year, 1764, they prevailed so much, that, in the year following, they formed an Association, called, "the Ketocton Regular Baptist Association."* From 1764, to 1774, the Baptists

* Ketocton, is the name of a water-course, in Loudoun county, that empties into the Potomac. Most of the Baptist churches, now in Virginia, take their names of distinction from the waters where they are.

spread over the greatest part of the state that was peopled. Several ministers, of that order came from Pennsylvania and the Jerseys, and settled in the northern parts of the state, and others were raised up in the southern parts, who travelled about, and preached like the old Baptist, John, "repent, for the kingdom of Heaven is at hand," and great numbers of the people went out unto them, and were baptized, confessing their sins. Many of the young converts caught the spirit of their teachers, and zealously engaged in the work. In a course of time, the fires from the northern preachers, and those in the south, met, like the two seas, in St. Paul's shipwreck, in Orange county, 1767. Two or three ministers, from each side, assembled in conference, but did not so happily unite, as candor desired. A division took place. The northern members called themselves, "Regular Baptists," and the southern members called themselves, "Separate Baptists;" and, if some alienation of affection did not attend this division, in some instances, it was because they were free from those temptations that have always mingled with religious divisions, and if there was not a little zeal discovered to proselyte, as well as convert the people, I have been wrongly informed.

The Regulars, adhered to a confession of faith, first published in London, 1689, and afterwards adopted by the Baptist Association of Philadelphia, in 1742; but the Separates had none but the Bible. Just upon the spot of ground where the division took place, the members knew something of the cause; but those who lived at a distance, were ignorant of the reason, and whenever they met, they loved each other as brethren, and much deplored that there should be any distinction, or shyness among them. The Separates, who also formed an association, increased much the fastest, both in ministers and members, and occupied, by far, the greatest territory. The Regulars were orthodox Calvanists, and the work under them was solemn and rational; but the Separates were the most zealous, and the work among them was very noisy. The people would cry out, "fall down," and, for a time, lose the use of their limbs; which exercise made the bystanders marvel; some thought they were deceitful, others, that they were bewitched, and many being convinced of all, would report that God was with them of a truth.

THE PERSECUTION OF THE BAPTISTS.

Soon after the Baptist ministers began to preach in Virginia, the novelty of their doctrine, the rarity of mechanics and planters preaching such strange things,* and the wonderful effect that their preaching had on the

* To this day, there are not more than three or four Baptist ministers in Virginia, who have received the *diploma* of M. A., which is additional proof that the work has been of God, and not of man.

people, called out multitudes to hear them—some out of curiosity, some in sincerity, and some in ill will.

Their doctrine, influence and popularity, made them many enemies; especially among those who value themselves most for religion in the Episcopal mode. The usual alarm of the *Church and State* being in danger, was echoed through the colony; nor were the Episcopal clergymen so modest, but what they joined the alarm; like the silversmiths of old, crying "our craft is in danger of being set at naught." Magistrates began to issue their warrants, and sheriffs had their orders to take up the *disturbers of the peace.* The county of Spottsylvania took the lead, and others soon followed their example. Preaching, teaching, or exhorting, was what disturbed the peace. A like work disturbed the peace of Satan, when he cried out, "let us alone." Sometimes, when the preachers were brought before the courts, they escaped the prison by giving bonds and security, that they would not preach in the county in the term of one year; but most of them preferred the dungeon to such bonds. Not only ministers were imprisoned, but others, for only praying in their families, with a neighbor or two.

The act of *toleration*, passed in the first of William and Mary's reign, afforded the suffering brethren some relief. By applying to the general court, and subscribing to all the thirty-nine articles, saving the thirty-fourth, thirty-fifth, and thirty-sixth, together with one clause in the twentieth, and part of the twenty-seventh, they obtained license to preach at certain stipulated places;* but, if they preached at any other places, they were exposed to be prosecuted.

Some of the prisoners would give bonds not to preach, and as soon as they were freed, would immediately preach as before. This was done, when they had reason to believe that the court would never bring suit upon the bonds. I have never heard of but one such suit in the state, and that one was dismissed. The ministers would go singing from the court-house to the prison, where they had, sometimes, the liberty of the bounds, and at other times they had not. They used to preach to the people through the grates: to prevent which, some ill-disposed men would be at the expense

* There are other parts of the thirty-nine articles, equally exceptionable with those parts excepted. If a creed of faith, established by law, was ever so short, and ever so true; if I delieved the whole of it with all my heart—should I subscribe to it before a magistrate, in order to get indulgence, preferment, or even protection—I should be guilty of a species of idolatry, by acknowledging a power, that the Head of the Church, Jesus Christ, has never appointed. In this point of view, who can look over the Constitutions of government adopted in most of the United States, without real sorrow? They require a religious test, to qualify an officer of state. All the good such tests do, is to keep from office the best of men; villains make no scruple of any test. The Virginia Constitution is free from this stain. If a man merits the confidence of his neighbours, in Virginia—let him worsnip one God, twenty God's, or no God—be he Jew, Turk, Pagan, or Infidel, he is eligible to any office in the state.

of erecting a high wall around the prison; others, would employ half drunken strolls to beat a drum around the prison to prevent the people from hearing. Sometimes, matches and pepper-pods were burnt at the prison-door, and many such afflictions the dear disciples went through. About thirty of the preachers were honored with a dungeon, and a few others beside. Some of them were imprisoned as often as four times, besides all the mobs and perils they went through. The dragon roared with hideous peals, but was not *red*—the Beast appeared formidable, but was not *scarlet colored*. Virginia soil has never been stained with vital blood for conscience sake. Heaven has restrained the wrath of man, and brought auspicious days at last. We now sit under our vines and fig-trees, and there is none to make us afraid.

THE REASONS OF THEIR DISSENT.

BUT why this schism? says an inquisitor. If the people were disposed to be more devotional than they had been before, why not be devout in the church in which they had been raised, without rending themselves off, and procuring so much evil unto themselves? This question may be answered in part, by asking a similar one. Why did the Episcopal church rend off from the church of Rome, in the Reformation? Why not continue in that church, and worship in her mode? What necessity for that schism, which occasioned so much war and persecution? If we are to credit Frederick, in his "Memoirs of the House of Brandenburg," the cause of the Reformation was, in England, the love of a woman—in Germany, the love of gain—in France, the love of novelty, or a song. But can the church of England offer no other reason for her heretical schism, but the love of a woman? Undoubtedly she can: she has done it, and we approve of her reason; but after all, she is not so pure in her worship, but what we have many reasons for dissenting from her. Some of which are as follows:

1. No national church, can, in its organization, be the Gospel Church. A national church takes in the whole nation, and no more; whereas, the Gospel Church, takes in no nation, but those who fear God, and work righteousness in every nation. The notion of a Christian commonwealth, should be exploded forever, without there was a commonwealth of real Christians. Not only so, but if all the souls in a government, were saints of God, should they be formed into a society by law, that society could not be a Gospel Church, but a creature of state.

2. The church of England, in Virginia, has no discipline but the civil law. The crimes of their delinquent members are tried in a court-house, before the judges of the police, their censures are laid on at the whipping-post, and their excommunications are administered at the gallows. In England, if a man cast contempt upon the spiritual court, the bishop delegates a grave priest, who, with his chancellor, excommunicate him. The

man thus excommunicated, is by law, disabled from being a plaintiff or witness in any suit. But for heresy, incest or adultery, the bishop himself pronounces the exclusion. The outcast, is not only denied the company of Christians, in spiritual duties, but also, in temporal concerns. He not only is disabled from being plaintiff or witness in any suit, (and so deprived of the protection of the law,) but if he continues forty-days an excommunicant, a writ comes against him, and he is cast into prison, without bail, and there continues until he has paid the last mite. Mrs. Trask was judged a heretick, because she believed in the Jewish Sabbath, and for that, she was imprisoned sixteen years, until she died; but a Gospel Church has nothing to do with corporeal punishments. If a member commits sin, the church is to exclude him, which is as far as church power extends. If the crime is cognizable by law, the culprit must bear what the law inflicts. In the church of England, ecclesiastical and civil matters are so blended together, that I know not who can be blamed for dissenting from her.

3. The manner of initiating members into the church of England, is arbitrary and tyrannical. The subject, (for a candidate I cannot call him,) is taken by force, brought to the priest, baptized, and declared a member of the church. The little Christian shows all the aversion he is capable of, by cries and struggles, but all to no purpose; ingrafted he is; and, when the child grows up, if he differs in judgment from his father and king, he is called a dissenter, because he is honest, and will not say that he believes what he does not believe; and, as such, in England, can fill no post of honor or profit. Here, let it be observed, that religion is a matter entirely between God and individuals. No man has a right to force another to join a church; nor do the legitimate powers of civil government extend so far as to disable, incapacitate, proscribe, or in any way distress, in person, property, liberty or life, any man who cannot believe and practice in the common road. A church of Christ, according to the Gospel, is a congregation of faithful persons, called out of the world by divine grace, who mutually agree to live together, and execute gospel discipline among them; which government, is not national, parochial, or presbyterial, but congregational.

4. The church of England has a human head. Henry VIII. cast off the Pope's yoke, and was declared head of the church, 1533; which title, all the kings of England have borne since; but the Gospel Church, acknowledges no head but King Jesus: He is law-giver, king, and judge—is a jealous God, and will not give his glory unto another.

5. The preachers of that order, in Virginia, for the most part, not only plead for theatrical amusements, and what they call civil mirth, but their preaching is dry and barren, containing little else but morality. The great doctrines of universal depravity, redemption by the blood of Christ, rengeneration, faith, repentance and self-denial, are but seldom preached by them,

and, when they meddle with them, it is in such a superficial manner, as if they were nothing but things of course.

6. Their manner of visiting the sick, absolving sins, administering the Lord's supper to newly married couples, burying the dead, sprinkling children with their gossips, promises, cross, etc., are no ways satisfactory, and, as they were handed to us through the force of law, we reject them in toto. These are some of the reasons we have for dissenting from the Episcopalians in Virginia, and though they may not be sufficient to justify our conduct, in the opinion of others, yet they have weight with us.*

THREE GREAT PRINCIPLES.

THERE are three grand, leading principles, which divide the Christian world: I say leading principles—for each of them is subdivided into a number of peculiarities; these three, I shall call *fate*, *free-will*, and *restitution.*

1st. FATE. Those who believe this doctrine, say, that God eternally ordained whatsoever comes to pass: that if the minutest action should be done that God did not appoint, it would not only prove a world of chance, but create an uneasiness in the Divine mind; that *providence* and *grace* are stewards, to see that all God's decrees are fulfilled. Sometimes a distinction is made between God's *absolute* and *permissive* decrees; that God *absolutely* decreed the good, and *permissively* decreed the evil. Other times it is stated thus: that upon the principle of God's knowing all things, every thing comes to pass of necessity. With this sentiment, most commonly, is connected the doctrine of *particular* redemption: that Jesus Christ undertook for a certain number of Adam's progeny, and for them alone he died; that those for whom he died, shall be called, by irresistible grace, to the knowledge of the Truth and be saved; that if one of these, whom he *chose* and *redeemed*, should miss of Heaven, his will would be frustrated, and his blood lost. And as this, at first view, seems to excuse the non-elect for not believing in the Mediator, it is sometimes said that Jesus died *virtually* for all, but intentionally for a few. Others, who disdain such pitiful shifts, say, that the want of the faith of God's elect, is no sin; that justice cannot require a man to have a more divine life than Adam possesed

* What is here said of the church of England, respects them before the late Revolution. Since the independence of the state, a great number of those who still prefer Episcopacy, have the most noble ideas of religious liberty, and are as far from wishing to oppress those who differ with them in judgment, as any men in the state. Experience proves, that while each man believes what he chooses, and practises as he pleases, although they differ widely in sentiment, yet they love each other better, than they do when they are all obliged to believe and worship in one way. The only way to live in peace and enjoy ourselves as freemen, is to think and speak freely, worship as we please, and be protected by law in our persons, property and liberty.

in Eden; that if we, as rational creatures, do not believe as much as Adam could have believed in innocency, when revealed to us, that we are guilty of the sin of unbelief; but that the law cannot require us to believe in a Mediator, and therefore, the want of *that* faith is not a sin. Those who adhere to this principle, are called, Fatalists, Predestinarians, Calvanists, Supralapfarians, etc.

2d. FREE-WILL. Those who adopt this principle, affirm that Ged eternally decreed to establish the freedom of the human will. That if men are *necessary* agents, the very idea of virtue and vice is destroyed; that the more angels and men are exalted in their creation, in the state of free agency, the greater was the probability of their falling; that sin could never have entered into the world, upon any other footing; that if man does what he cannot avoid, it is no rebellion in the creature; that God never offers violence to the human will, in the process of grace; that Christ has fulfilled the law, which all were under—bore the curse for all—spilt his blood for all—makes known his grace to all—gives to each a talent—bids all improve—and finally, that if men are damned, it will not be for the want of a Saviour; but for refusing to obey him, damned for unbelief, and that those who are damned will have their torment augmented for refusing an offered Saviour. Some, who adhere to this doctrine, believe that when men are once born again, that they can never perish, and others believe, that there is no state so secure, in this world, but what men may fall from it into eternal damnation. The advocates for the above sentiment, are called Arminians, Free-willers, Universalists, Provisionists, etc.

3d. RESTITUTION. Those who espouse this sentiment, declare that God eternally designed to save all men; that he made them to enjoy him for ever, and that he will not be frustrated—that Christ died for all, and will not lose his blood—that if more souls are lost than saved, Satan will have the greatest triumph, and sin have a more boundless reign than grace—that if even one soul should be miserable, world without end, the sting of death and the victory of the grave would never be destroyed—that Jesus will reign till all his foes, even the last enemy, shall be rooted up—that he will reconcile all things unto himself, and make all things new—that every creature in heaven, in earth, and under the earth, shall join in the celestial doxology. But those who hold this doctrine are equally perplexed and divided, with those who believe the two before-mentioned principles.

Some of them extend the doctrine to fallen angels, others confine it to the human race—some believe there will be no punishment after death, others conclude that torment will be infflicted in Hades, upon rebellious souls, even until the resurrection of the body; and others think that they will not all be restored, till the expiration of several periodical eternities.

Those who avow this doctrine, are called Universalists, Hell-Redemptioners, &c.

Whether it is a blessing or a curse to mankind, it is a certain truth, that the theoretic principles of men, have but little effect upon their lives. I know men of all the before-written doctrines that equally seem to strive to glorify God, in the way which they conceive will do it the most effectually. It is no novelty in the world, for men of different sentiments, to stigmatize the doctrines of each other, with being pregnant with dangerous consequences; but it is not the doctrine or system that a man believes, that makes him either a *good* or *bad* man, but the SPIRIT he is governed by. It is a saying among lovers, that "love will triumph over reason," and it is as true, that the disposition of the heart will prevail over the system of the head.

The third principle, mentioned above, has few, if any, vouchers among the Baptists in Virginia; but the two first spoken of, divide counties, churches and families, which, about the year 1775, raised a great dispute in Virginia, and finally split the Separate Baptists, which division continued several years; but, after both parties had contested till their courage grew cool, they ceased their hostilities, grounded their arms, and formed a compromise upon the middle ground, of "think and let think;" and ceded to each other its territory and liberty.

I am acquainted with men of all these principles, who are equally assured they are right. No doubt they are right in their own conceits, and they may be all right in their aims; but I am assured they are not all right in their systems; and far enough from being right, when they bitterly condemn each other.

OF MARRIAGE.

It is a question, not easily answered, whether marriage was appointed by the Divine Parent, merely for the propagation of the human species, or for the education of children. Whether one or the other, or both were reasons of the institution, it certainly was appointed by God, honored by Jesus, and declared to be honorable unto all by St. Paul. What lies before me at present, is to consider the mode of marriage, in Virginia, before the late revolution, and the alterations that have since taken place.

Under the regal government, the rites of matrimony were solemnized two ways. The first, and most reputable way, was this: From the clerk's office, in the county where the bride lived, a license was issued to the bridegroom, which cost twenty shillings, which was a perquisite of the governor; and fifty pounds of tobacco for the fee of the clerk, which raised the price to a guinea. This license was delivered to the clergyman on the wedding day, for his security; and for solemnizing the rites, he was entitled to twenty shillings. This way of getting wives, was too expensive for the poor, and, therefore, another mode was prescribed by law, as an alternative. The clergyman published the banns of marriage on three holy days, for which he was entitled to eighteen pence, and for joining such couples together he was entitled to five shillings. The Presbyterian ministers sometimes solemnized the rites; but if it was by a license, the parish preacher claimed and recovered his fee, as though he had solemnized the rites himself. After the declaration of independence, in 1780, an act passed the general assembly to authorise as many as four ministers in each county, of each denomination, to solemnize the rites; but the act was so partial that some would not qualify, others took what indulgence the act gave, and still petitioned for equal liberty. The Episcopal clergymen were allowed to join people together in any part of the state, while others were circumscribed by county bounds. In 1784, this partiality was removed, and all ministers were set on a level. By presenting credentials of their ordination, and a recommendation of their good character in the society where they are members, and also giving bond and security to the court of the county where they reside, they receive testimonials, signed by the senior magistrate, to join together any persons who legally apply in any part of the state. Publication is now abolished. From the county in whichh the bride resides, a license is issued out of the clerk's office, which costs the groom fifteen pence; this license is given to the preacher, for his security; and for joining them together, he is entitled to five shillings. The preacher is under bonds to certify the clerk, from whom the license came, of the solemnization; and the clerk, for registering the certificate, is entitled to fifteen pence more: so that it costs but seven shillings and six pence to get a wife in these days.

THE DECLENSION AMONG THE BAPTISTS.

A REVIEW of head eleven, informs us what persecution the Baptist preachers were subject to, which continued in some counties until the revolution. Upon the declaration of independence, and the establishment of a republican form of government, it is not to be wondered at that the Baptists so heartily and uniformly engaged in the cause of the country against the king. The change suited their political principles, promised religious liberty, and a freedom from ministerial tax; nor have they been disappointed in their expectations. In 1776, the salaries of the Episcopal clergymen were suspended, which was so confirmed in 1779, that no legal force has ever been used since to support any preachers in the state. But as they gained this piece of freedom, so the cares of war, the spirit of trade, and moving to the western waters, seemed to bring on a general declension. The ways of Zion mourned. They obtained their hearts' desire, (freedom,) but had leanness in their souls. Some of the old watchmen stumbled and fell, iniquity did abound, and the love of many waxed cold. But the declension was not so total, but what God showed himself gracious in some places; his blessings, like small showers in the drought of summer, were scattered abroad. Delegates from the churches assembled in association once or twice in each year; but so much of the time was taken up in confiding what means had best be used to obtain and preserve equal liberty with other societies, that many of the churches were discouraged in sending delegates. Many of the ministers removed from their churches, to Kentucky, and left their scattered flocks, like a cottage in the vineyard, like a lodge in a garden of cucumbers. In this point of view was the Baptist Society in Virginia, at the close of the war, and the return of auspicious peace.

October, 1783, was the last General Association the Separate Baptists ever had. They divided into four or five districts; but to maintain a friendly correspondence, and be helpers to each other, in a political way, they established a General Committee, to be composed of delegates sent from each distinct Association, to meet annually. Not more than four delegates from one Association are entitled to seats. This committee give their opinion on all queries sent to them from any of the Associations, originate all petitions to be laid before the legislature of the state, and consider the good of the whole society. It may be here noted, that the General Committee, as well as the Associations, exercise no lordship over the churches—all they attempt is advice, which is generally received by the churches in a cordial manner. Should they attempt any thing more, without legal authority, they would appear ridiculous; and with legal authority, they would grow tyrannical. Of this Committee, the regular Baptist Association became a member.

In 1784, the Episcopal society was legally incorporated, and such exertions were made for a general assessment, to oblige all the citizens in the state to pay *some* preacher, that a bill for that purpose passed two readings; but the final determination of the bill was postponed until November, 1785; when the time came, the Presbyterians, Baptists, Quakers, Methodists,* Deists, and covetous, made such an effort against the bill, that it fell through. In 1786, the act, incorporating the Episcopal society was repealed; but in 1788, their trustees were legalized to manage the property, which is the state of things at this time.

Several attempts were made, at different times, to unite the Regular and Separate Associations together, but all proved in vain, until August, 1787,

* Before this, the Methodists petitioned for a continuation of the established religion of the state; but being organized a distinct church, they vigorously opposed the assessment; and at the same time petitioned the legislature for a general liberation of the slaves. Although the petition was rejected, as being impracticable, yet it shows their resolution to bring to pass a noble work.

when they united upon the principle of receiving the confession of faith, before mentioned, as containing the great essential doctrines of the gospel, yet, not in so strict a sense, that *all* are obliged to believe *everything* therein contained.* At the same time, it was agreed, that the appellations, Regular and Separate, should be buried in oblivion, and that in future they should be called "the United Baptist Churches of Christ in Virginia."

THE GREAT WORK.

The first part of the last head gives an account of the declension of religion among the Baptists, which continued until 1785. In the summer of that year, the glorious work of God broke out, on the banks of James River, and from thence has spread almost over the state. In treating of this great revival, I shall not write as a divine, a philosopher, or an opposer, but solely as an historian.

In the greatest part of the meetings, when religion is low among the people, there is no unusual appearance among them; a grave countenance, a solemn sigh, or a silent tear, is as much as is seen or heard, and sometimes a great degree of inattention and carelessness: but in times of reviving it is quite otherwise, in most places. It is nothing strange, to see a great part of the congregation fall prostrate upon the floor or ground; many of whom, entirely loose the use of their limbs for a season. Sometimes numbers of them are crying out at once, some of them, in great distress, using such language as this: "God, be merciful to me a sinner—Lord, save me

* A union seemed so necessary and desirable, that those who were somewhat scrupulous of a confession of faith, other than the Bible, were willing to sacrifice their peculiarities, and those who were strenuous for the confession of faith, agreed to a partial reception of it. "United we stand, divided we fall," overcome, at that time, all objections; but had they united without any confession of faith, as they did in Georgia, perhaps it would have been better. In kingdoms and states, where a system of religion is established by law, with the indulgence of toleration to non-conformists of restricted sentiments, it becomes necessary for such non-conformists to publish a confession of their faith, to convince the rulers that they do not exceed the bounds of toleration; but in a government like that of Virginia, where all men believe and worship as they please—where the only punishment inflicted on the enthusiastical, is pity—what need of a confession of faith? Why this Virgin Mary between the souls of men and the scriptures? Had a system of religion been essential to salvation, or even to the happiness of the saints, would not Jesus, who was faithful in all his house, have left us one? If he has, it is accessible to all. If he has not, why should a man be called a heretick because he cannot believe what he cannot believe, though he believes the Bible with all his heart? Confessions of faith often check any further pursuit after truth, confine the mind into a particular way of reasoning, and give rise to frequent separations. To plead for their utility, because they have been common, is as good sense, as to plead for a state establishment of religion, for the same reason; and both are as bad reasoning, as to plead for sin, because it is everywhere. It is sometimes said that hereticks are always averse to confessions of faith. I wish I could say as much of tyrants. But after all, if a confession of faith, upon the whole, may be advantageous, the greatest care should be taken not to *sacradize*, or make a petty Bible of it.

or I must perish—what shall I do to be saved ?" etc. Others breaking out in such rapturous expressions as these : " Bless the Lord, O my soul ! O, sweet Jesus, how I love thee !—Let everything that hath breath praise the Lord !—O, sinners ! come, taste and see how good the Lord is !" etc.

I have seen such exercise, and heard such melody for several hours together. At Associations, and great meetings, I have seen numbers of ministers and exhorters, improving their gifts at the same time. Such a heavenly confusion among the preachers, and such a celestial discord among the people, destroy all articulation, so that the understanding is not edified ; but the awful echo, sounding in the ears, and the objects in great distress, and great raptures before the eyes, raise great emotion in the heart. Some of the ministers rather oppose this work, others call it a little in question, and some fan it with all their might. Whether it be celestial or terrestial, or a complication of both, it is observed by the candid that more souls get first awakened at such meetings, than at any meetings whatever, who afterwards give clear, rational accounts of a divine change of heart. This exercise is not confined to the newly convicted, and newly converted, but persons who have been professors a number of years, at such lively meetings, not only jump up, strike their hands together, and shout aloud, but will embrace one another, and fall to the floor. I have never known the rules of decency broken so far as for persons of different sexes, thus to embrace and fall at meetings. It is not to be understood that this exercise is seen in all parts of the state, at times when God is working on the minds of the people. No, under the preaching of the same man, in different neighborhoods and counties, the same work, in substance, has different exterior effects.

At such times of revival, it is wonderful to hear the sweet singing among the people, when they make melody in their hearts and voices to the Lord. In the last great ingathering, in some places, singing was more blessed among the people than the preaching was. What Mr. Jonathan Edwards thought might be expedient in some future day, has been true in Virginia. Bands go singing to meeting, and singing home. At meeting, as soon as preaching is over, it is common to sing a number of spiritual songs ; sometimes several songs are sounding at the same time, in different parts of the congregation. I have travelled through neighborhoods and counties at times of refreshing, and the spiritual songs in the fields, in the shops and houses, have made the heavens ring with melody over my head ; but, as soon as the work is over, there is no more of it heard. Dr. Watts is the general standard for the Baptists in Virginia ; but they are not confined to him ; any spiritual composition answers their purpose. A number of hymns originate in Virginia, although there is no established poet in the state. Some Virginia songs have more divinity in them, than poetry or grammar ; and some that I have heard have but little of either.

Candidates generally make confession of their faith before the whole assembly present; but, sometimes there are so many to offer, that the church divides into several bodies, each of which acts for the whole, and receives by the right hand of fellowship. At times appointed for baptism, the people generally go singing to the water-side, in grand procession: I have heard many souls declare they first were convicted, or first found pardon going to, at, or coming from the water. If those who practice infant baptism can say as much, it is no wonder they are so fond of it. Forty, fifty, and sixty have often been baptized in a day, at one place, in Virginia, and sometimes as many as seventy-five. There are some ministers now living in Virginia, who have baptized more than two thousand persons. It is said that St. Austin baptized ten thousand in the dead of winter, in the river Swale, in England, in the year 595. I have seen ice cut more than a foot thick, and people baptized in the water, and yet I have never heard of any person taking cold, or any kind of sickness, in so doing. And strange it is that Mr. Wesley should recommend *cold bathing* for such a vast number of disorders, and yet be so backward to administer it for the best purpose, viz., to fulfil righteousness.

THE NUMBER OF BAPTISTS.

There are in Virginia, at this time, about one hundred and fifty ordained preachers of the Baptist denomination, and a number besides who exercise a public gift; but in the late great additions that have been made to the churches, there are but few who have engaged in the work of the ministry. Whether it is because the old preachers stand in the way, or whether it is because the people do not pray the Lord of the harvest to thrust out laborers, or whether it is not rather a judgment of God upon the people, for neglecting those who are already in the work, not communicating to them in all good things,* I cannot say; but so it is, that but few appear to be advancing, to supply the places of the old ones, upon their decease.

There are also about two hundred and two churches. The exact number of members I cannot ascertain. Between Potomac and James rivers, are nine thousand; and as there is about the same number of preachers and churches, between James river and North Carolina, together with some good account, I judge there are as many as nine thousand south of James river. Upon the western waters, in Kentucky, there are thirty-one churches, divided into three Assaciations. In one of them, there were one thousand members, May, 1789. In another, there is about the same number; but, lest I should swell my numbers too high, I will add the little

* Gospel preachers are generally like the ass seen by Agelastus, loaded with figs, and feeding upon thistles.

Association, at the falls of Ohio, containing five churches, to make the round number of two thousand in Kentucky; and, as there are a few Baptists between the Alleghany and Kentucky, I conclude the sum of twenty thousand is a moderate estimate. These churches are classed into eleven Associations, nine of which correspond in the General Committee. For the ease of the eye, they are stated in the following table:—

1 General Committee.
11 Asssociations,
202 Churches,
150 Ministers,*
20,000 Members.

The number of communicants compose but a small part of those who commonly attend Baptist worship. It will not appear extravagant, to those who are generally acquainted in the state, to say that, taking one part of the state with another, there are more people who attend the Baptist worship, than any kind of worship in the state.

OF DRESS.

Upon the first rise of the Baptists in Virginia, they were very strict in their dress. Men cut off their hair, like Cromwell's round-headed chaplains, and women cast away all their superfluities; so that they were distinguished from others, merely by their decoration. Where all were of one mind, no evil ensued; but where some did not choose to dock and strip, and churches made it a matter of discipline, it made great confusion; for no standard could be found in the Bible, to measure their garments by. No doubt, dressing, as well as eating and drinking, can be carried to excess; but it appears to be a matter between God and individuals; for, whenever churches take it up, the last evil is worse than the first. This principle prevailed until the war broke out, at which time the Baptist mode took the lead. Those who went into the army, cut off their hair, and those who stayed at home, were obliged to dress in home-spun. Since the return of peace, and the opening of the ports, the uniformity between the Baptists and others, in point of clothing, still exists; notwithstanding the great work of conversion there has been in the state, but very little is said about rending garments; those who behave well, wear what they please, and meet with no reproof.

THE EXCESS OF CIVIL POWER EXPLODED.

The principle, that civil rulers have nothing to do with religion in their

* In England, are two arch-bishops, and twenty-six bishops. In Ireland, are four arch-bishops, and nineteen bishops. In Scotland, one general assembly, thirteen provincial synods, and sixty-eight presbyteries.

official capacities, is as much interwoven in the Baptist plan, as Phydias's name was in the shield. The legitimate powers of government extend only to punish men for working ill to their neighbors, and no way affect the rights of conscience. The nation of Israel received their civil and religious laws from Jehovah, which were binding on them, and no other; and with the extirpation of that nation, were abolished. For a Christian commonwealth to be established upon the same claim, is very presumptuous, without they have the same charter from Heaven. Because the nation of Israel had a divine grant of the land of Canaan, and orders to enslave the heathen, some suppose Christians have an equal right to take away the land of the Indians, and make slaves of the negroes. Wretched religion, that pleads for cruelty and injustice. In this point of view, the Pope offered England to the king of Spain, provided he would conquer it; after England became Protestant, and in the same view of things, on May 4, 1493, the year after America was discovered, he proposed to give away the heathen lands to his Christian subjects. If Christian nations, were nations of Christians, these things would not be so. The very tendency of religious establishments by human law, is to make some hypocrites, and the rest fools; they are calculated to destroy those very virtues that religion is designed to build up; to encourage fraud and violence over the earth. It is error alone, that stands in need of government to support it; truth can and will do better without: so ignorance calls in anger in a debate, good sense scorns it. Religion, in its purest ages, made its way in the world, not only without the aid of the law, but against all the laws of haughty monarchs, and all the maxims of the schools. The pretended friendship of *legal* protection, and *learned* assistance, proves often in the end like the friendship of Joab to Amasa.

Government should protect every man in thinking and speaking freely, and see that one does not abuse another. The liberty I contend for, is more than toleration. The very idea of toleration, is despicable; it supposes that some have a pre-eminence above the rest, to grant indulgence; whereas, all should be equally free, Jews, Turks, Pagans and Christians. Test oaths, and established creeds, should be avoided as the worst of evils. A general assessment, (forcing all to pay some preacher,) amounts to an establishment; if government says I must pay somebody, it must next describe that somebody, his doctrine and place of abode. That moment a minister is so fixed as to receive a stipend by legal force, that moment he ceases to be a gospel ambassador, and becomes a minister of state. This emolument is a temptation too great for avaricious men to withstand. This doctrine turns the gospel into merchandise, and sinks religion upon a level with other things.

As it is not the province of civil government to establish forms of religion, and force a maintenance for the preachers, so it does not belong to that power to establish fixed holy days for divine worship. That the Jewish seventh-day Sabbath was of divine appointment, is unquestionable; but that the Christian first-day Sabbath is of equal injunction, is more doubtful. If Jesus appointed the day to be observed, he did it as the head of the church, and not as the king of nations; or if the apostles enjoined it, they did it in the capacity of Christian teachers, and not as human legislators. As the appointment of such days is no part of human legislation, so the breach of the Sabbath (so called) is no part of civil jurisdiction. I am not an enemy to holy days, (the duties of religion cannot well be performed without fixed times,) but these times should be fixed by the mutual agreement of religious societies, according to the word of God, and not by civil authority. I see no clause in the federal constitution, or the constitution of Virginia, to empower either the federal or Virginia legislature to make any Sabbathical laws.

Under this head, I shall also take notice of one thing, which appears to me unconstitutional, inconsistent with religious liberty, and unnecessary in itself; I mean the paying of the chaplains of the civil and military departments out of the public treasury. The king of Great Britain has annually forty-eight chaplains in ordinary, besides a number extraordinary; his army also abounds with chaplains. This, I confess, is consistent with the British form of government, where religion is a principle, and the church a creature of the state; but why should these plans of proud, covetous priests, ever be adopted in America? If legislatures choose to have a chaplain, for Heaven's sake, let them pay him by contributions, and not out of the public chest. In some of the states, a part of each day, during the session of assembly, is taken up in attending prayers; and they may well afford it, for they are paid for the time; but whether they would pray as long, if they were not under pay, is a question; and whether the chaplain would pray as long for them, if the puplic chest was like Osiron's purse, is another.

For chaplains to go into the army, is about as good economy as it was for Israel to carry the ark of God to battle: instead of reclaiming the people, they generally are corrupted themselves, as the ark fell into the hands of the Philistines.* The words of David are applicable here: "Carry back the ark into the city." But what I aim chiefly at, is paying of them by law. The very language of the proceeding is this: "If you will pay me well for preaching and praying, I will do them, otherwise I will not." Such golden sermons and silver prayers are of no great value.

* A sheriff being sent to bring a Tartar to court, was a long time detained; when solicited to make his return, he replied, "the Tartar will not come." Come without him then, said the judge. "Yes sir," said the sheriff; "but the Tartar will not let me."

WASAING OF FEET AND DRY CHRISTENING.

WASHING of feet is practised by some of the Baptists, disused by others, and rejected by the third class, which breaks no friendship among them, each one acting according to his persuasion. Baptism and the Lord's supper, are neither of them used for the good of the body; but the first is significant, and the last commemorative. The question is, whether washing of feet is to be performed for the good of the body, or as a sacred rite? If for the good of the body, it should be done when, and only when, the feet are sore and filthy; but if as a sacred rite, people should do as they now do, viz., wash their feet clean before they meet together for the purpose of washing feet. A person being taken upon surprise at a *washing feet* meeting, made this confession: "If I had known that you would have washed feet to-night, I would have washed mine clean before I came from home."

Some of the preachers practice what is satirically called *dry christening*, and others do not. The thing referred to is this: when a woman is safely delivered in child-bearing, and raised to health enough to go to meeting, she brings her child to the minister, who either takes it in his arms, or puts his hands upon it, and thanks God for his mercy, and invokes a blessing on the child; at which time the child is named.

The Baptists believe that those who preach the gospel should live of it: that a preacher is as much entitled to a reward for his labor, as the reaper in the field is to his hire. It is a gross innovation from truth, to view the wages of a minister in the light of alms. That religion that opens the heart, unties the purse-strings. When souls are caught in the net of the gospel (like the fish that Peter caught) they have a piece of money in their mouths. If people will not give the preacher his due, they and their money must perish together.

Finally, the Baptists hold it their duty to obey magistrates, to be subject to the law of the land, to pay their taxes, and pray for all in authority. They are not scrupulous of taking an oath of God upon them to testify the truth before a magistrate or court; but reject profane swearing. Their religion also allows them to bear arms in defence of their life, liberty and property, and also to be friendly to those who differ with them in judgment, believing a cynick to be as bad as a sycophant.

THE VIRGINIA BAPTISTS COMPARED WITH THE GERMAN.

FROM this account of the Virginia Baptists, they appear to be a very different sect from the German Anabaptists. The grand error of those rioters, was founding both dominion and property in grace; which is the error of the church of Rome, and the church of England unto this day; and, indeed, the error of all established churches that incapacitate a man from holding his office and property, without he will submit to a religious test. The confusion in Germany was not of the religious kind, but the struggles of the people to get clear of the oppression of the princes. Their leader taught them, that if they would acknowledge their mission, they should be free from taxes, rents, and subjection; the prospect of which, drew multitudes of them, until, like the followers of Theudas and Judas, they were all dispersed. If the German fanatics were really Baptists, yet it is as cruel to impute their errors, by wholesale, to the Virginia Baptists, as it would be to impute all the cruelty of the church of Rome to those societies in Virginia that practise infant baptism. I have two histories of the German insurgents before me, one of which appears to be a scorpidium, written with the head of an asp, dipped in gall, the other is more mild. If these histories may be depended upon, neither Nicholas Stork nor Thomas Muncer, were Anabaptists; Melchoir Hoffman and John Becheold, were. They were called Anabaptists, because they repeated baptism; but they did not *dip* but *sprinkle*, so that the whole uproar belongs to other societies, and not to the Baptists. A late author, Rev. Mr. Pattilloe, in giving an account of the rise of other societies, says, "the Baptists made their appearance in Germany, soon after the Reformation began." Has the good Mr. Pattilloe got this by wrote, hearing of it so often? or has the judicious pen of Mr. Smith helped him out in a dead lift? or can the gentleman demonstrate his assertion and implication by real facts? Should I affirm that the Presbyterians made their appearance in London, in the reign of James I., on the fifth of November, 1605, in the gun-powder plot, it might perhaps raise the bristles of his meek heart; and this I might affirm with as much propriety, as he could affirm what he has. The names Papist and Presbyterian, are as much alike as Baptist and Anabaptist, and their modes of baptism far more uniform. I admire Mr. Pattilloe's writing in general; I was a subscriber for his book, and think my dollar well exchanged; but, let the Rev. gentleman remember, that the Baptists can produce sacred proof for their appearance in Judea, about fifteen hundred years before those tumults in Germany, and if he can produce more antiquated proof of the Presbyterians, then let him triumph; otherwise, be peaceable, as becomes him.

SOME REMARKS.

A retrospective view of this Chronicle, informs us that the number of religious sects in Virginia, is seven, viz., Episcopalians, Quakers, Presbyterians, Methodists, Tunkers, Mennonists, and Baptists. There are a few Jews, but they have no synagogue, nor is there any chapel for Papists. If men had virtue enough, it would be pleasing to see all of one mind; but in these lethargic days, if there is not a little difference among men, they sink into stupidity. It is happy for Virginia, in a political point of view, that there are several societies, nearly of a size; should one attempt to oppress another, all the rest would unite to prevent it. And the same may be said of the United States; more than twenty religious societies are in them, which render it almost impossible for one order to oppress all the others. This is a greater security for religious liberty than all that can be written on paper. If two or three of the most popular societies in the Union should unite together, the other societies would have cause to fear, from the consideration, that the *many* generally oppress the *few;* but if things in future, emerge as they have heretofore, we have more reason to believe, that the present societies will split and subdivide, than we have to believe, that parties, now at variance, will ever unite. O, Virginia! O, America!—a people favored of the Lord!—may the goodness of God excite our obedience. There are yet remaining some vestiges of religious oppression, but they are chiefly theoretical. It may be said, that in substance, the different societies enjoy equal liberty of thinking, speaking, and worshipping, and equal protection by law. Perhaps there is not a constitutional evil in the states, that has a more plausible pretext, than the proscription of gospel ministers; I say in the *states,* for most of them have proscribed them from seats of legislation, &c. The federal government is free in this point: to have one branch of the legislature composed of clergymen, as is the case in some European powers, is not seemly—to have them entitled to seats of legislation, on account of their ecclesiastical dignity, like the bishops in England, is absurd. But to declare them ineligible, when their neighbors prefer them to any others, is depriving them of the liberty of free citizens, and those who prefer them, the freedom of choice.

If the office of a preacher were lucrative, there would be some propriety in his ineligibility; but as the office is not lucrative, the proscription is cruel. To make the best of it, it is but doing evil, that good may come: denying them the liberty of citizens, lest they should degrade their sacred office. Things should be so fixed in government, that there should be neither degrading checks, nor alluring baits to the ministry; but as the proscription, mentioned above, is a *check,* so there are some *baits,* in the states, to the sacred work. In some of the states, the property of preachers is free from tax. In Virginia, their persons are exempt from bearing arms. Though this is an indulgence that I feel, yet it is not consistent with my theory of politics. It may be further observed, that an exemption from bearing arms, is, but a *legal indulgence,* but the ineligibility is *constitutional proscription,* and no legal reward is sufficient for a constitutional prohibition. The first may be altered by the caprice of the legislature, the last cannot be exchanged, without an appeal to the whole mass of constituent power.

THE RIGHTS AND BONDS OF CONSCIENCE.

The subject of religious liberty, has been so canvassed for fourteen years, and has so far prevailed, that in Virginia, a politician can no more be popular, without the possession of it, than a preacher who denies the doctrine of the *new birth;* yet many, who make this profession, behave in their families, as if they did not believe what they profess. For a man to contend for religious liberty on the court-house green, and deny his wife, children and servants, the liberty of conscience at home, is a paradox not easily reconciled. If a head of a family could answer for all his house in the day of judgment, there would be a degree of justice in his controlling them in the mode of worship, and joining society; but answer for them he cannot; each one must give an account of himself to God, and none but cruel tyrants will prevent their wives, children or servants, either directly or indirectly, from worshipping God according to the dictates of their consciences, and joining the society they choose; for as religion does not destroy either civil or domestic government, so neither of them extend their rightful influence into the empire of conscience.

The rights of conscience are so sacred, that no mortal can justly circumscribe them, and yet the conscience is so defiled by sin, as well as the other powers of the soul, that it may lead men into error. The word *conscience,* signifies *common science;* a court of judicature, erected by God in every human breast: and, as courts of justice often give wrong judgment, for want of good information, so it happens with conscience. The author of our religion said, "the time will come, when he that killeth you, will think that he doeth God service." And Paul verily thought that he ought to do many things against the Lord Jesus. So that conscience is not the rule of life, but the word of God. Though conscience should be free from human control, yet it should be in strict subordination to the law of God.

THOUGHTS ON SYSTEMS.

THAT devil, who transforms himself into an angel of light, is often preaching from these words; "contend earnestly for the faith once delivered to the saints." Whenever men are self-conceited enough to believe themselves infallible in judgment, and take their own opinions for tests of orthodoxy, they conclude they are doing God service, in vindicating his truth; while they are only contending for their particular tenets. By this gross mistake, the Christian world is filled with polemical divinity. I very much question, whether there was ever more sophistry used among the old philosophers, than there has been among divines. I never saw a defence of a religious system, but what a great part of it was designed to explain away the apparent meaning of plain texts of scripture. System writers generally adopt a few principles, which, they say, are *certain truths,* and all reasoning against those principles they strive to make sophistry, and all texts that seem to withstand their scheme, they endeavor to explain away; sometimes by mending the translation of the Bible. I have never yet known an instance of a man's altering the translation of a text that expressed his own sentiment, as it is translated.

When men are run hard to support their plan, they will appeal from scripture to the reason of things; and when reason fails them, they will fly back again to scripture; and when both disappear, they will have recourse to the *unsearchable ways of God.* There is no doubt in my mind, that the God of order acts consistently with himself; but it is a grand doubt, whether divine materials ever did, or ever will, submit to human standards. And, I think it much safer for a man to own his ignorance, and stand open to conviction, than to be too positive in asserting things that he himself may doubt of in his cool retired hours.

THE

FIRST RISE OF SIN*

NEITHER FROM A HOLY NOR SINFUL CAUSE;

UNAVOIDABLE WITH GOD, BUT AVOIDABLE WITH CREATURES.

EXHIBITED IN AN EXPOSITION OF THE FIRST THREE CHAPTERS OF GENESIS; IN WHICH A NUMBER OF CONJECTURES, CALCULATIONS, AND MATHEMATICAL OBSERVATIONS ARE MADE.

With novel *error* men engage;
At novel *truth* they always rage.——MERLUCIOUS.

* This piece was never before published, but was written in, or prior to, the year 1790. The appendix was probably written at a subsequent period, but *when*, we have no means of ascertaining.

PREFACE.

Longitude and *perpetual motion* have employed the prying thoughts of the ingenious for a long time; great premiums are offered to the man who shall first find them out. The apparent advantages of such discoveries would be great; but whether the world will ever enjoy those advantages or not, is a matter of present uncertainty.

The first rise of sin has also been a subject of much speculation. Orthodox divines, poets, and mystics have employed their pens to investigate the point; but not being satisfied with the elucidation of any piece that I have seen, I have presumed to offer the following tract to the public, which will speak for itself.

Those who have read Dr. Gill on Genesis, will see that I have borrowed some remarks of him; but, in some instances, I have dared to differ from that great man.

If the conjectures are considered extravagant, or futile, the reader may remember that he is at his full liberty to invent anything better. The whole of it is offered to the world in modesty and diffidence, by the author.

J. L.

AN EXPOSITION

OF THE FIRST THREE CHAPTERS OF GENESIS, &c.

The history of the world, before the flood, includes only one hundred and seventy verses: from the first of Genesis, to chapter vii., verse 11. It is very short, and, therefore, very sublime and significant. The term of time, that this short history treats of, is no less than sixteen hundred and fifty-five years, one month, and seventeen days.

From this history, we learn that there was one murderer, one man-slayer, one martyr, one prophet, and one preacher, before the deluge; and that the imaginations of men's hearts were, in general, evil, and only evil, continually.

No more than twenty-seven personal names are given us in this account, viz.: Adam, the first man, and Eve, his wife—Cain, and eleven of his posterity—Abel—Seth, and eleven of his descendants; and yet, we are told by some, that there were eleven, and some say, eighty thousand millions of people destroyed in the flood. No doubt but what there was a large number, but this account seems extravagant, beyond all reason; for this would be more than six souls to every acre of land on the face of the globe; which, perhaps, is eighty times as many as have ever been on the earth, living at one time, since the flood.*

The name, *God*, is used seventy-three times before the deluge, and the name, Lord, or *Jehovah*, thirty-five. No direct promise is given of the Messiah, in the whole history, but the conquering seed of the woman is made known in the denunciation of *Jehovah God* to the serpent.

But, what lies before me at this time, is to confine my observations to the first three chapters of Genesis, containing eighty verses.

---

* If, from the formation of Adam and Eve, to the flood, people doubled once in forty-five years, there had been on earth more than one hundred and thirty-seven thousand millions. And, if they have doubled as fast from Noah, to the present time, there have been in the world nearly forty thousand quatrillions; which would be more than one hundred thousand souls, for each square inch in the terraqueous globe.

CHAPTERS I. AND II.

In the first chapter, the phrase, *and God said*, is found ten times. A short account of creation is given, which is more fully explained, in a supplementary way, in the second; for which reason, both chapters are explained together; introduced by the words,

THE FIRST DAY.

In the beginning. Not of eternity, which had no beginning, but of time. If the history of Moses respects the whole creation, this clause destroys the notion of the pre-existence of angels, or the human soul of Christ; but if his history only treats of the solar system, and there are other worlds, and systems of worlds in existence, let their histories be produced, and they shall be regarded. Creation had, some time, a beginning; and no sufficient reason has yet been offered, that it ever had a beginning anterior to the Mosaic account. He who wrought in the beginning, was *God.* The Elohim, here used, is a noun of plural number, and seems to express a trinity of persons in the divine Essence: by this triune Creator were all things created, visible and invisible. The word Elohim, is said, by some, to signify *all Power*, to show that creation and formation were the effects of omnipotence; that the world, both as to matter and form, was the creature of God, and did not emerge by the fortuitous motion and conjunction of pre-existing matter. Others say, the word represents a being, in whom all fulness centres. This is true of the Creator; but as the same name is given to angels, and the rulers of this world, who are not centres of all perfections, the first signification seems best. The things that God made in the beginning, were, *the heavens and the earth.* All created heavens are here intended, at least in substance, though not as yet spread out like a garment, or tent. It is most likely that the Heaven for angels was first finished, and then peopled by angels; for it is certain that the heavens, earth, and seas, and all things in them, were made in the six days; and as angels were present on the third day, when the foundations of the earth were fixed, and sang for joy; where is a more likely time to assign for their creation than the first day? The word heaven, here used, signifies *above*, as the word earth does *below*, so that whatever is above or below, in substance, was made on the first day. But when the earth was first made, it was *without form and void.* Not without some form, which always attends gross matter, but void of the form which it now has—which it had when Moses wrote—which it had before the flood—and particularly which it had on the third day, when it was new-moulded and decorated by God. Had man been then formed, he could not have discerned what form it was in, for, *darkness was upon the face of the deep.* The particles of the earth being as much heavier than water as twenty exceeds twelve, of course, sunk the lowest, while the particles of water rose uppermost, resembling a deep sea; and as no light had then been made, (at least to appear,) darkness covered the whole mass; but it did not long remain in that predicament, for, *the spirit of God moved upon the face of the waters.* By the spirit of God, some understand the wind, which is volatile, like spirit, which they suppose moved on the face of the waters; if so, then the air was made on the first day. If this does not intend the wind, no account is given of its creation in the Genessian history; and as fire cannot exist in a visible manner without air, it looks as if the air must have been made before the light appeared. But it is more generally believed, that the infinite spirit of God is meant. The clauses before this, treat of the creation of all above and below, and the dark situation all was in; and this clause speaks of the working of God's power, to produce things and creatures out of what was already created: and, indeed, it appears most likely, that what the Hebrews call *To-kee* and *Bo-kee,* and the Greeks call *chaos,* was made in the beginning of the first day, and that out of this crude mass all things were formed. And when the spirit of God thus moved, *God said, let there be light,* which was the first time that God spake. It appears most probable, that God, the Son, was the speaker; from which it is said, in the beginning was the *Word*—all things were made by him—in him was light: and the first word was obeyed, for *there was light*; likely in the form of a pillar of fire, which answered the use of a sun, until the fourth day, when the sun was formed. *And God saw the light* that he had made, *and it was good* in itself, and would be useful to men. The almighty Architect examined his work, to see if it was well done, and pronounced it good. *And God divided the light from the darkness,* by causing the light to move round the rough mass of matter, or, more likely, the rough mass, to turn round the light. In either case, the shadow of the dark ball made darkness, and the light shining upon it made it lurid, and the division depended upon the diurnal motion, which has lasted to this day.

And God called the light day, and the darkness, he called night; which times are to continue, alternately, as long as the earth remaineth. *And the evening and the morning were the first day.* Darkness preceded the light, likely, about twelve hours, which was succeeded by twelve hours light, which evening and morning made the first day. Various philosophers say, that darkness was before light, and many nations, such as the Romans, Athenians, Druids, etc., began their days in the evening, as also, did the Jews their holy days.

THE SECOND DAY.

And God said, let there be a firmament in the midst of the waters. This firmament is called heaven; the visible heavens are intended, which were spread out like a curtain, on the second day. The use of this expanse was *to divide the waters from the waters;* from which, some have supposed that there are fountains of water above, and that these fountains of the great deep were broken up, in the time of the flood, when the waters descended in awful cataracts; or, it may signify nothing more than that the firmament was to divide the waters which were in the seas, lakes, rivers, etc., from the waters which were in the clouds. Obsequious to the Almighty fiat, *it was so; and the evening and the morning were the second day.* That the second day's work was well done, there is no doubt; but there is no account that God inspected it and pronounced it *good.*

THE THIRD DAY.

And God said, let the waters under the heavens be gathered together in one place. Before this, they covered over the whole face of the earth, but now God broke up, for the sea, the spacious channel, and ordered the waters to retire to their destined habitation, and said, "hitherto shalt thou come, and no further, and here shall thy proud waves be stayed." This was done that *the Lord might appear.* At this time the pillars of the earth were fixed, which made "the morning stars sing together, and all the sons of God shout for joy." *And God called the dry land earth, and the gathering together of the waters, called he seas.* The earth includes the two continents, and all the islands, but it is highly probable that the face of it differed widely, at that time, from its present position. There were seas before Moses wrote, and perhaps there were before the flood, and most likely before the fall, for God called the waters, *seas.* The seas at present have a communication with each other, but as they wash different shores, and for that cause, bear different names, the plural is kept up among us.

The earth and seas, together, form the terraqueous globe, supposed to be a spherioid, though generally treated of as a sphere. The ancients conceived the earth and seas to be as flat as a trencher, and those who believed in antipodes were called heretics.

The earth seems to be governed by the law of gravitation, subordinate to God; and though small, in comparison to some of the globes, is yet great and wonderful in itself, to show forth the mighty works of God. The diameter of the earth is computed at seven thousand six hundred and thirty-six miles; the circumference twenty-four thousand miles;* the superficial contents to be above twenty-eight millions of miles; which, if reduced to acres, would be above eighteen thousand millions: but, if a third part of the face of the globe is allowed to be sea, the acres of land would

* The general computation is twenty-one thousand six hundred, but some make it as great as twenty-six thousand; to form a medium therefore, and to give a round number without fractions, I compute it at twenty-four thousand miles. All my calculations, respecting the earth, are made upon that scale, except the foot-note in the introduction.

be more than twelve thousand millions: which would make about twenty-one such empires as that of the United States,* one hundred and seventy-five such states as Virginia, or four thousand five hundred and fifty such as Connecticut. And, if ten acres of land is sufficient for an individual, the earth will support more than a thousand millions of souls.

It is difficult to tell what is in the globular centre of the terraqueous ball, whether earth, water, rocks or mineral; and as difficult to put the point of a needle on any part of its ambit, which is not the superficial centre; nature having fixed it under such laws, that every part of it is central.

The annual motion of the earth determines the length of a year, which is about three hundred and sixty-five days, and six hours: and the diurnal motion fixes the length of a day, which is twenty-four hours. The surface of the earth is unweariedly moving, in her diurnal course, about the equator, the distance of one thousand miles an hour, and carries all her inhabitants with her: and as the distance between the earth and sun is ninety millions of miles, the earth is moving, with her inhabitants, in the direction of her annual circuit, about sixty-four thousand miles an hour. Does this surprise you, and make you cry out, impossible? If so, only consider, that if the earth stands still, according to the vulgar notion, and the sun moves round it, the sun must fly at the speed of above five hundred and sixty-five millions of miles each day, or, three hundred and ninety-two thousand eight hundred and fifty-seven miles each minute, in his diurnal course; which is about fifty-six thousand times as swift as a ball flies from the mouth of a cannon.

The earth is girt round with a girdle of circumambient air, which closely adheres to her in all her motions. Should a cannon be placed on the earth perpendicularly, and discharge a ball into the air, if the ball should be gone two minutes before it returned, the cannon would have removed, in that space of time, thirty-three miles, consequently the ball would return that distance from the cannon's mouth; but, as the air adheres to the earth, the ball would return to the very point from whence it went.

The solid contents of the terraqueous globe, is above three hundred thousand millions of miles, which, if reduced to inches, would be more than eight hundred thousand trillions. An inch of common sand weighs about an ounce, Troy, but an inch of water weighs only twelve pennyweights. Rocks and minerals weigh much more than sand. If sand may be considered as a medium, the globe weighs as many ounces (Troy) as there are inches in its contents. Fifty-one ounces, Troy, are equal to fifty-six, avoirdupois; and fourteen pounds avordupois, are equal to seventeen Troy. The earth, by this rule, weighs more than ninety-seven quatillions of ounces, Avoirdupois, or, above three hundred trillions of tons.

* The American empire contains six hundred and forty millions of acres, of which, fifty-one millions are water.

And God said, let the earth bring forth grass, herbs, and fruitful trees, yielding fruit after their kind, whose seed are in themselves, upon the earth. The spirit of God, that brooded upon the terraqueous globe on the first day, had, on the third day, not only separated the waters from the earth, but also impregnated the earth to produce vegetables for beasts and fruit-trees for man: and this provision was made before the creatures were formed to eat them. So, likewise, it is in the *new* creation, all spiritual blessings are provided in the New Covenant for men before they are new-made to receive them. The grass, herbs, and trees, had seed within themselves to produce their kind, which has continued in order down to this day. After God had made the earth, he made it vegetate and bring forth fruit; even so when men are created in Christ Jesus and put on the new man, they work for God and bring forth the fruits of the Spirit.

On this third day, *the Lord made to grow out of the ground every tree that is pleasant to the sight, and good for food; the Tree of Life, also, in the midst of the garden, and the Tree of Knowledge of good and evil,* though not spoken of until afterwards: from which we learn that creation furnished objects to please the senses, as well as to support the rational creature with food. Likewise, in religion, not only safety, but pleasure is found; the ways thereof are ways of pleasantness, and all her paths are peace.

And God saw all that he had done, on the third day, and it was good; no evil had yet appeared: angels retained their integrity, and filial subjection to their Maker.

THE FOURTH DAY.

And God said, let there be lights in the firmament of the heaven. This firmament includes all that space between the earth and third heavens; but that part of it called the starry heavens, seems to be particularly intended. No new light was made on this day; but that pillar of light, made on the first day, was, on this day, formed into the various luminaries, afterwards spoken of, *to divide the day from the night, to be for signs and seasons, for days and years.* Day and night are governed by the sun; while the sun shines on the face of the earth, it is day, and when it goes down, it is night. The length of the day is equal to the presence of the sun, and the length of the night equal to his absence. The moon, in her fulness, arises upon the setting of the sun, and enlightens the earth during his absence; and, therefore, is said, *to rule the Night.* When the moon fails us in her nocturnal visits, the twinkling stars pay their officious aid, and, by reason of their number, cast much light upon the inhabitants of the earth.

These lights were to be for *signs;* not for deluded necromancers to prognosticate by; no, those dull masses, ignorant of their own existence, can never foretel things future, respecting men; but for signs of good and bad weather, for the times of plowing, sowing and reaping. *And seasons* of summer and winter, spring and fall. *For days*, by the diurnal motion, in twenty-four hours; *and years*, by the annual circuit, in three hundred and sixty-five days and a few hours.

The greater light to rule the day; i. e., the sun, called by the ancients, *Ur*, which word signifies both light and heat; and, it is evident, that the sun is the fountain of heat as well as light. This stupendous orb may well be called great, being about nine hundred thousand times the bigness of the earth; placed at the distance of ninety millions of miles from the ball that we inhabit; yet capable of darting a ray of light to us in the space of seven and a half minutes.

This amazing luminary is the centre of the solar system, and once in twenty-eight years, all the worlds that play around it, come again to the same point and condition. This sovereign of nature, rules the day with such resplendent lustre, that no other orb is seen to shine in his presence: but instead of being an object of religious adoration, is but a speck of Jehovah's works, placed in the heavens, to show forth the wisdom, power, and goodness of the Almighty.

The smaller light (the moon) *to rule the night*. The moon is called a light, but she borrows all her bright ornaments of the sun. That the moon is an opaque body of some kind of matter, is evident, otherwise she would not eclipse the sun when she intervenes.

One entire day of the moon is almost equal to thirty of our natural days; consequently, the moon's night is nearly equal to fifteen of our days and nights.

If the moon is inhabited, it is matter of conjecture, whether her inhabitants sleep so long at a time, and work as long without sleeping: and how much the men of the moon must eat for supper, upon this supposition, is matter of speculation.

The moon in bulk, is as follows: diameter, two thousand one hundred and seventy-five miles; circumference, six thousand eight hundred and sixty-four miles; ambit, above three and a half million, which, if reduced to acres, would be more than two thousand millions. But, if one third part of the moon's surface, is allowed to be seas, it leaves upwards of one and a half thousand millions of acres in land: and, if ten acres of land are sufficient to support an individual, the moon will support above one hundred and fifty-eight millions of souls.

The size, complexion, dress, manners, language, laws, and religion of those people, we are ignorant of, (although the moon is called our neighbor.) *Swedenburgh's* account gains but little credit among us; the *air-balloons* have not yet answered the purpose of forming an acquaintance; what future experiments may do, is uncertain.

He made the stars also. Some, who believe in the existence of worlds and systems of worlds, prior to the solar system, suppose that this clause respects the creation of those stars, which are worlds or centres of worlds, and, that though by their inconceivable distance,* they appear to us but small points, like the diamond on a lady's ring, yet they are of themselves, globes of amazing magnitude. They conclude, that the same hand that made the sun and moon, on the fourth day, had made these stars long before. But it seems rather to respect those stars, that were made at the same time that the sun and moon were.

Others restrain it to the planetary stars, viz., Mars, Mercury, Jupiter, Venus, Saturn, and Herschel. Some of these stars have their moons, rings, and satellites playing around them, of which I cannot at this time be particular.

It is best, however, by these stars, to understand not only those already mentioned, but likewise Arcturus and his sons, Pleiades, and the chambers of the south, as well as all the constellations and stars in the heavens.

And God saw his work and it was good; free from evil, which had no being as yet, *and the evening and the morning were the fourth day.*

THE FIFTH DAY.

On the fifth day, God gave orders to the waters to bring forth living creatures. On the first day, gross nature was made; on the third day, vegetable life sprung out of chaos, and discovered itself in the grass, herbs and trees; and on the fifth day, animal life was produced. Fish of every kind were created, from the largest kraken to the smallest minnows; and fowls to fly in the open air, from the eagle to the fly. These, it seems, were produced out of the water, and yet, if we cast our eyes on Chapter ii., 19, it is pretty plain that they were made out of the earth. To reconcile both places together, and both to the nature of things, it is supposable that they were both made out of the earth at the water's side; or, more likely, out of the mud, under the water. It is also probable, that the fish were made in the fore part of the day, and fowls in the after part. There is a considerable likeness between these two species of creatures: both steer their courses by their tails; fins and scales to one, are as wings and feathers to the other, and both are oviparous. After God had made them, he blessed them with the power of procreation, and bid them be fruitful, and fill their destined elements.

This day's work, also, was well done: *God saw that it was good; and the evening and the morning were the fifth day.*

---

* The nearest fixed star is at such a distance from us, that a cannon-ball must fly at the rate of one hundred fathoms a second, and take nearly seven hundred thousand years to reach it: the distance being computed at almost two and a half millions of miles. A line of wheat-grains, from the sun to said star, allowing four grains to the inch, would form a mountain of wheat, more than sufficient to sow forty such globes as this, allowing a bushel to an acre.

THE SIXTH DAY.

And God said, let the earth bring forth the living creature after his kind: i. e., let the living creatures be made out of the earth, and live upon it; for, notwithstanding, the earth was impregnated by the spirit of God, and warmed by the sun, yet these causes could not create beasts without omnipotent power; and so it follows, God made beasts, cattle, and creeping things after their kind: by which is meant, wild beasts, tame cattle, serpents and reptiles; *and God saw it was good.*

Thus the earth was made for man to dwell upon, the heavens to cover over him as a canopy, the sun to enlighten him by day, the moon and stars by night, herbs and fruit-trees for his food, and every living thing for his service, before he was formed. Moreover, a garden of pleasure was planted in the east part of the land of Eden, with all kinds of useful and pleasant trees; and, to consummate his earthly enjoyments, a river of water went out of Eden, and ran through the garden, to water it, which spread out in four branches, as it left the garden, and formed the four rivers, Pison, Gihon, Hiddekel, and Euphrates. The first of these rivers is nowhere spoken of in scripture besides. The second is spoken of, 1 Kings, i., 33; 2 Chron. xxxii., 30, or, more likely, another river of the same name. The third ran through Persia, near Shushan, the palace, and the fourth ran through Babylon.

Almost all parts of the world have contended for this garden, and seem to be at as great loss about it as chronologers are about the time in which Job lived. Whether it was in Ceylon, Armenia, the land of Judah, Mesopotamia, or in any other place contended for, it certainly was a delightful spot, and seemed to invite an occupant; but as beautiful as things appeared, it had not rained upon the earth. But there went up a mist from the earth, being exhaled by the sun, from the seas, rivers, etc., in very small particles, and forming a cloud, sprinkled down water upon the whole face of the ground.

And God said, let us make man after our image and likeness, and let them have dominion over fish, fowl, cattle and creeping things. These words were not spoken to beasts, that could not understand; nor to angels, who were neither of the privy council, nor co-workers with God in creation; but the phrase bespeaks a co-operation of Father, Son and Holy Ghost in creating man: and man immediately was made in the image of God: not in the image of his deity: that God who cannot lie, could not make a being like himself, in that respect. Christ only bears the express image of his Father's person, as a natural son bears the image of his natural father; but the first man that was made, bore the image of God as the wax bears the image of the signet. He was also in the image of God, in this point of view: the Father, Word, and Holy Ghost are one; so soul, spirit and body, make one man; there is a trinity in man, as well as in God; moreover, he was made in the same human shape and dispositon that Christ was to appear in, a true figure of him who was to come; in these senses, he was made in the image of God, and was lovely in the eyes of his Maker. *Male and female created he them.* Both sexes were in one body. The man is not without the woman, nor the woman without the man in the Lord.

It is the opinion of some of the mystic writers, that Adam had power to propagate his own species before Eve was separated from him, having both the masculine and feminine natures in him; but it can hardly be credited, that sin has radically altered the shape of man; and how Adam could multiply with such a shape, without he had the power of creating, is unaccountable; and that he had power to create, no man pretends. It is best therefore to suppose that God made both natures in one body, with an intention of separating them before they procreated. Matter was first made, on the first day, afterwards it was remoulded; then Adam was made out of it; and cast the woman out of man; so that women are the most refined from dross matter—removed the furthest from clay of any of the lower creatures.

After God had made man, he put him into the garden to dress and keep it, and immediately constituted him a subject of moral government, by enjoining a law (not a covenant) on him, with a penalty annexed thereto. This indulgent father and divine legislated, or gave him free liberty to eat of all the trees in the garden, and regale himself with all the pleasures of paradise; but as there was one noxious tree,* he would have him avoid it; and said, " My son, you may eat of all the trees in the garden, save one, the fruit of which will poison you to death; and lest my caution should be ineffectual, I command you not to touch it; and to make my law forcible, I add the penalty of *death* to the breaker of it, which shall be inflicted the very day that the law is broken." This law therefore may be considered as a cautionary command, and it appears most likely to me that there was a poisonous quality, a physical evil in the tree, that would have mortalized Adam, if God had not prohibited it. This pro-

* Some suppose that the best way to clear the character of God from being the cause of every kind of evil, is, to imagine that Adam stood a representative of all the lower creation, human, animal, vegetative and the gross parts of it, and that when he sinned and forsook his moral order, it threw the whole creation into disorder. That as soon as sin raised a war of elements within him, the contagion ran through all the elements without him, and brought a curse upon the fire, air, water and earth. That briers and thistles and all poisonous weeds sprang up, as a consequent thereof; and that the infection rose up in the sap of the tree of good and evil, (which had not this quality before the fall, as they judge,) and that the animals received a cruel, venomous disposition from the source of Adam's sin, as well as the human world, a wicked stubborn nature.

hibition was also a test of Adam's obedience, to train him up in moral subjection.

After God made Adam and placed him in the garden, he did not choose idleness for him, but brought unto him all the beasts and fouls to name; and Adam gave names to them all, by which they were afterwards called. Some think that this is a great proof of Adam's primeval wisdom, in giving names to the creatures, the signification of which exactly agreed with the nature of the creatures to whom they were applied: but it is not likely that the names that Adam called them by, had been received into his dialect before, (for this affair happened within a few hours after his formation,) and if not, I cannot see how the signification of a name could exist before the name itself.

But among all the creatures that were brought before him to name, there was not found a *helpmeet* for him, not one that he could converse with; none to help him keep and dress the garden; nor any to help him procreate. This wonderous creature, man, of whom so much is said, was made out of the dust of the earth, in or near Eden; and after God had formed him in human shape, he breathed into him the breath of life, and he became a living soul. Vegetative and animal lives were made out of the earth, as distillers extract the spirit from grain, etc.; and therefore when they die, their spirits return to the earth from whence they came; but the soul of man was breathed out of the mouth of God, and therefore when men die, their souls go to God from whence they came. At the time when God quickened Adam's dust with animal life, he infused the immortal soul into him. Though Eve was in Adam, as has been said, yet it is not likely that the soul of Eve was in Adam's soul, much less in his rib.

And the Lord God said, it is not good that man should be alone, I will make an helpmeet for him. It may here be observed that the name *Lord* or *Jod-he, vah-he,* used in this clause, and indeed eleven times in the eleventh chapter, is expressive of the eternity of God. Gross nature, animals, and the mortal lives of men had a beginning, and will have an end; but there is one being who never had a beginning, and will never have an end; and this being is Jehovah, here translated *Lord.*

This eternal God saw that it was not good for man so to dwell alone. This clause has led some to believe that the defection had begun; but it designs nothing more than that God saw that man could not propagate by himself alone, nor be as happy as he might be with an associate. Moral evil is indefatigable here, because after this God pronounced all things very good.

The way in which the Lord God made Adam a helpmeet, was as follows: He caused a deep sleep to fall upon Adam, which was the first time that he ever slept: it was near the close of the sixth day, and perhaps, Adam was weary with his day's work in naming all the creatures, (as the second Adam often was in travelling,) and his senses were all locked up for rest. This was a *deep sleep* ; common sleep would not have kept the senses dormant enough to bear the operation that Adam went through; but this was so *deep* that Adam felt no pain while his side was opened, a rib taken from thence, and the flesh closed up again. This rib the Lord formed into a woman and brought her to Adam.

Anatomists say, that men have twelve ribs on each side; if so, we should judge that Adam had thirteen, at least on one side, and that the superfluous, unmated rib, was taken out for the purpose of a woman. The part of Adam that was taken to form a women, was neither from his head nor feet; to teach us that women should not attempt to *rule* their husbands, nor be trodden under foot by them: but the rib was from his *side*, under his arm, near his heart; to show that the woman is to be by her husband, under the arm of his protection, near the heart of his love.

It looks as if God carried off the rib to a little distance from Adam, while he formed it into a woman; perhaps to the same place where Adam was formed; and when God had formed this lovely creature, he brought her to Adam; who upon first sight knew her, at least from whence she came, and said, "this is bone of my bones, and flesh of my flesh." Her bones and flesh were taken from him, and this he knew. Perhaps while he was asleep, he was taught it in a dream; or God might reveal it to him by impulse; or we may suppose, that though Adam was in a deep sleep when the ribs were taken from him, yet he awaked before it was formed into a woman, and stood not far off to see God form it into a human shape; but let him come by his knowledge one way or another, he knew from whence she came, and called her name *woman*, because she came from man.

Even so, when souls are new made by divine grace, they are brought to the second Adam, the Lord Jesus Christ; being drawn by the father, not against, but with their wills; and when they come, Jesus knows them and calls them by a new name. *Therefore a man shall leave his father and mother and shall cleave unto his wife, and they shall be one flesh.*

If these words were spoken by Adam, at the time when he received Eve, they were either prophetic of, or preceptives for his posterity; for they were not applicable to Adam's case, who had no father but God, and no mother but the earth, neither of which was he to leave for his wife.

If they are considered as the words of Moses, they were not spoken at the time when Eve was brought to Adam, but between two and three thousand years afterwards, when the Hebrew historian wrote; and this he gives as a reason why men should cleave to their wives and take care of them.

But rather the words were spoken by God himself, who, at the time of instituting marriage, gave directions about it. In Mat. xix. 4, 5, where Jesus quotes this passage, he informs us that *he* who made the male and female at the beginning, *said* for this cause, etc.

And God blessed them with the tokens of his favor and love, and with the power of procreation, *and said unto them, be faithful and multiply and replenish the earth with your offspring, and subdue it,* by tilling the ground, sowing and reaping, *and have dominion over the fish of the sea, and over the foul of the air, and over every living thing that moveth upon the face of the earth.* As man was to be in subjection to God, so all the crertures below were to be in subjection to man, who was appointed vicegerent of the world. To the beasts, God gave every green herb, but to man he gave seed and fruit-trees. There is no account that God gave the beasts, birds and fish to man, for the purpose of eating, or that ever the antedeluvians did eat any of them before the flood; but it is certain that this divine charter gave man the dominion of them all, and very likely he and his children ate thereof, before the days of Noah.

In the day when they were made, *they were both naked and were not ashamed.* It is supposable that the air was temperate, and therefore they needed no clothing; and it is very doubtful whether the elements would ever have raged, and fomented storms, if sin had never entered the world. However, if it was the design of God to have them wear clothes in future, it is probable that he intended that they should manufacture for themselves.

As sin and guilt were strangers, so shame was unknown. Since the fall, God calls upon men to be ashamed of their ways; and grace teaches men to be ashamed of those things that do not profit; but that which is a virtue in a guilty man, would be mean and insignificant in an innocent being.

And the evening and the morning were the sixth day. Upon the close of each day before (the second excepted) the Lord pronounced all *good*; but upon the close of all his creation work, de declares all to be *very good.* Nothing sinful or disorderly had yet appeared; angels, man and beasts, all stood in their poper order and obedience.

Thus the heavens and the earth were finished, all the hosts of them.

THE SEVENTH DAY.

And on the seventh day God ended his work, or had ended his work, for all things were made in six days; *and he rested the seventh day from all his work which he had made,* not that he was fatigued with labor, as men are, but he ceased from his work, as it is expressed Heb. iv., 10. *And God blessed the seventh day, and sanctified it.* Although there is no account that ever man regarded the seventh day of the week more than any other, until the giving of manna in the wilderness, yet this is given as a reason, in the fourth commandment, why the nation of Israel should rest on the seventh day of the week.

If the decalogue (the ten commadments) is all of a moral nature, the injunction is binding on all nations; and if all nations were under the bond of regarding the seventh day in a holy manner, it is strange that St. Paul never had occasion to reprove the Gentiles, for the breach of it, as the Jewish prophet had to reprove their own nation; and besides, if the observance of the seventh day was a moral obligation upon all nations, God either designed that the poles of the earth should never be peopled, or the moral law required a natural impossibility; for, at the poles, there is but one day and night in a year. Yea, further; how is it possible for persons, under opposite horizons, being antipodes to each other, to keep the same day?

The most, therefore, that can be said, (at least proved,) is that God rested on the seventh day; and that after above two thousand four hundred years, he ordained that the nation of Israel should keep the same day of the week, throughout their generations. If, in the New Testament, Christians are commanded to keep the first day, by Christ or his apostles, that divine appointment is sufficient; human legislatures have nothing to do in ordaining fixed holy days, establishing creeds of faith, requiring religious tests, certificates, or anything of the kind.

Having made some remarks on the six days' work, and the seventh day's rest, the history of which includes the first and second chapters, I shall proceed to some observations on the third, which treats of the entrance of sin into the human world; but, as Satan seems to be a leading character in this chapter, it appears necessary to say something about angels, and by what means they were turned from celestial spirits to infernal devils.

But before I enter upon the dark arena, I shall premise a few things. First, on the nature of God, and secondly, on the nature of his decrees.

And who is sufficient for these things? Can man, by searching, find out God, or the Almighty, unto perfection? Clouds and darkness are round about him, yet righteousness and judgment are the habitation of his throne. Verily, he is a God that hideth himself, and giveth not a full account of any of his matters. Remember, O my soul, how vengeance fell on the Bethshemites, for prying too curiously into the ark. "Man was not made to question, but adore." Yet, with all submission to divine power and wisdom, let me attempt to speak of my God, and the glory of his works.

First. The Almighty exists of necessity, and yet willingly: he is of that nature that he cannot but exist, and yet that necessity does not destroy his infinite freedom; for he is under no necessity, but that of innate law.

Should I affirm that all God's works are works of necessity, it would convey this idea: that God *cannot* do anything, more or less than what he now does; which, perhaps, would be an idea unbecoming Omnipotence; and yet it may be safely affirmed, that many of his works are necessarily done. If God is under no necessity to speak, yet, when he speaks of choice, he is under necessity to speak truth, for he *cannot* lie. He is under a necessity of showing forth the glory of his perfections in his works, (when he works of choice,) for he *cannot* work beneath himself. And if creation was a deed of choice, and not of necessity, yet judicial works are works of necessity; God's nature being such, that he is under the necessity of innate law, to judge and punish for the glory of his perfections. If it should be thought presumptuous to say, that God *cannot* punish sooner, otherwise, or more severely than he does; if we consider that love and goodness counterpoise power and justice, and that, sometimes, mercy rejoices against judgment, it will not appear more presumptuous, perhaps, than true.

The great question is, whether God could have prevented sin or not? If the works of creation were works of necessity, i. e., if the nature of God was such, that he could not but have made the world *when* he did, and *as* he did, I conclude that it was not possible for God to have prevented sin; but if creation was a work of will, and not of necessity, then God could have prevented sin, by having not made the world, and creatures in it, to sin. But more of this hereafter.

Second. Did God decree that angels and men should sin, or not? A decree is the law of a court to accomplish some purpose. No such law was given to angels, to Adam, or to his children. The decree, through the Bible, is that creatures should not sin.

But I do not wish to criticise on phrases. The general idea of a *decree*, among Calvinistic writers, is the eternal design of God; the question is, therefore, whether it was the eternal design of God that sin should have birth, or not? If it was the design, decree, or secret will of God, that creatures should sin, how can it be sin? for sin is a transgression of his will. If God decreed sin, he decreed that which is opposed to his nature, contrary to his law, and what he could not effect himself, nor make his creatures effect. Some make a great difference between his *secret* and *revealed* will. Is not this charging God with duplicity? That there is a difference between the law that God works by, and the law given to his creatures, is granted. The rule of God's working, is either the law of his nature, or sovereign will; for there was no anterior existent to impose a law on him; but the law of his creatures, is his moral and absolute precepts; and simple obedience, without gainsaying, is indispensable from all rational intelligences. But the question is, whether it was the secret will of God, that sin should (in a direct or indirect manner) enter in among his creatures, and at the same time forbid it? If so, it is no wonder that all the philosophic divines are puzzled to reconcile the goodness of God with the misery of his creatures. But why do men talk so? Have they learned their theory from Scripture, or divine teaching? If from either, then it is *revealed* to them, and, therefore, is no longer his *secret* will. It has been observed, that the rule of God's working, was either innate law or sovereign will. That sin is agreeable to the law of his nature, I presume, no man vindicates; and if it was his sovereign will that sin should emerge, it was then *unavoidable*; either God or creatures must effect it: God could not, and, therefore, it follows, that creatures *unavoidably must*. If *sin* then is *sin*—the parent of sorrow—the cause of death and eternal misery, who can justify the goodness of God upon this principle? If sin is according to the secret, sovereign will of God, it is to answer some noble purpose; for all God's appointed works will praise him; but what angel or man can point out any general good effected by sin? If sin is the cause of general good, all creatures should love it; and if creatures should love it, why are they called upon to repent of, and hate it?

The first character that God ever discovered himself in, to Adam, (and likely to angels,) was that of a *moral governor*, and he treated him as a subject of *moral government:* first as a legislator, in giving a law; and afterwards as a judge, in punishing crimes. And as it was not possible for God to sin, or make creatures sin, so, likewise, (considering him in the character of a moral governor,) it was not possible for him to prevent it.

Should a legislator do anything more than make laws, forbidding crimes; should he make places of confinement, and shut up all his subjects, to prevent their crimes, what a kingdom of miserable subjects he would have; but if he makes them happy, with the freedom of thinking, speaking, walking and working, and only gives them a law of good behaviour, it is not possible for him to prevent their transgression: the only means that he could make use of to prevent it, would make them entirely miserable. So it was with God; he loved his creatures, and sought to make them happy; and, as rational creatures cannot be happy without the freedom of their will, this freedom was established in them by God; and, in this point of view, it was not possible for God to have prevented their sin; as the only means that would have secured them from sin, would have made them completely miserable.

Here, then, we see God, all goodness, seeking the happiness of his creatures, and the very essentials of rational happiness, by their inadvertence, proved their overthrow.

If the question then is asked, whether sin was *unavoidable*, or *avoidable*? the answer is, *unavoidable* with God, but *avoidable* with creatures. For creatures, in their moral agency, had sufficient power to stand and obey, as well as freedom to rebel. If, then, creation is acknowledged to be a good work, and that God had a right to command the creatures that he made, the character of God is clear in the apostacy of creatures; for his foreknowledge of their fall, had no influence on their wills, nor in any way occasioned their sin, any more than the foreknowledge of David made Judas sell his master.

The *new divinity*, (so called,) which declares God to be the efficient author of sin, and that sin, eventually, is the cause of great good, represents Jehovah as a cruel being, and cuts the nerves of repentance; for what idea must we form of a being, whose nature was such, that he could not discover the full glory of it, without the transgression of his creatures, which eventually brings on the damnation of many of them? And, if the truth of God is to abound more by the lies of his creatures, and the wrath of man is to work the righteousness of God, how can men be convinced and judged as transgressors? Every honest heart, unbiased by system, upon hearing "that God designed men to sin, and that sin will effect great good," will confess, that the natural conclusion is, *let men sin.*

That the Divine Legislator has given many laws to fallen creatures, which were not from the beginning, in which he, (in some sort,) accommodates himself to their condition, requires no proof but just to cast our thoughts on all laws of civil government, laws of war, and laws of putting away wives. These laws were not, and could not be from the beginning. In the execution of these laws, he makes use of one wicked man, or nation to punish another; and as the instruments act voluntarily from a wicked heart, (although their wrath, in action, praises God,) he punishes those instruments for what they do. Now, if from this consideration, it can be proved that God is more glorified, and men, (upon a large scale,) more happy than they would have been, if sin had never entered the world, then we may say, that *sin is the cause of great good:* otherwise, the circumstance of Joseph's being sold by his brethren, and Jesus being hated and crucified by the Jews will not prove it.

But to descend to the enquiry respecting angels. It has been observed, that no good reason has yet been given to prove that angels were made before the first day; but if they were made ten thousand years before, the difficulties are still the same in accounting for their first sin.

Beasts are all brutal, angels are all spirit; but men are part brute, and part angel. It is a point of dispute in these days, whether *materiality* belongs to all creatures or not; if so, then angels were made spiritual matter, but whether they were made spiritual matter, or spirit, distinct from matter, it is presumable that they were made beings that could neither procreate nor die: and yet it is certain that they were subject to moral mutability.

There is no way, in idea, possible to account for the entrace of sin among rational creatures, but by considering their wills entirely at liberty; as the contrary would destroy the very notion of vice and virtue, good and evil, right and wrong. It must, therefore, be supposed that angels, as subjects of moral government, were considered under a law, with the freedom of their wills, to obey or rebel. But how it was possible for sinless creatures, without a tempter, to *choose* to rebel, is a matter of great weight: yet, as difficult as it appears to us, it has certainly been the case with angels. The best way that I can conceive of it, is as follows, and which is partly conjectural.

One reason why Jehovah was six days in forming the worlds and their inhabitants, was, that angels might see what he could do; who stood by, as spectators, and sang together, and shouted for joy; and it looks most likely that not one of them had sinned before the *third* day, for they ALL sang for joy; which would not have been the case, if any of them had commenced rebellion.

And further, it is probable that none of them had rebelled on the sixth day; for God, at the close of that day pronounced all *very good*. It is a further conjecture, that sin had not raised any commotion in the universe until after the seventh day; for, on that day, God *rested;* seeing nothing out of order in all his works. But, soon after this, (perhaps on the eighth day,) the rebellion broke out.

The last of creation-work, was man; at the sight of whom, angels were filled with wonder, to see a body so noble, erect, and possessed with such endowments of mind; but while angels were wondering, said God to angels, "my Son shall assume the nature, and appear in the form, of that man, whom ye now behold; and I command all of you to worship him as an incarnate God." This was the first time that Christ was brought into the world, by name; and when Jehovah brought his first begotten into the world, he said, "let all the angels of God worship him." This appears to be the test of their obedience; and the trial was, whether they would worship a being in a nature inferior to their own, merely because God commanded them to. At this juncture, angels had full power to obey, and yet their wills were free to rebel; for God treated them as subjects of moral government, and exercised no coercion over them.

Angelic wisdom now began to reason. "What," said angels, "shall we worship a nature inferior to our own; why not worship a beast as well? It will be idolatry to worship a creature, and man is but a creature; our wisdom tells us, therefore, that it is best not to obey." Here rebellion arose. The wisdom of angels could not comprehend how divinity and humanity could be personally united; and, therefore, to prevent idolatry, they transgressed a divine command. Let our views be ever so good—let our reasoning be ever so fair—yet, if we refuse to obey a plain command, because we do not understand every thing contained in it, we are guilty of that crime which turned celestial angels into infernal devils.

To say that the first sin came from a sinful cause, is absurd; and to suppose that it came from a holy cause, is contrary to the order of nature. It is best, therefore, to conceive of it as arising from the limited wisdom and inadvertent conduct of sinless creatures. Sin, then, is the creature of beings, who are, themselves, the creatures of God. It is highly probable, from the order of God's works, that some angels were more noble and capacious than others, and that one of the high rank, perhaps the highest that God made, took the lead in the rebellion, and used his angelic oratory to persuade the rest to follow him, who, to this day, has a kind of subordinate government over others. When they are called *devils*, he is called their *prince*; and when he is called the *devil*, they are called his angels. But let it be observed, that angels acted personally for themselves; one was not a representative for another; and, as they do not procreate, corruption of nature is not communicated by generation.

If it should be objected, "that if the first cause of sin was the *limited wisdom* of creatures, it impeaches the goodness, or wisdom and power of God: for, if God was infinite in goodness, and sought the happiness of his creatures, he would certainly have made their wisdom so extensive that they could not have erred in judgment, provided his wisdom and power could have effected it."

The answer is, infinity belongs alone to God. Had angels been endowed with ten thousand times as much wisdom as they were, their wisdom would still have been limited to a point, infinitely inferior to the immense circle of Jehovah, and their trial would still have been the same. And will any man cooly say, that the great first cause—the cause of all causes and things, (sin excepted,)—is wanting in goodness, power, and wisdom, because he *did* not—*could* not, make things equal to himself.

The truth is, angels were endowed with wisdom, sufficient to make them as happy as the angels now in heaven are; and with power to do as much as God required them to do. And that creatures, as holy and wise as the angels, could be *inadvertent*, needs no proof, but to think of their fall.

It was an essential of angelical existence, that they should have the power of going through matter, and entering any material creature: and therefore, though they lost their moral excellences by the fall, yet they were not deprived of that power and wisdom, essential to their existence; had they been deprived of these—their hell—their very existence would have been extinguished. That Satan still retained these things after his fall, appears evident, by what follows.

CHAPTER III.

Now the serpent was more subtle than any beast of the field which the Lord God had made. The prince of devils, having been so successful among the angels, made his attempt upon man. The serpent here intends either that reptile, called a snake, or the devil in a real body of a snake, or else the devil in the form of a snake. Various Jewish authors say that animals had the power of conversing, before the fall, but this wants proof; without which, this seducer must have been more than a snake, for he spake: and further, the Scripture seems to hold forth that the seduction of our first parents was by the devil.

If this serpent was the devil in a snake, the question is whether the snake acted voluntarily and understandingly, or involuntarily in ignorance? If he understood what he was about, and formed a confederacy with the devil to go into the malevolent enterprise, he then deserved the judgment and punishment he met with; but if we acknowledge this, it proves too much, for by this rule the snake was a sinner before Adam or Eve was. If the snake acted involuntarily, i. e., if the devil assumed and used his body, merely as a machine, and the snake was ignorant of the intrigue, of course he must be innocent of the crime: why then should he be punished? To escape this difficulty, some have thought that the devil, only in the form of a serpent, was the seducer: the name that some serpents are called by, signifies *seraph*, and perhaps the devil might appear, at this time, in the form of a fiery flying serpent or seraph, which form good angels had appeared in before to Eve, and thereby transforming himself into an angel of light, might deceive Eve the more readily: and yet some of the denunciations to the tempter, seem to suit the snake better than the devil, and look as if God meant to punish the devil as the agent, and the snake as the instrument.

Supposing the snake guilty of no crime, yet he who made the earth, and all that is in it, for the use of man, might subject the snake to what he did, for the service of man, by putting enmity between them, that whenever men see a snake they may be put in mind of the fall, and be humble for it.

That God has ordered the death of beasts for the service of man, is evident from the sacrifices. If animal death was occasioned by the sin of man, surely the snake may suffer a little for his good; and if it is true that beasts would have been slain for the support of man, had man never sinned; that God made them purposely to lay down their lives for men; who can impeach the goodness of God for putting the serpent to a little disgrace for the profit of man, although he had been guilty of no crime? It is best therefore to suppose this serpent was the *devil*, in a real *snake*.

This serpent was subtle. Serpents are famed for their wisdom and subtlety, and, although the fox may be more crafty than serpents in general, yet *this* serpent, being actuated by the devil, *was more subtle than any beast of the field that God had made. And he said unto the woman,* who perhaps was a little distance from her husband, or if they were both together, he first attempted Eve, being the weaker part. The devil spake in the serpent, as the angel of the Lord did in Balaam's ass: the words he said, were, "*yea, hath God said, ye shall not eat of every tree in the garden.*" He begins with a *yea* to affirm it, yet speaks afterwards by an interrogation, in which his subtlety appears. Some suppose that the evil first arose when Eve wandered away from her husband in the garden, without his knowledge of it; but it is not certain that she was alone when the serpent accosted her, nor is it likely that the mutual love between them would admit of their being far apart, without the labor in the garden called for it: and if duty called for it, there could be no crime in it. Others think that the disease began when Eve gave the serpent audience, but it does not appear that she suspected him to have been a deceiver. If, as has been conjectured, the devil appeared in the same form that good angels assumed before, where was the imprudence of the woman in receiving him? And, even supposing Eve to have known him to be a deceiver, yet she answered him well, in these words, *we may not eat of the fruit of the trees of the garden,* freely. God is so far from restraining us, that he has given us free liberty to eat of all the trees but one, which is in the midst of the garden, which tree bears a poisonous fruit, of which God has bid us beware; and lest his caution should be disregarded, he has made it the test of our obedience, and threatened us with something awful, which he calls *death,* if we eat thereof. Some imagine that Eve was guilty of adding to, and taking from the words of God, in her reply to the serpent. The words that she added, were, *neither shall ye touch it:* and instead of saying, *ye shall surely die,* she said, *lest ye die.* But it may be observed, that Eve had orders second handed; when they were delivered by God to Adam, it is most probable that Eve was not formed, but Adam gave her information thereof, and if he had not been particular in detail, it was his error and not the error of Eve. But the words themselves convey no idea, (that I can see,) distinct from the words spoken to Adam by God himself: and, if men or women are guilty of a crime for not quoting words exactly, Peter, and Paul, and the Son of God, too, were guilty. Then said the serpent to the woman, *ye shall not surely die.* These words were in direct contradiction to the words of God; in them he gives God the lie. From this, he is said to be a liar from the beginning. These words, no doubt, shocked Eve to the heart, and I think the shock was fatal. The deception here began. Eve called in question the immutability of God, and supposed that this shining form had brought her some intelligence that God had revoked his threatening. But if the contagion had not yet taken place, it did before the serpent had done speaking; for when he had done, Eve was disarmed of all her confidence, and answered the serpent no more. The serpent proceeded. *For God doth know that in the day ye eat thereof, then your eyes shall be opened, and ye shall be as God's, knowing good and evil.* Here the devil speaks highly in commendation of the knowledge of God, but not so of his goodness. He had before insinuated that God withheld from them what might make them happier; and now he represents God as doing it designedly: that as he knew the quality of that tree to make them wise, he prohibited it to keep them in ignorance. It looks as if the devil, before this, had told Adam and Eve (the latter at least) that they were naked, and that it was very indecent; but, when they examined themselves, they saw no cause of shame in their nakedness, which the devil imputed to their ignorance, and told them that if they would eat of that tree, their eyes would be opened to see their shame as plainly as the Gods (the angels) did, and would know that what he had told them was true; or that they would be as *Elohim*, the divine Creator, and know abundance.

As Eve before suspected the immutability of God, she now had her ears opened to hearken to anything, and credited what the serpent said so far as to examine for herself. The deception had prevailed so far, that her mind was blinded. *For when the woman saw that the tree was good for food, and pleasant to the eyes,* her taste and sight took the lead of her mind, and preponderated against the divine prohibition: which proves that her senses were vitiated before she ate of the tree. And what mainly influenced her to eat, was that the fruit of the tree was *desirable to make one wise.* And surely, said Eve, God, who is so good, never wishes us to live in ignorance: what we know of God already makes us admire him; how great then will be our wonder and adoration, when our eyes are opened, and we are as God's, knowing good and evil. "Gold may be bought too dear." It is wisdom in creatures to live ignorant of those things that cannot be known but by rebellion; but false reasoning had so much weight on Eve, that she withstood the tempter no longer, but *took the fruit of the tree and did eat*; in which action she broke the divine command, and became culpable. And as soon as she had eaten, she used her voice to persuade her husband to do likewise; who, it seems, was near at hand, if not on the spot. St. Paul informs us, *that the man was not deceived, but the woman being deceived was in the transgression.* In which words the supplement first seems to be left out; for, without that supplement, the man was not in transgression at all. His meaning, therefore, is that the woman was *first* deceived and *first* in the transgression; for if Adam was not deceived by the words of the serpent to Eve, (who might stand by as a spectator and hear all that passed,) yet he was deceived by Eve. Some think that it was conjugal love that made Adam eat; who, rather than lose his wife, would disobey his God; if so, the excess of his conjugal love was his first depravity; so that the beauty and charms of Eve deceived him. But it is most likely that Eve, by extolling the sweetness of the fruit, and its excellent effects, deceived him.

As Eve was persuasive with her voice, so she was officious with her hands; for *she gave to her husband and he did eat.* If Eve was not a part of Adam, as federal head, then her transgression was only personal, for herself, and God could have killed her, and made Adam another helpmeet; and, if this was the case, then *our* fall depended upon Adam's transgression alone, and what Eve did in no way effects us; but I think that the whole man (Adam and Eve) was federal; and that when the defection began in Eve, the female part, the total apostacy was not to be prevented. And after they had transgressed,

The eyes of them both were opened; to see what good they had lost, and partly what evil they had incurred; to see themselves stripped of their original righteousness. Innocence was now gone, and guilt began to swell their breasts. *And they knew that they were naked;* by such a knowledge as to be ashamed of it. At first, they were not clothed with hair, feathers nor scales; their clothing was their moral virtue, and when that was gone, they saw themselves more naked than the animals, more vile than the beasts that perish. *And they sewed fig leaves together and made themselves aprons.* Not with needles, which were not then in existence, but either fastened them together with thorns, or, what is more likely, wreathed them together, and bound them around their waists, and let the longest leaves hang down before them, like aprons, to hide their nakedness. The fig-leaves they chose because of their large size. Equally foolish are men, who strive to make a clothing for their naked souls, with their own works. What follows, is the appearance of the Lord God in the garden—his arraigning Adam, Eve, and the serpent before his bar—their trial and respective dooms. But before I enter upon these heads, I shall inquire into the nature of the penalty, annexed to the law that was given to Adam. The law was: "Thou shalt not eat of the tree." The penalty threatened, in case of transgression, was: "Thou shalt surely die." The time in which the penalty was to be inflicted, was: "The day that he should eat thereof."

It is most commonly believed that the death of the body—the death of the soul—and the eternal death of both body and soul in hell are included in the threatening, and that all these would have been inflicted on Adam, on the day of his fall, if a mediator had not appeared; but these things require investigation.

By the death of the body, is understood the exit of the soul, the extinction of the animal life, and a putrefaction and rottenness of the earthy parts. This death, I believe, was contained in the threatening, under this restriction, that all of it was not to be inflicted on the same day. The words of the threatening are rendered, by some, *dying thou shalt die*; and seem to convey this idea: that in the day that Adam should eat of the tree, he should be mortalized—made subject to vanity, pain and sickness, which should never quit him till he should be reduced to death; and in this light God seems to explain it, when he says, *In sorrow shalt thou eat all the days of thy life, until thou return to dust.* This was fulfilled on Adam, and is fulfilled on his progeny. Whether the seeds of death were occasioned by the poisonous fruit, (which is probable enough,) or planted by God in a judicial manner, thay have certainly raised a war in the elements that compose man, that will not cease their rage till he expires—there is no discharge in this war.

The objection to this doctrine, is this: If the Death of the body was any part or all of the penalty annexed to the law, and Jesus, the security of his people, suffered death for them, with what propriety can justice punish them with death, when their security has paid it? To this it may be replied, that Jesus died, not to free men from it, but to follow death to his last retreat, in order to destroy death and raise men therefrom. Further, though Jesus laid down his life, yet he did not turn to dust, which seems to be the penalty annexed: this the real debtor pays, and not the surety; and besides, it is not certain that Jesus ever undertook to bear or palliate the penalty of that law; but it is most likely that the whole of the annexed penalty was inflicted on Adam and his posterity, and was no way mitigated by the Mediator. But more of this hereafter.

If by the death of the soul is meant alienation of affection and enmity against God, it is not rational to conclude that this death was any part of the penalty; for this reason: alienation and a carnal mind had taken possession of Adam and Eve before they broke the test of their obedience; and if spiritual apostacy preceded the transgression, it could not be the penalty inflicted for the crime. Nor would it sound very well to read the words of the Lord thus: "In the day that thou eatest the fruit of the tree, I will make thee an alienate, carnal, hardhearted enemy to thy Creator." Those who believe that spiritual apostacy was any part of the penalty, and that Jesus, the surety of his people, endured the penalty for them, would do well to ask themselves this question: Was Jesus ever made an alienate, carnal, hardhearted enemy to God? If not, how could he have borne the penalty, if spiritual death was included in the penalty?

But if by the death of the soul is understood simply its separation from God, the conclusion is not so absurd, that it was part of the penalty. The souls of Adam and Eve first wandered away from God, after Satan and sin, before they ate the interdicted fruit; and, therefore, God, in a judicial way, withdrew himself, and gave them up to the fury of Satan and sin as a just punishment. This Jesus endured for his people; he was forsaken of God, and given up to Satan, sin and sinners.

That something more than natural death came by the fall, is certain; and it is as certain that much sin was committed by Adam and Eve, exclusive of eating of the tree; it seems most elegible, therefore, to suppose that *morality* was the penalty, and that other evils arise, either as the attendants of sin, or the natural consequences thereof, many of which are communicated by ordinary generation.

It is pretty plain that many deaths spoken of in the Scripture, such as famine, pestilence, captivity; and the deaths that St. Paul and others were often in, as well as the death of Abel, Absalom, Haman, etc., were not contained in the threatening of God to Adam; because Adam and ten thousand times ten thousand besides never felt them: and yet it is certain that all the complicated miseries of this life, death and damnation, come in at the door of sin, either as the attendants or natural consequences of sin, or what are inflicted on men in a judicial manner, for the breach of the laws of nature and revelation.

How is it possible that corporeal and eternal death were both contained in the threatening? The first says, the body shall die and turn to dust, the last says, that the body shall endure eternal pain. It cannot be well supposed, that God told Adam, that if he should eat of the forbidden tree, his body should die, and that he would send his son into the world to die and destroy death, and raise up his body again to endure eternal pain: If so, then the whole plan of salvation was made known to Adam, in the precept given, and the penalty annexed; which would be strange divinity to imagine. The above observation therefore seems best; to consider damnation as the effect of sin, in a final issue, and as not being contained in the threatening.

Having made these observations, I pass on to the chain of history, which speaks of the Judge of all the Earth coming into the garden, and arraigning the criminals at his bar: which is introduced, thus:

And they heard the voice of the Lord God walking in the garden in the cool of the day. From which we learn that sin did not destroy the sense of hearing. By the voice of God some understand thunder, and suppose that sin having entered the world, set the elements at war in peals of thunder: but rather God spake with his usual tone, which Adam and Eve knew; and as he spake, he appeared to be walking among the trees of the garden, and drawing towards them. This was in the cool of the day. Satan's temptations and man's rebellion were both performed before on the same day; and in the cool of the evening, when the sun was nigh down, and the cool breezes began to blow, God came walking towards them.

And Adam and his wife hid themselves from the presence of the Lord God amongst the trees of the garden. As they had lost the image of God they could not be happy in his presence, and (if Adam spake the truth,) they were afraid of him, as well they might be, since they had broken the law which an omnipotent God had given them. *Guilty fear* appears to be the first evil that raged after the fall; and this still remains in all Adam's posterity, until they are reconciled by the blood of the Lamb, and are made partakers of that love which casts out fear. This fear made them *flee from the presence of the Lord*, which all men are prone to while unregenerate: they go astray as soon as they are born, giving God the back and not the face. *Blindness of mind* is seen in this procedure, that they should imagine that God was local, like themselves, and that they could hide from him: But of this error they were soon convinced, for *the Lord God called unto Adam, and said unto him, where art thou?* I placed you in the garden, and appointed you your labor, but where are you now? God knew where Adam was, but chose to make Adam confess what he had done. *And Adam said, I heard thy voice in the garden and I was afraid, because I was naked, and I hid myself.*

The sins that appear in Adam's answer, were *dissimulation* and *self-excuse*. His dissimulation is seen in endeavoring to conceal from God the real cause of his fear, which was his eating the forbidden fruit; whereas Adam represents it to be his nakedness; in which he would excuse himself, and charge God with the cause of it, in not making him with a covering.

And God said, who told thee that thou wast naked? Not I. When thou wast first made naked, I never accused thee with it; your nakedness did not prevent your access to me, nor cause me to reproach you; nor were you ashamed of it before: who then has told you of it in a sneering manner? If any one, he must be an enemy to me and my government, and a seducer to you; and therefore I ask you the question, *Hast thou eaten of the tree whereof I commanded thee that thou shouldst not eat?*

And the man said, the woman whom thou gavest to be with me, she gave me of the tree and I did eat. Here Adam makes use of nineteen words instead of saying *yes*. Fifteen of them are used as an apology, and four as a confession. Long apologies and short confessions have prevailed among men ever since. What Adam said, was true; and yet it is spoken with such an air as to cast blame on the woman, and finally upon God himself. He sought to screen himself by the seduction of the woman, and finally intimates that if God had not imposed *that woman* upon him, he should not have eaten.

The Judge then proceeded to examine the woman, and hear of her, whether she owned the charge of her husband, and what defence she had to make; and said unto her, *what is this that thou hast done?* If you acknowledge the accusation of your husband, what is *this* great wickedness that thou art guilty of? The woman did not deny the charge of Adam, but, like him, excused herself, by accusing her tempter, and said, *the serpent beguiled me and I did eat.* As fond as she was, before this, of the serpent, (as is supposed by many) being naked like herself; yet being beguiled by him, and exposed to punishment, she would fain excuse herself, and expose the tempter.

The serpent, who had received his doom before, was not interrogated at this time by the Judge; but was proceeded against with some denunciations in addition to his former punishment. In transgression, the Devil was first—next, the woman—and last, the man. The inquest began first with the man—and then the woman; no inquiry being made of the serpent. But judgment was denounced on them according to the order of their crimes,—first, on the serpent; next, on the woman; and last, on the man.

The judge addressed the serpent as follows:—

Because thou hast done this, i. e. beguiled the woman, *thou art cursed above all cattle.* Those that were tame, and to live among men, *and above every beast of the field,* such as were or should be wild; living in the forests and mountains, not to assist or be assisted by man. *Upon thy belly shalt thou go,* without wings or legs, and *dust shalt thou eat all the days* of thy life. As this respects the instrument (the snake) it strongly indicates, that before this, the serpent was the favorite of Eve, among all the cattle and beasts; but now it should be abhorred above them all: and also, that before this action, the serpent used to fly, go on legs, or creep erect; but now he should be degraded to creep his whole length on the ground, and lick the dust as long as he lived. And as it respects the agent (the Devil) it sets forth the abhorrence that he should meet with; being ever spoken of with contempt; that he should never soar to heaven or walk with majesty on earth, but be despised by all, and feed on the sordid lusts of men: and as he will live for ever, he never will rise from this abject state.

And I will put enmity between thee and the woman. Before this there was great friendship and intimacy between the serpent and woman; but now the friendship was broken, never to be restored again. Serpents are ever fearful of men, and men are at constant variance with serpents: women, in particular, cannot endure the sight of them. And with regard to the Devil, though men are fond of his ways, yet they are always averse to his name and character, and are prone to call every disagreeable thing that frets and plagues them, by his name: and the Devil is the common enemy of men, and cannot love them, even when they weary themselves to death in his vassalage.

And between thy seed and her seed. The whole serpentine race, and all the posterity of Eve are at enmity, as has been observed; but by the seed of the Devil, we are not to understand his angels, who joined him in the rebellion, but wicked men, who are called the children of the wicked one; and are said to be of their father, the Devil: particularly Cain, who was of that wicked one, and slew his brother; and all of his character. By the seed of the woman, is meant, not only the generation of the godly in every age of the world, between whom and the ungodly, there is always an irreconciliation, but principally the Messiah, who was a descendant of Eve, and the child of the Virgin Mary; who took not on him the nature of angels, but the nature of man; that through death he might destroy the Devil. At this *seed* the heathen rage, the kings of the earth set themselves at war, and all the ungodly are at variance.

It shall bruise thy head. When men encounter a snake, they are never contented till they have crushed his head; even after ever so many blows upon his back: so it was with Jesus; after all the blows of doctrine and miracles that he gave Satan, while he was living on earth, yet he never ceased till he bruised his head on the cross; where he destroyed all the projects, disconcerted all the schemes, and broke the power of the Devil, and took the wise in his own craftiness; and will never cease till he has levelled his kingdom to the ground, and brought down his horn to the dust.

And thou shalt bruise his heel. As this refers to the snake, by reason of his creeping on his belly, he can only strike the heel, at most, the lower part of man; and as it concerns the Devil, he could only bruise the heel of Christ; i. e. his human nature, which is inferior to his God-head. This heel Satan bruised with his temptations, and raised his instruments to bruise him to death on the cross.

The Judge next proceeded against the woman, and said unto her:—

I will greatly multiply thy sorrow and conception; or in thy conception; for it is not to be understood that Eve was to conceive more children for her transgression; but that her sorrows, in conception, should be greatly multiplied. It is not likely that women would have had *many* if *any* sorrows in bearing children, if sin had not entered the world; but now they bring forth their children with multiplied sorrows. But, notwithstanding their sorrows are so great in bearing and bringing forth children, yet, (said God)

Thy desire shall be to thy husband. That women in general have a desire to enjoy husbands and conceive by them, is evident, from the discontent of those who have no husbands; and those who have husbands and no children. But as the same word is used in the affair of Cain and Abel, chap. iv. 7, it seems rather to respect her subjection to her husband. Rulers address their subjects by command; but subjects address their rulers by desire, in a supplicative manner; and as Eve was first in the transgression, and a tempter to Adam, she, and all her sex are reduced to the subjection of *desiring* their husbands instead of commanding them. Indeed, by the order of Nature, the man being first made, the woman was to be in some subordination; but by reason of the order of sin, the woman being first in the transgression, this subjection is greatly increased; for so it follows,—

He shall rule over thee—In a lordly, cruel manner; which is the case of women in general, and a great curse it is; and when they meet with it they should remember that it is for their sin.

Next the man is called to the bar, and proceeded against as follows:—

Because thou hast hearkened unto the voice of thy wife. This shows that Eve used her voice to persuade Adam to eat. To hear the voice of a wife, as a counsellor, is becoming a husband; but to be enticed by a wife to transgress a divine command, is the first imprudence that Adam was charged with. It is no crime for a man to be tempted, if he withstands the temptation; but the guilt of the tempter will not expiate the crime of the man who is overcome by the temptation. And this was Adam's case. See what follows:

And thou hast eaten of the tree of which I commanded thee, saying, thou shalt not eat of it: meaning the tree of knowledge of good and evil, of which so much is said. It is not likely that this tree bore the same name before Adam ate thereof, but took its name from the crime of Adam: Adam and Eve knew *good* before the fall, but by eating of that tree they were brought to the knowledge of *evil.* It is true, that the tree is called by that name before the fall, but it is most likely it was so called by anticipation—Moses giving it the same name that it was called by after the fall. This tree stood in the midst of the garden, near the tree of life; but the fruits of the two trees differed widely: the first bore fruit to mortalize, the last to immortalize.

It is evident that Adam and Eve apostatized before they ate of the tree, but the prohibition of that tree being the test of their obedience, for the breach of that, God gives out the doom: *Cursed is the ground for thy sake.*

Some suppose that, if sin had never entered the world, the earth would have produced her increase spontaneously; but, in chap. ii., 5, it looks as if man at first was made to till the ground; and yet it is clear that sin has brought a great curse upon the earth. I conclude that a little labor for recreation would have been sufficient, had not sin marred the face of the earth: but now, says God, *In sorrow shalt thou eat of it all the days of thy life.*

Adam lived nine hundred and thirty years; and so many years he ate the fruits of the earth in sorrow, sweat, labor and pain; which grievous debt is entailed on his offsprings. The profit of the earth is for all—the king himself is served by the field—all live upon the fruits of the earth, and all eat thereof in sorrow. Let men live where they choose, follow what calling they please, yet sorrow attends them all the days of their lives.

Thorns also and thistles shall it bring forth to thee. The earth brings forth herbage for beasts spontaneously, but men have to till the ground, labor in the field, toil and sweat to kill the thorns and thistles, and noxious weeds in general, to raise vegetables and bread for themselves; and this fatigue lasts until they return to dust.

For dust thou art, and unto dust shalt thou return. Adam's body was made out of the earth, his animal spirit distilled from it; and when God recalled the soul that he breathed into him, the animal spirit was extinguished, and his body turned to dust. The same fate follows all his offsprings.

In this manner God explains the threatening that he gave to Adam before, and he is not a man that he should lie, but was as good as his word; and it appears to me, that whatever was contained in these words, "In the day thou eatest thereof thou shalt surely die," was fully inflicted on Adam, and was not mitigated by the Mediator; for God appeared as a judge to execute his law, and never so much as mentioned a Mediator to Adam and Eve in the whole process. I am also as well convinced that many evils befel Adam, and do befall us, that were never contained in the threatening, as I have observed before.

The *seed of the woman* was spoken of to Satan, not as a saviour, but as a destroyer; to convince him, and all his species, that though they refused to worship an incarnate God, and had prevailed over Adam and Eve, yet he should proceed from the woman, and wear a human form, and prove an over match for them all.

Adam and Eve, who stood by when God spake these words to the serpent, might yet hope at least of temporal life, and perhaps of eternal life, through the seed; but this no way diverted the threatening.

And Adam called his wife's name Eve; which name signifies *to live* or *she liveth.* As she was not annihilated, as he might expect, with himself, he gave her this name to perpetuate the action. Adam, before this, had given names to all the beasts, and the name of *woman* to his wife; but now, hearing that she was to bear a *seed,* and seeing her still alive, gave her a new name—*Eve.*

Because she was the mother of all living: i. e., of human kind. These words were added by Moses, which he offered as a reason why Adam gave his wife that name, or spoken by Adam, knowing that she was the only woman in the world, and that from her the whole human race would proceed. All nations upon the face of the earth, though bearing different colors and shapes, and in a multitude of conditions, must own Eve for their mother.

And the Lord God made coats of skins and clothed Adam and his wife. These skins were taken from beasts; but on what account the beasts were slain, is uncertain. It is the opinion of some, that before Adam fell the beasts came to him by instinct, and willingly offered their lives to serve him; and that, if sin had never entered the world, man would have lived upon animal food; and this opinion is supported, by observing that the earth would soon have been overstocked with beasts and fowls if none of them had died; and further, they remark that some beasts and fowls were made to slay others, and live upon them; that the very shape of some of them indicates that they were made to devour; that claws, long teeth and hooked bills, would have been useless and troublesome to creatures designed to live alone upon vegetables; and, finally, they cannot believe that the sin of man should bring death upon beasts.

If these things can be maintained, it is not difficult to say where God found these skins to clothe Adam and his wife with. Adam and Eve having killed these beasts to eat their flesh, flayed off their skins, in some such way as savages do, without knives, and laid them by as useless; but now God taught them that their skins were as good for clothing as their flesh was for food. But these things are questionable.

It is not certain that animal flesh was ever eaten by man till after the flood. The fruits of the garden, the herbs, and every tree yielding seed, are all that were given to Adam and Eve to eat, in their first charter; and after the fall, they were to eat their bread by the sweat of their brows. And how beasts could lay down their lives without pain, is inconceivable; and to suppose that they would have come instinctively and laid down their lives, without pain, for man, is strange.

But one thing further is certain, that the sin of man occasions the death of brutes; if not causally, in the first instance, yet it does eventually—the cruelty and wantonness of man reduce the beasts to death. And it seems to strike as directly against the goodness of God, to suppose that the species of brutes should toil, groan and die, to satisfy the pride, lust and cruelty of man, as it does to suppose that animals at first were made to be mortal, and die to satisfy the hunger of man.

But if beasts were not eaten before the fall, nor even before the flood, it is supposable that these beasts were slain for sacrifices, which ceremony was certainly in force in the days of Cain and Abel, and likely was ordained soon after the fall, but not before the beasts had begun to multiply; for if the first beasts had been slain, their species would have been extinguished. From this early institution of sacrificing lambs, Christ is called a Lamb, slain from the foundation of the world. How long it was after the fall before God clothed Adam and his wife with skins, is unknown; but the first clothing that he made for them was out of skins, from which, it is most likely, the hair was not taken off: so the Tartars, Laplanders, and various nations clothe themselves unto this day.

As the fig leaves that Adam and Eve sewed together to make themselves aprons of, were emblems of the vain ways, foolish hopes, and self-righteousness of the ungodly; so these coats of skins were figurative of the righteousness of Christ, that robe of righteousness and garment of salvation, with which the Almighty adorns the souls of penitents.

And the Lord God said, behold the man is become like one of us, to know good and evil. This phrase respects both Adam and Eve, though but one of them is mentioned. If these words were seriously spoken, the sense is, that now Adam and his wife had become like one of the divine reasons in knowledge. Before the fall, God knew good and evil, and good from evil; evil, not by possession, but by understanding its nature and consequences; but Adam and Eve did not; they knew good, by possession, but had no just idea of evil; but now being fallen into evil, and convinced of its nature and effects, in that respect they became as God. How applicable are the words of Solomon in this affair! "He that increases knowledge, increases sorrow."

Or else the meaning is, that *now*, since the Lord had graciously made known to them the Messiah, the seed of the woman, and brought them to a sense of their sin, and also clothed them with skins, (representing the righteousness of Christ,) that they were like the angels, being in favor with God, and ready and willing to obey him; or rather that they were like God himself, being created in Christ Jesus; having put on the new man, created in righteousness and holiness, after the image of him who created him.

But it seems best to understand the words, as spoken ironically; reproving while they seem to applaud. It was the vain hope and wish of Adam and Eve, that, by eating the forbidden fruit, they should be as Gods; and here God retorts upon them: "Now the man is become like one of us, is he? look and see his wretchedness! see what his pride has reduced him to! His knowledge is increased, it is true, but wherein is he the better? Innocence was far better: nor has his misfortune humbled his heart entirely; aspiring thoughts yet dwell within him."

And now, lest he put forth his hand, and take of the tree of life and eat and live forever. God first treated Adam as a free agent; he left him to his own choice, to eat or not to eat of the tree of knowledge, using no other means to keep him from eating, but a moral prohibition, as a test of his obedience; but not so with the tree of life. That tree was guarded with cherubims and a fiery sword. God, in the character of a legislator, never forces or prevents the human will; but in the character of a judge, dealing with culprits, he subjects them to afflictions contrary to their wills.

As it is probable that the fruit of the tree of knowledge was poisonous, and that it naturally reduced Adam to pain, sickness and death; so also it is likely that the fruit of the tree of life was of the nature to immortalize. And now, Adam having eaten of the first, by which he incurred death, (both physically and judicially,) was prevented from staying in the garden, lest he should take of the tree of life, and thereby immortalize himself and so live forever. Some have thought, that if sin had never entered into the world, yet men would have been subject to decay; to remedy which the tree of life was planted, and bore fruit of that quality to remove or rather prevent all weakness of the limbs, wrinkles in the face, and every thing of the kind.

Another reason assigned as the cause, why this tree was called the tree of life, is, that it was ever verdant, constantly circulating sap and bearing fruit all the year; and this seems probable enough from Rev. xxii., 2, where reference is had to this tree. And the Devil might have suggested to Adam, that there could be no malignity in the prohibited tree, which grew so near the tree of life, and if there was, they might easily take of the fruit of the tree of life, which would be a sufficient antidote; but to prevent all such vain hopes in Adam and Eve, and to convince them that they were not at liberty to follow the machinations of Satan, *The Lord God drove them out of the garden of Eden, to till the ground from whence Adam was taken.*

Before this, I conclude Adam had not begun to till the ground, but had lived upon the spontaneous fruits of the garden, what time he had lived, which was not long, as it seems. The garden was planted in the east part of Eden, and it looks as if Adam was driven entirely out of the land of Eden; for the cherubic guard was placed at the east of the garden, to keep Adam and Eve from returning to the garden and eating of the tree of life. The Lord drove them out of the garden (which they left with reluctance, as is probable) to till the ground from whence Adam was taken, and raise their bread in sweat, labor and pain. The ground that he was to till, was that out of which he was taken: from which it appears, that Adam was made out of the ground east of Eden, and *taken* from thence by the Lord, and placed in the garden of Eden; but as he was rebellious in the garden, he was driven back to the place where he was made, to spend his days in sweat, sorrow and pain, until he returned to dust.

From Adam's being taken from the spot where he was made and placed in Eden's garden, (if he had been obedient,) it is probable that he would have been raised, in gradual stages, to the same enjoyment that the glorified saints will eternally enjoy; but the life he possessed in the garden, did not capacitate him to rise any higher than he then was; nor had he any reason to believe that his best obedience would merit a higher station: yet, I conclude, it is not extravagant to suppose, that God would have exalted him to the same pinnacle of glory, that all the ransomed of the Lord will hereafter inherit; for, as sin will never prevent the purposes of God's *grace*, so likewise, it is never the *cause* of human exaltation, before God. Sin is the cause of pain and sickness, want and woe, horror and shame, hardness and impenitence, anger and rage, strife and contention, war and bloodshed, death and damnation. If sin had never entered the world, there would have been no cause of Christ's death; but sin was not the cause of the *incarnation* of Jesus Christ, nor does it cause the communication of eternal life into the human heart.

No man will ever return to the state that Adam was in while in the garden: those who are regenerated will rise much higher, and those who die in rebellion will sink much lower.

Or, perhaps, the meaning of the clause, *To till the ground out of which he was taken*, does not respect the particular spot where Adam was made and taken from; but the ground in general, out of which element Adam was formed.

And the Lord God placed at the east of the garden of Eden cherubims, and a flaming sword which turned every way, to keep the way of the tree of life. Frequent accounts, in Scripture, are given, both of living and lifeless cherubims. About the ark and mercy-seat, and on the walls of the holy place, in the temple, were lifeless images, called cherubims. The living cherubims are called seraphims, living creatures, four beasts, and cherubims. These creatures, in Scripture, generally intend gospel ministers; but not always. Where it is said that *Jehovah rode upon a cherub and did fly*, it is better to understand it of an angel, than of a human minister. Perhaps the name may be given, with propriety, to any messenger of the Lord, from the greatest angel to the smallest insect. In the text now under consideration, they seem to intend angels, and not ministers of the gospel. Angels were then in existence, but gospel ministers were not. These angelical ministers were made a *flame of fire*: streams of fire proceeded from them, resembling swords, like the beams of the sun, in every direction, to strike the rebel through who should dare to approach the tree of life.

Some think this wonderful appearance was designed by God, to convince Adam, and keep in his mind, that no life was ever after the fall to be had by the deeds of the law. That the flaming sword of justice stands pointed against every soul that seeks salvation by works of righteousness that he can do.

Others are of opinion, that as the tree of life was an emblem of Jesus Christ, (who is often compared to the tree of life,) so these cherubims were heiroglyphical of gospel ministers, who handle the word of God, which is quick and powerful, sharper than a two-edged sword; which turns every way to detect the hypocrite, alarm the profane, and point out to penitents the way of salvation, by faith in the Redeemer. But it appears to me, that these cherubims were not merely visionary appearances, but real subsistences, and therefore the first sense given seems most probable.

How long these angels continued there, as guards to the tree, is uncertain. If the tree of life died as soon as common trees do, (in about one hundred years,) or if they guarded the tree until the flood, when men were removed from that part of the world, they were happy in their post, doing the will of God. The flood has so altered the face of the earth (together with earthquakes and other causes) that no man can tell where the garden or any part of Eden lay; and what became of the trees in the garden, particularly the tree of death and tree of life; whether they were used for firewood or timber—whether they died with age or are now living—or whether the first was transplanted in hell, and the last in paradise, to me, is unknown.

APPENDIX.

MISCELLANEOUS.

THE nature of God is just, and therefore his ways are all equal; and as love and goodness proceed from him, consequently malevolence and sin cannot; otherwise, his ways would be unequal.

Some suppose that it was necessary that sin should emerge among the creatures of God, that the divine glory might be more effulgently displayed than otherwise it could have been. But is the supposition well founded? what idea should we form of a man who should charge his son not to run into the fire, and with one hand brace him from it, and at the same time, with the other hand, secreted by a screen, pull the forbidden child into the flame, that he might show his compassion to his little favorite in pulling him out of the burning coals? Would such compassion be amiable? But suppose the same man should serve ten sons in the same manner, and pull but five of them out, and leave the rest therein forever, that those five who were graciously delivered, and the five who were unfortunately forsaken might see his justice, could God or man love such a character?

If goodness, love and justice, cannot be displayed, known and enjoyed, without a previous knowledge and possession of evil, then Adam, in innocency, could not; angels in heaven, and the God of angels, cannot either know, enjoy, or display goodness, love and justice.

That sin adds anything to the glory of the Divine Essence, is inadmissible. If any beings, therefore, are profited by it, sinners themselves are; and if infinite wisdom could contrive no way to add to creatures, but a way that damns a great part of them, what shall we say of such wisdom? Could not justice shine to men as transpicuous without their guilt as it now can? Is it not as great justice to clear the innocent as it is to condemn the guilty? These things are so.

What has goodness to say, if the justice of God could not so fully be made known without the damnation of millions of millions? Is it possible for the best of creatures, yea, for God himself, to love such sovereign justice?

How can the mouths of the damned be stopped by *that* justice which could not be displayed without their exquisite torment? And how can the saints triumph in that character which wantonly glories in the misery of their fellow creatures?

Had sin never entered the world, the justice of God could have appeared as glorious as it now does, or ever will; and if creatures are to be raised to a higher state of glory than they could have been without sin, all the praise of this superabundant glory belongs to sin, and all creatures should love the *death of the wicked*, which the Creator takes no pleasure in.

The Lord God is omnipotent: nothing (consistent with his nature) is too hard for him to effect; but he acts upon a scale so exalted, from a principle so good, that he cannot do those mean, dirty things that men can. If it should be thought a pesumptuous impeachment of divine power to say that "God could not have prevented sin in the first instance," it certainly operates as much against his goodness, to say that he could have prevented it. The omniscient Jehovah made creatures without their own consent, and foresaw all the evils that ever they would fall into. Now, if he could have prevented their sin by one of his fingers, and would not put that finger forth, who can justify his goodness?

Eternal power is limited by nothing but the nature of the divine *Esse*, which is so good and benevolent, that Omnipotence could not make creatures miserable by destroying the liberty of their wills, which was the only way supposable to prevent their crimes.

"But was it possible for the Almighty ever to discover the attribute of *mercy* to his creatures, without their apostacy? Does not *mercy* always presuppose need or misery? If so, then sin, on the creature's part, has proved the way for the discovery of that perfection which otherwise would ever have been dormant."

This remark has real weight, and merits a fair investigation. It is a principal hinge for turning the disputes of the present day; and, therefore, is not to be slightly canvassed.

The word *attribute*, is as great a stranger in the Bible, as the word *moral;* and what two words are more frequently used by divines, or more variously understood.

If by an attribute is understood an essential property of Deity; *that*, without which the Almighty would be imperfect; and further, if it is supposed that all the attributes of Jehovah can have an ample circulation in the divine *Essee,* without the existence of creatures, so that the infinite God is independantly glorious: I conclude that *mercy* is not an attribute. For if *mercy* always presupposes need or misery, how could it circulate in a being where no need or misery was to be found?

Learned men say that the attributes of God are ever spoken of in the single number, thus: *love, power, holiness, &c.,* and will not admit of their plurals, *loves, powers, holinesses, &c.* If this observation has any weight in it, then mercy cannot be an attribute, for *mercy* is plural (mercies) in a variety of places in the Bible.

In the above view of things, if *mercy* is an attribute, God was dependant on creatures to do *that* which was contrary to his nature and law—*that,* which he could not do himself or tempt them to—to bring themselves into a situation in which alone he could make a full discovery of himself unto them. How dependant was God, in this point of view!

God is a spirit of light, life and love, and some think that his attributes are naught but the manifestations of himself to his creatures, in his word and works. The invisibility of the eternal power and godhead was made known in creation, and is clearly seen by the things that are made. Wisdom, power and goodness, were exhibited in creation, but grace and mercy were not. Here then the question arises: viz., was not sin necessary? etc. Can any man suppose that *fury, wrath* or *vengeance,* are essential properties of the God of love and goodness? Are they not the displays of justice on criminals? Just so *mercy* is the stream of love. God is love, and eternally loved his people; nor could all their sins either heighten or destroy it. And love, the fountain, could and would have raised them to the same enjoyment, that mercy, the stream, now will, if they never had sinned.

If, therefore, creation was a work of necessity, for a display of the perfections of God, yet sin was not; for no perfection of God is now made known to creatures, but what could have been made known as fully without sin: justice could have shone as effulgent, and love appeared as strong as they now do. The universe is as much worse for sin, as all the groans of the creation and all the damnation of men and devils amount to, and in no instance, upon a general scale, the better for it.

Those who go to heaven are raised entirely upon the scale of love and goodness, but saved from hell upon the scale of justice.

Another question arises, which is this: "Do not the saints in heaven admire *redeeming love* more than angels do, or more than they possibly could have done, if they had not sinned and been redeemed?"

Redeeming love, by that name, would never have been known on earth or in heaven, if creatures had not sinned; but from this it does not appear that creatures on earth or in heaven are happier than they could otherwise have been. That saints in heaven will be more exalted than angels, is what I believe; but this exaltation arises from the likeness of nature, and not from the redemption from sin; for Jesus Christ has done the human nature more honor than he has the angelic, in that he put on the first and not the last.

To solve the question, let me ask any godly man, who understands the nature of grace in his heart, whether (in times when his soul is most full of the love of God) he admires redemption from hell or the enjoyment of God's love the most? If I judge right when souls enjoy most ot God, they are the most swallowed up in admiring the perfections of God, without poring so much upon what he has done for them.

That the act of redemption calls loudly upon all on earth and all in heaven to adore the Redeemer is unquestionable; at the same time, if we trace things to their origin, the principle that this act proceeds from, is to be principally adored; and this principle could have been as well known and as fully enjoyed without sin, as it now can.

ALL the works of God are the effects of divine power and goodness, love, and justice in concert; and he always acts from motive in himself; and is noways biased by the conduct of his creatures: yet the actions of men vary the operation of his hand in numberless instances. A benevolent father loves his child, and always acts from a principle of love towards him; but as the behaviour of the child is sometimes filial and sometimes froward; the same stimulus of love that moves the father at some times to give a plaudit and bestow an encomium, at other times induces him to give a reproof and inflict a punishment. The application is easy.

To say that Jesus Christ did not die for sinners, but for the glory of God, is just as good divinity, as it is to say, that rain, and fruitful seasons, bread, and all the blessings of nature, are not given to men for their good, but for the glory of God. That Jesus shed his blood for the remission of sins, was wounded for transgressions, and bruised for iniquity, died for sins, and laid down his life for his sheep, is abundantly proven in scripture.

The nature of God, and the nature of sin are such, that *sin* must be punished somewhere, in some being; for it cannot be punished in itself: the criminal or the surety must smart for it. If the surety pays the whole debt, bears the full punishment, then the criminal is freed, upon the scale of law and justice; and the creditor cannot demand the sum, nor the law its penalty from both the debtor or criminal, and the surety. Now if the satisfaction of Christ consists in suffering for sin, (which is the light in which the New Testament holds it forth,) he either made universal satisfaction to God, for the sins of all Adam's race, or he did not. If the atonement is universal, how can any be damned, upon the scale of justice? If the answer is, "because men will not repent, believe, and return and submit to the deliverer." The next question is, are the acts of impenitence, unbelief, inattention and obstinacy, sins or no sins? If no sins, then men can be saved in them. If they are sins, then they were atoned for, or they were not; if they were atoned for, how can men be damned for them? If they were not atoned for, then the atonement was not universal. If, therefore, the atonement is proved to be universal, it follows, of course, that salvation is universal; but if the last is confuted, the first inevitably falls.

It is a question, whether Jesus the son of Mary went to heaven upon the scale of nature, obedience, God-head or grace. His nature was free from sin, but not spiritual enough for heaven, till after his resurrection. His obedience was as perfect as the law required; he magnified the law and made it honorable. The searching eye of omniscience could see no imperfection in him; but his obedience entitled him to no higher station than Adam was in before the fall. To suppose that he overcame and rose to heaven merely by his own God-head, would destroy the idea of his perfect human virtue, and represent the man of sorrow as having no trials at all: for what proof of a giant's skill would it be to conquer a pigmy, or what danger would a hero be in, beset only by a child. It seems best therefore to suppose that Jesus went to heaven by grace. That the babe that was conceived in the virgin's womb, was in the same predicament and texture of innocent Adam, we have great reason to believe; but without the grace of God, it is more likely that he would have fallen than that Adam should, as temptations had increased a thousand fold. That John the Baptist was regenerate in his mother's womb, is pretty clear; and likely it is the case with many others. So likewise the child Jesus, came into the world an innocent Adam and a regenerate soul, and in that character was proof against all the temptations that befell him, and perfectly obedient to the law; and after dying and suffering for sins, not his own, he was raised with a spiritual body capable of entering heaven, which was not the case of Adam's body before the fall. If these things are facts, then Jesus called God his father, as Christians do, being his son by regeneration, (I mean in some places,) and I shall leave the reader to judge, whether the words, "ye who have followed me in the regeneration of this life," are not applicable to the above sentiment.

It is the opinion of some, that depravity consists alone in the will, being the reverse to all that is good. That when the *blindness of the mind, and the darkness of the understanding* are spoken of, we are to form the idea, that the will is so perverse, that men will not attend to the means of information, and therefore the mind is left in ignorance. This observation is supported by great men and great argument; nor am I disposed, at this time, to call it in question; but one thing I shall contend for, viz. that moral agency and the violation of the will, have nothing to do in the work of regeneration. The reception of divine grace, or the new-birth, is not according to the *will* of man: it is not of him that *willeth* but of God.

To tell a congregation of people, that they may all come to Christ as a mediator, and receive eternal life, if they will, is incoherent divinity; Adam in innocncey had not that power. *Paul*, whose will was present, could not do as he would; and all the saints in every part of the world, when their wills are most swallowed up in the divine will, find the need of spiritual strength to perform things that they would.

That men are moral agents, since the fall, is evident; otherwise they could not sin at all; but let those, who believe that salvation turns upon man's acceptance, remember that the *tree of life* in the garden, was not to be eaten of at the will of man after the fall: and those who suppose that the promised seed, (or rather the seed of the woman, spoken of as a conqueror to the serpent,) restored fallen man to free agency, consider that the guardian prohibition of this tree, was after the seed of the woman was spoken of.

When will man duly consider, that the most perfect obedience of a moral subject entitles him to no higher station, than the state where he is fixed?

If Christ had died for all, and there is a fulness of grace for all; how comes it to pass that some are saved and not all? "because some will not come."

Are there not many who had this *will not* for a number of years, and afterwards *repented and went*? "beyond all doubt."

Was not their obstinacy of will atoned for as well as the rest of their sins? "To be sure."

Are the sins of obstinacy in other sinners atoned for or not? If they are, how can they be damned for sins already atoned for, upon the scale of justice? If they are not atoned for, how can such find pardon? "But the sins of men are atoned for conditionally."

What are those conditions?

"The conditions are, that every one that will repent of his sins and believe in Jesus Christ shall be saved; but every one that will not repent and believe, shall die under the curse of the law, and have an aggarvated damnation for refusing to submit to an offered Saviour."

Can men comply with those conditions? If one man can, so can all, except one is made better than another. If God has made one man better than another, how can he require as much of one as of another, in justice? If all men are in one predicament, then one can do what another can; and if all men have power to repent and believe, how comes it to pass that some do and others do not? "Because one uses the means and others do not." But why does one use the means and not another? "Because one will and another will not." But how comes one to have a will and not another ? Does this *better will* proceed from nature or from grace ? If from either, God is the author of it.*

If Jesus Christ was delivered up to *death* by an original statute, *sin* was certainly included in the moral system ; for on no other account did Jesus die, but for the sins of his people. That he was *delivered* by the determinate counsel of God, is evident ; but that this *delivery* includes *death*, is very questionable. There is no way supposable, that God could have raised human creatures to heaven, but by *delivering* his Son to become incarnate ; for the union of the two natures in the Mediator, is the ground-work of the exaltation of human creatures to the divine glory.

The best mode of thinking is this : That God *originally* determined to *deliver* his son to be incarnate ; and *secondarily*, from a knowledge of creatures' sin, *delivered* him to *death* ; the last being a consequence of the first, depending on the moral agency of creatures, and not arising from an *original statute.*

There is no kind of violence or cruelty under the sun, but what may be reconciled to *tyrannical sovereignty* ; but has the God of love and goodness a *sovereign right* to do *wrong?* "It must be *right* because God has done it," is not a sound as harmonical as to say, "It is *wrong*, and therefore God is not the author of it."

The whole universe is composed of a multitnde of units ; if the human world is therefore the better for sin, the advantage must be found among some or all these units ; but where is there a judicious individual in the universe, that can say, he is better for sin ?

That wicked men are physically impelled to sin, excited thereto by moral suasion ; or called upon to rebel by the dispensations of God's mercies and judgments, is inadmissible. But that their corrupt natures are in that predicament that they are under a *natural* necessity to sin until they are changed by grace, is incontestible. Consequently if there is a single action of *spiritual good* to be performed by them, prior to their receiving the grace of God, it will forever remain undone. The truth is, that in the simple work of regeneration, men neither assist nor resist.

In the foregoing exposition and apendix, there are a number of hints given, that the predicament of innocent Adam, was different from that of a regenerate saint on earth, and of a glorified saint in heaven ; and as this distinction is called in question by many, I shall say something more on the subject.

It is true, God may justly require more of his creatures now, than he required of Adam in the garden. The obedience and faith of a creature, should always be tantamount to the commands and revelation of the creator. If the creator, therefore, commands his creatures any thing more

*This mode of reasoning is just in the *plan of salvation*, but inadmissible in the *moral system.*

than he commanded Adam, they are under bonds to obey; and that creatures, since the fall, are commanded to make themselves new hearts and cleanse themselves from all unrighteousness, be unfeignedly sorry for their sins and love God with a pure heart fervently, admits of no doubt. And further, if God has revealed more to his fallen creatures than he revealed to Adam in the garden, they should believe more than he did, with an unshaken faith. When Jesus was on earth, he gave as full proof of his divinity and Messiahship, as the Almighty did of his God-head in creation; and therefore people who saw, and those who have heard of him, are as strongly bound to believe in him as the Almighty Saviour as they are to believe in the God-head of the creator.

But still the question is, whether grace does not raise men to a higher state than they fell from—do more for them than the law requires?

It cannot be supposed, that the law requires man to rise to a more exalted state than Adam was in, when in Eden: now if it can be demonstrated that grace raises men higher than Eden's garden, then the hypothesis is maintained.

Adam was on earth: saints will be raised to heaven. Adam was to propagate: saints will be like angels in respect of propagation. Adam was to dress the garden and eat thereof: saints will be fed by God without their hand labor.

The presumption is strong that Adam was made to till the ground: saints will live where there will be no ground to till. The point then is proved.

As for the predicament of Adam's soul, before the fall, it is as difficult to describe, as it is to describe where the garden of Eden was, for much the same reason. Sin drove him from that garden, and extinguished that life in his soul, that neither he, nor any of his progeny will ever regain. When wandering souls are brought home to God, it is not to Eden's garden, or to that life that Adam possessed in innocency; but to a place more exalted, to a life more sublime.

That Adam, while innocent, took complacency in the divine character, cordially submitted to the moral government of Jehovah, and cheerfully obeyed his God, is granted: anything short of this, would have been hypocrisy at best. This exercise is still enjoined on all men; for God has not lost his right to command, because men are depraved and fallen. But after all, the life of Adam's soul was mutable; it was not *eternal* life, it was not extinguished by sin, and ended in death; neither Adam nor any of his children will ever enjoy the same life again: but those who are changed by grace, are made partakers of an immutable, eternal life that can never be extinguished.

Another idea also contended for, is this, viz., that the grace of God, in regeneration, is bestowed in a sovereign manner: that God in giving that grace, works not according to the laws of nature, and treats with men, not as moral agents, but as recipient beings. The system of the Armenians merits regard, so far as it respects moral government; in this point, they have the advantage of those who suppose that sin, and all its consequences, emerge in consequence of some grand decree in Deity; but when they intrude the moral system into the channel of grace, and suppose that salvation depends upon the will and acceptance of the creature, prior to his being born again, they make wretched work.

In vindication of the first mentioned part of their system, it may be said, that if angels and men cannot act, but as they are acted upon; if spirits have no kind of self motion, but are always used as pullies, weights and wheels in a machine; and that they act voluntarily also, it not only represents *Jehovah* as the original agent of their wicked actions, but the author of their corrupt wills; by making use of motives behind the screen, to influence them to act. Should a monarch put a knife into a child's hand, and directing the child's hand with his own arm, thrust the blade into another and kill him, who would punish the child and exculpate the monarch? and if the monarch made use of motives visible or clandestine, to influence the child to act willingly, would the violation of the child clear the character of the monarch?

But in opposition to the last mentioned part of their system, viz., that salvation depends upon moral agency; let it be noticed, that if the grace of the gospel only re-Adams men, there is a thousand times as great reason to believe that all men will be damned, as there was to believe that Adam would fall. The sure standing or final falling of a soul, rests either upon the unchangeableness of God, or the unchangeableness of the creature; if on the unchangeableness of God, their standing is sure; for God changes not; but if their standing rests on the unchangeableness of the creature, their falling is not only possible, but probable; not only probable, but certain. In this point of sight, every argument that is brought to prove the possibility of falling away finally, operates with a thousand times as much weight, to prove that falling away is certain.

The truth is, that holy, mutable creatures had power to do evil, and evil creatures have natural power to do good; to do as much as the law requires, (so far as it respects their future conduct,) for sin has not destroyed their natural powers; but they have no more power than will, to perform spiritual services in a gracious manner. This spring of soul, Adam had not; this spring, sin never broke; this spring is effected in the work of grace; sin is not the cause of it, nor shall sin prevent its being formed in the heart, nor shall sin ever entirely break it.

To close the appendix, I shall observe, that sin arose at first, either from the agency of God, or the agency of creatures. If it arose from the agency of God, there is either no evil in it, or an eternal root of evil was in God, for nothing can arise in the agency of God, but what had root in himself; and if God is such a being, and by his power, mixed with love and hate, good and evil, he made creatures, and demands their admiration; then it must be given him: but one thing is certain, if this be the case, viz., the more holy creatures are, the less they love such a character, and when they are made like him, they will not be free from roots of bitterness. Let the wire-drawer, or the hair-splitter, who believes that sin was designed by God, and that it answers valuable purposes, show the difference between *cause* and *occasion*, if he can; and how he can maintain his point, without holding to two eternal opposite causes, I know not.

LETTER OF VALEDICTION,

ON

LEAVING VIRGINIA, IN 1791.

MEN, BRETHREN, AND FATHERS:

IN leaving the state, where I have contracted a large acquaintance—where I have spent fourteen years of the prime of my life; in which time I have baptized seven hundred persons (the chiefest of whom, God has graciously given me as the seals of my ministry,) it may reasonably be supposed that I feel an unusual perturbation of mind; especially when I consider the kind acceptance I have had among the people, as well as the confidence which the Baptist society have reposed in me. When all these endearing bonds present themselves before me, they strangely agitate my throbbing breast. A total dïvesture of these sensations would render me and odious stoic, among men formed for friendship: but an excess of these tender emotions, would appear too effeminate for a man of business, and inadmissable for the hazardous voyage before me.

I cannot say that I had any particular call to come to Virginia, like Paul to go to Macedonia; but came voluntarily, of my own accord; and hope kind Providence has overruled it for the best. Now I meditate a return to my native land, upon a principle as voluntary as I came. May Heaven send me good speed, and prosper me in every lawful undertaking. The thoughts of death, in general, are not as painful as the thoughts of living for nothing.

My friends in general, and those in particular who acknowledge my weak efforts as a means of their salvation, will receive this final valediction as a proof of my love; and as I cannot visit them all to take a formal parting, I hope this letter will be as pleasing and more profitable. When I came first into Virginia, I shared the common lot of strangers; many were afraid of me, that I was not sincere: and some better characters than myself, seemed to defame; but I always was prevented from retorting, by the words of David, "Who can stretch forth his hands against the Lord's anointed and be innocent:" and amidst all my troubles, these words were my support, "The Lord said, verily it shall be well with thy remnant of days; verily I will cause the enemy to entreat thee well in time of affliction, and in time of evil." No man can conceive the difficulty that a stranger in a strange land has to endure, but those who have tried it. Thus I was; in the day the draught consumed me, and the frost by night; my head has often been filled with dew, and my locks with the drops of the night. The love af my God, and the worth of immortal souls, has stimulated my heart and borne me up under all the pressure of mobs, tumults, reproaches, and contentions; and having obtained help of God, I remain until this very day.

The union that has taken place among the Baptists has been very pleasing to me, and a continuation of the same, is an object that engrosses my desire. For this desirable end, I have been willing to sacrifice a number of little peculiarities, and think myself a gainer in the bargain.

Ye are not strangers, my dear brethren and children, to the difference of opinions now subsisting among the Baptists in Virginia; some pleading for predestination, and others for universal provision. It is true that the schemes of both parties cannot be right; and yet both parties may be right in their aims, each wishing to justify wisdom, and make God righteous when he judgeth. He cannot be wrong, whose life and heart are right. He cannot walk amiss who walks in love. I have generally observed, that when religion is lively among the people no alienation of affection arises from a difference of judgment; and whoever considers that the Devil is orthodox in judgment, and that the Bible is not written in form of a system, will surely be moderate in dealing out hard speeches towards his heterodox brother. I conclude that the *eternal purposes* of God, and the *freedom of the human will*, are both truths; and it is a matter of fact, that the preaching that has been most blessed of God, and most profitable to men, is *the doctrine of sovereign grace in the salvation of souls, mixed with a little of what is called Arminianism*. These two propositions can be tolerably well reconciled together, but the modern misfortune is, that men often spend too much time in explaining away one or the other, or in fixing the lock-link to join the others together; and by such means, have but little time in a sermon to insist on those two great things which God blesses. I do not plead for implicit faith; let each man believe, speak, and act for himself; but when it is confessed that nine tenths of the scripture is best explained without descending to those cutting points, a man must appear contracted who spends all his time in disputing about them; and more malevolent when he finds it tends, not to promote love and union, but rather a rancorous spirit. Let us then follow after the things that make for peace, and the things whereby one may edify another, and strive who shall be the most humble, and love over the greatest affronts.

My children, I am afraid that after my departure, you will forget the weak advice that I have given you; and what is infinitely more the instruction of that gracious redeemer who bought you with his blood. Where fore watch, and remember that for the space of fourteen years I ceased not to warn you night and day, and taught you publicly, and from house to house. And now behold I go, with submission to Providence, to New England, not knowing what things will befall me there. Perhaps the faithless seas may be my tomb, or I may live to experience more severe trials than ever I have sustained.

I know myself to be a feeble, sinful worm. A retrospective view of my past conduct is not altogether pleasing, and perhaps it is owing to your partiality that I have not been publicly exposed; for my own part, I have nothing to fly to for defence, but the blood and righteousness of the dear Redeemer; but if my conduct has been such as to escape the censure of those men, who know what it is to struggle with a body of death, any calumny that may be cast on me after my departure, will be unnoticed.

I have preached about three thousand sermons since I came to Virginia; all of which have been too flat, and many of them so cold, that the sentences would almost freeze between my lips; and yet, many times, when I have attempted to instruct and comfort others, I have found the same blessings for myself. And now, brethren, I commend you to God and the word of his grace, which is able to build you up, and give you an inheritance among all those who are sanctified; hoping and praying that, if we meet no more on earth, we may meet in heaven, among all the redeemed of the Lord. Though the company is large, yet there is room, —"many mansions"—places for you, my brethren, a place, I trust, for worthless me.

Before I close, I wish to add a word in behalf of the poor, unhappy negroes, and speak a little for those who are not suffered to speak for themselves. I have generally been quiet on this head, for the following reasons:—1st. I have been a stranger among you, and, therefore, judged it indecent to meddle with the customs of the country. 2d. I have had no slaves of my own, and so concluded that if I said anything on that head, it would be construed to my disadvantage, without doing any good. 3d. It has ever appeared to me difficult to form any plan, even in idea, for their manumission; and, to expose the evil, without pointing out the way of escape, would be doing as the witch did to Saul. 4th. To say anything about it would raise the passions of a certain class of citizens; and from that they would abuse them worse than before, and so eventually make those in misery more miserable. But, as I am now about leaving the state, I can speak with more freedom.

I am heartily glad, that I can say that the spirit of masters has greatly abated since I have been in Virginia; it is now confessed, by many, that negroes can feel injuries, hunger, pain and weariness, and I hope this spark of good fire will be raised to a flame, in due time.

I confess, that I am not as much shocked to see them naked, gaunt and trembling, as I was when I first came into the state; the distance that they are kept in, the abject subordination, and things relative thereto, do not affect me as they once did: so fatal are bad customs; but I can never be reconciled to the keeping of them; nor can I endure to see one man strip and whip another, as free by nature as himself, without the interference of a magistrate, or any being or thing to check his turbulent will. And, as I am well convinced that many of my dear brethren have the same feelings with myself, I can unbosom myself with confidence. It is not my intention to drop the ministerial vest, and assume the politician's garb to-day; but, after adding that slavery, in its best appearance, is a violent deprivation of the rights of nature, inconsistent with republican government, destructive of every humane and benevolent passion of the soul, and subversive to that liberty absolutely necessary to ennoble the human mind, let me ask whether Heaven has nothing in store for poor negroes better than these galling chains? If so, ye ministers of Jesus, and saints of the Most High, ye wrestling Jacobs, who have power with God, and can prevail over the angel, let your prayers, your ardent prayers, ascend to the throne of God incessantly, that he may pour the blessing of *freedom* upon the poor blacks. If public prayers of this kind, would raise the anger of tyrants, or embolden the slaves in insolence, let the sable watches of the night, in lonely solitude, be witnesses to your sincere longings after the liberty of your fellow creatures.

How would every benevolent heart rejoice to see the halcyon day appear—the great jubilee usher in, when the poor slaves, with a Moses at their head, should hoist up the standard, and march out of bondage! Or, what would be still more elating, to see the power of the gospel so effectual that the lion and the lamb should lie together—all former insults and revenges forgotten—the names of master and slave be buried—every yoke broken, and the oppressed go free—free but not empty away.

And you, my black brethren, hear a word from your parting friend. It is not only a general complaint, but a general truth, that but very few of you will do your duty without a degree of severity. That your masters have the right to chastise you, while your are their servants, is undoubted. You cannot conceive what pain, what distress of soul, your masters endure for your sake. How glad many of them would be, if you would bear good usage. Their rest forsakes them at night, and their comfort by day, on account of your indolence and roguery. There is no way you can honor your profession, do a good part for yourselves, or move God to send you deliverance so effectually, as to obey those who have the rule over you in the fear of God. Though our skins are somewhat different in color, yet I hope to meet many of you in heaven; where your melodious voices, that have often enchanted my ears and warmed my heart, will be incessantly employed in the praise of our common Lord. In hope of this immortal joy, you may well be patient in your hardships, and wait till your change comes.

And now may the peace of God, that passeth all understanding, dwell richly in all your hearts. Amen.

THE RIGHTS OF CONSCIENCE INALIENABLE,

AND, THEREFORE,

RELIGIOUS OPINIONS NOT COGNIZABLE BY LAW;

OR,

THE HIGH-FLYING CHURCHMAN,

STRIPPED OF HIS LEGAL ROBE, APPEARS A YAHO.*

I know not to give flattering titles to men.—Elihu.

1791.

* First published in New London, Connecticut, on his return from Virginia.

THE RIGHTS OF CONSCIENCE, &c.

There are four principles contended for, as the foundation of civil government, viz., birth, property, grace, and compact. The first of these is practised upon in all hereditary monarchies, where it is believed that the son of a monarch is entitled to dominion upon the decease of his father, whether he be a wise man or a fool. The second principle is built upon in all aristocratical governments, where the rich landholders have the sole rule of all their tenants, and make laws at pleasure which are binding upon all. The third principle is adopted by those kingdoms and states that require a religious test to qualify an officer of state, proscribing all non-conformists from civil and religious liberty. This was the error of Constantine's government, who first established the Christian religion by law, and then proscribed the Pagans, and banished the Arian heretics. This error also filled the heads of the Anabaptists, in Germany, who were re-sprinklers. They supposed that none had a right to rule but gracious men. The same error prevails in the See of Rome, where his holiness exalts himself above all who are called gods, (i. e., kings and rulers,) and where no Protestant heretic is allowed the liberty of a citizen. This principle is also pleaded for in the Ottoman empire, where it is death to call in question the divinity of Mahomet, or the authenticity of the Alcoran.

The same evil has entwined itself into the British form of government, where, in the state establishment of the church of England, no man is eligible to any office, civil or military, without he subscribes to the thirty-nine articles and book of common prayer ; and even then, upon receiving a commission for the army, the law obliges him to receive the sacrament of the Lord's supper, and no non-conformist is allowed the liberty of his conscience without he subscribes to all the thirty-nine articles but about four. And when that is done, his purse-strings are drawn by others to pay preachers in whom he puts no confidence, and whom he never hears.

This was the case in several of the southern states, until the revolution, in which the church of England was established.

The fourth principle, (compact,) is adopted in the American states, as the basis of civil government. This foundation appears to be a just one, by the following investigation.

Suppose a man to remove to a desolate island, and take a peaceable possession of it, without injuring any, so that he should be the honest inheritor of the isle. So long as he is alone, he is the absolute monarch of the place, and his own will is his law, which law is as often altered or repealed as his will changes. In process of time, from this man's loins ten sons are grown to manhood, and possess property. So long as they are all good men, each one can be as absolute, free, and sovereign as his father: but one of the ten turns vagrant, by robbing the rest. This villain is equal to, if not an over-match for any one of the nine: not one of them durst engage him in single combat. Reason and safety both dictate to the nine the necessity of a confederation, to unite their strength together to repel or destroy the plundering knave. Upon entering into confederation, some compact or agreement would be stipulated by which each would be bound to do his equal part in fatigue and expense. It would be necessary for these nine to meet at stated times to consult means of safety and happiness. A shady tree, or small cabin, would answer their purpose, and, in case of disagreement, four must give up to five.

In this state of things, their government would be perfectly democratic, every citizen being a legislator.

In a course of years, from these nine there arises nine thousand: their government can be no longer democratic—prudence would forbid it. Each tribe, or district, must then choose their representative, who, for the term that he is chosen, has the whole political power of his constituents. These representatives, meeting in assembly, would have power to make laws binding on their constituents, and while their time was spent in making laws for the community, each one of the community must advance a little of his money as a compensation therefor. Should these representatives differ in judgment, the minor must be subject to the major, as in the case above.

From this simple parable, the following things are demonstrated: First, that the law was not made for a righteous man, but for the disobedient. Second, that righteous men have to part with a little of their liberty and property to preserve the rest. Third, that all power is vested in, and consequently derived from the people. Fourth, that the law should rule over rulers, and not rulers over the law. Fifth, that government is founded on compact. Sixth, that every law made by legislators, inconsistent with the compact, modernly called a constitution, is usurping in the legislators, and not binding on the people. Seventh, that whenever government is found inadequate to preserve the liberty and property of the people, they have an indubitable right to alter it so as to answer those purposes. Eighth, that legislators, in their legislative capacity, cannot alter the constitution, for they are hired servants of the people to act within the limits of the constitution.

From these general observations, I shall pass on to examine a question which has been the strife and contention of ages. The question is, "*Are the rights of conscience alienable, or inalienable?*"

The word *conscience*, signifies *common science*, a court of judicature which the Almighty has erected in every human breast: a *censor morum* over all his conduct. Conscience will ever judge right, when it is rightly informed, and speak the truth when it understands it. But to advert to the question, "Does a man, upon entering into social compact, surrender his conscience to that society, to be controlled by the laws thereof; or can he, in justice, assist in making laws to bind his children's consciences before they are born?" I judge not, for the following reasons:

First. Every man must give an account of himself to God, and therefore every man ought to be at liberty to serve God in a way that he can best reconcile to his conscience. If government can answer for individuals at the day of judgment, let men be controlled by it in religious matters; otherwise, let men be free.

Second. It would be sinful for a man to surrender that to man, which is to be kept sacred for God. A man's mind should be always open to conviction, and an honest man will receive that doctrine which appears the best demonstrated: and what is more common than for the best of men to change their minds? Such are the prejudices of the mind, and such the force of tradition, that a man who never alters his mind, is either very weak or very stubborn. How painful then must it be to an honest heart, to be bound to observe the principles of his former belief, after he is convinced of their imbecility? And this ever has, and ever will be the case, while the rights of conscience are considered alienable.

Third. But supposing it was right for a man to bind his *own* conscience, yet surely it is very iniquitous to bind the consciences of his children—to make fetters for them before they are born, is very cruel. And yet such has been the conduct of men in almost all ages, that their children have been bound to believe and worship as their fathers did, or suffer shame, loss, and sometimes life, and at best to be called dissenters, because they dissent from that which they never joined voluntarily. Such conduct in parents, is worse than that of the father of Hannibal who imposed an oath upon his son, while a child, never to be at peace with the Romans.

Fourth. Finally, religion is a matter between God and individuals: the religious opinions of men not being the objects of civil government, nor in any way under its control.

It has often been observed by the friends of religion established by human laws, that no state can long continue without it; that religion will perish, and nothing but infidelity and atheism prevail.

Are these things facts? Did not the Christian religion prevail during the first three centuries, in a more glorious manner than ever it has since, not only without the aid of law, but in opposition to all the laws of haughty monarchs? And did not religion receive a deadly wound by being fostered in the arms of civil power and regulated by law? These things are so.

From that day to this, we have but a few instances of religious liberty to judge by; for, in almost all states, civil rulers, by the investigation of covetous priests, have undertaken to steady the ark of religion by human laws; but yet we have a few of them without leaving our own land.

The state of Rhode Island has stood above one hundred and sixty years without any religious establishment. The state of New York never had any. New Jersey claims the same. Pennsylvania has also stood from its first settlement until now upon a liberal foundation; and if agriculture, the mechanical arts and commerce, have not flourished in these states, equal to any of the others, I judge wrong.

It may further be observed, that all the states now in union, saving two or three in New England, have no legal force used about religion, in directing its course, or supporting its preachers. And, moreover, the federal government is forbidden by the constitution, to make any laws, establishing any kind of religion. If religion cannot stand, therefore, without the aid of law, it is likely to fall soon, in our nation, except in Connecticut and Massachusetts.

To say that "religion cannot stand without a state establishment," is not only contrary to fact, (as has been proved already,) but is a contradiction in phrase. Religion must have stood a time before any law could have been made about it; and if it did stand almost three hundred years without law, it can still stand without it.

The evils of such an establishment, are many.

First. Uninspired, fallible men make their own opinions tests of orthodoxy, and use their own systems, as Pocrustes used his iron bedstead, to stretch and measure the consciences of all others by. Where no toleration is granted to non-conformists, either ignorance and superstition prevail, or persecution rages; and if toleration is granted to restricted non-conformists, the minds of men are biased to embrace that religion which is favored and pampered by law, and thereby hypocrisy is nourished; while those who cannot stretch their consciences to believe anything and everything in the established creed, are treated with contempt and opprobrious names; and by such means, some are pampered to death by largesses, and others confined from doing what good they otherwise could, by penury. The first lie under a temptation to flatter the ruling party, to continue that form of government which brings them in the sure bread of idleness; the last to despise that government, and those rulers, that oppress them. The first have their eyes shut to all further light, that would alter the religious machine; the last are always seeking new light, and often fall into enthusiasm. Such are the natural evils of the establishment of religion by human laws.

Second. Such establishments not only wean and alienate the affections of one from another, on account of the different usage they receive in their religious sentiments, but are also very impolitic, especially in new countries; for what encouragement can strangers have to migrate with their arts and wealth into a state, where they cannot enjoy their religious sentiments without exposing themselves to the law? when, at the same time, their religious opinions do not lead them to be mutinous. And further, how often have kingdoms and states been greatly weakened by religious tests! In the time of the persecution in France, not less than twenty thousand people fled for the enjoyment of religious liberty.

Third. These establishments metamorphose the church into a creature, and religion into a principle of state, which has a natural tendency to make men conclude that *Bible religion* is nothing but a *trick of state*; hence it is that the greatest part of the well-informed in literature are overrun with deism and infidelity; nor is it likely that it will ever be much better, while preaching is made a trade of emolument. And if there is no difference between *Bible religion* and *state religion*, I shall soon fall into infidelity.

Fourth. There are no two kingdoms and states that establish the same creed and formalities of faith, which alone proves their debility. In one kingdom a man is condemned for not believing a doctrine that he would be condemned for believing in another kingdom. Both of these establishments cannot be right, but both of them can be, and surely are, wrong.

First. The nature of such establishments, further, is to keep from civil office the best of men. Good men cannot believe what they cannot believe, and they will not subscribe to what they disbelieve, and take an oath to maintain what they conclude is error; and, as the best of men differ in judgment, there may be some of them in any state: their talents and virtue entitle them to fill the most important posts, yet, because they differ from the established creed of the state, they cannot—will not fill those posts; whereas villains make no scruple to take any oath.

If these, and many more evils, attend such establishments, what were, and still are, the causes that ever there should be a state establishment of religion in any empire, kingdom, or state?

The causes are many—some of which follow:

First. The love of importance is a general evil. It is natural to men to dictate for others: they choose to command the bushel and use the whip-row: to have the halter around the necks of others, to hang them at pleasure.

Second. An over-fondness for a particular system or sect. This gave rise to the first human establishment of religion, by Constantine the Great. Being converted to the Christian system, he established it in the Roman empire, compelled the Pagans to submit, and banished the Christian heretics; built fine chapels at public expense, and forced large stipends for the preachers. All this was done out of love to the Christian religion; but his love operated inadvertently, for he did the Christian church more harm than all the persecuting emperors ever did. It is said, that in his day a voice was heard from heaven, saying: "Now is poison spued into the churches." If this voice was not heard, it, nevertheless, was a truth; for, from that day to this, the Christian religion has been made a stirrup to mount the steed of popularity, wealth and ambition.

Third. To produce uniformity in religion. Rulers often fear that if they leave every man to think, speak, and worship as he pleases, that the whole cause will be wrecked in diversity; to prevent which, they establish some standard of orthodoxy, to effect uniformity. But, is uniformity attainable? Millions of men, women and children, have been tortured to death, to produce uniformity, and yet the world has not advanced one inch towards it. And as long as men live in different parts of the world, have different habits, education and interests, they will be different in judgment, humanly speaking.

Is uniformity of sentiments, in matter of religion, essential to the happiness of civil government? Not at all. Government has no more to do with the religious opinions of men, than it has with the principles of mathematics. Let every man speak freely without fear, maintain the principles that he believes, worship according to his own faith, either one God, three Gods, no God, or twenty Gods; and let government protect him in so doing, i. e., see that he meets with no personal abuse, or loss of property, for his religious opinions. Instead of discouraging him with proscriptions, fines, confiscations or death, let him be encouraged, as a free man, to bring forth his arguments and maintain his points with all boldness; then, if his doctrine is false, it will be confuted, and if it is true, (though ever so novel,) let others credit it.

When every man has this liberty, what can he wish for more? A liberal man asks for nothing more of government.

The duty of magistrates is, not to judge of the divinity or tendency of doctrines; but when those principles break out into overt acts of violence, then to use the civil sword and punish the vagrant for what he has done, and not for the religious phrenzy that he acted from.

It is not supposable that any established creed contains the whole truth, and nothing but the truth; but supposing it did, which established church in the world has got it? All bigots contend for it, each society cries out, "the temple of the Lord are we." Let one society be supposed to be in possession of the whole, let that society be established by law; the creed of faith that they adopt, be consecrated so sacred to government, that the man that disbelieves it must die; let this creed finally prevail over the whole world. I ask, what honor truth gets by all this? None at all. It is famed of a Prussian, called John the Cicero, that by one oration he reconciled two contending princes, actually in war; but, says the historian, "it was his six thousand horse that had the most persuasive oratory." So when one creed or church prevails over another, being armed with a coat of mail, law and sword, truth gets no honor by the victory. Whereas if all stand upon one footing, being equally protected by law, as citizens, (not as saints,) and one prevails over another by cool investigation and fair argument, then truth gains honor; and men more firmly believe it, than if it was made an essential article of salvation by law.

Truth disdains the aid of law for its defence—it will stand upon its own merit. The heathen worshipped a goddess, called truth, stark naked, and all human decorations of truth, serve only to destroy her virgin beauty. It is error, and error alone, that needs human support; and whenever men fly to the law or sword to protect their system of religion, and force it upon others, it is evident that they have something in their system that will not bear the light, and stand upon the basis of truth.

Fourth. The common objection, "that the ignorant part of the community are not capacitated to judge for themselves," supports the Popish hierachy, and all Protestant, as well as Turkish and Pagan establishments in idea.

But is this idea just? Has God chosen many of the wise and learned? Has he not hid the mystery of gospel truth from them, and revealed it unto babes? Does the world by wisdom know God? Did many of the rulers believe in Christ when he was upon earth? Were not the learned clergy (the scribes) his most inveterate enemies? Do not great men differ as much as little men in judgment? Have not almost all lawless errors crept into the world through the means of wise men (so called)? Is not a simple man, who makes nature and reason his study, a competent judge of things? Is the Bible written (like Caligula's laws) so intricate and high, that none but the letter learned (according to common phrase) can read it? Is not the vision written so plain that he that runs may read it? Do not those who understand the original languages, that the Bible was written in, differ as much in judgment as others? Are the identical copies of Matthew, Mark, Luke and John, together with the epistles in every university, and in the hands of every master of arts? If not, have not the learned to trust to a human transcription, as much as the unlearned have to a translation? If these questions, and others of the like nature, can be confuted; then I will confess that it is wisdom for a conclave of bishops, or a convocation of clergy to frame a system out of the Bible, and persuade the legislature to legalize it. No; it would be attended with so much expense, pride, domination, cruelty and bloodshed, that let me rather fall into infidelity; for no religion at all, is better than that which is worse than none.

Fifth. The groundwork of these establishments of religion is, *clerical influence.* Rulers, being persuaded by the clergy that an establishment of religion by human laws, would promote the knowledge of the gospel, quell religious disputes, prevent heresy, produce uniformity, and finally be advantageous to the state; establish such creeds as are framed by the clergy; and this they often do more readily, when they are flattered by the clergy; that if they thus defend the truth, they will become nursing fathers to the church, and merit something considerable for themselves.

What stimulates the clergy to recommend this mode of reasoning is:

First. Ignorance, not being able to confute error by fair argument.

Second. Indolence, not being willing to spend any time to confute the heretical.

Third. But chiefly covetousness, to get money, for it may be observed that in all these establishments, settled salaries for the clergy, recoverable by law, are sure to be interwoven; and was not this the case, I am well convinced that there would not be many, if any religious establishments in the Christian world.

Having made the foregoing remarks, I shall next make some observations on the religion of Connecticut.

If the citizens of this state, have anything in existence that looks like a religious establishment, they ought to be very cautious; for being but a small part of the world, they can never expect to extend their religion over the whole of it, without it is so well founded that it cannot be confuted.

If one-third part of the face of the globe is allowed to be seas, the earthly parts would compose four thousand five hundred and fifty such states as Connecticut. The American empire would afford above two-hundred of them. And as there is no religion in this empire, of the same stamp as the Connecticut standing order, upon the Say-Brook platform, they may expect one hundred and ninety-nine against one at home, and four thousand five hundred and forty-nine against one abroad.

Connecticut and New-Haven were separate governments till the reign of Charles II. when they were incorporated together by a charter; which charter is still considered, by some, as the basis of government.

At present, there are in the state about one hundred and sixty-eight Presbyterial, Congregational and Consociated preachers; thirty-five Baptist, twenty Episcopalians, ten separate Congregationals, and a few other denominations. The first are the standing order of Connecticut; to whom all others have to pay obeisance. Societies of the standing order are formed by law; none have a right to vote therein but men of age, who possess property to the amount of £40, or are in full communion in the church. Their choice of ministers is by major vote; and what the society agree to give him annually, is levied upon all within the limits of the society-bounds; except they bring a certificate to the clerk of the society, that they attend worship elsewhere, and contribute to the satisfaction of the society where they attend. The money being levied on the people, is distrainable by law; and perpetually binding on the society till the minister is dismissed by a council, or by death, from his charge.

It is not my intention to give a detail of all the tumults, oppression, fines and imprisonments, that have heretofore been occasioned by this law religion. These things are partly dead and buried, and if they did not rise of themselves, let them sleep peaceably in the dust forever. Let it suffice on this head, to say, that it is not possible, in the nature of things, to establish religion by human laws, without perverting the design of civil law and oppressing the people.

The certificate that a dissenter produces to the society clerk, must be signed by some officer of the dissenting church, and such church must be Christian; for heathens, deists, and Jews, are not indulged in the certificate law; all of them, as well as Turks, must therefore be taxed for the standing order, although they never go among them, or know where the meeting-house is.

This certificate law is founded on this principle, "that it is the duty of all persons to support the gospel and the worship of God." Is this principle founded in justice? Is it the duty of a deist to support that which he believes to be a cheat and imposition? Is it the duty of a Jew to support the religion of Jesus Christ, when he really believes that he was an impostor? Must the Papists be forced to pay men for preaching down the supremacy of the pope, who they are sure is the head of the church? Must a Turk maintain a religion, opposed to the Alkoran, which he holds as the sacred oracle of heaven? These things want better confirmation. If we suppose that it is the duty of all these to support the Protestant Christian religion, as being the best religion in the world; yet how comes it to pass, that human legislatures have a right to force them so to do? I now call for an instance, where Jesus Christ, the author of his religion, or the apostles, who were divinely inspired, ever gave orders to, or intimated, that the civil powers on earth, ought to force people to observe the rules and doctrine of the gospel.

Mahomet called in the use of the law and sword, to convert people to his religion; but Jesus did not—does not.

It is the duty of men to love God with all their hearts, and their neighbors as themselves; but have legislatures authority to punish men if they do not; so there are many things that Jesus and the apostles taught, that men ought to obey, which yet the civil law has no concern in.

That it is the duty of men, who are taught in the word, to communicate to him that teaches, is beyond controversy; but that it is the province of the civil law to force them to do so, is denied.

The charter of Charles II., is supposed to be the basis of government in Connecticut; and I request any gentleman to point out a single clause in that charter, which authorizes the legislature to make any religious laws, establish any religion, or force people to build meeting-houses or pay preachers. If there is no such constitutional clause, it follows, that the laws are usurpatory in the legislatures, and not binding on the people. I shall here add, that if the legislature of Connecticut, have a right to establish the religion which they prefer to all religions, and force men to support it, then every legislature or legislator has the same authority; and if this be true, the separation of the Christians from the Pagans, the departure of the Protestant from the Papists, and the dissent of the Presbyterians from the church of England, were all schisms of a criminal nature; and all the persecution that they have met with, is just the effect of their stubbornness.

The certificate law supposes, first, that the legislature have power to establish a religion; this is false. Second, that they have authority to grant indulgence to non-conformists; this is also false, for a religious liberty is a right and not a favor. Third, that the legitimate power of government extends to force people to part with their money for religious purposes; this cannot be proved from the New Testament.

The certificate law has lately passed a new modification. Justices of the peace must now examine them; this gives ministers of state a power over religious concerns that the New Testament does not. To examine the law, part by part, would be needless, for the whole of it is wrong.

From what is said, this question arises, "are not contracts with ministers, i. e., between ministers and people, as obligatory as any contracts whatever?" The simple answer is, yes. Ministers should share the same protection of the law that other men do, and no more. To proscribe them from seats of legislation, etc., is cruel. To indulge them with an exemption from taxes and bearing arms is a tempting emolument. The law should be silent about them; protect them as citizens, not as sacred officers, for the civil law knows no sacred religious officers.

In Rhode Island, if a congregation of people agree to give a preacher a certain sum of money for preaching, the bond is not recoverable by law.*

This law was formed upon a good principle, but, unhappily for the makers of that law, they were incoherent in the superstructure.

The principle of the law, is, that the gospel is not to be supported by law; that civil rulers have nothing to do with religion, in their civil capacities; what business had they then to make that law? The evil seemed to arise from blending religious *right* and religious *opinions* together. Religious *right* should be protected to *all* men, religious *opinion* to none; i. e. government should confirm the first unto all; the last unto none: each individual having a *right* to differ from all others in *opinion* if he is so per-

* Some men, who are best informed in the laws of Rhode Island, say, if ever there was such an act in that state, there is nothing like it in existence at this day; and perhaps it is only cast upon them as a stigma, because they have ever been friends to religious liberty. However, as the principle is supposable, I have treated it as a real fact: and this I have done the more willingly, because nine-tenths of the people believe it is a fact.

suaded. If a number of people in Rhode Island, or elswhere, are of opinion that ministers of the gospel ought to be supported by law, and choose to be bound by a bond to pay him, government has no just authority to declare that bond illegal; for, in so doing, they interfere with private contracts, and deny the people the liberty of conscience. If these people bind nobody but themselves, who is injured by their religious opinions? But if they bind an individual besides themselves, the bond is fraudulent, and ought to be declared illegal. And here lies the mischief of Connecticut religion. My lord, major vote, binds all the minor part, unless they submit to idolatry; i. e., pay an acknowledgement to a power that Jesus Christ never ordained in his church; I mean produce a certificate. Yea further, Jews, Turks, heathens and deists, if such there are in Connecticut, are bound, and have no redress; and further, this bond is not annually given, but for life, except the minister is dismissed by a number of others, who are in the same predicament with himself.

Although it is no abridgement of religious liberty for congregations to pay their preachers by legal force, in the manner prescribed above, yet it is anti Christian; such a church cannot be a church of Christ, because they are not governed by Christ's laws, but by the laws of state; and such ministers do not appear like ambassadors of Christ, but like ministers of state.

The next question is this, "Suppose a congregation of people have agreed to give a minister a certain sum of money annually, for life or during good behaviour, and in a course of time, some or all of them change their opinions, and verily believe that the preacher is in a capital error; and really from conscience, dissent from him, are they still bound to comply with their engagements to the preacher?" This question is supposable, and I believe there have been a few instances of the kind.

If men have bound themselves, honor and honesty call upon them to comply; but God and conscience call upon them to come out from among them, and let such blind guides alone.* Honor and honesty are amiable virtues; but God and conscience call to perfidiousness. This shows the impropriety of such contracts, which always may, and sometimes do lead into such labyrinths. It is time enough to pay a man after his labor is over. People are not required to communicate to the *teacher* before they are *taught*. A man, called of God to preach, feels a necessity to preach, and a woe if he does not. And if he is sent by Christ, he looks to him and his laws for support; and if men comply with their duty, he finds relief; if not, he must go to his field, as the priests of old did. A man cannot give a more glaring proof of his covetousness and irreligion, than

* The phrase of *blind guides*, is not intended to cast contempt upon any order of religious preachers, for, let a preacher be orthodox or heterodox, virtuous or vicious, he is always a *blind guide* to those who differ from him in opinion.

to say, "If you will give me so much, then I will preach, but if not, be assured I will not preach to you."

So that in answering the question, instead of determining which of the evils to choose, either to disobey God and conscience, or break honor and honesty, I would recommend an escape of both evils, by entering into no such contracts; for the natural evils of imprudence that men are fallen into, neither God nor man can prevent.

A minister must have a hard heart to wish men to be forced to pay him, when through conscience, enthusiasm, or private pique, they dissent from his ministry. The spirit of the Gospel disdains such measures.

The question before us, is not applicable to many cases in Connecticut: the dissenting churches make no contracts for a longer term than a year, and most of them make none at all. Societies of the *standing order*, rarely bind themselves, in contract with preachers, without binding others beside themselves; and when that is the case the bond is fraudulent; and if those who are bound involuntarily can get clear, it is no breach of honor or honesty.

A few additional remarks shall close my piece.

First. The Church of Rome was at first constituted according to the gospel; and at that time her faith was spoken of through the whole world. Being espoused to Christ, as a chaste virgin, she kept her bed pure for her husband almost three hundred years; but afterwards she played the whore with the kings and princes of this world, who, with their gold and wealth, came in unto her, and she became a strumpet. And, as she was the first Christian church that ever forsook the laws of Christ for her conduct, and received the laws of his rivals, i. e., was established by human law, and governed by the legalized edicts of councils, and received large sums of money to support her preachers and her worship, by the force of civil power, she is called the *mother of harlots;* and all Protestant churches, who are regulated by law, and force people to support their preachers, build meeting-houses, and otherwise maintain their worship, are *daughters* of this holy *mother*.

Second. I am not a citizen of Connecticut—the religious laws of the state do not oppress me, and I expect never will personally; but a love to religious liberty in general, induces me thus to speak. Were I a resident in the state, I could not give or receive a certificate to be exempted from ministerial taxes; for, in so doing, I should confess that the legislature had authority to pamper one religious order in the state, and make all others pay obeisance to that sheaf. It is high time to know whether all are to be free alike, and whether ministers of state are to be lords over God's heritage.

And here I shall ask the citizens of Connecticut, whether, in the months of April and September, when, when they choose their deputies for the assembly, they mean to surrender to them the rights of conscience, and authorize them to make laws binding on their consciences? If not, then all such acts are contrary to the intention of constituent power, as well as unconstitutional and anti-Christian.

Third. It is likely that one part of the people in Connecticut believe, in conscience, that gospel preachers should be supported by the force of law; and the other part believe that it is not in the province of civil law to interfere, or any ways meddle with religious matters. How are both parties to be protected by law in their conscientious belief?

Very easily. Let all those whose consciences dictate that they ought to be taxed by law to maintain their preacher, bring in their names to the society clerk, by a certain day, and then assess them all, according to their estates, to raise the sum stipulated in the contract, and all others go free. Both parties, by this method, would enjoy the full liberty of conscience, without oppressing one another—the laws use no force in matters of conscience—the evil of Rhode Island law be escaped—and no person could find fault with it, in a political point of view, but those who fear the consciences of too many would lie dormant, and, therefore, wish to force them to pay. Here let it be noted, that there are many in the world who believe, in conscience, that a minister is not entitled to any acknowledegement for his services, without he is so poor that he cannot live without it; and thereby convert a gospel debt to alms. Though this opinion is not founded either on reason or scripture, yet it is a better opinion than that which would force them to pay a preacher by human law.

Fourth. How mortifying must it be to foreigners, and how far from conciliatory is it to citizens of the American states, that when they come into Connecticut to reside, they must either conform to the religion of Connecticut, or produce a certificate? Does this look like religious liberty, or human friendship? Suppose that man, whose name need not be mentioned, but which fills every American heart with pleasure and awe, should remove to Connecticut for his health, or any other cause, what a scandal would it be to the state, to tax him to support a Presbyterian minister, unless he produced a certificate, informing them that he was an Episcopalian.

Fifth. The federal constitution certainly had the advantage of any of the state constitutions, in being made by the wisest men in the whole nation, and after an experiment of a number of years trial upon republican principles; and that constitution forbids Congress ever to establish any kind of religion, or require any religious test to qualify any officer in any department of federal government. Let a man be Pagan, Turk, Jew or Christian, he is eligible to any post in that government. So that if the principles of religious liberty, contended for in the foregoing pages, are supposed to be fraught with Deism, fourteen states in the Union are now fraught with the same. But the separate states have not surrendered that supposed right of establishing religion to Congress. Each state retains all its power, saving what is given to the general government, by the federal constitution. The assembly of Connecticut, therefore, still undertake to guide the helm of religion; and if Congress were disposed, yet they could not prevent it, by any power vested in them by the states. Therefore, if any of the people of Connecticut feel oppressed by the certificate law, or any other of the like nature, their proper mode of procedure will be to remonstrate against the oppression, and petition the assembly for a redress of the grievance.

Sixth. Divines generally inform us that there is a time to come, (called the Latter Day Glory,) when the knowledge of the Lord shall cover the earth, as the waters do the sea, and that this day will appear upon the destruction of antichrist. If so, I am well convinced that Jesus will first remove all the hinderances of religious establishments, and cause all men to be free in matters of religion. When this is effected, he will say to the kings and great men of the earth: "Now, see what I can do: ye have been afraid to leave the church and gospel in my hands alone, without steadying the ark by human law, but now I have taken the power and kingdom for myself, and will work for my own glory." Here let me add that, in the southern states, where there has been the greatest freedom from religious oppression, where liberty of conscience is entirely enjoyed, there has been the greatest revival of religion; which is another proof that true religion can, and will prevail best, where it is left entirely to Christ.

THE MODERN PRIEST.

Ignatius, born somewhere, no matter where,
Trained up in school, and taught to say his prayer,
Tired with his task at the academy,
Jump'd over all to university:
The books he read, and read, then laid them down,
But little wiser when his task was done;
But college pedantry bore such a sway,
That soon he gained a soaring diploma,
Dubb'd like a knight on a commencement day,
Gladly he quit his task, and went his way.
He thought of doctor, lawyer, prince and priest,
And made remarks in earnest or in jest,
"Should I turn doctor, I must stem the cold,
And break my rest, to gain the shining gold;
Must make my patients think their lives and blood
Are in my hands, or I can do no good.
When men believe in witches, witches are;
But when they don't believe there are none there;
When men believe in doctors, doctors heal,
At sight of whom their patients easy feel.
If I'm a lawyer, I must lie and cheat,
For honest lawyers have no bread to eat;
'Tis rogues and villains feed the lawyers high,
And sue the men that gold and silver buy.
Should I be statesman, I must use disguise,
And, if a priest, hear nothing else but lies;
State tricks, intrigues, and arts would me confound,
And truth and honesty nowhere be found.
This way of getting money is a risk,
I judge it better to become a priest.
Preaching is now a science and a trade,
And by it many grand estates are made;
The money which I spent at grammar school
I'll treble now by teaching sacred rule.
My prayers I'll stretch out long, my sermons short,
The last write down, the first get all by rote;
While others labor six days, I but one,
For that day's work I'll gain a pretty sum.
For fifty-two days labor in a year,
The sum of eighty pounds my heart shall cheer."
So asses heads for three score pieces sold,
When famines were severe, in days of old.

Ignatius thus resolved to rise by rule,
And to a grave divine he went to school,
The science of divinity engag'd,
And read the sacred volume page by page.
The Bible was so dark, the style so poor,
He gain'd but little from the sacred store;
Pool, Whitby, Burchett, Henry, Yorick, Gill,
He read, to find what was Jehovah's will,
Gravity, rhetoric, and pulpit airs
He studied well, and how to form his prayers.
At length his master gave him commendation,
That he was qualified to preach salvation.
And with his commendation gave him more
Than twenty notes that he had us'd before;
These for his models, and his learned guides,
Helped him to form his work with equal sides.
In composition he did pretty well,
And what he could not read, he'd softly spell.
A day appointed for him to perform,
Notice was giv'n and many took th' alarm.
At the appointed hour the people came,
To hear the will of God revealed to men.
At length Ignatius came all dress'd in black,
With sacerdotal bands and three shap'd hat.
Under his arm the holy book appeared,
And in it were the notes he had prepared:
He bow'd, and bow'd, and to the pulpit steered,
Went up the stairs, and in the desk appeared,
First he address'd the throne of God supreme;—
His master's prayer, new-moddled, did for him;
Fifty-nine minutes long, prays and repeats,—
He clos'd, and all the people took their seats.
The sacred volume next he gravely spread,
Before his eyes upon his elbow bed,
And so it happened, that Ignatius hit
The very place where all his notes were writ.
His text he told, and then began to read
What he had written, with a school-boys heed,
If he presumed to look upon the folks,
His thumb stood sentinel upon his notes.
Short were the visits that his eyes could pray;
He watch'd his notes lest he should miss his way.
At the conclusion, with an angry tone,
He said his gospel came from God alone.
From this, the preacher travell'd all around,
To see where glebes and salaries were found;
Many loud calls he had where land was poor,
People were indigent, and had no store.
The calls he heard, but gravely answer'd, 'no;
To other places God calls me to go!'

At length a vacant place Ignatius found,
Where land was good, and wealth did much abound:
A call they gave him which he did embrace,
'Vox populi, vox Dei,' was the case.
A handsome settlement they gave, a farm,
With eighty pounds, and wood to keep him warm.
All things were ready for his consecration,
A sacred council came for ordination.
The candidate was first examined well,
To see if he in knowledge did excel;
The first of John he hem'd and hammered thro,'
Some things forgot, but most he never knew,
But as he'd spent his time and money both,
To fit himself to wear the sacred cloth,
All things considered, 'twas believed that he
Was a proficient in divinity.
Lineal succession rites were then perform'd,
Their hands impos'd, Ignatius gravely warn'd
The sacred care of all the flock to take,
In love, *and not for filthy lucre's* sake.

CIRCULAR LETTER

OF THE

SHAFTSBURY ASSOCIATION, 1793.

Beloved Brethren: It is a leading characteristic of the Baptists, that without pope or king for head—without spiritual or civil courts established by law—without a conclave of bishops, or convocation of clergy—without legalized creeds or formularies of worship—without a ministry supported by law, or any human coercion in discipline, they are so far united in sentiment, respecting the New Testament, that a free correspondence and communion circulate among them. "They have no king, (on earth,) yet go they forth all of them by bands." The Bible is the only confession of faith they dare adopt—the final umpire they appeal unto for a decision of controversies.

But while we would felicitate ourselves with this infallible guide, we find ourselves boldly attacked by deists and infidels, who seek to sap the foundation of our religion, by asserting that Moses and the prophets were enthusiastical cheats, and that Jesus and his apostles were but pitiful impostors; that all their writings are like modern priestcraft—like the sublime nonsense of Jesuits.

Notwithstanding the variety of opinions, and discordance of sounds among those infidels, yet they are alike confident, and equally assiduous in declaring *what is not true,* and never tell us *what truth is.* With all their boasted illumination in the ground and laws of nature, they never tell us what natural religion is, nor how the God of nature is to be worshiped.

It can hardly be credited, that the Parent of the universe should leave his offspring in this dreary world to make their way to eternity without some guide—some sure word of prophecy, to direct their course. That the Bible is such a guide—a revelation of God's will, written by men divinely inspired—is attempted to be supported by the following remarks:

First. The antiquity of some of the sacred writings, is an argument in favor of the divine authority. The writings of Moses are several hundred years earlier than any profane writings now extant, which proves that he did not collect them from any records, but wrote by Divine impulse; nor could he, or any other man, have told how the worlds were made and peopled, (prior to the formation of Adam,) but by a revelation from God.

Second. The honesty of the penman has some weight in the argument. Moses, for instance, gives an account of his own sin, as well as the sins of his brother and sister, and is very full in pointing out the faults of his nation, and reproving them therefor, which things are not to be found in profane authors: and when he had the offer of being made great, and his family important, he declined the offer, and prayed for the pardon and preservation of that people that he had so plainly reproved for their sins. To these things we may add, that he says not a word about his learning, wisdom and honor in Egypt; all of which look as if he did not write to honor himself, but to reveal the will of God, and to do good to mankind. The same may be said of other sacred writers; they not only made verbal confessions of their sins, but left the same on record that others might fear.

Third. Notwithstanding the Bible was about sixteen hundred years in writing, by men in different ages and in very different circumstances, yet they all speak the same things. Some allowance must be made for the different dialects and customs of the people among whom the writers lived, and also for their own peculiar way of expressing themselves; but in substance they are uniform, infinitely more so than the human accounts of great events by many authors. Many of the apparent mistakes that are in the sacred volume, no doubt, are made by our own ignorance, but if there are a few of them that have been occasioned by a multitude of transcriptions, and other causes, yet they only respect numbers and places, and in no wise affect our faith and practice.

Fourth. The prophetic essays in the Scripture, together with their exact accomplishment, are wonderful. Josiah and Cyrus were prophesied of by name a long time before they were born, and the deeds they should perform, which exactly came to pass. The destruction of various kingdoms, and by whom, was foretold, and afterwards effected. The coming of John the Baptist—the conception of Jesus Christ—the place of his birth—the work of his ministry—the manner of his death—the effusion of the Holy Ghost—the gathering of the Gentiles—the destruction of Jerusalem, and a number of things besides, were not more expressly predicted, than fully accomplished. This leads us to believe that all prophecies that are behind the screen, will, in their times, be completely fulfilled.

Fifth. The sublimity of style in which the Scripture is written, bespeaks its author to be God. Some of the most lofty strokes were delivered by rustic men. Amos, for example, was not a prophet by birth, nor trained in the schools of the prophets, but was an herdman and a gatherer of sycamore fruit, yet some of his tropes are as lofty as the heavens; and the same is true of some others who wrote. How flat and insipid are the writings of Homer, Virgil, Xenophon, Cicero, and other Pagans, when once compared with the Bible. It is not a blind devotion that Jews have paid to the Old Testament, and Christians to both old and new, but a consciousness of their supreme merit. Longinus and Cyrus both acknowledged the sublimity of the style. To this may be added the chastity of diction through the sacred volume. When it was necessary to treat of things rather indecent, it is wonderful to see what euphonisms are used by the sacred writers, and throughout the volume gravity and chastity of dialect is found, and nothing to provoke obscenity, levity, or confusion.

Sixth. The wonderful effects that the reading and explaining of the Scriptures have had on the hearts and consciences of men, form an incontestable proof of the authenticity of the Bible. The Sybils, by the Romans, and the Koran, by the Turks, have been considered as coming from God: but their admirers have only received them as directions of life, (as we do codes of laws,) and have never pretended that those books affect the heart. Here, then, appears the pre-eminence of the Bible above all other books, for thousands of thousands can witness that the truth of the Bible has so affected their hearts as to make them love the divine character, and cordially submit to the government of heaven. And this same word of truth has borne up the minds of those who believed it under all their misfortunes, and made them triumph in the hour of death, so that if the faith of the gospel were a delusion, it would be the best delusion in the world.

Seventh. The patient sufferings of those who have received the Scripture as a revelation from God, is another argument in its favor. These sufferings they have endured, not with the sullen air of a disappointed usurper, or the obstinate spirit of a conquered hero, but with the meekness of a Christian, prizing life, if they could enjoy it innocently, but choosing suffering and death rather than sin. It is true that men will suffer much for their own wills, but such sufferers will recriminate when it is in their power; a quite different spirit has been seen among those who have suffered for the truth's sake, and it is not rational to suppose that they would have suffered so much for the defence of imposture.

Eighth. The great care that God has manifested in keeping these writings in existence amidst so many attempts to destroy them, is remarkable, and through the various translations that they have passed, to keep the sense so pure, still confirms the idea that God will preserve his own. And if we add to this, the rage that devils and wicked men have ever had to the Bible, the presumption is very strong that it is the Book of God.

Ninth. It cannot be that the Bible was written by bad men, for it condemns every branch of vice, and it cannot be supposed that designing men would form a system to condemn themselves in every respect. If it was written by good men, it is true, for liars are not good men; and if they spake the truth, then the Bible is of God, for the writers thereof declare that they wrote by the spirit of God.

Tenth. In addition to the grandeur and uniformity of that plan of truth which the Bible contains, we may further allege in support of its divinity, that in all parts it reflects the most transcendent honor on the character of God—it contains a perfect system of morality, answerable in all respects to the purity of God, and of course tends to the highest happiness of men.

Eleventh. The judgments that have been inflicted on those who have destroyed these writings are not to be forgotten, especially on Antiochus and Dioclesian, the first of whom vented his rage against the old Testament, and the last against the new. Both seemed to share nearly one fate, and the first owned it was for destroying the writings of the Jews. Because they took away from God's book, God took away their parts from the book of life, and from the holy city; that is, he did not suffer them to live to enjoy the blessings described in his book, and when they died, he did not admit them into heaven without a change of character.

Twelfth. If the miracles recorded in the Bible are not original arguments to prove the divinity of it, yet they must raise the wonder and confidence of all those, who, for other reasons, are persuaded of its veracity, to see what wonders God has wrought to preserve his people, establish his word, and furnish his ambassadors with bright credentials that they came and wrought in his name.

These are some of the reasons we assign, wherefore we receive the Scripture as the word of God.

Our faith is firm in the divinity of the Old Testament, as it is in the New, but as many things in the Old Testament are only historical, others form a code of political laws and moral precepts, while many things therein were typical and temporary, suited to the condition of a national church, we believe that Christians should have recourse to the New Testament for precepts and precedents to direct them in social worship.

By what we have written, our desire is, dear brethren, that your faith may be confirmed in the holy Scripture, in this day of infidelity, and that in all your conduct you may give heed thereto as unto a light shining in a dark place, and thereby prove to all that behold you, that you are *Bible Christians.*

A

SERMON,

DELIVERED AT THE INTERMENT OF

MRS. LYDIA NORTHROP,

WIFE OF

MR. STEPHEN NORTHROP,

WHO DEPARTED THIS LIFE

APRIL 26, 1794.

PREFACE.

THE following sermon was first delivered extempore, without much premeditation, or any expectation of publication; but, as the friends of the deceased have requested a copy of it, I have summed up the leading ideas, and present it to the mourners, in an abbreviated form. I am conscious of its deficiences, both as to depth of divinity, and beauty of diction; and the most that I can expect from the performance, is, that it may console the sons and daughters of sorrow, for the loss of a dear friend. J. L.

Cheshire, July 10, 1794.

SERMON.

THE solemn procession of the day brings to mind the following passage; Genesis, 53, 2: *And Sarah died in Kirjath-Arba, the same is Hebron, in the land of Canaan; and Abraham came to mourn for Sarah, and to weep for her.* We are taught to be followers of them, who, through faith and patience, inherit the promises. Ambition prompts aspiring souls to walk in the steps of those who gained the summit of honor, in hopes of obtaining a similar palm. If the examples of heroes, monarchs, and men of wealth, have so much magnetic force on the sons of earth, how much more should the virtuous actions of those "Elders, who have obtained a good report," influence the sons of heaven to follow their steps? "They do it to obtain a *corruptible* crown, but *we an incorruptible*." Our text presents us a couple of characters worthy of our attention. Abraham is declared to be the father of the faithful and the friend of God; and Sarah is held forth, by the sacred penman, as a pattern for wives, in her modest apparel, and subjection to her husband. When God called Abraham from Ur of the Chaldees, to forsake his native country of idolatry, and travel into a strange land, where the pure worship of Jehovah should be established, Sarah was not such an unbelieving idolater as to depart from her husband; but, true to her conjugal engagement, and firm in her faith in the providence and promises of the Almighty, she cheerfully forsook her country, her kindred and their gods, and travelled in a strange land, a pilgrim and sojourner, with her beloved husband.

When God made promise to Abraham, that he should beget a son, and become the father of many nations, he changed his name from Abram (a high father) to Abraham, (a high father of a multitude;) and when it was revealed to him that Sarah, his proper wife, should bear the son from whom the nations should arise, her name was changed from Sarai (my lady) to Sarah (the lady of a multitude.) But after these promises were made, their faith and patience were long put to exercise, before they received the promise; and after Isaac was born, the joy and delight of his father, Abraham was called by God, to perform a deed, the most strange and cutting that ever man was induced to, in the performance of which he gave the most unequivocal proof of his obedience to his God. Nothing short of his strong faith in God, in raising his son from the dead, sustained the old patriarch in offering his darling son, in whose line the promises of God were fixed.

While Abraham and Sarah were travelling from place to place, they were constantly protected by an omnipresent God, who suffered no man to do them wrong, "yea he reproved kings for their sake." How safe and happy are all those who constantly trust in Abraham's God, and cheerfully obey his commands!

The things which appear most imitable in Sarah, are

First. Her leaving all that was near and dear to her, to follow and obey the God of her husband. In this she acted the part of Ruth, the Moabitess, and stands forth as a bright example for her sex to go and do likewise.

Second. Her modest subjection to her husband. Men should love their wives, as Christ loved the Church, and confer honor on them as weaker vessels; neither abuse their persons, nor expose their weaknesses. But two reasons are given why the woman should be in subjection to the man. The first is taken from the order of nature; *the man was first made:* the second, from the order of sin; *the woman was first in the transgression.*

After Sarah had lived until she was one hundred and twenty-seven years old, our text follows,

And Sarah died. Death is the common lot of all. It is an article in the creed of the universal progeny of Adam. That the death of the body came in at the door of Adam's sin, is generally believed; but whether it is a penalty, sovereignly imposed for transgression, or was naturally occasioned by the poisonous fruit of mortalization, that grew on the forbidden tree, is not a point of present examination. But one thing is certain, viz: Christ never came to take off the curse, i. e. to save men from dying. Adam and all his offspring experience it; there is no discharge in this war —innumerable have gone before, and every man follows after; the rich, the wise and venerable, indiscriminately fall a prey to the monster. The innocency of Abel, the righteousness of Noah, the faithfulness of Abraham, the virtue of Joseph, the meekness of Moses, the strength of Sampson, the valor of David, the wisdom of Solomon, the piety of the prophets, the fervor of the apostles and the godliness of later saints, deliver none from death. Neither righteousness nor wickedness repel its force. In the single article of death, man has no pre-eminence above the beast.

Some die in infancy, some in youth; some are snatched away from their busy scenes and useful enterprizes; while others live long and wear out by the decays of old age. Death has a name, but no form; it is an article abstract by itself; it hardly belongs to this world or the next; but is a kind of imaginary line between the two.

> The pains that do reduce to death are great;
> But death is nothing but a change of state.

Death brings all upon a level, and shows no partiality among the sons of men. And that death yet fills its throne, and reigns with unrepelled force, over the sons of dust, requires no proof to-day, but the sight of our eyes. My hearers, lift up your heads, and if sorrow and tears do not forbid, look to yon coffin! see the affecting trophy of death's dominion! Voracious death has slain its prey and confines its boasts within those sable boards. Think, O my soul! Think, O beholders! what we must all be reduced to. O gracious God! if we must needs die and turn to dust, to fulfil the first great threatening of heaven, is there no kind support, is there nothing to take the *sting* of death away? Yes, thanks to God, through our Lord Jesus Christ, the sting is destroyed, the boast and the victory taken away.

Some die in one part of the world and some in another; as for Sarah, she died "In Kirjath-Arba, the same is Hebron." Kirjath-Arba was an ancient city, built seven years before Zoan, in Egypt. The name signifies *the city of four*. It took its name from Arba, which is *four*, or from four Anakims that possessed it, viz: Anak, Sheshai, Abiman and Talmai, or from some other cause, not very material for us to know; but in the days of Moses it was called Hebron, which word signifies *friendship*. Perhaps this name was given to the city by Abraham, on account of the friendship he received from the inhabitants; for at this place Abraham had been long before, see Gen. 13, 18. Little did Abraham and Sarah think, when they were at that place before, that it was to be the grave of Sarah, and the place of mourning to Abraham; and as little do we think, at least, as little do we know, when and where will be the time and place of our dissolution. O may we be prepared to give an account of our stewardship, whenever we shall be assaulted by the pale-faced visitant.

If I may be allowed the liberty of deducing matter from the import of the word, I will say, *Sarah died in friendship*. To die in friendship with God, and good will with men, is an inestimable blessing. How different the case of thousands in the world, who die in duels, or in the field of battle, whose main business through life has been to study human butchery, who die in non-subjection to God, and full of wrath towards their fellow-worms. Almighty God, we ask not for thrones and sceptres, supported by oppression and blood; we ask not for power nor disposition to recriminate injuries, and take guilty revenge on those who have abused us; we rather ask for some humble lot among the sons of peace—to live like Christians, at the feet of their Saviour, being perfectly reconciled to God and his government; and, should we be insulted or abused, we wish to submit ourselves to God in well-doing—take joyfully the spoiling of our goods, and breathe out such unfeigned prayers for our enemies as Stephen did: "Lord, lay not this sin to their charge;" or, if it would not be too presumptuous to imitate the Saviour of sinners when dying on the cross, say, "Father, forgive them, they know not what they do."

If any of my hearers wish to know how this friendship with God is obtained, the answer is, through the blood of the Lamb. This man is our peace—this peace he obtained by the blood of the cross; there is no other name under heaven, given among men, whereby we must or can be saved. Through Jesus, God is reconciling the world unto himself; therefore, behold the Lamb of God, who taketh away the sin of the world; for by him, all that believe are justified from all things, from which they could not be by the law of Moses.

This Hebron was in the land of Canaan. Canaan was given to Abraham by promise, and to his seed by possession. It was a land where God's worship was performed in a purer manner than it was in any other place; and let Canaan, at this time, represent the worship of God. How many people, of whom there have been the most comfortable hopes, that they were born of God, and reconciled to his government, have forsaken the worship of God, and conformed themselves to the world to such a degree, that they have not only been stumbling-blocks in the world, but pierced themselves through with many sorrows. On a dying bed, which is painful enough at best, they have the additional remorse of a sad apostacy, of negligence of duty and mis-spent time. The Christian who would die with comfort, should live in the fear of God, and learn to die while he is living. It is a fearful thing for a man to live longer than his religion exists; but when humble piety prevails more and more, heavenly-mindedness grows brighter and brighter. Though the outward man decays, the inward man is renewed day by day. Such a person bids fair to win the prize, and gain a crown of righteousness. May we all be so wrought upon by divine grace, so believe in the promises, and so conduct ourselves in life, that, like Sarah, we may die in friendship with God and man, persevering in the worship and service of Jehovah, that the same gracious Redeemer, who said to an expiring thief, "To-day shalt thou be with me in Paradise," might whisper like words into our ears, when our souls expatiate for eternity.

Though Sarah was dead, she had friends still living, who paid respect to her body after her soul had left it. She had been a partner with Abraham in sorrows and joys, nor was the friendship extinguished with her mortal life; for our text informs us that

Abraham came to mourn for Sarah, and to weep for her. He came, as some think, from the mount of God, where he had been to worship. If this was the case, then Sarah died in his absence, and upon his return he found his wife sleeping in the icy arms of death; but rather, he came from his own tent into Sarah's, to see the lifeless object of his love, and give full vent to his grief in mourning and weeping. Great souls are not insensible of losses, nor are gracious souls free from human sorrow. Old Testament saints mourned greatly for the death of their friends; and some spoken of in the New Testament, did likewise. "Devout men carried Stephen to his burial, and made great lamentation over him." Nor can mourning for the dead be reprobated, since the man of God's right hand, the God-man and Mediator, who was a perfect pattern for his followers, wept near the grave of Lazarus; and yet we are admonished by Paul to have proper bounds to our grief, especially when our godly friends make their exit, and not to mourn in sorrow, like those who have no hope in the resurrection, but to assuage our grief by believing that as certainly as Jesus died and rose again, so certainly will all those who sleep in Jesus be brought forth, and brought to see each other again. Our sorrows should never extend so high as to break out in murmuring against the dispensation, or to prevent us from the service of God, or even the duties of life. Of this we have an instance in Abraham, in the verse following the text. After the patriarch had mourned and wept a while for his dead, he cast the effeminate mourner off, and put the man of courage and conduct on, and said to the sons of Heth: "give me a possession of a burying-place with you, that I may bury my dead out of my sight." Fancy conjectures that, when Abraham lay mourning and weeping for his loss, after a severe contest, reason prevailed over passion, and triumphed in the following language: "Sarah, my wife, my beloved wife, the wife of my youth, is dead. She has lived with me until she was one hundred and twenty-seven years old. She has travelled, suffered, and rejoiced with me. She has been true to her conjugal engagement, and lived in the fear of God. Why should I mourn at my loss, since Heaven has thought best to call her away from me? Nay, it is not my loss; she was God's, and not mine. I gave my son, Isaac, up to God, obsequious to his order, and now I cheerfully resign my interest in my wife. But is Sarah dead? No; she yet liveth; she is living and adoring in heaven. Her body is dead, it is true, but her soul is in Paradise, basking in the sunny beams of noontide glory. Cease, then, all my passions: let my Sarah enjoy the beautific vision of her God, till he shall see cause to call me to his bright abode, to dwell with her and all the saints forever. In the meantime, I will serve my God on earth, and attend to the duties of my family; and the first thing that presents itself to view, is to purchase a burying-place, and bury my dead out of my sight."

The husband of the deceased, to-day, has to act the part of Abraham. This memorable day, you have to bury your dead out of your sight. Your amiable consort, the wife of your youth, is dead: she has breathed her last, and is now sleeping in death. The sorrow that sits on your brow, and the tears in your eyes, bespeak the anguish of your soul. The oratory of solemn silence breaks forth from your heart in the language of the eastern sufferer. "Have pity upon me! have pity upon me! O, ye my friends, for the hand of God has touched me." And, like the mourning prophet, cries: "Is it nothing to you, all ye that pass by? Behold, and see if there be any sorrow, like unto my sorrow, wherewith the Lord hath afflicted me." Or, like the man after God's own heart, in his complaint: "Both lover and friend hast thou put far from me, and mine acquaintance into darkness." Sir, your loss is great; deprived of the dear object of your love—of your domestic helpmeet, who guided the house, and governed her offspring, with subjection to her husband, in maternal fondness. But all the pleasing qualities of the mind did not secure her body from the pains and jaws of death. What still adds grief to the solemnity of the day, is her unexpected departure. Her debility was presageous to herself, of her approaching end, but no ways alarming to her friends, till within a moment of her dissolution, when she was incapable of speaking or answering to what was said. It is rational to suppose, on this occasion, that your language is this: "O, that I had been previously warned of her death, that I might have known how her hope of heaven was supported, that I might have received some counsel from her lips, and that the children might have obtained the dying charge and valediction of their mother.

Sir, your Lydia is dismissed from the troubles and cares of this life; and we have reason to believe that she has made a happy exchange of earth for heaven; if so, how much happier she is now, than ever she was before. She is now shining like the sun in the kingdom of heaven. She is now adoring before the throne of God, or flying through the vasts of heaven with messages from one choir to another; and, perhaps, is sometimes sent down to visit your abode, attend you in your solitary walks, and act the part of an official angel, though unperceived by you. Could you hear her heavenly voice to-day, she would tell you that she had lost all the doubts and fears that she had, when on earth, and had gained the celestial world, that she had heard little, and knew less of when she was on earth. Her longer stay on earth might have been pleasing and profitable to you; but surely her dismission from a world of sin and trouble, and her arrival at heaven, is her great gain. Then let it be the height of your ambition to live and die the Christian, that when you leave this world you may go where we hope your dear partner now is, and join with her in praise forever.

The children next claim my address; and surely the large tears flowing from their little eyes, their swelling breasts and pensive groans affect my heart. You have lost an indulgent mother, that bore you with pain, and raised you with care; no toil was too great for her to perform, to make your lives easy. It was not her ambition to prepare you for rioting, and teach you how to act your part on the dancing-floor; no, the religion she professed forbade it; but her anxiety was to train you up in the ways of virtue. How little do children imagine, when their parents restrain their youthful folly, or recommend the ways of religion to them, that they act out of good will to their characters and love to their souls; rather, they conclude it is the effect of a rancorous spirit, calculated on purposeto make them miserable. No one, without the experience, can conceive what excruciating pain fills the gracious souls of parents, to see nothing but pride and vanity in their children: it often leads them to cry to God, like Abraham, "O that Ishmael might live before thee." It is rational to suppose that your mother has lodged many prayers in heaven, for those very children that are now mourning over her corpse. I wish, and pray God, that your present affliction may be a lasting benefit to your souls. Funeral tears too often float away and leave no impression on the heart; but remember you all must die, and appear before God in judgment, where nothing will avail you short of the blood of the Lamb; no covering screen you from the storm of wrath, but the garments of salvation and the robes of Christ's righteousness; in fine, nothing will prepare you for heaven inferior to a gracious change of heart. Though you are now in youthful bloom, yet death is near, and may be nearer than we are aware of.

Survey the garden, where the fragrant rose,
In all the youthful pride of beauty glows;
Go pluck the tempting flower, and pensive say,
So cruel death may cut me off to-day.

'Tis often seen and known to be a truth,
That death first preys upon the fairest youth;
The flowers that bloom first, first fade away,
The fruit that first gets ripe, will first decay.

May that God, who is a father to the fatherless, be a father and Saviour to the motherless, and preserve you from sin and damnation, through Jesus Christ our Lord.

I shall now speak a word to the circle of mourners; to the aged mother, brothers, sisters, and all relatively concerned in the solemnities of the day. The present scene seems more affecting, when we consider how lately the family has been called together on a similar occasion. It is but a few days since a sister of the deceased followed her husband to the grave. Deep calleth unto deep; one stripe upon the back of another, this family receives, from the hand of the Almighty God. Surely the living are called upon to be ready to meet the Son of Man, in the dispensation of death. Ye are all uncertain which of the family will be next summoned; let each adopt the inquiry of the apostles, "is it I," and to practise myself what I preach to you, I shall say, "my merciful God, is it I?"

Brethren, members of this church, one of our sisters has left us; her seat will be empty in this meeting-house forever. While we have been busy here and there, she is gone—gone from a church in a militant, imperfect state, to the Church triumphant. She knows more now of the world of spirits, than ever she learned, or even heared from this pulpit; she no longer is confined to the partial knowledge, but knows as she is known; she looks no more through a glass darkly, but sees face to face. I have been happy, in seeing a considerable number join this church since I have lived among you; a few have moved away to other parts, and some few have been excluded from the communion; but this is the first mortal bereavement that the church has sustained since I have been resident in town. O may her vacancy be filled up with some of equal piety. Our expectation is from the youth. From close observation, I have noticed, that the greatest part of those who are born again, receive the gracious change between the years of sixteen and twenty-five; yet to this general rule there are many exceptions; so that those who are younger may hope, and those who are older need not despair. There have been several revivals of religion in this town, among the youth; but at present a great degree of carelessness and vanity is seen. How soon will this church dwindle away to nothing, by the removals and deaths of the present members, if recruits are not made up from the rising generation! O, thou lofty One, who inhabitest eternity, send thy good spirit down upon our youth, and turn their hearts to the love of the truth.

My hearers, one and all, I feel impressed with a sense of the uncertainty of all sublunary objects, the many ways in which death attacks the children of men, and the importance of our appearing before God, in eternity. Physicians have computed, that there are more than five-hundred ways, in which death assaults the offspring of Adam. Good God! are we yet living, when death, like a man of war, has so many instruments of mortality to reduce us to dust. It is owing to thy protective arm, Almighty Lord, that we are preserved from the terror by night, and the arrow that flieth by day; from the pestilence that walketh in darkness, and the destruction that stalketh at noon-day. When we consider the frailty of human nature, the wonder rises still higher; man has a vast number of vital fibres, infinately smaller than a hair, and dies if one of them is broken. "Strange that a harp of thousand strings, should keep in tune so long." Whoever studies human machinery, and calls in question the constant superintendency of God, must always live in the utmost fear of death.

It is as good a conjecture as can be made, that the earth is peopled, at present, with one thousand millions of souls. According to the bills of births that are taken, it appears that half that are born, die under seven years of age; but, as this may be questioned, we will suppose that half die under fifteen; the conclusion is, that in thirty years as many as a thousand millions leave this world. Now, if we suppose that a soul leaves the world every second, which is sixty for every minute, three thousand six hundred for every hour, at the expiration of thirty years, there will be left a surplus of about fifty millions, which I conclude is as great a surplus of living souls as thirty years produce. If we then contemplate the many ways that death invades our habitations, the frailty of human nature, and the amazing constancy of souls leaving this world, we shall naturally adopt the words of Paul, and say: "Having, therefore, obtained help of God, we continue unto this time." But let the careless sinner think that, when death dislodges his soul from his body, the yawning hell will be its residence. Notwithstanding the attempts of some to prove that the soul dies with the body, and of others to maintain that all souls will go to heaven on making their exit, yet Revelation assures us of the death of a rich man, and the existence of his something, I say soul, after his body was buried; and that this something was in hell, where a great fixed gulf forever separated him from Abraham and Lazarus. When the wicked, impenitent sinner dies, he goes to the generation of his fathers, and shall never see the light. He that made him will not have mercy on him, and he that formed him will show him no favor.

If there is not something pertaining to man that does exist in a separate state, after the dissolution of the body, what did our Saviour mean in his dying prayer—"Father, into thy hands I commend my spirit"? And how are we to understand Stephen, on a like occasion—"Lord Jesus, receive my spirit"? *Moses died, and the Lord hid him.* Moses had not been raised from the dead when our Lord was on earth, and yet he appeared on the holy mount when our Lord was transfigured; but how could this be, if there was nothing belonging to Moses that survived the death of his body? If souls know nothing when out of the body, why could not Paul tell whether he was in the body or out of it, when he was caught up into Paradise and the third heavens? and why should he give us to believe that he could be present with the Lord when absent from the body? If the souls of the martyrs do not live, sing, and pray, too, after their bodies are dead, and before their resurrection, how could John see, under the altar, the souls of them who were beheaded, hear what they said, and the answers made them? And how could the soul of a prophet bring him intelligence from heaven, if souls die with the body? Who can believe Paul, when he declared he was a Pharisee, if he did not believe their doctrine? which, in opposition to that of the Sadducees, was in spirits, angels, and the resurrection from the dead. The arguments that are brought to prove the mortality of the soul, will not admit of the existence of angels, and some of them strike directly against the existence of God.

But let souls continue ever so long in a separate state, yet the time will come—it hastens, when all will be raised from their graves, and souls and bodies will re-unite. The time is near, when we shall see a God in grandeur, and view a world in flames: when the Son of Man shall come in the clouds of heaven, and every eye shall see him. "A fire shall burn before him, and be very tempestuous round about him." Before his great white throne, all nations will appear to their final audit. Who can stand when God doth this?

It is not easy, if possible, to tell how many people have been on the earth since its first formation. If we suppose that from Adam to the flood, they doubled once in forty-five years, by births, there was born above one hundred and thirty-seven thousand millions. In the flood, all the threads of the web were cut off but eight. And if from the flood to this day, those eight souls have doubled in like manner, once in forty-five years, there have been born, since the flood, more than three hundred and ninety-seven thousand quatrillions, which, added to the antediluvians, make nearly four hundred thousand quatrillions. The surface of the whole globe would be as unequal to such a number, as a pepper-corn is to an empire; for if the whole solid contents of the terraqueous globe was reduced to square inches, there would be more than thirty-four thousand millions of souls to each inch. But if this earth could not contain them all, when the present is burnt up, God can make a new earth big enough; but it is not certain that resurrection bodies will require grass earth to stand upon. However these things may be, all rational creatures of Adam's line, will appear before God, and hear their final doom for eternity. May we all be prepared for the midnight cry—for the grand assize—for the solemn, righteous judgment of God; that we may hear the blessed plaudit—"Well done. Enter into the joy of your God." Amen.

THE

YANKEE SPY:

CALCULATED FOR THE RELIGIOUS MERIDIAN OF MASSACHUSETTS, BUT WILL ANSWER FOR NEW HAMPSHIRE, CONNECTICUT, AND VERMONT, WITHOUT ANY MATERIAL ALTERATIONS.

BY JACK NIPS.

By the life of Pharaoh, you are a SPY!——JOSEPH.

1794.

THE YANKEE SPY.

Question. Why are men obliged, every year, to pay their taxes?

Answer. To support government.

Q. What is government?

A. The government here intended, is the mutual compact of a certain body of people, for the general safety of their lives, liberty, and property.

Q. Are all systems of civil government founded in compact?

A. No: successful robbers and tyrants have founded their systems in *conquest*—enthusiasts and priest-ridden people have founded theirs in *grace*—while men without merit have founded their system in *birth;* but the true principle, that all Gentile nations should found their government upon, is, *compact.*

Q. Was civil government appointed by the Almighty from the beginning?

A. It was not; nor was it necessary until sin had intoxicated man with the principle of self-love. The law was not made for a righteous man, but for the disobedient.

Q. What form of government prevailed first among mankind?

A. Patriarchal. The father of a family used to exercise some sovereignty over his successors, until they moved from the city of their father, and became patriarchs themselves.

Q. How long did the world stand without any government in it but patriarchal?

A. There was no other kind before the flood, (which was more than one thousand six hundred and forty-five years,) nor afterwards till Nimrod, two generations after the flood.

Q. What was Nimrod?

A. He was the first that began to be a *mighty one* in the earth. He was a mighty hunter before the Lord, who hunted beasts to support his army with, and hunted men to reduce them to his will.

Q. What form of government did he adopt?

A. A kingly form; for the beginning of his kingdom was Babel, Erech, Accad, and Calneh. He was the first of those pretty cteatures called kings, who reduced others to subjection by hunting them like beasts.

Q. Did the Almighty ever give a code of political laws to any nation? or, are nations left to act at discretion in establishing forms of government and codes of laws?

A. The Almighty did certainly give the nation of Israel a complete code of laws on Sinai, and in the wilderness, for their rule of conduct in religious, civil and military life.

Q. Were those laws obligatory on other nations?

A. Laws, that are in themselves just, are binding on all men, but the particular form of many of those laws was peculiar to that nation. The transgression of many of those precepts was criminal in that nation, which the Gentiles were never accused of by their great apostle, Paul.

Q. What did other nations do, in point of government, while Israel was in the wilderness and under the regulation of judges?

A. When Nimrod usurped the monarch's crown, the spirit of domination ran through the world like a raging plague. Ashur went out to the land of Shinar, where Nimrod's seat was, and built Nineveh, and founded the Assyrian monarchy, and the contagion of having kings, and being kings, prevailed so greatly, that every little village had a king. Abraham, with three hundred and eighteen servants, conquered four of them and their hosts—Joshua destroyed thirty-one—and Adonibezek cut off the thumbs and great toes of seventy; also eight kings and eleven dukes reigned over Edom, before any in Israel.

Q. In what condition was the nation of Israel, after they left Egypt, before Saul reigned over them, in regard to their police?

A. They were in a state of theocracy, the best of all states when people have virtue enough to bear it.

Q. Were there no men among them who exercised dominion over the rest?

A. Moses and Aaron exercised divine orders among them; the princes of the tribes and the officers bore authority, and the judges, of whom there were thirteen, had some pre-eminence, but neither of them had the power of making laws; when God appointed them, they were to execute his laws, and no other.

Q. Was the code of laws, ordained for the government of Israel, sufficient to govern other nations by, in their very different circumstances?

A. It was not. Canaan was an inland country—the people were forbidden to trade with other nations, so that no laws were made for navigation, commerce, or union; all of which are necessary in Gentile nations. And, beside, their civil and religious laws were all blended together. The sabbath of the seventh day—seventh year, and fiftieth year—the three grand feasts, and a multitude of sacrifices, ceremonies, and oblations were enjoined on that people, which things Gentile nations have nothing to do with.

Q. Has the *political* part of that constitution ever been abused by Gentile legislatures?

A. Abundantly so, among Gentile nations that have become Christian; for by bringing Christian states upon the same footing with the commonwealth of Israel, they have supposed that Christian nations have a just right to dispossess the heathen of their lands and make slaves of their persons, as Israel served the Canaanites and Jebusites: for no better claim than this had the European nation to make a seizure of America. Nor is this all: civil rulers, in Christian countries, have taken the liberty of adopting such precepts of the Mosaic constitution as suited them, and punished those who would not submit, when, at the same time, they have left unnoticed a great number of the precepts of Moses which were equally obligatory.

Q. Has the *ecclesiastical* part of the Mosaic constitution ever been abused as well as the political part?

A. Yes, and that to a great degree. The church of Israel took in the whole nation, and none but that nation: whereas, Christ's church takes no whole nation, but those who fear God and work righteousness in every nation. But almost all Christian nations and states, since the reign of Constantine, have sought to establish national churches: in order to effect which, they have brought in all the *natural seed* of the professors into the pales of the church, making no difference between the precious and the vile; and from this foundation they have appealed to the laws of state, instead of the laws of Christ, to direct their mode of discipline. What a scandal it is to the Christian name to see church discipline executed in a court-house, before the judges of the police—to see censures given at the whipping-post, and excommunications at the gallows;* and for smaller breaches, to be admonished by a sheriff's seizing and selling cows, etc., or wiping off the admonition by a pecuniary mulct! Yet such has been, and still is the case, even in New England, that has made her boast of religion and liberty.† Circumcision, as to its first institution, was not of Moses, but of the fathers that lived before Moses, yet it was enjoined by Moses to be performed on all the males of Israel. From this a great number of ecclesiastics have changed blood for water, and sprinkle their children instead of bleeding them, in order to make the gospel church as extensive as the church of Israel was. Yet many of them will not admit a person to go back as far as John for the origin of baptism, because, say they, John's administration was under the law; yet they will run back two thousand four hundred years before John for a precedent of baptism.‡

* The Baptists and Newlights have been imprisoned, fined, and whipped, and witches and Quakers have been hung in Massachusetts.

† Seizing and selling, for ministerial tax, is still practised in many towns to this day.

‡ A Reverend Gentleman in the county of Worcester, who, like many of his brethren, views John's baptism under the law, contends for infant baptism from Genesis, ix., 27. That the laws of Moses was in force while John lived, and even to the death of Jesus, I

Q. Was not circumcision, to the church of Israel, the same that water-baptism is to the church of Christ?

A. If so, the following absurdities arise.

First. None but the males were circumcised: whereas, both males and females are sprinkled with water. To say that the females were *virtually* circumcised in the males, is just as good sense as to say the females are *virtually sprinkled* in the males.

Second. None were ever circumcised under eight days old, which was the general time appointed; but children are sprinkled sometimes before they are eight hours old. Midwives have been empowered to do it, in case death was nearer than a priest.

Third. Circumcision was never a priestly rite: fathers, masters, mothers, and friends did the work; but sprinkling is supposed to be a ministerial rite.

Fourth. Whatever circumcision figured out, it was something that was wrought in the *spirit* and done *without hands*; and as there is nothing done by men, that is called *baptism by water*, either sprinkling, pouring, or dipping, that can possibly change the spirit, so neither of them are effected without the hands of men. The conclusion, therefore, is, that the first did not figure out the last.

Fifth. None but those who were circumcised were to inherit Canaan; of course, then, none but those who are baptized with water can inherit heaven, which is a consequence inadmissible.

Q. What do you think of the British constitution of government?

A. There is no constitution in Britain. It is said, in England, that there are three things unknown, viz. the prerogatives of the crown—the privileges of parliament—and the liberty of the people. These things are facts, for although they consider the seventy-two articles of the Magna Charta as the basis of their government, yet from that basis they have never formed a constitution to describe the limits of each department of government. So that precedents and parliamentary acts are all the constitution they have.

Q. How does government operate in England?

A. A hereditary king of the Protestant faith, must always fill the throne, whether he be a wise man or a dunce. A house of lords, of the hereditary mould, must glways check the house of commons.

Q. What is the house of commons?

A. It is a representative body of a small part of the nation, chosen once in seven years. It is called the house of *commons*, because the house of lords is a house of *uncommons*, supposed to be a species of beings like the

---

do not deny; but that John baptized in Jordan and Enon, such, and such only, as brought forth fruits of repentance, by an order of the law, will be denied until it can be proved If no institution, appointed before the death of Christ, is imitable for Christians, the holy. supper should be neglected.

Genii of the Mahometans, between angels and men, born only to rule, without having a fellow-feeling with those whom they rule over.

Q. What condition has that form of government reduced the people to?

A. It has sunk them in a debt of more than two hundred and eighty millions, so that the interest of their debt, together with the support of the civil and military lists, imposes an annual tax on the people equal to thirty shillings sterling per soul, and at the expiration of the year the nation is a million of pounds more in debt than at the beginning.

Q. How stand religious concerns in England?

A. The thirty-nine articles and book of common prayer are established by law. No man can fill any office in the civil or military departments without taking an oath to support them, and upon receiving a commission he must seal his oath with the eucharist: this is true of all, saving the members of parliament, who are obliged only to take the oath of abjuration, *Curse the Pope and Papistry.*

Q. But are there none in England that dissent from the established religion?

A. Many of them, of various denominations.

Q. How do they fare?

A. They are deprived of such advantages as the conformists enjoy. In addition to all their proscriptions, the tenth part of all their income is taken from them to support priests that they never hear, and in whom they place no confidence.

Q. Is it supposed that the articles and forms of the church of England are so perfect that they cannot be mended?

A. They are always perfect when dissenters are handled. Edward Wrightman was burnt to death at Litchfield, by a warrant from prince James, for saying that the worship of God was not fully described in the thirty-nine articles and book of common prayers, and nearly eight thousand lost their property, liberties, and lives in the reign of the merciful king Charles, because they could not, would not say, that they believed what they could not believe, and so conform to the established worship.

They are also always perfect when a candidate enters into holy orders, for all of them do solemnly declare that they give their unfeigned assent and consent to all and every thing contained in that book, and yet, from the first formation of that book, it has passed above six hundred alterations, and to this day, many parts of it are complained of by many of the Episcopal clergymen.

Q. What have you to say about the Federal Constitution of America?

A. It is a novelty in the world: partly confederate, and partly consolidate—partly directly elective, and partly elective one or two removes from the people; but one of the great excellencies of the Constitution is, that no religious test is ever to be required to qualify any officer in any part of the government. To say that the Constitution is perfect, would be too high an encomium upon the fallibility of the framers of it; yet this may be said, that it is the best national machine that is now in existence.

Q. What think you of the Constitution of Massachusetts?

A. It is as good a performance as could be expected in a state where religious bigotry and enthusiasm have been so predominant.

Q. What is your opinion of having a *bill of rights* to a constitution of government?

A. Whenever it is understood that all power is in the monarch—that subjects possess nothing of their own, but receive all from the potentate, then the liberty of the people is commensurate with the bill of rights that is squeezed out of the monarch.

After the conquest of William, the government of England was completely monarchical, until the reign of king John, when the Magna Charta was given to the people: this has often been mentioned in America as a sufficient reason for a *bill of rights*, to preface each constitution: but in republican, representative governments, like those of America, where it is understood that all power is originally in the *people*, and that all is still retained in their hands, except so much as for a limited time is given to the rulers, where is the propriety of having a bill of rights? In this view, no such bill is found in the Federal Constitution.

But it is not my intention, at this time, to dispute the point of propriety or impropriety of a bill of rights, but shall only add that the liberty of the people depends more upon the organization of government, the responsibility of rulers, and the faithful discharge of the officers, than it does upon any bill of rights that can be named.

The illustrious patriots of Massachusetts, in framing their Constitution of government, in 1780, prepared a bill of rights, which is adopted in the state, on which I shall make some remarks. The bill contains thirty articles, upon a few of which I shall animadvert.

In the second article it is said, "it is the right and duty of all men publicly, and at stated seasons, to worship the Supreme Being." This article would read much better in a catechism than in a state constitution, and sound more concordant in a pulpit than in a state-house.

Suppose there are, in Massachusetts, a number of Pagans and Deists: the Pagans, upon hearing that it is their *duty* to worship *one* Supreme Being only, must consequently renounce all other deities whom they have been taught to adore; here their consciences must be dispensed with, or the constitution broken. The Deist, who believes all religion to be a cheat, must either act the hypocrite, or disregard the supreme law of the State. This duty is called a *right:* if every man has this *right*, then he has a *right* to judge for himself, and will hardly thank any body for turning his right into what they may call a duty. That it is the duty of men, and women too, to worship God publicly, I heartily believe, but that it is the duty or wisdom of a convention or legislature to enjoin it on others, is called in question, and will be, until an instance can be given in the New Testament, that Jesus, or his apostles, gave orders therefor to the rulers of this world.

It is the duty of men to repent and believe—to worship God in their closets and families as well as in public—and the reason why public worship is enjoined by authority, and private worship is omitted, is only to pave the way for some religious establishment by human law, and force taxes from the people to support avaricious priests.

What leads legislators into this error, is confounding *sins* and *crimes* together—making no difference between *moral evil* and *state rebellion:* not considering that a man may be infected with moral evil, and yet be guilty of no crime, punishable by law. If a man worships one God, three Gods, twenty Gods, or no God—if he pays adoration one day in a week, seven days, or no day—wherein does he injure the life, liberty or property of another? Let any or all these actions be supposed to be religious evils of an enormous size, yet they are not crimes to be punished by the laws of state, which extend no further, in justice, than to punish the man who works ill to his neighbor.

When civil rulers undertake to make laws against moral evil, and punish men for heterodoxy in religion, they often run to grand extremes. The eating of a potatoe for food, and using emetics for physic, were once considered in France as religious evils. Galileo was once excommunicated and banished by the Pope's bull, as a man of dangerous heresy, because he believed in the Copernican system. The ancients were treated as heretics, who believed they had antipodes. The court of Zurich made a law to drown Felix Mentz with water, because he was baptized in water. In short, volumes might be written, and have been written, to show what havoc among men the principle of mixing *sins* and *crimes* together has effected, while men in power have taken their own opinions as infallible tests of right and wrong.

The third article of the bill of rights is similar to the second in its structure. It is said, "The people of this commonwealth have a right to invest their legislature with power to authorise and require, and the legislature shall from time to time authorise and require the several towns, parishes, etc., to make suitable provision, at their own expense, for the institution of the public worship of God, and for the support and maintenance of public Protestant teachers, in all cases where such provision shall not be made voluntarily."

If the legislature of this commonwealth have that power to institute and establish that religion, which they believe is the best in the world, by the same rule, all the legislatures of all the commonwealths, states, kingdoms and empires that are in the world, and that have been in the world, may claim the same.

If dumb idols are called devils, and idolatry is the religion of the devil, this claim of power brings all the Gentile nations under the government of the devil. Idolatry was established by this pretended power in the Gentile nations, when the Christian religion was first sent among them; now if that establishment was right, then the apostles were wrong in separating so many thousands from the established religion. They were guilty of effecting a schism, and government was innocent in inflicting such punishment upon them and their adherents. In process of time, the religion of Christ prevailed so far that it was established in the empire of Rome; at which epoch it received a deadly wound, which gradually reduced it to superstition, fraud and ignorance; so that, in the sixteenth century, a number of kingdoms and principalities protested against the church of Rome; but this was a grand piece of obstinacy, if rulers have the power that the article under consideration says belongs to the legislature of Massachusetts. These Protestants, especially in England, retained so many of the Papal relics, that great numbers became nonconformists; here they repeated their crime, rejecting the English establishment, as well as that of Rome. Some of those nonconformists came into New-England, and soon began to exercise that power which the bill of rights says they have a right to.

Now, how shall all these evils be remedied? answer—all who have dissented from the established religion of New-England must return to that fold, and confess their errors; then all must return to the church of England, and submit to that establishment; then, joining with the Episcopalians, all must apply to the Pope for pardon, and submit to his uncontrolable authority; then, with the Papists, all must return to the Pagans, and submit to the Polytheism. If the power spoken of is right, then this mode of procedure is right; and, therefore, it is not the natural consequence of religious establishments by human law, to bring all men under the government and religion of the devil, it is because there is neither devil nor devilish religion in the world.

It is observed, that "the people of this commonwealth have a right to invest their legislature with this power." But where do they get this right? The universe is composed of a multitude of units; so this commonwealth is formed by a number of individuals. The confederacy is the sovereign, and rulers are agents; and how can the creature have more power than the Creator? *Propter quod unum quodque est tale, illud ibsum est magis tale.* Whatever is found in the commonwealth, in aggregate, is found in small, essential particles among all the individuals; if, therefore, this power is in the commonwealth, each individual has a little of it in his own breast; and has a right to exercise it towards his neighbor, and force him to worship God, when, where, and in such a manner as he himself shall choose; and if this be the case, what means the first article in the bill of rights; where it is said, "all men are born free and equal." To be consistent, either that clause should be erased, or the power contended for given up.

This power is to be used to oblige the people "to make suitable provision at their own expense, for the institution of the public worship of God." I have long been of the belief that Jesus Christ instituted his worship; and if my faith is well founded, then it is not left for rulers to do in these days; but, surely nothing more can be meant by it, than that the legislature shall incorporate religious societies, and oblige them to build houses for public worship. Parishes, precincts, and religious societies politically embodied, are phrases not known in the New Testament; convey ideas contrary to the spirit of the gospel, and pave the way for force and cruelty, inadmissible in Christ's kingdom, which is not of this world. If any number of real saints are incorporated by human law, they cannot be a church of Christ, by virtue of that formation, but a creature of state.

This power is further to be exercised, to require the people to be at expense "for the support and maitenance of public Protestant preachers."

Preaching by the day, by the month, by the year, annual taxes for preaching; what strange sounds these are! not strange in these days; but such strangers in the New Testament, that they are not to be found there. How insignificant would the federal government be, if it was dependant on the laws of the states to support its officers! That government that has not force enough in it to support its officers, will soon fall; just so with the government of Jesus. The author of our religion has appointed a maintenance for his teachers; but has never told the rulers of this world to interfere in the matter.

How much did John the Baptist, Jesus, Peter, James or John, ask per year? Answer: I know not. If a man preaches Jesus, he cannot talk enough for it; the gold of Ophir cannot equal it; if he preaches himself, it is good for nothing.

Strange it is, that men should pretend to be sent by God to preach to sinners, and yet will not do the work of the Lord, unless they can get men to be legal bondsmen for Jehovah.

To read in the New Testament, that the Lord has ordained that those that preach the gospel shall live by its institutions and precepts, sounds very harmonical; but to read in a state constitution, that the legislature shall require men to maintain teachers of piety, religion and morality, sounds very discordant.

We may next observe, that the legislature of Massachusetts have not power to provide for any public teachers, except they are Protestant. Pagans, Turks and Jews, must not only preach for nothing; but Papists, those marvellous Christians, cannot obtain a maintenance for their preachers by the laws of their commonwealth. Such preachers must either be supported voluntarily, support themselves, or starve. Is this good policy? Should one sect be pampered above others? Should not government protect all kinds of people, of every species of religion, without showing the least partiality? Has not the world had enough proofs of the impolicy and cruelty of favoring a Jew more than a Pagan, Turk, or Christian; or a Christian more than either of them? Why should a man be proscribed, or any wife disgraced, for being a Jew, a Turk, a Pagan, or a Christian of any denomination, when his talents and veracity as a civilian, entitles him to the confidence of the public.

The next thing to be noticed is, that the legislature of Massachusetts is invested with power and "authority to enjoin upon all the subjects an attendance upon the instructions of the public teachers, at stated times and seasons." By which stated times, no doubt, is meant the days called Sabbaths, Sundays, (Sondays,) First-days or Lord's-days. I shall not dispute the point about the holy-day, whether it was enjoined on men from the beginning, or never before the manna was given in the wilderness; whether the fourth commandment in the decalogue, was of a moral or ceremonial nature; whether it was binding on all nations, or only on Israel; whether the same day of the week is to be kept to the end of the world; whether the seventh part of time answers the end of the law, or whether the seventh day is changed for the first; but shall use the liberty of saying, that the appointment of such stated holy-days, is no part of human legislation. I cannot see upon what principle of national right, the people of Massachusetts could invest their legislature with that power; and as I cannot deduce it from the source of natural right, so neither can I find a hint in the New Testament, that Jesus or his apostles, ever reproved any for the neglect of that day; or that they ever called upon civil rulers to make any penal laws about it. And it is curious to see what havoc rulers make of good sense, whenever they undertake to legalize said day. No longer ago than 1791, the legislature of this commonwealth made a sabbatical law; wherein, for the groundwork, they say, that the seventh part of time is to be kept holy; but how do they calculate time? A man on a journey may travel until Saturday night, midnight, and begin again on Sunday at sundown; if eighteen hours is the seventh part of a week, then their calculation is good; but being conscious that it is not, they make it up (i. e. pay what they have borrowed) out of recreation; for such exercise must cease on Saturday at the going down of the sun, and continue to cease till Sunday midnight. It may further be observed, that the law of God, and the laws of men, differ widely in phrase; the law that enjoined the observance of the seventh day on the nation of Israel, which came from Jehovah, did not except the works of necessity and mercy; neither man, maid, nor beast were to work—but a little way were they to travel—a bundle of sticks was not to be gathered and laid on the fire—nor had they any orders to assemble on that day, in a stated manner, to read the law of Moses. It was to be a day of rest, which gave it the name Sabbath; but the laws of men have so many exceptions, that nothing, and anything, are done on said day.

But however these things are, the legislature of this state is to oblige the people to assemble on these stated times, to hear the instructions of these teachers of piety, religion and morality, if there be any on whose instructions they can conscientiously and conveniently attend. Here is a gap wide enough for any man to creep out. If neglecting to go to meeting is not justified by pleading inconveniency, his conscience will soon do it; but whether he goes to church or not, his pennies must go to the treasurer's purse.

It is true that one sect of Protestant Christians has as fair an opportunity to be incorporated as another, but there are many who justly despise the idea of religious incorporation by human law, and therefore those who do not, have an undue advantage over others. Supposing, in France, the National Convention should decree that all sects of Christians, that believed that kings, in certain cases, might wear their heads and crowns upon them, should have equal privileges in France, I ask, whether the Jacobin party would share equal favors with the royalists? So, in this case, all sects of Protestant Christians that choose to be incorporated, may elect their own teachers and contract with them for their maintenance, and assess it upon all within their respective precincts; but those who cannot, in conscience, accord with this legal religion, must pay their tax with the rest, and be at the trouble of drawing it out of the treasury again, which sometimes occasions vexatious lawsuits.

Now, if it should be argued that a great many in this commonwealth believe, in their consciences, that it is the best way to serve God, to have societies incorporated by law, and levy a tax upon all to support their worship and maintain their teachers, how easily the above evils might be prevented, and all enjoy liberty of conscience. If those only, who are conscientious in legal religion, are incorporated, and tax none but themselves, there will be no cruel distraining from those whose consciences dictate another mode of worship. A man can cheerfully work when he verily believes he is doing God service; a man, therefore, who believes in religious incorporation, can joyfully give in his name to be taxed; and he who believes that the law has nothing to do about religious worship, can as joyfully stay at home. The last of these have as good grounds to judge that the first plead conscience for cruelty, as the first have to judge that the last plead conscience for covetousness.

But there is no need for a constitutional clause about things of this nature; for if a number of men contract with a preacher, for a year, or for life, the bond which they give him, is as recoverable by law as any bond whatever; but the poison of such contracts is, including those who do not act voluntarily, and perpetuating them upon their successors or natural offspring.

The last clause of the third article reads thus:

"And every denomination of Christians, demeaning themselves peaceably, and as good subjects of the commonwealth, shall be equally under the protection of the law; and no subordination of any one sect or denomination to another, shall ever be established by law."

On this section I have several remarks to make:

First. The first part of it is very liberal, to a certain degree; but if it read *all men* instead of *every denomination of Christians*, it would be unexceptionable.

When the Pagans were favored by law, more than Christians, what devastation it made in the empire of Rome, in the first introduction of the Christian religion, until the reign of Constantine. In the first three centuries, almost two millions of lives were lost for conscience sake. These were men, women and children, who were as good subjects of state as any in the empire. After the change in the empire, when the Christian religion became established by law, the Pagans suffered in the same manner that the Christians had done in the ten preceding persecutions. Who can read the history of these sufferings without seeing the bad policy of establishing either of the religions in the empire?

Second. Although the clause now under consideration is some what liberal, indeed entirely so among Christians, yet it nowise accords with a former clause in the same article, where the legislature is forbidden to incorporate any Christians but *Protestants*, at least, are not vested with power to do it. *Protestants* only can be formed into religious societies and distrain for a maintenance for their teachers.

One of two things must be granted; either that Papists are no Christians, or that there is a partiality established. Among little souled bigots, who believe nobody right but themselves, who confine the Christian religion to their own sect, and conclude that they have the exclusive right to monopolize salvation, it would not be strange to hear that Papists, and all others who differed with them in sentiment, were no Christians; but this cannot be the case here. The framers of the constitution were men of information and acquaintance with the world; the result is, then, that there is a contradiction in the two clauses of the same article.

Such is the state of things in Massachusetts, that the legislature, according to the power vested in them by the first part of the third article, have made such laws as have effected a subordination of one sect to another, contrary to the last clause in the same article.

On March 23, and June 28, 1786, two acts passed; the first respecting towns, the other precincts, which effect the subordination just mentioned. These two laws were somewhat uniform in structure, and therefore a quotation from one of them may suffice in this place. Each inhabitant has the power of voting in town or precinct affairs, who pays two-thirds more in one tax than a poll tax; and then follows, "That the freeholders and other inhabitants, in each respective town, qualified as aforesaid, at the annual meeting for the choice of town officers, or at any other town-meeting regularly warned, may grant and vote such sums of money as they shall judge necessary for the settlement, maintenance and support of the ministry, to be assessed upon the polls and property *within the same*, as by law provided."

Now if any Christians but Protestants are thus incorporated, the constitution is violated ; and if none but Protestants, what may the Catholics say ? But this is not all ; by this act, property entitles a man to church privileges. A degree of simony is contained in the act. The wisest man that was ever born of a woman could not estimate *wisdom*, by all the gold and pearls on earth ; but here a little property procures it ; at least, an annual tax entitles a man to the rights of it. Whether these voters are spiritual, moral, or profane, they have an equal suffrage in the choice of spiritual teachers, who have, or should have, the cure of souls at heart.

It is well known, that there are a number of Baptists in this state ; in some towns they and their adherents form a majority ; but in the greatest part of the towns, those called the *standing order* are superior to all the rest. As the Baptists are Protestants, where they form a majority, they might be incorporated as well as others, and tax all in the town or precinct to part with their money for religious uses. But it is well known that they are principled against it. They do not believe that the legislature have any proper authority, upon the scale of good policy, to make any laws to incorporate religious societies and require a maintenance for the ministry. Now the question is, Do their sentiments prevent their demeaning themselves as peaceable subjects of state ? Let those who differ with them in judgment answer. Yet from their known and conscientious principles, how are they reduced to subordination in various places ?

In a town or precinct where the Baptists are a minority, the major part choose and settle a minister ; the expense is levied upon all according to poll and property ; the Baptists, in this case, must either part with their money to support a religion that they do not fully believe in, or be suborbinate enough to get a certificate to draw it out of the treasurer's hands. Some have condescended to the last mode, as being the best alternative they had ; while others have had such a disgust to submit to a power, belonging neither to the kingdom of the Messiah, nor the civil government on earth, that they would not bow let the consequences be what they would. The distraining law-suits and oppressions that have risen from this source, even since the ratification of the present constitution, need not be mentioned at this time.

One observation more shall close my strictures on this article. It is well noticed that none shall be protected by law, but those who properly demean themselves as peaceable subjects of the commonwealth. This, however should be extended to all men, as well as to Christian denominations.

For any man, or set of men, to expect protection from the law, when they do not subject themselves to government, is a vain expectation. Let a man's motive be what it may, let him have what object soever in view; if his practice is opposed to good law, he is to be punished. Magistrates are not to consult his motive or object, but his actions.

Without adverting to Bohemia, Munster, or any part of Europe or Asia for instances, we shall pay attention to a few recent transactions of our own. A Shaking-Quaker, in a violent manner, cast his wife into a mill-pond in cold weather; his plea was, that God ordered him so to do. Now the question is, Ought he not to be punished as much as if he had done the deed in anger? Was not the abuse to the woman as great? Could the magistrate perfectly know whether it was God Satan, or ill-will, that prompted him to do the deed? The answers to these questions are easy.

In the year of 1784, Matthew Womble, of Virginia, killed his wife and four sons, in obedience to a Shining One, who, he said, was the Son of God, to merit heaven by the action; but if the court had been fearful of offending that Shining One, and pitied Womble's soul, they would never have inflicted that punishment upon him which they did the October following. Neither his motive, which was obedience, nor his object, which was the salvation of his soul had any weight on the jury.

Should magistrates or jurors be biased by such protestations, the most atrocious villains would always pass with impunity.

I shall here add, that in Scotland, two women were brought before the sessions for fornication; one of them was a church member and the other was not. She who was a daughter of Zion was pitied, and the man who had defiled her was judged a vile seducer, and severely fined; but she who was not a member of the church, was judged a lewd slattern, and was driven out of the parish, that she might not deceive honest men any more.

Should a man refuse to pay his tribute for the support of government, or any wise disturb the peace and good order of the civil police, he should be punished according to his crime, let his religion be what it will; but when a man is a peaceable subject of state, he should be protected in worshipping the Deity according to the dictates of his own conscience.

It is often the case, that laws are made which prevent the liberty of conscience; and because men cannot stretch their consciences like a nose of wax, these non-conformists are punished as vagrants that disturb the peace. The complaint is: "These men, being Jews, do exceedingly trouble the city." Let any man read the laws that were made about Daniel and the three children, and see who were the aggressors, the law makers or the law breakers. The rights of conscience should always be considered inalienable—religious opinions as not the objects of civil government, nor any way under its jurisdiction. Laws should only respect civil society; then if men are disturbers they ought to be punished.

Among the many beautiful traits of the constitution of Massachusetts, the provision made for its revision shines with great effulgence.

Permanency and improvement should be mixed together in government. But few nations have ever had patriotism sufficient to remove the radical deficiencies of government, without falling into convulsion and anarchy. There are certain ebbs and tides in men, and bodies of men, which often break over all proper bounds, without a proper check. To leave government, therefore, so mutable that a bare majority can alter it, when under some prevailing passion, exposes that permanency that the good of the whole, and the confidence of allies, call for. In this last view of things, some real, confessed evils had better be borne with, than to make government too fluctuating. In the federal government, it requires two-thirds of the states, or two-thirds of the members of Congress, to change the constitution. In Massachusetts the same; but not till after the experiment of fifteen years. However this may appear to others, to me it appears one of the fairest lines in the constitution; a signal of a patriotic people, conscious of their liability of mistake, wishing to improve in policy, attached to energy and freedom. And there is no doubt but, in the year 1795, the citizens of this state may meet by their delegates, and coolly impove upon the constitution, and remove its defects, that time and experience have discovered, without the least danger of tumult or noise. Should that be the case, it is hoped that some things respecting religion will be altered, which is the chief end of the publishing of this small tract.

If the constitution should be revised, and anything about religion should be said in it, the following paragraph is proposed:—

"To prevent the evils that have heretofore been occasioned in the world by religious establishments, and to keep up the proper distinction between religion and politics, no religious test shall ever be requested as a qualification of any officer, in any department of this government; neither shall the legislature, under this constitution, ever establish any religion by law, give any one sect a preference to another, or force any man in the commonweatlth to part with his property for the support of religious worship, or the maintenance of ministers of the gospel."

CORRESPONDING LETTER

OF THE

SHAFTSBURY ASSOCIATION, 1796.

Beloved brethren: As the indulgent Guardian of men has preserved our lives, and brought us together at this our annual meeting, we have now an opportunity of addressing you in our collective capacity. It is a saying of the wise man, that "two are better than one, and a threefold cord is not easily broken." From which we learn that the great design of Heaven, manifested by nature's great law, as well as revelation, is that men should be helpers of each other. The feeble state of infants, the unwary paths of youth, the decrepitude of old age, the want in each sex of the other to make life agreeable, and, indeed, the inability of individuals to execute business of agriculture and arts of mechanism, all evince the utility of society in civil life. Nor are arguments less conclusive or pungent in matters of religion. But how are the laws of Heaven (in some sort) frustrated by sin! rather, we express it, the plum is gathered from the thorn, the rose from the brier, and the honey from amidst the stings. How has sin, how does self-love and self-importance, torment and chafe our minds among those very persons, our partners, our nearest connections, whom Heaven has appointed for our comforters, and without whom we are more forlorn than the beasts of the wilderness. But is there no antidote, is there no way to escape all the snarls of social life? O, gracious Heaven! show us the way—the hidden way, to obtain all the blessings of society without the disadvantages thereof. But here, again, we check the language of our hearts; for the voice of revelation promises, neither to individuals nor societies, in this world, good without evil, peace without contention, a crown without a cross, nor profit without incumbrance. Seeing, then, that this world is a mixture of good and evil, and men are in a middle state, between the consummate holiness of heaven, and the entire deformity of hell, let us wait patiently till our change comes; nor be so overcharged with the evils of life, as to neglect the use of those talents and means that God has assigned us in our pilgrimage here on earth. In this point of light, we joyfully embrace this opportunity of corresponding with you, by letter and delegates, wishing that we might suggest a little to you, (at least two mites,) for your furtherance in the gospel, and that, in return, we might receive much from you, for our reproof, instruction and comfort.

We conceive that the church of Christ, which is the kingdom of heaven, is not governed by the laws of men, but by the laws of Christ; not by the acts of parliament, but by the acts and epistles of the apostles; not defended by carnal weapons, and instruments of death, but by spiritual weapons, and instruments of righteousness. "Not by might and power, but by my spirit, saith the Lord." This kingdom forms no alliance with the kingdoms and states of this world, but is distinct from them, yet containing subjects in all of them, to be redeemed from among them. The negotiations, failures, violations, ratifications, or punctual compliances of treaties between earthly kingdoms and states, no wise affect the church in its spiritual standing, which is secured in the great treaty between Jehovah and the Mediator. "The council of peace was between them both;" in which covenant the persons and blessings of Christ's kingdom are both made sure. The offspring and vessels all hang upon this nail.

Dear brethren, if such is the security and happiness of the saints, oh, let us never forget the price of our redemption. The blessed Jesus came into this world, not to teach men husbandry, or the mechanical arts—not to instruct them in politics, or any of the branches of science or natural philosophy; he never taught man the use of the magnet, or the mariner's art. No; these things are good and profitable among men, but infinitely beneath the cause that Jesus came to espouse. He came to do the will of him who sent him, and to finish his work—to magnify his law, to clear his amiable character, to make a display of his excellent perfections, to build up truth, to expose sin, conquer Satan, and save sinners by his blood. Oh, how immense the love! how free the grace! how inexpressible the kindness! how painful the conflict! how interesting to us, and how triumphant to himself, the victory! The bleeding victim, slain under the Mosaic institution, the blood and smoke of the Jewish altars, but feebly pointed out the great offering of Christ, to make atonement for the sins of men.

Let Arians, Socinians, or any others, undervalue the bloody sacrifices and vicarious sufferings of the God-man, Christ Jesus, yet on this foundation we trust our souls, and humbly hope to spend a long eternity in finding out this knowledge of witty inventions, and adoring the wisdom, love and grace, which we never expect, nor ever wish to comprehend.

Since our last association, our dear brother, Rev. Joshua Morse, of Sandisfield, has departed this life. He began the work of the ministry in his youth, has followed it with unwearied zeal, solemn devotion and practical piety, to a good old age, and died in the triumphs of faith. We have gospel grounds to believe that, while we are associating here on earth, and see his seat empty among us, he is associating with the saints in heaven, and filling his seat among the servants of the Lord, and has heard and received the blessed plaudit: "Well done, good and faithful servant; because thou hast been faithful over a little, I will make thee ruler over much. Enter thou into the joy of thy Lord." Oh! may all of us, who are called upon to minister in holy things, be faithful unto death, that we may receive a crown of life. And may the Lord raise up and send forth able, wise, spiritual, and faithful laborers into his vineyard.

As to the state of our churches, there is nothing very flattering, nor is there anything peculiarly discouraging. A worldy, careless spirit too much abounds in general; but there are some revivings. Upon the whole, we can say "the Lord reigns," and his word of revelation recommends itself to us with satisfactory evidence. The preceding minutes will give any curious inquirer the number of our churches, and what alterations have taken place since our last anniversary.

In this present session, moderation and good order have presided, and some quickenings of the Holy Spirit. And may the word and spirit of the living God be our guide and comforter forever. Amen.*

---

* It is possible some alterations were made in this, and perhaps, also, the other associational letters, by the bodies for which they were prepared; but what these changes were, we have now no means of ascertaining.

A

BLOW AT THE ROOT:

BEING A

FASHIONABLE FAST-DAY SERMON,

DELIVERED AT

CHESHIRE, APRIL 9, 1801.

I will also show mine opinion.——ELIHU.
Shoot at her, spare no arrows, for she hath sinned against the Lord.——JEREMIAH.

A BLOW AT THE ROOT, &c.

MAN comes into the world *needy, dependent, frail, and polluted.* He is born without clothes and shoes, and with his mouth opened by a craving appetite. These needs have given rise to the various arts so studiously and gradually learned among men.

The *need* of a shirt has set the farmer to work to raise his flax, and the woman to spin and weave it: which again has set others to work to make tools for the farmer, spinner, and weaver to perform with, etc. The *need* of a jacket has taught men to raise sheep and manufacture their wool, which also employs a number of artisans beside, before the coat of a sheep is turned into a coat for a man. The *need* of shoes has discovered a use for the skins of beasts, and taught the tanner, the currier, and shoe-maker, with all others connected therewith, their respective arts. The open mouth and craving appetite, has given rise to the many agricultural arts, to raise food: and taught the butcher and cook, with a thousand others in train, to perform their parts in life. The surplus of necessaries, conveniencies, and luxuries, that are in one part of the world, and the want of many other articles, if they did not give rise to ship-building and navigation, employ abundance of men in carrying their exports and bringing home their imports. The need of shelter from the storm has formed the carpenter, mason, glazier, and a long list besides; and if the three sons of Cain, whose names were *Fire, Light,* and *Flame,* first found out fire by rubbing two sticks together, as some say, yet the tending, securing, and using of it, to warm and cook with, have employed a number of artists. The subject cannot be developed by me, I believe not by any man. To contemplate the rise of human nature, from its first state of barbarous ignorance in the beginning, to the present state of improvement in agriculture and the arts; to enquire how the first artisans got tools to execute their arts; together with the coincidence of all the parts, forming one great whole, is a subject so extensive and intricate, that no being but Him who teaches men knowledge, and who is infinite in knowledge himself, can comprehend it. These are parts of thy works, O Lord.

The doctrine so earnestly contended for, *that all men came into the world free and independent,* may, in a very small sense be true: indeed, it appears to be wholly true, in the sense intended by those who adopt the maxim, but in the view of things which I am now pursuing, freedom and independence are but little more than names. Man comes into the world more dependent than the quadruped—more helpless than the bird—more forlorn than the insect. As soon as he is born, he is involuntarily dragged from place to place by the sovereign arm of his nurse, and has one bitter thing after another crammed down his throat, entirely against his will: if he is in a serious mood, the fond mother will tickle him to make him laugh, and if he chooses to cry, she will stop his mouth with the pap. Pray where is the freedom of this child?

But further, when the child grows larger, if he chooses to pull the teacup off the table, his hand is confined, and if he chooses to put his fingers in the milk, it is moved out of his reach; if it is his will to run out in the mud or snow, he is called into the house, and if he chooses to stand in front of the fire, he is ordered to give place to his seniors; if it is his pleasure to set up at night he is ordered to bed, and if he desires to take a morning nap he is called up to work. When sent to school, he is often forced to be poring over his dull lesson or knotty sum, when he had much rather be at play. Now the question is, who speaks truth, the statesman or the child? The statesman says, that "man comes into the world free:" the child says, he "can never do as he pleases without being scolded at or controlled."

If we consider that freedom does not authorise one man to destroy the freedom of another, but that freedom is to be governed by the laws of good order, and that all beside is licentiousness, and tends to bondage in the final event, the seeming contradiction is reconciled.

The bondage just mentioned above, does not cease with our infantile or juvenile years, but remains with men through every stage of life. In riper years—in a connubial state—in parental concerns—in human society, both civil and religious—in short, in all their connections in life, they are bound to bear innumerable disappointments and crosses which are unavoidable.

The *dependence* of man further appears, in his inability to accomplish the works of husbandry or mechanism by himself, and in his entire incapacity, as a unit, to defend himself from a stronger man than himself, or a number of them in conjunction, who make an attack upon his life, liberty, or property. Hence results the propriety of human confederation, to effect the works of life, and defend the innocent from the depredations of villains.

Man is also *frail*—formed out of the dust—animated clay—possessing a heavenly spark that never can decay. That man is complex, to me is clear, but his immaterial, immortal part, is not an article of present animadversion: his material, mortal part is frail. Diseases, called the "first born of death," are in his tabernacle. The multitude of diseases, both internal and external, which men are subject to, have taught them the medical quality of roots, plants, minerals, barks, fruit, gums, etc. Hence chemists, apothecaries, physicians and surgeons have arisen. Accident and experiment have taught men, that in the growths of nature, there is both a medicinal and nutritive quality. What proficiency was made in the science of physic before the days of Æsculapius and Hippocrates, I cannot tell, but the first of these was worshipped in the form of a serpent, for his great skill in physic, the other reduced physic to a system, and it is now considered as one of the liberal arts.

Man is likewise *polluted*. That all rational creatures came from the hands of God pure, at first, is both reasonable and scriptural, but how these pure creatures could pollute themselves, is an intricate question: perhaps no man, in this period of existence, can fully illustrate, or even conceive of it, but one thing is certain, viz., God is always the same, infinite in love and in power. Now if sin and misery have arisen among the creatures of God, and have existed six thousand years, what argument can be drawn from the nature of God, to prove that sin and misery will not always exist.

This pollution may be considered both in a *moral* and *social*, or *political* point of light. Moral evil is the transgression of the moral law of God. This law is not confined to the prohibition that God laid on Adam, nor yet to the decalogue, or ten commandments, but it is that eternal rule of right, which took its rise in the scale of being, and runs through the Bible like a golden chord, enjoining on all rational creatures that which is right of itself, both towards God and man, in all places and conditions of life: any deviation from this rule is moral evil, commonly called *sin*. This pollution is that which all men, by nature, are in, and although this apostacy is not the cause of the eternal union that subsists between Christ and men, nor the cause of their being raised from earth to heaven, yet it was the cause of Jesus' agonizing in death, and of ministers being sent to preach repentance and forgiveness of sins to the children of men.

Social or political evil, consists in actions only—the philanthropy or turpitude of the heart, the motives, views, or designs of men, are entirely out of the question before this tribunal. The divine government of Jehovah takes cognizance of every exercise of the heart, as well as all external actions, but social government arrests visible actions only. Hence it appears that all political evils are moral evils, but all moral evils are not political evils. No evil, simply moral, is punishable by a political tribunal, yet every political evil comes within the jurisprudence of the Almighty, because it is morally wrong.

Social pollution influences men to work ill to their neighbors, to prevent which civil government was appointed. "The law was not made for a righteous man, but for the lawless and disobedient." "The powers that be, are ordained of God." Rulers are God's ministers. That civil government in the hands of men, is an evil of itself, admits of no doubt. The vast expense to the community—the pride and cruelty of those in power—the intrigue and chicanery made use of by aspiring, avaricious men to gain seats of importance, and the arts and dissimulation used to keep their real designs out of view, prove the hypothesis that government is an evil, but with all these horrid features, it is a choice among evils—in fact, a necessary evil, to prevent greater evils. In this case, one of those instances appear, where, of two evils, the least is a chosen good.

How extensive this government is, is a point in which legislators, philosophers, and men in general, are greatly divided. Some suppose, that when government is formed and organised, those in office have power to make all civil, municipal, sumptuary and religious laws, and that any disregard of those laws, is a moral evil: they seem to pin their life, liberty, property, body and soul on the sleeve of their rulers, and abundance of those in power, love to have it so. If rulers were infallible in wisdom and goodness, there would be no danger in this scheme, but as all Adam's children are a bad breed, the scheme is very exceptionable.

Perhaps the legitimate designs of government cannot be better defined, than by saying, "it is to preserve the lives, liberties and property of the many units that form the whole body politic." For these valuable purposes, individuals have, in certain cases, to expose their lives in war to defend the state—to give up a little of their liberty, and be controlled by the general will, and part with a little of their property to compensate those who should be employed to secure the rest.

Government is, when rightly understood, the most economical means that men make use of, to secure themselves and be happy.

When a constitution of government is formed, it should be simple and explicit, the powers that are to be vested in, and the work to be performed by each department, should be defined with the utmost perspicuity, and this constitution should be attended to as scrupulously by men in office, as the Bible should be by all religionists. For either of the departments of government to deviate from the constitution, with a view to do good, is criminal, for if the honorable servants of the people forsake their political Bible, for a supposed good, they will soon forsake it for a real evil. Let the people first be convinced of the deficiency of the constitution, and remove the defects thereof, and then, those in office can change the administration upon constitutional ground.

If men were now as virtuous as their great progenitor was at first, it is probable they would need some distributive laws; but the idea of a code of penal laws among such innocent beings, would be inadmissible.

But the idea of such innocent beings is not now to be realized in fact among men. "All have sinned." It would, however, be a great blessing to mankind, if they were so virtuous as to have a few laws sufficient to restrain and direct them; for where there is a vast number of laws in a political body, there will be but few of the people who have leisure to read, and capacity to understand them; in such a labyrinth, the legislature will almost inevitably injure one act by another; besides, where only a few are learned in the law, it gives those few an undue advantage over others; further, such a maze of laws, like a cobweb, will entangle the innocent flies, but support the venomous spiders. And yet, where many vices reign, if there are not many laws, there will be many cases left to the will of the judge, and this gives the judge such an amazing importance both to legislate and judge of the law, and fact, that all who are interested, will seek to bribe the judge. And, if his temptations of bribes and importance, do not overcome him, and induce him to pervert law and judgment, it will be because he is one of a thousand.

The conclusion is, that while men are so vicious, they must adopt the medium, between having too many, and too few laws; and above all, let them seek to become more virtuous, which is the direct way to escape the evils just pointed out; for when men observe the golden rule, of "doing unto all men as they would be done by," no just laws will do them any hurt.

But the means of procuring wealth, ease and comfort; the right of private judgment and free debate, and the liberty of conscience, are inalienable. These are not surrendered up to the general will, by individuals, when they enter into society; but each retains them in his own sovereign breast. The last of these, which is liberty of conscience, I shall now attend unto.

Whenever any right which men possess in a state of nature, is surrendered up to government, it is to be paid at least, with an equivalent: indeed, with something superior; but government cannot reward individuals with anything equally valuable with the liberty of their conscience.

He who is obliged by law, to sin against his own conscience, cannot have his loss made good.

To be definite in expression, by the liberty of conscience, I mean, the inalienable right that each individual has, of worshipping his God according to the dictates of his conscience, without being prohibited, directed, or controlled therein by human law, either in time, place, or manner.

If the worship of God is to be controlled by law, who shall make that law? Shall the Pope? Have not the long succession of Popes, given incontestible evidence that they have been fallible? And shall fallible men make laws to direct us how to worship an infalliable God? In all Protestant countries the idea is justly exploded; but kings, parliaments, and legislative bodies, have undertaken the solemn work, with but little solemnity. How have they succeeded? One year make a law, and the next alter, repeal, or add unto it. Does God annually, or periodically change? if not, these law makers change; and are changeable men competent to direct men how to worship an unchangeable God?

Before the late European revolution at Calais, in France, a man must have suffered for daring to call in question the infallibility of the Pope; at Dover, in England, a few miles distant, a man must take the oath of abjuration, curse Pope and prelacy, or be proscribed from all honorary and lucrative offices. In Connecticut, a man must quit all labor and recreation on Saturday, at the going down of the sun, and may resume it on Sunday at the same time. In Massachusetts, recreation must cease from Saturday sun-down, until Sunday midnight; but a man on a journey may travel until Saturday midnight, and resume it again on Sunday at the going down of the sun. In Virginia, under the regal government, all the Presbyterians were obliged to pay the Episcopal clergymen, as much as if they had heard them preach. In Massachusetts, all dissenters, so called, have had to pay the Presbyterian preachers, &c. &c. These things have been established by law. Query, do truth, righteousness, and the laws of God, change with the climes? or is it because men attempt a work which they are incompetent for, and therefore they are confused, like the builders of Babel; and while they seek to build the church by human law, they are only building up mystical Babylon, who is the mother of harlots.

How just is this remark, that "Religious opinions are not the objects of civil government, nor in any way under its control." If that part of the world which is become Christian, (so called,) had attended to this remark, what infinite evils would have been avoided? Had Spain hearkened thereto, two hundred thousand South Americans would not have been slaughtered as they were. For want of this, in France, in the reign of Charles IX. A.D. 1751, a persecution began, which in thirty years destroyed thirty-nine Princes, one hundred and forty-eight Counts, two hundred and thirty-four Barons, one hundred and forty-seven thousand five hundred and eighteen gentlemen, and seven hundred and sixty thousand of the common people; and in Ireland, in the days of Charles I. of England, above two hundred thousand Protestants were cruelly murdered in a few days.

I suppose that all Protestants, will unite in condemning this cruelty in Papists, because Papists are such blood-thirsty bigots; but pray have not Protestants done the same, whenever they have established their religion by law, and supported their preachers by a tax?

In the reign of the two Charleses, in England, two thousand preachers, and six thousand privates lost their livings, and the chief of them their lives, for non-conformity. But leaving these distant nations, let us turn our eyes on our own country.

The first settlers of Massachusetts had left the rod of oppression in England, and fled to America for freedom; but not fully understanding that religious opinions were not under the control of civil government, in

1635, they passed a sentence of banishment against Roger Williams, because he opposed the interference of law in matters of religion; and three months afterwards, they made an attempt to seize him, and send him back to England; but he fled to Providence, and obtained a grant of land from the Narraganset Indians.*

Governor Haines pronounced the sentence of banishment against Williams, but Haines soon got distressed in Massachusetts, and went to Connecticut; and when Mr. Williams saw him at his house, in Hartford, Haines said to him: "I must confess to you that the Most Wise God hath provided and cut out this part of the world, for a refuge and receptacle for all sorts of consciences." But had the fathers of Massachusetts believed the confession of Haines, they would not have proceeded, in 1652, and years afterwards, to imprison, whip, and pass sentence of banishment against the Baptists; and nail up their meeting-house because they built it without a license from the ruling powers. Nor would they have hung the Quakers, as they did in 1659, '60 and '61.

Had governor Haines extended his thoughts still further, and said "the Most Wise God has cut out the *whole world* for all sorts of consciences," it would have been a noble idea. Had this persecution ceased with the lives of our forefathers, (who are called our "*virtuous ancestors*" in every proclamation for a fast and thanksgiving,) I would not rake up the ashes of the dead; but much of it is still continued in this state until the present time.

About sixty years past, a very general revival of religion took place in New England; soon afterwards, a very considerable separation from the established religion followed, which occasioned abundance of distraints and imprisonments. For about forty of the last years, the Baptists have chiefly borne the lash; for no other society has arisen to any considerable importance. The point in debate is this: the law of the state says that, where the majority of a town, parish or precinct, choose a preacher, and contract with him for his hire, it shall be levied upon all within the limits of said town, parish or precinct, according to poll and property; and that it shall be collected in legal form, and distrained for, if not paid without. It also makes the same provision for building and repairing meeting-houses. It has hitherto been the case, that in most of the towns the Baptists have been the minority; consequently, they have been distrained upon, and imprisoned, because they would not pay their money voluntarily to preachers in whom they did not place confidence, nor approve of their sentiments; and to build meeting-houses where they did not choose to worship. He must be a poor logician, who does not trace this oppression back to its origin, to that rotten nest-egg, which is always hatching vipers: I mean

* He also held it unjust to take away the land from the Indians without purchase.

the principle of intruding the laws of men into the kingdom of Christ, which kingdom is not of this world.

But all the art and force that is used, neither effect uniformity nor stop the increase of the Baptists. In the beginning of the last century, there were but four Baptist churches in Massachusetts; but now there are one hundred and thirty-six churches, in which are eight thousand four hundred and sixty-three members, besides all their adherents; and in which churches there are one hundred and five ministers.*

The religious laws of Massachusetts are frequently varying, but the stump is always preserved with a band of iron. Legal force is always used in directing the worship of God, as if human law was the mainspring of the gospel.

In March, 1800, a law was made for the above purpose, by which former laws are repealed. This law is of so recent date, that it is difficult to tell how it will operate; but I shall take the liberty of making a few remarks on said law.

This law is a legitimate child of the constitution. The third article of the bill of rights authorizes the legislature to make such laws; and since the adoption of the constitution, in the year 1780, it is said, by candid men, that a sixth part of the time, during the sessions of the legislature, has been taken up in incorporating religious societies, and making other religious laws; and if the sixth part of the time of the judiciary is taken up in adjudging religious cases, then a very considerable part of the expenses of government is to support that root, that principle, which is the pillar of popery, and without which there could be no legal persecution, for conscience sake, in the world.

The law in view, enjoins on all towns, parishes, precincts, religious societies, and bodies politic, to have a teacher of morality, piety and religion, upon the forfeiture of a fine. If they are without such a teacher more than three out of six months, for the first offence, the fine is not to be less than thirty, nor more than sixty dollars; but for every offence committed afterwards, the fine is not to be less than sixty, nor more than one hundred dollars.

By these teachers of morality, piety and religion, I understand preachers of the gospel; because there is no order of moral and pious religionists, who undertake to teach men, in this state, except those who are called preachers of the gospel.

Let us first ask who sends forth men to preach, God or man? If ministers are furnished and sent by men, let them always remember their creators, and address their hearers in the name of those who gave them

* This account is taken from Backus's history, which was published in 1796. Since which time there have been very considerable additions, both of members and churches.

their commission. In this view of things, a consistent address would be as follows: "My dear hearers, I come to address you in the name of the authority of Massachusetts: the presbytery has approbated me, and the laws of the state have declared me learned and orthodox:——I am not one of them who vainly imagine they are moved by the Holy Ghost to preach, but I have entered in at the door of lineal ordination, succeeded from the apostles, through all the whoredom and murders of Rome: I am not of that class who harangue the people extempore, without sense or grammar; but I have my sermon all written down, and shall read it distinctly. It is true, I requested in my prayer that God would grant me his spirit, but what I meant, was that God would give me good eyesight and graceful pronunciation, so that, like Paul, I might please all men, everywhere. And now, my hearers, as the law obliges you to have a teacher, I exhort you to be subject to every ordinance of man, for the Lord's sake; and as it is our custom to wait for a call from the people, I shall observe the orders of Christ: 'If they receive you not into one city, go unto another.' But in this particular, I shall not regard so much the *size* of the *caul*, as the fat upon it. I first say, 'peace be unto you,' and I pray you all to be of one mind in my settlement and support. Schisms and contentions are dishonorary to God, and injurious to the salaries of preachers. I moreover inform you, that I intend to teach morality, piety and religion, and pray for all in authority, admire the goodness of our laws, and honor and respect all our rulers, so long as they continue to make laws to support preachers."

But if God sends men to preach, if Jesus thrusts forth laborers into the harvest, if the ministers speak as they are moved by the Holy Ghost, if none but the Almighty can fill the soul of man with love to God, to truth and to the souls of men, etc., etc., why should the law be left so lame?

If God sends men to preach to the people, then there are three parties concerned in the work of the ministry. I will therefore propose an amendment to the law now under consideration.

Be it enacted by the Senate and House of Representatives in General Court assembled, That the almighty God shall qualify and send forth a competency of teachers of morality, piety and religion, to supply all the towns, parishes, precincts, religious societies and bodies politic, within the commonwealth of Massachusetts, and on failure thereof he shall forfeit his moral government over the state.

And be it further enacted, That all those who are so qualified or sent of God, shall apply themselves to the work of the ministry; to teach publicly and from house to house; not as being Lords over God's heritage, but ensamples to the flock: that they shall preach in towns, highways, streets and hedges; and seek not their own profit, but the good of others, that they may be saved: that they shall constantly speak the word of God unto the people, whether they will hear or forbear; doing this not for filthy lucre, but of a ready mind; and on failure thereof for the first three months, they shall, each of them, be exposed to a fine, not exceeding sixty nor less than thirty dollars, but for every offence of three months neglect thereafter, they shall, in like manner, be exposed to a fine of not less than sixty nor more than a hundred dollars.

And be it further enacted, That every town, parish, precinct, religious society, and other bodies politic, shall have a teacher," etc.

Perhaps some may argue that the first section of the proposed amendment, is arrogant, presumptuous and blasphemous; and that the second section is cruel, binding preachers too tight by law.

This argument I shall not undertake to confute, because it is true, and the same may be said of the law that the amendments are proposed for; and, indeed of all religious laws of the kind that have ever been made since the Christian era began.

Reflect a moment how cruel it is, to fine a town or parish for not having a teacher, when none but God can make them teachers; and that those who are sent of God to preach, feel a necessity to preach, not only without the support of law, but in opposition thereto, obeying God rather than man.

It is so strange a thing, that in Massachusetts, where the people are so conversant with the New Testament, they should make and submit to such laws, that if I did not know it to be a fact, I would not believe a report of it.

There are three reasons offered, why religion should be established by the laws of men, viz:

First, *To prevent error.*

Second, *To effect and preserve uniformity of sentiment.*

Third, *To support the Gospel.*

I believe that all the arguments used in favor of such establishments, may be included in these three general heads. Some observations on each of them shall here be made.

First, To prevent error.

Have legal establishments done this? When did error prevail less, and when did truth prevail more than in the three first centuries of the Christian era? In no date since has truth prevailed and error fled as fast as in the above mentioned time; yet all this was before the Christian religion was established by law. Has not error fled as fast before truth in Pennsylvania, New Jersey, New York and Rhode Island, in which states there never have been such establishments, as in the other states? Further, is not ruth as well understood, and error as fully detected now, in the twelve other states, as in the four New-England states, where religion is supposed o be a principle of state policy, and ministers of the gospel creatures of the state? It is certain that the establishment of paganism, as truth, did not prevent the *error* of Christianity; nor did the establishment of Rome prevent the *error* of the reformation, in the sixteenth century, nor the late revolutions in papal countries, in the close of the eighteenth century. The establishment of the English church did not hinder the *error* of nonconformity, nor has the establishment of Massachusetts stopped the rise of a number of errors and sects in the state.* It is a fact, in the United States, that, in those twelve states where there are no religious establishments, there are not more sects or sentiments, than there are in the four states where such horned beasts dwell.

I now ask what proof can be given, that religious establishments prevent error?

Second, To effect uniformity. This is a counterpart of the first, and therefore the arguments there used, if reversed, will be applicable here; but I shall add something more. How easy it is for men to be deceived about the uniformity of sentiment in an empire. Dioclesian, who began and carried on the tenth persecution against the Christians, in the Roman empire, prevailed so far, that he struck a golden medal, with this inscription, "The Christian name is extirpated from the earth, and the worship of the Gods restored." Here he exulted in uniformity of religious opinions, but how great was his deception! for, within a few years, it appeared evident, that a majority of the empire, with Constantine at their head, were Christians. It is said, that in the days of Charles the first, of England, the kingdom seemed to be full of flattering addresses to his Majesty; but that there was pretty general discontent appears from the tumults which soon arose, which cost Charles his crown and the head that wore it.

Under the regal government of Virginia, the Episcopal religion was there established and conducted with all the force of law; but as soon as the revolution gave men a chance to speak freely, it appeared that two-thirds of the people were dissenters. In the great kingdom of France, the hierarchy of Rome triumphed in all its pontifical effulgence; but no sooner had they an opportunity to speak what they thought, than they convinced the astonished world that they were not uniform in the belief of the infallibility of the Pope. And I here ask, has the legal force that has been used in the four New England states, advanced men one inch towards uniformity?

In order for a uniformity in religion to be established by force, there must be a creed established by law, to measure, shape, and weigh the consciences of the people by. Now who shall frame this important creed? I presume there are a thousand different creeds in the Christian world; they cannot all be right, they may all be wrong. If we consider that all men are fallible, liable to err, it will not be illiberal to say, that some imperfec-

* In these remarks, every sentiment is called an error, that does not accord with the established creed.

tion is to be found in all of them. I question whether there now is, or ever was, a body of men, or an individual, who should coolly compose a creed of faith, or in short, a constitution of government, or code of laws, but who, upon examining the same once a year, would annually see cause to alter some parts thereof. Such is the school that men are in, such the theatre on which they act, so many the objects that pass before them, that he who says he never alters his mind, evidently declares that he is either very weak or very stubborn. Shall human creeds then, mixed at least with imperfection, be made a standard to measure the conscience by, which is God's vice-gerent in the human breast?

That the late law of Massachusetts is a religious creed, admits of no doubt, because it describes the character of religious teachers, and fines religious bodies from thirty to one hundred dollars, every six months, if they do not have such teachers. The question, therefore, is, whether the legislature of the commonwealth is infallible? This court has been perpetually making and altering religious laws, from the first settlement of Boston down to the present day. If all those laws, previous to that of March, 1801, were infallible, then the last law was fallible, for it differs from all before; if the last was infallible, the former were imperfect, and while things are thus, it is doubtful whether there is much divinity in any of them. If, therefore, infallibility is not claimed by the legislature of Massachusetts, it has no more right to make religious laws than other similar bodies: consequently all legislatures have a right to make such laws, or none of them have. If all of them have such right, then the Pagan legislatures had it when they established the worship of the gods, and made provision for the priests, and the apostles and first Christians were guilty of a criminal schism. The same is true of all the Mahometan, Papal and Protestant hierarchies, that have been, or now are, and consequently all the legal persecution for conscience sake, that has been in the world, is justifiable, and all the sufferings that have been from that source have arisen from the stubbornness and self-will of the sufferers.

But if no legislature has a right to make such creeds, and yet some creed must be established, to effect a state uniformity in religion, then it follows that legislatures have a right to do what they have no right to do—to effect that which they never can effect. But,

Third. To support the Gospel. That is, to raise money by law, equalized upon all the people, for the purposes of building meeting-houses, paying preachers, etc. Building temples for religious worship seems to be a prudential thing, and rewarding preachers for their labors of love, is both reasonable and scriptural; but the question is, whether this money is to be collected by *legal force* or *moral obligation*. If by legal force, then the principle is supported, that the cause of God is to be directed and supported by the laws of man, and, of course, all the persecutions mentioned before, are justifiable. The people of Massachusetts boast of their religious knowledge; to them I appeal. Pray tell me where Jesus, or the apostles, ever called upon the rulers of state to make any laws to oblige people to part with their money to hire preachers or build meeting-houses. I am serious; I am in earnest: if our present edition is not complete, search the original, and put your finger on the passage. I have not yet seen it, and until I do, I shall call all such laws anti-scriptural and anti-Christian.

How often have I wished, that when rulers undertake to make laws about religion, they would complete the code—not only make provision for building meeting-houses, paying preachers, and forcing people to hear them, but also to enjoin on the hearers, repentance, faith, self-denial, love to God and love to man—that every one who did not repent of his sin, should pay five pounds—that all those who did not believe, should pay ten pounds—that every soul who did not deny himself, and take up his cross daily, should pay fifteen pounds—that whoever did not love God with all his heart, should be imprisoned a year—and that if a man did not love his neighbor as himself, he should be confined for life.

That all these duties are taught in the New Testament is certain; if, therefore, the laws of man are to enjoin moral duties, these important ones should not be neglected: but, on only hearing of them, our minds are struck with the absurdity of reducing them to civil legislation and jurisprudence, and had not the poison of anti-christ infected the minds of men, they would be equally struck with the idea of making human laws about any religious article.

It follows, then, that the money necessary in the Christian cause, is to be raised by moral obedience.

The gods of Egypt could not speak for themselves, and therefore Pharaoh spoke for them, and made a law to assign the priests a portion, by which means they saved their lands in the seven years of famine. Baal was asleep and could not provide for his prophets, and therefore Jezebel fed them at her table; but Jehovah, being a living God, made a law for the maintenance of the priests in the Mosaic economy, but he never empowered magistrates to execute that law. It was a *divine* and not a *human* law, and when the people neglected it, they had to answer to God and not to man. And when two of those priests grew lordly and said, "thou shalt give us now, and if not we will take it by force," their sin was great, and they were both slain in one day. Even so has the Lord ordained in the New Testament, that those who preach the gospel should live of it. God has ordained it, but has not ordained that rulers should enforce it. Whenever, therefore, money is given for religious purposes, it is given in obedience to the law of God, and not in obedience to the laws of men: I mean when it is *rightly* given.

The word *religion*, properly signifies *to bind again:* sin has rent us off from God, and rent our hearts from virtue, but religion binds up the breach, turns our hearts to God, and our minds to virtue. Religion may be considered as comprised in three parts: first, internal; second, practical; third, social. Internal religion, is a right exercise of soul towards God and man. By practical religion, I mean those righteous external actions, which men, as individuals, perform towards God and their fellow-creatures. Social religion includes the various duties of religious society.

All the gold and property of the world cannot purchase religion, and yet the practical and social parts of religion have never been executed without money, or its worth, from the days of Abel to the present time. They cost Abel his lambs, and the patriarchs their beasts: the nation of Israel had a religion, very expensive, and the Christian church have administered much for the cause of their God. The nation of Israel received their orders from God, and the Christian church from the mouth of Him, who has been faithful in all his house, as a son. And the same spirit that influences men to love God, and their neighbors, also influences them to give willingly to those who preach the word, and for other necessary uses. Legal force is here inadmissible.

I have said before, that the times, places, and manner of worshipping God, were inalienable rights, not subject to legal control. What holy-days soever God has appointed in his word, each individual must judge for himself, and be fully persuaded in his own mind, and act accordingly, as each must give an account of himself to God. But no legislature, uninspired by the Holy Ghost, has any right to appoint fixed sabbaths, or decades for religious purposes, and bind the people to observe said days.

A legislature that believes in the Christian system, and from that system believes that one day in seven is to be kept holy, have just as good a right, and no better, to make a law to force all the people whom they legislate for, to observe those days, as another legislature has, who believe in the god of reason, and from thence deduce, that one day in ten should be a decade, and force all the people within their power, to worship the god of reason on those decades.

Nor is it within the legitimate power of civil government, to direct the place where men shall publicly worship their God. To fine a man because he does not attend worship at a definite place, definite times, is illegitimate, and to force men to build temples for public worship, against their consent, is a piece of religious oppression, and yet this act is carried on, with all deceivable arts and force, in this commonwealth. In the year 1800, about six hundred dollars were taken from the Baptists, in Partridgefield, for the building of a meeting-house in said town, for another denomination. The case is now in law, hung up, and what the event will be, we know not. But abundance of property, heretofore, has been taken in the same way, for similar purposes, within this commonwealth, and no redress has ever been granted.

The *manner* of worshipping God comes next in course. If it is a truth, as has been suggested, that the design of government is only to protect the life, liberty and property of the community; and if religion is, at all times and places, a matter between God and individuals, and also, that religious opinions are not objects of civil government, nor under its control, it then follows that government has no right to describe the god which the people are to worship. The reason why legislators and legislatures have forced the people to worship Lama, Osiris, Jupiter Ammon, Bel, Baal, etc., is because they professedly believed those gods to be the most deserving; and the same is true of Christian legislatures, in obliging people to worship that god whom they prefer. Now, where an empire is composed of Heathens, Turks, Jews, and Christians, how cruel it must be to all those whose consciences cannot be formed, like a nose of wax, into that form of adoration which the legislature esteems best. Whose life is in danger—whose liberty is curtailed—whose property is destroyed—by considering each individual inalienably free to worship the god whom he esteems the most deserving, in the way which he judges to be the most acceptable to him?

Perhaps an objector may say, "these observations are not applicable to Massachusetts, where the people generally believe in the Holy One of Israel, and in the divinity of the Christian scheme. That the people of this state generally believe in the Holy One of Israel, may pass for truth, but that they generally believe in the divinity of the Christian scheme is not so true. As a religionist, I wish both articles were believed through this state, and throughout the world; yet, as a statesman, let me ask, why do they not learn to imitate their God, and regarding the scheme of his government, in which they professedly believe, reason thus with themselves: "God bears with wicked men, and so must we: God does not force all to believe alike, nor should we attempt it: Jesus never forced any man to pay him for preaching, and we must imitate him. The New Testament never calls in the aid of the magistrate to carry folks to prison, or take away their cows, or other property, to pay men for preaching, or build temples, and therefore, we will not. The apostles never taught the churches, which they planted, to be incorporated bodies politic, to make use of the civil law to regulate their concerns, nor will we. The New Testament nowhere says, that towns, parishes, precincts, etc., shall have a teacher of morality, piety and religion, three months in six, or pay a fine of sixty dollars, and, therefore, we will have no such laws. The New Testament churches were formed by the laws of Jesus, and the acts of the apostles only, and so it shall be among us." These observations show, that men wish to avil themselves of the advantages of religion, without regarding the laws thereof.

I now return to the chain of the argument, to show that the manner of worshipping God is not under legal control.

Those who call themselves Christians have but a contemptible opinion of Christ, if they call in question the sufficiency of the New Testament to govern the churches in all places, at all times, and in all cases. If he was infallible, infinitely wise, and universally good, his laws must be tantamount to the exigencies of his disciples in every circumstance; but if this is called in question, let his followers live up to all the rules which he has given, and see if there is any want. It is observable that those who live the most according to the New Testament, make the least complaint of its deficiency. After all, if it still is maintained that there is a deficiency in the New Testament, who is to supply that deficiency? Not ecclesiastical officers; for they are not to be lords over God's heritage. Not civil rulers; for, in their official capacity, they have nothing to do with religion. Let those who attempt it remember one text: "If any man shall *add* unto the words of this book, God shall add unto him the plagues therein written."

If the constitution of government for Massachusetts is all divine, I confess that civil officers have this right; for it is so expressed in the third article of the bill of rights. But where do they get this right? Our rulers have no power but what they receive from the people, and the whole body of the people, in aggregate, have no power but what is found in small constituent parts among the individuals. Now, if each individual has a little of this right to force his neighbor to worship God, when, where, and as he pleases, then, by adding all these little parts together, in the representative body, the legislature has that right; otherwise, it has not.

Supposing there should be fifty religious sects under one government, and each sect should build temples as they please, to worship the God whom they adore, in the manner which they believe most pleasing to him, I ask, who is injured by this free variety? If all these sects are uniform in the support of the government for its proper uses, what danger is the state in? None are injured, the state is in no danger, but all would be friendly to that government which secured them in their liberty.

This seems to be the happiest state that a nation can be in, so far as it respects government; yet it is possible that difficulties might arise, from two sources, viz., mobs, and legal process. One of these sects might arise in a mob, and rob, confine, or kill others. Here then is work for the magistrates; the lives, liberties, and property of the people are destroyed, which the government was formed and supported to protect. Whether this lawless sect should plead that they were influenced by their God, or by the devil, or neither of them, it would not alter their case in the least; for the court would not judge of their motives, but of their actions. Governments, where religion is established by law, do not escape such evils.

The other difficulty might arise in this wise:—One of these sects being ambitious, and fearing the importance of the rest, might make use of art to flatter the officers of state, to bestow partial favors on them, and, finally, establish the religion which they esteem, as the religion of the state.

When this is done, peace, confidence in each other, and respect for government, take their flight. If the depressed party retain any patriotism, contention, imprisonment, confiscation, war and bloodshed will follow; if they have no spirit of patriotism, they sink into ignorance, vassalage and misery. Here let it be noticed, that these last evils did not arise in the supposed government, in its pristine state of religious liberty, but after it had apostatized into a state of established religion.

If the manner of worshipping God is not under legal control, then for religious societies to be forced by law to have a teacher among them, at least half the time, is an abridgment of religious liberty.

The golden rule is: "Do unto *all men* as you would they should do unto you." If Christians were in Turkey or Algiers, would they not wish to enjoy the liberty of their consciences without control? Would they not say, in their hearts at least, "We wish to be freed from paying the Turkish priests, and supporting the Turkish religion, which is only an imposture, and that we might be respected according to our conduct, while we enjoy our religious opinions, as an inalienable right?" If so, then let them grant these favors, or rather, let them not deprive others of these rights, or give up the name of Christians.

I shall now proceed to offer a number of reasons why religious laws and test oaths should never be woven into constitutions, or mixed with the laws of state.

First. It makes a constitution, or statute law book, look more like a catechism than a rule of political life. Some have placed Apocrypha in the Bible, where it should not be; but, in this case, religion becomes prostitute among the laws of state.

Second. It makes the opinions of fallible men, the test of orthodoxy for all the people. View such laws in the most favorable light, they are but the opinions of their makers; and shall the judgment of one man in a thousand, be the rule for the faith and worship of the whole thousand?

Third. A religious establishment, reduces religion to a level with the principles of state policy, and turns officers of the church into ministers of state.

Fourth. It holds forth a tempting bait to men to embrace *that* religion which is pampered by the law, without searching after truth conscientiously.

Fifth. It checks all rational conviction of the errors in the national creed; for if those errors are arrested and condemned by a man, he must be proscribed and legally persecuted.

Sixth. It raises the uniformists to arrogance and superiority, and sinks the non-conformists into disgrace and depression; and, thereby, destroys that confidence and friendly equality, which is essential to the happiness of any state.

Seventh. It creates and upholds a power, which Jesus Christ has never ordained, either for the civil or ecclesiastical department.

Eighth. It tends to keep people in ignorance. By implicitly believing what the ruler and the priest says, they give up their own judgments, and suppose it is a crime to think and speak for themselves.

Ninth. It is the parent of all the legal persecution, for conscience sake, that has been on earth, and has drenched the world in blood.

Tenth. It is every way calculated to destroy those peaceable, harmless, amiable qualities among men, which religion, in its simplicity, inculcates.

Eleventh. It tends to make Deists, and support infidelity, more than any one cause. Nothing tends so much to convince candid spectators, that there is nothing in a religion, as to see the disciples of that religion inattentive to its rules. I will here confine myself to the Christian religion. It is confessed by all, in our land, that the precepts of the New Testament exceed everything that ever appeared among men, of the kind. The common failings of the professed followers of Christ, greatly weaken the faith of serious inquirers; but, when those who profess to be his greatest friends, break over all the bounds of justice, humanity and pity; and, because they have the power in their hands, will proscribe, imprison, banish, rob, hang, and burn all those who differ with them in judgment; and all this, under pretence of serving the meek, harmless, just, holy and compassionate *Prince of Peace*; what strong arguments these are to convince men, who are not void of all humanity, that the religion of Jesus is only a mask to cover the most atrocious crimes that ever were committed.

It is no wonder to me to see so many literary characters—so many men of great information and candor, in the world, so strongly beset with infidelity. The chief, if not all that they have seen, which is called religion, is nothing but haughtiness and cruelty; and to see men, under religious pretences, do those things that common sense blushes at, must cast a deadly aspect on that which they say authorises them to do those things.

In Masssachusetts, the religious laws oblige people to hire preachers, and build meeting-houses; yet there have been some laws, which exempted some of the people, under certain restrictions. But is there a single article in the state, in which so much deceit, fraud, and cruelty have been used, as in the article of religion? How often have ministerial taxes been mixed with town taxes, that the man taxed might pay the ministerial tax without knowing it? How often have men, who have made use of the law to draw their money back, been flung out of it, under one pretence or another? and if they have gained their cause, being in the town, they have had their proportionate part of the costs to pay. How many times towns have hired ministers to preach, not being ordained over them; and if the dissenters have been exempted from paying the stipulated salary, yet the charge of the committee, and the boarding of the priests, have been put into the town rate. Where meeting-houses are built for one society to worship in alone, because the house is in a town, and sometimes used for town meetings, what specious arguments are made use of to make all pay for building them. Can an honest man look on all this, and much more, and not feel his heart rise with indignation against that religion which gives birth to all this? The late destruction of the king's evil, and especially of the plague of priestcraft, has made a great noise in the world. Established clergymen take the alarm, and, like the merchants and captains, cry, alas! alas! our craft is in danger. The ministers of the established religion, in Massachusetts, are greatly alarmed at the growth of infidelity in France, and use all their art to prevent French influence in America. Reverend gentleman, if you wish to stop the spread of Deism, seek to remove the cause. Come forth upon the plan of the gospel, and trust God and his word for your support. Renounce the scheme that Mr. Cotton first introduced in Massachusetts, to support preachers by law; and let it never be said, that a cow, or a dollar, or a cent, is taken from any widow, or man, by the constable, to complete your salaries, or pay for your temples. Convince the world that the religion of Jesus will stand upon its own basis, without law or sword; so will you contribute more for the destruction of Deism, than all the arguments of Leland, Lock, Addison, Steel, Tennys, Wesley or Gill; or of those later writers, Watson, Winchester, Ogden, and the Mendon Association, etc.; but

To these a twelfth clause may be added. Religious tests, required by law, to qualify men for state offices, is a main pillar of state-established religion, and a curse to a nation. Bishop White observes, that the articles and forms of the Church of England, had passed through a great number of alterations, from the days of Queen Elizabeth. One month they solemnly declare that they believe all and every thing therein contained, and swear to support them; the next month they alter these forms, and then declare and swear as before, and so on. This is trifling with oaths at a shocking rate. Test oaths are calculated to make hypocrites, effect perjuries, and keep from office the best of men. Sychophants and hopocrites will take any oath to obtain offices; but honest men will not; their firmness and talents entitle them to the confidence of the people; but because they cannot believe what they cannot believe, and will not swear that they believe what they do not believe, they are kept from office, and the people are deprived of their services.

The constitutional test of Massachusetts is, protestant Christianity. Every denomination of christians peaceably demeaning themselves, shall be protected by law; and provision is to be made for protestant teachers.

Jews, Turks, Pagans and Deists, are not to be protected by law, and no kind of Christian teachers can have legal provision made for them, except they are protestants. From this we learn that the government of Massachusets, is a protestant Christian government. The same cannot be said of our national government; nor of several of the state governments; and it is a pity that it should be said of any of them, for no body politic can form a Christian government and administer the same, without breaking the rules of pure Christianity.

How much better the constitution of this commonwealth would read, if it was thus formed, "All men peaceably demeaning themselves, shall be protected by law, in worshiping the Deity according to the dictates of their consciences; but the sentiments and creeds of none of them shall be protected by law, but be left to argument and free debate for their support; nor shall there be any provision made by law for any teachers of religion, nor any religious test required, to qualify an officer for any department of government."

Some circumstances that I am personally acquainted with, may add confirmation to the doctrine contended for in these pages. The Episcopal party, in Virginia, was paramount, in law, to all others in the state, anterior to the revolution. The Presbyterians, as well as the Baptists, had to pay obeisance to that party. In the year 1776, the work began, to set all societies on a level; but it was twenty-two years before it was finished. During these twenty-two years there were many debates in the Legislature. In the year 1786, Mr. Zachariah Johnson, of Augusta, made the following speech in the assembly, when the house was in committee of the whole, on the state of the Commonwealth: "Mr. Chairman, I am a Presbyterian, a rigid Presbyterian, as we are called; my parents before me were of the same profession; I was educated in that line. Since I became a man, I have examined for myself, and I have seen no cause to dissent. But, sir, the very day that the Presbyterians shall be established by law, and become a body politic, the same day Zachariah Johnson will be a dissenter. Dissent from that *religion* I cannot, in honesty, but from that establishment I will." While I lived in Virginia, and heard such speeches, I used to wish that they might be heard by the Presbyterians in Massachusetts. In 1780, Col. J. Innis spoke as follows: "Gentlemen, I wish that religion may be as free as the air in which we breathe, as uncontrolled as the waters of the boundless sea; that it might extend to the Heavens, to which it tends, and with one universal embrace, within its fostering arms, enclose all the progeny of Adam." How noble! How evangelical such speeches sound, when once compared with the little pigmy *shall bes* and *shall not bes* of Massachusetts.

I close my address, by adding, that in the beginning of the eighteenth century, there were no more than fifteen Baptist churches within the limits of the United States; but now at the beginning of the nineteenth century, there are twelve hundred, which include about eighty thousand members, among whom are between eleven and twelve hundred preachers.

I have not documents sufficient to state the number of communicants belonging to any other order among us precisely; but very much question whether the Presbyterians and Congregationalists together, throughout the nation, can produce an equal number of churches, members or ministers, notwithstanding what Dr. Styles has published in his election sermon, and Dr. Morse hints at in his geography. I mean not to boast of numbers, but love to see truth published.

Finally, gentlemen, we have great cause of thanksgiving on this public fast; what wonders has nature's God been doing in America, in the course of twenty-five years. A vast empire, of sixteen United States, has risen out of a number of feeble, depressed colonies. These states, from being in a feeble band of confederacy, have formed one national government, which, like a Colossus, is above the whole; at the same time guaranteeing to each its proper sovereignty. But ah! the lust of power and importance! Designs to screen men and measures from public animidversion; forsaking the good old simple maxims of republicanism, and adopting the maxims of monarchical courts, have crept into our councils. During this period, the genius of America has been slumbering and sleeping, while from the presses and pulpits, we have been alarmed with the undescribable hobgoblins of illuminatism. But heaven above looked down, and awakened the American genius, which has arisen, like a lion, from the swelling of Jordon, and roared like thunder in the states, "we will be free; we will rule ourselves; our officers shall be honorable servants, but not mean masters."

This exertion of the American genius, has brought forth the *Man of the People*, the defender of the rights of man and the rights of conscience, to fill the chair of state; who, in his inaugural speech, cries out, "America, be free, be happy, guard your own rights, and leave them not to the disposition of officers."

Pardon me, my hearers, if I am over-warm. I lived in Virginia fourteen years. The beneficent influence of my hero was too generally felt to leave me a stoic. What may we not expect, under the auspices of heaven, while JEFFERSON presides, with *Madison* in state by his side. Now the greatest orbit in America is occupied by the brightest orb: but, sirs, expect to see religious bigots, like cashiered officers, and displaced statesmen, growl and gnaw their galling bands, and, like a yelping mastiff, bark at the moon, whose rising they cannot prevent.

Let us then adore that God who has been so favorable to our land, and nation—praise him for all that is past—trust him for all that is to come, and not ascribe that to man which is due to God alone.

AN

ORATION,

DELIVERED AT

CHESHIRE, JULY 5, 1802,

ON THE

CELEBRATION OF INDEPENDENCE:

CONTAINING

SEVENTEEN SKETCHES,

AND

SEVENTEEN WISHES.

ORATION, &c.

GENTLEMEN:

The creation of the world, the deluge of the earth, the deliverance of Israel from Egypt, the founding of Rome, the birth of Christ, the flight of Mahomet, and other important events, have given rise to certain eras, from which dates have been fixed, ceremonies instituted, and days appointed to perpetuate the remembrance of those interesting events.

The revolution of America has been an event which, (simply as a human revolution,) has promised more for the cause of humanity, and the rights of man, than any revolution that can be named.

The revolution of France yet hangs in awful suspense; whether that enterprising people are to gain anything at last, after all their unparalleled exploits, except the change of riders, either in the civil or ecclesiastical department, is very uncertain, according to present appearances. Should it finally terminate on the side of liberty, and right, still the change in America, may be considered as the first vital spring of that reform. Their alliance and communication with Americans, enkindled the spark of liberty among them, which had long been covered with the ashes of despotism, and superstition.

The American revolution, therefore, may be justly esteemed the returning dawn of long lost liberty, and the world's best hope. Here the people decide their controversies by their voices, and not by the cannon's awful roar—by small pieces of paper, and not by the instruments of death. Here our chief magistrate resides in his house, and rides abroad without a guard of armed soldiers; being shielded by the affections of the people. Well may the day be celebrated on which the iron bands were broken, and liberty to America was proclaimed. Well may the man be viewed in an endearing point of light, who drew the declaration, and fills the highest post of honor and trust.

To-day this august assembly have convened to reflect on the past and the present condition of this growing empire; and in order to assist that reflection, I shall submit the following sketches.

First. When the much admired policy of Britain had sunk the nation into a debt of two hundred and eighty millions sterling, she claimed the right of governing the trade of America for her own profit, and of taxing the American colonies at pleasure, without the consent of colonial representatives. To force the Americans to this subjection, their ships and troops were sent to our coasts, to burn our towns, and shed our blood. America had nothing to plead but her right, and the help of her God. Twenty-six years, this very day, have elapsed, since that instrument was formed, (the Declaration of Independence,) which separated the United States from Great Britain, her policy, her debts, and her fate. This just, modest, bold, decent declaration, was made at a time when the British lion was roaring on our sea-coasts, and the war-hoop and hatchet were infesting our frontiers. Feeble and presumptious as the United States appeared to foreign nations, yet, after a seven years' struggle, they gained the point for which they fought; and Britain lost the American empire, and augmented her debt to three hundred and twenty millions. Since that period, by their splendid victories, their debt has been increased to seven hundred millions. Were the United States at this time British colonies, add the five millions in America, to the twelve millions of Great Britain and Ireland, and the debt equally distributed among all ages and sexes, would be about one hundred and eighty dollars per soul, or nine dollars for every finger, and every toe. This debt, in silver, would amount to more than ninety-six thousand and seventy-eight wagons would carry, allowing a ton to each wagon,* which would fill the road in a string about nine hundred miles, allowing three rods to each wagon.

Second. But to return; during the seven years' struggle, there were some such manifest interpositions of divine Providence, that to pass them by in silence, would be a crime. In the middle states, the scene at Trenton is one. The American army was reduced to a handful; the British had but little to obstruct them; and to all appearance, the cause of America was lost. But, behold, the scale turned in a short time. The Hessians became prisoners—the British generals were foiled—Princeton felt the prowess of American troops—the spirit of America revived, and hope gleamed through the land. Let our chief commander have his due—let the troops have their reward; but give unto the God of armies the ultimate praise.

Third. In the northern states, the check at Bennington, and the conquest at Saratoga, were most notable. Burgoyne, with the flower of the British army, had pushed his conquests from Quebec to Skeensborough, and all things bid fair for him to establish a line of posts from Canada to the city of New York, and thereby cut off all communication between the southern and eastern states. A detachment from the main army was sent to Bennington, near which place they were met by Americans and defeated. The scene was tragical. While the roads were crowded on one side by the inhabitants, fleeing for their lives, they were occupied on the

* This calculation is made upon the scale of £3 sterling being 1 *lb.* Troy; and 17 *lb.* Troy are equal to 14 *lb.* Avoirdupois.

other side by the militia, flying to meet the foe. The defeat, near Bennington, was soon followed by the surrender of the whole army, at Saratoga. Those who never look beyond second causes, may ascribe the glory to Warner, Barnum, Stark, Arnold, Lincoln, or Gates, but those who believe in the superintendence of Providence, will render the glory to America's God.

Fourth. The southern states exhibit a like picture. Charlestown was taken and in possession of the Britons—Gates was defeated at Camden—the enterprising Tarlton flew over the Carolinas like an Eagle—the tories were numerous and vindictive. But soon a change took place. King's Mountain seems to have been a pivot, on which the scale turned, after which, the defeat of Tarlton, at the Cowpens, took place. How nearly the prisoners taken by Morgan were retaken, and how singularly they were twice secured from Cornwallis, by the swell of the rivers, is remarkable. After this, Cornwallis dearly bought a piece of ground at Guilford, with British blood, which yet he could not hold, but abandoned his post, and, with a circuitous route, came into Virginia, and left the Carolinas as a field for Greene to display his military skill in, who, in a short space, cleared those states of every Briton, and silenced every tory. After Cornwallis had traversed a considerable part of Virginia, he took his stand at Yorktown. Several things appeared providential at this place. First, Degrass came into the Chesapeake with a French fleet, so that his lordship could not retreat with his vessels. Second, when he attempted to cross York River, to escape by land, if possible, a remarkable storm of wind prevented him. Third, during the siege, in that sickly season of the year, had the rains been as usual, it is highly probable, that great death would have been in the camp, but not one drop of rain fell during the whole siege.

"Ye clouds of heaven distil no rain,
The great Jehovah said,
'Till haughty Britons all are slain,
Or bow the stubborn head."

Soon after his capture, proposals were made, and preliminaries of peace were drawn, which were finally ratified. America was now acknowledged as an independent republic, composed of democracies in confederation, to hold rank among the nations of the world.

Fifth. Since that memorable era, in 1783, America has experienced two semi-revolutions. In the time of the contest, the support of the army and securing the independence of the states, absorbed almost all things, but when the contest closed, it was found that the articles of confederation, were entirely too lax to secure those blessings that were bought with blood. Hence arose the necessity of altering the political system. This reform of police, established a national government in all its parts, restricted however to certain specified articles. In these articles, where the national government was to operate, it was complete: legislative, executive, and judiciary powers were contained in its provisions. And on all other objects, each state retained its sovereignty. This change was effected without war or bloodshed, and without any alarming confusion, and renders memorable the year 1788.

Sixth. Nothing is more common than to see parties in governments. The *ins*, generally, are grasping after more power, while the *outs* are complaining of oppression. Deprive an *in* of his office, and he cries out, "the church and state are ruined." Put an *out* into office, and government grows better and better every day. These remarks are too often verified, but very far from being universally true. In America, where land is abundant, and labor very lucrative, the temptation to be in office greatly decreases. There are few, if any gifts or offices in these states, (considering the necessary drawbacks,) which exceed the profits of labor. It is, therefore, reasonable to suppose, that there is a greater proportion in America, who form their judgment of government from reason, and not from interest, than is the case in Europe. Yet, in these states, men of equal talents and opportunities, have, and still do differ in opinion, and this difference is so radical, that the two parties have lately appealed to the sovereign people to decide the controversy, which has effected a kind of revolution.

Seventh. When men in private life or public office err, in rare instances, charity will cast a veil over those errors; but when the fixed course of conduct is wrong, neither charity nor candor should be silent; even granting that while they pursue the course of error, they sometimes hit upon that which is right. That our national administration, for several years anterior to March, 1801, was wrong in its career, admits of no doubt in my mind. Notwithstanding the immense sums collected by external and internal taxes, yet the debt increased. An army and navy were raised, when there was no more prospect of war, than there is at the present moment. And that rigor and distinction, which has cursed the old world, cast a malignant aspect upon the new. Had the ruling party been forty years, instead of four, in making their advances on the rights, liberties and purses of the people, they might have gained their point; but happily for us, they sung lullaby too loud, and startled the drowsy child before it was fast asleep.

If we compare our present administration, with what preceded for several years, we shall see economy instead of extravagance—saving in the room of wasting—diminishing taxes and not increasing them—lessening salaries and not swelling them—recalling foreign agents, and not sending them where they can be of no service—disannulling useless courts and not creating them for their own profit, when they have nothing to do—a regard for the rights of the people, and not a design to trick them out of their native blessing—freeing labor, as much as possible, from burthens—securing the liberty of speech and the liberty of the press, instead of the reverse, etc. When these things are considered, we may, with propriety say, "that the late chauge has been as radical in its tendency, as that which took place in 1776." And that these things have taken place, is undeniable: confessed by all, except those who are determined to confess nothing good, but what accords with their high notions of aristocracy.

Eighth. There is a foible among men, expressed by the words, "*I told you so.*" When any occurrence turns up, if a man can say, "I told you so," he supposes he establishes his character as a man of sagacity and forecast. The high toned party have been telling us for several years, that themselves were the only friends of our government—that the Republicans complained, on purpose, to get the ins out and get in themselves—that, should it be the case, there would be no more economy in government—no lessening of taxes—no sinking of the debt: they are therefore determined not to believe that there is any change for the better, for if they believe it, they cannot preach, "I told you so."

It looks as if every friend of his country would rejoice to see that debt, which was created to gain our independence, honestly and wholly paid. While Britain boasts that her credit is good, let the boast of America be, that she has *no creditors.*

Ninth. If editors of newspapers were genuine friends to their country, they would be fair and impartial, but such papers are rare, hence the readers of them are duped to party zeal. There are but a few men in the states, who have access to the official documents, or the laws that are enacted, except what teem through party gazettes, where they are so mutilated and commented upon, that the readers are biased and held in ignorance. Jackalls hunt the prey for the Lions, by whom they are rewarded with the offal, so some printers are hunting for their employers, by whom they are supported.

Tenth. The federal party are constantly exclaiming that the republicans are all deists, or if not, yet they all unite to undermine religion, law, steady habits and good order. Let these charges be fairly examined. The federal party includes the old tories—those who admire a state-established religion, and a few others. The republican class contains those who fought, not only to be independent of Britain, but also from that policy which governs her—those who contend for the civil and religious rights of all men, and some beside. As Deism is an opinion about religion, and not so much connected with government, the Deists might be left out of the question. However, as they are not omitted, they shall here be considered. The federalists and Deists agree in one point, viz: they both believe that if Christianity is not protected by law, it will fall to the ground. But then they disagree in their wishes: the federalists wish that what they call Christianity, may stand, but the Deists wish it might fall. The republicans and Deists agree in the counterpart, viz., that it would be delivering the world from one of its greatest curses, to have all legal establishments of religion abolished: but their conclusions are diametrically opposed to each other. Republicans believe that pure Christianity would gain much by such a dissolution, but the Deists suppose it would utterly fall. As for a religion of cruelty, laws to enforce it, and the steady habits of persecution, the republicans do wish to undermine them, and if Deists unite with them in this wish, they are so far right. It is true, there are some who call themselves republicans, who suppose that religion is an object of civil government, and under its control, but such men hold with the hare and run with the hound, and how they can reconcile the business of fighting with the dog, and whipping the cat, at the same time, I know not.

It is almost enough to tickle sobriety itself, to hear the clamor of some of the federalists about good order and religion, when, at the same time, their disorder is such, as to be no great commendation to any religion: so peacocks raise their shining feathers, but walk on shameful feet. It almost makes us believe, that they are conscious of their sins and dangers, and, therefore, wish others to have religion to prevent their own damnation: so a man once gave his parson a guinea a year, that he himself might freely swear.

Eleventh. The late marvellous work of God in Kentucky, has been echoed through federal and republican papers: it is well attested, and cause of rejoicing. There are, in that State, four Baptist Associations; to one of them, (the Elkhorn,) three thousand and eleven joined in one year, and I have pretty good authority to say, that as many as ten thousand joined in all the Associations, besides the vast numbers that joined the Methodists and Presbyterians. But what shall we say to these things? Kentucky was settled at first upon the plan of religious liberty, like Pennsylvania and Rhode-Island, and has continued so until the present time. Kentucky has been a democratic state, and boldly cried out against the measures of the late administration. Kentucky had no laws to support *teachers of piety, morality, and religion*, and yet the Lord of Heaven has blessed them marvellously. That God blesses sinners, is acknowledged with humble praise, but when he blesses them with his grace, he makes them virtuous, and that this change has been evident in Kentucky, is owned by all. How then comes it to pass, that Kentucky is still a democratic, disorganizing, unconstitutional state? Mr. Brackenridge is a senator from Kentucky, and the whole representation of that state is democratical. We are, therefore, reduced to the necessity of believing that democrats can be religious, or that the accounts of the great reform in Kentucky are all false. Can there be an instance given where there has been a like display of God's power in any state in the Union, which has left the people as generally federalists?

Twelfth. Under the late administration, if a man called in question the constitutionality, or expediency of any law or measure, he was charged with irreligion and sedition, but now, forsooth, it is become virtuous to condemn all that is done by government. Some say, that if the President had acted according to his inaugural speech, they should have had nothing to object; but I know not of an instance wherein he has transgressed the sentiments of that speech. Had he retained all the officers which he found in office, he would have disappointed that majority which promoted him, and likewise committed himself to the opposition party, to reproach him for being too cowardly to change men or measures, or stick to his friends. The truth is, the federal *ins* made their calculations to be eternal *ins*, and those three letters, o, u, t, have been made a handle of to raise a mighty fog. Notwithstanding several millions of dollars have been saved and appropriated to the payment of the debt, yet they condemn, because they were determined to condemn, the present administration.

Thirteenth. The late session of Congress has dismissed about five hundred officers, by the modification of the judiciary and the dismissal of the internal taxes. While other Congresses, and the former administration, talked about economy and sinking the debt, the present reduce those words to practice. Can the citizens of the United States be so blind to their interest, as to reprobate the only line of conduct, which can make and keep them a free people? They cannot—they will not. The President wishes to have the discretionary power of the executive department limited by legislative acts. The Secretary of the Treasury recommends the same. This is language almost new to the world, and will surely meet with the approbation of the people, just as fast as the false gloss of federal newspapers is removed. When we contemplate, that nearly all the unimproved land, belonging to the United States, lies in the republican hemisphere, populating exceeding fast, we have rational ground to believe that the republican interest will continue to triumph. But who can look into futurity? The depravity of human nature—the restless propensity of men after novelty—the fate of other nations—and the maxims of Revelation, all conspire to check our soaring prospects, and warn us to be still, and know that the Lord reigns king of nations. I shall, therefore, close this part of the address, in the words of the wise man: "Fear God, and keep his commandments, for this is the whole duty of man: for God shall bring every work into judgment, with every secret thing, whether it be good or bad.

Fourteenth. When equitable laws are administered by a magistrate, in whom the people place confidence, their yoke is easy and their burden is light. The satisfaction which they feel, will stimulate them more to part with their property for public uses, than rigor and force will from a tyrannical administration, unless the tyranny is so complete as to prevent all means of opposition. A striking instance we have of this in the history of

David, and his grand-son, Rehoboam. The liberality, in the days of David, is astonishing. The provision funded for the building of a superb temple for Jehovah, was immense. David, as king, contributed (exclusive of timber, stones, iron, brass, costly and glittering stones, etc.) one hundred thousand talents of gold, and one million of talents of silver. If a talent is sixty-two pounds, Troy, the offering exceeded two thousand millions of dollars. The princes likewise cast into the fund five thousand talents of gold and ten thousand talents of silver, which surpassed seventy-four millions of dollars. Besides this, David, of his own private property, advanced three thousand talents of gold, and seven thousand talents of silver, more than forty-five millions of dollars: which sums form a total of more than two thousand two hundred and sixty millions of dollars. But when Rehoboam (at the instance of the young men, who were swarming in his court like locusts, gaping for the *loaves and fishes*) undertook to stop the remonstrances of the people, and subject them to his sovereign will, by sedition whips, and excise scorpions, the people revolted: and when the provisional army was raised to force obedience, for want of guns, the people made use of stones, and stoned the excise officer, who was over the tribute, to death. It may be added, that the building of the tabernacle, as well as the temple, and the repairing of the temple, were done by free-will offerings, and not by force.

Fifteenth. Gentlemen, you have taken notice that some men are always contending for the *energy of government*, while others are pleading for the *rights of the people*. On this I shall remark, that man has no *right* which stands in opposition to his *social duties;* no right to exercise his liberty to destroy the right and property of his neighbor; no right that frees him from his proportionable part of the burdens of government, and the restraints of just laws. Those who are always contending for the energy of government, generally have some office under that government, either in their own hands or the hands of their friends, which makes the government a profit to them, rather than a burden; and they wish that profit to be secured by energetic laws. While many, on the other hand, who plead for the liberty of men, too often use their own liberty for an occasion to the flesh.

Generally, in a revolution, for a time, the laws are too lax, which often drives the people to the opposite extreme; not stopping at the proper centre. Soon as ever government is energtic enough to protect the lives, liberty and property of the community, the people should use the utmost vigilance to prevent the intrusion of officers. I would as soon give my vote to a wolf to be a shepherd, as to a man, who is always contending for the energy of government, to be a ruler. I conceive our national government to be strong enough, and yet provision is made therein, to counterpoise all the powers that may be abused. Let the people keep awake, and danger flies. It is not long since the people of these states were becalmed in their spirits: they left government in the hands of their servants, and reclined on the bed of domestic ease; but, thanks to kind Providence, the servants fell out about the loaves and fishes, and contended so loud that they awaked the people from their slumbers. Let the dangers which we have just escaped make us more watchful, with lead, line and lookout. And when our hoary heads shall lie slumbering in death, may our sons and successors take warning, and never forget the inactive folly of their ancestors.

Disdain mean suspicion, but cherish manly jealousy; be always jealous of your liberty, your rights. Nip the first bud of intrusion on your constitution. Be not devoted to men; let measures be your object, and estimate men according to the measures they pursue. Never promote men who seek after a state-established religion; it is spiritual tyranny—the worst of despotism. It is turnpiking the way to heaven by human law, in order to establish ministerial gates to collect toll. It converts religion into a principle of state policy, and the gospel into merchandise. Heaven forbids the bans of marriage between church and state; their embraces, therefore, must be unlawful. Guard against those men who make a great noise about religion, in choosing representatives. It is electioneering intrigue. If they knew the nature and worth of religion, they would not debauch it to such shameful purposes. If pure religion is the criterion to denominate candidates, those who make a noise about it must be rejected; for their wrangle about it, proves that they are void of it. Let honesty, talents and quick despatch, characterise the men of your choice. Such men will have a sympathy with their constituents, and will be willing to come to the light, that their deeds may be examined. Remember that the genuine meaning of republicanism is self-government; if you would, then, be true disciples in your professsion, govern yourselves. The man who has no rule over his unruly passion, is no republican. He who will swear profanely, drink to excess, cheat his neighbor, speak falsely and scandalize his fellow creatures, is no republican, let his profession be what it will. Such republicans, like ferry-men, look one way and row the other. If you are republicans, indeed, you seek the public good. Be looking out, then, for objects of charity. Let the widow and the fatherless meet your kind assistance, and the blessing of him that is ready to perish fall upon you. Let the naked and hungry share your favors; the sick and afflicted, your hospitality; and let the case of poor prisoners and slaves excite your pity and stimulate your prayers.

Sixteenth. I already anticipate an objection to the method which I have pursued in this oration. The objection is, that "the subject has been too frequently changed." I own the subject has frequently changed; but king Solomon changed his subject seven times as often, in the book of Proverbs;

and yet that book is justly esteemed so highly, that the golden verses of Pythagoras, and the morals of Seneca, claim no comparison with it. I have also a later example. The honorable senate of Massachusetts, in the late session, when answering the governor's speech, suddenly elope from their subject, and take that opportunity to declare "that the freedom of the people is best secured by the independence of the judiciary." If kings and senators give the example, the present speaker hopes for indulgence. But why should the senate take that opportunity to declare their opinion? I know not; ask them, they are of age, and can answer for themselves. It was, however, no great compliment paid to Vermont, Rhode Island and Connecticut; in which states all the judges are annually chosen. But I conclude that the butt-end of it was aimed at Congress, for repealing the judiciary law of midnight darkness. As kings and senators hop, I will skip, and, in my turn, say that the late repeal of the judiciary law was constitutional, and expedient; and has given a tone to our government, worth more than all the gold of Ophir. The language is, that *all* officers, directly or indirectly, are amenable to the people. If the repeal of that law destroyed the constitution, as some said, why did not every man return home? What had they to do there, if the constitution was lost? They knew better—they acted otherwise. Not a single Fed of two thousand has quit his post; all stick like horse leeches at the veins, and will stick as long as there is a drop of money—blood in the body, unless they are removed; and when that is the case, they roar and yell like greedy wolves. Pause! pause! for heaven's sake, pause! and behold the inconsistency of Federal folly.

Seventeenth. As kind Providence has been so propitious, in appearing in behalf of America, so often, and so wonderfully, we have ground to hope that it will still interpose, again and again. A great number of thousands of people, within the United States, are still held in lasting slavery. The poor creatures have made several attempts to gain their lost liberty, but have failed, like the Poles. This evil chiefly abounds in the middle and southern states. Poor creatures! is there no liberty for them? must they forever drag the galling chain of vassalage under their despotic masters? How would every benevolent heart rejoice to see them all emancipated from slavery, and enjoy that little pittance of freedom, by nature due to them. May Heaven move on the minds of their masters, and open a way in Providence to bring them out of bondage, with the consent of their masters, and consistent with good policy. As personal slavery exists chiefly in the southern states, so religious slavery abounds exclusively in three or four of the New England states. Here the rights of conscience are made articles of merchandise, and men, who differ in opinion from the majority of a town, have to buy them. Here the majority vote away the money of the minority, for religious uses, at pleasure; and the legal relief, provided for the minority, is so intricate in its nature, and so precarious in its final issue, that, generally, heavy costs fall on those who strive to regain what usurpation has taken from them. Tyranny is always the same. Pharoah said to Moses, "Go ye and serve the Lord, but let your flocks and herds be staid." Massachusetts says, "Go ye and serve the Lord, but pay for building the parish meeting-house, and the salary of the teacher of piety, morality and religion." And men must pay their money according to a *legal* assessment, and draw it back again by a *legal* process, in order to be freed from the society which is dissented from; because they govern their religious concerns in a *legal* form. The most explicit language of the Pharoah of Massachusetts is, "Go ye and serve the Lord, but serve him as the majority do." Be incorporated by law, and become bodies politic; make use of the tool which we are so fond of; kill yourselves and we will not kill you. Oh! that the day—the halcyon day, may come, when the chains of personal slavery, and the manacles of religious despotism may be broken asunder, and freedom and religion pervade the whole earth.

GENTLEMEN: As it is my custom, on our anniversaries, to retire from company as soon as the public exhibition is over, I shall now express a number of wishes, in the form of toasts, which voluntarily flow from my heart—then conclude and retire.

1st. *The world at large.* May truth and friendship overspread the earth; and may all nations be freed from war, oppression, personal slavery, and religious tyranny.

2d. *The people of the United States.* May they be virtuous, industrious and wise; free from the intrigues of lawyers, the deception of doctors, the holy fraud of priests, and the imposition of lying printers.

3d. *The United States.* May the sixteen links be all of republican gold, and form an indissoluble chain. Let them adopt the policy of no nation, but improve upon them all.

4th. *The President.* May the first consul of France learn wisdom of the President of the United States, for a finishing stroke to his victories. As for old and foolish kings, they will not be reproved.

5th. *The Legislature.* Short sessions, few laws, and good customs.

6th. *The Judiciary.* Let judges know that they are as amenable to God, to law, and to the people, as other men.

7th. *The Treasury.* May the treasury be supplied with a frugal sufficiency for the exigences of government; but let the great treasure be in the hands of the people; each man being the treasurer of his own earnings.

8th. *The Revenue.* Let the resources of the nation run freely, when necessity calls; but let private right and public economy secure the dam and the gate.

9th. *The Navy and Militia.* May the time quickly come, when there shall not be a ship of war on the seas—till then, let every vessel be allowed to arm in its own defence, and let the same be extended to voluntary companies, that may see cause to build navies for trade. But why should government be at the expense to guard the speculation of individuals? However, if the condition of the world justifies an American *navy of war*, may it bring the piratical states, on the coast of Africa, to national justice.

May the malitia always be in readiness, but never be needed.

10th. *The Debt.* May the debt of the United States be discharged with speed and punctuality; and let not the people be deceived, by having the funds, established for that purpose, put to other uses.

11th. *Commerce.* May our exports be so great, and our imports so small, that the balance of trade may be in our favor.

12th. *Agriculture.* Let Americans improve the extensive, fertile land which the Almighty has given them, and not amuse themselves with the whimsies of circumscribed Islands.

13th. *Literature.* May our schools, academies and universities, diffuse abundance of light and knowledge abroad, and produce a long list of sages and patriots, whose souls shall so widely expand, that they shall know something more than just how to decline a noun and conjugate a verb.

14th. *The American Indians.* May the scalping-knife and hatchet be intered in the earth, and their fertile soil be cultivated by themselves. May they excel their white brethren in honesty, liberality and religion.

15th. *The Territory of Ohio.* May the new state be properly organized by the year 1804, and cast four republican votes into the box at the next presidential election.

16th. *The Gospel.* The only hope of man: may it prevail everywhere in its virgin purity—free from the legal apparatus and traditional complexion which have long covered its native beauty. May the combination of rulers and priests, church and state, be dissolved, and never re-unite.

17th. *The Day.* May it be kept as the birth-day of independence, with that gratitude and joy that become free-men and Christians.

Gentlemen: I conclude—I retire. I hope nothing will be done this day, that will disgrace the republican or the Christian.

CORRESPONDING LETTER

OF THE

SHAFTSBURY ASSOCIATION, 1803.

DEAR BRETHREN: Amidst the carnage of war, the revolutions of empire, the spasms of contending parties, the jarring interests and turbulent passions of infuriated men, which have deluged the world in confusion, it has been the privilege and delight of the saints, that they have a God to apply to in every time of need—a God, who has been a present help, a refuge from the storm, a strong tower, a munition of rocks, and a hiding-place.

This all-puissant Jehovah, self-glorious in his nature, and independent in all his works, has not confined his glory to the heavens, nor his goodness to the angels of light; but the inhabitants of *this* world have largely received of the fulness of his grace. Though the Lord be high, yet hath he respect unto the lowly. He who has the high heavens for his throne, and the earth for his footstool—before whom all the nations of the earth are as drops of the bucket, or small dust of the balance, in infinite condescension and boundless love, receives and protects every broken heart and contrite spirit; and, for their encouragement, has given them many precious promises, by which they are made partakers of the divine nature. If these foundations are destroyed, what can the righteous do? The saints have an omnipotent God on their side, who has promised, with an oath, to be a God unto them, and bless them. With an *Almighty Friend*, they may triumph over all their *mighty foes*, and say, "We will not fear what man can do unto us."

Brethren, while the world is emblazoning the virtues of valor, policy and industry, in agriculture, mechanism, and science, we, who are not of the world, wish to treat those virtues as the pigmy valor of game-cocks, the policy of bees, and the industry of ants; and display the noble valor of a Christian, to resist Satan, conquer sin, and destroy error; to be wise in the policy of Christ's kingdom, and industrious in the vineyard of the Lord: that what part soever we are called upon to act in the civil department, we would always esteem the high calling of God, in Christ Jesus, infinitely paramount.

We are not disposed to eulogize the period in which we live, as the only day of light, reason and liberty; nor to despise the pittance of time allotted us, as worse than former days; for the same contest between truth and error, right and wrong, which has been in the world from the beginning, still exists. But it is truly pleasing to the children of light, to consider that all the error and wrong of creatures, can never destroy the truth and rigteousness of the Creator.

The day in which we live, is neither dark nor light; not the darkness of sin, superstition and idolatry, nor the clear light of heaven; but at "*evening* time it will be light;" at the evening of life, as it respects individuals, and the evening of the world, as it applies to all the saints,—then it will be light without darkness.

In some of our churches there have been painful trials, since the last meeting of our association; others have escaped such trials; while some have received showers of heavenly grace.

It is with pleasure we receive your messengers, minutes and letters, from time to time, being confident such a procedure tends to edify the whole body; and, on our part, we shall pursue the same measures, for similar purposes.

Since our last meeting, one of our ministerial brethren (Elder Nathan Haskins, of Savoy,) has departed this life. Help, Lord! for the godly man ceaseth. We hope, however, that our loss is his gain.

Brethren, farewell. May a gracious God preserve us from every evil, and bring us, at last, into the full enjoyment of himself, through a blessed Mediator. Amen.

THE GOVERNMENT OF CHRIST A CHRISTOCRACY.

FIRST PUBLISHED IN 1804.

THE MAIN QUESTION.

Is the government of Christ according to the genius of the Monarchical, or like Democratical government; or is it distinct from both, being unlike all the governments on earth?

In answering this comprehensive question, I shall, first, consider the genius of Monarchical government; secondly, elucidate the nature of Democratical government; in the third place, I shall endeavor to state the difference between the universal government of the Almighty, the Theocracy of Israel, and the government of Christ, intended in the main question; fourth, I shall attempt to show, that although there are some parts of this government which resemble monarchy, and other parts, democracy, yet it is, upon the whole, different from all other governments, forming, of itself, a Christocracy.

First, I am to consider the genius of Monarchy. The origin, use, extent and abuse of government, are not articles of present investigation, but the genius only, which may be thus described. The monarch on his throne is the fountain of power and honor. His will is law for all his subjects; their privileges are his favors; he is responsible to none of them for his conduct; he appoints and commissions all officers for every department, who are accountable to him alone; he confers honors and pardons on whom he pleases, and takes away the lives of his subjects at pleasure. Some monarchies are absolute, and some are qualified, while others have the monarchical power distributed among a number of nobles, forming what is called aristocracy; but whenever it is understood that men are born to rule, that government is founded in birth, that, by some inconceivable, inexpressible mystery, some are born with a right to rule over others, with out the choice or consent of those ruled, whether this right is held by one king, or a number of nobles, it is monarchical government.

Secondly, I am to elucidate the nature of Democratic government. It is simply this: that men have the right, and exercise the power, of governing themselves; that all men are born equal, and that government is founded in compact, by mutual agreement for general good. It is most likely that there never was an unlimited democratical government on earth; for among American savages, the women and children have no choice in framing their laws, nor have the hunters as much influence as the chief. Nor does democracy suppose that all the body politic must be present on every legal occasion; but it supposes that all men, ripe in years, have a voice in the choice of their agents, and that they are themselves eligible to office. That all officers are amenable to those who appoint them, and must, at a certain period, return to private life. That those in power, have not and cannot have, any power but what they receive, in small constituent parts, from all the community. It disclaims allegiance to any foreign tyrant, and to every domestic usurper.

Thirdly, I am to state the difference which exists between the universal government of the Almighty, the Theocracy of Israel, and the government of Christ, intended in the main question.

1st. The great Jehovah is the moral governor of all rational beings. His law is binding on all of them. He requires reasonable service of them all, and they are all accountable to him for their conduct. All the angels in heaven and hell, all men, in the body and out of the body, are under obligation to love and obey God, and acknowledge the Messiah, and their opposition and rebellion have no excuse. Yea, further, in some sort, his government extends over all creation. The material world, which arose at his command, exists by his power, and will be destroyed at his word. In the intermediate time, the seas roll, the winds blow, the clouds fly, the thunder roars, the rain and snow descend, and the earth brings forth her increase in obedience to his will. The beasts of the field, the birds of the air, the fish of the sea, and all the creeping things, were made, are preserved and fed, and will decease by the hands of the Almighty.

2d. The nation of Israel, at Mount Horeb, were formed into an ecclesiastico-political government, and as they received all their laws of religion and government from God alone, their government is called a Theocracy. All the nation, whether good or bad, belonged to that church, for the bounds of the church and the state were commensurate. Those who sinned away their lives in the wilderness, all the sinners of God's people until the time of Christ, together with those in his day, called serpents and generation of vipers, belonged to that Theocracy, as well as the righteous. In the days of Samuel, the government was altered in some respects; kings were appointed instead of judges; but still the Theocracy continued, for those kings were to execute the laws which God had given to the people, and make none themselves. When David was on the throne, the state of the people was considerably changed from what it was when their code of laws was given them; yet the alterations which David made, were done by the *Spirit of God* which was upon him.

3d. The glorious Mediator is spoken of under the most dignified titles, according to the highest sense of the words. He is called Leader, Commander, Captain, Counsellor, Ruler, Governor, Prince and King; and it is said of the increase of his government and duration of his kingdom, there shall be no end. This government, or kingdom, is not of this world; the subjects are not of this world, but are called out of it. Those that fear God and work righteousness, are the only persons that belong to it. No man can understand the nature of, or enter into this kingdom, unless he is born again. And such may say, "*We are thine; thou never bearest rule over them,* (the men of the world,) *they were not called by thy name.*"

I proceed, in the fourth place, to show that, although some parts of this government resemble monarchy, and other parts of it a democracy, yet, upon the whole, it is different from all other governments, forming of itself, a Christocracy.

There is some likeness between the government of Christ, and a monarchy.

1st. Christ is absolute legislator. His will is law. He consults not with angels or men, in framing his orders. He is king, without a privy council, and judge, without any associates.

2d. He appoints and commissions all the spiritual officers in his government. The ministers of the gospel receive their orders from Christ alone.

There is also some likeness between the government of Christ and a democracy.

1st. Liberty and equality, the boast of democracy, is realized in the church. The saints are set at liberty from the prison of sin, and freed from the curse of the law. They are all one in Christ; the poor are exalted, and the rich brought low.

2d. The saints on earth are Christ's subjects, forming his kingdom below. When Christ went to heaven, and left his house below, he gave authority to his servants, and to every man his work; and as far as church government on earth is the government of Christ, it is of democratical genius. Church government is congregational, not parochial, diocesan, nor national. Each congregated church disclaims the power of Popes, kings, bishops, parliaments, kirks, or presbyteries, and claims the right and power to govern itself according to the laws of Christ. And it must be confessed, that the spirit and rule by which the subjects of Christ's kingdom are to live one among another, greatly resemble the genius of a republic, and as greatly confronts the inequality and haughtiness of monarchies. So far as Christ's government may be compared to governments on earth, we may say, that as many democracies as there are chuches, form one absolute empire. But such a government was never on earth.

The difference that exists between Christ's government, and all others, I shall now attend unto.

1st. Christ's laws are spiritual, reaching to the hearts, thoughts, and motives of men, and requiring truth in the inward parts; whereas, the laws of state take cognizance of actions only, and of those actions only, whereby one man injures another, in life, liberty, or property. So that a man may be a good citizen of state, and at the same time be an enemy to God, and not worthy to be numbered among the subjects of Christ. His laws, moreover, reach to every case, taking into view all actions, temptations, circumstances, and motives, which the laws of men cannot do.

2d. The government of which I am treating, admits of an atonement for transgressions, by the vicarious sufferings of the innocent for the guilty; which is not, and ought not to be allowed in any government of this world. In civil cases, if one man owes another, the surety may pay the debt, and set the debtor free; but not so in criminal cases, for if a man is guilty of an overt act and exposed to the penalty of corporeal punishment, no government on earth admits of a substitute; the criminal, and the criminal only, must suffer. Here, then, appears that mystery which philosophy and state policy never found out,—the mysterious way how sin could be atoned for, and sinners saved. Yes, men have sinned, and incurred the divine displeasure, but the blessed Jesus died for sinners,—died, the just for the unjust, that God might be just, and justify the ungodly who believe. This atonement, unlike any thing seen in all governments on earth, is the sinner's only hope of acceptance before God.

3d. In all other governments, whenever grace is administered to a criminal, it is done at the expense of the law; the law dies, that grace may reign. I mean this: when a criminal is condemned to death by a legal process, if he is pardoned, both law and adjudication are overruled. But, in the kingdom of Christ, sinners are pardoned and the law honored—pardoned, not in the light of benefit of clergy, but through satisfaction made to the law by the suffering of another—pardoned, not by an absolute proclamation of grace, but by the price of blood.

4th. Another singularity of Christ's kingdom, is this; characters, as well as facts, are noticed. If my words are not well chosen, I will explain thus: In the governments on earth, if two men, say A. and B., are proved guilty of one and the same crime, and adjudged to the same punishment, if A. appears hard hearted and furious, and B. discovers all the symptoms of sorrow and reformation, still they must equally suffer, for the law has nothing to do with characters, but facts. But, in the divine government, in the name and by the atonement of Christ, all those who repent, receive remission of sins, while those who harden their hearts, fall into mischief.

5th. All monarchies, empires, kingdoms, and states, on earth, have their limits and boundaries. Seas, lakes, rivers, mountains, or lines of latitude, form the boundaries, and mark the division among them, so that no place or people is under the control of two of those governments at the same time. But Christ's government has no territorial bounds—it is not located, but general—it runs into all the kingdoms and states on earth, and claims all those who fear God and work righteousness for its subjects, and at the same time does not deprive any kingdom or state of a single subject or citizen. For the hundred and forty-four thousand, the vast multitude of Christ's subjects, which no man can number, are scattered over every kingdom, nation, tongue and people, and while they are the devoted subjects of king Jesus, they are, at the same time, the most loyal subjects and best citizens in the kingdoms and states where they reside.

6th. The kingdom of Christ is a kingdom of *truth, righteousness,* and *peace,* without error, injustice, or discord. When Pilate asked Jesus if he were a king, he said, "I am; for this end was I born, that I might bear witness unto the *truth.*" And St. Paul informs us, that the kingdom of God is *righteousness* and *peace*. Truth, righteousness, and peace, have but little to do in the kingdoms of this world, but without treating them with any severity, it will not be denied, that abundance of corruption, partiality, oppression and fraud, creep into, and proceed from the best governments on earth, but none of these attend the kingdom of Christ. Justice and judgment are the habitation of his throne, mercy and truth go before his face. He sits upon a great white throne, free from every stain of error. The conclusion of the whole matter, therefore, is, that the government of Christ is radically different from all the governments on earth, forming, of itself, a divine Christocracy. By a Christocracy, I mean nothing more than a government of which Christ is law-giver, king, and judge, and yet so arranged, that each congregational church is a complete republic of itself, not to be controlled by civil government or hierarchy. Let this government be called by what name soever, it is not of the world, and therefore, the rulers of this world have nothing to do with it, in their official capacity. It is distinct from the government of state, and consequently, should never be mixed with it. It is complete of itself, and disdains the assistance of human laws.

Civil government is designed to protect the lives, liberty, and property, of the community, but the divine government is adapted to pardon the guilty, reform the heart, instruct the mind, and improve the morals of the wicked. The promotions and punishments of civil governments, are all this side of the grave, but those of the divine government, are in the succeeding world. Blood, warlike valor, and state policy, raise men to high rank in the governments on earth, but self-abasement, love to enemies, simplicity and humility, are the characteristics of those whom the King delights to honor. The great names of Alexander, Cæsar, Washington, or Jefferson, will be no more regarded in the judgment day, than the names of their meanest servants, unless they possess that moral excellency which their servants do not.

Whenever churches, (the little republics which form the empire of Christ,) are formed according to the gospel, acknowledging Christ for their head, and his laws for their rules, all that such democratical societies expect, wish for, or are entitled to, from civil government, is the protection of their rights to worship God as they judge best, without the molestation of others. But whenever churches are formed by civil law, whether they are national, diocesan, or parochial, and become bodies politic, and appeal to any authority, either civil or ecclesiastical, higher than the authority of a church, for a final decision of controversies, such churches wish for, receive, and exercise a power over the rights of others, which is inconsistent with the genius of Christianity. Such societies may call themselves churches of Christ, but in reality, they are creatures of state. Let there be more or less of the subjects of Christ in such societies, (who are held there through ignorance or by force,) yet, as bodies collective, they are not those democracies which form the divine Christocracy; for the reason why the nation of Israel was called a Theocracy, was, because they received all their laws from (Theas) God alone, so churches must be governed by the laws of (Christos) Christ alone, to form the Christocracy here spoken of. I am not, however, tenacious for a name; let the church be called a kingdom, empire, republic, or commonwealth, and let the saints be called subjects, servants, or fellow-citizens, yet keep up the idea that the government is complete of itself, and no gap is left for magistrates to interfere, and also that it is different, in many particulars, from all the governments on earth, as has been shown. Experience, the best teacher, has informed us, that the fondness of magistrates to foster Christianity, has done it more harm than all the persecutions ever did. Persecution, like a lion, tears the saints to death, but leaves Christianity pure: state establishment of religion, like a bear, hugs the saints, but corrupts Christianity, and reduces it to a level with state policy. Magistrates frequently love the advantages of Christianity more than the precepts of it, and flatter themselves that they are doing much for God, and themselves, when they make laws to protect what they esteem the truth of Christianity, and to reward the preachers of that truth, but every law which they make of that complexion, proves their aversion to the scheme of pure Christianity: for, by such a procedure, they arraign either the wisdom, or good will of Christ, the Lord, for not giving enough, and the best of laws for the government of the church, at all times, and in all places. And further, they arrogate to themselves a lording over consciences, which is God's prerogative, and a favor which is not attached to their civil office. They, moreover, lead the preachers to trust in them, and not in the Lord: at least, they become the legal bondsmen of Christ.

The exercises of Christ's government are moral excellencies which force can never effect. The freedom of the will, and volition of choice, are so essential to moral virtue, that it cannot exist without. We must, therefore, give up the idea of legal force in matters of religion, or own that there is no moral worth in them: hence the conclusion is, that religion, in all its parts, is distinct from civil government, or, otherwise, Deism will triumph. For, if there is no moral virtue in religion, the cost and contention about it, sink it far below Deism.

While I am reflecting on these things, it strikes my mind that the religion of Massachusetts is somewhat dissimilar to the religion of the gospel, in the following particulars.

First. Whoever consults the third article of the Bill of Rights, in the Constitution of Massachusettss, together with sundry existing laws, will find that Protestant Christianity is the established religion of the state. Pagans, Turks, Jews, and Papists, are minor departments; whereas, the primitive Christians had no such establishment—no such preference—and they were so tenacious of the laws of Christ, that, before they would submit to traditions of elders, (among the Jews,) or the established religion among the Gentiles, they exposed both property and life. There was no Pope to protest against in those times, nor ever would have been, had Christianity never been established by law. It is true, that the Christians, at first, were but a feeble band, but Christ, as a prophet—as a God—certainly knew that the Christians by name, would, thereafter, become so numerous as to form a majority in the empire which then claimed universal sway; why, then, did he not give some hint, that, when that should be the case, the Christians should regulate their religion by law? This he has not done,—this the apostles are silent about. They understood better the will of their Master, who had said, "my kingdom is not of this world."

Second. This state is formed into a great number of ecclesiastico-politico, major-vote parishes. Some of these parishes are personal, but most of them are territorial. They are religious societies, made bodies politic, and governed by major vote. Let any man read the New Testament, and find any account of such societies among primitive Christians, if he can, or any orders for Christians to be formed in that manner, whenever they should be numerous enough.

Third. These Pharisees are now exposed to a fine of from thirty to a hundred dollars for every six months that they are destitute of a teacher of piety, morality, and religion, which is a little different from New Testament times. Now, the laws of state impose fines upon the people if they are destitute of preachers; then, the laws of Christ imposed prayers: "Pray ye the Lord of the harvest, that he would send forth laborers into the harvest."

Fourth. When a territorial parish have chosen a minister by major vote, and contracted with him for his salary, the sum is levied upon all within the limits of the parish, according to poll and property, and collected by a legal officer. If all within the parish are acquiescent, I have only to say, it is putting the law to a use for which it was never designed by Him who rules above, and sinking religion to a level with worldly articles. But, when any are dissentients, such force and cruelty follows, as to disgrace the religion of the meek and lowly Jesus. Disgrace it, did I say? It is as foreign from gospel religion, as darkness from light. Some relief, however, is provided for a certain description of deficients, by giving in certificates, or suing their money out of the treasury, but the mode is so intricate, and the event so uncertain, that, in many cases, where the deficients have exerted themselves, they have gained only heavy costs upon the back of the original sum. In many cases, also, the deficients are not allowed to sit upon the jury, because they are parties concerned, but their oppressors, not being interested, judge the case alone. The expense of building meeting-houses, has the same course as ministerial salaries. Now, where shall we find the chapter or verse in the New Testament, that coincides with such proceedings?

Fifth. The framers of our state Constitution, and the makers of our canonical laws, seem to have been conscious that the hierarchy which they were forming, was distinct from the gospel, for they uniformly give it other names. The privileged order of preachers, which these laws are designed to foster, are never called ministers of the gospel, but invariably, "teachers of piety, morality, and religion." Peter gave the following definition of piety: "But if any widow have children or nephews, let them learn first to shew piety at home, and to requite their parents." Piety, then, consists in relieving distressed widows, and not in taking away their property to pamper the teachers. James explains religion thus: "Pure religion, and undefiled before God and the Father, is this, to visit the fatherless and widow in their affliction, and to keep himself unspotted from the world." But how can the saints keep themselves unspotted from the world, when they get the world to define their religion, and, by worldly power, force the people to attend their worship, build their temples, and pay their teachers?"

The word morality, is not in the Bible: it is a word, however, of common use, but of somewhat indefinite signification. The Armenians use the word to express those actions of men which tend to the good of families, societies, etc., when there is no gracious disposition in the men who perform those actions. The Hopkinsianists, and Calvanists, make use of the word to describe the quality of actions, or the motives which stimulate. Others, again, say, there is a legal honesty, and there is also a moral honesty; supposing that a legal honesty consists in conducting so to ourselves and others, that the laws cannot impeach us, but that moral honesty is from a sense of God's laws, and a love to his ways; doing that which is right of itself, whether the laws of men enjoin it or not. But so far as my acquaintance extends, all parties agree that the words of our Lord give the best description of morality that ever was given: "Whatsoever ye would that men should do unto you, do ye the same to them." Taking this to be a just description of morality, I wish to ask whether the hierarchy of Massachusetts teaches men this lesson? Let the ruling party in the state answer. Gentlemen, were you the minor part, should the Quakers, Methodists, or Baptists, form a majority in the various towns and parishes in this state, and tax all those of the standing order to pay their preachers, build their meeting-houses, endow their colleges, etc., or, in order to get relief therefrom, that you must give in a certificate, or sue your money back out of the treasury, and that none of your order could be admitted jurors, but the case must be decided solely by them, would you not in such cases say, (if you are allowed to speak,) "you know, in your consciences, that you are not doing as you would be done by?"

The question then arises, whether the establishment of religion is friendly to piety, morality, and religion, or whether it is not rather, in its nature and tendency, sapping the foundation of all of them? "I speak as unto wise men, judge ye what I say."

To myself, there remains no doubt, that the religious establishments of Massachusetts, and all state establishments of Christianity in the world, are all of them, ANTI-CHRISTOCRACIES.

AN

ELECTIVE JUDICIARY,

WITH OTHER THINGS,

RECOMMENDED IN A

SPEECH,

PRONOUNCED AT

CHESHIRE, JULY 4, 1805.

There is none that holdeth with me, in these things, but MICHAEL, your Prince.——DANIEL.

AN ELECTIVE JUDICIARY.

In family registers, and biographical writings, the birth-day, the wedding-day, and the dying-day of individuals, are noticed with peculiar emphasis: so, with regard to nations, the rise, alliances, and downfall of empires and states, are articles of great notoriety with historians. In this point of light, this fourth of July is the birth-day of the United States. Twenty-nine years have elapsed since the British colonies, in North America, cast off the tyrant's yoke, and assumed a rank among the nations of the earth.

The American revolution has opened a scene—is the beginning of a drama, which will not close until time shall be no more. While we celebrate the day, the birth-day of long-lost freedom returning to visit the earth, and take up her abode among men, we will not be unmindful of the agents which the Almighty has used in his hand to effect that work, for which nations will arise and call them blessed.

When the distresses of our country called forth a deputation from each colony, who convened in Philadelphia, in the year 1776, their cry to heaven, in behalf of their constituents, was, " Lord, what wilt thou have us to do?" It was a bold attempt, in Richard H. Lee, to make the motion of Independence; which was no sooner done, than the intrepid Samuel Adams seconded it. The motion was carried—the declaration was made, which forever separated the United States from Great Britain, from her policy, her corruption, and her debts. But Lee is gone to his long home—Adams sleeps in dust—Randolph is no more—Hancock is gone the way of all the earth—Henry's all-persuasive voice no more is heard—Franklin commands the shafts of heaven no more. These worthies, with most of the fathers of the revolution, having served their generation, according to the will of God, have fallen asleep and seen corruption.

But after the declaration was made, arduous was the struggle to support it. Warren, Montgomery, Worcester, Mercer, Nash, and others, lost their lives in the field of battle; with thousands of our sons, equal, perhaps, in virtue, though not in rank. Those who survived the contest, and saw the return of peace, found that mortality was not conquered. Yes, a Washington and a Greene, the boast of Virginia and Rhode Island, and the triumph of America, are no more. They were swifter than eagles, they were stronger than lions; but they are fallen by death. The quinsy was an overmatch for Washington—a stroke of the sun too powerful for Greene. "How are the mighty fallen, and the weapons of war perished." But, notwithstanding the great destruction of those who made destruction of tyranny, some of the fathers and patriots remain. Jefferson yet lives —may he long live—may he outlive all his enemies—may he live till the debt of the nation is entirely defrayed. Clinton, the friend of man, the persevering republican, the long guide of New York, is yet on the stage of action.

It is pleasing to contemplate, that though most of the fathers of the revolution have closed their eyes in death, yet their sons have risen up to maintain the same cause; so the young Elisha caught the mantle and a double portion of the spirit of Elijah, when, with a whirlwind, he rode to heaven in a fiery car. Among these, a Bidwell is the boast of this district; like Barnabas of old, a son of consolation, meek in temper, and amiable in manners. His talents and integrity, which have appeared so conspicuous, as a writer, an advocate at the bar, a treasurer, a senator, etc., in the small circle of one state, will shine with a longer tail, and more effulgence, in the large orbit of the Union. May he ever lighten, but never scorch.*

While I am eulogizing character, not for their names', but their works' sake, I feel under some obligation to reply to several charges lodged against the president. His flight to Carter's mountain, his attempt to cheat Mr. Jones, his intrigue with Mrs. Walker, and his sending from France after black Sall, are the four topics of censure. These crimes, it is said, were all committed between the years 1776 and 1790. I do not absolutely know but all the charges are true; but one thing I know to be true. I lived in Virginia, from December, 1776, until April, 1791, not far distant from Monticello; yet I never heard a syllable of either of those crimes, till I read them in these eastern newspapers; said to be extracts from Calender & Co. I shall, therefore, be an infidel in these reports, until I have better evidence.

That his public administration has been just and enconomical, I think no candid man will deny. Some, however, attribute the *means* to the former administration; and say that Jefferson & Co. rise upon the revenue which was left by the former administration in bank. The truth, I conceive to be this. The avenues of revenue were opened before the funding system, and other collateral measures, split the nation into two parties; after the split, the Federal party, being paramount, added to the revenue by internal taxation. The internal taxes, at the close of Mr. Adams' administration,

* This patriotic wish was not realized. The "scorching" effects of Bidwell's subsequent defection were severely felt by the republicans of Berkshire.

formed one-eleventh part of the revenue; but, with all the imposts and internal taxes, the debt of the nation was so far from being diminished, that it increased about one million of dollars per year. That the federal Congresses understood how to levy taxes and swell the revenue, no man denies; but that they put the money to the right use, is denied; so that, if we give them the credit of procuring the *means*, we must certainly give to the present administration the praise of applying those means to their proper *ends*. One-eleventh part of the taxes are taken off the people, and with the ten-elevenths, more than twelve millions of dollars of the national debt was reduced during the first four years of Mr. Jefferson's administration.

The auxiliaries in the executive department merit some attention, at this time. Mr. Madison is secretary of state. From a child, he has been a pattern of sobriety, study, and inflexible justice. From an intimate acquaintance with him, I feel satisfied that all the state of Massachusetts, for a bribe, would not buy a single vote of him. A saying of his is fresh in my memory. "It is ridiculous for a man to make use of underhanded means to carry a point, although he should know that the point is a good one: it would be doing evil that good might come." This saying of his, better describes the man than my pen can do. He has been in public life from the beginning of the revolution until now; and is at this time assisting to administer that government, which he (the first man in the United States) made a motion to call a convention to form. Should Jefferson die, or resign, on whom would the office of president fall with as much propriety and safety, as on Mr. Madison?

In the treasury department, Mr. Gallatin is principal. A foreigner by birth, but by naturalization an American. Having filled many important officers in Pennsylvania, he was sent a delegate to Congress; and was an able opposer of all those measures which were so abhorrent to the people as to cause a change of administration. In the Congressional debates, when the souls of men were tried, he discovered such financial talents, that his enemies prophesied, that if Jefferson became president, Gallatin would have charge of the treasury; which is the only part of the federal prophecy that has ever come to pass. With propriety he may be called the American Neckar. Never did Sir Isaac Newton search into the laws of gravitation, or explore the starry heavens, and give to each star its magnitude, distance and orbit, with more depth of thought, accuracy, and despatch, than Albert Gallatin surveys all the sources of revenue, and points out the proper mode of collecting and applying the same, in a manner highly economical, making just allowances for contingent events, and closing his statements to the tenth part of a cent. We know he is wise—we believe he is honest. May his fiscal arrangements be such, as will sink the debt of the nation in a short period.

But, while I am passing encomiums, it strikes my mind that the same reason which forbids us to write the history of a man, while he is living, warns us against being too lavish of eulogium on men, until they leave the theatre where so many play the worst part of their lives in their latest days. Arnold was the song of '77, and many of the quondams of our country were famous for a while; yet Arnold betrayed his trust, and the quondams have fallen into disgrace, or sunk into the state of doubtful disputation. The saying of a citizen of Tarsus, "it doth not yet appear what we *shall be*," is applicable to statesmen, in the point of light before us. We have a recent instance before us, which proves that a man may be one day contending for liberty and equality—the next be a qualified consul—then consul for life—after that emperor—and with that have the crown of another kingdom placed on his head.

Let gratitude swell our bosoms, to render the tribute of praise to all who deserve well of their country; but let inflexible patriotism inspire us to withhold our suffrages from all the unworthy. By unworthy characters, I mean those who wish to plunge the nation into debt; make offices permanent, and destroy responsibility; make government a mystery, and induce the people to call neither men nor measures in question; use others as a ladder to climb the tree of eminence with, and when once risen, kick down the ladder; join churches, and make a great noise about religious qualifications in rulers, and, at the same time, be as void of them as an ice-cake is of fire; plead much for the constituted authorities and the laws, while they themselves are in office, but speak evil of dignities when themselves are neglected. In such men place no confidence; for they that are such, serve not their country, but their own bellies, and, with good words and fair speeches, deceive the hearts of the simple.

Men who are best qualified for office, are generally the least ambitious after it; so it was with Moses, David, Seranus, Cincinnatus, Washington, and others. Being furnished with rectitude and variety within, they court not the trappings and tinsel without: yet, when duty calls, they will hazard their all to serve their country. Pleased, however, when the object is gained—when the period arrives that they can, with true honor, quit the noisy world to enjoy themselves. But I close my encomiastic, and characteristical preface, and proceed to objects more sentimental.

The sages of America declared, in the Declaration of Independence, that government was instituted for the good of the people, and not for the aggrandizement of a few; and therefore, whenever the form of government did not preserve the lives, liberties, and property of the people, they had an indubitable right to amend it, so as to answer those valuable purposes. This sage opinion, in the year 1776, was eagerly adopted by the people of the United States. In 1787, the patriotic fathers, in general convention, held the same sentiment as dear as the ligaments of their hearts. Possessed of this right, in behalf of their constituents, they changed the then existing government; and in the machine of government which they formed, great care and wisdom were used to secure the same right to their children. The provision made in the constitution, for peaceable amendments, whenever defects are discovered, is one of the brightest ornaments of that model of policy.

Men in political, as well as in agricultural, mechanical, and scientifical life, are prone to conceive themselves nearly infallible, and often seek to erect barriers to prevent their children from forsaking the opinions and pursuits of their fathers; but, with wonder and gratitude, we behold the American fathers assiduously engaged to leave to their children the golden legacy of choosing their own form of government, and making their own laws, without any danger of noise or convulsion. Hitherto, it had been supposed, that no government could be altered or amended, without war and carnage abroad, and national injustice and bankruptcy at home; but the people of the United States have acquired the art of changing their mode of government, as often as experience dictates the utility thereof, with as little danger as they repeal a law. Nor do, nor can any men wish to deprive the people of this privilege, except those who are something, or conceive themselves something, in the existing order of things, and fear they shall be nothing, should a change take place.

As a number of amendments have been made to the national constitution, since its first adoption, and others are now before Congress, with great diffidence, I shall here propose one, which is an *Elective Judiciary.* Pagans have a notion, that certain gods or godesses preside over certain limited countries. Whether their notion is substantial or fanciful, it appears very evident to me, that the election of all officers, to fill all parts of the government, is the natural genius that presides over the United States, and if my conviction is just, there will be spasms, and commotions in the states, until such amendment takes place. I have labored under this conviction for a number of years; but as I have never borne any office in state, to try my theory by experiment; and, as my calling in life is in another department, I have quieted myself in silence; waiting, in the mean time, for some to plead the cause of an *Elective Judiciary*, or overcome the reasonings of my mind, by demonstrating the impropriety of such an establishment; but neither, as yet, has taken place.

All the arguments which I have yet heard, to prove that judges must hold their office for life, or during good behaviour, in order to make them independent, honest, and impartial, have been as inconclusive, as the arguments are which are adduced to prove that a national debt is a national blessing. If the arguments, however, are more conclusive than I have conceived them to be, and support the doctrine that judges once appointed, should have a life-lease of their office, except for high crimes and misdemeanors, they also prove something more; they equally prove, that the executive and legislative officers should hold their office by a coeval tenure, to make them independent, honest, and impartial.

The objections that are made against an *elective judiciary*, may be summed up under two general heads. First, "the body of the people have not wisdom and sedateness enough to select from among themselves, those who are the best qualified to be judges." Secondly, "if judges hold their office by the tenure of periodical elections, they will have such strong temptations to please the strongest party, in order to secure their next election, that they will not judge uprightly."

The first of these objections, applies with all its force against the two other departments of government; for if men have not wisdom enough to choose the judges, they have not enough to choose presidents, governors, or legislatures; which notion saps the foundation of all representative governments, and supports the monarchical. If men are incompetent to elect their judges, they are equally incompetent to appoint others to do it for them.

Government, originating among men, is the cool result of reason against vicious passion. Men find within themselves, and discover in others, a number of vicious propensities, which reason condemns; to prevent these propensities from breaking out into overt acts, reason fixes a standard containing a number of rules, which all have to submit unto; and pray, have not the people, whose sovereign voice declares all these rules, wisdom enough to designate the agents to enforce them? If the people, however, make an unwise choice, the catholicon of suffrage will correct the error; but, when they are appointed for life, (in substance,) there is no remedy in the hands of the people.

Judges are above all the laws that the legislature can enact; being under oath to adhere to the constitution, any law to the contrary notwithstanding. In one point of light, this power is proper; for legislatures may forget their political bibles, in a gust of passion, and make laws unconstitutional and pernicious; the judiciary, in such cases, have the power to prevent the mischief: but, though the people have this judiciary check against the usurpation of the legislature, what check have they against the usurpation of the judiciary? When judges set up their opinion on the constitution, in opposition to the legislature, and in opposition to the great mass of the people, who can check them? The people cannot, for they have no direct voice in setting them up, or taking them down. The legislature cannot, except by impeachment, which, in such cases, would be no more than a whistle. The executive cannot, for they hold their office by a tenure, which the executive cannot destroy.

These remarks are applicable to our national government, and to some of the state governments; but not to all of them, for in some of the states, the judges are chosen annually by the legislature, &c. In New York they cannot serve after they are sixty years old.

The second objection is, that if judges are chosen by the people, at periodical elections, they will have such strong temptations to please the strongest party, in order to secure their next election, that they will not judge uprightly; and therefore, they must be appointed three or four removes from the people, and hold their office by a tenure, that neither the two other arms of government, nor the people, can disannul; with an invariable salary attached to the office, in order for them to judge uprightly.

This doctrine appears to be founded on the opinion, that perfection is attached to the judicial office; but the opinion is fallacious, for once there was an unjust judge in a city, that feared not God, nor regarded men; and I will appeal to candor itself, if there are not judges to be found, who are deaf, sovereign, insulting, and superannuated. Is the board of appointments—is the legislature—or are the body of the people, satisfied with the talents and conduct of all, who are now in office? If all were satisfied with them at their first appointment, must the present inhabitants bear with them as long as they breathe through their nostrils? My age authorises me to say, that the leading doctrine of the American revolution has been, "that responsibility was the best expedient to keep men honest." And why this maxim should be inverted in the judiciary establishment alone, I never could see.

The more permanent and lucrative an office is, the more self-important and avaricious characters seek after it. And yet, it is said, that, "if offices are not permanent and lucrative, men of talents will not accept of them." But if experience is to be our guide, we shall find such offices too much filled with aspiring, unfeeling men; while those places of trust, which are more precarious, more responsible and less lucrative, are filled with better characters.

Trial by juries, is held as a sacred right in these states; on their verdicts hang suspended life and death, poverty and wealth, in many cases. If judges cannot judge uprightly without a permanent appointment, how can jurors?—Why not have standing juries for life, with honorary salaries secured to them?

If judges should be elected by the people, common sense would dictate that all over whom they should have jurisdiction, should have a voice in the choice. This being the case, there would be but a very few cases, in which the parties, between whom they were to judge, would be so large as to affect their next election materially. Should a judge, in such cases, discover partiality, it would disgust even his friends. Nothing would make him so popular, in his district, as a constant, uniform adherence to justice; whereas, in the present mode of appointing judges, they are under no obligation, (except their oath,) to be just to any man, or even to treat him with civility.

Judges should be independent, and feel important enough to keep order in court, direct the jury in matters of law, keep the witnesses to the proper point, prevent the lawyers from eloping from the direct subject, etc., which could be done as well by men who were chosen by the people for a limited term, as by those who are appointed by the executive or legislature for life; and, if the necessary work could be done as well, the evil of having superannuated, tyrannical, heady, unsociable judges would be prevented. In this case, judges would not only feel the importance of judicial officers, but also the salutary obligation to be *men*. A judicial monarch is a character as abhorrent as an executive or legislative monarch, in my view.

Considering the habits and prejudices of my country, I have but small hopes that an elective judiciary will take effect very soon, unless the state of Pennsylvania, (which state has taken the lead in many of the American improvements,) should introduce it. Well, if the judiciary establishment must continue as it is—must be monarchical, while the executive and legislative departments are representative—let us make the best of it, and have nothing to do with courts of judicature, that we can possibly avoid, but settle all our controversies by mutual arbitration, then the host of lawyers, who infest our land like the swarms of locusts in Egypt, and eat up every green thing, will have nothing to do, but apply themselves to that happy vocation, which they now recommend to others, "plough, hoe, go to meeting and learn good things."

Laws—government—courts of judicature must exist, otherwise the injured could not arrest the guilty and bring them to the standard of justice; but when controversies arise between man and man, he who is unwilling to have the dispute amicably settled by mutual arbitration, manifests a desire to injure his neighbour. In this particular, I am happy that I agree with the founder of Rhode Island, Roger Williams, who, through his life, and with his last breath, recommended arbitrations as the best mode of adjusting variances.

The right of suffrage is more fully and equitably enjoyed in the United States, I believe, than in any part of the world, and still it is a question, whether that right may not be extended farther with safety. Place *all* men on a level, and the poor, who pay little or nothing for the support of government, can vote away the money of the rich; proscribe the poor from voting, and the rich can vote away the labor of the poor. The rich have often oppressed the poor, by laws which they have made, but I have met with no account in history, neither have I known any instance, where the poor have legally oppressed the rich. Government is designed to protect the life, liberty and property of individuals; the poor have life and liberty to be protected, but no property; here, then, is two arguments against one, in favor of the poor. Should every man, who is of age, be allowed the right of suffrage, without any of those prerequisites which are required, in almost all the states, the citizens would be more free, equally safe, and much more economical in the redemption of time.

I have noticed, several times, the proceedings of congress, which I conceive to be erroneous. The proceedings which I have in view, are, the confounding of justice and mercy together, in a manner to destroy both of them, by forcing the people, under the authority of law, to be merciful to those who had suffered by fire. Human laws reach no farther than to force a man to be just to his neighbor. The divine law enjoins on men, bowels and mercies. Mercy is a moral duty, but not a legal one. No man can perform moral virtue when forced against his will. The volition of the will is essential to moral exercises. If men are forced to relieve the distressed, it cannot be mercy. To force a man to part with his hard-earned property, to relieve the needs of another, cannot be just. When men suffer by fire, or otherwise, and are reduced to distress, let the members of congress, as individuals, have compassionate hearts and liberal hands, and let the same glow of good will spread far and near, then it will be mercy. I see no clause in the constitution which authorises congress to dispose of the money in the treasury for the relief of any sufferers by fire; therefore, such laws must be unjust, for whenever money is taken out of the national chest, without a constitutional key, the nation sustains a fraud.

From a small error in government, great mischief may, and often does arise. "Behold how great a matter a little fire kindleth." At first it is so small that great men hate to meddle with it, while little men do not perceive it, but, like a nest-egg, it does not continue alone, it becomes a habit—a precedent—a plea for other errors of the same kind, but more fatal. Six hundred dollars a year is a trifle, far less than the three pence on a pound of tea: distributed among the inhabitants of the United States, it would not be the tenth part of a mill per soul. It cannot, therefore, of itself, ever be oppressive to the people. But the very principle upon which this money is given, has drenched the world with blood, and made fiery havoc of the most virtuous citizens.

The two chaplains to congress, have about that sum annually. This money they receive for religious services, by the force of the laws of the national legislature. That a legal compensation for religious services, is a species of religious establishment, will not be denied, it is presumed, and to what extent this little horn may grow, is a matter of uncertainty.

The rulers of the earth are under obligation to serve the Lord with fear, as much as other men, and if they are disposed to have chaplains, it is not to be reprehended; but to support them by law, and make the nation pay for their devotion, is the thing to be reprobated.

This error, however, is perfectly congenial with the constitutions and laws of Massachusetts and New Hampshire, and with the old habits and laws of Connecticut, in which states religion is considered an object, and religious societies creatures of state policy.

The evil of blending religion and property—religion and education—religion and commissions—religion and politics together, has been abundantly exposed, but not yet forsaken. In addition to all the arguments which have been used to dissolve the firm, I shall here subjoin two, which I have seldom or never seen brought into the debate.

First. Every article, which is so mysterious and subtle in its nature, that natural men, as such, cannot understand it, must be excluded from legislation, otherwise men would be called upon to legislate about that which they cannot understand. Now, the Christian religion, "is not of this world—is hidden from the wise and prudent—the things thereof are not received and cannot be known by natural men." These sayings are prominent in the scheme itself. If, then, the Christian religion be true, these sayings are true; and if these sayings are true, then natural men cannot understand what religion is; and, if they cannot understand it, they are utterly incompetent to legislate about it.

But, if the Christian religion be false, it cannot be right to make laws to support it, for, in so doing, government would undertake to support a lie. Whether, therefore, the Christian religion be true or false, it is not an article of legislation. In this case, Bible Christians, and Deists, have an equal plea against self-named Christians, who (because they are void of the spirit, and ignorant of the precepts of the gospel) tyranize over the consciences of others, under the specious garb of religion and good order.

To avoid the force of this argument, some undertake to support the idea, that none but saints should bear rule, and such characters do understand, and, therefore, are competent to legislate in matters of religion.

If this argument has any weight at all, it proves that government is founded in grace, and I appeal to the truth of history, if any governments have ever been so unjust and cruel, as those which have claimed a gracious foundation. With this pretence, the mad-men of Munster esteemed, it lawful to kill and plunder all the wicked princes. In the same view of the subject, the Spaniards justified themselves in the massacre of two hundred thousand South American idolaters. In the same point of light, the Pope offered to give America away the year after it was discovered, to his Christian subjects. On the same foundation crusades have been formed (i. e., armies raised under the cross of Christ,) to kill and take possession of all the property of ungodly infidels. And I appeal to experience, if any of the governments of the United States are so cruel, in matters of conscience, as these eastern states, where there is the greatest noise made about religious qualifications for rulers.

These consequences always have, and, I believe, always will follow the erroneous idea, that "government is founded in grace." But

Secondly. If the affairs of the souls of men and eternity are articles of legislation, of course they are cognizable before the courts of judicature.

A few years past, a criminal was tried for his life, at Newport. The counsel for the prisoner at the bar, addressed the jury thus: "Gentlemen, you have the life of the prisoner in your hands, and with that, in some sense, the disposal of his soul; for, should you condemn him to death, and his soul be unprepared, he would go to eternal woe." "Hold! hold!" cried the judge, "the jury have nothing to do with his soul and eternity." "I know it," replied the crafty attorney, "but the thought was so impressive that I could not forbear." The spectators beheld the art of the barrister to affect the jury, which, in the event, produced a verdict of not guilty. In this case, the great judge and great lawyer both agreed that courts of justice had no cognizance of the affairs of souls and eternity, and I conclude that all who hear me to-day, approve of their judgment. Well, if courts of justice have nothing to do with those affairs, of course legislatures have not; otherwise there would be no correspondence between the judiciary and legislative departments. I know men often make use of that little, indescribable something, which is made anything, everything, and nothing of, (I mean conscience,) to assist them to do that which reason condemns, and nature shudders at.

In the year 1780, when the constitution of Massachusetts was formed, the third article of the bill of rights occasioned a long and close debate. A gentleman, at the head of his party, said: "We believe in our consciences that the best way to serve God, is to have religion protected and ministers of the gospel supported by law, and we hope that no gentlemen here will wish to wound our tender consciences." The plain English of which is: "Our consciences dictate that all the commonwealth of Massachusetts must submit to our judgments, and if they do not, they will wound our tender conscience." Had a Jew and a Turk been in the same convention, and founded a plea on tender conscience—the first, to abstain from hogs' flesh, and the last, to abstain from wine, would the gentleman have been so careful of hurting the soft feelings of the son of Isaac, and the son of Ishmael, that he would have abstained from pork and wine all his days? And yet the Israelites were forbidden to eat swine's flesh, and the Nazarites and Rechabites were forbidden to drink wine, in the sacred volume, the Bible; but where shall we turn to the page, in that blessed book, which gives orders to the rulers of this world, to make any laws to protect the Christian religion, or support the preachers of it?

Why is my liberty judged? and why am I condemned by another man's conscience? Condemned for that for which I give thanks. But I forbear—I must suppress the feelings of my heart—to dwell longer on this subject, would not correspond with the arrangements of the day.

Gentlemen: this town, Cheshire, has been famous for republican principles. In those times, when no timber was put into the building but Federal oak, and when no sentimental currency passed but that which came from Federal mints; when it was sedition to question the infallibility of those in authority, and disorganization to dispute the divinity of every part of the administration; even then, the inhabitants of Cheshire were firm, and almost unanimous in their suffrages, for a change of measures. With placid patriotism, they saw their lands valued, and their glass numbered, which let in the light of heaven to their houses, together with their paper stamped; all to support an army, which was raised for a war, that existed nowhere, but in the heads of those who adopted the measures; yet no mean murmuring was heard among it all; but when your voices were constitutionally called for, you were decided for a change. Your exertions, with the exertions of others in the United States, have been crowned with success. A change has taken place—a change for the better—a change which, without the internal taxes, has sunk millions of our debt, and added to the United States an extensive empire, without a drop of blood, which can be paid for without recourse to taxes, by continuing the sinking fund but three years longer than the time first allotted for the redemption of the debt.

In view of all these things, the words of an illustrious gentleman, who resided on the fertile banks of the Nile, to his brethren, are applicable:—"See that ye fall not out by the way." "Let us divide and conquer them," was the doctrine of Great Britain, in the revolutionary war. "Let them be divided, and we shall yet conquer them," is the doctrine of the Federalists. "United we stand, divided we fall," was the song of the Whigs, through the war. "United we stand, divided we fall," is still the watchword for Republicans. In high Federal times, we were assured that the men who were then in office were the exclusive friends of the people and of the constitution, and that all the measures of government were pure—that no other men in the nation were equally able to wield the sceptre, and that a different line of administration would ruin the people. A change of men and measures, however, has taken place, notwithstanding the hideous outcry. Upon this change, the hopes of the Federalists were, that the people would not be eased of their burthens, and that the debt would not be diminished, that the hearts of the people might be weaned from the Republican agents, and be turned to themselves. But herein their hopes have been blasted. At present, their only hope seems to be, that the Republicans will fall out by the way, and that they themselves shall rise upon the ruins of the divided house. Hence, the propriety of the text, "see that ye fall not out by the way." Sacrifice a thousand little electioneering quibbles, rather than lose sight of the great importance of union. Gentlemen, I plead for the rights of men to-day, against the insatiable thirst of ambitious mortals, to subjugate their fellow creatures to the lowest grade of vassalage. I plead the cause of my own life; for, should the Federal party once more gain the ascendency, it is beyond calculation to tell at what point they would stop. From principle, and from the chagrin which they have had, it is reasonable to suppose that the measures of '98 would be no more than the first stair in the case. I honestly declare, that if that inauspicious day should come, I should esteem my life very insecure—I should hardly value my head at a cent; and, empty as it is, I am fond of it. Should it be cut off, I question whether there is a head in the United States, that would suit my shoulders as well.

My words may be rude, but they are full of meaning—they flow from the centre of my heart. For more than twenty years, the rights of men, civil and religious, have been fostered in my bosom; and (next to the salvation of the soul) have called forth the exertion of my small talents in their defence, against the attacks of tyrants, bearing what name soever. It is not the prospect, nor the desire of any office, that makes me take a decided part in the laws, and modes of administration, but principle alone.

Let the people be sovereign—let their earnings be secured to them by law, deducting therefrom what is necessary for the protection of the rest—let their alienable rights be defended by government, and their inalienable rights be sacred as the holy ark—too awful for government to meddle with. Then, so far as happiness is to be expected from government, the sacred benediction is applicable: "Happy is the people that is in such a case."

Government is frequently blamed for those evils which arise from other sources. Where people are indolent, profligate and quarrelsome, given to tattling, drunkenness, dissipation and debauchery, no government on earth, nor, indeed, in heaven itself, can make them happy. The habits of industry, frugality, friendship, sobriety and morality, must, therefore, be cherished among a people, or all the proficiency which they can make in constitutions and laws will not help them.

Here let me recommend to your view, as a model of life, the simple, balmy precepts of the gospel. I grant the gospel has, for its main object, the state of the soul in a succeeding world; yet the precepts of it are wonderfully calculated for the good of men in this present life. A few of them I will here extract. "Lie not one to another—let every man speak the truth to his neighbor—see that ye love one another—live peaceably with all men—do good unto all men—owe no man anything but to love one another—let not the sun go down on your wrath—use not your liberty for an occasion to the flesh, but by love serve one another—be courteous and tender-hearted, forgiving one another—render unto all their due—remember them who are in bonds, as bound with them—study to be quiet, and do your own business, and to work with your own hands—be patient towards all men—see that none render evil for evil—speak evil of no man—be not overcome of evil, but overcome evil with good—whatsoever ye would that men should do unto you, do ye also unto them—be not forgetful to entertain strangers—husbands, love your wives—wives, obey your husbands—parents, provoke not your children to wrath, lest they be discouraged—children, obey your parents—masters, give unto your servants that which is just and equal—servants, obey your masters—let every soul be subject to the higher powers—thou shalt not speak evil of the ruler of thy people. Finally, whatsoever things are true, whatsoever things are honest, whatsoever things are just, whatsoever things are pure, whatsoever things are lovely, whatsoever things are of good report; if there be any virtue, and if there be any praise, think on these things."

These extracts contain a few of the maxims and precepts of the New Testament, written with amazing simplicity and perspicuity, enjoining a temper of mind and correspondent behaviour towards men, superlatively excellent, which every man must own, whether he believes in the atonement of a mediator, and a consequent pardon of sin, together with the resurrection from the dead, or not. No treatises on heathen morality, nor any code of ethics, drawn by human pencil, unassisted by inspiration, that I have seen, bears any comparison therewith. How different the picture of virtue, given in the gospel, from that which is given by pagan authors, which consists only in heroism, love of country, revenge and suicism. Let, then, these sacred essays be cherished among you; they will greatly assist republicans—they will reform Federalists, and make something of nothingarians—they are calculated to amend the hearts of the vicious, and reform the lives of the profligate.

Let me also recommend to you, a line of proper decorum on days of election and at all your town meetings. If any thing on earth would disgust me at popular government, the disorders and confusion that too often attend such meetings, would do it. How painful it is to the presiding officer of the day, to grow hoarse calling to order. How mortifying to a man of wisdom and prudence, to be interrupted by the loud, unmeaning words of another. It is true that men sometimes carry their points against wisdom and experience, by loud, insignificant declamation. In such cases, the wise had rather lose their object than to contend for it in a manner so impolite and clownish; so, stronger beasts yield their path to the skunk, rather than to contend with a combatant so disagreeable.

The laws of this state give almost universal right of suffrage to men of age; seeing then that ye have all an equal voice, strive to be equal, strive to excel in civil virtue. The good rule, laid down in ancient book, is, "ye may all speak one by one, that all may hear, all learn and all be edified." A man has no excuse, in the rules of good manners, to interrupt another, when speaking, in common cases; yet such interruptions are not only common, but the intruder often wins fame, as a man of public spirit, contending for his right.

There is a respect due to age; the ancient should be treated as fathers. What can be more unseemly than for young men, with fierce spirits and voices, to drown the voice of that wisdom which is gained alone by age and experience. To this, however, there is a counter evil. Old men often grow sovereign and sour, self conceited and dogmatical. Their natural powers have failed, they will own, but their moral powers are in bloom; their judgment, in particular, is in its meridian; and young men are but upstarts, hardly fit to be set with the dogs of their flocks. Such men do not rejoice that others increase, while they themselves decrease; nor exult that *Sparta* has fifty men more virtuous than they; but strive to crush youthful ingenuity, lest it should supplant superannuated importance.

Let this fiend of society have no habitation among you, but cherish every appearance of talents in young men. Information is the very lungs of republicanism; for want of it, free governments languish, and give way to despotism. It would be a laudable strife among the towns in Berkshire, to produce the best statesman. By a statesman, I do not mean the man who will be most noisy at town meetings, nor he who publishes most egotism in newspapers; not the man who is always pleading for the prerogatives of government, and forgetting the rights of the people, nor the crouching sycophant, who will fish all day for a royal nibble, or a lucrative office. But the man who understands the laws of nations, and the constitution and laws of his country—who can draw the proper line between the alienable and inalienable rights of men—who has distinct ideas of those objects which are legal and those which are moral—who can trace effects up to their causes, and follow causes down to their effects—who conceives government to be a national compact, a simple agreement among the citizens, and not a mysterious monster—who can pursue the sly arts and arguments of monarchists and aristocrats, those curses to the world, through their various windings, and drive them from their intrenchments—who will not be decoyed by the flowery sophistry of a courtier, but abide firm by simple, fundamental principles—who will not buy an office by flattery and deceit, and then sell the people to pay for it—who loves responsibility, and is aiming to give rulers power enough to do good, and yet have it so counterpoised that they can do no hurt. Such men would be precious as gold, yea, more precious than a golden wedge of Ophir. Young gentlemen, here is a copy for you, and

"Tho' of exact perfection we despair,
Yet ev'ry step to virtue's worth our care."

Let the vices and follies of the age shift for themselves, while you apply your hearts to the acquisition of wisdom. While you think with the wise, you will often find it expedient to speak with the vulgar.

Veritas in puteo; as truth lies in a well, you will have to dig deep and draw long to get it. "How dark! how intricate the road that leads to intellectual light." As you gain wisdom you will grow in modesty, for modesty is the child of wisdom, and impudence the offspring of ignorance. Let your conclusions be the result of much study—form your judgments upon a preponderancy of evidence—let your arguments be dispassionate, and the reasons you offer exceed your assertions—never betray the smallest trust reposed in you—discharge every office you are entrusted with, with fidelity and despatch—husband well your time, while your powers of body and mind are active—remember it is beneath the dignity of human nature to be employed about trifles—never foul your hands or spot your garments with the dirty contentions, scandals and prejudices of the age—finally, be men—add human dignity to the genius of the mind, candor to information, and bestow pity on ignorance. Never, with keen reply, consume the affections of those who stand astonished at the copious lustre of your arguments. Were a young Randolph, that prodigy of genius, present, I would deal out the same lecture, nor think the admonition either unfriendly or ill-timed.

The fundamental principle of republicanism is this; "that all powers of government are vested in, and consequently derived from, the many individuals that form the body politic; and therefore all those who are raised to power, are responsible to their constituents for their conudct." With this sage maxim before your eyes, you will rarely err in your pursuits; and if this principle does not justify an *Elective Judiciary*, it is because there is no logical force in argument.

If my address, young gentlemen, appears too dictatorial, the habits which I have contracted, by my calling, the furrows in my cheeks, and the desire I have for you to excel, are my only apologies.

SERMON

PREACHED AT ANKRAM, DUTCHESS COUNTY, N. Y., AT THE ORDINATION OF REV. LUMAN BIRCH.

JUNE 17, 1806.

Isaiah, vi., 6, 7.—"Then flew one of the Seraphims unto me, having a live coal in his hand, which he had taken with the tongs from off the altar: And he laid it upon my mouth, and said, Lo, this hath touched thy lips; and thine iniquity is taken away, and thy sin purged."

With more than eastern pomp of diction—in language sublime, beyond the power of art—the sacred poet here represents the Almighty, in awful emblems of divine majesty. Uzziah, the king of Judah, with a complex character, had reigned upon the throne of the house of David for more than fifty years: but kings, as well as slaves must die. In the year that Uzziah died, the prophet Isaiah had a vision of the King, the Lord of Hosts, sitting upon a throne, more resplendent than the ivory throne of Solomon—higher than the heavens—with a train which filled the superb temple of glory, while the dazzling seraphims, with veiled faces, clapped their golden wings, and proclaimed, "the whole earth is full of his glory."

Whoever reads the visions of Isaiah, Ezekiel and John, will not hesitate to pronounce them the same in substance. Isaiah calls these winged songsters *seraphims*. Ezekiel calls them *living creatures* and *cherubims*. John calls them *four beasts*, but their appearance and employment is the same in all their accounts, except the more particular description given by some, which is omitted by the others.

Various are the opinions of men respecting these seraphims, and perhaps no man can certainly tell what or who they represent. The greatest number of expositors, however, that I have read after, conclude that the angels of God are intended. They seem to imagine that their appearance and employment are too celestial to be accommodated to any beings on earth. But one insurmountable difficulty attends their comment. In Revelations, v., 9, they sing to the Lamb, "Thou wast slain and hast *redeemed us* to God by thy blood." If Angels in light were *confirmed* by God in a Mediator, which is highly probable, yet, as they never left their first estate, it cannot be admitted that they were ever *redeemed* by the blood of the Lamb. Of course then angels cannot be intended.

With all the embarrassments that attend the interpretation, yet, with Dr. Gill, it appears most likely to me, that the ministers of the gospel are to be understood by these singular creatures. In this light, therefore, I shall consider them. And, as there is the most minute description given of them in the first chapter of Ezekiel, I shall make many of my bearings upon that chapter.

They are there said to be *Living creatures*. Ministers are creatures, made by God, and poor feeble creatures they are—earthen vessels, subject to human passions and frailties. But yet they are *living* creatures, being raised from the death of sin to the life of holiness. Though they die daily, and are crucified with Christ, yet they live, and the life which they live is by the faith of the Son of God, who lives in them. Their number is

Four. Reference may here be had to the four principal standards of the Hebrew camp in the wilderness, on which it is said, the four emblems of a lion, ox, man, and eagle, were inscribed: or to the four evangelists who wrote the gospel, and all their successors in the four quarters of the world.

And every one had four faces. First, the *likeness and face of a man*. Ministers are men, not angels—their work is among men, unto whom they are sent, and they should ever remember that they are but men. To prevent Ezekiel from being self-exalted through the abundance of sublime revelations, he is called the *son of man* about ninety times.

Second. *The face of a Lion*. The righteous are bold as a lion, and surely ministers, who are clothed with the garments of salvation, and the robes of righteousness, may, ought to be, and are, bold as lions. Peter and John, though unlearned and ignorant, by their boldness, made the rulers and elders of Israel marvel. They spake the word of God with boldness. The religion of Jesus makes men bold, but not impudent—modest, but not shamefaced and hypocritical.

Third. *The face of an Ox*. The Israelites were not to muzzle the ox that trod out the corn, which Paul says, was written for the ministers. Much increase is by the strength of the ox. Ministers are patient and laborious, like oxen, bending their neck in obedience—bearing the yoke of the gospel on their shoulders—drawing the plough of God's word, to break up the fallow-ground of the heart.

Fourth. *They four had the face of an Eagle*. As lions are the strongest among beasts, and turn not aside for any—disdaining all subtle arts, and trusting alone to their strength—so eagles are kings of the air, taking the loftiest flight of all birds, having the keenest eyes of any, which can gaze on the sun without winking, and fixing their eyes on the sun, will steer their course upwards, until they lose sight of the earth. So the ambassadors of Christ take their lofty flights to the throne of God—have their conversation in heaven—gaze on the Son of Righteousness by faith—and are so allured by heavenly objects, that they lose sight of earth and earthly things; and, like the eagle, where the slain are, there is she: where Christ, the slain lamb—the sacrifice for sin, is revealed in the gospel—there the preachers dwell.

It is moreover said, that these living creatures *were full of eyes within—before and behind*. Ministers have *eyes within*, to see their own corruption and weakness; *eyes before* to look unto God for instruction and strength; *eyes behind*, to see the world lying in wickedness, and also have an eye over the saints, who are following them, as they are following Christ.

These Seraphims *had every one of them fixed wings*. Ezekiel speaks of but four of them, but Isaiah and John describe six. *With twain he covered his face*. Repentance and humility cover the face of the minister of Jesus, and, indeed, the face of every human saint. As creatures, we are needy—as sinners, we are guilty; as creatures, we should be humble—as sinners, repentant; that, as creatures we may be supplied, and as sinners be pardoned. The call to the ministry does not exalt the preacher to be Lord over God's heritage, nor deliver him from the internal mass of corruption, or the outward adversities of life: hence humility and repentance ever cover his face.

With twain he covered his feet. That is, he runs as if he flew: at least, like the ostrich, his wings assist his feet. Fervency and resolution are subservient to his feet. When the preacher turns his course to heaven, with what fervency does he pursue the road of prayer, and with what resolution does he resist the fiery darts of the wicked—the accusations of Satan—his inbred unbelief at the delays of divine beneficence. When he steers his course among men, with what fervency does he run to and fro; being fervent in spirit, he speaks and teaches diligently the things of the Lord, with a resolution so great that neither entreaties nor threats can prevent him from finishing his course with joy.

And with twain he did fly. Faith and love are the two wings with which he flies. Faith in God—in the mediation of Christ—in the divinity of the Scriptures—in the accountability of all rational beings—in the resurrection from the dead, and a future state of rewards and punishment; together with love to God—to the gospel, and to the souls of men, constrain him to preach and bear him up as on wings. By these six wings the heralds of Christ fly through the midst of heaven, having the everlasting gospel to preach to them that dwell on the earth.

When they went, their wings were lifted up, but when they stood, they let down their wings. When ministers are engaged in preaching, and repentance and humility, fervency and resolution, faith and love are all in lively exercise, how charming is their voice, how beautiful their feet; but when they cease, and attend to the lawful callings of this life, to provide necessary things for their own houses, and those heavenly accomplishments do not appear, how different they seem to be: a bystander, with difficulty believes them to be the same men.

And their feet were straight feet. It is required of stewards that a man be found faithful. A bishop must be blameless—must have a good report of them who are without—must be an example to the flock—a pattern of them that believe—must make straight paths for his feet, and walk uprightly without crooking in conversation or practice.

In some preachers, there is so great discordance between their preaching and conduct, that when they are in the pulpit we wish they would never come out, and when they are out, we wish them never to ascend it again: but the true ministers of Jesus have straight feet. The sense of the phrase, however, seems to be, that they were cloven-footed like an ox or calf. Beasts of prey have crooked feet, at least crooked claws in them, with which they devour the lives of others; but the ministers of Christ carry neither mental or material weapons to deceive the souls, or destroy the lives of men with. Like the clean beasts of Moses, they chew the cud of God's precepts and promises, and are cloven-footed, without claws to devour.

And they sparkled like the color of burnished brass. Ministers like John the Baptist, are burning and shining lights, and, like the prophet, are like iron pillars and a brazen wall. It is further added, *their appearance was like unto burning coals of fire,* to consume the chaff and stubble of error and hypocrisy, sin and self-righteousness: and also to warm the affections and soften the hearts of the saints, as well as to frighten and drive off the wolves and dogs, and all the enemies of the flock. *And like the appearance of lamps, it went up and down among the living creatures.* From this it seems that each cherub had a lamp in his hand, and as they sometimes were rising on their wings, and at other times standing on their feet, the lamp of each went up and down among them. The word of the Lord is a light to our feet, and a lamp to our path, and preachers hold forth this word of life, the entrance of which giveth light: preach the word, the sure word of prophecy, which is a light shining in a dark place, and thereby enlighten the children of God to walk on in this world of darkness.

And the fire was bright, and out of the fire went forth lightning. The light of scripture is *bright.* All the mighty volumes of philosophers are trifling to the Bible. They give no account how sin can be pardoned, or the dead raised, but the sacred volume informs us how the first can be, and assures us that the last shall take place: and from this fountain of bright light, lightnings proceed. When ministers have their wings up—full of burning love—holding up the lamp of the gospel, and succeeded by the Holy Ghost, the effect on the hearers is frequently like a flash of lightning. Lightning will burst the strongest wall—break down the loftiest tree—follow the vein of a tree from top to bottom—melt the buckle in the shoe, and spare the man who wears it—kill the child unborn without injuring the mother, etc. All which seems to be expressive of the power of the gospel in the hand of the spirit, when ministers are proclaiming the truth. This word of God is quick and powerful, sharper than a two-edged sword, piercing even to the dividing asunder of soul and spirit, joints and marrow, and is a discerner of the thoughts and intents of the heart. It tears off the veil of the heart—rends the stupor from the conscience—removes the film from the eye of the soul—lays death naked, and destruction without a covering—destroys self-righteous props, and hypocritical hopes, and teaches the sinner that he must perish forever unless he repents of his sin, believes in the Saviour, and submits to his laws.

When preachers are thus assisted, and thus succeeded, it may with truth be said, *the sound of the cherubim's wings is heard, even to the outer court, as the voice of the Almighty God, when he speaketh.*

When Isaiah had this vision of the King, the Lord of Hosts, on his dazzling throne of glory, and saw the splendor of his attendants, and heard their celestial doxology, he cried out, *wo is me.* Unlike those shining songsters—unfit to dwell among them! this body of sin renders me obnoxious, and sinks me beneath a heavy wo; nor can I extricate myself, *for I am undone.* Undone in character, for I have risen in rebellion against the Lord of Hosts, and am guilty of high treason. Undone in health and strength, for the first born of death is in my tabernacle. I am reduced to perfect weakness, and my obstinate disease will reduce me to the caverns of death. Undone in interest, being a fugitive and bankrupt, owing ten thousand talents, and having nothing to pay; nor can I solicit remission from my creditor, in a manner that becomes his majesty and my own wretchedness, *for I am a man of unclean lips.* Out of the abundance of the heart the mouth speaketh. My heart abounds with corruption, which vitiates all I say and do. Had I the hallowed lips of these seraphims, how would I address the throne of glory, and plead for my life! but now, like a crane or a swallow, so do I chatter; I mourn sore, like the dove; nor can I expect relief from any around me, for *I dwell among a people of unclean lips,* who are in a state of apostacy, like myself, none of whom can, by any means, redeem a brother, nor give to God a ransom that he should still live, and not perish. But, ruined and unclean as I am, and vile as all my fellow creatures are, I did not perceive it till of late. While I only heard of God with the hearing of the ear, and was ignorant of the nature of the divine law, I conceived myself to be better than my neighbors—

worthy of heaven, and peculiarly interested in the favor of God. But now *mine eyes have seen the King, the Lord of Hosts,* which discovers to me how wretchedly I am fallen from that image in which I was created. Now I see the holiness, justice and goodness of the divine law, whereby sin revives, and I see how unclean I am. In presence of the Lord of Hosts, and the holy throng of seraphims, I abhor myself, repenting in dust and ashes. (The text follows.)

Then flew one of the seraphims. By special commission from the Lord of Hosts, he came, not reluctantly, but of a ready mind—he flew on wings to my relief. I did not go to him, nor meet him half way, but he came *unto me,* not empty handed, but *having a living coal in his hand.* An emblem of the promise of eternal life through the Mediator; which promise God made, ere time began, to Christ the Lord, and revealed it unto men in ancient times—which runs through the Old Testament like a golden cord, and which was sent unto them that believed, by the apostles. But this coal, which ever lives, ever glows, and never burns out, cannot be taken by merely human hands, but *with the tongs* —the dispensation of the gospel. Though men, as such, cannot lay hold of, carry, and apply this coal to its designed use; yet, by the dispensation of the gospel, committed to their trust, the ministers of Christ can and do. This promise comes to penitent sinners, through Christ; who, through the eternal spirit, offered himself to God, who was himself priest, offering and altar. Hence this coal is said to be *taken from off the altar.*

And he laid it upon my mouth. Which encouraged him to pray—enabled him to offer the calves of his lips in praise, and prepared him to speak to the people, unto whom he was now sent. *And said, lo, this has touched thy lips.* For the purposes just mentioned. *And thine iniquity is taken away,* through the atonement of Christ, who was made sin for us, that we might be made the righteousness of God in him. *And thy sin purged,* by the grace of God, which is shed abroad in the hearts of men, by the Holy Ghost, through the righteousness of Jesus Christ.

It is probable that the narrative, which I have been animadverting upon, is a history of the first conversion of Isaiah to God; if so, then, like Paul, he was called to the prophetic work at the time when he was called out of darkness into the light of truth. He began his prophecies in the days of Uzziah; and, if not until the last year of his reign, this vision was his inauguration. But, if he had begun before the year in which Uzziah died, then this vision was made to him, to prepare him for greater usefulness.

At the close of this vision, Isaiah *heard the voice of the Lord, saying, whom shall I send? and who will go for us?* To which the prophet answered, *here am I, send me. And he said, go.* And as the seraphim has done to you, so do you to all humble penitents. Whenever you find any person lamenting thus, "wo is me, for I am undone," fly with all speed to administer relief, and say unto the penitent, "thine iniquity is forgiven, and thy sin purged."

In this view of the subject, the character of an humble penitent, and the work of a gospel-preacher, solicit the attention of this august assembly.

Though repentance can never atone for the crime, yet it is an essential characteristic of the sinner who shall find pardon and salvation. There is one excellency of mind which is preferable to repentance, and that is innocence. It is better to be innocent, free from any crime, than it is to repent of a crime committed. But when men have become criminal, repentance may be considered a qualification of the first grade. That all have sinned, is certain, and, therefore, to expect salvation by innocency, is out of the question.

Such is the relation between the Creator and rational creatures, that, whatever the Creator reveals and commands, the creatures are under obligation to believe and obey; and no place or condition that the creatures can be in, does in any wise free them from this obligation. The apostacy of men, therefore, forms no good excuse for them to disbelieve or rebel, either in this life or in that to come. That all men, everywhere, are commanded to repent, is certain; and he who does not obey this command, condemns the law and lawgiver, and pleads for the usurpation of sin. Such, however, is the apostacy of men—so great is their obstinacy, pride, rebellion and love of sin, that neither the precepts of the law, the threatenings of God, the lashes of conscience, the pangs of death, nor the torments of hell, will bring them to *that* repentance, to which is annexed forgiveness of sins. Until the Lord works *first* in the human heart, by his gracious influence, nothing is to be expected, to purpose. In the change of mind, commonly called *conversion*, or the *new birth*, there are three distinct things to be conceived of.

First. *The communication of divine life.* Not the same life that Adam possessed in innocency, for that was lost, whereas this which is given is called *eternal life*. In some respects, it is like the Adamic life, in that it makes us love holiness, and take complacency in the character and government of God. In other respects, it is inferior, not delivering us from all moral evil; but, in other respects, vastly superior, being eternal in its nature, and tending to a station far more exalted. Whether this grace is called living water—incorruptible seed—new creation—an unction from the Holy One, or by what name soever, it comes down from God, through the Mediator, and rectifies all the powers of the soul. This lays a foundation for spiritual instruction; for, as well may a lifeless corpse understand natural things, as a natural man understand spiritual things. In this detached part of the work, the preachers and preaching are out of the question, Christ having reserved the power to do this in his own hands. It should be carefully noticed, that a *change of heart*, is one thing, and the information of the mind, another. When the soul is renewed, then follows

Secondly. *An active and voluntary turning to God.* In this stage of the work, nature and grace, sin and holiness, truth and error, darkness and light, ignorance and information, hope and fear, desire and languor, Christ and Satan, all assail the soul. Some are held years in this restless state, and others but a short time. But, notwithstanding all embarrassments, the soul is willing, and comes to Christ voluntarily, and chooses the good part. After men repent and believe, and before they are sealed with the holy spirit of promise, their views are accurately described, by the prophet, in my context. "Wo is me, for I am undone; for I am a man of unclean lips, and I dwell among a people of unclean lips." Or thus: "Lord, I am a sinner, and deserve to perish. Thy character is good, thy law is just, but I am carnal, sold under sin. If thou sendest me to hell, I cannot impeach thy righteousness; but, oh! spare me, if pardon may be had. My sins are many and great, and my best works need to be washed, as well as my soul. I have no hope, but in thy mercy, through the mediation of Christ. At the feet of Jesus, I cast me down, and, if I must perish, I will perish there."

The Bible is full of encouragements, invitations and promises, to such gracious penitents; all these promises of God are in Christ Jesus. From this altar, the preachers may take their living coals, and ministerially apply them to all such humble mourners. For, if preachers and preaching are excluded from the first part of the work, yet in the stage, of which I am now speaking, they are workers together with God.

But, Thirdly. *Free pardon*, which is graciously bestowed by God, and gratefully received by the returning, humble penitent. It is not to be wondered at, that those who believe that pardon of sin is the change of heart, that men are not renewed until they obtain sealing deliverance, should have so high opinion of the self-exertion of natural faculties, to forward them on to a change of heart; for they well know that before they obtained pardon, they had sorrow for sin, longings after God, love to the saints, and a regard for the worship of God, and perhaps found the pardon of sin, while they were praying and striving for it. Taking it for truth, that they were not graciously changed, before they obtained pardon and deliverance, they suppose that others, in their natural state of mind, can do what they did. Hence the opinion, that self-exertion of the natural powers greatly helps the sinner, and lays God under obligation to bestow pardon. I cannot by any means concede to this opinion, for a multitude of reasons; but am full in belief that the exercises of humble penitents, before they receive a sealing pardon, are as acceptable to God as the exercises of those who have had the forgiveness of sins sealed to them, and equally bring them within the compass of the promise, "if we confess our sins, he is faithful and just to forgive us our sins." For I cannot conceive of any difference of internal character between them. No difference in the subjects; the difference is objective; one having the comfort of believing his sins pardoned, and the other without that comfortable hope. Men are either for Christ or against him, enemies or friends, dead or alive; no medium can be conceived of. To say that a sinner has spiritual light, but not life; that he is quickened, but not renewed; that he mourns for sin, but does not love holiness; that he feels the burden of sin, but has no gracious sensation; that he loves the saints, but is not born of God, &c., to me is perfectly absurd.

From the moment a sinner receives the grace of life (infants and those who are incapable of reflection excepted) he begins to cry like the leper, "unclean, unclean." Or like the prophet before us, "wo is me, for I am undone." And not only continues this cry, until he obtains pardon, through Christ, but on thereafter as long as he draws mortal breath. For when a penitent receives pardon of sin, it only gives him new and pleasing views of his state, not of his internal character. Of course repentance is not an exercise, confined to the period between being changed and pardoned, but continues to operate in the soul of a saint through his whole pilgrimage on earth. The complaint of Isaiah, "wo is me" etc., was not the complaint of a backslider, fallen from grace; for these things said Esaias when he saw his glory and spake of him. Now, as the saints are constantly sighing and crying, repenting and lamenting, (at least these complaints mingle with all their heavenly joys,) ministers, like the seraphim, are sent by God, with a "comfort ye, comfort ye, my people, saith your God—feed my lambs and sheep—let your profiting appear to all; teaching them to observe all things whatsoever I have commanded you," etc.

Nor is the preacher to confine his addresses to penitents alone, but is commanded to preach the gospel to every creature. There is no article in Christendom, in which ministers are more divided, than in that of addressing a congregation of sinners, as such. Most of the addresses of the prophets, were unto the children of Israel, a people in circumstances dissimilar from all other nations, or unto other nations in their political capacities; for which reasons, a gentile gospel preacher cannot find a sure sample in the Old Testament. Jssus Christ, who spake with authority, spake as man never spake, confined his ministry to the twelve tribes, which still continues the difficulty of finding a sure precedent in the four evangelists. But when we come to the tenth chapter of the Acts, we find something direct. Peter was called by a heavenly vision to go and preach to a gentile congregation, the principal of which was warned by a holy angel to send for Peter; and who, with the congregation, presented themselves before God, to hear all things which God commanded Peter to preach. Here the drama opens.

Here the first gospel sermon was preached to the Gentiles. From this instance we may expect the best pattern. And what is it?

After Peter had introduced the subject, of declaring his conviction that God did not respect the Jews more than the Gentiles, but equally accepted those of all nations, who feared him and wrought righteousness; and spoken a little of the word which God sent to the children of Israel, preaching peace by Jesus Christ, who was Lord of Jews and Gentiles; that this word was published from Galilee, through all Judea; testifying that God had annointed Jesus Christ with the Holy Ghost and with power, who went about doing good, and healing all that were oppressed with the devil; he then proceeds to the main business of his mission. "And we are witnesses of all things which he did, both in the land of the Jews and in Jerusalem; whom they slew and hanged on a tree. Him God raised up the third day, and showed him openly, not to all the people, but unto witnesses chosen before of God, even to us, who did eat and drink with him after he rose from the dead. And he commanded us to preach unto the people, and to testify that it was he who was ordained of God to be the judge of quick and dead. To him give all the prophets witness, that through his name whosoever believeth in him shall receive remission of sins." This short sermon was delivered extempore. Without abstruse questions or metaphysical niceties, the preacher gave a detail of important facts and doctrines, in the most simple manner, in which we discover the following truths:

1. That God does not respect the person, rank or national character of one man more than another.

2. That he accepts of such, and only such, as fear God and work righteousness.

3. That the word of the gospel, which was first sent to the Jews, by John, and afterwards prevailed ahundantly, proclamed peace to men, through Jesus Christ.

4. That Jesus Christ is Lord of all worlds, nations and beings.

5. That the work of Christ on earth was doing good, and healing all that were oppressed of the devil.

6. That the miracles, precepts and examples of Christ were incompetent to save men. That without the shedding of his blood there could be no remission. That the Jews contrived his death—slew him and hanged him on a tree; they meant it for evil, but God meant it for good. That he died both as a martyr and Mediator.

7. That he was raised from the dead on the third day; being the first born from the dead; thereby, opening the way for the resurrection of all men.

8. That ministers are commanded to preach and testify, that this same Jesus, who died and rose again, is ordained of God to judge the world, both those who are living and those that are dead.

9. That the prophecies of the Old Testament united in the truth of Christ's character; that whosoever believeth in him, shall receive remission of sins.

10. That ministers are only witnesses, to declare the truth, Christ having reserved the power of changing hearts in his own hands.

These seem to have been the main topics of Peter's sermon, the language of which, to all gospel ministers, among the Gentiles, is, "go ye, and do likewise."

As Peter spake these words, the Holy Ghost fell upon all those that heard the word. While the truth fell from Peter's lips, the Holy Ghost fell from heaven, which, when Peter beheld, he commanded them to be baptized in the name of the Lord. The baptism of the Holy Ghost is not an essential prerequisite to water baptism, but repentance towards God, and faith in the Lord Jesus, are essential characteristics; but the baptism of the Holy Ghost does not exempt the possessor from the duty of water-baptism: hence the injunction of Peter.

On the whole, may all of us, who are ministers of Christ, take Peter for our model in preaching, and may we meet with at least a portion of the same success.

Another article, which the foregoing discourse, and the solemnities of this day seem to call for, is a description of a MINISTERIAL CALL: that is, how men are called to the ministry.

First. The call to the ministry does not depend upon the brilliancy of natural talents. The mysteries of the gospel are hidden from the wise and prudent. The world, by wisdom, know not God, etc. Natural talents furnish men for usefulness in the things of this world, but do not qualify them for gospel ambassadors.

Second. Nor does it depend upon the acquisition of schools. By some, the striplings of genius, or striplings without genius, are sent to school with the avowed purpose of preparing them for the ministry; as if the preaching of the gospel was but the declension of nouns, or the conjugation of verbs, with the knowledge of a little Greek and Latin. Supposing, however, they excel, and equal Newton, Milton, or Jefferson, they are but prepared for the study of astronomers, the closet of the poets, or the chair of state. Amos was a rustic herdsman—John the Baptist was brought up in the wilderness—and the apostles, for the most part, were ignorant Galileans, who followed the trade of fishing; yet these were called by God, while the learned among them were neglected.

Third. It is not included in a gracious call out of darkness into the marvelous light of the gospel; this call is experienced by all the saints, but all the saints are not preachers.

Fourth. It is not subservient to the will or choice of men. Where preaching is a lucrative business, the avaricious may choose it—where it is honorable, the proud may desire it—where it is attended with ease, the indolent may covet it; but all theseare ignorant of it.

Fifth. It is not miraculous. It is true that miracles have sometimes attended the commission, as in the case of Moses, Jeremiah and Paul. But the commissions to the twelve, and to the seventy, were without miracles, which proves that miracles are not essential to the call. If the call was miraculous, we should have as good reason to believe that God would call infants, idiots or dumb men, as any others; but this we know is not the case.

Sixth. The call is by *special mission.* Men, who have the common use of their senses—who are delivered from darkness, and translated into the kingdom of the Son of God, receive a *special gift* to qualify them for the work of the ministry. When Christ ascended on high, he received gifts for men, and these gifts he bestowed on them; and he gives to some apostles, to others prophets, evangelists, pastors and teachers, for the work of the ministry, etc. This *spiritual gift* includes two things. First, the *furniture of the mind:* and secondly, a *constraint* to improve. By the furniture of the mind is not meant extraordinary endowments of talents or science, but a gift bestowed with the commission. It is a treasure given to earthen vessels—a dispensation of the gospel committed in trust. When Jesus was on earth, he called to him whom he would, and sent them to preach; so, in every age, the call depends on the will of God. Whether the persons called excel in science or not, when they are sent, they have a roll given them to eat. The great plan of salvation is opened to them, and words and arguments given them to communicate it to others; and yet what they thus receive is but a small part of the treasure, for they have the key of the kingdom of heaven given to them, to unlock the treasure-house (the Bible) and constantly draw things new and old out of that sacred treasure, as occasion calls, in their ministration. When they have eaten the roll and received the key, they feel such *constraint* to run and point out to men their ruin, and the way of recovery, that, like the prophet, they say, "here am I, send me." They have such love to God—to the Mediator, to the gospel, and to the souls of men, that like Paul, they declare, "the love of Christ constraineth us." And like him, they will neither be disobedient to the heavenly vision, nor confer with flesh and blood.

The customary address to the candidate elect, I shall pass by, reserving that part of the solemnities for my worthy brother, who is assigned to administer the charge, and whose age and experience qualify him in an eminent degree for the task. But when I look around me, and see nearly one thousand souls assembled in this grove, to hear and see what is said and done to-day, it affects my heart. Pardon the falling tear, I learned to weep over a multitude, of Jesus. Seeing the multitude, I feel compassion swelling my aching breast. Were my talents equal to my wishes, I would bring forth the riches of the gospel, and hold them up in all their winning forms. But (applying the words of the prophet to myself) by whom shall Jacob arise, for he is small?

Without attempting to solve the questions, how it was possible for sin to take its rise among sinless creatures; whether sin was necessary or otherwise; whether God decreed it or not; what part of Adam's transgression and corruption of nature is attached to us; whether the atonement of Christ is infinite or limited; whether apostacy has affected the will only, or equally all the faculties of the soul; whether the debility of a sinner is moral, natural, or both; whether the want of the holy unction is a crime or not; I say, passing these questions, and a thousand more, which puzzle the minds of men, I would aver, that my hearers, in their natural estate, are such guilty rebels and bitter enemies to God, and a life of holiness, that notwithstanding all the warnings of God; the reproofs of ministers; the laws of state; the sword of the magistrate; the ethics of philosophy; the pangs of sickness; the fears of death; the threatenings of future torments, and the glories prepared for the righteous, they will choose the road that leads to death. "The wicked will do wickedly." The same disposition, which neglects the love and service of God for one minute, would for one eternity. I, therefore, utterly despair of ever seeing a single sinner in this attentive assembly ever turning to God, until the Lord touches his heart with the finger of his gracious power.

If men are ever honest, they will be honest when they pray; and it is a matter of notoriety, that, whenever good men pray for themselves, or for others, their language is: "Lord, have mercy on me, or I shall perish—Lord, have mercy on sinners, or they will perish." Such prayers express the truth; and, while I speak the truth, I would use the prayer to-day: "Lord, have mercy on these poor, needy, guilty sinners; turn them, O Lord, and they will be turned; open their eyes to see, their ears to hear, and their hearts to understand. Grant them repentance and remission of sins, in the name of Jesus Christ." How would my poor soul rejoice to see the goings of my God and King; to hear the sound of his going in the top of these oaks, or rather from the mouths of these people.

It is possible, yea, (from the attention of all, and the tears of some,) it is probable, there may be some broken-hearted, heavy-laden penitents in this assembly; some, who see the extent and propriety of God's law, and the evil nature of sin; who feel the plague of corrupt nature, and the painful load of guilt; who see the imperfection of all their works, and the vitiation of all their powers; who discover the excellency of true religion, and long to possess it; who entertain no scruples about the power of Christ to save, but question his willingness to receive themselves, who are so vile; who do not hesitate to bear all reproaches that attend religion, but fear they shall perish at last, for want of it. If such there be among you to-day, in addition to the complaint of the prophet, "wo is me, for I am undone," you make the inquiry, "what shall I do to be saved?" and suboin the prayer of the publican: "God, be merciful to me a sinner." To such I would address myself, and fly, like the seraphim, with a promise of eternal life, to administer relief. Your case is very uncomfortable, but not desperate. Had God been disposed to slay you, he would not have shown you such things as these; and, as he has begun to teach you, you will see greater things than these. Verily, you are Galileans, for your speech agreeth thereto: and he that has begun the work will finish it. He that has raised you out of the grave of carnal security, will loose you and let you go. He that has opened your eyes to see your dungeon and chains, will also bring you out of the prison-house, and set you free. To-day he is willing to receive you; he calls you to come; he commands you to believe. Nor is there any danger of your being damned, if you see yourselves bad enough to be saved wholly by grace. Then, like the blind and the lame, come to Jesus, and he will heal you. If your father and mother forsake you for your religion, the Lord will take you in. His promise stands thus: "Him that cometh unto me, I will in no wise cast out." Then stretch out the withered hand, and touch the hem of his garment; cast away your clothes, and come unto him begging, and you will receive the sight of pardoned sin.

LINES

INTRODUCED AT THE CONCLUSION OF A DISCOURSE PREACHED ON THE OCCASION OF THE DEATH OF REV. SAMUEL COVELL, 1806.

AH! my dear brother Covell, art thou gone?
Hast thou forsaken earth for worlds unknown?
And hast thou found those mansions, far above,
Where every bosom glows with sacred love?
And hast thou found the disembodied throng,
To sound thy harp in their triumphant song?
And dost thou, now, with angels vie in praise,
And sweep the golden harp, in high seraphic lays?
Is Jesus in thy view? dost thou behold
His sacred head, adorned with radiant gold?
Doth he appear as lovely in their eyes,
As revelation saith, as faith descries?
Yes, thou art gone—thy better part is fled—
Thy body only is among the dead.
Before thy mortal limbs were stiff and cold,
Thy soul was gone ten thousand leagues twice told.
The news from Canada has reached our ears,
Which grieves our hearts, and fills our eyes with tears.
The news declares that Covell's spirit's fled,
Just twenty-seven days he's been among the dead.
Should some departed souls to earth return,
On messages of love of vast concern,
To warn the wicked, comfort the distress'd,
Strengthen the feeble, and relieve the oppress'd;
Should Covell's soul appear with us to-day,
And fill this desk instead of worthless me,
How would the people feel to hear him tell
The joys of heaven and awful pains of hell!
Fancy conjectures, should he come to preach,
He'd deal a double portion out to each.
As spirits cannot speak without the help of clay,
I'll lend him my mortal tongue to-day;
Then hark! and hear what Covell has to say:
"My wife! the partner of my former bed,
Our conjugal enjoyments now are dead;
We bound ourselves for life, but life is gone;
Those who had wives are now as tho' they'd none.
Fleshly connections never can abide
Within these mansions where I now reside;
Yet friendship dear, and fellowship divine,
Are heavenly things which never can decline.

"O Clarissa! weep not for me—'tis vain;
My face you never will behold again.
A widow's hardships you must bear awhile,
Expos'd to injury, distress, and toil,
Always remember what the Lord hath said;
'I'll be the widow's God, the orphan's aid;'
Trust in his word; he never spake in vain;
He'll guide and guard you thro' this world of pain;
Then, in full glory you shall live and reign.
"My first-born, Deidamia, hear your father's voice;
In youthful days, oh, make the Lord your choice.
All things beneath the burning sun are vain;
But Christ is life, and heaven is boundless gain,
Repent of sin, believe in gospel grace,
Then when you die, you'll see your father's face.
"Sally, my lovely Sally, you must die;
Let youthful charms give way to piety.
Tho' I am dead, like Abel now I speak;
O fall, like Mary, at your Savior's feet,
For sinners Jesus bore exquisite pain;—
Let not his blood be spilt for you in vain.
"Cordelia, know thy father loves thee still,
Though, cheerfully resigned to the Almighty's will,
My station now forbids all earthly care,
To feed your body, or your dress repair;
Yet one grave warning I am sent to give,—
Look at your Savior, and your soul shall live.
"Julia, my youngest daughter, charming child,
Be not, by wicked customs e'er beguil'd.
The virtuous pattern; let the virtuous throng
Govern your passions, and command your tongue.
Regard your mother; still her counsels hear;
Keep from her eyes the parent's painful tear.
"Alanson, my son, my lovely, only son,
Farewell my babe, thy father's glass is run;
Whose hand may guide you, what your lot may be,
Is only known to the great Deity.
Know then, thy father's God, my son, in youth;
Receive the Savior; trust the word of truth;
Out of the mouth of babes, God can ordain
Surprising strength to stop the mouths of men.*
"Brethren and neighbors, when I left the town,
I little thought I never should return;
But God, who governs all things, did ordain
That you and I should never meet again,
Till time shall be no more, and Christ shall come to reign."
Thus far my Covell speaks, with Leland's tongue;
Now Leland speaks with sentiments his own.

* The child here alluded to, an infant at the time of his father's decease, became afterwards a preacher, at the age of 21, and died, seemingly in the midst of usefulness, at the early age of 33.

Brethren, the preacher of your choice is dead;
His soul from earth and earthly things has fled,
And the cold ground has now become his bed.
Alas! what shall poor weeping Zion do?
Zion, whose foes are many, friends are few?
The sadness of your hearts your eyes betray,
You weep as Jesus did o'er Lazarus' clay,
And say 'our friend and pastor's called away.'
But let not funeral tears alone be shed;
Mourn for your sins as for a brother dead:
Mourn for your sins which have provoked your God
To send this token of his vengeful rod.
Cheer up! ye saints, the blissful Jesus knows
What's best for you, and that his hand bestows;
Though prophets die, and fathers dwell in dust,
He will preserve the souls who in him trust.

EXPERIENCE.*

Come old, come young, and hear me relate
My life and adventures, and my present state;
I pray you all give ear, to what you now shall hear,
For my story will pleasure and sorrow create.

My childhood and youth in vanity I spent,
Regardless of truth, and to folly intent,
For more than eighteen years, I shed no mourning tears,
But pleaded for my sins, and refused to relent.

Inflexibly hard, and impenetrably blind,
The pleasures of sense bewildered my mind;
To me it did appear, God's law was too severe,—
To the cross of the gospel I was not inclined.

But oh! that love—the love of God to man,—
That everlasting love, that drew the saving plan,
That love pursued my soul, when I was sick and foul,
Too great to resist, and too strong to withstand.

Sin then appeared vile,—the law appeared right,
And justice and grace and holiness shone bright;
The word of God was true, and lovely to my view,
But a pardon for sin was out of my sight.

I languished and mourned, how long I cannot tell,
I saw God was just, if he sent me to hell,
My heart was dreadful hard, and the door of grace seemed barred,
And my soul with the devil forever must dwell.

* Written about the year 1807.

The way of salvation thro' Christ I did spy,
How God could be just and his law magnify,
And yet bestow his grace on sinful Adam's race,
But those blessings, I feared, were not for such as I.

But when all my hopes had nearly fled away,
And hell from beneath was gaping for its prey,
My Saviour did appear to dissipate my fear,
And washed all my sins in a moment away.

What freedom I felt, what joy I did receive!—
'Twas easy to repent—'twas easy to believe;—
I freely gave him all, and at his feet did fall,
And the glory—all glory to him I did give.

His voice then I heard, in sweet majestic sound,
"I've loved you—I've sought you, and closed up your wound,
I've a work for you to do—be faithful, just and true,
And proclaim to the world what a Saviour you've found."

Not money nor fame, did e'er send me forth,
But love to his name, and love to his truth.
I girt my armor on, and ventured forth alone,
Trusting only in God to preserve me a youth.

O'er mountains and waters, as duty led me on,
Through snow storms and tempests, and hot burning sun,
I ran with all my might, and labored day and night,
To proclaim a dear Saviour to sinners undone.

But little have I done, but what was done wrong,
Revivals have been short, and apostacies been long,
After six and thirty years, I am greatly in arrears,
And have nothing to plead but pardoning love alone.

And now I'm growing old, my powers all decay,
I wander and grovel, and stumble in the way,
My sun is going down, my work is almost done,
I yield up my life, and return to my clay.

A BIOGRAPHICAL SKETCH

OF THE

LIFE AND CHARACTER OF THE REV. PETER WERDEN,

Who died at Cheshire, on Lord's day, the 21st of Feb. 1808. The funeral was attended the Wednesday following by a large assembly of people. An appropriate discourse was delivered on the occasion, from Acts xiii. 36, 37, by the Rev. John Leland; at the close of which, the following lines were exhibited:—

Howl, fir tree, for the cedar is fallen!

Help, Lord, for the godly man ceaseth; for the righteous is taken away from among men.

My father, my father, the chariots of Israel and the horsemen thereof. Let me die the death of the righteous, and let my last end be like his.

Elder Werden was born June 6th, 1728, and ordained to the work of the ministry, at Warwick, Rhode Island, May, 1751, in the 24th year of his age.

When he first began to preach, he was too much of a New-light, and too strongly attached to the doctrine of *salvation by sovereign grace*, to be generally received among the old Baptist churches in Rhode Island, which had been formed partly upon the Armenian plan, until the following event opened the door for him. A criminal, by the name of Carter, was executed at Tower Hill. This occasion collected abundance of people from all parts of the state. While the criminal stood under the gallows, young Werden felt such a concern for his soul, that he urged his way through the crowd; and being assisted by the sheriff, he gained access to Carter, and addressed him as follows:—"Sir, is your soul prepared for that awful eternity, into which you will launch in a few minutes?" The criminal replied, "I don't know that it is, but I wish you would pray for me." In this prayer, Mr. Werden was so wonderfully assisted in spreading the poor man's case before the throne of God, that the whole assembly were awfully solemnized, and most of them wet their cheeks with their tears. This opened a great door for his ministrations, both on the Main and on the Island.

He preached at Warwick, Coventry, and many other places with good success, about nineteen years, and then moved, in 1770, into this place, where he has lived and administered almost thirty-eight years.

In his first religious exercises, he was led to dig deep into his own heart, where he found such opposition and rebellion, that when he obtained pardon, he attributed it to sovereign grace alone; which sentiment, so interwoven in his own soul, he ever proclaimed aloud to a dying world. Nothing appeared to be more disgustful to his mind, than to hear *works* and *grace* mixed together, as the foundation of a sinner's hope. To hold forth the Lamb of God as a *piece* of a Saviour; or to consider the self-exertions of a natural man, to be the *way* unto *Christ*, the true and *only way*, were extremely displeasing to that soul of his, which delighted so much in proclaiming eternal love, redeeming blood, and matchless grace.

Sound judgment, correct principles, humble demeanor, with solemn sociability, marked all his public improvements, and mingled with all his conversation in smaller circles, or with individuals.

In him, young preachers found a father and a friend; distressed churches, a healer of breaches; and tempted souls a sympathizing guide. From his first coming into this place, until he was seventy years old, he was a father to the Baptist churches in Berkshire and its environs, and in some sense an apostle to them all.

His many painful labors for the salvation of sinners, the peace of the churches, and purity of the ministers, will never be fully appreciated, until the time when he shall stand before his Judge, and hear the words of his mouth, "Well done good and faithful servant."

The character which I have drawn of the life and labors of the man, who now lies sleeping in death before our eyes, many of you know to be true. From the sternness of his eyes and the blush of his face, a stranger would have been led to conclude that he was sovereign and self-willed in his natural habit of mind; but on acquaintance, the physiognomist would have been agreeably disappointed. He has so much self-government, that he has been heard to say, that, except when he had the small-pox, he never found it hard to keep from speaking at any time, if his *reason* told him it was best to forbear; and no man possessed finer feelings, or treated the characters of others with more delicacy than he did. He had an exalted idea of the inalienable rights of conscience; justly appreciated the civil rights of man, and was assiduous to keep his brethren from the chains of ecclesiastical power.

His preaching was both sentimental and devotional; and his life so far corresponded with the precepts which he taught, that none of his hearers could justly reply, "Physician, heal thyself."

A number of revivals have taken place in the town and congregation where he has resided and preached, and a number of ministers have been raised up in the church of which he was pastor.

For about ten years his physical and mental powers have been on the decline, and how many times have we heard him rejoice, that others increased though he decreased; but his superannuation was not so great as to prevent the whole of his usefulness, and his hoary head was a crown of glory unto him.

A number of times he has been heard to pray, that he might not outlive his usefulness, which has been remarkably answered in his case, for the Sunday before he died, he preached to the people—he preached his last.

The disease which closed his mortal life, denied his friends the solemn pleasure of catching the balm of life from his lips, in his last moments. He had finished his work before, and nothing remained for him to do but to die. Socrates, the patient philosopher, said to have never been angry in his life, when dying, was vexed. The cause was this: his pupils asked him what he would have them do with his *body* after he was dead. To whom he sternly replied, "have I been so long with you, and taught you no better? After I am dead, what you see will not be Socrates. Socrates will then be among the gods." The improvement which I now make on the words of this philosopher is this: what we see here lying before our eyes, is not Werden, this is but the shell: his soul is now among the angels and saints in light, before the throne of glory. I will not say that his soul is under the altar with others, crying, "how long, O Lord, holy and true, dost thou not judge and avenge our blood on them that dwell on the earth," because he did not offer his life on the altar of martyrdom; but I have an unshaken belief that his soul has left all its tribulation, being washed and made white in the blood of the Lamb, and is now basking in the sun-beams of immortal noon.

Let the inhabitants of Cheshire reflect a moment on the dealings of God towards them. Within about three years, three ministers, belonging to Cheshire, have departed this life. The pious Mason took the lead—the pleasing Covell followed after—and now the arduous Werden, who has been in the ministry a longer term than any Baptist preacher left behind, in New England, has finished his course, in the eightieth year of his age, while Leland remains alone to raise this monument over their tombs.

The ten following hymns were published as early as 1809:—

EVENING HYMN.

The day is past and gone,
The evening shades appear;
O may we all remember well
The night of death draws near.

We lay our garments by,
Upon our beds to rest;
So death will soon disrobe us all
Of what we've here possessed.

Lord, keep us all this night,
Secure from all our fears;
May angels guard us while we sleep,
Till morning light appears.

And if we early rise,
And view th' unwearied sun,
May we set out to win the prize
And after glory run.

And when our days are past,
And we from time remove,
O may we in thy bosom rest,—
The bosom of thy love.

INVITATION TO PILGRIMS.

Wand'ring pilgrims, mourning Christians,
Weak and tempted lambs of Christ,
Who endure great tribulation,
And with sin are much distressed;
Christ hath sent me to invite you,
To a rich and costly feast;
Let not shame nor pride prevent you,—
Come,—the rich provision taste.

If you have a heart lamenting,
And bemoan your wretched case,
Come to Jesus Christ repenting;
He will give you gospel grace;
If you want a heart to fear him,
Love and serve him all your days;
Come to Jesus Christ and ask him;
He will guide you in his ways.

If your heart is unbelieving,
Doubting Jesus' pard'ning love,
Lie hard by Bethesda waiting
Till the troubled waters move.
If no man appear to help you,
All their efforts prove but talk,
Jesus, Jesus, he can heal you,
Rise, take up your bed and walk.

If, like Peter, you are sinking
In the sea of unbelief,
Wait with patience, constant praying,
Christ will send you sweet relief;
He will give you grace and glory,
All your wants shall be supplied;
Canaan, Canaan, lies before you,
Rise and cross the swelling tide.

Death shall not destroy your comfort,
Christ will guard you thro' the gloom;
Down he'll send a heavenly envoy,
To convey your spirit home;
There, you'll spend your days in pleasure,
Free from every want and care;
Come, oh come, my blessed Saviour,
Fain my spirit would be there.

THE INTERCESSION OF CHRIST.

Now the Saviour stands a pleading,
At the sinner's bolted heart;
Now in heaven he's interceding,
Undertaking sinner's part;
Now he pleads his sweat and blood-shed,
Shows his wounded hands and feet;
Father, save them, though they're blood-red,
Raise them to a heavenly seat.

Sinners, hear your God and Saviour,
Hear his gracious voice to-day;
Turn from all your vain behaviour,
O repent, return, and pray;
Open now your hearts before him,
Bid the Saviour welcome in,
O receive and glad adore him,
Take a full discharge from sin.

Now he's waiting to be gracious,
Now he stands and looks at thee;
See, what kindness, love and pity,
Shine around to you and me;

Sinners, can you hate that Saviour?
  Can you thrust him from your arms?
Once he died for your behaviour,
  Now he calls you by his charms.

O be wise, before you languish
  On a bed of dying strife;
Endless joy or endless anguish,
  Turn upon th' events of life;
Come, for all things now are ready,
  Yet there's room for many more;
O ye blind, ye lame and needy,
  Come to grace's boundless store.

Blessed be God for all,
  For all things here below,
For pain, and grief, and joy and thrall,
  To my advantage grow.

Blessed be God for shame,
  For slander and disgrace;
Welcome reproach for Jesus' name,
  And his redeeming grace.

Blessed be God for loss,
  For loss of earthly things;
For every scourge and every cross,
  Me nearer Jesus brings.

Blessed be God for want
  Of raiment, health and food;
I live by faith, I scorn to faint,
  For all things work for good.

Blessed be God for pain,
  Which tears my flesh like thorns,
It crucifies the carnal man,
  To God my soul returns.

Blessed be God for doubts,
  Which he has overcome;
My soul in full assurance shouts,
  Of being soon at home.

Blessed be God for fears
  Of sin, and death, and hell;
When Christ, who is my life, appears,
  I shall in glory dwell.

Blessed be God for friends;
  Blessed be God for foes;
Blessed be God whose gracious ends,
  No finite creature knows.

Blessed be God for life,
  Blessed be God for death,
Blessed be God for all he sends;
  I welcome all this faith.

THE CHRISTIAN'S CONSOLATION.

Come and taste, along with me,
Consolation running free,
From my Father's glorious throne,
Sweeter than the honey comb.

Wherefore should I seek alone?
Two are better still than one;
More that come, of free good will,
Make the banquet sweeter still.

Saints in glory sing aloud,
To behold an heir of God,
Coming in at grace's door,
Making up the number more.

Goodness running like a stream
From the New Jerusalem,
By its constant breaking forth,
Sweetens earth and heaven both.

Sinful nature, vile and base,
Cannot stop the run of grace,
While there is a God to give,
Or a sinner to receive.

When I go to heaven's store,
Asking for a little more,
Jesus gives a double share,
Calling me a gleaner there.

Then, rejoicing, home I go,
From this feast of heaven below,
Gleaning manna on the road
Dropping from the mouth of God.

Heaven there, and heaven here,
Comforts every where appear,
This I boldly can declare,
Since my soul receives a share.

THE PREACHER'S LIFE.

How arduous is the preacher's fight!
  What pangs his vitals feel!
To preach the gospel day and night,
  To hearts as hard as steel.

While some blaspheme and show their spite,
And mock at all they hear,
Others, in chase of vain delight,
Like adders, stop the ear.

To heaven he turns his weeping eyes,
To antidote despair,
With broken heart, and longing eyes,
He tries the effect of prayer.

If God, propitious, hear his cry,
And some small fruit he see,
How soon the hopeful prospects die,
How short the jubilee.

When sinners hear the Saviour's voice,
And feel the power divine,
The preacher's heart and soul rejoice,
To see the gospel shine.

What courage, faith, and holy zeal,
Transport his ravished breast,
What inward joy his spirits feel,
To see his labors blessed.

But ah! how short the shining day;
How soon the night appears!
All those of Asia turn away,
How gloomy then his fears!

Good God! he cries, with anxious breast,
Are all my labors vain?
Must all the lambs and sheep of Christ,
Turn goats and wolves again?

THE PREACHER'S ENQUIRY.

Brethren, I have come once more,
Let us join and God adore;
Joseph lives, and Jesus reigns,
Praise him in the highest strains.

Many days and years have passed,
Since we met, before the last,
Yet our lives do still remain,
Here, on earth, we meet again.

Many of our friends are gone,
To their long, eternal home,
They have left us here below,
Soon we after them shall go.

Brethren, tell me how you do,
Does your love continue true?

Are you waiting for your King,
When he comes, his saints to bring?

If you wish to know of me,
What I am, and how I be,
Here I am, behold, who will,
Sure, I am a sinner still.

Weak and helpless, lame and blind,
All unholy, still I find,
Worse than ever, all may see,
Yet the Lord remembers me.

THOUGHTS ON THE JUDGMENT DAY.

THINK, O my soul, the dreadful day,
When heaven and earth shall flee away,
When Christ in solemn pomp shall come,
Upon his white majestic throne.

Then Gabriel, at the King's command,
Shall take the trumpet in his hand,
And sound alarm, so shrill and clear,
That heaven, and earth, and hell shall hear.

The grand assize will then take place,
On every soul of Adam's race;
Both saint and sinner must appear,
And all their final sentence hear.

The saints, in glittering robes, shall stand,
In that great day, at God's right hand;
The Lamb's rich blood shall be their plea,
And they his smiling face shall see.

"Come, all the bless'd of God," he'll say,
"My blood hath wash'd your sins away;
"Come, take your golden harps and sing,
"And make the heavenly arches ring."

But what will guilty sinners do,
When all their sins appear in view?
How will they tremble, cry, and groan,
To see their Judge upon his throne!

"Depart from me, ye sinful race,
"Ye broke my laws, abused my grace;
"Go down to darkness and despair,
"And dwell eternal ages there."

The occasion on which a part of the following Hymn was composed, is related in his biography. The last three verses appear to have been afterwards added.

CHRISTIANS, if your hearts be warm,
Ice and snow can do no harm;
If by Jesus you are prized,
Rise, believe, and be baptized.

Jesus drank the gall for you,
Bore the curse for sinners due;
Children, prove your love to him,
Never fear the frozen stream.

Never shun the Saviour's cross,
All on earth is worthless dross;
If the Saviour's love you feel,
Let the world behold your zeal.

Fire is good to warm the soul,
Water purifies the foul;—
Fire and water both agree—
Winter soldiers never flee.

Every season of the year,
Let your worship be sincere;
When the storm forbids you roam,
Serve your gracious God at home.

Read his gracious word by day,
Ever watching, always pray;
Think upon his law by night;—
This will give you great delight.

I SET myself against the Lord,
Despised his spirit and his word,
And wished to take his place;
It vexed me so, that I must die,
And perish too, eternally,
Or else be saved by grace.

Of every preacher I'd complain;
One spoke thro' pride, and one for gain,
Another's learning small;
One spoke too fast, and one too slow;
One prayed too loud, and one too low;
Another had no call.

Some walk too straight to make a show,
While others far too crooked go;
And both of these I scorn;
Some odd, fantastic motions make;
Some stoop too low, some stand too straight—
No one is faultless born.

With no professor I could join;
Some dressed too mean, and some too fine,
And some would talk too long;
Some had a tone, some had no gift;
One talked too slow, and one too swift;
And all of them were wrong.

I thought they'd better keep at home,
Than to exhort where'er they come,
And tell us of their joys;
They'd better keep their gardens free
From weeds, than to examine me,
And vex me with their noise.

Kindred and neighbors, too, were bad,
And no true friend was to be had;
My rulers, too, were vile;
At length, I was reduced to see
The fault did mostly lie in me,
And had done all the while.

The horrid load of guilt and shame,
The inward consciousness of blame
Did wound my frighted soul;
I've sinned so much against the Lord,
Despised his goodness and his word,
How can I be made whole?

"Why, there is balm in Gilead,
"And a physician may be had,
"And balsam too most free;
"Only believe on God's dear son,
"Thro' him the victory is won—
"Christ Jesus died for thee."

O, Christ's free love, a boundless sea!
What! to expire for such as me?
"Yes, 'tis a truth divine."
My heart did melt, my soul o'er-run
With love, to see what God had done
For souls so vile as mine.

Now, I can hear a *child* proclaim
The joyful news, and bless the name
Of Jesus Christ, my king;
I scorn no sect—the saints are one;
With my complaints I now have done,
And God's free grace I sing.

BUDGET OF SCRAPS.

The following essays were published in 1810, in a pamphlet entitled "A BUDGET OF SCRAPS." Several of the original essays are omitted for want of room.

A MAN MUST HAVE SENSE TO JUDGE OF SENSE.

THIS trite sentence is entitled to a good degree of credit, but is subject to many exceptions.

Infantus could count one hundred, but knew nothing more of arithmetic. His preceptor told him that ten times ten were one hundred: this the child could not understand, but placing ten grains of corn by themselves, in ten different places on the table, and counting them altogether, he found the total amount to be one hundred. The preceptor then told the lad, that ten times one hundred would make one thousand, on which the pupil reasoned as follows: "In the first instance, I know my master knew more than I did, and in the last, I have good reason to believe, that he knows more than I do."

Servitus entered an apprentice to architecture. The master-builder prepared and framed each stick for the house, in a separate place, in the forest, and after collecting them together, reared up the house in regular squares and altitudes: at sight of which, the astonished Servitus exclaimed, "I know the master-builder knows more than I know."

Neptunus resolved to try his fortune at sea, though ignorant of navigation; freighted a large ship for Canton, and committed himself to sea, at the direction of a pilot. In the lapse of a few months, the ship doubled the cape of Good Hope, and came to her moorings before Canton. After Neptunus had adjusted his business in the East Indies, he returned a different route, but, at length, landed at the same port, whence he took his departure: on landing, he said, "My sense tells me that the pilot has more sense than I have."

When Simplemus first read the prophetic calculations of Astronomous, respecting the eclipses of the sun and moon, he treated them as essays of chimerical folly, but when he saw them all accomplished, he radically changed his opinion, and now he believes all such prophecies, by a faith, grounded on reason: notwithstanding, he is still as ignorant of the science of eclipses, as he is of the first vital pulse of his heart. Simplemus has now adopted the maxim, that "it is *reasonable* to believe a *fact*, when supported by *rational evidence*, although the *fact* still continues to be *inconceivable* or *incomprehensible*.

As I am much pleased with the maxim of Simplemus, I wish to accommodate it to a theological use.

The incarnation of Christ—the personal union of the divine and human natures, commonly called the hypostatical union, is one of those *facts* which admits of *rational evidence*, yet is *incomprehensible* by men—by angels—by every being except Ubiquity, the great Eternal.

That Jesus Christ was properly and truly God, his *names*—his *claims*—his *works*, and the *testimonials* of inspired witnesses, all confirm.

His *names* are, King—King of kings—Lord—God—Everlasting Father, the First and the Last—the Beginning and the End—Alpha and Omega—the true God and Eternal Life—the Light of the world—the Life—the Creator and Upholder of all things, etc. Some of these names are given to angels and magistrates, it is true, but others of them are given alone to Jehovah.

It is moreover to be observed, that the Hebrew *Adonia*, or *Jodhe vau he*, which occurs more than six thousand times in the Old Testament, (translated Lord,) and which is a peculiar name of the Almighty, and never given to angels or kings, is frequently given to Christ, both by the apostles, who quote and apply such passages to him, and by the prophets when manifestly speaking of the Messiah.

His *claims* to Godhead are also manifest. Hear his words: "I and my Father are one; that all men should honor the Son as they do the Father, even so the Son quickeneth whomsoever he will; I am the resurrection and the life; he that seeth me seeth the Father also; I know you, that ye have not the love of God in you," etc.

His *works* were many and marvellous. The prophets wrought miracles in the name of the God of Israel. The apostles wrought in the name of Jesus of Nazareth. If Jesus, in some instances, wrought by prayer to his Father, to establish his character as a prophet of the Lord, and set an example for the apostles, yet, for the most part, he spoke authoritatively, not in the name of another, but in his own name. In his casting out devils—controlling the winds and the waves, and raising the dead, very little doubt can remain, he wrought as an independent, self-sufficient God.

By Christ all things were created: he is the only Redeemer of men: by him all the dead will be raised. What works can evince godhead, if creation, redemption, and the resurrection do not? The two first of these works, however, have been done by Christ; the last, also, partially, and will be completed by the same hand, according to the Sciptures. Now, if Christ does all these works by a *delegated* power, which, as an exalted creature, he receives from God, what difference can we possibly conceive exists between the Creator and the creature? Has the Creator made a creature equal to himself? Or, are the works of creation, redemption, and the resurrection, no proof of Omnipotence?

The *testimonials* which Christ has received from inspired witnesses are explicit, viz: "The word was God—all things were made by him—He thought it no robbery to be equal with God—the express image of his person and the brightness of his glory. Thou, Lord, in the beginning, hast laid the foundations of the earth, and the heavens are the work of thine hands; they shall perish, and wax old and be changed, but thou remainest the same, and thy years fail not; this is the true God, and Eternal Life—the only wise God, our Saviour," &c.

That Jesus Christ was real man, as well as truly God, is also evident. His flesh, bone and blood—his hungerings, thirstings and weariness—

His weeping, praying and sighing—
His groaning, bleeding and dying—

all unite to prove him human. But notwithstanding the whole force of evidence that is given to prove the fact of this hypostatical union of two natures in Christ, yet the fact itself, of God manifest in the flesh, is declared by Paul to be a great mystery, not to be controverted.

If I understand the import of *enthusiasm*, it consists in *believing without evidence*, but it is no part of enthusiasm to believe an article incomprehensible in its nature, when we have all the evidence of the truth of the article, that its nature admits of.

It is, therefore, my devotion, my joy and my glory, to adore an incarnate Jehovah. Should I refuse this adoration, I should act an *unreasonable* as well as a wicked part.

A LITTTE CAKE FIRST.—1 KINGS, XVII.

ELIJAH, the Tishbite, was very jealous for his God, but a man of passions like other saints. He was led, by the spirit, to pray for a sore judgment to fall on the people of Israel, that those who had despised the goodness of God, might be reclaimed by his severity. He prayed earnestly that it might not rain, and it rained not on the earth for the space of three years and six months. The drought was followed by a want of bread and water, and the prophet, who prayed for judgment, had, in common with his own countrymen, to combat the evils, which arose from the answer of his own prayer.

"And the word of the Lord came unto Elijah, saying, get thee hence, and turn thee eastward, and hide thyself by the brook Cherith, that is beyond Jordan, and it shall be, that thou shalt drink of the brook, and I have commanded the ravens to feed thee there."

In obedience to these orders, the prophet went and dwelt by the brook, which was one of the tributary streams of Jordan. And the ravens, that live upon prey, contrary to the laws of their nature, brought the lonely saint bread and flesh in the morning, and the same at evening, which, with the water of the brook, formed the sustenance of Elijah.

But in process of time, the brook dried up, and the ravens neglected their charge, which reduced the prophet to perfect want, without the least ***human*** appearance of relief: but "the word of the Lord came unto him, saying, Arise, get thee to Zerephath, which belongs to Zidon, and dwell there: behold, I have commanded a widow woman there to sustain thee." I do not send thee to king Ahab, nor any of the princes of Israel, for they are idolaters, and seek thy life: nor do I send thee unto the rich, who have wealth, but no hearts to communicate: I send thee not to any man or woman of Israel, for they are so self-conceited of their own advantages, and their pre-eminent virtue, above other nations, that they neglect all humane and benevolent actions: but to a *widow woman of Zidon* I send thee.

In compliance with those instructions, Elijah arose and came to Zerephath; and when he came to the gate of the city, behold! the widow woman was there, gathering sticks for oven-wood, and he called to her, and said, fetch me, I pray thee, a little water in a vessel, that I may drink. The woman (who had not been civilized to barbarity, nor gospelized to covetousness,) very courteously went to bring him the water for which he prayed: but as she was going, he called to her again, and said, Bring me, I pray thee, a morsel of bread in thine hand.

The Lord had given commandment to the woman to sustain Elijah, but had not given him any legal orders on the woman; hence he *prayed*, both for water and bread. Water had not yet grown scarce in Zidon; with this request the woman could easily comply, but when a *morsel of bread* was called for, it touched the tender feelings of her heart. "And she said, as the Lord thy God liveth, I have not a cake, but a handful of meal in a barrel, and a little oil in a cruise, and behold I am gathering two sticks, that I may go in and dress it for me and my son, that we may eat it and die."

The Zidonian woman swore by Elijah's God, that her case was extremely pitiable and indigent, and we have every reason to believe her narrative was true. She had no prospect of any future supply, but expected that after herself and son had eaten one little cake more, they must both of them die.

And Elijah said unto her, "fear not; go and do as thou hast said; but make me thereof a little cake *first*, and bring unto me; and after make for thee and thy son." How radically different is the doctrine of the text, from the conduct of most of the ancients and moderns! "Let me *first* get wealth, and *then* I will be liberal—*first* lay up enough for myself and my children, and *then* I will communicate to the servants of the Lord," is the pactical language of men and women in general; but the injunction of the text is, "Give the prophet of the Lord a little cake *first*, and *then* prepare for thy family." This precept perfectly coincides with the instructions which Solomon has given us: "honor the Lord with thy substance, and with the *first fruits* of all thine increase."

Some suppose the prophets of the Lord will perish, unless *legal* provision is made for them: *this* provision, however, was not made for Elijah.

Others imagine that when men are called to the holy and public service of the Lord, that the Almighty will support them by miracles. This is sometimes the case: by ravens, this same Elijah had lately been fed; but in the instance before us, the miracle was not wrought so much for the prophet, who *received*, as it was for the woman, who *gave*.

A certain class of men have strong faith, that God will provide for the laborers in the vineyard, and their good faith is all they have, for they never communicate; but in the case before us, the woman did not speak the language that many do in these days: "Never fear, Elijah, your God will feed and preserve you; for my own part, I should never be afraid to trust him: I have but a little, and that I need for myself and my son: no doubt but others will give you, and you will do well enough." No, her language, her conduct was different. She reasoned thus: "I have a little meal and oil, and but a little; the Lord who gave me this *little* store, has a right to it. He now commands me to give a *little* out of my *little*, and I must obey: otherwise I should be worse than the ravens, who checked their own appetites, to bring bread and flesh to the prophet. Obedience is my work; events belong to God, who can make all grace abound. The Lord has not only commanded me to give a little cake *first* unto the prophet, but has also promised that my store shall not be exhausted. I will, therefore, trust his promise and obey his command. If my son should ever reproach me, for giving that to the prophet which was his patrimonial or matrimonial right, I will read him a lecture, of what befel old Eli for honoring his sons more than his God, and what judgments likewise fell on his sons."

The widow, therefore, obeyed—made the cake *first* for the prophet and carried it to him—invited him into her house, and entertained him all the time of the drought, and the barrel of meal wasted not, neither did the cruise of oil fail, according to the word of God, which he spake by Elijah.

In process of time, the son of the woman sickened and died. All the human prospect of succor in old age, was now taken away. How pitiable her state! yet she did not murmur, but acquiesced like a saint. She said to the prophet, "O, thou man of God! art thou come hither to call my sin to remembrance and to slay my son?"

It is supposable, but not certain, that this was an illegitimate son, and that now the Lord punished her for her former sin by the death of her son, as in the case of David and Bathsheba. In either case, the woman viewed this stroke as a just punishment for her sins. Elijah was also extremely afflicted, that the woman who had been so hospitable to him, should be thus deprived of her only son. He, therefore, mourned and prayed to his God, until the soul of the child returned to its clay. The woman was now greatly comforted and confirmed in the word of the Lord, which was spoken by Elijah.

Here we see that the woman was supplied through a long famine, and had her son raised from the dead, because she gave the servant of the Lord a *little cake first.* Let others learn to do likewise. And let all the servants of the Lord learn from Elijah, to be not greedy of filthy lucre, but content themselves with a *little cake.*

MANY MEN OF MANY MINDS.

How various are the opinions of men respecting the mode of supporting gospel ministers.

A thinks that preachers of the gospel should be qualified, inducted and supported, in a mode to be proscribed by the statute laws.

B is of opinion that a preacher is not entitled to any compensation for his services, unless he is poor and shiftless, and cannot live without the alms of the people.

C says, that it takes him as long to go to meeting, and hear the preacher, as it does for the preacher to go and preach, and their obligations are therefore reciprocal.

D believes a rich preacher is as much entitled to a reward for his labor as if he was poor.

E believes that a preacher should give the whole of his time to reading, meditating, preaching, praying and visiting, and therefore he ought to be liberally supported ; not in the light of alms, but in that of a gospel debt.

F joins with *E*, with this proviso ; that the liberal support be averaged on all the members of the church, according to property and privilege.

G also agrees with *E*, provided the liberal support be raised by a free, public contribution, without any knowledge or examination what each individual does.

H chooses to tax himself, and constable his own money to his preacher, without consulting any other.

I loves the preachers, and pays them with blessings, but the sound of money, drives all good feelings from his heart.

When *J* hears a man preach that he does not believe is sent of God, he feels under no obligation to give him anything; and when he hears a preacher, that gives him evidence, that he is in the service of the Lord, and devoted to the work, he forms the conclusion, that the Lord pays the preacher well for his work as he goes along.

K likes preachers very well, but preaching rather better; he feels, therefore, best pleased, when the preacher fails coming, and a gap opens for himself; for he had rather work his passage, and take his turn at the helm, than pay a pilot.

L argues like a man, that the preacher ought to receive something handsome for his services, and laments that himself is in debt, and cannot communicate any thing, without defrauding his creditors: at the same time, he takes special care to keep always in debt for cheap farms, wild land, or some other articles of an increasing nature.

M is a man of a thousand. He argues that the mode of supporting ministers is left blank in the New Testament; because no one mode would be economical in all places; but that the deed itself is enjoined on all who are taught by an ordinance of heaven. If, therefore, a contribution is recommended, *M* will be foremost to the box. When a subscription is judged most advisable, his name will be first on the list. If averaging is considered most equitable, he will add a little to his bill, lest others should fail. And if no mode at all is agreed upon, still *M*, as an individual, will contribute by himself; for he reasons, that if others are remiss, it is neither precedent nor excuse for him. He does not give to be seen of men, but because his heart is in it; and these gospel debts (as he calls them) he pays with as much devotion, as he spreads his hands in prayer to God. The creed of his faith, which seems to be written on his heart, is "That, although all the money in the world cannot purchase pardon of sin, or the smiles of a reconciled God; yet religion always has cost money or worth, from Abel's lamb to the present day. And that the man who will not part with a little money, for the sake of him who parted with his blood for sinners, is a wicked disciple."

N approves of the faith and profession of *M*, in every particular, but reduces nothing of it to practice.

O, like his make, believes nothing, does nothing, and is as near nothing as anything can be.

THE BIBLE.

The Bible contains 66 books—1,189 chapters—31,114 verses. The name Lord is found 6,062 times in the Old Testament. The name God, 2,725 times. The name Jesus occurs 925 times, in the New Testament, and the name Christ, 555 times. The word Selah, is found 74 times in the Bible. The word Eternity, in only one place.

There are in the Old Testament, 607,207 words: in the New Testament, 179,476; which numbers, added together, make 786,683. In this enumeration, the titles of books and contents of chapters are excluded.

The head-pieces, however, prefixed to 115 of the Psalms, and the 22 words in the 119th Psalm, are included. The number was found out, by counting one by one, pointing every 100, and then adding up: which countings employed me 130 hours, and yet, after all the pains and care taken, some mistakes may have been made; but it is believed but small.

The Bible seems to be self-divided into six parts, viz:

	BOOKS.	CHAP.	VERSES.	WORDS.
I. *The Law of Moses*, beginning with Genesis, and ending with Deuteronomy; it contains........................	5	187	5853	155,767
II. *The history of the Jews*, beginning with Joshua, and ending with Esther, containing,...........................	12	249	7024	203,303
III. *A book of poems*, beginning with Job, and ending with Solomon's song, including,.............................	5	243	4794	84,358
IV. *The prophecies of sixteen prophets*, beginning with Isaiah, and ending with Malachi, containing,.................	17	250	5491	163,780
V. *The evangelical part*, containing the history of Christ and the Apostles, embracing,............................	5	117	4785	107,093
VI. *The epistolary writings* of Paul, Peter, James, Jude and John, together with the book of Revelations, comprising,.....	22	143	3171	72,383
Total,	66	1189	31,118	786,683

The middle chapter in the Bible, is the 117th Psalm. The middle of the verses, is between the 102d and 103d Psalms. The middle word is in the 60th Psalm, the 4th verse: "To them that fear thee."

The double asseveration, verily, verily, is found twenty-five times in John's gospel, and no where else. The words, Lord, God, are not found in Esther, nor Solomon's song; so, likewise, the names, Jesus, Christ, are not in the 3d epistle of John. The word baptism, with its relatives, is found one hundred times in the New Testament.

The Bible was more than sixteen hundred years in writing. It contains a history of the world's whole age; partly in narrative, and partly in prophecy; yea, more, it assures us of some things which took place before the mountains were made, or the hills brought forth: it also reveals unto us many things that will take place after the world, and all its works are burnt up; and yet the whole of it can be read over in sixty hours. It is written in a style that no man on earth can imitate; which will forever keep it from being incorporated with human composition.

The Bible is in its parts, historical, poetical, allegorical, prophetic, receptive, and promissory. It claims the merit of being a revelation from God unto man. Of revelation, there are two kinds; oral, and written.

Oral revelation was first. In this, God revealed his will unto men; but as letters were not in use, men had no way of preserving those revelations, but by their memories; these records were so treacherous, that the revelations were greatly mutilated and perverted. It is from this source, however, that those nations, who are destitute of written revelation, got their belief of the future existence of departed souls; for I can see nothing in all the pages of nature, that proves that men have immortal souls, but what equally proves the same of beasts.

Whether the use of letters was taught at once, or whether the science was gradual, the result is equally amazing; that with twenty-two letters, all the thoughts of the human heart can be expressed. After letters came in use, the Almighty directed the hands of men to write down those revelations of his will, which he made known unto them; and such writings are called written revelations. These writings, collected together in one book, form the Bible, or Holy Scriptures.

THE LONG-ISLAND INDIAN——IMPROVED.

About sixty years past, a very considerable revival of religion took place, on the east end of Long-Island, and some of the Indians of that place were made partakers of the grace of life. Several years afterwards, one of the natives gave the following account of himself, in his own way of speaking:

"When me first converted, me was a poor, vile, black Indian; but me love all the Christians, and all the ministers like my own soul. Afterwards me grow, grow, grow, but me no love Christians. Then me grow, grow, grow very big; then me no love ministers. But one day, as I was in the swamp after broomsticks, I heard a voice saying, Indian, how comes it to pass, that you no love Christians and ministers? Me answer, because I know more than all of them. The voice say unto me again, Indian, you have lost your humble. On this I began to look, and behold! my humble was gone. I then go back, back, back, but I no find my humble. Me then go back, back, back a great way, and then me find my humble; and when me find my humble, I was poor, vile, black Indian again. Then me love all the Christians and all the ministers, just as I love my own soul."

This simple narrative of the native, reminds me of the sayings of some of those illustrious worthies, whose names and characters shine with dazzling refulgence in the sacred volume.

Job was a perfect and upright man, who excelled all men on earth in his day; yet he experienced a great sight of affliction. In defending himself against the illiberal charges of his three friends, he lost sight of his wretchedness before God. But, when the Almighty summoned his attention to behold the marvellous works of the Creator, and drew his mind near the immaculate throne of divine glory, he cried out: "behold! I am vile—I abhor myself, repenting in dust and ashes."

When Isaiah, the sublime prophet, saw the Lord on a throne of glory, and the heavenly host adoring before him, from a deep sense of his own pollution, the pensive confession flowed from his lips: "wo is me, for I am undone; for I am a man of unclean lips."

The knowledge which St. Paul had in the mysteries of God, was exquisite—his labors in the ministry were abundant—his sufferings, for Christ's sake, above measure—his tour to the third heavens, very friendly for the health of his soul—and yet, long after this, we hear him lamenting in piteous groans, "O, wretched man that I am! who shall deliver me from the body of this death? I yet find a law in my members, bringing me into captivity, to the law of sin."

How very different these confessions are, from the protestation of some in these days, who affirm that they live in such obedience to the laws of God, and walk so fully in the divine light, that they have attained to the state of sinless perfection.

JEMIMA WILKINSON AND THE INDIAN——IMPROVED.

The high claims of Jemima Wilkinson (that Christ has descended the second time, and dwells in her,) are generally known. Her place of residence is in the town of Jerusalem, Ontario county, and state of New York.

A few years past, a religious Indian paid her a visit, with intention to find out wherein her great strength lay. After discoursing with her some time, in English, he changed his dialect, and spake in his own mother tongue; to which Jemima replied, in her plain manner of speaking, "thee must not speak to me in Indian language, for I do not understand it." "Ah!" said the Indian, "then I know you are not my Saviour; for my blessed Jesus understands poor Indians." How significant the words, and how marvellous the idea of the Indian!

More than a thousand different dialects now exist, among the various nations of the earth, which bear so little affinity to each other, that the people who speak one of them understand little or nothing of another. Supposing a thousand congregations, belonging to a thousand distinct nations, should assemble in some spacious plain, and the whole number of individuals, in each congregation, should lift up their voices in prayer and praise to God; is it probable that Jesus would understand them all? Like the Indian, I believe he would. Should any individual, in the vast assembly, hear all the voices, what a din of confusion would assail his ears; but all would be order and significance with the dear Redeemer. If this conclusion is just, it is presumptive evidence that Jesus Christ is omniscient God. If it should be objected, however, that it is possible for Omnipotence to make a creature of such extensive faculties, that he can understand all that is said by all, it will not hastily be denied.

But, supposing the public worship of this great assembly should close, would Jesus then know the temper of each heart? Can an inarticulate prayer of the heart rise to God, through the mediation of Christ, and at the same time the Mediator know nothing of it? It cannot be admitted. He must then know the hearts of men.

When he was on earth, he perceived the thoughts of the people, and knew what was in man. If we consider Solomon's address to Israel's God, "Thou, even thou only, knowest the hearts of men," it will be substantiated that Jesus, who knew the thoughts and hearts of men, is Israel's Lord and Saviour; for it is not possible for Omnipotence to make a creature of co-omniscience with himself.

ONE THING LEADS ON TO ANOTHER.

In the year 1788, a term of great religious awakening in Virginia, a negro man, by the name of Peter, belonging to a Mr. Steward, of Culpepper county, came forward to declare the dealings of God with his soul, in order for baptism. As he had been imported from Africa, his language was very broken; but he gave a satisfactory account of himself, and appeared to be in the then present enjoyment of precious faith. Soon as he had finished his detail, he boldly broke out in whistling. The minister, who presided, asked him what he meant by whistling? To which Peter made answer, "let those sing the praises of Jesus who can; I cannot sing, but I can whistle for my blessed Jesus."

Notwithstanding whistling is supposed to be the exercise of a thoughtless clown, yet, in the case of Peter, it naturally leads the mind to contemplate the various ways in which religious adoration is performed.

Prayer is made by crying, weeping, lifting up the eyes, groaning, sighing, panting, breathing, etc. Self-abasement is also expressed by veiling the face, rending the garments, kneeling and falling on the ground.

This again leads us to treat on falling religion, so common in these days. As I have lived among such exercises a considerable part of my life, I have formed a diffident opinion for myself.

Some take it for undeniable evidence, that a man is converted if he has fallen, by the slaying power of God, under the preaching of the word, singing or praying. Others seem as well convinced, that all such exercises are parts of hypocrisy.

When Paul and his company drew nigh to the gates of Damascus, a great light shone around them. If we examine the three accounts given of this vision, in the book of Acts, we shall find that they all saw the light, heard the voice, and fell to the earth; and yet there is no account that any of them received the grace of life but Paul alone. It is not absolutely certain, however, but what all of them received a heavenly blessing, though not recorded. But one thing is certain, viz., when the guard went to take Jesus, with Judas at their head, and heard the Saviour preach a sermon three words long—I AM HE—they went backward, and fell to the ground. That those who fell down at this time, received a gracious change, we have every reason to believe in the negative; for, as soon as they recovered strength to rise, with malevolent hands, and cruel bands, they bound the harmless Jesus, and led him away to the place of unhallowed judgment.

Making no strictures on those falling downs which are hypocritical, and others, which are evidently mechanical, performed on purpose to alarm and proselyte, it is rational to believe that men may be, and sometimes are, so much impressed with the majesty and truth of God, as to fall to the earth, and yet continue in their enmity to him. That this will be the case of all the wicked, at the last judgment, admits of very little doubt; and that it should be so, with some of them, in this life, will appear credible, when we consider the two systems in which God deals with the children of men.

These two systems, some call *law* and *grace;* others term them *the covenant of works* and *the covenant of grace.* I am in the habit of treating them as *the system of moral government,* which God exercises over all rational beings, and *the scheme of grace, through a Mediator.* That God first treated man as a moral subject—allowing him the freedom of his will to act—at the same time accountable for the right use or abuse of his will—bound, by a law of perfect order, to do all that was commanded, and believe all that was revealed, to me appears evident; otherwise, it was not possible for sin ever to have entered the human world. And that he still treats with men in the same system, is also as evident; for, without it, sin could not be repeated, nor guilt exist.

Perfect obedience to this law, secured from blame, but did not entitle the obedient subject to any advanced station; nor was there any means provided in this system to expiate guilt, or regain lost favor.

The works of creation are so evincive of the natural perfections of Deity, that heathen have no excuse for worshipping any other being. But the word and worship of God, which reveal his *moral* character, and the influence of his spirit, are clothed with solemn majesty.

It is not, therefore, to be wondered at, that guilty men, (still holden in the moral system,) not only by beholding the works of God, but by hearing his word dispensed in the power of the spirit—that word, which reveals the wrath of God against the wicked, and the sinner's doom; it is not, I say, a wonder, that they should tremble, smite their knees, and fall to the ground. Let it rather be wondered at, that any sinner can hear and remain unshaken. Were not men hardened in unbelief, through the deceitfulness of sin, they could not endure what is commanded them; no, this terrible sight would overcome their physical powers.

Balaam and Saul were black characters, yet both of them fell before the Lord or his angel; particularly Balaam, was taught much—saw much—fell into a trance, having his eyes open—and was greatly restrained by God; when, at the same time, he was so abandoned, that he wished to curse a whole nation, to get the money in Balak's coffers.

In the system of which I am now treating, the Almighty works abundance *in* men, *by* men, and *for* men; all which works are distinct in their natures from the *work of grace in the heart*; there is no gradation from one to the other, nor any lock-link that unites them together.

The scheme of grace, through a Mediator, was not formed on sin, nor on a *foreknowledge* that *sin* would arise, but on *eternal love*, by infinite wisdom, to be accomplished by Omnipotent power, in a way of divine favor. *Sin* was not the cause of this scheme, nor can sin prevent it. It was formed to secure those who are included in it, and raise them to a higher station than they were placed in at first. All spiritual and eternal blessings are included in it, which are communicated to men by the Holy Ghost. Children may receive this grace before they are born of their mothers, like John the Baptist, or in their infantile days, when their capacities are so small that they cannot discover it; yet it lives and reigns in them.

When this grace (which is called incorruptible seed—an unction from the Holy One—Water of Life, &c.) is given to those who are grown to years of reflection, it discovers unto them the holy, just and gracious character of God—the propriety and extent of the holy law—the evil nature of sin—the insufficiency of all legal and ritual works to justify—the justice of God in the damnation of sinners—and the sufficiency of the blood and righteousness of Christ to atone for sin and secure the soul.

And as these things are discovered to the subject, so also his heart and disposition are new formed to love God—delight in his laws—hate sin—renounce his own righteousness—love that justice which condemns sinners, and heartily embrace the salvation of God, through the blood and righteousness of Christ.

Where these discoveries and dispositions are found in the heart they denominate a man *a true Christian.* But void of that spirit, which produces these views and inclinations, all the fears, horrors, visions, raptures and falling-downs that a man can experience; yea, all that God does in him, by him, or for him, are no evidences that he is a subject of that precious faith which saves the soul.

A DIALOGUE BETWEEN PHILO AND JUBAL.

Philo. My dear brother Jubal, I have come to pay you a Christian visit this afternoon, and if you are not pre-engaged, I hope to spend the time in profitable conversation.

Jubal. I am glad to see you, my brother Philo. Please to take a seat, be at perfect ease, and all your wants be on me. Now, my brother, as time is precious, and should be put to the best possible use, I wish to know, in the first place, whether you come to talk to me, with me, or to hear me talk?

P. Why is my brother Jubal so particular in the first essay of the conference?

J. Because, if you come to talk to me, I will place myself in the attitude of hearing, and patiently receive all your discourses. But if you come to talk with me, I shall expect half the time, without interruptions. On the other hand, if you wish to hear me discourse, I will entertain you as well as I can.

P. I perceive you are for rule in all things; but can it be disorder to break in upon a speaker, if he speaks wrong, too long, inexplicit, or with barbarous words?

J. Should I break in upon a speaker before he closes his sentence, I should talk into his mouth and not into his ears, (to use a vulgarism,) and should also trespass against the good rule, "Ye may all speak one by one." —If anything be revealed unto another, let the first hold his peace, before the other speaks. If a speaker has anything to say worth hearing, give attenton until he has done: if he has nothing worth hearing, let him hold his tongue voluntarily. If a speaker speaks wrong, it may be a comparatively harmless error; if, however, it is a malignant error, I am not obliged to receive it. When a man speaks too long, it is painful to a nimbler mind; but not so painful, to a man of delicacy, as it would be to check him. If, moreover, his discourse is destitute of explicit ideas, or clothed with barbarous words, it is quite enough to have one fool in the play; it would be barbarous to expose him; and if I interrupt him, while he is speaking, my words will certainly be inexplicit to him. What can be more supercilious! what can show more vanity, than for me to help the speaker to better language, or stop him, to show how well I can explain his ideas?

P. I can assure you, my good friend, that I came here to converse to you, with you, and to hear you discourse: nor have I any objection to the rules of conversation, which you have given: but knowing a little what I am, I fear I shall act like a ferryman, who looks one way and rows another; or like a professor, who believes like a Christian and lives like a pagan; or like a Christian who has given all up to God, and would give the world if he had it, for Christ's sake; yet never gave a dollar to the poor, nor a cent of what he really has, to forward the gospel among men.

J. Well, my dear Philo, I am anxious to hear; please to proceed.

P. My tutor, with whom I studied divinity, adopted the maxim, to "explain every passage of scripture literally, if the phraseology would anywise admit of it; and riveted in my mind, that the preacher who would allegorize narratives, and spiritualize moral precepts, would thereby prove anything and everything, and at the same time prove nothing to the purpose. With the maxim of my master before me, and his just observations sounding in my ears, I have read the Bible ever since I left him; but until the present time, I am unable to give a literal exposition on many passages in the Bible. In the ninth chapter of the Revelations, the four angels were loosed to destroy the third part of man, and raised an army of two hundred thousand thousand. The earth never contains, at one time, more than a thousand millions of living souls: not more than one-fifth of them are soldiers. The army here spoken of, contained two hundred millions, which includes every soldier on earth. Now, if all the soldiers on earth were in this one army; who formed the other army, which was destroyed, called the third part of men? Also, in the 14th chapter, when the earth was reaped, and the vine of the earth was cast into the great wine-press; blood came out, it seems, in every direction, the distance of two hundred miles, as high as the horse-bridles. The lowest part of the bridle is four feet from the ground. Now here is a blood-pond, spoken of, four hundred miles in diameter, and four feet deep; which would contain 235,615,018,905,600; more than two hundred and thirty-five billions of cubical inches. Men in general are said to possess twenty-five pints of blood; which is about seven hundred cubical inches: making no deduction for children, who have less blood than men; all the blood of all the living would amount to 700,000,000,000 of cubical inches. Of course, it would take all the human blood of more than three hundred and thirty-six such worlds as this, to form the blood-pond spoken of.

I now wish, secondly, to converse with you, my dear Jubal: and to lead on thereto, I ask, what allowances are we to make for the phraseology of the Bible, and yet hold it divinely authentic?

J. It is not likely that the original copies, written by the prophets and apostles are now in existence: the most, therefore, that any can boast, is transcription: and we, from transcription, have a translation. Our Bible was translated in the days of Prince James; when the English language, was differently spoken from what it is now. Of course, many passages will not admit of a grammatical construction. Prepositions, moods, tenses and numbers are used in a barbarous manner (according to modern taste) and yet a clue will be found, which unveils the meaning to the sincere seeker, in all essential cases. It was not written at first, nor has it been so wonderfully preserved since, in transcriptions and translations to teach men the arts and sciences; but to instruct them in the will of God, respecting their duty and the ground of their hope.

P. Will you give an instance, wherein you take the liberty of changing mood and tense.

J. I will. Take your Bible and look over Acts iii. 19, 20, 21, and I will repeat it, as I think it is to be understood.

"Repent ye, therefore, and be converted, that your sins may be blotted out; for the times of refreshing are come from the presence of the Lord; and he has sent Jesus Christ, who before was preached unto you, by the prophets: whom the heavens did receive until these times of restitution of all things, which God has spoken by the mouth of his holy prophets since the world begun."

P. You have taken great liberty, indeed, in this passage; much greater than I should dare to do, lest I should be guilty of adding to and taking from the sacred book.

J. I grant it. The context, however, seems to invite it; and if the text itself will not admit of the transposition which I have given; still, this new versification conveys no corrupt idea.

P. Well, my brother, in the third place, I wish to hear you converse.

J. I have been frequently called upon to give an exposition of Matt. v. 25, and will now avail myself of the auspicious moment, and do it. The text referred to, reads; "Agree with thine adversary quickly, while thou art in the way with him; lest at any time the adversary deliver thee to the judge, and the judge deliver thee to the officer, and thou be cast into prison: verily I say unto thee, thou shalt by no means come out thence, till thou hast paid the uttermost farthing." Some, by the adversary, understand God—others the justice of God, or the law of God; which they suppose the sinner is to agree with. Others, again, are of opinion that the Devil is the adversary intended: But all these opinions seem to be utterly groundless. Those who apply it to the church discipline, bid much fairer to be in the right; were it not applied to magistracy, by St. Luke. "When thou art in the way to the magistrate," &c. Now, as church discipline has no affinity with magistracy, the sense given cannot be admitted. The text is introduced thus: *When thou bringest thy gift to the altar.* The Jews brought their lambs and other offerings to the altar; and Christians bring their prayers, praises and gifts of improvement into the church and offer them before God. *And there rememberest that thy brother hath aught against thee.* Either a natural brother, national brother, spiritual brother, or human brother. When thou comest before the Lord with thy gift, and rememberest, that thou hast given any man just cause of offence, which is actionable by law, *leave there thy gift before the altar and go thy way; first be reconciled to thy brother, and then come and offer thy gift.* This offended brother is the *adversary;* and I tell you my disciples, if you have given offence, make it your *first* business to effect a reconciliation. If your offence calls for confession, restitution or other costs, pay all immediately before a prosecution begins. If you do not, the adversary may, at any time bring you before the Judge; and being found guilty before him, he will deliver you to an executive officer, who will inflict on you such punishment as the law directs; and if your crime is debt or trespass, you will be cast into prison; and when once you are imprisoned, all your repentance, faith and prayer will not deliver you; for I came not to destroy civil law, or save men from these legal penalties which they have incurred: Of course, they must remain in prison, until they have paid debt and costs. The doctrine of this text, in part, is exemplified in the case of the dying thief. Our Lord forgave his sin; promised him admission into Paradise; but did not deliver him from the penalty of the law, but let him hang on the cross until he had paid the last farthing, with his life.

SELF-EXCUSE.

In the year 1785, there lived in the city of Richmond, (Vir.) a free negro woman, who by her parsimony obtained money enough to purchase her husband, who was a slave. The woman being a member of the Baptist church, in that city, was complained of before the church, for allowing of lewd conduct in her house. She did not deny the truth of the charge, but excused herself thus, "Pray, how can I help it? My husband is the head, and does as he pleases; and I, who am his wife, cannot help it." At the same meeting, another charge was brought against her, for whipping her husband; to which she replied, "I bought him with my own money—he is my legal property, and he shall mind me; otherwise I will whip him."

* * * * * * * *

Excuse—the doctrine of the fall,
From Adam first we hear;
The roots are found within us all,
No mortal man is clear.

When God commands him to appear,
And answer to his case—
Just *nineteen* words from him we hear,
Instead of saying *yes.*

* * * * * * *

LABECULA, OR LITTLE SPOT.

Now Naaman, captain of the King of Syria, was a great man with his master, and honorable; because by him the Lord had given deliverance unto Syria: he was also a mighty man in valor; BUT he was a leper. Dr. Ashly is an accomplished divine, BUT he cannot admit of an equal. Rev. Mr. Benson is an excellent preacher; BUT his discourses are more declamatory than sentimental. IF he was as full of ideas as he is of words, he would shine like a star of the first magnitude. Elder C——, is a good preacher, BUT he is too often telling of what great things he has done. "I had three thousand hearers—I baptized forty in a day—I was moderator of the council," &c. Elder D——, is a man of talents, BUT, like Cæsar, he had rather be the first man in a village than the second man in Rome. IF he was not so much like Diotrephus; IF he was willing that other preachers should have more praise and fame than himself, he would much more resemble the chief Shepherd. IF the writer of this number did not partake of a large share of the vices of these Rev. gentlemen, and but a small part of their virtues, he would be a better man than he is; BUT he is a chip of the old block—a degenerate plant of a strange vine---a bottle in the smoke.

* * * * * *

The virtues of the low we tell,
With elevated strings;
But those we fear will us excel—
We strive to clip their wings.

THE RETURNING PENITENT.

Once there was a precious season,
When my Saviour smiled on me;
Ev'ry groan his grace did sweeten,
Ev'ry bond his love set free.
Patient, I could bear affliction,
Never murmur at the pain;
Just conception, resignation,
Cheerfully did me sustain.

Joyfully I heard his preaching,
Read his word with vast delight,
While his spirit, gently teaching,
Was my comfort day and night.
Sweet was Christian conversation,
Christ and grace was all my theme;
Oh! these days of consolation!
How delighted I have been!

Had I guarded every passion,
Watching daily unto prayer,
Of each sin made just confession,
I had never felt this snare;
Now my Saviour's smiles are wanting,
Now my groans perpetual rise;

Ev'ry hope of joy is falling,
  Now I vent my fruitless cries.

  Just conception, resignation,
  From my breast are far removed;
Now I murmur at affliction,
  Doubting whether e'er I loved.
Oft I hear the gospel sounded,
  Oft I read my Saviour's name;
Yet my heart, most deeply wounded,
  Still remains unmov'd, the same.

Now I've fearful apprehension,
  Whether Christ I ever knew;
Tho' I made a great profession,
  Yet 'twas rather false than true.
Oh! that Jesus was my saviour!
  This is all my soul's desire!
A portion, Lord, within thy favor,
  Tho' I enter here thro' fire!

PRAYER BETTER THAN LAW-SUITS.

Colonel Samuel Harriss, of Pittsylvania, Virginia, was converted, and called to preach, about the year 1758; on which he quitted all his honorary and lucrative offices, and applied himself to the work of an evangelist. A train of seriousness followed him; and, for a number of years, he was more blessed of God than any man in the southern states. His preaching was not much fraught with the wisdom of man, but so full of simplicity, zeal and the Holy Ghost, that judgment and eternity would seem to be present before himself and hearers. His heart was so full of burning love to the souls of men, that his domestic concerns fell into derangement, while he was seeking to pluck them as brands out of the fire. Finding, at length, the absolute need of providing more grain for his family than his plantation had produced, he went to a man (whose name I do not retain) who owed him a sum of money, and addressed him thus:

Harriss. Sir, I should be very glad if you would let me have a little money.

Man. Mr. Harriss, I have no money by me, and, therefore, cannot oblige you.

H. I want the money to purchase wheat for my family; and, as you have raised a good crop of wheat, I will take that article of you, instead of money, at a current price.

M. I have another use for my wheat, and cannot let you have it.

H. What will you do?

M. I never intend to pay you until you sue me, and, therefore, you may begin your suit as soon as you please.

H. To himself, "good God, what shall I do? shall I leave preaching for a vexatious law-suit? Perhaps a thousand souls will perish in the time. I will not. Well, what will you do, Harriss? This I will do: I will sue the man at the court of heaven."

Having resolved what to do, the colonel retired into the woods, and, falling on his knees before the Lord, opened his mouth to this effect: "Lord Jesus, thou hast redeemed my soul from hell and sin, and thou hast called me to preach faith and repentance to my fellow men; but, while I am doing it, my family is like to suffer. Blessed Jesus, a man owes me, and will not pay me unless I sue him. I am in a great strait—O, Lord, teach me what to do."

In this address, the colonel had such nearness to God, that (to use his own words) Jesus said unto him: "*Sam,* I will enter bondsman for the man—you keep on preaching, and omit the law-suit—I will take care of you, and see that you have your pay." Mr. Harriss felt well satisfied with his security; but thought it would be unjust to hold the man a debtor, when Jesus had assumed payment. He, therefore, wrote a receipt in full of all accounts which he had against the man; and, dating it in the woods, where Jesus entered bail, he signed it with his own name. Going the next day by the man's house to attend a meeting, he called a little negro to the gate, gave him the receipt, and bid him deliver it to his master. On returning from meeting, the man hailed him, and said—

M. Mr. Harriss, what did you mean by the receipt which you sent me by the boy?

H. I mean just as I wrote.

M. You know, sir, I have never paid you.

H. Yes, sir, I know it. I know, moreover, that you said you never would, except I sued you. But, sir, I sued you at the court of heaven, and Jesus entered bail for you; and I thought it would be unjust to hold you in debt, when I had got so good security, and, therefore, I sent you that receipt.

M. I insist upon it, it shall not close in this manner.

H. I am well satisfied—Jesus will not fail me. Farewell.

A few days after this, the man loaded his wagon with wheat, and carried it to Mr. Harriss.

HE THAT DWELLS IN A GLASS HOUSE SHOULD NOT CAST STONES AT OTHERS.

Having heard more than three hundred preachers exhibit in my life, and some of them a great number of times—without ill will or vanity, (for pray, who will own himself wrong ?) I have noticed that the most brilliant, as well as the most obscure, have their hobby-horses—I mean words or sentences, which they use, in preaching, to great disadvantage. If these by-words or sentences, were used only in rare instances, they would not only be appropriate, but harmonious; but when they are repeated again and again, without thought, and, indeed, in many instances, to supply the lack of ideas, no apology can be admitted, on the principle of ingenuity.

Mr. Y. was a good man, and felt the importance of the doctrine which he preached; on account of which, he contracted the habit of saying *depend upon it;* which sentence would not only be heard in a great part of the observations through his sermon, but would sometimes mingle in his prayer. The writer once saw him on his knees at prayer, at the close of a meeting, and heard the following words flow from his lips: "O, Lord! look down in mercy on these poor sinners, and convince them that if they are not converted, they must be damned, *depend upon it.*"

Mr. B. is a good divine, and an excellent preacher, but he has so much apostolical benevolence, that he not only introduces every section with, *My dearly beloved brethren,* but often uses the address in the middle of a sentence. He was once observed to use his favoritism more than two hundred times in one sermon.

In one section of the United States, a great part of the preachers were exceedingly fond of the note of similitude, *as it were.* The note frequently occurs in the New Testament. But among these preachers, the note was used so much in course, that it lost all comparison, and was made to substantiate facts. Without holiness, no flesh shall see the Lord, *as it were.*

But, among all the vulgarisms that find the way into the desks of learned and polite preachers, none appears more clownish than the old adage, *I've often thought.* When we meet a farmer in the road, we expect his first remarks will be on the weather; or, if we see a merchant, we calculate to hear the din, hard times and little money. But when we hear preachers, who are in the habit of composition, telling us so often what they have thought, it naturally makes us wish that they would think a little better.

But surely, a man guilty of all of these errors, and seven times as many more, ought to be careful of casting stones, and withhold his criticisms, till he first casts the beam out of his own eye.

A LITTLE GOOD THING.

The little epistle to Philemon is fraught with good things. In composition, it exceeds all the efforts of the learned. Simplicity and benevolence are its characteristics. The tragic scene, therein contained, is drawn with more than human pencil.

The cause of the epistle follows:

Philemon was the disciple of Paul, and owed himself to him as the instrument of his salvation. Philemon had a servant, Onesimus. This Onesimus, not liking his religious master, instead of paying him a debt which he owed, wronged him still more, by pilfering his property, and then running away. Making his way to Rome, where Paul was prisoner, he fell in with the apostle, at his own hired house, which stood within the limits of the prison, where Paul was preaching the gospel with all readiness, and receiving all that came unto him. Here the preaching of Paul arrested the conscience of Onesimus; and the prisonor Paul begat the fugitive servant, by the word of truth to a lively hope.

Onesimus, on this change of character, gave Paul a true account of his conduct towards his master; on which information, Paul wrote the epistle to Philemon, and sent it by Onesimus to his master, to effect a reconciliation between them. So intent was Paul to gain his point, that he wrote a bond and signed it with his own hand, to make good to Philemon, whatever injury he had sustained by Onesimus. His words are—

"For perhaps he therefore departed for a season, that thou shouldest receive him forever. Not now as a servant, but above a servant, a brother beloved, specially to me, but how much more to thee, both in the flesh and in the Lord. If thou count me therefore a partner, receive him as myself. If he hath wronged thee or oweth thee ought, put that on mine account. I, Paul, have written it with mine own hand—I will repay it: albeit, I do not say unto thee, how thou owest unto me even thine own self besides. Yea, brother, let me have joy of thee in the Lord: refresh my bowels in the Lord."

When Onesimus returned to his master, by his own confession of his error and the letter of Paul, a reconciliation was soon effected between the returning servant and his pious master. Philemon frankly forgave him all that he owed; and in addition thereto sent him back to Paul with a liberal offering to supply the necessities of the prison. After which Onesimus tendered his services to Paul, to bear the epistle from Rome to the Colossians; and some say that he became a preacher of the gospel thereafter.

Query. If the great apostle Paul wrote and signed a bond, that he would pay an unknown sum to Philemon, can any man be scrupulous of signing a subscription to pay money for religious uses?

OLD THEY——EXPOSED.

Of all the villains that haunt the world, not one of them is more mischievous than *Old They*. He is generally treated as a noun of multitude, followed by a single verb, (*They say*,) which makes it exceedingly difficult to identify the vagrant. Whether he is an individual, bearing as many titles as a Spanish Don, or a monster, having as many heads as a Hydra, is hard to ascertain.

If a man wishes to spread a false report, to injure his ruler, priest or neighbor, he has nothing to do, but to add, *They say so*, and all passes currently.

If any, however, are incredulous, and back the evil report, after passing many hands, which gave the report publicity, and drawing the ideal residence of *They*, he then plays the game of a talisman before them, or dissolves himself in air.

Others, who have been often foiled in their pursuits after the fugitive, and yet are in the habit of believing that *They has said so*, instead of fixing the blame on the infamous tatler, who is retailing the slander, conjecture a substitute for *They*, and ever afterwards consider the substitute as an enemy, when, at the same time, the poor suspected man, knows not for what. If it will not be considered too dictatorial, I will here suggest a salutary expedient.

When a man begins to retail the libellous reports of others, or vend his own choleric manufacture, on the credit of, *They say so*, if he will not identify his author, hold the man responsible for all he says, and let *Old They* shift for himself.

THE GENEALOGY OF CHRIST—POSSIBLE—PROBABLE—NOT CERTAIN.

Levi, the son of Melchi, married a woman and begat Matthat. He then died, and Eleazar married the same woman and begat Matthan.

Matthat married a woman, who bare him Heli; then dying, Matthan married the widow and begat Jacob.

Heli married a wife, but dying childless, Jacob married the same woman, and begat Joseph (the husband of Mary) who succeeded to Heli; according to Deut. 25, 5, 6. Agreeable, therefore, to St. Matthew's account, Eleazar begat Matthan, and Matthan begat Jacob, and Jacob begat Joseph. And according to St. Luke, Joseph was the (ceded) son of Heli, Heli was the son of Matthat, and Matthat was the son of Levi.

SPEECH

DELIVERED IN THE HOUSE OF REPRESENTATIVES OF MASSACHUSETTS, ON THE SUBJECT OF RELIGIOUS FREEDOM, 1811.

MR. SPEAKER: The right of private judgment, like sight and hearing, is inalienable in nature. Should an individual attempt to surrender it to society, it, nevertheless, would remain with him still in all its vigor. Whatever individuals, from the source of private judgment, might be led to say on the subject now before the house, provided the house was in the capacity of a convention, assembled for the purpose of framing a constitution, I cannot determine: but at the present time, the house is on legislative ground, under the solemnity of an oath, to legislate according to the meaning of the constitution in their best judgments. The part of the constitution, sir, which the subject before the house has particular bearing upon, is contained in the second and third articles of the Declaration of Rights. It is well known, Mr. Speaker, that the inhabitants of this commonwealth, were, when the constitution was framed, as well as at the present time, divided in sentiment about religion, and the mode of its support. From the face of the constitution, as well as from a knowledge of those times, there exists no doubt, that a decided majority believed that religious duties ought to be interwoven in the civil compact—that Protestant Christianity was the best religion in the world—and that all the inhabitants ought to be forced, by law, to support it with their money, as a necessary institute for the good of the body politic, unless they did it voluntarily. While a respectable minority, equally firm in the belief of the divinity of Christianity, and still more Protestant in their views, conceived it to be a measure as presumptuous in a legislature, as in a Pope, to lord it over consciences, or interfere either in the mode or support of Christianity. This minority, Mr. Speaker, did *then*, and do still believe that religion is a matter between individuals and their God—a right inalienable—an article not within the cognizance of civil government, nor any way under its control. In this discordance of religious sentiments, the second and third articles of the Declaration of Rights, are evidently a compromise of parties, in which mutual concessions are made for a general union. The language of the convention, in the constitution, appears to be as follows: "Let those towns, parishes, precints and other religious societies possessed of corporate powers, support their religion by force of law, but if there be any one residing within the limits of those corporate bodies, who attends other worship, and yet has no scruples of conscience in being *legally* taxed, his money when paid, if he requests it, shall be paid over, by the collector, to the minister of his choice. And, whereas, there are many religious societies, who have scruples of conscience about availing themselves of corporate powers; if such societies, voluntarily, in their own mode, make suitable provision for the maintenance of their ministers, all such societies of Protestant Christians, properly demeaning themselves as peaceable citizens, shall not be forced by law to support the teachers or worship of any other society. But as we cannot well know how these principles will operate on experiment, we lay down one fundamental maxim, as a polar star, for the legislature—*no subordination of one religious sect to another should be established by law!*" Taking this, sir, to be a good translation of those two articles, which seem to be somewhat obscure, the question is, whether the laws, made since the adoption of the constitution, or more particularly, whether the interpretation of that part of the constitution and laws, have not effected a subordination of one religious sect to another? The Congregationalists, sir, have no scruples about supporting their worship, in its various parts, by law, but some other societies have—some, indeed, have availed themselves of corporate powers for no other purpose but to defend themselves from being taxed to support a worship in which they had no faith. In such instances they have been subordinate in time and expense to extricate themselves from the clutches of the Congregationalists. Others are so well convinced of the all-sufficiency of Protestant Christianity, and the completeness of its code to govern in *all* things, that they will not—they cannot in good conscience submit to a power, which they believe, in their best judgments, was never given to government to be exercised. These are peaceable subjects of state—ready to arm in defence of their country—freely contribute to support Protestant Christianity, but cannot pay a *legal* tax for *religious* services; this, sir, is one of the essentials which constitutes them a distinct sect: and what have these endured since the adoption of the constitution? Have they not been reduced to subordination? How many law-suits—how much cost—and how much property has been taken from them to support other societies? Mr. Speaker, is not this subordination?

According to a late decision of the bench, in the county of Cumberland, which, it is presumed, is to be a precedent for future decisions, these non-incorporated societies are nobody—can do nothing, and are never to be known except in shearing time, when their money is wanted to support teachers that they never hear. And all this must be done for the *good of the state.* One hundred and seventeen years ago, wearing long hair was considered the crying sin of the land: a convention was called, March 18, 1694, in Boston, to prevent it; after a long expostulation, the convention close thus: "If any man will now presume to wear long hair, let him know that God and man witnesses against him." Our pious ancestors were for bobbing the hair for the *good of the colony,* but now, sir, not the hair, but the *purses must be bobbed* for the *good of the state.* The petitioners pray for the right of going to heaven in that way which they believe is the most direct, and shall this be denied them? Must they be obliged to pay legal toll for walking the king's high-way, which he has made free for all? Is not this a greater subordination than to sail under British licenses, or to pay three pence on every pound of tea? In Rhode Island, New York, New Jersey, Pennsylvania and Delaware, of the old colonies, and in Kentucky, Tennessee and Ohio, the new states, there has never been any legal establishment of religion, nor any assessment to support Protestant Christianity, for the *good of the states,* and yet, sir, these states have stood and flourished as well as Massachusetts.

Since the Revolution, all the old states, except two or three in New England, have established religious liberty upon its true bottom, and yet they are not sunk with earthquakes, or destroyed with fire and brimstone. Should this commonwealth, Mr. Speaker, proceed so far as to distribute all settlements and meeting-houses, which were procured by public taxes, among all the inhabitants, without regard to denomination; it is probable that the outcry of sacrilege, profanity and infidelity would be echoed around; and yet, sir, all this has been done, in a state, which has given birth and education to a Henry, a Washington, a Jefferson and a Madison, each of which contributed their aid, to effect the grand event; for which event the Presbyterians and others prayed and gained. It is there believed, sir, that God hates robbery for burnt offerings, and ought not Massachusetts to pay a decent respect to the voice of fifteen of her sister states? We should imagine that laudable pride would prevent any one religious society from forcing another to pay her laborers, and that the same principle would not admit a public teacher to take money, collected by distraint, from those who did not hear him; but in this particular, we find that religion is made a covert to do that which *common honesty blushes at!*

Sir, it is not to disrobe towns of their corporate powers; no, let them go to heaven in such turnpike roads, and pay legal toll at every ministerial gate which they choose, and what can they wish for more? According to our best judgments, *we* cannot pay legal taxes for religious services, descending even to the grade of a chaplain for the legislature. It is disrobing Christianity of her virgin beauty—turning the churches of Christ into creatures of state—and metamorphosing gospel ambassadors to state pensioners. If my information be correct, the town of Boston has enjoyed the liberty which we plead for, more than one hundred years, yet the inhabitants increase and are virtuous. Fifteen states, now in the Union, have all that we ask for, and is religion demolished in those states? Mr. Speaker, let gentlemen turn their eyes to the religious magazines, published in this state, by those who plead for law-regulated religion, and they will find, that while the editors in one page plead for the old firm of Moses and Aaron—ruler and priest; where the language is, "you comb my head and I'll scratch your elbows—you make laws to support me, and I'll persuade the people to obey you;" in the next page, they will narrate the wonderful works of God in those states wherein there are no religious laws, and indeed, wherein the inhabitants know that religious establishments and assessments, serve only to make one part of the community fools, and the other hypocrites—to support fraud, superstition and violence in the earth.

Let Christianity stand upon its own basis, it is the greatest blessing that ever was among men; but incorporate it into the civil code and it becomes the mother of cruelties.

It is questioned, Mr. Speaker, by good judges, whether it is possible for the legislature to execute the power vested in them, in the third article of the Declaration of Rights, without defeating the provision in the same article "that no subordination of any one sect or denomination to another, shall ever be established by law." I know not, sir, what can be done, but one thing is certain, it never has been done since the adoption of the constitution. Supposing, sir, it *cannot* be done, to which part of it ought the legislature to adhere?—to that which supports partiality and injustice, or to that which secures right and equality; can any gentleman be at a loss?

Tyranny, Mr. Speaker, always speaks the same language. The tyrant of Ammon would be friendly to Israel, if he might put out their right eyes. The tyrant on the Nile would let his subjects go free, provided they would leave their flocks and herds behind.

Go serve the Lord, proud Pharaoh said,
But let your flocks and herds be staid—
Go serve the Lord, says Massachusetts,
But bow to Baal with your certificates.
You all may worship as you please,
But parish priest shall have your fees;
His preaching is like milk and honey—
And you shall pay *our* priest *your* money!

Mr. Chairman, if Christianity is false, it cannot be the duty of government to support imposture; but if it be true, the following extracts are true: "The natural man receiveth not the things of God, neither can he know them; the world by wisdom know not God; none of the princes of this world, know the genius of Christ's kingdom." If, sir, Christianity is true, these sayings are true; and if these sayings are true, natural men, as such, with all the proficiency of science, cannot understand the religion of Christ; and if they cannot understand the subject, they must be very unfit to legislate about it. If, to escape this dilemma, we adopt the Papal maxim, that government is founded in grace, and, therefore, none but gracious men have a right to rule; and that these gracious rulers have both right and knowledge to legislate about religion, we shall find, what other nations have found, that these divine rulers, will be the most cruel tyrants: under this notion, Mr. Chairman, the crusades were formed in the eleventh century, which lasted about two hundred years, and destroyed nearly two millions of lives. In view of all this, and ten thousand times as much, is it to be wondered at, that the present petitioners, should be fearful of attaching corporate power to religious societies? These petitioners, sir, pay the civil list, and arm to defend their country as readily as others, and only ask for the liberty of forming their societies, and paying their preachers, in the only way that the Christians did for the first three centuries after Christ: any gentleman upon this floor, is invited to produce an instance, that Christian societies were ever formed, Christian sabbaths ever enjoined, Christian salaries ever levied, or Christian worship ever enforced by law, before the reign of Constantine; yet Christianity did stand and flourish, not only without the aid of the law and the schools, but in opposition to both. We therefore hope, Mr. Speaker, that the prayer of thirty thousand, on this occasion, will be heard, and that they will obtain the exemption for which they pray.

The second section of the bill before the house, I object to. It recognizes principles which are inadmissable—invests all non-corporate societies with corporate powers—puts the mischievous dagger into their hands, which has done so much mischief in the world, and presents no balm for the wounds of those who cry for help.*

The petitioners do not ask to be known in law, as corporate bodies, but, to be so covered, that religious corporate bodies shall not know, and fleece them; but, this section puts the knife into their hands against their wills; a knife, sir, which is more pestiferous than Pandora's box. The interference of legislatures and magistrates, in the faith, worship, or support of religious worship, is the first step in the case, which leads in regular progression to inquisition; the principle is the same, the only difference is in the degree of usurpation.

The bill has its beauties, and its deformities. One prominent defect of the bill, is, a crooked back; it makes a low stoop to his high mightiness, town-clerk, to pray for the indulgence of worshipping God; which is, and

* After the delivery of this speech, the bill passed some radical amendments.

ought to be guaranteed a natural and inalienable right; not a favor to be asked by the citizen, or bestowed by the ruler. It has also a disagreeable squinting; it squints to a purse of money with as much intenseness, as ever a drunkard does at the bottle, or as ever Eve did at the apple. Yes, Mr. Speaker, if there was no money to be got, we should never hear of these corporations. How strange it is, sir, that men, who make such noise about Christianity, should be afraid to trust the promise of God, unless they can have legal bondmen, bound by incorporation.

Government should be so fixed, that Pagans, Turks, Jews and Christians, should be equally protected in their rights. The government of Massachusetts, is, however, differently formed; under the existing constitution, it is not possible for the general court, to place religion upon its proper footing; it can be done, however, much better than it is done, either by the late decision of the bench, or by the adoption of the present bill, in its present shape; and the best which the constitution will admit of, is all that I seek for at present. I shall therefore take the liberty, at a proper time, to offer an amendment to the bill.

I shall no longer trespass on the patience of the house.

A

SHORT NARRATIVE

OF A

FIVE HOURS' CONFLICT,

ON THE NIGHT FOLLOWING THE 17TH OF OCTOBER, 1811.

I am the man that have seen affliction by the rod of his wrath.—JEREMIAH.

IN the summer of 1811, there appeared to be a gracious work among the people in Cheshire. I had my trials to bear; yet the circle which I trod, on the whole, was pleasant. My outward man was affected with a jaundiced debility, but my inward man was renewed day by day. By the last of September, I had baptized twenty-eight, and the work seemed to be prevailing; when suddenly I was stopped from my ministerial labors, and called to pass through a scene very afflictive. Whatever the disease might be called, it shocked my whole nervous system, and assailed my head with such pain that it deprived me of a great part of my hearing and power of speech. Whether my sickness was brought on by latent causes—by imprudent conduct—or by unavoidable events, is immaterial to my narrative. I was sorely attacked. When first seized, I had an impression riveted in my mind that I should be given up of the Lord, to pass through a doleful conflict; how long I could not tell. But whether this affliction was to come upon me for specific crimes committed, for a trial of my faith, or to prevent me from being exalted with pride, or falling into some other sin, I could not suggest. On entering this valley of the shadow of death, I seemed to be stripped of all my armor, which so lately I had gloried in. The God whom I had addressed and confided in; the Mediator, through whose blood and righteousness alone I hoped for pardon; the gospel of salvation, which revealed the only foundation of trust; and the spirit of prayer, which I preferred to all riches, were removed from my grasp; nor could I conceive that there was any happiness in the universe. In this state, however, I had a small hope, that God, in his own good time, would bring me back again to that circle which I had lately walked in;

and notwithstanding my distress of body and mind were great, yet I had some acquiescence in the affliction. The language of the prophet became mine; "I will bear the indignation of the Lord, because I have sinned against him, until he plead my cause and execute judgment for me." But when I had waited more than a fortnight, my sickness still prevailing, and no deliverance granted, it struck my mind that the Lord would never bring me back again to that state where I enjoyed my armor and happiness, and that I must begin in *hell's belly*, where I was, to call upon the name of the Lord. Memorable time! dark and doleful night! let it never be forgotten by me! My mind was arrested, by some invisible power, and my soul seemed suspended on a point, that unless I could solve a number of questions, all would be lost. How did my poor heart tremble! It was ten o'clock at night; all was dark, without and within! On entering the contest I felt like a feeble child cast into a pit to combat with dragons. The first question propounded to me, was, "Is there a harmony in the universe becoming a God?" The immensity of the universe I could form no idea of. How many worlds and systems of worlds there were I knew not; and what an infinity of space surrounded those worlds, was beyond my stretch of thought. The visible heavens and earth were all that I could contemplate to any advantage; and indeed the *condition* of rational and animal creatures was the subject that summoned my attention. Among rationals, war, famine, pestilence, earthquakes, plagues, personal slavery, despotic oppression, sickness, pain and death, &c. Among beasts, fear, hunger, cruelty, killing and living upon each other, bearing the abuses of men, and slain by them to feast upon, &c. Here the reasoning of my mind was this—"Why did the Almighty make creatures subject to all this? If he is the parent of all, why does he suffer one of his children to inflict so much injustice and cruelty upon another? Could he not have made things otherwise? If not, why create at all? After he had created, could he not have prevented sin and misery? If he could, who can justify his goodness in withholding aid? Can it possibly be pleasing to God to see darkness, wrath, sin, misery and death rage in his dominions? If his will is otherwise, why did he not, why does he not prevent it? But this he does not do. These destructive evils have always existed since I can remember; at least, do still exist, and I can see no end to them. How did my aspiring and arrogant soul struggle against believing self-evident facts, when I could not comprehend the great constitution, (or the events that took place under the constitution,) whence all those evils arose! At length it was suggested to me, that I was utterly incompetent to understand the mystery that was enfolded in the smallest insect or grain of sand; that there was a principle, known to exist, by which to pour cold water upon a cold stone* would raise fire to burn up the house. That I could not tell

* The burnt limestone is here intended.

why the water ran down hill; why the wind did blow; or what that angry spirit, called fire, was, that ate up the wood and warmed the flesh. That I could not account for the voluntary or involuntary motions of my own body; nor did I know why or what the pain was which I felt. And if I could not understand the least of God's works, I must be more insufficient to understand the whole system than the smallest fly was to understand the greatest piece of machinery. This kind of reasoning had a little weight in my mind, but effected no real subordination in my spirit. Creation was all in disorder. Darkness, wrath and confusion reigned through the whole; and happiness did not exist. And here this subject was left.

The next question which arrested my mind was this, "there is no God. If so, who is he?" On the first part of this suggestion, my reflections were as follows. There either is a God, or there is not. If there is a Supreme Deity, he must be increate, himself uncaused; and this I can form no idea of; it seems impossible. But if there is no God, whence arose all creatures and things, which I know exist? To suppose that the visible heavens and earth are eternal; or that the first man on earth had never a beginning, is equally impossible to sense, and less likely to be true. Of course then, to escape a greater dilemma I must believe that there is a God, and that his eternal power and Godhead are seen by the visible things which he has made. If, then, there is a God, who is he? Here my thoughts were exercised thus. Whoever God is, he must be *eternal*, without beginning—*sovereign*, under no law—and *omnipotent*, to create all things. The gods many and lords many of the heathen world, were, some of them, ideal and others of them material beings; but none of them that I have ever read or heard of, claimed the character, nor have any of their worshippers ever given them the character of *creating all things and raising the dead*. The heathen accounts of creation are chimerical enough: but they never ascribe it to any of their gods. And the *resurrection from the dead* is looked upon as a thing incredible by them; in it they have no hope. But the Holy One of Israel, who is the Christian's God, claims the works of creation and the resurrection as his own. Here many texts occurred to my mind; such as, "Thus saith the high and lofty one that inhabiteth eternity—I am God and there is none else—I am the Lord, that is my name, and my glory I will not give to another, nor my praise unto graven images—Give ear, O ye heavens, and I will speak; and hear, O earth, the words of my mouth; I have made the earth and man upon it; my hands have stretched out the heavens, and all their hosts have I commanded—Mine hand also hath laid the foundation of the earth, and my right hand hath spanned the heavens; when I call unto them, they stand up together; I clothe the heavens with blackness, and I make sackcloth their covering; I kill and I make alive; Thy dead men shall live; All that are in the graves shall hear his voice and come forth; they that have done good to the resurrection of life, and those that have done evil to the resurrection of damnation, and many more beside; for never did the scripture flow into my mind as it did that night. Now, if creation certainly has taken place, (which none can deny,) and the resurrection also in a few instances, and will be universal according to history and prophecy; and none of the heathen gods claim the work; to whom can it be ascribed better than unto him who claims it? Surely Jehovah he is God! the Lord he is God! It is not to be understood that my convictions of the Godhead of Jehovah were so clear and absolute as to prevent all scruples; they seemed but to hold me up with a little help, while the horrors of atheism and black despair, like billows, were dashing round my trembling soul.

The following thought next bolted into my mind: "Jesus Christ was not truly God, nor the Saviour of men." This was no new suggestion to me; it has often assailed me in my life; but it came now with great force, when I had but little strength to withstand it. In health, I had given up the point, that the mystery of the trinity, and of the union of two natures in Christ were incomprehensible; and here it struck my mind that the Creator and Saviour of men must be too exalted in nature for men or angels to scrutinize; that a being must be just as incompetent to create and redeem, as the creatures were competent to understand. But the question arose in my mind, "Is there not rational evidence within the comprehension of men to prove *facts*, which are, in their nature, inconceivable?" The answer was, yes. For proof, I have evidence to believe that my eye can see, my ear hear, and my tongue speak; but *why* these organs have that power, and others have not, I cannot tell. The question then followed, "Is there rational evidence to believe that Jesus Christ was truly God, and the only Saviour of lost sinners?" This evidence I then sought after. It here occurred to me, that Jesus bore all the names and titles of Israel's Holy One, and did godlike works by inherent power, and, therefore, must be the true God and eternal life; and that salvation was in none other; for there was no other name under heaven, given among men, whereby we must or could be saved. But here I got headed. It burst into my mind like a torrent, "That I was bringing my evidence from the Bible, which was a fictitious book—that the history of Jesus was not true, and the gospel was only an imposture." How this sunk my spirits! The only prop which my feeble soul had to rely on, must now be taken away. "If the foundations be destroyed, what can the righteous do?" In the course of my life, I have read all the deistical books that came to hand, and have had many difficulties in my mind about the divinity of the Bible, which no Deist that I have read after has availed himself of. I have also read the replies to the Deists, and have had some arguments of my own in defence of revelation. But now, when I was weak, and my life hanging in suspense, to go over all the ground of debate, was so elaborate, that it was not practicable. Some shorter way of relief I must find, or plunge. The divinity of the New Testament—the truth of the gospel, was now the point at issue. On which I reasoned thus: the New Testament is in existence: it was written either by bad men or by good men: to believe that bad men wrote it, requires a faith more marvellous than it does to believe the truth of any article contained in it. For bad men to form a book that condemns every species of sin—that lays the honors, pleasures, and wealth of the world in the dust—that enjoins patience under injury, and good for evil—in short, to sacrifice everything that is pleasing to bad men: who can believe it? The New Testament is written in a style peculiar to itself. In it, there is such majesty and simplicity, united with such force to arrest the conscience, that all the wise men aud wits on earth cannot imitate it. The belief of the gospel never makes good men worse, but often makes bad men better. If the gospel is not from heaven, who can account for the impression that it has had on the hearts and lives of thousands in our day, and we cannot deny it. ? The presumption is, then, that the gospel was written by good men; if so, they spake the truth, for a liar is not a good man. And, if they spake the truth, their writings are divine; for they assure us that "holy men of God spake as they were moved by the Holy Ghost."

So I reasoned with myself. But, notwithstanding the arguments in favor of the divinity of the gospel overweighed those against it, yet, I found logical reasoning to be but feeble support for a desponding soul, verging on eternity. I wished to know, *without a doubt*, that Jesus was a Saviour, and that the gospel was from heaven. The prayer of Moses came to mind, "I beseech thee, show me thy glory." How did I long to see Jesus, either in a trance, like Paul, or to have the heavens open that I might see him, like Stephen; but this I was not favored with. At length, I corrected myself thus: But few of Adam's children, for four thousand years, ever saw him, and those few only saw him in vision. When he was on earth, but a small part of men, then living, saw him; and, since his ascension, he is not to be seen without a miracle; and, therefore, is not my prayer tempting the Lord? But is it necessary, or any ways advantageous, for me to see him? Many saw him, and believed not. Should I now see him, perhaps I should not reverence him; and, if I did, perhaps I should as soon doubt the truth of that appearance as I should the gospel. Here the following words occurred: "If they hear not Moses and the prophets, neither will they be persuaded although one rose from the dead." But neither Scripture nor reason would still the tempest in my soul. The suggestions, "hearsay will not do; history may be false; you must have ocular evidence to convince you," would break over my head like mighty billows. Words cannot express the distress of my heart at that time. An instance recorded of Abraham was appropriate to my case. "Lo! a horror of great darkness fell upon him." While musing on my state of misery, of which I could see no end, the plaintive language of Jesus came to mind. "My God! my God! why hast thou forsaken me? Now is my soul exceeding sorrowful, even unto death. If it be possible, take away this cup from me. Being in an agony he prayed more earnestly, and his sweat was, as it were, great drops of blood."

Never did I before have so great a sense of the agony of Christ—never such fellowship of his sufferings. But he agonized and resisted unto blood; I did not. He bore his afflictions for others; I for my own sins. Indeed, his sufferings appeared so much greater than mine, that my own hardly deserved a name, and yet they were severe.

While thus tossed to and fro in my spirit, the words of Paul and Silas to the jailer fell into mind. "Believe on the Lord Jesus Christ and thou shalt be saved." This text caused a pause in my thoughts. I remembered that the words were spoken to a man, who, but a few minutes before, to prevent impeachment and disgrace, would have killed himself. Surely, thought I, this is short work, indeed. This too was after Christ left the earth; and is he the same now? If so, O, that I might believe! What is it to believe? How must I come and bow before him? The answer was, "he that cometh to him must believe that he is, and that he is a rewarder of them who diligently seek him." While I was querying with myself whether I believed or not, the words of a man (who was desiring and doubting) flowed into my thoughts with great force. "Lord, I believe, help thou my unbelief." Never did words suit a man's condition better. I felt as if I believed a little, but was surrounded with surges of unbelief. If words had been made on purpose for me, they would not have been more applicable than was the text, "Lord, I believe, help thou my unbelief." But the thought followed, "you have not seen him, and, therefore, your faith in him is no more than fancy." On which the words of Peter seemed to strengthen me: "Whom having not seen ye love; in whom, though now ye see him not, yet believing, ye rejoice with joy unspeakable and full of glory." And also the words of Paul: "We walk by faith and not by sight." Together with the saying of Jesus: "A little while and ye shall not see me, and again a little while and ye shall see me." But the text which was most impressive, was, "Blessed are they which have not seen and yet have believed." By this time my soul was full; like Jacob, I could say, "It is enough." Or, like the apostles, "We believe and are sure that thou art Christ the Son of the living God." It really appeared to me that, when I breathed, my soul drew in the water of life, or "breathed her native air." But rest was not for me yet. It was next presented to me, "that if ever the texts were spoken in which I had rejoiced, they were spoken to others, and bore no relation to me."

Here I plunged again, and sunk in the mire, where there was no standing. And is the Bible false? Is it compatible with the goodness of God, to leave all his creatures without any directory to guide their feet—any foundation to encourage their hope? Have all the martyrs and saints suffered so much in vain? If, however, the history of their sufferings is false, or if they suffered from sinister views, what shall we think of what we know has taken place in our days? Thousands, in our days, have been so impressed by the gospel, as to have their principles changed, and their lives reformed, which I cannot impute to any cause but its divinity. It must be true. My soul then rose up again in faith, and I fled, as before, to my refuge. "Blessed are those who have not seen and yet have believed—Lord, I believe, help thou my unbelief." I cannot say how many times, but I believe more than twenty, in the course of my conflict, I had these triumphs in believing and plunges in unbelief. I compared myself sometimes to a child riding on the end of a beam fixed on a pivot; sometimes his end would be up, anon it would fall, and bruise and break him. At other times, to a man cast into the ocean in the night, feeling with hands and feet for some support; at length, he finds a solid rock to stand upon, but the rolling billows, beating around, and breaking over his head, almost sweep him from the rock.

The next attack which I had was this. "Man is all mortal and has no soul that will survive his dissolution, but his death is the close of his existence." This suggestion has greatly assaulted me for twenty years. Notwithstanding the scripture proves the contrary so abundantly, yet a spirit has been fluttering around me, and whispering that the complexity of man was chimerical. (Those who know how hard it is to realize, as Christians, what they believe as rationalists, will understand me.) Here my spirits played again. My nerves were grievously attacked; and this close thinking on abstruse questions I knew was injurious to me. Fain I would have stopped thinking to save my life, but I could not do it. Some invisible power impelled me to it. Well, thought I, if myself and all others die like brutes, there will be an end of us all; I shall fare as well as any, and all of us shall certainly escape future pain, and lie in dust unconscious of our existence. But this state of passivity looked horrid to me. And besides, I did not see as the decay of my health, flesh and strength impaired my thinking faculties, nor could I believe that death would extinguish them. But I did not long continue here; my thoughts were arrested by another subject, viz: "Will the dead ever be raised?" It is remarkable that all the most potent objections that are ever advanced against the divinity of Christianity, should appear in all their front, in battle array against me, in one night, when I was so poorly prepared for the attack, both in body and mind. Whether it can be accounted for or not, so it was. The Deist admits that if the resurrection in general, or that of Christ in particular, can be proved, Deism must fall. The Christian agrees, that if there is no resurrection from the dead, the gospel is a lie—men believe in vain and are yet in their sins. It then struck my mind, that the way in which great events were perpetuated, was by history, periodical days and emblems.

The resurrection of Christ was handed down to us by history; and if the history was no more authentic than other histories, yet, at least, it deserved equal credit. And no man disputed but what Augustus Cesar and Tiberius Cesar had lived and reigned in Rome. Now, as it is said Christ was born in the days of one of them, and died and rose again in the days of the other, why not believe in the resurrection of Christ, as well as in the reign of those emperors? To me it appeared unaccountable, if the history of Christ's resurrection was a forgery, that, at a time when it was so easy to detect the cheat, it should nevertheless gain such credit among every class of people, that in less than three hundred years it should overturn an empire which claimed universal sway. A periodical day has also been observed to perpetuate the event; and every first day of the week gave us as good proof of the resurrection of Christ, as every 4th day of July gives our children, under thirty-five years old, when the American revolution took place. Baptism has also handed down the same fact; this commemorates the burial and resurrection of Jesus; but if the dead rise not, why are they baptized for the dead. But I could not reason much. To me, however, it appeared, that if Jesus arose from the dead, there was no difficulty in proving or believing that all men would be raised. But my thoughts ran fast. When I had got one difficulty removed, before I had any time to receive consolation, another would present itself. I was like the troubled sea which has no rest. The next blow I had was this: "Well, if Christ was the Son of God, and rose from the dead, yet no man of talents, who is candid in his researches, will ever believe in the divinity of Christianity. Let him only survey the errors, contentions, fraud, cruelties, banishments and bloodshed that have been among Christians, and this too under a pretence that they were doing the will of their master, and he will not hesitate to reprobate it. I noticed through the whole conflict, that it was never suggested to me, that any annals, history or traditions handed down to us were questioned, except what was in the Bible; all other accounts were genuine. I had read so much, and believed so much of what I had read, and seen so much, that I felt the force of the last blow to purpose; it struck me to the ground, and I lay bleeding in the dust. I knew, from scripture, that the first Christians were not perfect, and I knew, from history, later Christians had been worse. And from experience among men, I knew that modern Christians were far out of the way. The amazing divisions and splits that had taken place among them, and that still existed; the various and uncertain solutions on scripture points among them, &c. appeared very formidable before me. At length the following text came to mind: "What if some did not believe, shall their unbelief make the faith of God without effect?" And another, "Let God be true, but every man a liar." And a third, "When they shall say lo! here, or lo! there, go ye not after them." Here I saw that Christ did not trust his cause to the goodness of his followers, but rested it on his own shoulders. That he had foretold of all these errors among them who called themselves by his name; and that all those divisions, wars, &c. served to prove the authenticity of the scripture and the divinity of its author. By this time the gospel of salvation appeared true and lovely; and Jesus was without doubt the Saviour of men. But the question was suggested, "will he save you?" At this time my soul was plunged into the utmost agony. Never did I feel such concern about my own soul in my life. "Will Jesus save me? How shall I know it, unless I see him and hear the gracious word from his mouth?" The world was then presented to view; I concluded that seven-tenths of Adam's children had lived and died without ever hearing of a Mediator: and what had become of all these? The words of Jesus then occurred. "Him that cometh unto me I will in no wise cast out." At this time there seemed to be a concurrence of several things. The end of the beam loaded with doubts was down; my belief in the truth of the gospel and mediation of Christ was up. There was a strong cry in my soul after relief, and a Saviour bidding me, "come." I left the heathen world to settle the affair with God, without me. With the Jews, Turks, Christians, and indeed every human creature, I did the same, and felt myself as one alone in the world summoned before the mighty God. My heart was drawn out to my Saviour, and I felt him my friend. With what voice I had I proclaimed, "here is *one* Saviour, Jesus, for *one* sinner, Leland." Nor had I, at that instant, any thought of another creature in the universe. Christianity then appeared to me to be the religion of sinners. I thought the law, under some restrictions, was the religion of holy creatures. Do this and thou shalt live—transgress and there is no forgiveness. How sweetly the following text flowed into my mind. "This is a faithful saying, and worthy of all acceptation, that Christ Jesus came into the world to save sinners, of whom I am chief. I am come to save that which was lost. He was wounded for our transgressions, he was bruised for our iniquities; the chastisement of our peace was upon him, and by his stripes we are healed. Christ died for our sins according to the scriptures. He washed us from our sins in his own blood;" and many more beside, which made it appear that Christianity was not adapted to holy beings, but to sinners. "I came not to call the righteous, but sinners to repentance."

Here a query arose in my mind, whether Christ had re-Adamed men by the atonement which he had made, and did no more for them; that is whether Christ had only redeemed men from the curse of the law, and, given them a self-determining power over their own wills; and now their salvation depended upon their choosing or refusing; or whether he, in addition to dying for them, wrought effectually in their hearts, and drew them to himself. As a branch of this query, I was led to contemplate the internal state of a world of sinners. That all have sinned—there is none that seeketh after God, no, not one—he hath concluded all in unbelief; the heart is deceitful above every thing, and desperately wicked—none calleth upon God—the carnal mind is enmity against God, it is not subject to his law, neither indeed can be, &c. From these, and similar passages, it appeared to me, that all men, in their natural state, were so blinded, hardened, deceived by satan, and opposed to God, that if the scheme of salvation left any thing depending on the will of man, as a condition of his acceptance with God, at best, every thing was precarious; and as it respected myself, I should certainly fail. The plan, therefore, of softening salvation by grace, to make it acceptable to sinners, neither met my case, nor relieved my soul. I felt the need of an almighty agent to work in me, to rectify my soul, as well as to work without me, to suffer for sin. Here the following passages came into my mind, with life and force. "It is not of him that willeth, nor of him that runneth, but of God that sheweth mercy." Every good and perfect gift cometh down from the father of spirits and light. A man can receive nothing, except it be given him from heaven. Which were born, not of blood, nor of the will of the flesh, nor of the will of man, but of God. And you hath he quickened, who were dead in trespasses and sins; even when we were dead in sins hath he quickened us, together with Christ; by grace ye are saved. For by grace are ye saved, through faith; and that not of yourselves, it is the gift of God. Not of works, lest any man should boast; for ye are his workmanship, created in Christ Jesus, unto good works. It is God that worketh in you, both to will, and to do, of his own good pleasure. Lord, thou wilt ordain peace for us, for thou also hast wrought all our works in us. To give repentance, and remission of sins unto Israel. Then hath God also unto the Gentiles granted repentance unto life. I will put my fear in their hearts, and they shall never leave me." These passages came with such evidence to my heart, that I was reminded of the words of Jesus. "The words which I spake unto you, they are spirit, and they are life." The Saviour now appeared all complete, not only in paying the price of man's redemption, but in new forming the apostate soul, and preparing men for the kingdom of God. My soul felt so enlivened, and the Saviour appeared so competent to save, that I spake as before, "Here is one Saviour, for one sinner;" and this I repeated a great number of times, and at every breath, (as I said before,) my soul drew in the water of life. But soon this query arose, "Are you right? is he competent for you only? is he not the Saviour of the world?" Here I paused, and reasoned thus. Some say that he is the Saviour of all men, not only in redeeming all with his blood, but, also, in that he will bring all to heaven. Others say, that he is the Saviour of all men, in making an atonement sufficient for all, so that all may come if they will; yet, he limits the displays of his grace, and draws none to himself but the elect. A third class say, that he died for all—has taken away original sin—given all a talent—calls and strives with all—and has elected those who turn to the Lord, repent of their sins, and believe in the Saviour. While a fourth party say, that election was personal, and eternal; not characteristical and conditional—that for the elect alone he died—that these he will restore by grace, and bring to glory. These points, I knew, had been the strife of ages; and, thought I, they cannot all be right; but they may all be wrong. I dare not trust any of them. But the blessed Jesus, and not systems or creeds, is the foundation which the prophet and the apostles laid and built upon, and I will do likewise. Here is one Saviour, for one sinner. It followed in my mind, every man shall give an account of himself to God. The words of Jesus were also impressive. When Peter was inquisitive to know what John should do, and what should be done to him; said Jesus, "what is that to thee? follow me." However, at this time, I remember, I desired to live and revive, that I might tell to all around, that I had found one Saviour for one sinner, and that every one that came to him by faith, I believed would find him a Saviour, as well as myself. Here the words of the poet occurred:

> The faith that unites to the Lamb,
> That brings such salvation as this,
> Is more than mere notion or whim,—
> The work of God's spirit it is.

My mind was next arrested, to survey the Scripture proof of the existence of disembodied spirits, as follows. Moses died, and was buried; but fefteen hundred years afterwards, Moses, with Elias, was seen and heard by James, Peter, and John. If the body of Moses was raised immediately after Christ's resurrection, (of which there is no certain proof,) yet it had not been raised when the apostles saw him. Hence the argument, that the soul of Moses lived when his body was dead. Jesus Christ spake of himself, as having a spirit distinct from his flesh. "The spirit is willing, but the flesh is weak;" and when he was dying, he commended that spirit to the hands of his father. He also told the dying thief, "to-day shalt thou be with me in paradise." None can imagine that the body of that thief went to paradise that day. Hence, more proof of the existence of disembodied spirits. Paul said, while he was at home in the body, he was absent from the Lord—he had rather be absent from the body, and present with the Lord. What can be plainer? The author to the Hebrews, speaks of the spirits of just men made perfect. John saw under the altar, the souls of them that were beheaded, and they cried, "how long, O Lord, holy and true," &c. The narrative given of the rich man, and Lazarus the beggar, proves, that the soul of the bad man, and the soul of the good man, existed after death. But, notwithstanding this, I was not contented; I wanted ocular evidence. Never did Moses long more to see "that goodly mountain, and Lebanon," than I longed to have heaven opened to me, that I might see if there were spirits, and if they were happy; for the universe still looked in disorder; creation in dark confusion, and happiness out of existence. At this time, it appeared to me, that three or four angels or spirits, in a cluster, came and took their stand a few feet from my bed-post; light was dazzling around them, and they appeared pleasant and happy. I saw no real shape, and heard no voice, but the Saviour seemed to be near them, and the heavenly world was full of light. To me, it was then plain, that there was a boundary between heaven and this world, where so much wrath, horror, and misery reigned. If it could be supposed, that all this was nothing but heated imagination, arising from enfeebled nerves, yet the effect was amazing. For seventeen days I had been without any idea, that any part of the universe was free from darkness, distress and confusion, or that any creatures possessed pleasure. But now the boundless regions of heaven opened to view, where light and serenity displayed their beams, and where the inhabitants seemed pleased and happy. This so diverted my mind, that all the horrors of being dead, and part of the horrors of dying, were removed. When I reflect on the weak state of my nerves—the distress and close thinking of my mind for four hours, without a moment's respite, this appearance did then, and does still, look to me, as if it saved me from total distraction. For, after I have found a heaven of light, with happy beings in it, the lower world appeared much better; I could then see a mixture of goodness in creation, and the glory of God shining through the whole. This, however, gradually prevailed on my mind, for it was several days, before I got entirely reconciled with creation. I will here add, that the little band of angels, or supposed angels, continued in their charge three days and nights and then withdrew.

Notwithstanding the deliverance which I obtained from this real or supposed appearance, yet dreadful clouds and darkness were round about me; but the little strength which I had received assisted me in what followed. The next attack was this: "You are firm in the faith that Jesus Christ was the Son of God, and the only Saviour of sinners, and that the Christian economy is true; but according to that belief, what evidence have you in your own mind, that you are one to be saved by Christ?" This called my attention to several things. I admitted that all men (myself among the rest) by nature were unprepared for heaven, and that no exercises of ours, while in that state of enmity could be pleasing to God; that unless men were *born again* they could not be saved; that Christ saved men by the washing of regeneration and the renewing of the Holy Ghost. Granting this, have I ever experienced this change? I knew that almost nineteen years of my life, from infancy on, was exceeding vain; that for several of the last years of that time dancing and merriment was superlative pleasure; that some change then took place in my mind, which not only stopped my career, but made those exercises abhorrent, so that I could not remember that I ever had had a single desire to return to them again. That change turned me to religious exercises, in which I had taken delight, and that I had continued, more or less, in them until the then present moment. This seemed encouraging. But then considering the weakness of my views at the time of that change, the unsanctified nature that was left, and the evils that had mixed with my religious exercises all along through the whole, I was at some loss what conclusion to draw. I next took a survey of my ministerial life. On which my reflections were as follows. When I began the work, I was so well covinced that a gracious change of heart and an internal call were essential to form a minister of Jesus, that nothing would have tempted me to undertake the work, short of a belief that I had both; but though I believed I had, and undertook for fear of offending the Lord, yet I might have been deceived. Since I undertook, I have travelled through many fatigues, over mountains and waters, through storms and tempests, with little or no prospect of getting a penny for my pains. Yea, many hundreds of miles, pinched with hunger, sometimes for want of the means of supplying the wants of nature, and at other times to save what little I had, to supply the wants of my family, that I might travel and preach the more. It has not been rare to preach six months successively, without receiving six dollars for it. But was it not from curiosity, to see the world and those in it? Was it not the effect of ambition, to be taken notice of by others, as a man of talents? Add to all this, such languor of soul and indifference of mind have attended me, that the evidence seems against me. But, to do myself justice, I have many times felt such travail of soul for the conversion of poor sinners, such a constraint to point out to them their ruin and recovery, that I could boldly say, "the love of Christ constraineth me." And often, when I have been preaching, I have felt such pain, pity and desire for the people, that the tears have run from my eyes. At such times I have felt as if my preaching *was with power, with the Holy Ghost and much assurance*, as if I was certain that the word of life in my mouth was eternal truth. Add to this, the heart pleasure which I have felt when sinners have turned to the Lord, and it seems to form an argument that I am in the work and favor of God.

My life, as a moralist, I next examined, thus. I have had but little dealing and few contentions with men, since the time I professed religion. I have ever thought that little sacrifices were the cheapest settlements; yet I have found covetousness and ill-will in myself towards others. Indeed, my thoughts, my words and actions (having a little good in them, as I hope) have had a preponderance of moral evil, so that the scale turns against me. How then can I be justified and accepted with God? Here a number of texts seemed to volunteer themselves to solve the query.

"To him that worketh not, but believeth on him who justifies the ungodly, his faith is counted for righteousness. In whom we have redemption through his blood, the forgiveness of sins, according to the riches of his grace. Blessed is the man to whom the Lord will not impute sin. David describeth the blessedness of the man unto whom God imputeth righteousness without works. Therefore, being justified by faith, we have peace with God, through our Lord Jesus Christ. It is God that justifies. The just shall live by his faith," &c. These texts seemed to breathe the spirit of life into my soul, and constrained me to say as before, "here is a Saviour for a sinner." And if any man sin, we have an advocate with the father, Jesus the righteous. Summing up the whole and judging as well as I could, I formed the conclusion, that my soul was interested in the salvation of God. Fleeing, however, to those texts which were my city of refuge, through all the conflict, "Lord I believe, help thou my unbelief, Blessed are they who have not seen and yet have believed." From this, and from the view of those happy spirits, which seemed to stand sentinels over me, just after the clock struck three, I fell asleep. So that my conflict, such as I never had before, lasted five hours. When I awaked in the morning, I found my body and mind very feeble, corresponding with the words of David, "I am feeble and sore broken—thou hast sore broken us in the place of dragons." In the year 1791, I was tossed in a tremendous sea storm about fifteen hours. The wind assuaged about the appearance of day-light. I knew not whether to rejoice for my safety, or tremble at the boisterous ocean which was beating all around. So it was with me at this time. Notwithstanding the signal deliverances which I received the night before, yet dark boding fears, clouds and malignant suggestions were all around me. Several texts of scripture seemed, however, to be whispered in my ears by the Holy Spirit. "The joy of the Lord is your strength. Father, I will that they whom thou hast given me, be with me where I am, that they may behold my glory. I will not leave you comfortless. Because I live ye shall live also. Thou shalt guide me by thy counsel, and afterwards receive me to glory."

ADDRESS

TO THE ASSOCIATION OF THE SONS OF LIBERTY, CHESHIRE, MARCH 4, 1813.

Young Gentlemen: From the epoch of the *funding system*, until the present moment, there have been strong exertions to turn our elective government into a government of *confidence* and *perpetuity*. These exertions had prevailed so far, that in 1798, the friends to the rights of man exhibited their mourning weeds, at the symptoms of death in the pulse of the genius of liberty. But that kind Providence, which produced a Washington to deliver us from the invading foe, presented a Jefferson, as a mound of our liberties, who snatched the constitution from the talons of its enemies, and turned the government into its natural channel. This day, young gentlemen, you assemble to commemorate the inauguration of the man who saved his country from the curse of despotism. Yes, ye Sons of Liberty, ye celebrate the virtues of Jefferson, which secured to you the blessings that Washington achieved. High and doubtful was the contest between the imitators of monarchy, and the advocates for a representative democracy, in 1800. The latter prevailed by only seven electoral votes. But now, after trying the Republican administration twelve years, notwithstanding the combination of Federalists and Clintonians—the discontented and disappointed—and notwithstanding the unfavorable events of the campaign, on the line of Canada, on an appeal to the people, there are thirty-nine electoral votes more for Madison and war, than there are for Clinton and submission, and the choice of members for the thirteenth Congress, about the same majority. This majority includes about one and a half million of inhabitants, and (leaving out the territories, which are not incorporated into states) the eleven states, which are republican, and approve of the administration of Madison, contain three times as large an extent of territory as the seven states in opposition. The self-named *peace party*, who are always at *war* with their own government, are so far in the back ground, that they are one and a half million in the minority, and possessing but one fourth part of the soil. The majority on the republican side is more than five times as large as it was when Mr. Jefferson was elected in 1800. And when we consider the vast extent of south-western territory, rapidly populating, lying entirely in the republican climates, the prospect brightens before us.

If there were causes of resistance and war in 1775—if the three-penny act on tea, and a claim to tax the colonies without the voice of their representatives, justified the war of the colonies; there is seven times the justification for the present war. These causes I shall not enumerate at this time; they are fresh in all your minds. But hark! do you not hear the groans of your brethren! How do the cries of seven thousand of them, confined in British floating prisons, rise to heaven, and cry to you! The voice sounds, "help, help, for God's sake, help!" Spend not your time in unmeaning parade, like the militia of Massachusetts, in drinking toasts of patriotism—in volunteering to stay at home—in striving for offices or disputing about politics; but arise and avenge our wrongs, and never sheath your swords, or stack your arms, until the soil and shores of North America are freed from British cruelty.

The two first campaigns in the revolutionary war, were so disastrous by the camp fever and defeats, that thirty thousand soldiers were lost, yet success smiled at last. The idependence of the United States, cost eighty thousand lives: and after the destruction of much property, in addition to all that was paid to the army, the states were involved in a debt of about seventy millions of dollars. This debt, in the first twelve years of our general government, was increased to eighty millions. During the eight years of Mr. Jefferson's administration, the debt was reduced to about forty millions of dollars; and but for the unjust attack on our commerce, by foreign powers, it is morally certain, that by this time the debt would have been reduced to a trifle. But a continuation of these attacks on our commerce and seamen, with other causes, have imperiously called to war; of course our debts must increase. But, young gentlemen, it is expected, that, while, like Spartan youths, you learn to know and plead for your rights, so also, like them, you will patiently bear that burden which is the price of your liberty. Those of you who are not rugged enough to bear the burdens of the camp, will be pursuing some lawful course with industry and prudence, for vain is the pretence of patriotism in the man who wastes his time in useless parade, and neglects to act well his part in life to support society.

Notwithstanding the difference of the administration of our general government, in respect to laws and measures for ourselves, yet the Presidents have alike, and uniformly, treated all other powers with justice and impartiality. I know not of an instance to the contrary; the demands of our government have always been reasonable, and their measures conciliatory. War, and all the causes of it, were shunned with the utmost vigilance, but all would not prevent insufferable outrage on moral right, and the laws of nations. Our cause, then, is just, for the support of which, we rely on the Disposer of all events.

Since the declaration of war, our privateers have taken many prizes, and many of our vessels have been taken by the enemy. I am not in possession of any documents that determine on which side the balance is, but all the prizes taken may be viewed as nett gain, for before the war, the hostilities of Great Britain were nearly as great as they have been since. Our naval officers and crews have immortalized their names, in gaining an amazing ascendency over the enemy. Our land forces have been, at Detroit and on the Niagara, unsuccessful. Time alone must develop the cause: yet the north-western army has had success as well as disaster.

Should any of you, young patriots, enter the army in defence of your country's rights, while your aged fathers would let the paternal tear run down their furrowed cheeks, and give you their prayers and blessings, each would exclaim, "my sons, let me never hear that you are shot through the back."

It is matter of regret, that so few specimens of Elder Leland's style of preaching can be offered to the public. Of the thousands of sermons which he preached, a very small number only have been preserved, and some, even of these, it has been impossible to obtain. The following syllabus of that preached in Philadelphia, on the evening of the 17th of April, 1814, (referred to on page —— of the Autobiography,) was communicated, by one of the hearers, for the Memorial, from which it is here extracted. The author of the communication remarks:—

"After singing, he engaged in prayer, which was devout, interspersed with some phrases that I had not been accustomed to hear. One was—while adoring Jehovah for his divine perfections, and admiring his condescension to sinful, mortal worms, in bowing his ear to their supplications, he spoke of the privilege, importance, and efficacy of fervent, humble prayer; and added: 'It is a long prayer that reaches heaven, and a long sermon that reaches the heart of the sinner; and all prayers are too short which do not reach heaven, and all sermons are too short which do not reach the heart of the sinner.'"

The text was in Isaiah, x., 27, last clause: "And the yoke shall be destroyed because of the anointing." He proceeded as follows:

Without any introduction, I shall attempt to show what we are to understand by *the yoke*—by whom it was imposed—upon whom laid—and lastly, how it was destroyed. After which I shall put an evangelical culture upon it. By the *yoke*, several things in Scripture are represented—the yoke of legal ceremonies—the yoke of afflictions—the yoke of chastisement for sin—the yoke of profession; but that which is particularly intended in the text, is the yoke of bondage or slavery. In every age, the tragedy is upon record, that the fortune of war has laid one party tributary to the other—the weaker to the stronger. As the world advanced in age, it advanced in pride and wickedness; and men were disposed to assume power and authority over man. Ever since the days of Nimrod, the mighty hunter, who is supposed to be the first to set up a separate kingdom, there have been kings on the earth, ruling with a rod of iron, and swaying their sceptres over an enslaved people, and putting the yoke on their necks. Kings multiplied, and soon became very numerous; for we read of the five kings of Sodom, Gomorrah, Admah, Zeboim and Bela, defending themselves against the encroachments of the four kings, Amraphel, Arioch, Chedorlaomer and Fidal, as early as the days of Abraham. There were the five kings who confederated against Gibeon, whom Joshua pursued, and they fled into a cave—whom he caused to be brought out, and all the men of Israel were commanded to put their feet upon their necks, after which he slew them. And, also, of the thirty and one kings which Joshua and the people of Israel smote on this side Jordan, on the west. And the three score and ten kings, which Adoni-bezek had caused to have their thumbs and great toes cut off, and who gathered their meat under his table. And, while the nations of the earth had their kings, and nobles, and mighty men of valor, the tribes of Israel thought they must be like the nations around them: they wanted a king to rule over them; and, although Samuel expostulated with them, and described the manner of king they might expect, yet they insisted upon having a king. Very like the people now-a-days; they form societies, and they must have a president and two or three vice-presidents, to be like their neighbors around them. Samuel was directed to anoint Saul, the son of Cis, to be their king, who was head and shoulders higher than any of the people. After him, the stripling David, who was a man after God's own heart; then his son, Solomon, renowned for wisdom, who was succeeded by his son, Rehoboam, in whose reign ten tribes revolted, and the kingdom was divided, and Judah had twenty kings, and Israel had eigtheen, until they were carried captives to Babylon, under Nebuchadnezzar. The whole period, from Saul down, being about five hundred years, during which time, there were two and forty kings, besides an interregnum of ten or eleven years, and queen Athaliah, who reigned six years. The period of their captivity was seventy years, according to Jeremiah's prediction; so that the Jews were put under the yoke to Nebuchadnezzar, and other kings of Babylon and Chaldea.

We come, now, to show how the yoke was destroyed because of the anointing. Cyrus was foretold, by this same prophet, upwards of a hundred years before he was born, that he should be the deliverer of the Jews out of their captivity; and, at the time specified, he opened the two-leaved gates, and entered the city, the same night in which Belshazzar was feasting with his princes, his wives, and his concubines, where the hand appeared writing upon the wall, "Mene, Mene, Tekel, Upharsin;" and, in that same night, was Belshazzar slain, and the deliverance of the Jews was effected, and the yoke destroyed.

I proceed now to put an evangelical culture upon it. Man, though made upright, was deceived by the subtle serpent, and enslaved, and brought under the yoke, and is in bondage to sin, Satan, and the law; and, consequently, left in a wretched, forlorn condition, and without any power to deliver himself from that state of thraldom, but must forever lie under the curse of God's righteous law which he had violated, had not God, of his mercy and grace, provided a deliverer, which is described in the text—"the anointing"—"and the yoke shall be destroyed because of the anointing."

The Lord Jesus Christ is God's Anointed One, whose coming was foretold hundreds of years before his nativity, as that of Cyrus was told many years before he was born. Cyrus's father was Cambyses, king of Persia, and his mother was Mandane, daughter of Astyages, king of the Medes; so that he was Medo-Persian, parta-king, part of both. So Christ possessed a divine nature, and partook also of the human nature. In Cyrus, the kingdoms of Media and Persia became united in one; so, by Christ, the middle wall of partition was broken down between Jew and Gentiles, and believers of all nations are united in one kingdom, and under one head, even Jesus. Many marvellous things are said to have been foretold concerning Cyrus, whether true or fabulous, I leave; but many very wonderful things were foretold concerning Jesus Christ, which really came to pass. It is said that Cyrus was much exposed in his infancy; so Christ was much exposed in his infancy. Cyrus was foretold as God's anointed; so Christ was emphatically the Lord's anointed. Cyrus was called by his name by the prophet; so Christ, the true Messiah, was designated by many glorious names and titles, which meet in no other persons. Cyrus was a great commander; so Christ is given to be a leader and commander of the people; he is wise in his counsels, and commands with authority. Cyrus, it is said, knew all his soldiers by name; so Christ knows all his people, and calleth them by name. Cyrus is called God's shepherd; Christ is God's shepherd, and is called the "great shepherd and bishop of souls." It is said that Cyrus rode on a white horse; so Christ rides on the white horse of the gospels. Cyrus effected a miraculous deliverance for the captives in Babylon; the Lord Jesus Christ effected a much greater deliverance for his people, and in the most wonderful manner. He, "through death, conquered him that had the power of death." Cyrus made proclamation to the Jews that deliverance was wrought, and they were at liberty to return to their own land, and rebuild Jerusalem and the temple; Christ was announced to proclaim liberty to the captives, and invited the laboring and heavy laden to come to him, and find rest for their souls.

Some of the Jews were contented in Chaldea, and did not choose to regard the proclamation to return. So, many poor sinners are contented in their bondage, and disregard the proclamation of the gospel, etc.

I come, now, to show more particularly how the yoke is destroyed "*because of the anointing.*" Christ delivers by *power*, as well as by *price*. There is no intrinsic merit in the gospel, in and of itself, to convert sinners, but by the power of the Spirit accompanying the word. Men sometimes profess to have great power; they will make laws to fine and imprison people, if they will not have their children christened, or if they will not pay towards building meeting-houses, or the support of the ministry, or if they refuse attending a place of worship. If they possess so much power, would to God they would employ it to purpose. That if a man would not repent, he should pay five pound; if he would not believe the gospel, he should pay ten; if he would not love the Lord Jesus Christ with all his heart, might, soul and strength, he should pay fifteen; and, if he would not deny himself, take up his cross, and follow the Saviour, he should be put in the state prison for life.

The power of the gospel consists in the authority with which its author is invested, who said, "All power is given unto me, in heaven and on earth." Christ promised to be with his faithful servants unto the end of the world. When he sent out his disciples by two and two, he sent them into the towns, cities, and villages, *whither he himself would come.* So he sends his Holy Spirit with his word to convince of sin, to discover the glories and fulness of Christ, to apply the blood of sprinkling to the wounded conscience, to lead the soul to Christ, and to his precious promises. He is, also, a spirit of prayer and of supplication, as well as a spirit of grace, to sanctify and prepare his people for glory. God is always as good as his word, and his promises never fail; his word that goeth forth out of his mouth, shall prosper in the thing whereto it is sent. So, when the gospel is preached in its purity, sinners are converted, and turn to the Lord. Great things have been achieved by the gospel, through the power of Christ. Witness its effects on the day of Pentecost, and during the apostolic age, and in subsequent periods, down to the present time. There is still the same promise and the same power, and Christ is riding forth majestically in the gospel chariot, from conquering to conquer. I have been endeavoring to recommend this gospel for nearly forty years, and have not grown weary in the service; and I have witnessed the truth of God's word, in the conversion of many precious souls to the obedience of faith—to God be all the glory. Amen.

"The foregoing," says the writer, "is but a sketch of the discourse, which occupied nearly an hour in the delivery. In a few places, I have employed words to fill up the skeleton, that the thread may not be broken; but, of far the greater part, the language is verbatim as delivered, and the sentiments and train are Leland's, particularly in the history of the kings."

THE

JARRING INTERESTS OF HEAVEN RECONCILED

BY THE

BLOOD OF THE CROSS.*

* First published in 1814.

JARRING INTERESTS OF HEAVEN RECONCILED, &c.

COLOSSIANS i. 20.—And by him to reconcile all things unto himself; by him, I say, whether they be things in earth, or things in heaven.

THE reconciliation of *Things in Heaven*, is the part of the text which I shall attend to.

Let reverence and humility possess my heart, while I develop the character of the Deity—and let all who hear me, at awful distance bow.

All the changes that have taken place from the beginning until now, and all that will take place hereafter, give to the Almighty no new ideas—furnish him with no novel matter for consideration. Things which are past, present, or to come, with men, are all in the *eternal now* of the great Jehovah, and yet he speaks of himself (in anthropopathia) as if thoughts and designs entered his mind in a train of succession.

The Divine Being is not composed of parts, or possessed of passions like men; he, nevertheless, in condescension to our weakness, speaks of himself as having head, eyes, ears, face, mouth, nostrils, shoulders, arms, hands, fingers, feet, bosom, back, heart, soul, etc., as also being jealous, angry, contrary, pacified, reconciled, having his anger turned away, etc.

Our text implies a contention in heaven, and that the Father of our Lord Jesus Christ undertook to reconcile the contending parties to himself, by Jesus Christ, and that Jesus obtained a peace among all the jarring interests in heaven, by the blood of the cross. The particulars to be attended to, are,

1st. To explain the cause of this contention.

2nd. To nominate the parties at variance, together with their respective pleas.

3rd. To point out the person by whom, and the means by which this reconciliation was effected.

First. I am to explain the cause of this contention.

The Creator of the heavens and the earth, and all things therein, is a *free, sovereign agent.* He owes neither existence nor obedience to any other being. He is under obligation to nothing which we can conceive of, except the innate law of his nature, and the voluntary words of his mouth, neither of which stand opposed to his infinite freedom.

But all rational creatures owe their existence and obedience to their Maker; of course they are not *free agents*, any further than that they are left *free* in their *wills*, for they are all of them accountable to God for their works and words.

The law of God is the *eternal rule of right*, binding on all rational creatures, and is, in all periods, places and conditions, that which is proper for them to do, and that which tends to their own happiness. It may, therefore, be called, with propriety, the moral law of perfect order. It prohibits nothing but what is injurious to men—it enjoins nothing but what leads to their felicity.

Any transgression of this perfect rule is *sin*, for *sin* is said to be a transgression of the law. No action of man, which is not contrary to the holy law, can be called *sin*. Man, did, at first, by some cause, as unaccountable as inexcusable, abuse the freedom of his will—pervert his moral agency—break over the law of due order, and sin against his God. *By one man sin entered into the world.*

Man, by sin, not only commenced rebel against his God, but, like an electric shock, it affected all his mental and physical powers, so that his transgressions increased like arithmetical progression.

Angels were placed upon a footing of such independence, that neither the guilt nor misfortune of *one* could be transferred to *another*. But all the human race were to proceed from one progenitor, in a succession of procreation. If, therefore, the guilt of a crime, committed by a father, cannot be transferred to his child, yet the *misfortune* can, and generally is. In the case now before us, it is universally transferred.

This rebellion of man, against his God, is that which gave rise to the contention in heaven, implied in the text.

When this contention began in heaven, (to speak after the manner of men,) the great I AM arraigned the criminal *man*, and summoned all the contending parties to appear and make their pleas, before the great white throne of divine glory. Which leads me,

Secondly. To treat of the contending parties and their pleas.

The holy Law began. "My rise is not from revelation, although that does me honor: throughout the sacred volume I hold conspicuous rank, and have been magnified and obeyed by the son of God. But my origin is from the great scale of being itself, so that, if there had been no revelation among men, honor and regard would have been my due.* Yet with all the sacred majesty due to my character, man, the dependent creature, has risen in rebellion and disregarded my voice: not only in one instance, but

---

* Though I am treating of events which took place before the world was peopled, and the law given to man, yet my arguments run through time, and treat of men and things. So God calls things that are not as though they were.

sin, taking advantage by me, has wrought in him all manner of concupiscence, so that the imagination of his heart is only evil continually.

Now we know a *law* is nothing without a *penalty* to enforce it, and a penalty threatened is but a piece of mockery, unless it is executed. In this case, therefore, should man escape with impunity, the divine government would be reduced to contempt, and every fugitive vagrant would be hardened in his wickedness. My demand, therefore, is, that man should die without mercy."

Truth next approached the throne, and, after attending to and confirming all which the holy law had said, added, "The soul that sins shall die—cursed is every one that continueth not in all things which are written in the law—he that offends in one point is guilty of the whole—the wicked shall be turned into hell—in the day thou rebellest thou shalt surely die. These are true sayings of God: sentences which came from the mouth of that Being who cannot lie: the veracity of the Almighty is therefore pledged, that the sinner, *man*, be speedily executed, without delay; for, if sentence against an evil work be not speedily executed, the hearts of the vicious will be fully set on mischief, and nothing but anarchy and confusion will be seen in the empire."

Justice then advanced with piercing eyes, like flaming streams and burning tongue, like the devouring fire, and made his plea, as follows: "My name may sound inharmonious to the guilty, but that which is *just* must be right, and the least deviation therefrom must be wrong. I plead for nothing but what is just. I come not with an *expost facto* law, to inflict a penalty which was not known at the time the sin was committed, but I come to demand the life and blood of the rebel, man, who sinned with eyes epen; for guilt will always stain the throne of glory, till vengeance is taken on the traitor."

Holiness then addressed the sovereign arbiter of life and death in the words following: "My name and nature forbid the continuance of the sinner, man, in the empire. He is full of wounds, and bruises, and putrifying sores; from the crown of his head to the sole of his foot, there is no soundness in him: among all his helpers there is no healing medicine, and if there was, yet he is so stubborn that he would not apply it. Therefore, as two can neither walk nor live together, except they be agreed, either the polluted sinner or consummate Holiness must quit the regions."

By this time, darkness and smoke filled the temple, and seven thunders uttered their voices:

"The flashes of vindictive fire
Broke out impatient from the throne;
And the angelic messenger
Wav'd his dread weapon, which, high brandished, shone,
Thirsting for human blood;—while hell grew proud,
In hopes of prey, and laughed profanely loud."

The sun became black as sackcloth, and the heavens were all in angry convulsion—the earth shook to its centre, and the everlasting hills trembled. Angels stood astonished at the awful emblems of divine displeasure, expecting each moment to see the rebel hurled to eternal darkness, as they had seen their fallen brethren, who left their first estate, in a former period.

Omnipotence appeared as the executioner of the criminal clothed in panoply divine—robed in awful majesty—thunders roared before him—the shafts of lightning darted through the etherial vault—the trumpet sounded—the mountains skipped like rams, and the little hills like lambs : even Sinai itself was moved at the presence of the Lord. At the brightness that was before him His thick clouds passed, hailstones and coals of fire. In one hand he had an iron rod, with which he could dash his enemies to pieces like a potter's vessel, and in the other, a sharp sword with two edges. He set one foot on the sea, and the other on the earth, and lifted his hand to heaven. His face was awfully majestic, and his voice as the roaring of a lion, but none could learn, from his appearance, whether he chose to strike the vengeful blow, or interest himself in behalf of the criminal. At length he spoke.

"I am able to destroy as I was mighty to create; nothing is too hard for me to do. All worlds were spoken into existence by my word, and all material worlds hang upon nothing, through my power; yet I have no will, no choice of my own. Let all the contending parties agree, and I am at their command, all acquiescent. The charges against the criminal as they now stand, will call for my vindictive stroke; but, if any expedient shall be found to overrule the pleas which have been made, when the final result is made, then I shall act. Vicious beings feel power, and forget right; but omnipotence is governed by right. The works which I perform, are those which all perfections of Deity, in concert, point out."

Wisdom then arose, and spake to the following effect: "Why is the decree so hasty from the king? the matter is of the first importance. One soul is worth more than all the world. The pending decision not only effects this one criminal, but the millions and millions of human kind. I, wisdom, dwell with prudence, and find out knowledge of witty inventions. I, therefore, object to the execution of the criminal, not to controvert the pleas of the law, truth and justice, but to wait until it shall be known whether man has any friend at court, who is wise, powerful, and good enough to relieve him in a way that law, truth and justice, will be satisfied with."

Love then comes forward in all its winning forms; his bosom swelled with philanthropy, and his eyes bespoke the benevolence of his heart In mellifluent accents he began, "My name is love; no one in heaven claims higher rank than myself, for God is love; of course, none deserves to be regarded more than I do. My love to man is everlasting, and neither death nor life, angels, principalities, nor powers, things present, things to come, nor any other creature, shall ever extinguish my love.

Mine is an unchanging love,
Higher than the heights above,
Deeper than the depths beneath,
Free and faithful, strong as death.

Should the rebel, therefore, be doomed to perdition, with all his vast progeny, the cross of my love would cause eternal mourning in heaven: to prevent which, my fervent cry is, let the rebel live.

Grace also appeared on the side of the criminal, and made the following plea; "if a creature receives from a fellow creature, or from his God, a compensation for any services rendered unto him, it is reward, and not grace; but, if he receives a favor, for which he has no claim on the donor, it is grace. If, moreover, a donor confers a favor, not only on a needy creature, who has no claim on the donor, nor any thing to buy with, but on one, who, in addition to his need, has contracted guilt, and is an enemy to the donor, this is grace of a marvellous kind. This is my name, and this is my memorial, and shall be through all ages. To do good for evil, is God-like. My plea, therefore, is, that all the transgressions of the criminal may be blotted out—cast behind the back of his God—sunk in the midst of the sea, and he himself raised to a station far more exalted than he possessed before he sinned. If this should not be the case, grace would be a word without meaning, and the benevolence of Jehovah would be obscured forever."

Mercy, in concert with Love and Grace. was all divine oratory in favor of the rebel, and proceeded, "I cannot claim the same rank among the attributes of Deity, that wisdom, power, holiness, goodness, truth and justice can, but, am myself the child of love; or rather a new name given to love, since sin and misery have entered the moral system. All the essential attributes of Jehovah, can have a free and full circulation in the Divine Being, detached from all creatures; otherwise, divinity itself would not be self-glorious; but mercy, (which always presupposes want and misery,) can have no seat in that divine circle, because there is no need or misery in the Almighty.

The attributes of God are always spoken of in single number, thus: love, power, truth, justice, &c. and will not admit of the plural, loves, powers, truths, justices, &c. Now as the name mercy, admits of the plural, mercies, the conclusion is, that mercy is not an attribute.

All the attributes of God can, not only have a free circulation in Deity, but, also, a full display to sinless creatures; but, mercy cannot show her pitying face where need and misery are absent.

If mercy is an attribute, then, sin and misery, were necessary among the creatures of God, otherwise, mercy must have continued dormant forever; useless in the Creator, and unknown to the creatures.

If mercy is an attribute, then the Creator was dependent on the creature to do that for himself, which his maker could not do for him, himself, nor make the creature do, that which he forbid him to do, in order to reduce himself to a condition where he could have a discovery of mercy.

If sin was necessary, then, creatures should love that necessary something; and, if neccessary sin should be loved, why are men called upon to hate it and repent of it?

That sin adds anything to Jehovah, is inadmissible in idea. If any beings, therefore, receive any advantage from sin, creatures must; but, where is there an individual in the universe, that can coolly say for himself, or of whom it can be said, in truth, that he has received an advantage by sin? If it cannot be said of an individual, it cannot be said of the universe; for the universe is composed entirely of a multitude of units. Had sin never entered the world, love could, and would have raised creatures to a state exalted as mercy can expect or wish for; and all the intermediate evils would have been avoided. This would not have been the case, supposing love, grace and mercy, gain their suit, in behalf of the rebel man; but, should he, or any of his progeny fail of deliverance, all their misery must be fathered upon sin.

What idea can be formed of a being, whose essential attributes are such, that they cannot be revealed without the sin and misery of those to whom they are revealed.

Justice is an essential attribute of Deity, which can shine as effulgent among the innocent as among the guilty, but when creatures are become guilty, the display of justice is *punishment*. So *Love* is an attribute which pervades the bosom of Jehovah, fills the angels with rapturous joy, and is the delight and companion of all that are innocent: but when innocent creatures fall into need and misery, the display of Love assumes my name, *Mercy*. As I, therefore, have a name in heaven—as *Mercy* is magnified above the heavens—as Jehovah is rich in mercy—and is the Lord God, gracious and merciful, I plead for the life of the criminal at the bar."

Here the pleas closed for a season, and profound silence filled the temple of God.

One thing appeared very remarkable in their pleadings: not the least ill will was to be seen personally existing among the disputants; no false coloring, or black consequences were cast upon the arguments of each other. Law, Truth, and Justice never accused Love, Grace, and Mercy of disorganization or anarchy, because they pleaded for the life of man; nor did the latter reproach the former with cruelty because they demanded his death, or represent the character and desert of the criminal less vile and obnoxious than the former. Perfect agreement had always existed among them, and nothing that ever emerged, except the transgression of man, made them take different sides at court.

After a solemn pause, the great I AM, the sovereign judge, delivered the following speech: "The statements and demands of Law, Truth, and Justice, against the criminal are well supported. Love, Grace and Mercy have discovered abundance of goodness and good will toward the sinner, but they have not shown any expedient how the law can be honored, truth supported, and justice satisfied, in the forgiveness of the rebel; and unless such an expedient can be produced, man must die without mercy. If any of the celestial angels, or any being in the universe can suggest the expedient, the sinner lives—if not, he dies."

He spake——he closed——but all was still, and silence reigned in Heaven!

The elect angels knew how Love, through a Mediator, could confirm innocent creatures in their innocency, but had no idea how criminals could be pardoned.

At the instance of *Justice,* Omnipotence arose, like a lion from the swelling of Jordan, made bare his thundering arm; high raised his brandished sword; waved his iron rod and advanced toward the rebel with hasty strides.

Love cried forbear, I cannot endure the sight.

The *Law* replied, cursed is every one that continueth not in all things written in the law to do them. The soul that sins shall die.

Grace exclaimed, where sin hath abounded, grace shall much more abound.

Truth said, in the day thou transgressest thou shalt surely die.

Mercy proclaimed, Mercy rejoiceth against judgment.

Justice, with piercing eye, and flaming tongue, said strike! strike! strike the rebel dead! and remove the reproach from the throne of heaven.

At this the angels drooped their wings, and all the harps of heaven played mournful odes. The flaming sword, to pierce the criminal came near his breast, and the iron rod, to dash him to pieces, like a potter's vessel, was falling on his head; when lo! on a sudden, the voice of *Wisdom* sounded louder than seven thunders, and made the high arches of heaven ring and reverberate. The voice said, deliver him from going down to the pit, for I have found a ransom.

In that all-eventful crisis the eternal Son of God, in *mediatorial, form* appeared, clothed with a garment down to the foot, and girt about the paps with a golden girdle. Angels paid him profound reverence, the great I AM placed him at his right hand. He saw the ruined, guilty man,

"And oh! amazing grace! he loved;
With pity all his inmost bowels moved."

He said, I was set up from everlasting, my goings have been of old, and my delights are with the sons of men. The sinner shall live.

The *Law*, in awful majesty, replied, I am holy, just, and good, my injunctions on the rebel were perfectly proper for a human being, and my penalty, which the rebel has incurred, is every way proportionate to his crime.

Mediator. All you say is true. I am not come to destroy the law, but to fulfil. Heaven and earth shall pass away, but not a jot or tittle of the law shall fail.

Truth. The lips that never spoke amiss, have said, that the wicked shall be turned into hell. My veracity is therefore pledged to see it executed.

Mediator. That part of truth which was proper to reveal unto man, as a moral agent, has said as you relate, with abundance more to the same effect; but that part of truth which the great Jehovah, my heavenly father, spake unto me, in the covenant of peace, which is made between us both, has declared, that, on account of an atonement which I shall make, sin shall be pardoned and sinners saved.

Holiness. I am so pure that I never can admit a sinner into heaven. Nothing unclean or that worketh a lie, shall ever enter there.

Mediator. Provision is made in the new covenant, whereof I am the Mediator and Messenger, to remove the *pollution* as well as the *guilt* of sin. I have guaranteed that sinners shall be washed in my blood and made clean, and come before the throne of glory without spot or wrinkle, or any such thing.

Justice cried out again, strike.

Mediator. Not the sinner but the surety.

Justice. Can heaven admit of a vicarious suffering?

Mediator. It is that which no government on earth ever will admit of, or ever ought to do, but is the singular article agreed upon in the scheme of salvation, which will astonish the universe in its accomplishment.

I now appear in human form; but in the fulness of time, I shall assume the nature, which I now appear in form of, shall be born of a woman, be made under the Law, and perfectly obey and magnify it; which is all that the Law can require of human nature, in reason; shall suffer that penality for sinners that justice will be pleased with, and God accept of; shall die and follow death to its last recess; shall rise again with the same flesh and bones, and thereby obtain the victory over death; shall continue a while in the lower world after I rise, to give incontestible proofs of the resurrection, and then reascend the throne of glory.

I have engaged to do everything in behalf of the sinner, that law, truth and justice can ask for, in a way of holiness, which will reflect the greatest honor on wisdom.

Unchangeable love, grace and mercy will stimulate my heart, and Omnipotence will execute my designs.

In the mean time, the creature man is to live and propagate his species to an immense host; but in succession, one after another, all of them must die, and rest in death for a season; for I have not undertaken to save them from dying, but to rescue them from death.

Between this and the time fixed upon, when I am to pay the dreadful debt, make the great atonement and bring in everlasting righteousness, those of the human race, who repent of their sins, believe in my character, and obey my voice, are to be admitted into paradise, upon the dissolution of their bodies, on account of what I am to do, at the appointed time.

After that period, when I shall do all that is necessary to be done to make an atonement for sin, the world will continue for a season; but the day of days will commence, the "*great day of dread*, for which all other days were made," will arrive: on that day, the dead shall all be raised, and those who are living on earth shall be changed from a mortal to an immortal state, and all of them shall come to judgment before my bar. Those who are like goats among sheep, like tares among wheat, who are unclean and polluted, who are lovers of transgression and haters of obedience, who have broken the law—wantoned with atoning blood, and done despite against the work of the Holy Ghost; shall be expelled the kingdom—cast into outer darkness and knaw their galling bands forever.

But the righteous, both those whose souls have been in Paradise, and their bodies sleeping in the dust, and those also who never shall have died, shall be admitted into the kingdom prepared for them—shall enter into life eternal.

Now, if any one in heaven has ought against this plan, let him speak; for I have undertaken to reconcile all things and beings in heaven, to the salvation of man. He closed! but O what rapturous joy beamed forth on every face in heaven! Law, Truth, and Justice cried out, "It is all we want or wish for." Love, Grace, and Mercy shouted, "It is the joy of our hearts—the delight of our eyes, and the pleasure of our souls." The great I AM said, "It is finished—the expedient is found—the sinner shall live—deliver him from going down to the pit, for a ransom is found!" The angels, filled with heavenly pity and divine concern, who had been waiting in anxious suspense, through the important contest, now swept their golden harps and sang, "glory to God in the highest, peace on earth and good will to man. Thou art worthy, O, thou Son of God, to receive glory, and honor, and riches, and power, forever and ever. Man, though a little lower in nature than the angels, shall be raised a little higher, being in likeness of nature, more like the Son of God. While angels will be ever adoring *confirming love* through a Mediator, men will be extolling the riches of redeeming blood and the freeness of boundless grace."

The great I AM then said to the Mediator, "For as much as thou hast undertaken to reconcile *all things in heaven and in earth to me*, and hast proposed a plan of reconciliation, in which all contending parties are agreed

—in which mercy and truth meet together; righteousness and peace kiss each other; justice and judgment surround my throne; and mercy and truth go before my face: And whereas I am perfectly satisfied that thou wilt, at the time appointed, fulfil all thy engagements, at the expense of thy blood; therefore, behold I give thee a name which is above every name—that at the name of JESUS every knee shall bow and every tongue shall confess. Thou shalt have dominion from sea to sea, and from the river to the ends of the earth. I will divide thee a portion with the great, and thou shalt divide the spoil with the strong. I will give thee the heathen for thine inheritance, and the ûttermost parts of the earth for thy possession. I will glorify thee with myself, with the glory which thou hadst before the world was."

I now proceed, thirdly, *To point out the person by whom, and the means improved to effect this reconciliation.*

This I have already done, so far as it respects the new covenant agreement; but the appearance of the person among men, and the means actually administered, are yet to be considered.

In the foregoing observations I have personified the perfections of God, and used arguments rather in an allegorical, visionary way, which I shall have no occasion to do in the subsequent remarks.

Leaving, therefore, the great transactions which took place before the world was, (of which, however, many hints are given in scripture,) I turn my attention to those things which have taken place in time, on the face of the earth; being assisted by that guide which God hath given to men, the sure word of prophecy, which is a light shining in a dark place.

Of revelation there are two kinds, *oral* and *written.* Oral revelation was first; in this God made known his will to men, but left them no means of preserving it, only their memories: This register was treacherous; and the communication from father to son, down through a succession of generations, greatly obscured and perverted what was first revealed. It is from this source, however, that those nations destitute of *written* revelation, get their ideas of the future state of the soul, after the body is dead. After letters became of use among men, Moses, and many others were inspired, to record what God, at various times and in various manners, revealed unto men. From this source men obtain information, that God can pardon sin, and that he will raise the dead, &c.

The Grecians, with all their improvement in philosophy, gained no evidence that the dead could be raised. This appeared to them a thing incredible. Hence, when their friends died, they gave themselves up to excessive sorrow, having no hope in the resurrection. Their philosophy could no more account for the resurrection, than it could for creation. Upon the reduction of the Greeks, the Romans arose to the pinnacle of fame; but with all their military conquests and political maxims, they never found out how crimes could be pardoned. In their government, they did not admit of an innocent man suffering stripes or death for the crimes of one who was guilty, and had no idea that their gods would admit of it. The Jews, to whom were committed the oracles of God, read and believed that the Messiah would come; but they formed an idea that he would appear an *illustrious potentate*, and restore the *civil kingdom* of the house of David, again to Israel. The rest of the nations were as barbarous and cruel in their laws and customs, as they were ignorant and superstitous in their religion.

In this condition the world was, when the *due time*, appointed by the Father of all worlds, arrived for the Mediator to appear on the earth, and make reconciliation to God by his own blood, for the sins of the people, according to the great plan which was formed before the world was.

That there was such a person on earth as Jesus Christ, we have as good reason to believe, as we have to believe that there was such an emperor of Rome as Augustus Cæsar, in whose reign it is said, the child Jesus was born; as sacred and profane history treat of both. And that Jesus said and did that which is recorded of him, we have no more reason to doubt, than we have to doubt whether Demosthenes, Cicero, Alexander, and Julius Cæsar said and did the things recorded of them.

That the four Evangelists gave a true history of Jesus, is a rational conclusion; for when Constantine established Christianity in the empire, and received Christ Jesus as a God to adcre, greater than Jupiter, he caused no other history of him to be written, than that which was extant.

That the Bible in general, the New Testament in particular, is *as true* as other histories are, not to say more true, we have abundant reason to believe; it has been as much contested by its enemies as any history has, and has hitherto triumphed.

For the sake of argument, and to lead on to that which I have in view, let it be conceded, that the New Testament stands on a level with other histories, not written by inspiration; true in its prominent features, but subject to error in some circumstances. On this footing, how far it exceeds all other histories, because it details facts infinitely more important.

Should a messenger come to any of our houses, with intelligence that a sparrow had dropped a feather in the field, and produce such evidence that we should believe him, without any kind of doubt, the report, though *true*, would be of very small consequence. Let another messenger arrive and inform us that the earth had taken fire at the seaboard—that the mountains were melting, and all was consumed one thousand feet deep—that it raged with amazing velocity, in a direction towards our dwellings, and that, within a few hours, it was morally certain, that we should share the same fate in the conflagration, that thousands already had done. If the evidence which the last messenger produced, was equally good with that of the first, his report would certainly concern us much more.

So in the present case. The histories which come before us, treat of the boundaries of countries—their natural curiosities—their mountains, streams and bays—their produce and animals—the manners, laws, government, and religion of the inhabitants—the talents and exploits of their first rate men, etc.

But when we turn our eyes to the Bible, we are there informed how the world was made, and by whom—how apostacy, disease and death entered the world—how Christ came into the world and died for sinners, that they might live. Here we learn the moral character of God, and the accountability of all rational creatures. In this book, we are informed how sin can be pardoned, and how the dead can be raised. This book assures us that the earth will be dissolved, the dead raised, the general judgment commence—the righteous taken from the wicked and placed in life eternal, and the wicked cast into everlasting fire.

The history of the late French revolution may contain a thousand false statements; but there are four facts so well supported, that no men question them.

1. They revolutionized from their former government.
2. They beheaded Louis, their former king.
3. Their conquests have been extraordinary.
4. Bonaparte is now their emperor.

Now, if we suppose the Bible is fraught with many mistakes, and as full of error as the history just alluded to; yet, allowing it *equal* credit, there are four facts, at least, which admit of no doubt.

1. That all men have apostatized from God, and thereby exposed themselves to misery, death and hell.

2. That Jesus Christ was God incarnate, and made such an atonement for sin, that all those who repent and believe in him shall obtain pardon and life everlasting.

3. That Jesus Christ did rise from the dead, and will, in the fulness of time, raise the bodies of all the dead.

4. That God has appointed a day, in which he will judge all rational beings by Jesus Christ; when every one will receive a reward, according to the deeds done in the body.

The Bible is reprobated by many on account of the many contradictions which it is said it contains. But are these contradictions *certainly* contained in the Bible? How many absurdities and contradictions are found by a young student in the mathematics, which age and experience dispel; and, as the scholar grows sage, he condemns his former ignorance and rashness. In this case, also, many things which appear contradictory, to a novice in divinity, in greater maturity, appear, not barely reconcilable, but as harmonious links in the great chain. The great age of the Scriptures—the different habits, customs, and dialects of the ancients from ours, may account for many seeming contradictions which are to be met with in them. But, if there are are some *real* contradictions in the Bible, respecting places, names and numbers, (occasioned by the many transcriptions and translations which the writings have passed through,) must the *facts*, therein detailed, be considered as false accounts? As well may the four things respecting the French nation be considered forgeries, on account of the mistakes in the history of the French revolution.

It is true, that there are some things recorded in the Bible, of which the laws of nature afford no parallel. This is the case in the *creation of the world*, and in the *resurrection of the dead;* nevertheless, the first has taken place, and the last will. Let those who disapprove of the last, confute the first. To believe these facts, I confess, requires faith of the *marvellous kind;* but, not to believe the divinity of the Scriptures, requires a *more marvellous faith.* For sublimity, majesty, picturesqueness and politeness, no book besides bears any comparison to it.

For sublimity, read Solomon's prayer, at the dedication of the Temple, and the prayer of Jesus, in the seventeenth chapter of John. For majesty, see the eighteenth Psalm, and the third chapter of Habakkuk. For picturesqueness, observe the figures in Job, the tropes in Isaiah, and the rhetoric in Paul's Epistles. For politeness, look over the book of Ruth, and the precepts of the New Testament, which, on the subject of good manners, as far exceed any of the writings of Greece, Rome, France, England or America, as the brightness of the sun surpasses the rays of a candle; and, therefore, to believe that they are of human invention, requires a faith more marvellous, than it does to believe any article therein recorded.

The existence of the New Testament, proves that it was written by some hand. The writers must have been either bad, designing men, or good, honest historians.

If the writers of it were deceivers, it is unaccountable that they should form a book to condemn themselves. The world affords no parallel to this. Surely the writers of it would have omitted their own errors, and covered their own crimes, if they had been evil inclined; but this they have not done.

To suppose that bad men should ever have formed such a book, which condemns every species of wickedness, requires faith so *marvellous,* that it must be unreasonable.

The conclusion, therefore, is, that the writers of the New Testament were true men, and wrote, as they pretended, by the finger of God. From this history, therefore, I now proceed to state and support the things which remain to be canvassed.

The appearance of the person on earth, by whom, and the means by which the reconciliation of all things in heaven is effected, are yet to be considered.

That Christ, the Mediator, is the *person*, by whom, and what he did and suffered, particularly the blood which he shed on the cross, is the *means* of this reconciliation, our text declares.

I shall investigate the subject, by examining what the great errand of Christ to this world was; and the works which were necessary to be performed by him to accomplish his embassy. His errand into this world, may be briefly summed up, by extracting a few texts of Scripture.

"The father sent not his son into the world to condemn the world; but that the world, through him, might be saved."

"For this purpose was the son of God manifested, that he might destroy the works of the devil. I am come to seek and save that which was lost. The Son of Man is not come to destroy men's lives, but to save them. I am come that they might have life, and that they might have it more abundantly. Forasmuch as the children are partakers of flesh and blood, he also himself took part in the same, that through death he might destroy death, and him that hath the power of death, that is the Devil; and deliver them who, through the fear of death, are all their life time subject to bondage."

From these, and many coincident texts, it is evident that the *salvation of men*, was the object of the embassy of Christ.

Some, however, conclude that it is beneath the dignity of God, ever to act from motives beneath his glory; and, therefore, the glory of God was the highest motive that Christ could have in coming into this world, and dying on the cross.

I feel no disposition to dispute the point with those good souls who are jealous for the *glory of their God;* but would just reply, that the *essential* glory of God cannot be added unto, by all that God and man can do; nor can his declarative glory appear more conspicuous in his own view, on account of anything done by him, or by his creatures. What, therefore, displays the glory of the divine character most among his creatures, is most for his glory. Now, as nothing ever done among men, made equal display of the moral perfections of God, with the death of Christ for sinners, we may safely say, that God has his own glory always uppermost, and yet the very object of Christ's mission, was the *salvation of men*.

The works, which were necessary for him to do to accomplish his great undertakings, were:—

1. To keep the precepts of the law.

2. To give evidence of his complex character, and show forth his glory.

3. To suffer for sinners, and make an atonement for sin.

4. To disconcert the schemes of Satan.

5. To conquer death.

Of these, I shall treat particularly.

First. To keep the precepts of the law.

I can form no idea of human nature being free from the obligation of the law; consequently, when the Word was made flesh, manifested in flesh, Immanuel was under the same bonds to keep the law, that Adam, Abraham, Moses, or any of us are. Perfect obedience he owed to the law; and this obedience was necessary for *himself*, as a failure would have been fatal to the last degree. If this statement is just, then his perfect obedience to the moral law formed no part of that merit by which we are justified. When a man pays his debt, he does a good deed, but nothing meritorious. So the obedience of Christ discharged what he owed to the law, but formed no part of the atonement.

Two advantages, however, we receive from this moral obedience.

1. We have him as a perfect example, and see what human nature is capable of.

2. As he was entirely free from sin, he was a proper lamb, without spot, to be offered for a sacrifice to take away sin.

But, as Jesus Christ was made under the law—that law which was equally binding on him and on us—so hewas under another law, which none of us are. I call it a law, because it had the force of law in it: I mean the stipulated articles of agreement, which he voluntarily engaged to fulfil in the great covenant of peace. His obedience to this law was meritorious, and by this obedience many are justified. This law included all his mediatorial works and sufferings, "for he learned obedience by the things which he suffered."

It is sometimes said, "that Christ obeyed all the precepts of the moral law, and bore the penalty, or curse of the same law, for us." But the propriety of the saying is difficult to conceive of. If Christ obeyed all the precepts of the law for us, then for us there was no penalty due; otherwise punishment would be inflicted where there was no crime. It is best, therefore, to say, that he obeyed the law for himself, and suffered the penalty for us. "He bore our sins in his own body on the tree."

Second. It was necessary that Christ should give evidence of his complex character, and show forth his glory.

That Christ was the "true God and eternal life," the Scriptures declare, and his word and works confirm the same. The winds and the seas obeyed his word.

The works which he did, in healing the sick and raising the dead, are works that none but God can do, or otherwise they must be done in the name of the Lord. The prophets and apostles did these works in the name of the Lord, by faith and prayer, but Jesus did them, not in the name of another, by prayer, but authoritatively, in his own name, which proves that he was God.

Both Jews and Christians believe that "none can forgive sins but God only;" and Pagans have the same notion of their gods: but Jesus wrought a miracle, to prove that "the Son of Man had power on earth to forgive sins." Now, as God would not have assisted him to work a miracle to support imposture, it follows, of course, that he could forgive sins, which none but a God can do. Hence the evidence that he was God.

No being but God is omniscient; *He only knows the hearts of all men:* This knowledge, however, Jesus had; He knew his enemies, that they had not the love of God in them; He perceived their thoughts, and knew what was in man. Surely then he was God.

The incommunicable name of the Almighty, *Jod he vau he*, translated Lord, is found more than six thousand times in the Old Testament. The word comes from a verb, which signifies *to be*, and is expressive of the external existence of the great Supreme. Many of the texts in the Old Testament, where this word is found, are applied to Jesus, in the New Testament. If, then, the New Testament writers understood themselves, Jesus is *Jehovah*, God eternal.

The names, in general, by which the *Holy One of Israel* is called, in the Old Testament, are also given to Christ, either in the New Testament, or in those prophecies, which manifestly treat of the Messiah: such as the First and the Last—the Everlasting Father—the Creator—Deliverer—Redeemer—only Saviour—Shepherd—Husband, etc.

As Jesus Christ, in the beginning, laid the foundations of the earth—as by him all things were created—as the creative word was God—as he upholds all things by the word of his power, he must be God *essential.* "In him dwells all the fulness of the God-head bodily."

We cannot form a higher idea of Deity, than that he is the Creator and Preserver of all worlds—the Redeemer and Saviour of men, and these works are the works of Christ. Now, if we suppose he was only an exalted creature, and that he, by a delegated power, has done and still does all these mighty works, we are entirely at a loss how to conceive any difference that can exist between the Creator and the creature—the Author and the agent, and must consequently form the conclusion, that the Almighty Creator has made a creature equal to himself.

But as he was God essential, so he was man real.

The assumption of Christ in human nature, was a new thing in the earth which the Lord created. That a woman should compass a man—a virgin conceive, by the power of the Holy Ghost, and bring forth a holy thing, which should be none other than the Son of God, is a mystery of godliness so great, that we can no more account for it than we can account for the creation of the world, or for the resurrection of the dead; and yet, with the two last articles, is equally true. The hungering and thirsting of Jesus—his weariness and sleeping—his weeping, praying, crying, sighing, bleeding, groaning, dying, flesh and bones, all declare that he was *man.*

As man he was sorely tempted: as God he could not be tempted. As man, by grace, through striving and praying, he withstood every temptation, and thereby gave the fullest evidence of his human virtue.

Had the attacks of the enemy been at his God-head, they would have had no impression, and therefore would not have made the soul of Christ "exceeding sorrowful, even unto death." And if the conquests which the Saviour obtained over Satan, had been solely by the Deity, it would have been like the conquest of a giant over an infant, and not like the conquest which virtue gains over vice, in long and doubtful contest, to the last exerting every effort, and triumphing at last, to the wonder and astonishment of all that behold. That the sufferings and victory of Jesus are spoken of in the Scripture, in this last sense, is very evident.

As Christ was, in truth, God and man, so he gave the fullest evidence of his complex character, and calls upon men to believe in him as such a being, upon the rational evidence which he has given—evidence of an hypostatical union, which creatures cannot comprehend, and has said, "if ye believe not that I am he," the promised Messiah, "ye shall die in your sins."

Third. He came also to suffer for sinners and make an attonement for sin.

It would be extremely improper to admit of a vicarious punishment in the governments on earth, for by it the innocent would be punished, and the guilty be hardened to repeat their crimes: whereas, the very design of civil government is, to protect the innocent in their rights, and punish the guilty, and the guilty only.

But in the divine government, where the actions and motives of all men are perfectly known, without evidence—where He that suffered death for the guilty, had power to rise again, and thereby prevent any loss of subjects in the state—where He, who suffered for the guilty, had the power to change the hearts of the transgressors, and make them true men, and thereby prevent future crimes—the objections which forbid a vicarious suffering among men lose all their weight.

That Christ Jesus suffered, groaned, bled and died for sinners, is abundantly proved in scripture; and that his sufferings, in soul and body, were exquisitely painful, beyond what we can conceive of, seems evident from the expressions used by himself, and his historians, when he was in his agony.

The nature of his sufferings, in some respects, is exceeding difficult to form an idea of.

I once believed that the sufferings of Christ were exactly such as damned souls endure, but have seen cause to question my former belief. Wherein do the torments of damned souls consist? Are they sovereignly imposed, or are they naturally incurred, or both? I mean, do they all arise from the pressures of guilt and shame, or does the righteous Judge inflict stripes on them, besides what torments they feel within? When a criminal is exposed and condemned, his personal guilt is a severe scourge for his crime, but still he has the lash of the law to bear besides. And is this the case with the guilty sinner? When a sinner is given up to the fury of Satan and sin, his torment must be exquisite, for sin seems to form the quintessence of hell. And yet the language of the Bible, which is to be preferred above all logical arguments, is, that sinners shall be beaten with stripes.

It appears as safest, therefore, to conclude, that part of the sufferings of miserable souls arise from the dominion and guilt of sin, which is torment of itself, and part proceeds from the judicial hand of the righteous judge, and yet it is difficult to conceive how instruments of torture can be found in that being, who is essentially Love: but as difficult as it is to conceive of, if we do not admit of the idea, we are entirely at a loss to conceive of the nature of Christ's sufferings, for he did not assume a guilty nature; he never transgressed the law, and therefore he could not feel the personal remorse that sinners do, when given up to the dominion and guilt of sin. Yet his sufferings were extreme, as his words, his agony, and his bloody sweat declare.

Some have supposed that the sufferings of the Saviour consisted in *the fear of death* and in *dying*. But this supposition, if true, would render the mighty conqueror void of courage, and more timorous than thousands of thousands who have braved death without a groan.

On the whole, it may be concluded, that the part of a sinner's torment, which is judicially imposed, the Saviour could and did endure; but that part which arises from guilty remorse, from the dominion and fury of sin, he could not and did not endure. I say he *could* not; for it is beyond my comprehension, to conceive how *guilt* can be transferred from *one* to *another*.

The *weakness* of Christ must ever be in view, as well as his *strength*. The prophecies and history which treat of the sufferings of Jesus, represent his sorrows as rising and falling like the tide. As a God he knew, and as a prophet he foretold of his conquest over death; but if he did not (through the weakness of human nature) sometimes doubt about *the resurrection of the dead*, it is not easy to conceive how he could be tempted *in all points like unto his brethren*. None had ever been raised from the dead, with immortal bodies, when Jesus was on earth. The regions of death had never been explored by himself; and the certainty of his rising from the dead, at times hung exceedingly gloomy on his mind. All was here at stake! On this pivot the beam turned for eternity! By man came death; and if by man death could not be destroyed, then an enemy would triumph, Christ fail of his crown, be crossed in his love, and all the human race be eternally lost. When all this was at a risk, we may easily conclude, that every doubt in the mind of the Saviour of his obtaining a complete conquest over death, filled his soul with exceeding sorrow.

With the light which I now have, I consider this struggle in the mind of the suffering Mediator, to have formed a very essential part of his sufferings. Nor do I know any light in which Heb. v. 7, can be so naturally understood: "Who, in the days of his flesh, when he had offered prayers and supplications, with strong crying and tears, unto him that was able to save him from death, and was heard in that he *feared.*"

But whether this mode of reasoning does honor to the subject or not, one thing is certain, viz., Christ has suffered for sin, for sinners, for the ungodly; and made such atonement for sin as the great JEHOVAH is pleased with, and on account of what Jesus has done, he can be just, and justify the ungodly who believe. Though, as a lawgiver and judge, he was angry with men, yet, through the mediation of Christ, his anger is turned away, and he comforts them; and he will give eternal life to all who obey him.

Peace is obtained by the blood of the cross—the blood of Christ speaketh better things than the blood of Abel. We have redemption through his blood, even the forgiveness of sins. Ye that were sometimes far off, are made nigh by the blood of Christ. He hath washed us and made us clean in his own blood. His blood he sprinkled o'er the burning throne, and turned the wrath to grace. The Father lays his thunder by and looks and smiles, and loves.

Fourth. Another object of Christ's mission was, *to disconcert the schemes of Satan.*

The early attacks of Satan on the parents of the human race, were successful in their seduction. As it is criminal to sin, either with or without temptation, so likewise it is criminal to tempt the innocent to commit sin. The Devil first sinned himself, and then tempted and deceived Eve to transgress, which finally brought on the rebellion of Adam.

When the Lord God came into the garden, and summoned the tempter and the tempted to appear at his bar, he said unto Satan, "because thou hast done this, I will put enmity between thy seed and the woman's seed; it shall bruise thy head and thou shalt bruise his heel." Christ Jesus was the seed of the woman, whose heel, the inferior part, the human nature, was bruised to death by Satan and his auxiliaries. But the head, the wisdom and deep concerted schemes of Satan, were all to be disconcerted by Christ. And for this purpose was the Son of God manifested, that he might destroy the works of the Devil. The Devil sinned from the beginning; was the first sinner, and therefore *sin* is called his work. The Devil is a liar, a deceiver, and a sinner. But Jesus destroyed his lying, by speaking the truth; his deceit, by sincerity; the sin which he introduced, by holiness of life, and by suffering for sin; bearing sin in his own body on the tree, and thereby making an end of sin in one day.

As the Devil introduced sin among men, which brings on death; and, as Satan lives and reigns in the department of death, it is said that he has the power of it; but Christ has assumed the nature of man (flesh and blood) that he might destroy death, and him that had power of it, that is the Devil.

By the conquest that Christ obtains over the Devil, we are not to understand that the Devil will be annihilated, nor yet that his enmity will be destroyed; but, the usurper will be bound in chains, and confined in the bottomless pit; and, all who are ultimately deceived and ruined by him, instead of honoring their leader, will reproach him for his folly, usurpation, and temptations.

It should be noticed, that Satan has his synagogue, as well as his palace; his religion, as well as his politics. The golden calves of Jeroboam, are called devils; and idolatry is a work which Satan has instituted for religion; but Christ came to destroy this work from among men, and turn them to the worship of the true God.

I proceed to show,

Fifth. That it was necessary for Christ to conquer death.

Persecutions, captivity, and anarchy, are called death, as well as the dissolutions of the body, the apostacy of the soul, and the punishment of both soul and body in hell. These deaths all entered among men at the door of sin. But, that all these deaths were contained in the first threatening of God to man, viz. *In the day that thou eatest thereof thou shalt surely die,* is more doubtful. It is pretty evident that the depravity of the soul took place before the test of Adam's obedience was broken; for, if his mind had not first been corrupted, he would not have rebelled. Lust did first conceive, before it brought forth the action of sin. If, therefore, the internal depravity preceded the transgression of eating of the prohibited tree, it could not be the penal consequence thereof.

And further, it is difficult to distinguish between moral depravity, (often called spiritual death,) and sin itself. Now, with what propriety could God have said unto Adam, "In the day thou sinnest, thou shalt surely die."

Nor is this all. To be carnally minded, is death; the carnal mind is enmity against God, &c. Here the inspired description of spiritual death, is, to be under the government of a carnal, envious, irreconcilable mind. If spiritual death, therefore, was included in the threatened penalty, God must have said, "In the day that thou eatest thereof, I will make thee a carnal, irreconcilable enemy to myself."

Supposing a father should lay his injunction on his child, not to leave the place where he was, and go to a certain tree: to make this injunction effectual, he should, moreover, threaten him with stripes if he disobeyed. The child, however, should break over the prohibition of the father, and run to the interdicted tree: on his way a poisonous adder should leap at him, and inject a deadly poison into his flesh and blood. In this supposed instance, it could not be said that the deadly poison was any part of the father's threatening, nor could the calamity of the child exempt him from the threatened stripes.

From these remarks, it is safest to conclude, that, although the world is in a deplorable state of depravity, yet *moral depravity*, which is called *spiritual death*, was no part of the threatening of God to Adam.

There is a doleful state of existence frequently spoken of in the Scriptures: hell, hell-fire, everlasting fire, eternal fire, everlasting punishment, everlasting destruction, the second death, etc. In common conversation, it is most frequently called *eternal death*, and this death is supposed, by many, to be included in the threatening of God to man, which we are treating of.

But, if *moral death* is excluded, eternal death cannot be included, for moral death is such an essential part of eternal death, that the last cannot exist where the first is absent.

Furthermore, the death which was threatened, was to take place on the day of transgression; whereas, Adam and Eve did not experience eternal death on *the day* in which they fell; if they had experienced it their bodies must have been immortalized, and, with their souls, have been in a state and condition in which they could not have propagated their species.

But natural or corporeal death was included in the threatening. Whether there was a poisonous quality in the fruit which grew on the forbidden tree, which mortalized Adam and Eve, from which death immediately began to prey on them, by *disease*, or whether disease was a penalty inflicted on them for transgression, are questions attended with some doubt.

If the fruit was poisonous in its nature, and tended to mortalization and death, then the prohibition of God was only cautionary, to preserve the new made pair from poisoning themselves to death: and, if this was the case, then, if there had been no prohibition, and they had eaten of it by mere accident, it would have had the same effect. But, if all this was true, (which, to me, is highly probable,) still the prohibition was made the test of Adam's obedience. So the rainbow, though depending on a natural cause, was made a token of the covenant made with Noah.

If, on the other hand, there was no poisonous quality in the fruit, but it was prohibited, simply, as a test to Adam, then, by eating, he did not mortalize himself, but only rebelled against his God, and for his rebellion, mortal disease was that day implanted in him, which neither food nor physic can remove.

In either of the cases, death began his career on the day of the transgression: a career, which, if I may be allowed to personify death, he has unweariedly been pursuing ever since, and which he will pursue, until Adam, in all his offspring, shall fall before him.

The first great threatening of God to man, has its full accomplishment without abatement. In this instance, the Almighty does not recede from his word. The coming of a Mediator into the world, has in no degree mitigated it, for the blessed Saviour did not come to save men from dying, but leave them all to die, as universally as though he had not come; but he came to destroy death and raise the dead—to swallow up death in victory—to take captivity captive, and deliver those who are appointed to die. As death came by man, so by man shall death be destroyed, for, as in Adam, all died, so, in Christ, shall all be made alive.

My proposition is, that Christ came to destroy death.

He first destroyed death in himself: he had power to lay down his life and take it again; he died through weakness, but rose again by the power of God.

The resurrection of Christ, is abundantly proved in the Scriptures, and let the man who can comprehend eternity, and mete out immensity—who can conceive of the mode of external existence, and account for the creation of the world—who can tell where the winds began to blow, together with their destination, and measure the depths of the sea—who can fill the high heavens with loud thunder, and dart the shafts of lightning through the ethereal vault—who can shake the earth to its centre, and swell the seas into raging fury; let such, and none but such, contend with their Maker, exalt reason above revelation, and deny the resurrection of the dead.

I have now briefly attended to what was first proposed, and considered:

1st. The cause of the contention in heaven.

2d. Spoken of the parties at variance, together with their respective pleas.

3rd. Treated of the person, by whom, and the means by which a reconciliation was obtained.

These particulars were drawn from the text: *That God undertook, by Christ, to reconcile all things in heaven, to himself; and that Christ effected the work by the blood of the cross.*

Two things more present themselves to view, on repeating the text. First, by all things in heaven, we may understand the spirits of the just which were in heaven, when Christ died on the cross. By virtue of the ancient engagement of the Mediator, these souls were admitted to heaven, but the price of their reconciliation was not paid until Jesus died on the cross, and thereby made remission for sins that were past. The sins of Abel, Noah, Abraham, &c, were as much atoned for by the sufferings of Christ, as the sins of any who were then living; so that whether his people were on earth or in heaven, Christ obtained peace for them, by the blood of his cross.

Secondly. By all things in heaven, we may also understand the angels in heaven. These angels, it has been suggested, were confirmed in their innocency, through a Mediator; but, as they never apostatized into a state of opposition to God, they could not be reconciled in the same sense that sinners can be; but, in another sense, they could be. Angels are holy, and could never be reconciled to dwell with unholy sinners in heaven; and, especially, to see them rise to heaven at the expense of God's law, justice, and government. But, when they saw how peace could be obtained by the blood of the cross, how the law could be honored, justice satisfied, and the divine government supported, in the pardon of sinners; and, also, how sinners could be delivered from the dominion of sin, and cleansed from all pollution, they were entirely reconciled to the plan of God, and to the accession of sinners into heaven for their companions. These things the angels desired to look into, and are so well pleased therewith, that there is joy in heaven among the angels of God, when one sinner repenteth.

Now unto the king eternal, immortal, and invisible, the only wise God, be glory and honor, world without end, Amen.

MISCELLANEOUS ESSAYS,

IN PROSE AND VERSE.*

NUMBER ONE.

WHICH IS BEST, THE HYPOCRITE OR THE CLOWN?

THE precepts of the New Testament as far exceed the maxims of Lord Chesterfield, on the subject of *good manners*, as the light of heaven exceeds the feeble taper of a glow-worm. Those infallible precepts paint hypocrisy, in all its horrid forms, with the blackest shades, and affirm that men-pleasers cannot be the servants of Jesus Christ. At the same time, they enjoin on us, to be courteous—to study to be quiet—to do good for evil—to give offence to none—to be patient towards all men—to follow after the things that make for peace—to do all in our power to live peaceably with all men, etc., etc. From these, and such like observations, it looks as if virtue lay in the medium between the *parasite* and the *cynic*—the *flatterer* and the *clown*. The customs of this world are not altogether friendly to moral virtue; nor are individuals entirely in the habit of it. Individuals are prone to call their *misanthropy* by the name of *honesty*, *candor*, or a *sacred regard for truth*; while they christen their *hypocrisy*, by the name of *gospel courtesy*. They give their vices the names of virtues, that others may esteem them such. On the other hand, when individuals are as nearly right as the state of things admits of in this world, their best exercises are abused by the censorious many. When the individual is solemn, he is said to be churlish—if he is sociable, it is vanity—if he is recluse, he is monkish—if he mingles with others, he is as bad as any of them—if industrious and frugal, he is a servant of mammon—if devotional, he is indolent—if he pleads for his just right, he is a knave—if he gives up his right, for the sake of peace, he is a fool.

But, to come closer to the question at the head of this number. Sir Isaac Newton was persuaded by his friends to marry. He excused himself, by saying he had no time to court a wife. His friends said they would assist him, by sending to his apartment a woman of worth. He

* Published some time since 1810, the precise year not known.

thanked them for their offer, and promised to receive a visit from her. His friends applied to the woman, and requested her to dispense with the usual ceremonies of courtship, and wait on the philosopher, which she consented to do. When she came to his apartment, and produced her letter of recommendation, he received her very politely—filled and fired his pipe—sat down by her side—took hold of her hand, and conversed on the subject. Before they had brought points to a close, some question about the magnitude and motion of the heavenly bodies struck his mind with such force, that he forgot what he was about—turned his eyes up to heaven—took the pipe out of his mouth with his left hand, and, being lost in study, without design, took the lady's hand, which he held in his own, and, with one of her fingers, crowding down the tobacco in the bowl of his pipe, held it there so long, that her heart, as well as her finger, took fire, and she, in a huff, sprang and went off, leaving the philosopher to finish his study alone.

In this case, had Sir Isaac been as great a hypocrite as many are—stopped his studies for female charms, as many collegians do—flattered and praised beyond his judgment, as is common in such cases, it is likely he might have obtained a wife; and he that findeth a wife, findeth a good thing, and obtaineth favor of the Lord. So said a wiser man than Sir Isaac.

By this, we should think that the hypocrite is better than the clown. But when, in the opposite scale, we calculate the immense advantages which the world has received from the clownish studies of Sir Isaac, it still leaves the question unanswered.

Mrs. Sandy is very polite. "Pray, come and visit me—I am exceedingly gratified in your company—I cannot part with your good company so soon—you must do me the honor of coming again," and such like expressions, are constantly flowing from her mellifluent lips; but, among her confidents, she is frequently telling how often she grows weary of company—animadverting severely on the conversation and behaviour of her visitants, and extolling the pleasures of retirement. Notwithstanding the fine education of Mrs. Sandy, which she adheres to, as she says, to overcome the rusticity of nature, yet, among her sober friends, she owns herself a hypocrite, and her conscience condemns her for her hypocrisy.

Mrs. Vatel is a different character. She has the bad custom of censuring the custom of the times—glories in her singularity—so fearful of being a flatterer, that she affronts all—under pretence of being plain-hearted, she squeezes out the bile of her heart on all whom she converses with or about, and makes a righteousness of her unrighteousness. Her conscience never reproaches her for hypocrisy, but is constantly gnawing her heart-strings for her misanthropy.

Neither the hypocrite nor the clown can lay any just claim to moral virtue; but, in human life, I should give hypocrisy the preference—for this reason, it makes a person more exceptable among the foolish, and the proportion of the foolish to the wise is as nineteen to one.

As no precepts are equally philanthropic with the precepts of the gospel, so, likewise, nothing in the universe is equal to the spirit of grace to ennoble the soul with benevolence. So far as the religion of Jesus triumphs in the human heart, so far the man steers between Scylla and Charybdis—hypocrisy and ill will. The most refined rules of education never describe more love of country, love of all the world, benevolence, bowels and mercies, kindness, sympathy, and, indeed, every virtue, human and divine, than naturally flowed from Paul, Peter, John, etc., and, indeed, from the hearts of all the saints, in proportion to the reign of grace within them. From other sources, we may get information what we ought to be; but from the reign of grace alone are we made such as we should be. All the kind affection and benevolence that a mere man of the world excels in, flow in higher streams, a more steady current, with impartial diffusion, from a better fountain, more durable, from the humble heart where grace reigns. Kindness and faithfulness, are the internal characteristic of the real saint, which the hypocrite and the clown but poorly ape.

EXTRACTS FROM NUMBER TWO.

A LITTLE SERMON, SIXTEEN MINUTES LONG.

Text.—*Schools, Academies and Colleges, are the inexhaustible fountains of true piety, morality and literature.*

THE text, in substance, occurs as frequently in the constitution, laws, usages, governors' speeches, and election sermons of Massachusetts, as the phrase, "And the Lord spake unto Moses," does in the pentateuch. But I am as hard put to it, to find anything like it in the New Testament, as I am to find out who Cain's wife was, or where Tubal Cain got his first hammer to work with. If I do not believe it, I shall be called a Deist; and, if I do believe it, as far as I have yet seen, I must believe without evidence. Instead, therefore, of dividing my text into propositions, I shall, in the first place, examine its divinity. The authenticity of the text is questioned, on the following grounds:

First. It is contrary to evident fact. The absolute precepts of Jehovah have varied with the times and dispensations in which men have lived, but the *essentials* of *piety* have always been the same. A dedication of the heart to God, and obedience to his voice, have been, now are, and ever will be, the quintessence of piety. That righteous Abel possessed this true piety, is certain; and who can imagine that schools, academies and colleges, were in existence in the days of Abel. Yet, according to the text, they must have been the fountain whence the stream of piety flowed to the first martyr.

But further, when Christianity was introduced among men, John was the harbinger—Jesus the King, and the apostles were heralds and ambassadors. John was brought up in the wilderness—Jesus, (as the Jews said,) was not learned—the apostles, for the most part, were ignorant Galileans. And was there no true piety in them? No morality in the system which they taught? The questions answer themselves.

The primitive Christians were not only without the aid of law and the assistance of the schools, but had to combat both, for about three hundred years; during which period, more true piety and morality was seen among them, than has ever been at any period since, which could not have been the case, if the text is true.

Second. True piety proceeds from a fountain, distinct from schools of learning. That true piety in the heart is the gift of God, all confess, who possess it; and every good and perfect gift is from above, and cometh down from the Father of Lights. "Ye have an unction from the Holy One, whereby ye know all things. I will pour out my spirit upon all flesh," &c. Who can read such passages, (which abound in the scripture,) and believe them, and at the same time believe that schools of learning are the *fountains* of *true piety?*

Third. The text, with its usual comment, defeats itself. Individuals, associations, and legislatures, are said to found such schools from pious views. Now, if the founders have true piety in their hearts before the academies or colleges are founded, how can such schools be the fountains of *all* true piety? Piety before schools, and schools before piety. Strange logic.

Fourth. That seminaries of learning are preservatives and improvements of literature, is true; but to call them the fountains of it, is not proper, without there was a seminary to instruct the preceptor who established the first seminary, which would not have been possible. But why should true piety and literature be classed in the same grade, when they are radically different in their natures? The greatest scholar, is often at the greatest distance from true piety; and the most pious saint as far from the embellishments of literature. Science informs the mind in things of this life—piety gives knowledge of, and prepares the soul for the life to come. And as well may cold iron and hot be welded together, as piety and literature. It is true, a man may possess both; but if he does, he knows they proceed from different fountains—have a different tendency to different ends.

* * * * * *

First. By way of enquiry. What are those people to do, in this state, who have a regard for the civil and religious rights of men, and are borne down by a hierarchal clergy—a despotic judiciary—an aristocratic host of lawyers—a great majority of the presses—the influence of the colleges—and the superstition of the ignorant?

* * * * * *

Second. A word of advice. Evils in government had better be borne with, as long as they are sufferable, than to make government too changeable: but the representation of this state is so large, that it loudly calls for a constitutional reform. Should the legislature make and appeal to the towns, either to choose a convention for, or prescribe, in their municipal capacities, a revision of the constitution, it is hoped that they will not be restricted to the article of representation only. It is believed that one hundred and fifty representatives, would be better than six hundred; and that, if the judges were made a little more responsible to men, they might feel themselves a little more accountable to God; and that the third article of the declaration of rights, should be blotted out, taking the constitution of the United States for a pattern in this particular. If these amendments could take place, with the addition of a new article, similar to the fifth article of the United States constitution, my advice would be answered.

Third. Some observations. Nothing is more plain, than that the Almighty has set up the government of the United States in answer to the prayers of all the saints, down from the first proclamation of the gospel. *The earth,* at last, has *helped the woman.* Had such a government existed, from the beginning of the Christian era, what rivers of blood—what shocking havoc—how much imprisonment, confiscation, exile, torture and burning, would have been prevented! "Rome was not built in a day." Great events arise from small beginnings. The notion of excluding religion from legislation, first arose in Rhode Island, New York, New Jersey, and Pennsylvania, in their colonial capacities; and has, since the revolution, been interwoven in the government of the United States. The clergy in New England, were champions in the revolution; but, to justify the separation from Great Britain, they were obliged to establish maxims, (respecting the rights of men,) which they are *now* loth to abide by.

Fourth. A word of experience. When I was about twelve years old, I constantly attended the preaching of Mr. H., one of the standing order, so called. On every Sunday afternoon, in his prayer, (which was about fifty-nine minutes long,) he would repeat the following words: "Pity Mahomedan imposture—pagan idolatry—Jewish infidelity—papistry and superstition: bring the downfall of anti-Christian tyranny to a period." I knew not the meaning of the words, but I heard them so often that I committed them to memory, and have not yet forgotten them. My minister was in the habit of changing with other ministers, of the same faith and order, to economise upon notes, (as was supposed,) to save the time of writing so much. These changelings (not hirelings) used the same expressions in their prayers, or what amounted to the same, with Mr. H. Many admonitions were given me, in those days, about the tyranny and wickedness of the Pope, and the papal clergy. All was awful! all was true! because their high reverences said so.

But *now*, since the French Revolution began, and the Pope is humbled, and the papal clergy set at nought; how the note is changed among the clergy in New England. Their present language is this: "We did not mean so; the Lord has not understood our prayers: We meant, that the papists should all turn congregationalists, as we are; having no Pope over them, but the collective clergy over the people; and that our national and state governments, might all be *Christian* governments; and not deistical, to leave every man at liberty, as is now the case, except in three of the New England States; and even in them, the clergy are not honored and implicitly believed, as they once were. O tempora! O mores!!!"

Fifth. Encouragement. Nearly all the states are, at this time, republican: indeed the atmosphere south and west of the North River, is mild and friendly to the growth of representative democrats. Religious liberty has no manacles in those extensive regions. Population, and of course representation, will ever place the balance where it now is: and the New England *old Grin*, RELIGIOUS BIGOTRY, will gnaw his galling bands, in his small cavern, until his teeth are broken. Upon his decease, I volunteer myself to preach his funeral sermon, and publish his biography, gratis. He is yet living, and struggling for existence.

Conclusion. My text contains *six* prominent words, viz:

Schools, Academies, Colleges,
True Piety, Morality, Literature.

On which I have made *six* strictures, and *six* articles of improvement; which, added together horizontally, make the number six hundred and sixty-six. Here is wisdom—here is understanding—the number of the beast is counted, and it is the number of a man. I will not say that my text is the beast, of which so much is said in the Revelations: but I do not hesitate to pronounce it one of his claws. Some divines, by the beast, understand Louis XIV. Others find his name in the Pope; a third class believe that Napoleon is the beast; while others believe it to be the transformation of the Christian church into a tyrannical body, in the year six hundred and sixty-six. All of them have to divide, multiply, substract, and add perpendicularly and horizontally too, as well as myself, to make out their beast. If these divines, who differ so much in opinion, can obtain the degree of Doctor of Divinity, it is to be hoped that the exposition, here given, will not prevent the author from the same diploma, provided he can get money and friends enough. Should that ever be the case, then with *little thought* and *copious extracts*, he could form a body of divinity, to adorn the shelves of libraries and eternize his own name. Amen.

NUMBER THREE.

FACTS AND QUESTIONS.

Jews, Christians, and Deists, all believe in the *unity* of God. Jews have Jehovah—Christians have Immanuel, and Deists have their Deity. The Jews believe in Jehovah, and receive the *Old Testament* as a revelation from God; but do not believe that Christ was the promised Messiah, nor that the *New Testament* is of divine inspiration. The Christians believe in Jehovah, and in the divinity of the *Old Testament;* they also believe in Immanuel, as Jehovah incarnate, and receive the *New Testament* as divinely authentic. The Deists believe neither in the God of Moses, nor in the God of Christians; but (borrowing language from the Bible, a book which they detest,) speak very sublimely of Deity.

Query. Is there a man on earth, (where the gospel of Christ is known,) who gives any evidence, by the temper of his mind and his external conduct, that he loves the Supreme Deity and rejoices in his government; who, at the same time will satirize the Christians' God, and reprobate the *New Testament?* I believe not. And if my faith is well founded, *infidelity* takes its rise in the baseness of the heart.

Again. If a company of men had a vast and valuable inheritance, secured to them by a writing as well authenticated as the *Bible*, would they not feel well satisfied with their charter? The inheritance of pardon of sin and a resurrection to eternal life, is chartered in the scriptures, and no where else. The light of nature and the laws of nations—philosophy and state policy have no concern in it.

NUMBER FOUR.

POETIC LINES, ON THE DEATH OF REV. JOHN WALLER.

Come heav'nly muse, inspire my heart,
Thy gracious agency impart,
And teach my pen to write;
Direct my pencil to proclaim
The life and death of the dear man,
In whom I took delight.

'Tis no slain hero I bemoan,
No patriot of high renown,

Whose death I now lament;
When gen'rals fall—when statesmen die,
I often heave the solemn sigh,
And mourn the black event.

But when a bright and shining light,
A blazing star, a lamp of night
An envoy from the skies;
Commission'd from the throne above,
To treat with men, in terms of love,
And make the nations wise.

When such a friend of God and man,
Is called to quit his mortal stand,
And fill a higher post;
'Tis then I feel the keenest pain,
My loss exceeds a hero slain—
'Tis then I sorrow most.

Such is the anguish now I feel,
Waller is dead! what pointed steel
Could wound my heart as deep!
Waller, the friend of God and man,
Has left this needy, guilty land,
And I survive to weep.

Like Saul, he spent his youthful days,
In riot, oaths and wicked ways,
The leader of a pack—
His birth, and education good,
But sin did so effect his blood,
They called him swearing Jack.

When vengence, near the throne of God,
Impetuous drew the flaming sword,
All dreadful to employ!
Almighty goodness cried "forbear,
Wisdom shall better means prepare
To conquer—not destroy."

"Waller is not ordain'd to wrath,
But to employ his vital breath
In the Redeemer's praise;
His sins, thro' Christ, shall be forgiv'n,
And he shall ever reign in heav'n,
Thro' free and sov'reign grace."

When persecution reign'd,
And magistrates were unrestrain,d
To punish in their borders;
When Lewis Craig was apprehended,
And to the county court presented,
For preaching without orders:

Waller was one of the grand-jury,
Yet not so fill'd with rage and fury,
But what he'd reason hear;
Craig's meek defence and calm repose,
Disarm'd the fury of his foes,
And open'd Waller's ear.

The meetings then he did attend,
Not as a foe, but as a friend,
And sought the Lord with tears;
The pardoning love of Christ he found,
Which prov'd a balsam for his wound,
A cordial for his fears.

Soon he began to tell around,
What a dear Saviour he had found,
And call on all to fly;
" Sinners, repent and turn to God,
Trust in a mighty Saviour's blood,
And you shall never die."

How oft I've seen the envoy stand,
Imploring mercy for the land,
With eyes uplift to heav'n;
" Father, forgive the stubborn race—
Subdue their hearts to sov'reign grace,
That they may be forgiv'n."

Then turning from the upper skies,
With glowing heart and wat'ry eyes,
Would eager gaze around;
The listening croud, like wandering sheep,
He'd warn and woo, embrace, intreat,
In heart affecting sound.

All round the land the herald ran,
Proclaiming life to dying man,
While heav'n his words apply'd;
Thousands obeyed the voice of God,
And found salvation in the blood
Of Jesus crucified.*

Waller, intrepid for his God,
Would ne'er confer with flesh and blood,
But put his all at stake;
Come life—come death—praise or disgrace,
Naught could impede him in his race;
He ran for Jesus' sake.

---

* He baptized more than two thousand before he removed from Virginia, which was in or near 1794. A few years afterwards, he died in South Carolina.

But while superior to all fear,
He pushed his conquests far and near,
To conquer or to die;
By mobs and courts, and laws unjust,
The dragon made a deadly thrust,
With expectation high.

Four times to prison he was sent,
Where many days of grief were spent,
With ardent prayers and tears;
His wife alone was left to sigh;
His children had no father by,
To sooth their anxious fears.

But here behold his gracious mind,
While in the prison walls confin'd,
He'd pour his soul abroad;
Thro' iron grates he'd sound aloud
The gospel to the listening crowd,
Who came to hear the word.

When Independence was declar'd,
Waller was Whig—a valiant bard
To blow the trump of jubilee;
The change brought freedom to his cause
And banished all religious laws,
And set the sons of Zion free.

Language would fail to figure forth,
In equal shades, his real worth,
And all his virtues tell;
As husband, parent, friend and neighbour,
As preacher of incessant labor,
Bvt few did e'er excel.

From house to house—from place to place,
He'd tell the wonders of that grace
Which ransomed dying men;
With melting heart and balmy tongue,
Kindly persuade both old and young,
To strive to enter in.

But nature's laws will never fail,
The mortal powers of men are frail
And must dissolve and die;
Prophets and kings—heroes and saints,
Are subject to the same complaints,
And in one ruin lie.

Sometimes death makes a sudden storm,
Sometimes the siege continues long,
But always gains the fight;
The strongest constitution fails—

Physics are vain, when death assails
The soul must take her flight.

Twelve months before he quit his clay,
Waller was lingering in decay
And sufferings did endure;
Preaching with all the strength he had,
Exorting all, both good and bad
To make salvation sure.

Seven weeks before he did expire,
He preach'd his last from Zechariah,
"Run speak to this young man,"
His soul glow'd high with heav'nly zeal,
His outward man began to reel,
He fell—he could not stand.

His friends conveyed him to a bed—
He lay as dying, or as dead
For sev'ral tedious hours;
But when his spirits rose again,
Redeeming love—his fav'rite theme,
He prais'd with all his powers.

Some days before he lost his breath,
When stiuggling in the war with death,
He raised his eyes to heav'n;
With smiling face and joyful eyes—
"O God of grace the sufferer cries,
My sins are all forgiv'n.

"Ready, my Lord, to come to thee,
Mine eyes do thy salvation see,
Oh! send thy chariot down;
If any angel can be spar'd,
O send a kind celestial guard
To bear my spirit home.

"But if I longer must remain,
To prove my patience in my pain,
Thy will, O God be done;
If angels cannot now attend,
When I on Jordan's banks shall stand,
I'm sure they will come down."

Some hours before his clay was dead,
His children knelt around his bed
And asked a benediction;
His hands upon their heads he laid,
And for his weeping offspring pray'd,
And gave his valediction.

"O God of mercy, God of truth,
The widow's help—the guide of youth,
I die at thy command;
My wife and children stay behind—
O God, be merciful and kind,
And keep them in thy hand.

"May heav'nly grace on them be shed,
And earthly blessings crown their heads
Long as their lives remain;
When ripe for heav'n, may all remove,
And meet me in the world above
And never part again.

"Remember Zion, O my God,
The costly purchase of thy blood,
Her rights and cause defend;
May she awake, arise and shine
In robes and ornaments divine,
Enduring to the end.

"May all my neighbours hear thy word,
For this I pray, my gracious Lord,
With my last dying breath."
This said, his mortal life expir'd,
His joyful soul to heav'n retir'd,
And left his clay in death

So Jacob's sons, at his bed-side
Receiv'd the blessing when he died,
Prophetic from the Lord;
So Moses, when his life deceas'd,
Bless'd the twelve tribes and was releas'd,
And charm'd to heav'n, by God.

Jesus, the Saviour of mankind,
When on the cross his head reclin'd
Pour'd out his soul to God;
He cried aloud for friends and foes,
"Lord visit these, and pardon those,
Since I have shed my blood."

So Stephen, fill'd with faith and love,
Saw heaven open'd from above,
And Jesus on his seat;
"Jesus, receive my soul," he cries,
"And pardon all mine enemies;"
Upon his knees, the martyr dies,
And joyful falls asleep.

NUMBER FIVE.

REPUBLICANISM, THE BEST GOVERNMENT; BUT NOT WITHOUT ITS EVILS.

A republican government secures to the people the greatest portion of happiness that any government can; yet *noise* and *change*, from the nature of man, are interwoven in its institutions. Ambition is a shade of human nature; it is scarcely more natural for men to breathe, than it is for them to wish to control; at least to be free from the control of others. When in authority, men have a little of both; i. e. a little power to control others, and a little refuge from the control of others; hence the station of office is courted.

It is always easier to see defects in others, than to avoid them ourselves; add to this, government itself is but a choice among evils; and very frequently cases occur, in which the best possible mode of administration will be attended with glaring inconveniences. At such times, those who are out of office, and perhaps out of the confidence of the people, and at the same time wish to secure the *last* that they may gain the *first*, will avail themselves of every embarrassment, which those in the administration have to encounter, give every measure the most unfavorable, if not a false coloring, to render the laws obnoxious, and supplant those who are in authority.

As men are ambitious, so they are avaricious; and as *offices* are pre-eminent, and generally more lucrative than husbandry and mechanism, it is not to be wondered at that men fish for them.

But the noise and tempests in a republic, generally proceed from those who have no power to injure; whereas the noise of a monarchy is clothed with awful majesty. Hence the *calm of despotism*, so called, is like the calm silence of the people when the thunders roar. Which, then, is to be preferred? The joys of a public feast, attended with a little noise and riot, or the profound silence that reigns, when the shafts of lightning fly and the people are afraid to speak?

The contentions that arise among individuals and parties, in a republic, frequently remind me of an instance that happened among the domestic animals of the good old Mr. Pebody. His whole stock consisted of a goose, a sow, and a dog. The industrious goose in painful labor, without the aid of the others, had laid herself a nest of eggs, and was brooding over them with patient inquietude, in hopes of a good reward for her labor. The *avaricious* sow attacked the goose, and devoured half of her eggs. The *ambitious* dog, seeing the defenceless goose suffer so unjustly from the sow, grew big with patriotism and benevolence, and was moved with choler against the sow, that had committed such an assault and battery upon a goose, and ran upon her in the fury of his might, and drove her from the nest. He then reasoned like other ambitious dogs, that an *old worn out soldier*, in the service of the goose, ought not to go unrewarded; and therefore enacted a new fee-bill for himself, which consisted in the other half of the eggs. These two quadrupeds were no friends to each other, but agreed that the goose might live and qua, qua, qua forth her rights and liberties, and lay eggs for them to eat.

Offices should be decently honorable; otherwise government falls into contempt; but if they are too pompous, the liberties and morals of the people are ruined. Salaries should be competent; if otherwise, none but the rich can discharge offices; but if they are very lucrative, the republic will always be haunted by office-hunters.

In the United States, where land is abundant and fertile, and where long habit has rendered the husbandman honorable, where the greater portion of the people are better informed than in other countries, and with the experience of all former ages before them, it is hoped they will escape the rocks on which former republics have split. Under this head, I would remark, that there is a common saying, "that a republican government is the best in the world if people only have *virtue* enough to bear it." If people had *virtue* enough, there would be no need of *any* government. Government becomes necessary on account of the *vices* of men. Can a royal monarch, or a splendid junto of nobles, make the people happy without virtue? The great empires of the earth have crumbled into atoms for the want of virtue, as well as the most flourishing republics. How subject we are to place our eyes on the pomp and splendor of the court and overlook the miseries of the people. Those who so frequently are making the above observation, should do all they can to save and foster that government which they own is best; but for the most part, the remark is made by men who are wishing to sap the foundation of a republican government, trick the people out of their liberties, and raise themselves to a state of pre-eminence above the control of others.

NUMBER SIX.

AGE AND EGOTISM.

A man's *judgment* is his *standard*, by which he measures and weighs his own talents, words and actions, and those of other men. By this standard, he may know when his physical powers fail, when his hearing, sight, voice and memory decline; but when his judgment falters, he has no *standard* to try it by, and therefore never knows its depreciation. His language therefore is, "I know my physical and sensitive powers fail, but thank God, my *reason* is as good as ever it was." If a friend suggest to him that he is on a decline, he takes it unkind, and calls his friend an upstart. If his friend appeals to his age to enforce the suggestion, the man concludes that he himself is one of those rare constitution that does not sink with the burthen of seventy years. Let the younger pity the older, but not laugh at them, for we are all in one row.

Nothing appears more fulsome, than the egotism of men in their superannuacy, dilating so proudly of what *they* have said or done, and what *they* know, in their *now* improved station. But is it always a proof of superannuacy, for men of years to speak or write in the first person? I think not. *Moses* was taught in all the learning and wisdom of Egypt. When he first began to write, he was meek, to a proverb: most of his writing was in the third person. But after the experience of forty years, as prophet and first magistrate, his addresses were somewhat different. What he had seen and known, he declared with great assurance: but this was not the effect of dotage, for *his eye was not dim, nor his natural force abated.*

That *Paul* was a polite scholar, equal to any of his day, is not denied by any; yet with all his logical reasoning, there is mixed abundance of detail about himself, what he had said, done and suffered. If it should be objected, that *Paul* had become the *aged* before he wrote his epistles, the reply would be, that his pen was governed by an unerring agent, whose dictates are to be preferred above all our notions of diction.

We come into the world ignorant. To a child, every thing is new and impressive, and more so to a young man, than to one of a greater age. The young man of genius, is charmed with the logic of his author, and feels impressed with his own arguments. He lays down his thesis, supports it with metaphysical arguments, forms his sylogism, and draws his conclusion, with little or no doubt of the reality of the whole. Not having lived long enough to see any broken links in his chain, he has no occasion to advert to what *he has seen or known* to support or qualify his thesis. But with the man of years, thought and observation, the case is different. He has found that many opinions exist in idea, that will not bear experiment. He knows that he has often been drawn aside from *simple truth*, by metaphysical arguments. Things which he once felt confident of, he is now obliged to qualify, if not entirely to abandon. The safe road to intellectual light he finds to be difficult. When he considers questions in all their bearings, he finds that much can be said for and against. He has considered opinions, and their tendencies, causes and their effects; and forms his conclusions (with a trembling heart,) from experience. In the speeches and writings of such men, there will be much in the first person: they will advert to what *they have seen and known* to illustrate and enforce their opinions. Nor do I think this a criminal or indelicate piece of diction; but contrarywise, the most instructive, and the most impressive of any.

NUMBER SEVEN.

HAWK AND BUZZARD.

If I rightly understand the meaning of the phrase, *between hawk and buzzard*, it is used to express a certain suspense of mind, when the person is in *bivio*, which may be illustrated by the following instances. Young Fabius was brought up to learning, and graduated at the university. It then became a question with him what branch of business to pursue. The calling which promised the least fatigue, and the most profit, he sought for. Law, physick and divinity, all presented themselves before him. Troubles, as well as profits, seemed to be attached to each of them, and for a considerable time his mind hung in suspense, *between hawk and buzzard*. He finally made choice of the sacred gown, and, after the usual studies and examinations, was licensed to preach as a candidate. Many places he visited, and many calls he received, but the rewards promised did not meet his wishes. Five hundred dollars per annum was the highest bid that any parish made for him, on which he reasoned thus: "If I accept of this call, I shall never expect to get more, and I think eight hundred dollars is not more than I ought to have, each year, considering my talents, and what expense it has cost to improve them by education; but still, if I do not acccept of this call, I am not sure of getting so much in any other parish. On the whole, I am at a loss about my *sacred duty:* whether the Lord calls me to accept of this call, or has a *greater call* for me in another parish." While Fabius was thus reasoning, he stood *between hawk and buzzard*.

All things considered, he accepted the call, and took the charge of the people, over which the Holy Ghost made him overseer, not for filthy lucre, but of a ready mind, and served them several years to good satisfaction: *like people, like priest*. But lately, an unhappy circumstance has turned up. A very wealthy parish, having a fund of one thousand dollars a year, with other valuable perquisites, has become vacant. Fabius is greatly affected towards the people of that parish, that they should be as sheep without a shepherd, and is constantly praying, hoping and longing that the Lord will make it clear to him, that he must remove among them. The people to whom he now administers, are confident, that if Fabius leaves them, it will be *all hawk* on their side, but the thousand dollars keep such a buzzing in his ears, that the good soul of Fabius is constantly between hawk and buzzard; or like the creature, less than a mule, spoken of in the Gospel, tied where two ways meet.

That these instances illustrate the common use of being *between hawk and buzzard*, it is presumed none will deny. I own myself at a loss about the origin of the proverb, and am rather inclined to believe that it is pu to a use somewhat different from its original design. In the middle and southern states, there is a bird, which, from its colour and size, is called the Turkey-Buzzard. This bird is carniverous, but radically differs from the hawk, in one particular: while the hawk assails and devours the living, the buzzard feeds alone on what it finds dead. To stand between hawk and buzzard, according to the natures of these flesh eaters, is to stand between a foe that would destroy your life, and another that would devour your body. Viewing the subject in this point of light, it needs no particular instances of illustration. Let the hawk represent death, and the buzzard the grave, and all the living men on earth are between them. Death seeks to destroy their lives, and the grave is waiting to consume their bodies. That men must die, is an article of the universal creed, to which Pagans, Turks, Jews, and Christians, all subscribe. Death is spoken of, in the Scripture, as having a name, but it has neither shape nor substance.

> The pains, which, do reduce to death, are great,
> But death is nothing but a change of state.

All nations are in the habit, however, of personifying death under some horrid figure, like the grim-faced king of terror, who always stands ready, in an infinitude of forms, to destroy the lives of men—from whose assault neither the king nor the beggar—the wise nor the ignorant—the virtuous nor the vicious, is secure. Upon the dissolution of life, the grave, which is never satisfied—which never says, "it is enough"—arrests the body, and cries over its prey, "dust thou art, and unto dust shalt thou return." The thought of this, inspires the following soliloquy. O, my soul! leave the busy scenes—the vain amusements of life, and, like the dove, fly to the rock of safety, and build thy nest by the side of the hole's mouth. There, and there only, canst thou sing the triumphant song, "O, death where is thy sting! O grave, where is thy victory! Thanks be to God, who giveth me the victory, through our Lord Jesus Christ."

NUMBER EIGHT.

A THOUGHT ON SYSTEMS.

SENEGAL, was a man of talents and profound education, but living a sedentary life, was attacked with the hypocondria. In his study, he embraced the idea that his body was crystalline glass: of course, in all his garden walks, he took great care to preserve his body from being broken to shivers. He was first a fool to believe what was false, then wise, as Daniel, to preserve the result of folly.

I am frequently reminded of Senegal, when I observe the measures of religious theorists in these days. Infallibus is one of those theorists. A *system of consistency* is his boast. He has fixed a number of monuments, in a straight line, from earth to heaven, but, in steering from one monument to another, the road is not so smooth as he wishes for. The plain phraseology, and apparent meaning of texts of Scripture, do not volunteer themselves to his service as he desires: he, therefore, forms an imaginary monument, which, he says, lies in a direct line, between two unquestionable monuments. This ideal monument he believes in, as much as he believes in his own existence. And the reason why he believes it with a faith so firm, is because he *must* believe it, or abandon his boast of consistency. Having laid down his thesis, (which, to others, appears very problematical,) he then exerts all his powers and learning to support it. The more doubtful his thesis is, the more he labors to maintain, and the greater his talents are, the greater is the prospect of making many disciples. Hence, the greatest errors often arise from the weakness of great men, for little men have neither character, to give their opinions a hearing, nor arguments to defend them, but great men have both. It is a saying among barristers, that "plain cases need no elaborate defence." So the essentials of religion are made as plain in the Bible, (not to say more so,) as they can be made in any book.

Rusticus is a marksman: he levelled his rifle at a buck: the sight, on the muzzle, varied but the forty-eighth part of an inch, from the true line to the neck artery; but in the distance of one hundred yards, the ball declined so far from the line, that it never touched the game. So it is with metaphysical reasoning: the smallest error, in the outset, though undiscovered by the writer or reader, if pursued, under the pretext of consistency, will lead to an amazing distance from the truth.

The Bible is not written in systematical form; but heavenly truths are interspersed in it, in a manner somewhat promiscuous, and he that simply reads will generally gain more to instruct his mind, and warm his heart than he who reads to find supports for his system.

After all, I am convinced that a fondness for systematical consistency is interwoven in our nature, and has its advantages in a religious life. Without it, the student in divinity will never be a close thinker—he will be too licentious in his conclusions—he will, too much, feel the impression of every moment, and, of course, pull up stakes too soon, and be driven about with every wind of doctrine. We may, with certainty, argue, that God is a God of order, equal in all his ways, and that a consistency runs through all his works. With equal certainty we may reason, that our own capacities are limited—that divine materials will not submit to human standards—that we may be most in the wrong when we think ourselves to be nearest right. With such reflections in our minds, we ought to follow the clearest light—hold fast that which we believe to be true, but always stand open to conviction—willing to part with error when we can gain truth for it, and remember that the great characteristic of a disciple of Jesus, is to be a little child, possessing an honest heart.

These reflections involuntarily bring my own exercises into view. It has ever been a hard lesson for me to know how to address an assembly of sinners, as such, in gospel style. That the salvation of the soul is from the Lord, and the destruction of the soul is from ourselves, is evident. Nothing is better supported than that men are *saved by grace*, and *damned for sin*, but to reconcile these two evident axioms together, and clear the Almighty from being a respecter of persons, involves such difficulties in my mind, that neither Gill nor Wesley—Hopkins nor Fuller—Winchester nor Paine, can relieve me from them, and the reasoning of my own, are as inefficient. But, when the Lord pleases to quicken me by his holy spirit, and fill my soul with the fulness of the gospel of Jesus, I can, at such periods, address the ungodly without any hesitancy of a deception. *Then* the words flow from my heart—feel important in my mouth, and fall on the audience. No whispering *then* in my heart, "perhaps you are wrong;" no fiery dart to make me blush in the pulpit; what before seemed irreconcileable, *now* becomes plain. My own soul finds pleasure in the truth, and I feel a confidence that God approves the words of my mouth. But when the heavenly gale ceases to blow, the vision closes, nor can I, with all my reasoning powers, retain that view of the harmonious scheme of salvation.

This circumstance is additional proof to me, that the plan of God is better understood by the influence of grace, than it can be by all moral reasoning on the fitness of things. I here subjoin, I have often sat with pleasing wonder and solemn awe, to hear men of small capacities, (when preaching in a full tide of heavenly love,) address the ears, judgments and consciences of the assembly, while men of much greater accomplishments, destitute of the divine influence, do but mangle heavenly things.

"Without me, ye can do nothing," says Jesus.

NUMBER NINE.

NO HOLY ORDERS, BUT GOOD MINISTERS.

It has been the misfortune of most governments, to have *holy orders* of men among them. The more *holy and just men* there are in a state, the stronger and better the state is; but where there is an *order* established by law, by a charter of exemptions and pensions, such orders will, in a good measure, be filled with the most *unholy* men. Whether such privileged orders are called Davids, Priests, or Clergy, the amount is the same. To traverse the subject, would be a boundless task; a few instances must suffice.

According to Nizbet's history, an opinion prevailed through christendom, in the tenth century, that the world would close its existence with that century. The clergy availed themselves of this opinion, and worked it to their own advantage. Near the close of the century, men would give, first, all their money, and next, all their lands, to the priests, for their prayers. The century at length closed, but the world still existed—existed—but the chief of it belonged to the priests.

In the eleventh century, a Christian clergyman, called Peter the Hermit, crept out of his cell, and, going on pilgrimage to Jerusalem, he saw the holy land in the hands of Infidels; he returned, and taking a crucifix, ran to the European princes, and inflamed them to commence the crusades and holy wars, which lasted a century, and destroyed the lives of two millions of people, to take the country where Christ lived and died, out of the hands of those who did not believe in him. These orders of men are exempt from taxes, and their lands with them—freed from bearing arms, and all the burthens of government. And it is candidly believed that they inflame the people to commit more cruelty and injustice than they restrain them from. But nothing is here intended to invalidate the characters or usefulness of that number of individuals, who are the ministers of the meek and lowly Jesus. Let such individuals be left where they ought to be, in relation to the laws, without partial indulgence, and without legal proscriptions; and, as citizens, they will feel the common burthen of government, and thereby be led to seek the good of their country, and, as ministers of Christ, will exert their powers to save the souls of men from the wrath to come. Constitutions of government, and the laws of the land, should never know religious officers, by placing golden baits and exemption from social burthens before them, nor by proscribing them from any civil offices in the state. Either of these establishes them as a *holy order;* the first rewards them as such—the last reserves them because they are such. The first is calculated to make hypocrites—the last to encumber virtue.

NUMBER TEN.

OLD PIGS WANT TEATS AS WELL AS THE YOUNG.

It is become fashionable to consider the body politic under the emblem of a sow; the lucrative offices of state, as teats; and place-men, who hold those offices, to be pigs. Pigs will squeal and nuzzle until the milk comes; but the freer the milk flows, the more easy and silent the pigs are; but, when the sow has exhausted her treasury, and drives them off, they squeal and bite like furies. If there are more pigs than teats, it is attended, at least, with noisy consequences, for no pig will willingly give up the teat, which he is in possession of, to another. The truth is, pigs had rather live on the milk of the sow, than root the clods for a living.

Some time past, the writer sold a barrel of cider to a couple of laborers; after they had finished their labor, they were invited into the cellar to choose their barrel: they concluded the best way was to take a quill, and choose by taste. But the musical part of the whole, was the impatience of each when the other had the tasting quill. "You've had it long enough—do let me taste," reverberated the subterraneous cavern, as much as the like sound does a republic by office wish-fors.

To see young men wishing to rise and shine, is natural; but what shall we think of old men, who employ all their friends to solicit for them, and after they gain the appointment, will declare that the office was unasked for, and undesired? Does not this look as if *old* pigs wanted teats? And does it not look as if old men would say that which is not true, to cover their ambitious and avaricious views? It is a matter of notoriety, that many old men behave as if they believed that a possession of an office for some time, gave them a life lease of it; why else should they be so chagrined when they are dismissed?

From these observations, it is not to be concluded that *all* men, either old or young, are hungry pigs. No; there are many men, who are so rich and happy in the furniture of their own minds—who so far prefer retirement to the noisy stage of office, that they make a great sacrifice of inclination whenever they accept of any appointment; nothing but imperious duty will move them to do it.

NUMBER ELEVEN.

NIMROD, MOSES, CHRIST, AND THE UNITED STATES.

As Nimrod was the great grandson of Noah, he founded his government not far from the beginning of the nineteenth century, A. M. His government is called a *kingdom*, and yet it speaks the language of a *commonwealth*. "*They* said, go to, let *us* make brick—let *us* build *us* a city, and let *us* make *us* a name." These expressions do not accord with the language of an absolute monarch. It is probable that, in the first founding of this government, there was a general consent—that a majority, if not of numbers, yet of affluence, agreed to the measure; for fancy itself cannot invent how government could take rise against the consent of the people. After the government was formed, Nimrod, by his exploits and deception, gained an ascendency over the rest.

In the twenty-fifth century, the twelve tribes of Israel were formed into a government, at Mount Sinai. This people received all their laws, both civil and religious, from Jehovah; consequently, they had neither legislature nor executive in their institutions. The judiciary only was established among them. Judges over thousands—over hundreds—over fifties and over tens, were appointed; but no salaries were provided for them; the expense, therefore, of the civil list was nothing. The term in which the judges ruled (from the inauguration of Moses to the death of Samuel) was about four hundred and fifty years. While the stationary judges performed their work, a number of extraordinary judges was raised up, who judged and ruled the whole nation. Of this last description, there were sixteen. During this period, they had no king, "but every man did that which was right in his own eyes." That they sometimes did wrong, is certain; but they did worse after they became a kingdom.

There were two intervals, of forty years each, in which there was no war, while the judges ruled, and one interval of eighty years, which was never the case after their regal modification. Religion, in all its forms, was established among this people—the line of priests was fixed—and their salaries appointed, which consisted of the tenth part of all the products of the people. This, I say, was appointed—God commanded it; but, if men did not obey, they were accountable to God alone—the judges had no orders to take cognizance of it.

This people, at length, (to get clear of wicked judges, and have a general stated among them to fight their battles,) changed their government into a qualified monarchy. A king they would have—a king God gave them in his anger. The king, however, was to make no laws; but rule them according to the laws given by Moses. The theocracy, therefore, still existed. Four kings reigned over the twelve tribes; and then ten of the tribes separated, and formed a distinct kingdom. Over these ten tribes, reigned nineteen kings in succession; and over the two tribes, on the throne of Judah, reigned twenty. The ten tribes were, at length, captivated by the Assyrians; and, some time after, the two tribes shared the same fate by the Chaldeans. The length of time, from the royal modification of the tribes, unto the close of the dynasties of the two lines of kings, was about four hundred and seventy years. Over the two tribes, the crown was hereditary in the house of David; but over the ten tribes, he who was the most ambitious and fortunate wore the crown. In short, all the qualifications of many of those kings were comprised in killing the one who reigned before them.

About the middle of the fifth millennium, the kingdom of Christ was set up. Jesus said he was a king, born to bare witness unto the truth—that his kingdom was righteousness and peace, but not of this world; of course his servants were not to fight for it with carnal weapons. The cause of Christ, without coercion by law or sword; by appealing to the reason and judgment of men, gained such evidence of its divinity, that in three hundred years, it overturned the empire, which claimed universal sway. Let it carefully be observed, that Jesus claimed no civil preogatives among men —has set no example—given no code of laws for the government of state;

but left all such affairs to have their course in Providence, while he pursued his object, *the eternal salvation of men.* It should here be noticed, that when Christianity overturned empire, as mentioned before, in a great measure, it overturned itself. Government, which before had opposed it, now flattered it. Learning, which till then had used all its force against it, now sought to support it by the aid of reasoning, and by the court and the college, Christianity was disrobed of her native beauty, and prostituted to the basest purposes. Christianity being established in the empire, it opened a large door for Christian officers: to fill the civil offices, the ambitious would be Christians; and to get a fat living, many would be called to preach.

Strange to relate! It was left for the United States of North America, to give the example to the world; to draw the proper line between church and state, religion and politics. Yes, from the beginning of Christianity, down to the close of the eighteenth century, A. D. it never prevailed among a people, of any considerable consequence, but they would either punish or pamper it almost to death: either proscribe it, or make it a principle of state policy. To say that the government of the United States is perfect, would be arrogant; but I have no hesitancy in saying, that the Constitution has left religion *infallibly* where it should be left in all government, viz: in the hands of its author, as a matter between God and individuals; leaving an open door for Pagans, Turks, Jews or Christians, to fill any office in the government, without any religious test, to make them hypocrites: securing to every man his right of argument and free debate: not considering religious opinions objects of civil government, or any ways under its control: duly appreciating that Christianity is not a scheme of coercion; but only calls for a patient hearing, a dispassionate examination and a rational faith.

NUMBER TWELVE.

FAITH.

In reading and hearing, I have discovered a considerable variety of opinion, among divines, respecting *faith.*

Some consider it to be the *simple assent* of the mind, to a declaration or fact which is supported by rational evidence. Others suppose that faith is expressive of the *exercises of a gracious soul,* believing and embracing what God reveals to men; and that it is the duty of all men, who hear the gospel, to exercise faith. In this view of the subject, they boldly call on all their hearers to *believe* and be saved. A third class will have it that faith is the gift of God, that it intends something *received,* and not anything *done* by men.

To me, nothing appears more evident, than that faith is an indefinite word, admitting of a variety of significations. That faith frequently intends the exercise of the soul; and that men are under the strongest obligations to *hear* and *believe* all that God reveals, admits of no doubt; but that faith *always* has that meaning is not so clear. Eph. vi. 2, 3. Peace be to the brethren, and love with *faith*, from God the father, and the Lord Jesus Christ. II. Thes. i. 11. We pray always for you, that our God would count you worthy of this calling, and fulfil all the good pleasure of his goodness, and the work of *faith* with power. I. Tim. i. 14. And the grace of our Lord was exceeding abundant, with *faith* and love which is in Christ Jesus. Heb. xi. 1. Now *faith* is the substance of things hoped for, the evidence of things not seen. Heb. xii. 2. Looking unto Jesus, the author and finisher of our *faith*. II. Peter, i. 1. To them that have obtained like precious *faith* with us, through the righteousness of God and our Saviour Jesus Christ. Let any man divest himself of the prejudices of system, and dispassionately reflect on the texts here quoted, and it is probable he will confess that *faith* sometime bespeaks *the work of God in man*, and not always *the work which God requires of man*. Nothing is here intended to chill the burning zeal of those, who so pathetically call on all to repent and believe the gospel, and deal out the vengeance of God and the wrath of the Lamb to unbelievers: but let them at the same time remember, that there is a faith superior to all duty, called, sometimes, the spirit which God pours out upon them; at other times, the water of life; an unction from the Holy One; the word of God which liveth and abideth in the saints; Christ in them the hope of glory, &c. *This* kind of faith, Adam, in innocency, had not; this faith came not by Abraham or Moses, but by Jesus Christ, and is life eternal.

It is hard to believe that a righteous God, requires *us* to be inherently more rarified and celestial than innocent *Adam* was; but if the saints of Jesus are not so, what mean such texts as these? "I am come that they might have life, and that they might have it *more abundantly*. But where sin abounded grace did *much more* abound. We are *more* than conquerors through him that loved us." Christ did not come to re-Adam the sons of men; he does not restore them to the garden of Eden. The flood and other causes, have blotted out of existence the garden of Eden, and sin has done the same to the pristine innocence of Adam; neither of them are in existence, and of course cannot be described. But Christ, in the new covenant, raises men to a station more exalted than the genesian paradise —to a life more sublime than Adam possessed. "His flesh shall be *fresher* than a child's." It is not unreasonable for God to require men to be as good as Adam was; to believe what he did, and as much more as is revealed to them; (for the faith and obedience of men should always keep pace with the revelation and commands of God,) but if the saints of Jesus are made partakers of a divine nature, and are more celestial than Adam was, as has been suggested, then there is *one faith* which is not a *duty*; not a work of man; not an exercise of the soul: the want of this faith constitutes no crime: the possession of it meetens us for heaven.

If the scheme of salvation is nothing more than a *remedial law*, and men are only re-Adamed by grace, they may fall away as Adam did. As temptations have increased a hundred fold, it is a hundred times as likely that all gracious souls will fall, as it was that Adam should fall: every argument, therefore, drawn from Adam's fall, to prove that saints *may* fall from grace, proves that they all certainly *will*. But if we consider the new covenant as established upon better promises, that Christ is the author and finisher of faith, in men; and that faith is eternal life; we may conclude that the saints are kept by the power of God, through faith, unto salvation.

NUMBER THIRTEEN.

SADDLE-BAGS JOURNAL.

Growing weary with the objects within the smoke of my chimney, I fixed myself as decently as I could, and made my tour through the adjacent country. The first man that saluted me was a hard-handed laborer, with his sickle in his hand. After the usual remarks on the weather, without any solicitation of mine, he proceeded to give the following history of himself.

"I am a laboring man, and get my bread by the sweat of my face. I began the world with nothing, but by labor and frugality, have gained a considerable property. I make it my practice, when I am in company, to talk as loud, and as much, as any of them. If I hear a man reading, I often interrupt him, and make my remarks on the subject; if I see a man writing, I look over his shoulder to see what he is about. On politics, I give my opinion with independent freedom, for I carry no velvet mouth in my head. I have heard, that in the southern states they give a man time to think, without forcing him to speak or to hear, and conceive it a great rudeness to interrogate a stranger, or interrupt the student or speaker; but, thank God, I am no Buck-skin, Tuckahoe, or Vandalian, but a true born Yankee, and interrogate and animadvert constantly, keeping the wind-mill and clatter always in motion, when I am in company, and *think* when I have leisure: by these means I have gained more information than many of those who make such a bustle about *education*, as if bookish knowledge was every thing. Such men read books, but I read men and facts: such men talk much of the advantages of literature, but if the laborers did not support them, they would soon "be as poor as Job's turkey."

Sir, said I, will you be pleased to give me some information of your discoveries?

"Ah! you need not *sir* me," said the man, "but, if you have got a head for it, I can easily do it, for the Almighty has made a good turnpike from my brains to my mouth. I have found that two hundred and seven thousand, three hundred and sixty rails, each noting eleven feet, will enclose a square containing two hundred and seven thousand, three hundred and sixty acres of land, with a fence six rails high, and I question whether many of the soft fingered tribe know it. This I did not learn from Sir Isaac, but was self-taught, myself original.

"Again. One penny at simple interest, five per cent, from the birth of Christ to 1800, would be no more than seven shillings and seven pence. But the same penny, at compound interest would amount to the amazing sum of nearly one hundred and thirty five thousand quatrillions of tons of gold, avoirdupoise: which ball of gold would be heavier than four hundred and forty-four millions of such globes as this."

I then bid the man adieu, remembering what I had read, that a pearl is found in an oyster-shell, and in a toad's head.

I had not traveled far, before I was overtaken by a gentleman, neatly clad, well mounted, with a very small pair of saddle-bags. Remembering that I was in a country where questions would not be unpleasant, I asked the gentleman his occupation and destination. To which he replied with a smile, "sir, I am a doctor of physic, and am going to visit a circle of patients; the season is sickly, and I have abundance of custom; not less than forty are now indisposed; and, notwithstanding, it is an evil day among the people, yet it is fine times for doctors. 'Every dog has his day.'"

"Are your saddle-bags large enough to carry medicines for so many patients," said I? "Plenty large," said the doctor, "I have medicine enough in them for three hundred people. Once there was a time, when physicians studied the difference of constitutions, as well as the difference of diseases: but in these days of improvement and patent rights, it is become obsolete. Mercury, mercury is now the catholicon: nearly all other medicines are in disuse, and he who differs from the mercurial line, is cried down as a quack: and it certainly has one preference, being so energetic, a small quantity answers; hence little saddle-bags, and a small horse, will do."

"Are all your patients willing to be quicksilvered so much," said I? "They are not," said he, "but we know how to work it with them. We use our technical phrases, to raise their admiration, and have so many preparations of mercury, that we get it down before they know it; and when we get them well charged, their resistance leaves them. And, besides, if they were only spleeny before, the mercury makes them sick, and when they revive, we get the praise of being skilful physicians. We have established a great importance among the people, especially those who are superstitious: if we direct them to give seven drops once in seven and a half minutes, they durst not measure in the tea-spoon, nor intermit eight minutes, believing that life depends on the exact quantity and time which we prescribe. If nature triumphs over the disease, we impute it all to medicine; but if nature sinks, we preach up the foreordination of God. The clergy and lawyers have a great ascendency over the people, and we endeavor to keep up our end of the yoke. We studied as long as they did before we began practice—we know how to make our charges as well as they do—we love money, like them, and are as intent to get it."

On saying this, the doctor outrode me, and left me behind to reflect on this query: "does the devil and doctors know any thing about the *inside* of men?"

Soon after this, I overtook a man, affecting genteel gravity, with a huge pair of saddle-bags: he soon opened the conference in the following manner: "Where do you live sir? What sort of religion is most fashionable in your parts? Are there any vacant parishes that you know of? Are there any ministerial funds and perquisites in those parishes? What do preachers generally have by the year among you?" etc.

"Pray sir," said I, what mean your huge saddle-bags?" "My saddle-bags," he replied, "contain a valuable treasure; I am a minister of the gospel, and go to sojourn where I can find a place. I am now on a mission to visit the destitute, and the heathen, but while I am performing my missionary labors, I am looking out for a settled place of abode. St. Paul could leave his cloak, books and parchments behind him, and when winter was approaching, could send word to Timothy, to bring them along with him; but I have no Timothy to do the like for me; I, therefore, carry all along in my saddle-bags. I have, therein (besides my clothes,) my diploma, my license, my Bible, and psalm book—many necessary assistants, and notes enough for one whole year, provided I settle myself; if not, they will suffice for seven years. I am now in the fulness of the blessing of the gospel of Christ, having stocked myself before my departure. If I can find an opening that pleases me, I shall engage with the people, but if not, I shall turn my attention to law or merchandize, for the expense of my education must some how or other be reimbursed." Here he closed, and here we parted. He pursued his course, and I returned home, musing on some of Paul's words. "I conferred not with flesh and blood, for whom I have suffered the loss of all things—necessity is laid upon me, yea woe is me if I preach not the gospel."

NUMBER FOURTEEN.

OLD MR. WELL'S YOU CAN.

In my travels, and among my acquaintance, I have heard much said about a Saviour, by the name of *Well's you can;* but have never yet seen him—the house where he lives, nor the man who entertains him: and am almost in despair of ever finding him below the sun. The accounts of him are these: "If I do as *well as I can,* I believe the Lord will accept of me, and if you do as *well as you can,* you will be saved." If the salvation of the soul depends upon our doing as *well as we can,* who then can be saved? If a man faulters once in his life from doing as *well as he can,* the chance is over with him; and where is the man to be found, who can lay his hand upon his breast and conscientiously declare, that he has at all times, and in all cases done as *well as he could?* If such a man cannot be found, it follows that *well as you can* is only an ideal, not a real Saviour.

It is a saying replete with truth, that those men, who place the greatest hope for heaven on doing as *well as they can,* are more negligent in good works, than those who detest themselves as the vilest of the vile, and trust alone in the mercy of God, through the blood of the cross. Pharisees may boast of good works, but humble penitents perform them. Men, who are taught of God, instead of doing one good work to make atonement for a bad deed, see so much pollution in their best works, that they implore the pardoning blood of Christ to wash their works as well as their souls. There cannot be anything meritorious in the performance of dependent creatures: the righteous law of God requires, of all rational creatures, the unceasing exertion of all their powers in loving and obeying their Maker. If any part of their time is otherwise employed, sin is committed, and guilt is contracted. If, after the failure, creatures could do more than the law requires, by this extra work (which would be meritorious) they might make amends for former deficiencies; but this extra work cannot be done, because the law requires the constant exercise of all their powers in his service. If, therefore, perfect and perpetual obedience is due to God, neither the whole, nor any parts of obedience, can be meritorious. And, as no after obedience can make satisfaction for a former failure, so, likewise, repentance for sin committed will not atone for guilt contracted. The conclusion of the whole is, that, when creatures have sinned, neither after obedience nor repentance will save their souls.

NUMBER FIFTEEN.

ANTEDILUVIAN AND PATRIARCHAL.

THE first child ever born of human parents was a murderer, and slew his brother. It was two hundred and thirty-five years after creation, before men began (socially) to call on the name of the Lord. No mention is made of *fire* before the flood, nor of a *knife*. Enoch, the seventh from Adam, was born A. M. 622, and about sixty-five years afterward, (as it seems,) delivered his prophecy of the last and general judgment. As Adam lived two hundred and forty-three years after Enoch walked with God, it is highly probable that the *first* man heard of the *last* judgment.

No direct promise is made of the Messiah unto men, in the whole antediluvian history; but the conquering seed of the woman, is revealed in the denunciation of the Lord God to the serpent. Noah, the tenth from Adam, was born A. M. 1056. He was a preacher of righteousness, and the builder of the ark, into which he entered when he was six hundred years old, *and the Lord shut him in*. And here ends the history of the antediluvians. Peleg, the fifth in descent from Noah, was born one hundred and two years after Noah went into the ark. In the days of Peleg the earth was *divided*.

Some think that, before the days of Peleg, Europe and Asia joined with Africa, but, by some tremendous shock, the chasm of the Mediterranean sea was formed in his days, which *divided* Africa from Europe and Asia. Others conclude that Peleg was the first surveyor, who *divided* the earth by lines.

Perhaps there was a great agreement among the families descending from Noah, about their territorial claims and boundaries, in which Peleg acted a distinguished part. Or, it may be, the inhabitants of the earth got so divided, that they committed great hostilities upon each other; the hunting, wars and arrogance of Nimrod and his associates, being at this time.

Ten generations from Noah, and twenty from Adam, Abraham was born, A. M. 1946. Fourteen generations after Abraham, David was born; and after fourteen generations of royal government, (exclusive of Saul and Ishbosheth,) the Babylonish captivity commenced. And fourteen generations afterwards, which made the sixty-second from Adam, the Saviour, Jesus Christ, was born. From this, we learn that the generations, in average, from Adam to Jesus Christ, were not far from sixty-five years.

How many generations have been since the Christian era began, I know not. Indeed, the genealogy in the Old Testament was only in *one line* from Adam to Jesus. Whether they were longer or shorter in other branches of the same families, I cannot tell.* It is probable enough, that the Jews are very particular in their genealogical tables, of the house of David at least, as they are looking for their Messiah yet to come; but, of this I have no assurance.

NUMBER SIXTEEN.

THE PARCHMENT. AN ALLEGORY.

As Meslucius was digging in the earth after golden ore, he found an iron chest, which, to all appearance, had lain there a number of centuries. Opening the chest, he found therein a parchment, preserved entire from the waste of ages, and every line thereon written legibly plain. In composition, it exceeded everything he had ever seen. The boldness of the figures—the pomp and sublimity of the style, surpassed all the writings of the oriental regions; but, in detailing facts, and describing moral precepts, such artless simplicity appeared, that a child would unavoidably feel the force of the narratives and injunctions. By the face of the parchment, it appeared that it was written by a number of hands, impelled by one and the same spirit. It detailed events which had taken place before the writers lived, in part; and gave an account of the condition of the world, in the days when they lived and wrote; and, likewise, foretold what future events would take place. But, what was most surprising, it gave an account of a certain *disease* which had raged among men, and how they found a cure. It particularly pointed out a plague that would prevail at the time when Meslucius found the chest, and prescribed a certain, and the only balsam which would restore to health. On the whole, Meslucius reasoned as follows: "At what time, or by whom, this parchment was written, I cannot ascertain. Whether the great events therein related, took place or not, is uncertain. And whether those future events will ever emerge, I know not. But one thing I know, it gives a true account of the condition which the world is *now in;* with a number of peculiar circumstances, which puzzle me to ascribe to any calculation, short of the foreknowledge of God.

"The plague foretold in the parchment, I not only see raging with all its horrors among all my acquaintance, but feel its ravages in myself. All medicines have proved unavailing, and I will try the prescription of the parchment."

---

* From David to Jesus Christ, in the branch of Solomon, were only twenty-eight generations. See Matt. i., 17. But in the branch of Nathan, the son of David, to Christ, were forty-two generations. Luke, iii., 23—32. For a solution of this seeming contradiction of genealogies, see *Budget of Scraps*—article, *Genealogy of Christ.*

Meslucius made application of the balsam, and received immediate cure. He then recommended it to others, and all who touched it were made perfectly whole. After this, neither Meslucius, nor any who were healed, entertained any unconquerable scruple of the truth of all the facts related in the parchment. The intention of this allegory is easy to conceive of.

The present inhabitants of the earth, came into the world seventeen hundred years since the last part of the sacred Parchment (the Bible) was written; at any rate, all of us found it in existence, at the time when we were first capable of knowing. Let it have been written by whom, and at what dates soever—or let it have been preserved by whom, and by what means, we neither know nor imagine; still, one thing we know, the Bible does exist. And is there any reason in man, or any book written by man, that reveals precepts equal to those in the Bible—that describes a mode of life as harmless and useful as the sacred Parchment? The plague of moral evil, in all its stages and windings, is drawn with more than human pencil. Both flattery and effrontery are avoided, and naked truth shines in all her virgin beauty.

After all the reasonings of men, guilt, with her iron talons, seizes their consciences; nor can they evade the assault with all their vain surmises. Where then shall a guilty sinner find relief? The light of nature, philosophy, and state policy are all silent: neither of them can give a gleam of hope beyond the grave, nor show one sin forgiven. But the gospel of Jesus, is loaded with such blessings as guilty sinners need. Yes, through the blood of the cross, and the resurrection of Christ, pardon of sin is administered and eternal life made known. When sinners are made sensible of their pollution, and feel the plague of sin, on applying to the Saviour, and receiving the balsam of his grace, they obtain a perfect cure. All whoever apply, are received; all who look, do live; all who touch, are made whole. Though Christ crucified, is to the Jews a stumbling-block, to the Greeks foolishness, to the men of worldly wisdom scorn; yet to them who believe, he is the wisdom of God, and the power of God. O! that all my dear countrymen might apply to this balm; then would they joyfully believe in the truth of the scriptures.

NUMBER SEVENTEEN.

SUPERFICIAL THOUGHTS ON ANGELS.

THAT Creation, at some period, had a beginning, is necessarily believed; but where to fix this period, is a matter of some doubt. Some astronomers seem confident, that many of the fixed stars, must have existed long before the creation which Moses relates, and therefore confine the genesian history to the solar system. Others are equally confident, that angels were formed at some period far anterior to the formation of the first pair of the human family. With the first of these I am not competent to dispute; with the last I am not disposed. I have never yet been convinced, however, that creation began at an earlier date than the time which Moses narrates.

That angels were in existence on the third day, appears pretty evident; for on that day the Almighty formed the cavern—fixed the boundaries of the sea, and caused the dry land to appear: at sight of which, "the morning stars sang together, and all the sons of God shouted for joy." It is most likely that angels were created on the first day. "In the beginning God created the heavens," (and their inhabitants.) Let this supplement be admitted, and the sense is complete. In six days the Lord made the heavens and earth, and *all* that is in them: Angels, being in the heavens, were certainly made within the six days, (if the history of Moses includes *all* creation,) and as they were songsters on the third day, where is a better place to fix their creation, than on the first day? In creation, two orders of intelligent beings were made, angels and men. The race of men were all to proceed from one complex parent by procreation; but angels were more independent in nature; all of them were created, none are procreated: the whole family of them were created at one time. Whether we call them spiritual matter, or spirit distinct from matter; in either case, they are not subject to natural decay, but are immortal: age, sickness and death never prey upon them. That they were subject to moral decay, is certain, for many of them have left their first estate, and turned themselves into devils. How long the angels, which are now fallen, retained their obedience in their first estate, is not certain.

The Almighty spake all creation into existence on the first day; and on that day, and the five days following, he formed creatures and things out of the mass, (*tohu* and *bohu*,) which he made on the first day. Angels stood wondering to see what their God could do. On the sixth day man was formed, with a body so erect, and a soul so capacious, as to raise the highest admiration among the angels; but, said God to the angels, "Do ye wonder at what ye see! know ye that my first begotten shall assume the nature and appear in the form of Adam; and I command you all to worship him as God incarnate." This was the first time that the Messiah was named; and when God brought his first begotten into the world, (by naming him,) he said, "let all the angels of God worship him." This was the test of angelic obedience: and the trial was, whether they ought to worship God in a nature inferior to their own, in obedience to the command; or whether they ought not rather to withhold their adoration. "What," said angels, "shall we worship a nature inferior to our own—why not worship a beast as well? We cannot understand the union of an incarnate God; and it would be idolatry to worship a creature: our reason tells us, therefore, all things considered, that it is best not to obey." If these suggestions are well founded, the first sin in the universe, arose from the limited wisdom and inadvertent conduct of sinless creatures. And further, if this is truly descriptive of the entrance of moral evil into the angelic department, then angels did not transgress before man was made, for angels to see.

At the close of the sixth day, God pronounced all very good, and on the seventh day he rested, which expressions seem to carry an idea, that no disturbance, as yet, had fallen out among his creatures, to "grieve him to the heart," and make him "repent that he had created man upon the earth." But, soon after this, perhaps on the eighth day, the rebellion broke out.

It is highly probable that some high angel, (likely the tallest which God had made,) took the lead in this rebellion, who, after he had become self-fallen, used his infernal address to deceive and ruin others, and who, to this day, has a kind of supremacy (under God) over those angels who followed his pernicious ways. When they are called devils, he is called Belzebub, their prince; and when he himself is called devil, they are called his angels.

An innumerable multitude of the angels have kept their first estate, and retain their innocency until this day. These are not sent by God to be preachers of the gospel among men, but are, all of them, ministering spirits, to minister unto the saints in the kingdom of Providence.

From the days of Abraham down, about two thousand years, the angels of God frequently appeared among men, to bring intelligence from heaven—feed and rescue the saints, and destroy the wicked: but from the close of the apostolic age down until the present time, the appearance of angels—the spirit of prophecy—and the working of miracles, have been more rare. That angels, however, still exist—guard the saints unseen—smite the wicked—escort the souls of the saints to Abraham's bosom, when they die—and will come in awful pomp with Christ at the last judgment—gather the elect from the four quarters of the earth—sever the righteous from the wicked, and dwell forever with the saints in heaven, we have abundance of evidence to believe. Of this innumerable company of the heavenly host, there are not more than the names of two handed down to us, if any name at all. Michael, (who is as God,) seems to intend Christ, the angel of the covenant, who has often appeared in angelic form:—with him Jacob wrestled, and to him Abraham prayed, etc. Whether the name, Gabriel (strength of God,) is peculiar to any one angel, or whether the name is given to any of the angels, when they are sent of God to accomplish grand events, is not certain; besides these two, no angelic names are found in our translation of the Bible.

The seraphim of Isaiah—the living creatures and cherubim of Ezekiel, and the four beasts of John, seem to be the same. Abundance of expositors, by them understand the angels, but in Revelations, v., 9, they are said to sing unto the Lamb, " thou wast slain, and hast redeemed us to God by thy blood," which is not a song for angels to sing.

The Mahomedans hold to genii, a race of beings between angels and men—that they bear higher offices than men, but are mortal and die: from this opinion, we should think, that aristocrats got their notion, that to rule over others is a right which some families are born to inherit.

All those creatures which are more exalted in nature than men, who are (dependently) possessed of immortality, I call angels. Let there be ever so many grades or orders, they form but one race.

I have said that angels were not sent to preach the Gospel. It is to be understood, however, that an angel first preached to the shepherds, the birth of the Saviour, who is the essence of the Gospel, but the doctrine of the gospel among men, which consists of *law* and *grace*—repentance towards God, and faith towards the Lord Jesus, contains essential articles which angels cannot well explain. The guilt of sin—repentance for sin—pardon from sin, and striving against the law of sin, are articles which the apostles preached, and are essential parts of the Gospel: but should angels undertake to preach, they must either omit these articles, or preach what they never experience.

ON SABBATICAL LAWS.

Of the pamphlet (published in 1815) entitled, "Remarks on Holy Time—on Moral Law—on the changing of the Day—on Sabbatical Laws"—the ideas contained in the first three divisions, are, for the most part, comprised in other pieces on the same subject, and in a more condensed form. It has, therefore, been deemed advisable to omit, in this place, all except the last head.

The Mosaic institution, which formed the tribes into a theocracy, was very different from the government of any other nation, and from the government of Gospel churches.

The Israelites had no legislature, but received their laws from Jehovah; they had no executive, God was their king. Judges they had, but no salaries provided for them; of course their civil list did not cost them a cent per annum.

Exclusive of their "divers washings and carnal ordinances," which were typical of good things, they had many laws to regulate them as a body politic, peculiarly adapted to their circumstances, and binding on no other nation. Their laws for trying jealousy by bitter water; for deciding the cause between the man-slayer and avenger of blood, at the gates of the cities of refuge; against taking usury; to oblige a man to marry the widow of his deceased brother; to release lands at the jubilee, etc., no other nation has seen cause to adopt, nor felt themselves bound to obey. The incompleteness of the political part of the Mosaic code to govern other nations by, requires no other proof, but just to observe, that the people were forbidden to have commerce with other nations, of course had no commercial laws. Any laws, therefore, which the Jews had to enforce the observance of the sabbath, or punish the sabbath-breaker, give no grounds to Christians to exercise like force. The king of Israel gave that people their laws and orders, but Christ has given laws for the regulation of Christianity. Now, if there be any account in the New Testament, that Jesus called upon the rulers of state, to make and enforce laws, to oblige the people to keep the first day of the week holy, and fine or punish them if they did not; such an account would be direct in point, but such an account we have not.

It has been noticed, in a foregoing page, that the evidence was so clear, that the first Christians assembled in course on the first day of the week, that it hardly admitted of a doubt, and the evidence is about as clear, that it was done voluntarily, as a matter of prudence, without any divine command; hence a disregard of the day was not esteemed a matter of offence. In Galatians, iv., 10, 11, Paul *reproves* the Galatians for observing days, months, times and years, as the Jews did; for Jewish times, no doubt, are intended. But in Romans, xiv., 5, a day is spoken of, which some regarded, and some regarded not, but none of them were *reproved* by Paul. It is probable the day here spoken of was the Lord's day, for if it had been a ceremonial day of the Jews, he would have *reproved* them for regarding it, as he did the Galatians; but, in the case before us, a regard, or disregard to the day, was not to be a cause of judging and setting at nought a brother, whom the Lord accepted. If, then, a disregard to the Lord's day was not censurable by the church, can we possibly suppose that it ought to be punished by the laws of state?

For the first eighteen centuries of time, there was no government among men but patriarchal, which took its rise in nature. Next, a more extensive government was formed, by mutual agreement, (Genesis, xi., 3, 4,) but, by the address of an ambitious hunter, the government was soon turned into a kingdom. The government of the tribes of Israel was a theocracy (from *Theos*, God,) because they received all their laws from God. The government of the Christian church is from heaven, and not from men.

Among the nations of the world in general, that government which does not rise in compact, is usurpation and tyranny. When men associate, it is for specific purposes, viz., to protect life, liberty and property, and not to prepare them for heaven. Souls and conscience are inalienable. The gracious and ungracious, all belong to the body politic, and are equally eligible to posts of authority. The work of the legislature is to make laws for the security of life, liberty and property, and leave religion to the consciences of individuals. If the sacred code, in the New Testament, is not sufficient to govern Christians in all their religious affairs, either the wisdom or goodness of Christ is deficient.

Much confusion arises in government, when sins and crimes are blended together. Every state crime is a moral evil or sin, (provided the laws of state are legitimate,) but every sin is not a crime to be punished by law. Malice, guile, hypocrisy, envy, pride, impenitence, unbelief, etc., are sins, but not crimes. Suppose, then, that a disregard of the first day of the week is a sin as flagrant as enmity, bigotry or ill-will, yet it is not a crime to be punished by law; for I would here request an instance where Jesus, or the inspired apostles, ever called on the civil rulers to punish sabbath breakers, or those who disregarded the first day of the week. If there is such an instance, let it be pointed to; but, if not, let clamor cease. When God, by Moses, gave law to the tribes, they had no king, nor any thing that looked like one, but the Almighty, knowing what would take place about four hundred and fifty years afterwards, gave them the character and administration of a king: (Deuteronemy, xvii., 14, 20.)

When Christianity was first set up in the world, it was small. The power of making laws was in the hands of the enemies of Christianity. Laws to guard the Christian religion could not have been expected, but Christ knew what would come. He knew that about three hundred years thereafter Christianity would rise triumphant; why did he not then give some precept, at least some small hint, that when Christianity should become so general, that *then the rulers of state should make laws to establish Christianity, and force the observance of the first day of the week?* We look in vain to find any thing like it in the New Testament, and it is generally confessed, that when the event did take place—when Constantine the Great established Christianity in the empire, and forced an observance of the first day of the week, Christianity was disrobed of her virgin beauty, and prostituted to the unhallowed principle of state policy, where it has remained in a criminal commerce until the present moment.

Men of little reading, and less thought, conclude, that if there is no law of state to force the observance of the sabbath, (for so they name the first day of the week,) it would entirely run out, and not be regarded at all. Why did it not then run out in the three first centuries? How came it to be regarded all that time as purely as it has ever been since? There were no sabbattical laws during that period. Why has it not run out in Pennsylvania, New Jersey, and New York? They have no holy laws in those states, and yet the sabbath, so called, is not run out, but meeting-houses and public worship in those states are not inferior to those of New England. Those states abound with Quakers, who never thank a legislature for making religious laws, and yet they keep the first day of the week as regularly as the Presbyterians, and the fifth day of the week beside.

The Jews, and some of the Christians, would keep the seventh day—most of the Christians would keep Sunday—the Turks would hallow Friday—Infidels no day. Shall that sect, which is most numerous and ambitious, direct the sceptre of government to interpose, and force all to submit to one standard, and fine, punish and burn non-conformists? Such has been the course of things, it must be confessed, but does not human nature shudder at the thought, and the spirit of Christianity flee from the sight! Let each sect enjoy their own rights and freedom, in respect of the God whom they wish to adore, the days on which they would pay that adoration, and the modes of performing it. If one sect has the liberty of worshipping whom, when and as they please, why should that sect wish to force other sects to worship whom, when and as they would not?

Legal force is not the armor with which the Captain of our salvation clothes the soldiers of the cross. An honest appeal to the reasons and judgments of men, is all the force that Christians should use to induce others to believe in and worship God as they themselves do. All the punishment that pious Christians inflict on the irreligious, is pity, forgiveness, and prayer, unless the irreligious man breaks out into overt acts, in which case he is to be punished according to his crime. If labor or amusements, on the first day of the week, may be considered as the foulest sins, yet they were no crimes to be punished by law, for the first three hundred years after Christ, nor are they, at this time, crimes in several of the states in our country, and, if laws were fixed as they should be, they would not be crimes any where. If those who keep the first day of the week, in remembrance of the resurrection of Christ, believe themselves to be right, (as they have cause to,*) let them "beseech others, by the mercies of God, to present their bodies a living sacrifice to God, which is a reasonable service," (Romans, xii., 1,) and not make use of legal force to do it, which will only prejudice others against the day and against themselves.

Where Jews (of which there are eight millions in existence) and seventh-dayrian Christians reside, they must either sacrifice conscience, or lose a day in each week. The majority of Christians in our country keep the first day of the week; but if there was a majority who kept the seventh day, and should oblige all others to regard the day, would those who now make the law and plead for its utility, bear the privation of one-seventh part of their labor, or change their day? If they did the first, they would justly complain of partial oppression—if the last, discover the rottenness of their consciences.

It has been observed before, that government should guarantee the rights of conscience to all; consequently if an individual or an assembly should be interrupted by assault, on Sunday, Monday, or any other day or night, either at the meeting-house, a private house, market, field or grove, where he or they should be conscientiously paying devotion to God, the law ought to be open, as it is, to punish the assailants, as disturbers of the peace; for the design of the law is, to punish him who works ill to his neighbor. This law is sufficient for all, every day of the week. It is no assault upon one man's right for another to refuse to unite with him in his devotion. Those who keep the first day of the week, will work in their fields and travel roads, where Jews assemble in their synagogues, and sevendayrians meet in their meeting-houses on Saturday, and never suspect that they are interrupting them in their worship; why, then, should it be looked upon an interruption for sevendayrians, or those who regard no day, to work in the field or drive their team in the road upon the first day? Yet, in many

* See remarks at the close of "The Sabbath Examined."

places, tything-men, or wardens, are chosen as legal officers to prevent labor and recreation on the first day of the week. When I see men turn their backs upon public worship, and pursue their labor or recreation in preference to the service of God, either on Sunday or on any other day, my heart beats in poetic strains,

"O might they at last, with sorrow return,
The pleasures to taste, for which they were born,
The Saviour receiving, the happiness prove,
The joy of believing, the heaven of love."

Or breaks out in the language of the Hebrew prophet, "Oh that they were wise, that they understood this, that they would consider their latter end!" Or vents itself in the words of Paul, "I pray you in Christ's stead, be you reconciled to God."

But when I see a man with the insignia of his office, arrest a fellow-man for non-attendance on worship, or labor or amusement on Sunday, it strains every fibre of my soul. Who that ever read the New Testament, which describes the meekness, patience, forbearance and sufferings of the first Christians, would ever have expected to see those who call themselves Christians, avail themselves of such weapons to suppress vice and support Christian morality? The spirit seems to be the same that influenced Peter to draw his sword and cut off the ear of one who did not reverence Christ; or, like that which stimulated James and John to command fire to come down from heaven and consume those who would not receive the blessed Saviour. The first was ordered to put up his sword; and the last were rebuked, with "ye know not what manner of spirit ye are of." It reminds me of an instance which took place with one of Burgoyne's men, who professed to be a zealous Christian. The man, hearing an American speak irreverently of religion, exclaimed, "How I hate him—I will kill him, because he does not love my blessed Jesus." About two centuries past, the spirit of witchcraft and witchburning ran through a considerable part of the world, like a raging plague. The rulers used to reason thus: "God will burn wizards and witches in the next world, and we who are God's representatives, must burn them in this world." But it is thought that the following reasoning would have been better: "God is merciful to the poor, deluded creatures, and lets them live, and we will imitate him." So in regard to those improperly called sabbath breakers. If they commit overt acts—if they assault the life, liberty or property of any man, let them be punished by law. But if their only error is not worshipping where, when, and as you do, your only weapon is fair reasoning with them. If God lets them live, though in disregard of Sunday solemnities, let not man kill them.

But how must a tything-man feel? The day he conceives to be holy: no civil or economical business must bedone on the sacred day; devotion must employ his time and his thoughts; and yet his office is civil; he receives his authority from the acts of the legislature, and not from the acts of the apostles, and his oath obliges him to profane the day which he conceives to be holy, by performing civil actions, for he has no authority to officiate, except on the time which is holy. When he rises on Sunday morning, instead of having his mind disentangled from earthly things, he is watching the fields and the roads; when going to meeting, instead of watching to prepare his heart for the solemnities of the day, he is watching how others behave; when at meeting, his eyes and his ears, which should be open alone to God, and to his word, are constantly looking and harking to prevent the errors of others. And thus, by law, he is obliged to do evil that good may come. However others may seek to regulate religious societies by law and by force, to me a man cannot give greater evidence that he is ignorant of the precepts and destitute of the spirit of Christianity, than by calling the aid of the civil arm to legalize religious days and modes, and punish those who will not submit.

I shall close this part of the subject, with a few reflections on some late events. When the British, (who are called the bulwark of religion,) landed near Saybrook, it was Sunday. The good people of Connecticut would not assemble to drive them off, because it was holy time, until the enemy had burnt the shipping at Pettipague. The God whom they served did not protect them from the depredations of the old "Bulwark." But on Lake Champlain, the "Bulwark" attacked McDonough on Sunday. McDonough solemnly prayed for success, and then fought with astonishing bravery. The signal victory which he obtained over the "Bulwark," together with what was achieved by the land forces, under General Macomb, have met with the thanks and rewards of more states than one. I have not yet heard, however, whether the pious apathy of Connecticut, or the profane heroism of the northern fleet and army, meets with the most applause from those who conceive Sunday to be holy time. It is highly probable, however, that there were no tything-men aboard McDonough's fleet.

The public assembling of Christians for religious worship, is certainly appointed in the New Testament by precept, and abundantly by example. And, as has been noticed, the evidence is nearly conclusive, that the first Christians generally assembled on the first day of the week, not with a view that it was of moral obligation—not in obedience to the fourth command of the decalogue, which enjoined the observance and rest of the seventh day—nor in obedience to any command given them by Christ, but voluntarily, as a prudential thing, to perpetuate the event of Christ's resurrection. Their public assembling, however, was not confined to the first day of the week, but daily, in the temple and other places, both day and night, as opportunity served, they assembled for Christian worship. There were some among them, who did not discover any advantages in their assembling on the first day more than on any other day, and, as the day was not divinely appointed, those who regarded it, did not judge and set at nought those who regarded it not, but left every man to be fully persuaded in his own mind.

SUMMARY.

1. God, for once, rested on the seventh day.

2. No proof that God commanded men to rest on the seventh day during the patriarchal age.

3. About two thousand four hundred years after creation, the holy sabbath was enjoined on the tribes of Israel.

4. The fourth commandment was not moral, but absolute.

5. The sabbath was not a day of public worship, but of rest.

6. After the return of the Jews from Babylon, of their own accord they built synagogues, and assembled in them every sabbath, to read and hear the law of Moses and the prophets, for which they had no command, and received no reproof.

7. The Gentiles were never reproved for sabbath-breaking.

8. The first day of the week was never appointed by Christ, to be kept different from other days.

9. Proof, nearly conclusive, that the first Christians paid particular attention to the first day of the week; those who did not regard the day, were not judged and set at nought by those who regarded it.

10. The observance of the first day of the week, perpetuates the resurrection of Christ.

11. The appointment of religious days, no article of legislation.

12. The observance of the first day of the week was never enforced by law until the reign of Constantine, in the beginning of the fourth century.

13. Tything-men are obliged, by their oaths, to profane the time which they conceive to be holy.

14. The public assembling of Christians for religious worship, enjoined by New Testament precept, and abundant examples.

JUNE 15, 1815.

MR. PRINTER—In the reign of Queen Elizabeth, when wizards and witches were abundant, her majesty established a court for the trial of witches. An ignorant peasant, (not rightly conceiving of the design of the court, and concluding that the honorable bench were only to inform persons who suspected themselves, whether they were witches or not,) took a journey of about sixty miles, when the court was in session, to be examined. Entering the solemn hall, he addressed the court as follows: "May it please your worship! I am come to be examined whether I am a wizard or not. My wife tells me that I am a witch; and, I have a mole on my breast, which my mother said was a witch-teat; and having strange cogitations of mind, I am suspicious of myself, and have come to be examined whether I am a wizard or not." The decision of the court, and the reception which the old peasant received from his wife, on his return, I shall not detail; but, with all the honesty of the old peasant, shall relate to you my moles, marks, and cogitations, and request yourself, or some of your readers, to tell me what I am.

In the administration of Mr. Adams, the democrats, by publishing a great deal of truth, and a little falsehood, completely run down the stupendous system of administration, which greatly disturbed me, and I took the holy, patriotic resolution, that by publishing a great deal of falsehood, and a little truth, I would run down the democratic administration; which resolution I have pursued ever since, but have not yet succeeded. When the act that established the court of sixteen judges was repealed, I boldly declared that the constitution was destroyed; which declaration I have repeated in every essential measure of government, from that time until the present. And, yet, I fully approved of the Hartford convention, which owned that the constitution did exist, and resolved to have it amended in seven particulars. The constitution, I know, bears the signature of Washington; but those who stick to it, are under the influence of Bonaparte, and I am a Washingtonian to the back-bone.

When Mr. Jefferson presided, my constant cry was, "protect our trade, secure our naval rights," &c. When the embargo was laid, I pronounced it "worse than war." When war was declared, I said it was unjust, impolitic and unnecessary. The disasters of Hull, Van Rensselaer, Winchester, and Wilkinson, gave me pleasure under the jacket, but, with a sanctimonious grimmace, I would say, "poor creatures! how my fellow men suffer the fault lies somewhere! Our government were wicked in declaring war, and incompetent to manage it." Such sermons I often preached, with a view to disparage those in power, and get myself and my partizans into their seats. I sometimes doubted the moral rectitude of my conduct for a moment; but, when I reflected that the ends I had in view were sufficient to justify the most deceitful means, it eased my conscience from such childish scruples. The bravery of the American troops at Niagara—the victories of Erie, Champlain, and New Orleans, I am obliged to own, have not been exceeded since the age of miracles ceased. That the war was justly waged, I will not believe. That God would succeed an unjust war, I dare not say. However, I ease myself of this dilemma, partly by saying it was done by the genius of the people, distinct from government, and partly, by hoping that the democrats are so stupid that they will not discover any inconsistency in my sayings and doings. The victories and captures on sea, have given me pleasure and pain. Pleasure, to see naval defence successful. In this particular, I can say, "I told you so; which establishes my character as a man of forecast. Pain, to think that our best friends who have done us no essential injury, the very bulwark of our religion, should lose sixteen hundred of their ships, with their rich cargoes.

When Bonoparte was sent to Elba, and Louis ascended the throne, I grew fat; the jig I concluded was nearly over; and the movements of the British army at Washington, exactly corresponded with my wishes. Had that army succeeded in catching Madison and sending him to Elba, my joy would have been full; I should have burst all the buttons from my jacket; but, to my chagrin, Madison made his escape. My joy, however, was considerable in blasting Madison for cowardice, and complimenting him with smoky walls; this joy, nevertheless, was somewhat allayed, when the British, near Baltimore, (the nest of democrats,) were repulsed, and lost a thousand men, including their commander and Sir Peter Parker. What a pity that lords and sirs must fall by the barbarous hand of low-bred democrats! Notwithstanding all, I rejoiced, and kept thanksgiving for the downfall of Napoleon, and chanted forth, "How art thou fallen, Oh Lucifer, son of the morning." The return of Napoleon, it is true, has astonished the world, but I hope his triumphs will be short. I trust that the combined powers, with their armies, will soon destroy him; for it is not war that I am principled against, it is only war with Great Britain.

The late treaty of peace is an unkind affair to me. I once said that the government could not be kicked into war, and did all in my power to prevent, not the aggression of Great Britain, but the declaration of war, to fulfil my prediction; but I failed—war was declared. I then said that Great Britain would never make peace while Madison presided; and used to tell my neighbours, at election terms, that the democrats had plunged them into a ruinous war; but, if they placed the Federalists in power, peace would immediately follow; but peace is made while Madison presides, without the aid of Federalists, or the Hartford convention. But even here, I find some food to cheer me. Great Britain has not agreed to desist from a single thing that the war was declared for; the democrats, therefore, I say, have lavished blood and treasure for nothing.

There is one staff that supports me more than all the rest, viz. taxes. At the close of the revolutionary war, the national debt was about seventy millions of dollars, which increased to eighty millions in twelve years. This increasing debt was a very popular argument for the democrats; and, as that debt was diminished more than forty millions of dollars in the eight years of Mr. Jefferson's administration, democracy wore a bold front; but now, thank my stars, the scale is turned. The late war has greatly increased the debt, and this I am resolved to play off against the government, and all those that support it. No doubt there will be different statements of the amount of the debt; but, I am determined to believe the largest, which will strengthen my arguments the more: for have the art of believing and saying whatever appears most ikely to supplant the democrats, all under the garb of religion and good order; and never intend to quit the pursuit, until the object is gained; for, as long as Mordecai sits in the king's gate, everything else avails me nothing. One cogitation more I have to communicate, viz., I am resolved to blacken the characters of Monroe, J. Q. Adams, and Gov. Tompkins, and eulogize King, Pickering, and Strong.

Now sir, if yourself, or any other man will tell me what I am, you will much oblige your humble servant. BROKEN-LEG.

CATECHISM.

Q. Which is the eleventh commandment ?

A. The eleventh commandment is, "Remember the first day of the week, and keep it hypocritically : the six following days *may* labor, laughter, lying, cheating, drinking, gaming, revelling and oppression, be done, by day or by night, according to the inclination of the individuals ; but, on the first day of the week, shall no labor or recreation be done, save only that men may salt their cows in the morning, sleep in time of service, talk about politics, fashions and prices, at noontime ; read newspapers after service, and pay their addresses at night. To redeem time, however, a traveller, on a journey, may continue his travel until Saturday midnight, and resume it on Sunday at the going down of the sun, losing but eighteen hours in a week ; but recreation must cease on Saturday at sun down, and not commence again until Sunday midnight, losing thirty-six hours each week. The law, morever, commands towns, precincts, and parishes to have teachers of morality, piety and religion, at least six months in a year, on the penalty of from thirty to one hundred dollars. It also enjoins it on the people to attend on the instruction of said teachers, if they conveniently and conscientiously can."

This is the eleventh and great command ; on the observance of which hang all religion and good order.

Q. Is there any precedent in the New Testament for all this ?

A. Christ's kingdom was not of this world : he claimed no civil prerogative ; consequently, he could not make any law of state, with pecuniary or corporeal penalties to sanction it ; nor did he give any divine orders to the rulers of this world to make such laws. But Constantine loved the Christians, who supported his imperial dignity, so much, that he made a law to enforce the observance of the first day of the week, and pay the teachers of Christianity. And, as every generation grows wiser, by experience of former generations, when our virtuous ancestors fled from Europe, and came to America, Mr. Colton, in Massachusetts, and Mr. Davenport, in New Haven, like Haggai and Zechariah, instructed the rulers how to proceed. Mr. Davenport, in particular, and his company, had high notions of a Christian commonwealth ; that government should be administered in an ecclesiastico-political mode. When the assembly met at New Haven, they took up the subject; but, as the season was busy, they adjourned, with the resolution that they would take the laws of God for their rule until the winter session, when they should have leisure to amend them; and, consequently, at their leisure session, they culled those parts of Moses's law they chose to preserve, and Christianized them; and, by little and little, have made the law as perfect as the state of society will admit of. In Massachusetts, they progressed in the same manner; in Connecticut, they begin their holy-day at the sun's setting, and end it at the same time; and, also, the Connecticut laws are *blue*, while some of Massachusetts' were *red*.

Q. Does not the New Testament forbid Christians to judge, and set at nought, those who differ with them about the observance of days? If so, are not all penal laws, on that subject, cruel persecution.

A. Christians, as members of churches, are not to judge them that are without; nor judge, and set at nought, those who differ with themselves, respecting meats and days; but every man is to be fully persuaded in his own mind. Every man must give an account of himself to his Maker, and, of course, ought to be free to act as conscience dictates. Nor should Christians, as citizens or magistrates, ever quit the weapon of fair reasoning, and assume legal force, to coerce and reform others from what they suppose to be religious errors. All laws, therefore, that describe the God—the day—or the mode of worship, are usurpative and oppressive—contrary to the genius of the gospel, the dictates of grace, and the kingdom of Christ; which laws have done incalculable evil among men. But times are altered so much—New Testament, meek and humble religion, grown so unpopular—and men have become so much wiser, (especially in the New England states,) that laws to force people to keep the first day of the week holy, and oblige them to have teachers, and pay them, are absolutely necessary. Without such laws, Sabbaths would be neglected and forgotten, the sanctuary forsaken, the priesthood disgraced, and Christianity demolished. Leave religion as unguarded by law as the New Testament leaves it, and the New England states would soon fall into the same licentiousness of manners, and error in politics, that many of the states are now involved in.

Q. If such laws are necessary, what is the best mode to carry them into effect?

A. The path is plain, but requires a little disguise. Let a society be formed with all pharisaic pomp, for the ostensible purpose of promoting good morals; let this society have a president, vice-president, and executive officers; and let as many auxiliary societies be likewise self-created as is necessary with their presidents and company. By this method, there will be a number of presidents, who, otherwise, would live in obscurity. Let all these societies, by their executive committees, make a bold stand against vice ; but let them be cautious not to criminate covetous and fraud among the aged, nor balls and revelling among the youth, for that would be unpopular ; but let them bend their whole force to prevent travelling on the first day of the week. This will make people believe that the *whole* of good morals consists in keeping the day abstemiously. Let the executive committees call on justices, sheriffs and tything-men, to aid them in the laudable work. Let the justices fill their writs, and sheriffs pursue and arrest the traveller, and bring him to trial till he pays seven dollars, and then let him travel on. Half of the money will be for the prosecutors ; and here the society will get money, as well as presidents. Indeed, this course of proceeding will give the society boldness in the faith—many honorary officers, and a quantum of that which answers all things, and all gained by the pure motive of suppressing vice, and promoting good morals. And, by making the day more sacred, it will make a better market for the sons of these officers, if any of them choose to be teachers of piety, morality and religion. One thing must be carefully attended to, viz., in rare instances, the fines must be relinquished after they are awarded ; and these acts of generosity must be published abroad, otherwise, the people will judge that the society acts for filthy lucre's sake ; whereas nothing is sought for but the good of the souls of the poor deluded travellers. Another advantage arises from this method of procedure ; should arrests and law suits attend it, which is highly probable, it will be a harvest to the attorneys, who fatten on the glorious uncertainties of the law, and the distresses of their fellow creatures.

Q. Is the law, which sanctifies the first day of the week, made for all of the community, or for a part only ? If binding on all, can it be executed in the mode just described, without defeating itself ?

A. On a superficial glance, the answer is no. Lying in wait to detect others—watching houses, roads and fields—gazing around in the meeting-house—filling writs—pursuing travellers, and arresting them—holding courts of trial, and awarding fines, are as radical infringements on holy time, as labor, travelling or recreation. But, when justices, sheriffs, and others, through great self-denial, undertake the holy and meritorious work of promoting good morals, by preventing disorder on the first day of the week, they receive another heart, like Saul ; old things are done away, and all things are become new ; so that, like a goose, they can have one eye to heaven, and the other to earth ; they can keep their hearts with all diligence ; pray, love and forgive ; esteem others better than themselves, and follow every good work, while they are prosecuting profligate and abandoned men. If this is not altogether the case, yet the *end* is so laudable, that it would justify the worst *means* that could be used. And, further, if the very *bulwark of religion* would lead on to battle, on Lake Champlain, and at New Orleans, on Sunday, to overthrow Democracy, who can hesitate to attack Democrats for sabbath-breaking? Likewise, Procrustus made an iron bedstead to measure his subjects by: those who were too long he would lop off, and those who were too short he would stretch, so that all might be of a length; just so we must lop and stretch the opinions and consciences of others, for *we know that we are right.*

Q. With all submission, I will state a certain case, and ask a question upon it. Some years past, a certain Indian was arrested and carried before a justice for sabbath-breaking, as it was called, and was fined a quarter of a dollar for his crime. The Indian very peaceably paid the fine to his honor, and then requested a certificate. Why would you have a certificate? said his honor. Because, said the Indian, bye and bye I die, and go before the Great Spirit for breaking the law, and, if I have no certificate to show that I mended the law, I shall have to go all the way down to hell for you, Mr. Justice, to come as a witness for me that I have mended the law. From this stated case, I ask the question, what will be the future destiny of justices, sheriffs, tything-men and others, who take their own judgments (perhaps their interest) for a test of orthodoxy and good morals, and must stop, keep in custody, and fine others, as good men as themselves, because they do not believe what they cannot believe, and are too honest to be hypocritical?

A. The prospect is gloomy. When they are asked by him who judgeth righteously, "who hath required this at your hands?" their mouths will be shut. The hope and the prayer of the pious is, that they may repent of the evil of their way, and be saved.

FREE THOUGHTS ON WAR.*

If Christianity forbids national war—if the precepts of Christ, "I say unto you that ye resist not evil," etc., were intended for the nations of the earth, and are binding on them, as political bodies, it follows, of course, that all the wars that have been since the introduction of Christianity, have been in direct rebellion against God.

Taking this to be the case, what ought to be done to remedy the evil, and make an atonement for the long perpetuated crime? Those nations of savages, who have never heard the precepts of Christ, are excepted from present animadversion, but those nations that have been favored with the gospel, and now call themselves Christian nations, are particularly addressed.

A reformation, acceptable to God, consists in a disavowal of crimes—turning to the way of future righteousness—and restoring to the injured that which was wrongfully taken away. In this view of the subject, it becomes the kings and rulers, kingdoms and states, of this world, to confess the sin of war—turn to a course of perpetual peace—and restore all the dominion and territory, that has been taken by war, to those from whom they wrested them. Anything short of this would be hypocritical reformation. It is true, that this procedure, in a retrospective chain, would carry most of the nations and territories back to Rome, with Tiberius Cæsar at their head; in which condition the world was when Christianity was introduced.

This would be utterly impracticable. But the now existing kings and rulers, kingdoms and states, have it in their power to make restoration of the dominion and territory, which they now possess, that were taken from others by the horrid crime of war. And for such rulers and states to plead for peace without a restoration, is like the felon who wishes all others to be at peace, that he may quietly possess his stolen goods.

When two men are in single combat, and one casts the other, and holds him, he cries, "Will you be peaceable?" But if the master was in the place of the underling, he would think more of extricating himself than he would of peace.

* First published in 1816.

It is now rumored that the great powers of Europe, particularly Russia and Great Britain, are for giving peace to the world. Russia is the strongest power, by land, in Europe, and likely in the world. Great Britain commands the sea, with her navy, which is far superior to that of any other nation, if not to all other nations. Should these nations, therefore, unite to extirpate war from the earth, and establish universal peace, the poor and needy would resound their praise—the widows and fatherless would bless them. But while they proclaim peace, is it their intention to keep their navies, armies and garrisons in such repairs, that other nations cannot effectually resist them? If so, it is but the boast of complete despotism. The plain language of it is this: "We are masters, and intend to be so; we command you all to be peaceable one with another, and with us in particular; if not, see the rod in our hands, by which we will scourge you until you are peaceable, for we are determined that all others shall be in peace, on the conditions that we prescribe." Did Napoleon ever wish for more? Can a tyrant ask for more? If this state of the world is desirable, why did not Russia, Great Britain, Austria, Prussia, and other powers adopt it seventeen years past? What scenes of horror, and seas of blood it would have prevented.

If the now triumphant kingdoms are convinced of the moral evils of war, and wish to make an atonement for the treasure which they have consumed, the powers which they have overturned, and the lives which they have destroyed, let them now confess, reform, and restore all that they can; but, if they justify their past wars, under the pretence that they were necessary, in order to free the world from the tyranny of Napoleon, and bring it into the happy state which it is now in, other nations may justify future wars, to deliver the world from its present masters, and bring it into a happier state than it is in at present. But if the conviction of the now triumphant kingdoms is genuine, and their desire is to free the world from the cause of war, without seeking their own supremacy, then let them disband all their troops, and dismiss their military officers—demolish all their garrisons—destroy every ship of war—and convert every implement of war into instruments of mechanism and husbandry. Let them, moreover, restore the provinces and territories, with their respective jurisdictions, which they have taken from others, and make declaration that every section of the world shall attach itself to what government they choose, establish that form of government which is most congenial to their wishes, and have those to administer it whom they prefer, and that every man shall be free in his religion, to worship whom, when, and as he pleases, without any interruption. Let this proclamation be made, and put into effect by the great powers, and followed by all the smaller dominions, and all but tyrants, pensioners, and covetous priests, who make merchandise of what they preach, and of the souls of men, would hail the halcyon day. For princes to talk about peace, without coming to this standard, is but mocking the people—seeking to be emblazoned for noble generosity after they have killed and taken possession, without restoring to nations their liberties, and guaranteeing to individuals their inalienable rights.

If the period has arrived when the lust of power, the love of supremacy, and the thirst for wealth, are so far extinguished, that men are willing to be on a level with men, and the Lord alone be exalted by them, universal peace may be expected; otherwise, strife and war are likely to continue.

For a number of centuries a political project has been thought of to prevent the evil of war, which project is now considerably agitated. The project is, "that a great congress shall be formed, by representatives from all the powers of Europe, and by as many more as choose to unite. That no one power shall proclaim war, or commit hostilities against another, but that the cause shall be common. That this congress shall adjust the controversies that may arise between two or more of those powers, and if any one will not submit to the decision, all the rest shall unitedly join to compel them."

As the project has never assumed the character of system, and been put in operation, it is unknown whether the members that are to compose this congress are to be chosen by the people, or appointed by the sovereigns—whether they are to hold their offices for life, during good behavior, or for limited terms—whether each kingdom and state shall have an equal number of members, or whether kingdoms and states shall be represented according to their numbers—whether, in all cases, a majority shall rule, or in some cases more than a majority should be necessary to carry a point—whether the non-submission of a single power, or several of them in concert, shall be suppressed by force of arms, or by non-intercourse only.

Should all these questions, and all others that might arise, be cordially adjusted, and a congress assemble in style, it would remind one of what a barbarian said to the senate of Rome: "My own countrvmen are hydras, but the senate is an assembly of the gods."

In a congress thus formed, it is presumed that every member would have the views and wishes of their respective governments at heart. So long as unity continued among them, so long harmony would remain among the confederate nations; but in case of disagreement, the same evils that now infest the world would arise in all their baleful aspects. From a knowledge of the physical strength of the greater powers ,the smaller ones would feel afraid, as they now do; but supposing the decrees of congress should be contrary to the will of Russia or Great Britain, or against both these powers in connection, would those great powers succumb to the little states for the sake of peace, or would they not more naturally resist? If war is declared to subject the powers that will not acquiesce, the design of the congress, which is to prevent war, will be defeated. If an embargo is appealed to, that none of the confederate nations shall buy or sell any article to the obstinate states, could they enforce it? Would not the avarice and enterprise of the merchant defeat all the laws of congress? It is hard to conceive of any advantage that would arise from a congress thus formed, that does not now exist by friendly embassy, but it is easy to foresee what pomp and expense would attend it.

To prepare the way for a congress to be appointed, to prevent the horrors of war, peace societies are forming to facilitate the grand event. If these societies lay the foundation of their appeal upon this condition: "That on the day of in the year all nations, by their agents, shall meet at for the purpose of affixing the day, when all armies shall be disbanded—all ships of war be sunk in the sea—all forts and garrisons be destroyed—all the instruments of war broken to pieces—all territory and dominion, taken by force of arms, restored to their best claimants—all legal establishments of religion repealed, with a pledge that war never shall be appealed to for any purpose, and that no law shall ever be made to regulate religion, all good men, who understand the genius of Christianity, will give them their support. But if their exertions tend only to prevent the military exertions of one nation of the world, while other nations are waxing stronger and stronger, they must not judge that all those who withhold their support are enemies to human happiness.

The remarks already made originated from the supposition that the precept of Christianity, "resist not evil," was a prohibition of national war; but the precept, connected as it is, looks as much like a prohibition of legal resistance, as it does of military force. If you are compelled, stripped of your coat, persecuted or smitten, never make use of the law to resist the evil, or get redress. Rather than go to law, why do ye not take wrong? Why do ye not rather suffer yourselves to be defrauded?

To see the criminal arrested, dragged before the judge, condemned to the dungeon for life, or hanged—his wife left a sorrowful widow, and his children hungry, naked and destitute orphans—does not the spirit of Christ recoil as much at this as it does when a man is slain in battle?

It is strange that any man should pursue his fellow-men in a legal course that will inevitably kill him, and yet be so scrupulous in his conscience about pursuing any in a military course, which does but kill him. What is the law without the sword? Let a criminal be found guilty by the jury, and condemned by the judge: let it be known by the criminal that the court cannot use the sword to execute the decision, and he would laugh at the sentence. The ministers of God (magistrates) bear not the sword in vain. It is by force and arms that the penal laws are executed. Government, without the sword, is but a cypher, and if the sword is not to be used, all is but a bubble—the powers that are ordained of God are vain.

If Christians, then, in the character of citizens, or in their national compact, are not to resist any kind of injury, what are they to do? Physical strength, and universal uprightness, are all their weapons; if the first is not to be used, the last only can be resorted to: and is a reliance on *right* a sufficient guard for men in a *wrong* world? In a kingdom or commonwealth of Christians—if an individual, Jew, Turk, or Pagan, or a small number of them, should arm themselves with clubs and knives, and begin to kill and plunder at one end of the kingdom or commonwealth, and proceed from house to house with their depredations, must the many ten thousands sit still, and see themselves robbed and killed, and use no resistance, but faithfully preaching unto them, "my friends, ye are wrong?"

Erasmus describes the horrors of war among men, in high shaded colors, but seems to justify it among brutes. For man ne shows great benevolence, but for the whole creation, which groan in painful travail, he discovers no pity. Would the Almighty arm all the animals with weapons of war, and also allow of war in heaven between Michael and his angels, and the Dragon and his angels, and prohibit man alone from self-defence? If men are to learn wisdom from the ant, industry from the bee, and a reliance on Providence from the birds, why not learn more? The brutes have natures and clothing to live without shelter, store-house or barn, but men possessed of reason, which the beasts have not, are to provide these things for themselves. Beasts are clad with a natural armour, men are not; but from reason and experience find it necessary to arm themselves.

That the precepts of Christianity, which enjoin non-resistance on the disciples, were not intended as maxims of state policy, or civil law, appears pretty evident, from the consideration, that Christ never assumed the character of a worldly king, or civil judge. He said his kingdom was not of this world, and he refused to act as judge, in dividing the inheritance of two brethren, and in pronouncing the penalty of the law against the adulterous woman. The direct tendency of Christ's kingdom was the eternal salvation of souls; but the systems of civil law and national war, have nothing to do with souls and eternity. In the case of the dying thief, both governments show their nature and distinctness. The government of men condemned him to death, which he himself said was just, and the government of Christ pardoned his sin. Christ did not deliver him from the penalty of the law, and the decision of the law did not interfere with the government of Christ, which was wonderously displayed, in saying, "This day shalt thou be with me in paradise." The civil judge is not to question whether the cirminal is saint or sinner, or how it will fare with him in the world to come; but these characteristics are all important in the kingdom of Christ.

In war, also, which is the same among nations that courts of trial are among individuals, the moral state, and worth of the soul is out of the question, and national justice is all that is (or ought to be) in view. Nothing can be more preposterous and presumptuous than to declaim, or conceive that all who fall in battle, will undoubtedly go to heaven. The agriculturist, the mechanic, the merchant, the sailor, the scholar and the soldier, in this respect, stand on even ground. The truth is, those who fear God and work righteousness, will be accepted of their Maker, and all others will not. The soldier, therefore, who is a devout saint, if he falls in battle, will go from the field of battle to the regions of glory; but he who is a hardened sinner, falling in battle, will sink where he will lift up his eyes in torment.

Christianity was not designed by its author, to be characteristic of the nations of the earth, in their political state; nor was the name given in the days of its purity, to any but the meek disciples of Christ. The name, however, has been filched by the enemies of Christ, and Christianity has been prostituted to the vilest purposes. Since Christianity became national, Christian nations have been equally cruel and bloodthirsty, and more unjust and perfidious than Turks or heathens. Nevertheless, Christ has a people among these nations, whom he redeemed and washed with his blood—a peculiar people, zealous of good works; they are not of this world, and the world knows them not. These are his disciples indeed. And to these disciples, there are so many commands of non-resistance, patience, forgiveness of offences, praying for enemies, rendering good for evil, and blessing for cursing, that if these disciples are not to be considered in a two-fold capacity, it is notoriously wicked for them to bear arms and go to war, prosecute any one for smiting or robbing them, suing any man for debt, or applying to any legal office to secure the titles of their lands.

By their two-fold capacity, is intended, first, their being members of Christ's body, which is the church; and secondly, their being subjects of the government where they reside.

As members of Christ's body, or kingdom, their weapons are all spiritual. Force and recrimination are forbidden them. Their law is love. Their armor is the word of God for a sword—faith for a shield, and hope for a helmet. Where legal force, and carnal weapons are used among nominal Christians, to convert heathen, punish heretics, establish creeds of faith and forms of worship, collect money, compel attendance on worship, etc. under a religious covert, the commands of Christ to his disciples are broken. If they think they are serving God in it, they know not what manner of spirit they are of.

In the government of Christ among his members, commonly called church discipline, no force or resisting of evil is to be used. The church is to restore such as are overtaken with faults, in the spirit of meekness, warn the unruly, with all the gentleness of Christ—admonish and reject heretics, and cast from among them wicked persons; but church censure extends no farther than non-fellowship. Fines, imprisonments, punishments and civil incapacities, are not imposed by church censure. A declaration of *who* and *what* is fellowshipped, and *who* and *what* is not fellowshipped, is all that the church is to do.

But, if the disciples of Christ are considered in the second capacity that has been suggested, members of civil society, other things may be said. Civil society (which takes its rise from the weakness of individuals to defend themselves from other individuals more daring and villainous than themselves) is a society of force and arms. Rules are formed for the government of this society, called laws, which are either writen or sanctioned by custom; and the whole physical strength of the society is pledged for the execution of those laws, both against the villains among themselves and foreign invaders; and the club, the stone, the knife, the tomahawk, the gallows, or the sword, is the last appeal. It is in vain for men to plead for the use of the law, and deny the utility of the sword; for it is a truth as self-evident as a sun-beam, that the decision of a magistrate, a court or a monarch, would be no more than the song of a nightingale, if the whole military force did not stand ready to support the decision. In this capacity, the saints, in common with others, share the advantages, and ought to bear the burdens of the society proportionably.

War, famine, and pestilence, are the three scourges with which the Almighty chastises rebellious creatures.

War, for the most part, involves in debt, spreads sore distress around, gives place for ambitious knaves to rise, imposes partial burdens on the citizens, is merciless to parental, conjugal and fillial affection, tends to harden and demoralize the people, seldom gains its object, increases the number of widows and orphans, and is a species of human butchery.

Famine, in besieged cities, is often produced by war; but extensive famines are caused by drouth. Famine creates impatience, fosters covetousness, provokes theft and robbery, extinguishes parental affection and social intercourse, preys upon the vitals, gnaws upon the bowels, and ends in painful death. When the whole staff of bread, and the whole stay of water is taken away, the description of famine, by skilful writers, is as follows: "Our skin is become black as an oven, by reason of the terrible famine. The garners are laid desolate, the barns are broken down, for the corn is withered. How do the beasts groan! the herds of cattle are perplexed, because they have no pasture. The fire hath devoured the pastures of the wilderness, and the flame hath burned all the trees of the field. The beasts cry, for the rivers of water are dried up. The hands of the pitiful women have sodden their own children, and eaten them for meat. They that be slain with the sword, are better than they that are slain with hunger, for these pine away for want of the fruits of the earth."

Famine is not only very distressing for the time being, but sometimes leads on to lasting evils. The famine in the days of Joseph, (not to mention the calamities of other countries,) cost the Egyptians all their money and cattle, their liberty, and the fee of their lands; so that afterwards, they were ever servants and tenants of Pharaoh.

Pestilence seems to be descriptive of all the calamities that befal mankind, that are affected by water, fire, wind, disease, or any strange phenomena contrary to the usual course of things. In this sense, however, I shall use the word.

When one thousand six hundred and fifty-six years had elapsed from creation, all the inhabitants of the earth, except eight, were destroyed by a flood of water. The number of souls destroyed in the deluge cannot be well ascertained. Some have said there were eleven, and others eighty thousand millions. The great longevity, health, and prolificacy of that age, suggests the conclusion, that there were more people drowned in the flood than have been slain in all the battles that have been since that time. Half a million is the greatest number of men slain in one battle, that we have an account of in the Old Testament. John, in his visions, gives us an account of a cavalcade of two hundred millions, who slew the third part of men; but whether all these troops paraded in one day, and slaughtered so many, or whether they were all that were called forth and killed during the dynasty of some warlike and triumphant kingdom, he has not told us.

As the old world was destroyed by *water*, so Sodom and Gomorrah, Admah and Zeboim, were consumed by *fire*; not kindled by a wicked incendiary, but rained down from heaven, mixed with brimstone.

The pestilence in Egypt, besides destroying the necessaries of life, cut off the first-born in every house, and drowned Pharaoh, and all his host, in the Red sea. The earth opened her mouth, and swallowed up Korah, Dathan and Abiram, with their rebellious company. Fifty thousand Beth-shemites were smitten to death, for prying too curiously into the ark. One hundred and eighty-five thousand Assyrians were slain in one night, by an angel of the Lord, etc., etc. Add to these the calamities by earthquakes, the eruption of burning mountains, hurricanes on land, and destructive gales at sea, epidemical diseases and raging plagues. If all these are placed with the havoc of war and famine, it will force us to say, "The misery of man is great upon him."

Should any object to the justice of national war, on the principle that it places the burdens on those who have no hand in it—no voice in declaring it, and no ill will against those with whom they fight, let them reflect a moment, and they will find that famine and pestilence are uniform with war, in this respect. Infants, virgins, and the aged fall indiscriminate victims to the ravages of one as well as the other.

Kingdoms and political bodies, like human bodies, contain many members; and, if one member of the body suffers, all the members suffer with it; and, very frequently, for the sin of one member, other members, if not the whole body, bear the punishment: for the sin of the hand, or the tongue, other members suffer, and often the whole body is imprisoned or hanged.

When David sinned, in numbering the people, and not offering a ransom for their souls, the pestilence destroyed seventy thousand of them, of whom David said, "As for these sheep, what have they done?" When Saul, in his wrath, had slain the Gibeonites, three years' famine fell upon Israel, nor could it be assuaged but by the heads of seven of Saul's sons. The blood of all the prophets, from Abel the first, to Zacharias the last, was required of a generation, which had risen many thousand years after some of the murders were committed.

The thing contended for is this, that war was, in the days of the Old Testament, as much used by God, to punish wicked men and wicked nations, as famine or pestilence; and, that the mode of punishing by war, coincides as much with divine justice, equity and goodness, as punishment by famine or pestilence.

That God called Joshua, David, and many others of his favored nation (the Israelites) to wage war, is not more true, than that he called Cyrus, the king of Assyria, and Nebuchadnezzar, to do likewise.

But the great question is, whether national war is appointed by Christ, or can be justified from the New Testament?

That war, famine and pestilence, have continued their ravages among men, since the introduction of Christianity, as much as they did before, will be generally granted, it is presumed; and the same is true of earthquakes, eruptions, etc. But for Christ, in his mediatorial character, to direct national war, would be meddling with the government of this world, which does not appear to be included in his mission. He did not come into the world to teach men the arts of husbandry, mechanism or science. He gave no code of laws for the government of nations, nor pointed out the best mode of administration. He left no orders, whether all nations should adopt the ancient Theocracy of the Israelites, or whether they should govern themselves as reason and justice dictate. He came into the world with the avowed purpose, "To glorify God on earth—to seek and save that which was lost—to lay down his life for his sheep—to wash sinners from their sins in his own blood—to magnify the law, make an atonement for sin, and bring in everlasting righteousness—to abolish death, and open a new and living way into the kingdom of glory—to save men by the washing of regeneration and the renewing of the Holy Ghost," etc. Having these great works to finish, (all of which tended to the *eternal salvation of the souls of men,*) he did not intermeddle with the affairs of this world, but left the wheels of commerce and government to roll on as Providence led the way.

The *great silence*, however, in the New Testament, about war, has more signification than words could have. Had Christ given a precept that, in certain cases, it was the duty of kingdoms and states to wage war, every nation would make such cases their own, though the war which they waged was ever so unjust. Had he, on the other hand, given a precept that every species of war was criminal, the whole would have been exposed by robbery and death, by the cruelty of an individual, or a few, at most. But, although there is no direct precept in the New Testament, for or against national war, yet there are some useful hints given to direct our minds in research.

John was the forerunner of Christ, and his ministry is called "the beginning of the gospel of Christ." He admitted those to his baptism, who repented of their sins, and gave evidence of their repentance, by bringing forth its fruits. Some of these were soldiers, who asked the divine teacher "what they should do?" John never suggested to them that a military life was incompatible with the gospel, and that they must quit the sword, if they would follow the Lamb of God who stood among them; but prudently answered them, "Do violence to no man, (who is a private citizen,) neither accuse any falsely, (for a pretence to kill him,) and be content with your wages." If your work was unjust, your wages would be unrighteous; but, while you do your duty, be content with your pay, and not covet more.

A centurion (captain of an hundred men) sent to Christ, requesting him to speak a healing word, that his favorite sick servant might live. The condescending Saviour answered his request—healed his servant—gave him no reproof for bearing the sword—no orders to relinquish the army; but said of him, "I have not found so great faith in Israel."

Another centurion we read of, who was a devout man, that feared God with all his house, who gave much alms to the people, and prayed to God always. The character given him is excellent; but he had not, as yet, heard of the gospel way of salvation. As he was at prayer, he was warned of God, by a holy angel, to send for a New Testament preacher; and the preacher was also warned by a vision to go to the centurion, and tell him the way of salvation, and *what he ought to do.* Peter came, accordingly, and preached to him the forgiveness of sins, in the name of Jesus; and, when the Holy Ghost fell on him, and those that were assembled with him, Peter commanded them to be baptized in the name of the Lord; but gave him no reproof for bearing a military commission—no orders to resign his command of the Italian band.

The parable of the marriage made for the king's son, and the dinner made ready, is so self-evident in its meaning, that all interpreters are agreed about it. The king's son, is Christ. The sumptuous dinner, intends the blessings of grace in the gospel, including forgiveness of sins and eternal life. The first bidden guests were the Jews, who made light of it, and murdered the servants of the king: they both killed the Lord Jesus and their own prophets—persecuted the apostles—pleased not God, and were contrary unto all men. For their opposition to the truth, and malice prepense against the messengers of it, He (the king) *sent forth his armies, and destroyed those murderers, and burnt up their city.* That these armies intend the Roman legions, these murderers, the Jews, and the city, Jerusalem, there seems to be no real doubt. This event took place more than three score years after the beginning of the Christian era. Here, then, is one instance in which the Almighty made use of war, after the gospel dispensation took place; and wars and rumors of wars have been in the world ever since. Many of the sore calamities, which God inflicts on wicked nations, (spoken of in the book of Revelations,) are evidently effected by the scourge of war.

But one thing should be particularly noticed, viz., that war was never appointed by God, by an *original statute.* Laws of civil government—putting away wives—war and such like precepts, *were not from the beginning.* As they all presuppose SIN in creatures, they could not have been appointed until sin had taken place. But after rebellious creatures had kindled the fire of hatred and war, the Almighty varied his precepts to meet their condition, and of course appointed war, which rebellious creatures had made, to punish them for their rebellion. This was the case in Old Testament times, and is as true in these days.

The Old Testament seems to be a kind of accommodation of God to fallen barbarous men, containing the best rules that the conditon and general good of the world would admit of, having its special bearings towards the Jews.

The New Testament is not fraught with a code of civil laws, or national maxims, but has the salvation of souls for its object.

It appears, therefore, proper to examine the rise and rage of war among men, and whether any or all wars can be justified, on the principle of *eternal right and wrong.* Acknowledging this, however, in our examination, that the principle of eternal right and wrong, like a golden cord, runs through the Old and New Testaments, and shines with a thousand times more effulgence, than human reason can paint it with.

It is reasonable to conclude that the parent of all rational beings allots to each of them a certain degree of national right and independence, which no other individual, nor many individuals, in concert, ought to deprive him of. If this was not the case, individuals would never feel guilt for what they do, nor be accountable to their Maker for their deeds; but society must bear the whole. But as guilt preys upon individuals for overt acts, and as every one must give an account of himself to his Maker, the argument is conclusive that each has a measure of original right, of which he cannot justly be deprived. In this measure of natural right, exist *life, liberty and property*. Should one individual, therefore, be attacked by another individual, or a number of them in connection, in quest of life, liberty or property, the injured individual has a just right to use his weapon to defend himself, and if blood and life are lost in the contest, the guilt falls upon the assailants.

If no resistance can be justly offered to repel violence, it would follow of course, that one or two individuals might arm themselves, and destroy whole nations.

This kind of assault began with the first man that ever was born of a woman. His works were evil, and he slew his brother, and has ever since been called a murderer.

In process of time, individuals found it necessary to form into collective bodies, to withstand the aggressions of daring individuals and banditti. And what was unjust or expedient among individuals at first, became unjust or expedient among these collective bodies, now called governments and nations of the earth.

As an individual who assaults and kills another, is a guilty murderer, so the nation that wages war, out of vain glory, from enmity, through covetousness, or from any other motive than *self-defence*, is guilty of murder, and will be treated by the King of kings as such. For notwithstanding any use that the Almighty may make of war, as a scourge to wicked nations, yet the nation that plunges voluntarily into it, is always criminal. Let all unrighteous, offensive wars cease, and there cannot be any righteous defensive wars on earth : for, if there is no assailant, there can be no defendant.

When one nation or government encroaches upon the territory or property of another government, dictates the other about her laws or rulers, or sheds the blood and enslaves the persons of her citizens, whether it is done under a proclamation of war or not, it is offensive war. And after the injured government has remonstrated and exercised all becoming patience, if a cessation and restitution do not follow, a *defensive war* seems not only justifiable but imperious ; for the nation that does not contend for its own *right*, contends for the *wrong* of the encroaching nation.

Although Christianity, in its purest state, was not national, but personal and ecclesiastic, yet it is now become a national characteristic, to distinguish those nations where Christianity is professed, from Pagans, Turks and Jews.

Granting the propriety of the title, (which in fact is very disputable,) these nations, as bodies politic, may wage war upon the same footing as other nations, and on no other, viz., to defend their lives, liberty and property from the hands of those who assault them without cause. Nothing can be more horrid and wicked, than for these Christian nations to form their crusades and holy wars to convert the heathen, violently take away the land of the savages and make slaves of the prisoners.

But supposing there was a kingdom or commonwealth, of not only nominal Christians, but of real disciples of Jesus, whose hearts and practices were as perfect as this state of the world admits of, would it be lawful and duty for them to proclaim war, on any account?

This question is predicated upon a supposition which has never existed, it is presumed, since Christianity was introduced among men. The tares and the wheat have grown together, and will continue to do so until the harvest. Some colonies, however, have been settled by companies that made some advances towards it; but Roger Williams, Mr. Davenport and William Penn, with their respective associates, in Rhode Island, New Haven and Pennsylvania, found so many tares among themselves, that they were obliged to have civil law (which is always sanctioned by the sword) to govern by. And notwithstanding Williams and Penn were great favorites of the savages, yet those colonies were involved in war.

There is no doubt but many of those good people, who condemn national war of every description, are *sincere* in their profession; but should there be a commonwealth, in which all the leading characters, who control the destinies of bodies politic, were real saints, and conscience bound against all war, should that commonwealth be invaded by a hostile army, of less physical strength than the commonwealth possessed, is there any doubt but what the citizens of said commonwealth would *sincerely* change their opinion? Would they not be guilty of neglecting the means which were in their hands, to defend themselves from the *wrong* of others, if they did not? Could not the most pious saint meet the hostile foe, in such a case, with the high praises of God in his mouth, and a two edged sword in his hand? Could he not do as a venerable old man did at Deerfield, in an Indian war? Said he, "I met an Indian, and I loved him; but to defend my *right* from his *wrong*, after praying the Lord to have mercy on his soul, I shot a bullet through his heart."

In the first settlement of Hartford, the inhabitants lived in a fort; but a young woman going out of the fort, was taken by two Indians and led to their canoe in the river. As soon as she was missed, two of their gunners took their guns and ran to the river, accompanied by Mr. Hooker, their preacher. The Indians had placed the young woman in the canoe, and were rowing off, keeping the canoe in such direction, that the gunners on shore could not well hit them without hitting the young woman. The gunners saw that in a short time the canoe would be out of gunshot, and cried out, "Mr. Hooker, what shall we do?" The venerable man stretched his hands and turned his eyes towards heaven, and answered, "Take good sight, and heaven direct the balls." They shot and killed both the Indians and the girl rowed back to the shore.

In this case, I ask whether the war, proclaimed by Mr. Hooker, and carried on by the two hunters, against the Indians, was according to the spirit of Christ, or not? I think the question answers itself.

We may reason from a unit to a universe: that which is right or wrong in an individual, would be the same in a government. Such kind of defensive war, is the only war that can be justified upon the principle of eternal right; all other wars are robbery, piracy and murder. And yet, the misanthropy and barbarity of fallen men are so great, that wars waged in avarice, on purpose to plunder—in ambition to rise high in esteem—or through hatred to a rival, are called honorable wars; and the more they can slaughter, the more splendid is the battle; while those who fall of their own, are said to be covered with glory; and, if they succeed to deprive the nation with whom they are at war, of all its sovereignty and rights, *Te Deum* is chanted, and the leaders of the war are led in triumph.

Military force, whether armed with staves, stones, battle-axes, swords or fire-arms, should never be called forth, but to repel invasions, suppress insurrections, and enforce the laws. The words of Washington, in his last will and testament, breathe forth the spirit of a good citizen. In bequeathing his sword to his kinsman, he adds, "Never draw it but in defence of your country's rights; and, when drawn, never sheath it until the object is attained."

It is a melancholy thought, that, in all ages, men, as individuals and as nations, have been so ungrateful, covetous, and full of misanthropy, that justice and goodness could not restrain them without the scourge of severity; but, when the King of kings gives orders to "loose the four angels, which are prepared to kill the third part of men," it is "in righteousness—HE doth judge and make war." So individuals, in prosecuting other individuals, and nations, in warring with other nations, should do it out of *love to right*, and not from a *spirit of hatred.*

The man who prosecutes his neighbor before a legal bar, does, in fact, declare war with him, as much as one nation does with another when it commences military hostilities. How happy it would be for the world, if there was so much virtue in it, that no kind of war would be necessary! If every man and every nation would do right to their neighbors, there would not and could not be any war on earth. But the reasoning is irrefutable, that those individuals who conduct in a manner that justifies a legal prosecution against them, when collected together in a political body, would conduct so as to justify a war of hostilities against them.

The path is plain before us: let no individual work ill to his neighbor, and let no nation be unjust to another, and war will cease forever.

As things are managed at present, if not an individual, yet a few control the destinies of each nation. The mass of the people are so ignorant that they know not why war is proclaimed, or so circumstanced that they cannot help it. In such cases, some fight for a living, and others because they are forced to. To conquer or to be conquered leaves them in the same predicament. This is a sore evil under the sun, but it is common among men.

The religion of Jesus, in its genuine course, fills men with such meekness and philanthropy, that, if it was *universally* possessed, there would be no prosecution at law, nor any wars among men. But, when Christianity is prostituted, to be the characteristic of an unhallowed nation—a principle of state policy—a test to office—a footstool to promotion—a sinecure to religious orders, and a piece of merchandise, it ever will be, as it ever has been, followed by war and slaughter.

Among nations, as among individuals, it frequently happens that each party has injured the other; and, if they plunge into war in that predicament, it is like the potsherds of the earth striving with the potsherds of the earth. Innocency has nothing to plead; justice has nothing to hope. If they mutually make confession and restoration, war will be prevented. If one party only makes all reasonable concessions, and the other party makes none, but rushes into war, the offence lies on the side of the last party, and the first is the defendant.

In this wrong world, right does not always take place. "Truth faileth in the streets, and equity cannot enter;" hence, victory and triumph often attend the basest tyrant, while the unoffending are trodden down like the mire of the street. The king of Babylon conquered and subjugated more than twenty-five kingdoms (see Jeremiah xxv.) and made them drink the bitter cup. The Lord used him as a scourge to those wicked nations; but, as they had done the king of Babylon no harm, he was wicked in his offensive wars upon them; and, therefore, in his turn, the king of Sheshach (Babylon) was made to drink after them.

RIGHT will finally take place. Though the contest between truth and error, right and wrong, is long, and, to appearance, very doubtful in its issue, yet truth and right must triumph at last.

A RAY FOR THE SUN.*

In a parody between Dean Swift and Alexander Pope, the following fracas took place. Swift was a Churchman, and Pope was a Papist. The Dean offered Pope twenty pounds to change his religion, to which offer the ingenious poet replied: "the Dean of St. Patrick's cannot be serious! twenty pounds to change my religion! it is more than any clergyman ever gave for any religion, from the days of Moses until the present time."

In the Mosaic economy, the Levites lived on tythes, but a tenth part of their tythes they gave to the Aaronites: this was the tax which the Levites paid. But is there not too much truth in the implication of Pope, in these days, that ministers stimulate others to honor the Lord with their substance, but touch not the burden themselves with one tip of a finger? To accuse them of covetousness would be illiberal; perhaps the whole defect arises from the want of system. I would, therefore, propose a scheme to raise a fund for the relief of the indigent, by items which the people will never feel. Let every minister retrench his expenses so that he may give a tenth part of his salary, including what he gets from parish votes, donations, and marriage fees. And let him labor in the field one day in ten, (Sundays excepted,) the wages to be applied to benevolent uses. Moreover, as ministers are exempted from bearing arms, and paying taxes, some returns to the public are due therefor, otherwise they would be partially eased, while others would be partially burthened.

Suppose there are four hundred settled ministers in Massachusetts, (which is a moderate estimate,) and that in average they receive five hundred dollars per annum, this would make a sum of two hundred thousand dollars. The tenth part of which would be twenty thousand dollars, which might be considered as the first item.

The tenth part of the days of labor, in a year, is more than thirty, but let thirty be accepted of. Each of the four hundred ministers laboring thirty days in a year, would be twelve thousand days. State the wages of each day at twenty-five cents only, (for it is possible that some of them would make but awkward work with the hoe and pitchfork,) and the amount will be three thousand dollars.

---

* Published in the Pittsfield Sun, 1818.

The benefit which they receive from the exemption of taxes and bearing arms I have no data to judge by. I will fix it, therefore, at ten dollars for each, and if any of them think it is too much, let them equip themselves and perform military duty, and pay their taxes and work at the highways, and this shall exempt them, otherwise the sum arising from this source would be four thousand dollars, making in all a sum total of twenty seven thousand dollars.

Let this fund be appropriated to the assistance of young men who have no interest. Their fathers labored hard to support the ministers, educate pious youth for the ministry, and to send out missionaries, and they, with their fathers, sweat in the burning sun, and shivered with the cold to aid their fathers to make those benevolent donations, but now, when they come to an age when they must shift for themselves, how gloomy is the prospect before them!

Their fathers have neither land nor money for them, and being thus destitute, they fall into an indolent despair, and relapse into the course of violating the sabbath, frequenting the taverns and gaming table, and end their days in the state prison, or on the gallows. Whereas, if they had only had the assistance of two hundred dollars to start with, it is reasonable to suppose that they would have pursued a course more reputable to themselves and more beneficial to their country.

The fund, already described, would annually assist one hundred and thirty-five, distributing to each of them the sum of two hundred dollars, and how many blessings would they pour on the heads of their patrons for the relief! How strong their conviction that their fathers had been disposing of their money to educate and support an order of men who did not wish to grind the faces of the poor, and take from them burdens of wheat, and prepare war against every one who did not put into their mouths, but an order of men, who, from the purest motives, sought to make their fellow-creatures virtuous and happy.

As a fund of this kind, wisely distributed, would relieve and save many every year, so, likewise, it would be a salutary check to prevent unworthy characters from crowding into the ministry. The drawbacks and duties necessary to form the items of this fund would check those who have filthy lucre or indolent ease in view. It would, moreover, be the most effectual defeat of all such sarcasms as Pope complimented the Dean with, and leave the ministers more affluent than Paul was, who endured hunger and nakedness, and far more so than HE who went about doing good, but had not where to lay his head.

MISSIONARY SOCIETIES.*

A CORRESPONDENT in Palestine, in a late letter to his friend in this country, dated at Nazareth, in Galilee, writes thus:

"By a great number of pamphlets, said to be Evangelical Magazines, and a great variety of other writings, purporting to be of a religious nature, forwarded to this country, we have received correct and authentic knowledge of numerous missionary societies, and other societies of a like kind, formed and very zealously supported in New England, and adjoining parts, in North America. Believing that these zealous societies wish for useful assistance in the great work they have undertaken, we are happy to inform you—which information you will please to communicate to these societies—that, about seventeen hundred years ago, a missionary society was formed and instituted in this country. Having had access to the records and minutes of this society, we are able, with great pleasure, to state to you, that the great design and objects of this society were not of this world. The chairman, or president, or more properly speaking, the founder of this society, was a person whose character is divine, and altogether lovely; his name, according to the records, is Jesus Christ. The more effectually to accomplish the great objects in view, he associated to himself twelve assistants, taken chiefly from that class of men known by the appellation of fishermen, and constantly going about doing good, was, himself the most self-denying and laborious of all in promoting the all-important ends of the mission. The missionary work increasing greatly, a meeting of the society was called and holden about the year thirty. Present at this meeting, the president and the twelve assistants. After considering the extensiveness of the missionary ground, and the importance of thoroughly promoting the missionary work, seventy missionaries were appointed and sent out into a great variety of places, which the president himself designed afterwards to visit. Their instructions, with orders to report after they had accomplished their mission, were these: "Go your ways, and, as ye go, preach, saying, the kingdom of heaven is at hand. Provide neither gold, nor silver, nor brass in your purses, nor scrip for your journey, neither two coats, nor yet shoes, for the workman is worthy of his meat, and that they should eat such things as were set before them." Having fulfilled the duties of their appointment, they made their report

* First published in 1818.

with great joy in the success of their mission, not that they had gained money in great or small sums, but that even the devils were subject to them through the name of the president. The president highly approved their fulfilment of their mission, and congratulated them on their success; but, at the same time, informed them that their highest cause of joy was, that their names were written in heaven. About three years after this, on a very trying occasion, in the midst of a vast concourse of people, he addressed his missionaries, and said, 'When I sent you without purse and scrip and shoes, lacked ye anything?' And they said, nothing. It is the unanimous opinion of the people of Galilee, that, had the president and members of this society, together with their missionaries, declined engaging in the labors of their mission, until ample funds for their abundant pay and support had been collected and fixed on permanent security, the work, which they so remarkably performed, would never have been entered upon, even to this day.

"When the people of Galilee consider the unceasing solicitations, and that in a great variety of shapes, which are made for money, by your missionary societies; the numerous and continual collections and contributions that are made for them; the amazing sums they have funded; and the presidents and directors of the New England, and other missionary societies, almost wholly taken up in managing money matters; even descending to obtain from the unsuspecting little children, the few cents which are given them by their friends; and, at the same time, a few young and inexperienced persons, with great salaries fixed upon them, sent out as missionaries; (and, at the same time, probably, parish-hunting;) they are strongly persuaded that your missionary societies are unacquainted with this ancient Galilean society; or, if they have heard of it, they pay little or no attention to its example. The inhabitants of Galilee, to be sure, after being made acquainted with their schemes and practices, wish to be excused from having a branch of the New England missionary society, or any of the missionary societies of their neighborhood, established in Nazareth, or in any part of their country; being altogether better satisfied with the missionary society anciently established in this country, and which we ardently wish to see flourish in its power and purity, not only in Palestine, but in America, and in all the earth."

SHORT ESSAYS ON GOVERNMENT,

AND THE PROPOSED REVISION OF THE CONSTITUTION OF GOVERNMENT FOR THE COMMONWEALTH OF MASSACHUSETTS.*

THE first seventeen hundred years of the world's age elapsed, without any kind of government in it, but parental and patriarchal, that we have any account of.

The Genesian history is short, and, to us, rather obscure, which leaves the enquirer to the fertility of his own conjecture. As the inhabitants of the earth increased, a number of them journeyed westward, and finding a beautiful plain, they formed themselves into a kind of political body, and said, "go to, let *us* build *us* a city, and a tower, whose top may reach unto heaven; and let *us* make *us* a name, lest *we* be scattered abroad upon the face of the whole earth." Nothing monarchical in this language—all is confederate. These confederates were scattered abroad for their pride and impiety; and Nimrod, the unblushing sinner before the Lord, who formed a party in his favor, and hunted down men like beasts, laid the foundation of his kingdom in Babel and the adjacent country. If it may be supposed that Nimrod was one of the confederates, and by his address gained an ascendency over the rest, or that he formed a banditti and came and scattered the confederates abroad, and took possession of their territory; however this may be conceived of, one thing is certain: The character of these confederates, and of Nimrod in particular, is such, that the thing is certain, that DOMINION WAS NOT FOUNDED IN GRACE.

From this rise of government, in the eighteenth century, until the introduction of Christianity, which was more than two thousand years, all kinds of dominion were tested, from the most absolute monarchy, to the most licentious mobocracy.

In the twenty-fifth century the Almighty established the Sinai government, which was afterwards new modified, to meet the conditions of the Israelites, which government is commonly called the Jewish Theocracy. In the first establishment of this government, there was neither executive nor legislature. Judges only were appointed, but no salaries provided for

* Published in 1820.

them. It was not then understood that judges must have honorable salaries, to qualify them to give righteous decisions.

The Romans tried kings, consuls, dictators, decemvirs, tribunes and emperors, and had shut the temple of Janus, and quietly submitted to the imperial dignity of Cæsar Agustus, when Christ was born. All other powers were then subordinate to Rome.

It cannot be supposed that the Almighty had the same agency in forming codes of laws for all the nations as he had in the Jewish code ; yet he endowed all with reason and the principle of self-defence, to seek their own safety and happiness, and raised up Phareoh to show forth his power, Cyrus for his shepherd, the Assyrian for his rod, Nebuchadnezzar for his servant, &c., and frequently rebuked the nations for their pride, injustice, idolatry and cruelty, and is, therefore, with propriety called the king and governor of *all* nations. The conclusion is, that the *powers* that were in existence when Christianity was set up, *were of God*, although in the hands of heathens. To these powers, the Christians were commanded to submit: not to speak evil of dignities, but pray for all in authority, knowing that magistrates are God's ministers, set for the punishment of evil doers, and the praise of them who do well. How undeniable the fact, that civil government is not founded on Christianity.

The greatest civilians, who equally contend for the *rights* of individuals and the *energies* of government, are in the habit of enumerating certain *rights* of which the citizens cannot be deprived, but by despotic tyranny. And nations that are wise, form their constitutions of government as charters of *rights* retained, and of *powers* granted. Indeed there are some rights which may or may not be surrendered, and the quantum of sacrifice depends upon the exigence of the time and the object to be obtained. But there are other *rights* which individuals possess, so inalienable in their nature that they *cannot* be surrendered. The tyrant himself cannot acquire them, nor can individuals grant them. Like sight, hearing, thinking and breathing, they are always attached to individuals. Of this description are the *rights of conscience and private judgment.* Men will have an opinion of what is right and wrong, and their consciences will accuse or excuse themselves for what they do. But notwithstanding conscience and private judgment are both inalienable, yet they are radically distinct in their exercises. Conscience never goes abroad, but opinion ranges the world over. One man's best judgment may dictate what God his neighbor ought to adore, on what days or hours he should adore him, what creed he should believe and what ceremonies perform, but conscience has nothing to do with all this. The liberty and duty of one man is not judged by another man's conscience. One man has his reasons to believe that another man believes and does wrong ; the last has the same opinion of the first ; which of the two is to be umpire ? To their own master each of them stands or falls. Conscience takes cognizance of the home department, but meddles not with foreigners. How improper, how unjust, how anti-Christian it must be, for one man or one party of men to get that kind of religion interwoven into the civil constitution, which they believe is best, under the pretence that their consciences are wounded if others do not believe like themselves. The plea of conscience, in such cases, is the art of ill design, or the effect of imposition, which none but tyrants or bigoted enthusiasts will make.

Pure Christianity is the only religion, ever known on earth, that met the guilty sinner's needs, and relieved his woes. It brings pardon for the rebellious—cleansing for the polluted, and life for the dead. Ten thousand times ten thousand and thousands of thousands have felt its divine efficacy, and are now drinking of rivers of pleasure, where their God is their glory. But still a question arises, whether Christianity, as a national characteristic, or political institute, has ever been of any advantage to the nations and governments on earth, in their collective capacities ? Was Rome more virtuous or prosperous after Christianity was established there, than it was when Paganism was their religion ? Are the papal kingdoms, now subject to the see of Rome, governed by Christian princes, and directed by the successor of Peter, more honest, peaceable, chaste, brave in war, or renowned for just maxims of jurisprudence, than they were under Pagan rulers ?

Can Christian nations produce greater geniuses than Greece and Athens —more superb cities than Babylon and Nineveh—or more flourishing commerce than Tyrus ? Was there ever a more unjust and cruel conquest than that of Spain over South America ? Or when was there ever a confederation of Goths, Vandals and Moors, more unreasonable, mischievous and disasterous, than the crusades, etc., etc.

If simple Christianity is all innocent and interesting, and yet the most horrid evils have existed, and do still exist, in Christian kingdoms and states, the cause should be sought for, and shunned.

The kingdom of Christ is not of this world—all parts of it are unlike everything in state policy. He never interfered with Cæsar's dues—would not act as civil judge in dividing the inheritance between two brethren, or in giving judgment on the adulterous woman. He claimed no civil prerogative, and had no civil promotion to bestow on his followers. When he pardoned the sin of a criminal, and promised him admission into Paradise, he yet left him to bear the penalty of the law, which he had broken. And he told his disciples that, if they had given offence to any other, which was actionable at law, to settle the matter quickly, lest a civil process should bring them before the judge, who, finding them guilty, would deliver them to the executive officer ; and, if that should take place, the religion which they professed would not deliver them until they had paid the last farthing.

Had the rulers of this world been as cautious of intruding on Christ's prerogative and government, the evils complained of would never have existed.

Christianity was introduced in a peaceable, harmless manner: it asked only for a dispassionate hearing, with a correspondent faith, grounded on facts and undeniable evidence. And, by appealing to the reason and judgment of men, without being armed with royal edicts, military force, or aided by the college, and the wisdom of this world; but, in opposition to all of them, it prevailed with that astonishing rapidity, that, in less than three hundred years, it overturned an empire that claimed universal sway. The founding of a Christian college in Alexandria, to polish the Christians like rubies, and make Christianity itself mechanical; and the establishment of Christianity, by Constantine, to be the only religion tolerated in the vast empire—allowing none but Christians to fill offices of state—building and ornamenting temples for their use—providing fat salaries for the ministers—appointing the first day of the week for Christian sabbath, or auction day, for the mechanical Christian auctioneers to vend their wares, etc.

All these things together made the Christians shine like carbuncles. The error of Constantine did not exist in his delivering the Christians from the bloody hands of Pagans. So far he was right. But his great error was giving the same fatal dagger, which the Pagans had used, unto the Christians, who soon used it with as bloody hands.

That Constantine founded his government on Christianity, is certain; for he allowed none but Christians to bear rule. That Christianity was disrobed of apostolical order, and ravished of her virgin chastity, by this establishment, cannot be confuted. By the *imperial Christian* establishment, arose the shocking monster of *Christian nation*.

When Christianity becomes national, a majority who govern the church will be ungodly men, and have recourse to law and coercive measures to regulate religion; and, as all men are not stamped in the mill of uniformity, the strongest party will oppress the weakest.

Government is the formation of an association of individuals, by mutual agreement, for mutual defence and advantage; to be governed by specific rules. And, when rightly formed, it embraces Pagans, Jews, Mahometans and Christians, within its fostering arms—prescribes no creed of faith for either of them—proscribes none of them for being heretics, promotes the man of talents and integrity, without inquiring after his religion—impartially protects all of them—punishes the man who works ill to his neighbor, let his faith and motives be what they may. Who, but tyrants, knaves and devils, can object to such government?

It follows, of course, that a man has a *civil right* to believe that which is *erroneous*, and do that which is *morally* wrong. Nor can this liberty be taken from him, without supporting the doctrine, that a man's religion affects his civil capacity; which doctrine has occasioned the persecution and bloodshed of all the saints and martyrs on earth.

Who is to be judge, whether a man believes truth or error, or whether his exercises (that no wise effect the civil compact) are right or wrong? The decision belongs not to the body politic; for neither legislators, judges nor jurors, in their official capacities, have anything to do with consciences, souls or eternity.

It is the glory of the United States, that, after Christian tyranny had raged with savage fury for fifteen hundred years, its progress should be arrested in this land of liberty. Rhode Island, New York and Pennsylvania, produced the first fruits of delight, that abound in a state where persons, property and equal right are protected by law, and Christianity left in the hands of its author, and conscience free in the hearts of each possessor.

The new experiment succeeded beyond their calculation, and rose so high in esteem, that the framers of the constitution of government for the United States, interwove the sacred principle into the body of that charter of rights retained and powers granted, by which the states in union are now governed. And the benign influence of this state of things has prevailed in almost all of the states, in their local government, either in the first formation of their constitutions, or by revisions afterwards. In Massachusetts, however, the priniciple is not recognized. A religious test is required. The legislature is empowered to make laws to oblige the people to support Protestant teachers of piety, morality and religion. Papal Christian teachers cannot be provided for like Protestants. Pagans, Jews, Turks and Deists cannot be promoted to office, except they declare and subscribe a lie. But, as there is *now* legislative provision made for the revision of the constitution of government for the commonwealth of Massachusetts, a few strictures will here be made on the *religious* parts of the existing constitution, with a proposed amendment annexed.

According to the existing constitution, all the members of the executive and legislative departments, must make and subscribe the following declaration, viz.: "I do declare that I believe the Christian religion, and have a firm persuasion of its truth." This reminds us of ancient sayings: "If thou believest with all thine heart, thou mayest, but he that doubteth is damned." But, supposing God has hidden the mystery of the truth from the wise and prudent, and revealed it only unto babes: that none of the princes of this world know these things, and that the world, by wisdom, cannot find them out; must men of talents be proscribed, because God has has not given them the like gift of faith? The declaration is a good one for man to make when joining a Christian church; but in this place, his Christian confession is prostituted to civil purposes. When a man is elected to fill those places, the question is, "has he talents—is he honest?" and not whether he is a firm believer. A very ingenius author has informed us, that God has concluded all Jews and Gentiles in unbelief; from which interpreters tell us, that all men, in their natural state, until they are renewed by the Holy Ghost, are unbelievers. If this is true, no unregenerate man can make the declaration, without giving God the lie. The conclusion is, that government is founded on Christian grace; and consequently, where this grace is wanting, there can be no government.

When I look over the declaration of rights, the second and third articles remind me of the last will and testatment of a dying man, who prefaces his will with a creed of his faith. Perhaps, in countries where heresy works corruption of blood, it is proper to confess an orthodox creed; but in the United States, such testimonies, make the legacies neither larger nor surer. If a like creed was to preface every bond, note, or any instrument of writing, the loss of time and paper, would be the only injury sustained. But, where such creeds grant powers and jeopardize rights, they are of more consequence. The articles under consideration, were evidently formed as a compromise of conflicting parties, and as the powers granted militated against the provisions made, all was clothed in ambiguity, to give each party hope. A man once wrote a letter to his attorney, but after he had written he could not read it. He then handed it to his son to read it for him, but his son could not. The man then folded up the letter and sent it to the attorney, saying, "Never mind it, my son, the lawyer is a better scholar than we are." I have conversed with a number of the sages who formed the constitution, and they could never reconcile the conflicting parts of those two articles, either to my conception or their own satisfaction.

When I read of the investure of the legislature, and how the power invested in that body is to operate, (treated of in the fore part of the third article,) and compare it with the last clause in the same article, I am involuntarily led to reflect on the prayer of a man, who sometimes prayed for the Lord to reign, and at other times, that the devil might triumph. When he was asked, why he prayed both ways, he answered, he did not know which of the two would prevail, and therefore chose to keep friends on both sides.

One thing is certain, that a number of distraints have been made, and many lawsuits commenced for ministerial taxes since the adoption of the constitution; and courts have given interpretation of some parts of the article, that common sense could never have thought of. The part of the article alluded to, reads thus: "And all monies paid by the subject, to the support of public worship, and of the public teachers aforesaid, shall, if he require it, be uniformly applied to the support of the public teacher or teachers of his own religious sect," etc. The personal he, refers back to a governing substantive of the same number; it cannot, therefore, take *teachers* for an antecedent, for that is plural, and the following pronoun would be *they*; it must, therefore, refer back to the word *subject*. The sense is, then, that when the money is paid by a subject, to the support of public worship and public teachers, the money shall be given to the *teacher*, that the *subject* requires.

This exposition, however, is generally overruled by courts of law, and the personal *he*, is interpreted to intend the *teachers*. Hence, when a man has paid his ministerial tax, the *teacher* of his choice must bring suit to draw the money out of the treasury.

What shocking work is all this, in the eyes of a Bible Christian, and the more so, as it is done under the cloak of befriending the gospel of Jesus Christ.

Of all instruments of writing, constitutions of government should be the most plain and free from ambiguity; and, if articles of religion must be crowded into frames of government, they should be so simple that the most illiterate part of community may understand them.

For heathen to persecute, hang and burn Christians, is horrid barbarity; but, for one Christian sect to torture another, is worse. This, however, always has been the case where Christianity has been made a national characteristic, and religion a political institute, and, (without the spirit of prophecy,) I am confident it ever will be.

For the good of man, therefore, I hope that in the contemplated revision of the constitution, the following amendment will be made to supply the place of the second and third articles in the declaration of rights.

Amendment.—The legislature of this commonwealth shall have no power to establish any kind of religion, either in the object of adoration, creed or faith, forms of worship, or times of service; but all men shall be left free to worship their God according to the dictates of their consciences.

No man shall be considered a member of any religious society, or any way bound to support the worship or teachers thereof, until he has voluntarily joined himself therewith. And, if he sees causes to leave the society which he has joined, by lodging a written cirtificate with the clerk of said society, of his intentions, he shall not be holden to pay anything for the support of that society, or the teacher thereof, which shall be assessed after the date of his cirtificate.

No man's religious opinions, shall, in any wise, effect his civil capacity; but every man shall be encouraged to declare his sentiments, and by argument, support them.

No religious test or declaration shall ever be required to qualify a man to fill any post of office or trust in the commonwealth.

If any man, under religious pretence, disturbs the peace, or commits any overt act, he shall be punished by law for his transgression, and pitied for his heresy.

OLD THUMPER.

APPENDIX

TO A PAMPHLET WRITTEN BY REVEREND JUSTUS HULL, CONTAINING A COMMENT ON ROMANS XI., 16, 17, PUBLISHED 1822.

First. The Jews circumcised their male children only, but the Christians baptize (rantize) both male and female.

Second. The Jews never circumcised a child under eight days old. In ordinary cases, no other day would answer. A weekly sabbath might be profaned, that the law of Moses (respecting circumcision) might not be broken: but the Christians baptize their childen at any age. If they are sick, and likely to die, a priest is called to baptize them before they are half eight days old.

Third. Circumcision was never a priestly rite among the Jews, but fathers, mothers, masters, and neighbors, did the work; but infant baptism is supposed to belong to the priests. Gospel baptism is certainly to be performed by those who are sent to teach.

Fourth. Circumcision was performed by drawing blood from the subjects, but infant baptism by applying water to them. Gospel baptism, by burying the candidate in water.

Fifth. Circumcision left a mark in the flesh, but baptism leaves none.

Sixth. Circumcision was not performed on the faith of the parent, but by the express command of God; but infant baptism is done on the faith of the parent, without any command of God.

Seventh. Circumcision distinguished the church from the world, but infant baptism unites them together.

Eighth. All that were circumcised ate of the passover, but baptized infants do not eat at the Lord's table.

Ninth. If native innocency entitles them to baptism, as some think, why does not the same innocence entitle them to the eucharist?

Tenth. If infants are fit for heaven, and, therefore, fit for baptism, why not fit for church-fellowship and communion.

Eleventh. If children are innocent, they are not proper subjects for baptism; for baptism, in every case, but that of Jesus, presupposes repentance, Christianity being a religion for sinners, and not for holy beings.

Twelfth. But, if infants are sinful, how can they be entitled to baptism before they repent of their sins, and bring forth the fruits of repentance?

Thirteenth. Whatever circumcision, under the law, figured out in gospel times, it was something to be done without the hands of men: "Being circumcised with the circumcision made without hands," says Paul. Now, as all kinds of water-baptism are performed by the hands of men, the conclusion is in point, that baptism is not the antitype for circumcision.

Fourteenth. If children, by being baptized, are brought within the covenanted mercies of God, as is often said, the covenant is either conditional or unconditional. If the covenant is unconditional, all of them will be saved, for God never fails; but if the covenant is conditional, the conditions rest either with the parent or the child. If with the parent, it stands thus: if the parent does his duty, the child will be saved. This grounds the salvation of *one* upon the obedience of another, and not on the atoning blood of Christ. And, besides, if Noah, Daniel, and Job, could save neither son nor daughter by their own righteousness, can any others do it? How would every humble man, who loves the souls of his children, shudder, if he knew that the salvation of them depended on his own obedience. But if the conditions rest with the baptized child, I am at a loss to know what duties he owes to God or man, more than those children that were never baptized.

Fifteenth. The circumcised Jew, though he knew not *when* he was circumcised, yet knew that he *was* circumcised, by the mark in his flesh, and therefore had not to depend on what others told him; but the baptized infant has no mark, and has to rest his faith on human testimony.

Sixteenth. Gospel baptism is said to be "the answer of a good conscience," but what conscience a young infant can have, about that which he knows nothing of, I cannot tell.

Seventeenth. Is there an error in christendom, which has prevailed as extensively as infant baptism, and yet admits of so feeble support?

Eighteenth. If God made that covenant of grace with Abraham, which secures the salvation of souls, it follows of course, that all who died before the covenant was made, are lost.

Nineteenth. When a minister dips his hand in water, and sprinkles the face of a child, would there be a greater correspondence between his words and his actions, to say, "I baptize my hand," than to say, "I baptize this child?"

Twentieth. Should an angel descend from heaven and address a man as follows: "Some baptize infants without their consent, or knowledge, by sprinkling water in their faces. Others baptize adults on a confession of their repentance for sin, and their faith in the Lord Jesus, by burying their bodies in water. Now, which of these modes is according to the will of Christ? The salvation of your soul depends upon a right judgment. Judge right, and you shall live—judge wrong, and you shall be damned." Should a man be thus addressed, with the Bible in his hand, what answer would he make? Or would it be in this case, as in many others, that men think more of will and wealth than they do of the salvation of their souls!

Twenty-first. When a heathen forsook his idols, and was proselyted to the Jewish religion, all his males were to be circumcised, before he could eat the passover: but is there any account in rabbinical or Christian history, that the Jewish priests ever baptized the proselytes with water at their admission? If there is, the important question follows, what orders to do it had they from their great law-giver?

Twenty-second. That John the Baptist was of the priestly line, is certain, but that he was consecrated, or officiated as a Jewish priest, is denied with almost the same certainty. He was as great a stranger to killing sacrifices, burning incense, lighting lamps, etc., as the Jewish priests were to preaching repentance and baptizing believing penitents in Jordan, and other waters.

Twenty-third. None but Aaron, and his sons, could be priests in the Jewish church. It was miraculously decided by the budding of Aaron's rod. King Uzziah was of the tribe of Judah, and for assuming the priest's office, to burn incense, he was smitten with leprosy. Jesus Christ was of the tribe of Judah, of which Moses spake nothing concerning the priesthood. Now, if the Christian church is the same as the Jewish, how could Christ be the great High Priest forever, after the order of Melchisedec? On assuming the office, would he not have been smitten, like Uzziah?

Twenty-fourth. The Grecian church baptize their children in fonts. The Latin church imitate them, with the addition of chrism, (an unction made of oil and balsam,) which the bishop consecrated at Easton, and sells to the parish clergy for the year. The church of England enjoins dipping, unless the priest is informed that the child is unable to bear it, and then sprinkling is to suffice.

The various sects of Protestant pedo-Baptists, sprinkle their children for baptism, without chrism or god-fathers. Some do it to wash away original sin, and others do it because they are sinless. Some will baptize none but the children of church members, others baptize all that are presented. Some ground their right on the Abrahamic covenant of circumcision, and others on the household baptisms of the New Testament. Some do it because they are in covenant with God, and others to bring them into covenant with him, etc. The Baptists, unlike all others, baptize those, and only those, who make a credible profession for themselves, that they are believing penitents, and these they baptize by burying their bodies in water, in the name of the Father, of the Son, and of the Holy Ghost.

There is something so harmless in water, that were it not for other causes, there would have been no strife in the world about baptism.

Those who adopt the sentiments of the Baptists, have been complained of, in all countries, as dead weights in the church. The truth is, the Baptists are such *Bibleists*, that they are always opposed to monarchy in state, and hierarchy in church, while infant baptism, by uniting church and world together, tends to promote both. This makes the strife.

WHICH HAS DONE THE MOST MISCHIEF IN THE WORLD, THE KINGS-EVIL OR PRIEST-CRAFT?

By the *Kings-Evil* is not intended the necessary rules which men adopt by their prudence, in the hours of reason, to control the unruly passions of themselves and others, which sometimes break out like an overwhelming torrent. No: such rule or government, whether administered by kings or any others, is a blessing to mankind; attended, however, with some evil, like every other blessing below the sun. But by the Kings-Evil is meant the lust of arbitrary power—the unjust strides to gain it—the disguise to retain it, and the cruelty inflicted by it.

By *Priest-Craft*, no contempt is designed to be cast upon any of the Lord's priest's, from Melchizedeck to Zecharias, nor upon any of the ministers of Christ, either those who have been remarkably endowed with power from on high, to work miracles, &c. or those of ordinary endowments, who have been governed by supreme love to the Saviour, and benevolence to mankind. These, to the world, have been like the stars of night. But by priest-craft is intended, the rushing into the sacred work for the sake of ease, wealth, honor and ecclesiastical dignity. Whether they plead lineal succession or divine impulse, their course is directed for self-advantage. By good words and fair speeches, they deceive the simple; and by solemn threatening of fines, gibbets, or the flames of hell, to those who do not adhere to their institutes, they drive the people from the ground of reason and common sense, and establish their own importance beyond the reach of investigation. These remarks are intended for the priests of Pagan, Mahomedan and Christian countries, different indeed in their creeds, but uniform in their exertions, each class pleading the super-excellence of their religion; and alike compassing sea and land by their missionaries, to proselyte others to their faith.

The question now returns, "which has done the most mischief in the world, the *Kings-Evil* or *Priest-Craft?*"

The first man, Nimrod, who was affected with the Kings-Evil to a dangerous degree, was an impious wretch, who cruelly hunted down men in slaughter, and made sport of it as if they were beasts. After the disease broke out, it ran like a raging plague, and kings became as plenty as the locusts in Egypt; who sported themselves in cutting off the thumbs and great toes of each other. Indeed, among ten of the favored tribes, was a line o kings; and the character which raised many of them to the throne, was murdering their predecessors. History has detailed the destructive effects of this malignant disease in the world, for about four thousand years. What destruction of property! what torrents of blood! In the late contest in Europe, between Bonaparte and the Hereditaries, it is said that more than one million of lives were sacrificed.

Strong symptoms of this disease are found in representative Republics as well as in Monarchies. "Pray hold the ladder that I may climb the tree," says the ambitious Democrat; and when he has ascended, he kicks the ladder down that no others may climb but himself. Out of office he talks like a Whig, but in office he plays the tyrant. This predominant love of arbitrary power, has been the bane and ruin of many flourishing Republics. A plural tyrant is as mischievous as an individual despot.

To consider Priest-Craft in all its ramifications, would be a herculean task, that would make Olympus sweat. The game which it plays with *power* and *deceit* is all that will here be attended to. In ancient times, the servants of the priests, like modern constables, used coercion, and said, "Thou shalt give me now; and if not, I will take it by force." But their sin was great before the Lord. In later days, the public teachers of piety, religion and morality, cried, "Peace," (be all united in our support: let there be no division, partyism, or bigotry among you,) "and he that put not into their mouths they declared war against." These same teachers prophesied for reward and divined for money.

On the introduction of Christianity, "three shepherds (scribes, priests, and prophets,) were cut off in one month;" since which time, the ministers of the gospel have never been called priests, in the New Testament, in distinction from all the saints; but as words are but air, and bear the meaning which the speakers attach to them, let them be called priests.

It is the boast of Christianity, that in an enlightened period of time, (so far as it respects science and state policy,) it should be promulgated; and that without the aid of law, sword or college; but contrarywise in opposition to all of them; by simply appealing to the reason and judgments of men, it should gain such conviction among every class of citizens, that in three hundred years it should overturn an empire, which claimed universal sway.

Excepting imperfections and imposters, priests were then servants of the people, and not lords over God's heritage. They had a missionary spirit and practiced upon it, without missionary societies and missionary funds. They labored to collect free-will offerings, which they themselves carried to the poor; but did not oppress the poor to fatten themselves. They trusted to Providence for their food and raiment, laboring and working with their own hands, and had nothing to do with town votes and subscription bonds for their living. They did not esteem the civil law, the very *sinews of the gospel*, but the *sinner's gospel*. They never appealed to the laws to establish their holy days; confirm their creeds of faith; or punish any man that did not observe their days of worship, or pay the preacher of the parish. In short, they behaved as if they understood the will of their Master, that *his kingdom was not of this world*. That legal rewards should never be given for religious services; and that civil incapacities and legal penalties should never be inflicted on men for religious heterodoxy, or evils simply moral.

But after the founding of the Christian college, in Alexandria, and the mechanical form which Christianity assumed, Constantinus Magnus established it as the religion of the Empire, and made all others pay obeisance to that sheaf. What a melancholy reverse has followed! Churches invested with corporate power by the *Acts* of Legislatures, and not by the *Acts* of the Apostles. Ministers supported by the *laws* of men, contrary to the *laws* of Christ. And all this brought about by the craftiness of priests who profess to be the followers of Christ, and the imitators of the apostles; who estimate the excellency of their religion by its popularity, splendor and dignity. The living Jesus was but meanly clad with swaddling bands, with straw in a manger for his bed; but the dead Christ was wrapped in fine linen, and laid in a magnificent tomb.

The strife for power and pre-eminence was long and violent among the priests, till at length the Bishop of Rome prevailed: and there have been one hundred and eighty popes in succession, from A. D. six hundred and six, until the present time. That popes, with their triple crowns, standing armies, thundering bulls, high claims and bloody cruelty; together with their legions of priests to support the papal throne by signs and lying wonders, are inverted followers of the meek and lowly Jesus, and his humble apostles, all protestants attest.

In the tenth century, an opinion prevailed all over Christendom, that with the close of that century, the world would be burnt up; which the crafty priests worked to their own advantage. Near the close of the century, men would give first all their money, and then all their land to the priests for a single prayer. At length the century closed; the world still continued: but the money and land were in the hands of the priests.

Soon after this a priest, called Peter the Hermit, crept out of his cell, and with a crucifix in his hand, ran to the princes of Europe, and inflamed them with holy ardor to raise their armies, and go and take Jerusalem and the holy land out of the hands of infidels. This memorable frenzy of crusade, lasted more than a century; and some say as many as two millions of lives were sacrificed in the religious farce.

In protestant countries, where the civil arm triumphs over the ecclesiastical, the Kings-Evil rages among kings and prelates, who in the disease, like Procrustus of old, forge their iron bedsteads, (creeds of faith,) and stretch or lop off all that are too long or too short for their measure. He, who in the preface of the English Bibles is compared to "the Sun in its strength," claimed infallibility as much as the Roman Pontiff. He ascended the Star-Chamber and preached, "That to call in question the infallibility of the king, was to wade into the weakness of princes." His infallible tyranny, however, drove our forefathers from the bosom of their country, into the wilds of America. The same high claim cost his son Charles his crown and the head that wore it.

As it respects the bearings on society, all the difference that exists between a papal church, with a pope at the head, and a prelatical church, with a king or legislature at the head, lies in this, viz: the first is infallible, and the last is always right.

The first settlers in New England had been oppressed by the prelatic church in England, and fled to Holland; but not finding things among the Dutch to please them, Mr. Robinson's Congregation came to Plymouth, and set up their government and religion, in sixteen hundred and twenty. But all the art of their priests could not bring them into the measure of supporting the preachers by legal tax, until Governor Bradford was dead, which was more than thirty years afterwards. Those who settled at Boston, adopted the measure sooner. Priest Cotton, with his amazing influence, led the General Court to place *Lord Majority* in the pontifical chair in each town, and assume to itself the right of judging of the orthodoxy and tendency of every man's doctrine. This high claim of power soon banished Roger Williams—persecuted Mrs. Hutchinson and Co., and hung several Quakers. This beast, though diverse from the beast of Rome and that of Great Britain, has been wondered at and followed by a majority of Massachusetts, until this time; "who is like unto this beast? who is able to make war with it?"

The late Convention, called to revise the Constitution, still retain the same principle. Strange, indeed, that Massachusetts, all alone, in opposition to all the other states, should still view religion a principle of state policy —the church a creature of state, and ministers in the light of state pensioners! That the legislature should have the power to clothe the majority of each town or parish with authority to compel the people, by a legal tax, to support the religious teachers among them. What a pity! When will men realize that a Constitution of civil Government, is a charter of *powers* bestowed, and of *rights* retained; and that *private judgment* and *religious opinions* are inalienable in their nature, like sight and hearing, and cannot be surrendered to society. Consequently it must be impious usurpation for ecclesiastics or civilians to legislate about religion. Things should be so fixed in government, that neither a *tempting bait*, to exempt from burdens and reward for services on one hand; nor any civil incapacities or proscriptions on the other, may either flatter or deter men in the work of the ministry. The first would draw into the ranks of the ministry indolent and avaricious men, who would follow for the loaves ; the last would cast an unequal and cruel burden, on those who feel a woe if they preach not the gospel of Christ.

Admit of the principle that religious opinions are objects of legislation, or any wise subject to the control of jurisprudence, and there remains no effectual barrier in the hands of the people against legislative oppression. The disposition of the legistature is all the defence that remains ; and this disposition is as variable and changeable as the moon. The freedom here contended for, is not founded on the toleration or benevolence of those in authority, but in *nature, inalienable right,* of which individuals cannot be deprived, but by impious tyranny. I call it *impious* ; for a man cannot give greater evidence that he is ignorant of the precepts and spirit of Christianity, than when he resorts to legal coercion to compel others to perform what he himself believes to be religious duties. If a man works ill to his neighbor, punish him according to his crime : whether he plead religious impulse or devilish instigation, the fact alone is to be attended to. But where conscience begins, empire ceases.

This religious liberty is one item among others that has given the states of New York and Pennsylvania, such an amazing ascendency over Massachusetls. Foreigners, with their arts and wealth, bend their course to those climes where they can enjoy their religion without legislative chains ; nor can all the pharisaic boast of the *conscience-slave-holding* state divert them from their choice.

The pretence for a legislative interference in religious affairs, is thus stated.

1st. Christianity is the best religion on earth, and is essential to good society.

2d. All men ought to support the best good for society.

3d. As many men will not contribute voluntarily, they ought to be compelled by law.

Was I capable of analyzing and elucidating this pretence, with the wisdom of a statesman, the politeness of a gentleman, and the skill of a logician, my strictures would appear to better advantage. With such talents as I have, however, I will make a few remarks ; keeping in mind the words of a popular author, "If the truth is not as plain as the nose on the face, but few men will poke long in the dark to find it."

That Christianity is the best religion on earth, has my unqualified assent, and I will add, that it is the only religion that ever was on earth that brings pardon to the guilty, and brings a sure prospect beyond the grave. Granting this, a question arises, whether it is not possible for the best things to be perverted to the worst of purposes ? The faith of Rome was once spoken of throughout the whole world, but when Christianity became the national characteristic of the empire, and was modulated as a political institute, it became an engine of cruelty. The inquisition in Spain, the horrid murders in South America, with the rivers of blood that have flowed in Asia, Africa and Europe, all done under the mask of Christianity, answer the question in the affirmative.

That Christianity is essential to good government, requires some animadversion. The nations of the earth from the eighteenth century, A. M. down, had recourse to civil government, and many famous law-givers among them, such as Solon, Lycurgus, &c. In this condition the world was, when Christianity was introduced, and whatsoever was true, virtuous, lovely and of good report, was selected and enjoined by the precepts of the New Testament, and the important doctrine of remission of sins by the blood of the Lamb, and the resurrection of the dead, (which heathen philosophy and state policy knew nothing of,) were revealed. Moral precepts of right, whether they are found in the golden verses of Pythagoras, the maxims of Socrates, the sayings of Seneca, or in the Bible, are essential to the peace and good order of society. But to suppose that Christianity must put on a legal robe, and dictate either by a pope, a king, a prelate, a kirk or a major-vote, as essential to good government, is far, very far, from being true.

The New Testament is written *multum in parvo*; the whole of it can be distinctly pronounced in fourteen hours. It is an easy matter, therefore, to test the following questions.

Did the Lord Jesus Christ ever call in the aid of civil rulers to defend his doctrine, force an attendance on his ministry, and support the twelve and the seventy whom he sent out to preach? Did he ever ordain that his followers should be formed into bodies politic, and have legal authority to assess and distrain to support the gospel? Did he ever intimate that colleges should be endowed with funds, to prepare pious youth for the ministry, or prescribe any other measure, saving this, "Pray ye the Lord of the harvest, that he would thrust forth laborers into the harvest?" Did he ever institute that one day in every seven should be religiously observed by his followers, and that those who would not observe the day, should be arrested by a publican and fined by a magistrate? Did he leave any orders, that parishes, in their ecclesiastico political capacity, should contract with a preacher for life, and give him a sum per annum, and that this sum should be levied upon all, according to poll and property? He certainly ordained that those who preach the gospel, should live of it; but is the duty of communicating binding on the disciples in their social compact, or on them as individuals?

Granting Christianity all its merit, (which, as it respects the salvation of of men, is incalculable,) still the question returns, "ought all men be compelled by law, to support it by tax."

The New Testament is the code of laws which Zion's king has given to his subjects; to which nothing is to be added, and from which nothing is to be taken away. In that code, there is no account that Jesus or the apostles ever appealed to civil law, to aid them in their ministry, or ever desired it. Nor is there any precept given, that when Christianity should become more general in the nations, then magistrates should interfere. They asked for nothing but a dispassionate hearing and a correspondent belief, on rational evidence. All that preachers, in right, ask for from government, is to be protected as citizens, and let alone as religionists.

It is not only a supposable case, but a case that exists in fact, that in many parts of the world, Pagans, Jews, Turks and Christians, all have the bounds of their habitation fixed within the limits of one government. These several sects unite and form one body politic; for mutual advantage and defence, each sect pays its part of the civil list, and all arm equally alike for mutual defence. In such a case, what reason can be offered, why the three last should all be compelled to support the temple and worship of Jupiter? or why the other sects should be forced to be circumcised and abstain from swine's flesh, etc.? or that all the rest should subscribe to the alcoran and worship the great prophet? Every Christian would say, "the demand is unreasonable and cruel." If the Christians should gain the ascendency and tax all the other sects, to support the religion of Christ, would not the other sects have equal cause to plead injustice and cruelty? and would not the religion which they profess to admire, meet them in the face, and cry, "Whatsoever ye would that men should do unto you, do ye even the same unto them?"

In the United States, the above case has but small bearings, where the number of Pagans, Jews, and Mahometans is so small; but, there are thousands of Deists, who cannot be convinced of any revelation from God to man, except that of nature; and a thousand thousand who cannot conscientiously join with any religious society, from an honest conviction in their own judgments, that they themselves are not fit for Christian fellowship; or that the religious societies among whom they live, are not sound in faith. Now, what is to be done with all these? shall Christians compel the Deists to support that which they believe to be delusion? As well might they call for fire to come down from heaven and consume them, because they do not receive Christ! It is a horrid work for infidels to persecute Christians, but, for Christians to oppress and persecute those who own themselves unbelievers, has no excuse. Men of common honesty, have judgments, though they may be void of the holy unction; and in their best judgments, thousands of them conclude, that while they are destitute of the spiritual anointing, it would be a presumptuous crime for them to join a religious society, which is composed of living stones. Others there are who entertain a hope for themselves that their sins are pardoned; but with the sects of religionists, among whom they live, they cannot in conscience unite. In such cases, ought the ruling party to compel such honest souls to act the hypocrite, or support that order of worship, in which they have no faith? If it should be suggested, that such men make their pleas only to save their money, and act hypocritically, (which no doubt is the case with some,) the answer is, that their hypocrisy originates from the compelling power, which always has a tendency to create hypocrites, and distress honest men. But, pray, who has given the ruling sect a patent right to all the hypocrites, and all honest individuals? It is enough for societies to tax their own members, who have voluntarily joined them and wish to be taxed; but, for them to send a press-gang of assessors and constables, and press all within their limits to enter their service or be put in irons, may be justified on the principles of sovereign tyranny, but it is certainly anti-Christian.

If all men ought to be taxed to support religion, why are the priests themselves exempted? Paul enforced his precepts by his example. "I have coveted no man's silver or gold, or apparel. Yea, ye yourselves know that these hands have ministered unto my necessities, and to them that were with me. I have showed you all things, how that so laboring, ye ought to support the weak, and to remember the words of the Lord Jesus, how he said, it is more blessed to give than receive." These words were directed by the apostle to the Elders of Ephesus. And why priests should be exempted from civil taxes and military duty—and why they should lay grievous burdens, hard to be borne, on the shoulders of others, and not touch them with the tip of one of their fingers, I know not.

The most popular argument, used by the priests and company, in Massachusetts, to justify legislative interference and a compulsive power in religious taxation is, "that religion and education are placed on the same footing in government; and, therefere, as all men of interest ought to support education, for the good of the commenwealth, so, likewise, all ought to be compelled to support the priests. That, as ignorance and barbarism will prevail, if education is not supported, so superstition and heresy will abound, unless legal provision is made for the priests."

If this is a correct principle—an axiom in politics, it is as necessary among Pagans and Mahometans as in Christian countries. If there should be ever so respectable a minority of Christians among the Hindoos or Turks, according to this principle, they must all unite with heathen and musselmen, to support the priests of Jupiter, and missionaries of the great prophet. Where this takes place, and the Christians complain of their burden, would they like to hear this doctrine from the ruling party—"religion and education are placed on the same footing; and, as you share the protection of government, you must bear the burdens with us, to support both for the good of society."? The question answers itself.

Where do Christians learn the lesson, that religion and education stand on the same footing? The first originates in heaven, the last arises among men. The first, no natural man can receive or know—none of the princes of this world understand it—there is a way which no bird (common man) knoweth; the vulture's eye (philosophical research) hath not seen it; the lion's whelps (princes and rulers with all their proficiency in policy) have not trodden it; nor the fierce lion (the warrior with all his military skill) passed by it. It is hidden from the wise and prudent, and revealed to babes. What is more common than for men of the greatest science to be the farthest from Christian piety; while the most illiterate are filled with the spirit? It was said, by some, that Jesus never learned—John was in the deserts until he began his ministry—many of the apostles were brought up in fishing-boats: where do men get the idea that religion and education, like a pair of columns, stand on the same pedestal? The scheme of uniting believers and unbelievers together in religious society—of having some in the pales of the church, who are not in the church—of being incorporated by law, and becoming bodies politic—of levying money for building meeting-houses and paying the priests, as is done for the state and county tax, etc., may be justfied on the principle of enlarging society and getting money; but meets with no support from the New Testament.

It should never be forgotten, that there is no *object* of legislation, but what natural men, as such, can understand and legislate upon; but the things of the spirit, which belong to the Messiah's kingdom, are out of the reach of merely wise men, and, therefore, do not come within the compass of legislation. Every attempt of a legislature to interfere about Christianity, is to impeach the *wisdom* of Christ, as not knowing how, or his *goodness*, in not giving a sufficient code to his subjects. Those, who are in reality the followers of Christ, will not—durst not—and know they cannot make any addition to the code which Christ has given. But those who, under a pretence of friendship to Christ, as spiritual lords, have presumed to dictate, to their consummate hypocrisy have added complete tyranny. Religion and education do not, therefore, stand on the same ground; for education is an article which natural men can legislate upon with understanding. Whatever may be said of those governments that contend for the divine right of kings—that they were born to rule—that they are the fountains of honor and power—that *rex lex*, is a true maxim, and that the subjects enjoy their privileges as favors from the throne, and not of native right; yet, surely, in the United States, where *lex rex* is believed in—where it is understood that all power is originally in the people, and, by them, given to their agents, there can be no plea for a legislative interference in religious concerns; for the many units in a government cannot invest their legislature with any power which they themselves do not possess in small constituent parts. If each individual has this power and right to dictate and compel his neighbor what God to adore—what homage to pay—what times to pay his homage, and how much to contribute, then, by adding all these little items of rightful power together, the whole body of the people may invest their legislature with power to interfere, but not without.

If the Almighty had appointed legislatures for it, and they would take the responsibility upon themselves to answer for all the people at the judgment day, it would be reasonable that they should have the control of them in this life. But this is not the case: every man must give an account for himself; surely then he ought to be left free to act for himself. Legislatures, judges and jurors, in their official capacities, have nothing to do with the souls or consciences of others, or eternity.

The introduction of pure Christianity into a nation, is an immense blessing, so long as it operates in its native channel; which is to make known the good will of God to men, through a Mediator, and teach them to do justly, love mercy, and walk humbly before God. But, wherever it has been made the characteristic of a whole nation, and treated as a principle of state policy, it has been the worst hag above hell. Heathens and Turks shudder at the perfidy, fraud, cruelty and thirst for blood, which prevail in Christian nations. Hence, the appearance of Christian missionaries, in barbarous nations, is dreaded. Those nations look upon them as the precursors of war. And stubborn fact proves that colonization, war and extermination have followed them in many instances. What a pity that the only religion on earth, worth having, should be perverted, by *priest-craft*, to a trade of emolument—an article of merchandise—a science of the schools—a sanctuary for crimes—a pretence for extermination—a claim for power, and a speculation for money. Christianity must, necessarily, be the best thing on earth; otherwise, it could never have been a covert for the worst abominations.

Notwithstanding a compulsive power exists in the constitution of government, and laws of Massachusetts, to force people to pay the priests, yet the principle has been rebutted with so much address, that it is greatly weakened. The spirit of so respectable a minority rises so high against it, that the majority hesitate to use it on every occasion. Recourse is therefore had to the formation of societies—charitable appeals, etc., to raise funds to make preachers—support them that are made—and furnish the missionaries with money to carry the gospel to remote regions. In these exertions a great degree of philanthropy, or a great degree of craft is manifested. The images of the gods of India are literally held to view, and the immolations of the Hindoos are painted out in all the horrors of language. Children are exhorted to cast in their mites, with encouragements that every cent may save a soul, and young men are solicited to labor a part of their time to supply the ministerial treasury. Restraints on drink and superfluities are recommended, and every conceivable measure pointed out, (except the unpopular method of ministers waiting until they are endued with the spirit—taking neither purse nor scrip with them when they go—being willing to die daily that others may live—to labor, working with their own hands to supply their necessities, etc.,) as if the salvation of the world depended upon a *priest-fund* as much as it did on the promise made to Abraham. Good God! are these thy ways?

To honor the Lord with our substance—to contribute for the relief of the poor and widows—to administer to the saints, and communicate all good things to those who teach the word, are sacrifices with which the Lord is well pleased. But to create large funds in advance, for the declared purpose of educating young men for the ministry, and supporting missionaries, lays a temptation before them which may be too strong for many to withstand, that are not inwardly moved by the Holy Ghost to the work of the ministry.

When Jesus was on earth, he called unto him "whom he would," and sent them forth to preach, nor is there any good reason to believe that the same Jesus does not now use the same method: if so, it is not for parents, friends, churches, presbyteries, or bishops to designate the candidates. If certain grades of education, beyond what men in common possess, are more necessary now than at the first times of the gospel, the Lord of the harvest can thrust such forth. I have not yet been able to find any command or precedent, in the New Testament, for the churches to be at expense for the preparatory stages of the preachers. No, nor indeed any preparatory stages at all, until it pleases God to separate them from their mother's womb, und call them by his grace to preach, without conferring with flesh and blood.

The subject of producing preachers, is treated by many as a mathematical question. "There are so many vacant parishes—so many old preachers will die in a year. These vacancies must be supplied, and so many must annually be raised for foreign and domestic missions. And as preachers cannot be raised without money, money must be collected in every devisable way, or souls will perish for lack of knowledge." If my conceptions are just, St. Paul would treat such mathematical and mechanical stuff with an indignant smile; and well he might, for he, himself, labored abundantly, and travelled from Jerusalem round about to Illyricum, fully preaching the gospel, without such parade of reasoning.

The exemptions which students receive, from military duty and civil taxes, while in the stages of preparation, together with the prospect of a support through life, are strong temptations to many, who are no great friends to sun-burnt faces and hard hands. This suggestion will not appear invidious, when many of them confess, that their motive is to get an easy and genteel living.

The missionary plan, formed with great ingenuity, is now in operation, and will soon test its own merit. Like the great Amazon, it receives its tributary streams of thousands of auxiliary societies, and draws revenue from every spring. Whether this great exertion is the travail of Zion, to be delivered from Babylon, and usher in the latter-day glory, or whether it is only a piece of ostentatious pomposity, and will finally burst like a bubble, as the crusade and armada did, is yet uncertain. To me it appears more like religious parade than humble piety. The predominant spirit seems to speak, "come, see my zeal for the Lord of Hosts." It opens a door for writers to paint fables and exaggerate facts. It is a lucrative business for printers, and a large field for preachers, who cannot find employment at home.

I close with an anecdote, between James Manning, president of Brown University, and Sam Niles, an Indian preacher, in Charlestown, Rhode Island. Mr. Manning paid Niles a visit, and addressed him thus: "How do you do brother Niles?" To whom Sam replied, "Ah, who are you?" Mr. Manning replied, "I am James Manning, a preacher of the gospel of Christ." "Ah," said Sam, "do you preach for Jesus Christ or *old ten?*"*

---

* When dollars passed at forty-five shillings, the currency was called *old ten.*

EXTRACT OF A LETTER FROM J. L. TO HIS INQUISITIVE FRIEND.

THE Unitarians will not believe that one is three and three are one, when the terms are applied to God; but who can deny the truth of the saying, when applied to man?

That man has a rational soul, capable of reasoning logically upon moral subjects, (which none of the brutes can do,) is pretty generally believed. That he has a spirit which animates his matter, (which can be extinguished,) no one disputes. And that he has an organical body is self-evident. Soul, spirit, and body: these *three* make *one* man, and *one* man possesses all *three*.

Some, however, deny the triple nature of man, and say he is only duplicate—matter and spirit. In this light, two are one and one is two. Why will then the Socinians deny that two can be united in one, in Christ Jesus. If he is not God essential, and man real, what or who is he? Does it require a faith more marvellous, to believe that he was Jehovah-Jesus, than it does to believe that he was born of a virgin, without an earthly father?

I take it then for granted, that I am a trinity; possessing soul, spirit and body. But what my soul is—of what form, size, and complexion, I know not. My spirit is equally invisible and undescribable. My body, it is true, is tangible; but so curiously wrought—so wonderfully made, that I should be worse than a madman, to deny that the author of my existence was infinitely wise and powerful.

And dost thou set thine eyes upon such a one, and inquire after my health! * * *

What a wonderful phenomena is sleep. Our senses all locked up—unconscious of our own existence, in a death-like posture we remain. Anon, our senses all resume their former functions with fresh vigor, and past events and pursuits flow into our minds.

Is the death of the body and the resurrection from the dead, attended with wonders more unaccountable than this? Yet Hymeneas and Philetus, and many besides, experience the last every night and morning, and boldly deny the possibility of the first.

I cannot please myself better, nor entertain you with anything more interesting, than to quote some observations on this subject, made by the ingenious Dr. Rush, in conversation. Said he, "Sir, I can prove that the dead never will and never can be raised. Philosophy and the laws of nature forbid it—*and yet they will be*. So, likewise, I can prove that *creation* never could have taken place: all that we know of the laws of nature and the reason of things, declare it impossible—*and yet it did take place*. I mention these things, sir, to show the incompetency of the wisdom of man, to comprehend the works of him who is infinite." * * *

Some men seem to gain considerable advantage from the loss of memory. If they have promised to pay a sum, or remit a charge, and it does not suit them afterwards to comply—or, if they have told the age of a horse, or quality of a cow, which is not true—or, if they have defamed another person, &c., when those who are injured call for an explanation, their reply will be, "we have no remembrance of saying the things which are tacked upon us." If their declaration is true, one would think that a poor memory makes an easy conscience. * * *

When I read in a Constitution, that all power is originally in the people; and that it is, by them, vested in the several magistrates, whether legislative, executive, or judicial; and that all these magistrates, are at all times accountable to the people; and then turn my thoughts to the organization of the judicial department, and see how the judges are made without the voice of the people—at no time accountable to the people—that the power which made them, cannot without aid dismiss them; and that their responsibility is so remote from the people, that a riddance of them is almost impossible, my judgment says their is a contradiction between the declaration and organization: and a *judiciary despotism* is likely to be our ruin.

So, likewise, when I read in a catechism, that baptism is not to be administered to any who are out of the visible church, till they profess their faith in Christ—connected with the exception—but the infants of those that believe are to be baptized; my judgment determines, that the exception radically defeats the principle.

When a missionary solicitor exerts all his powers to frighten, flatter and deceive the people, and works so effectually upon the passions of a Christian congregation, as to sell them an Indian god, for money to support missionaries, (which has been the case,) my judgment tells me that the congregation thus gulled, have exchanged Gods with the Hindoos, and given their money to boot.

SHORT REFLECTIONS.

Immense exertions have been made to find out *perpetual motion*. That a mass of dull matter, governed by gravitation, should have a principle within to move itself, is strange; but that it should have energy enough to move another mass of equal size, or superior bulk, is more surprising. It is possible, however, that such a principle exists in matter, for many things have been found out, that once were supposed impossible; but if it does exist, and is ever found out, it will put a new face upon the world. All kinds of machinery will then be in operation, without wind, water, fire or steam.

That nature has fixed an universal standard for weights and measures, is very doubtful: for different nations establish different standards; and each nation establishes its standard upon an undefined standard.

It will remind a man of an article in Alcoran; that the world stands upon a great ox—the ox stands upon a great stone—the stone rests upon the shoulders of an angel—and the angel stands upon God knows what.

In Great Britain, the half-bushel must contain one thousand and eighty-nine cubical inches; which requires a round vessel fourteen inches in diameter, and in the clear, seven inches and one-fourteenth of an inch deep. In Massachusetts, the half-bushel must contain sixteen Winchester quarts; which is intended to accord with the British standard of a half-bushel. But what is the length of an inch? Do all rules agree? if they disagree, which of them is the perfect standard? We are told that an inch, is the length of three barley grains; but how would a child hiss at this last resort for a standard, when he sees the unequal lengths of the grains. The same may be said of all kinds of standards for measures and weights.

And yet, where the first settlers of a place fix their weights and measures, their posterity imitate—and by comparison, can detect a cheat—and all the purposes of commerce are accomplished, without any material injury. * * *

After the Lord Jesus arose from the dead, he gave orders to the apostles to teach and baptize in the *name* of the Father, Son and Holy Ghost. That he meant to be understood, and that the apostles did understand him, can hardly be questioned. After this commission, there are three or four accounts of the name used in baptism. Acts viii. 16. *They were baptized in the* NAME *of the Lord Jesus.* Acts x. 48. *And he commanded them to be baptized in the* NAME *of the Lord.* Acts xix. 5. *They were baptized in the* NAME *of the Lord Jesus.* Acts xi. 38. *Be baptized every one of you in the* NAME *of Jesus Christ.*

In neither of these places do we find the words *Father, Son and Holy Ghost* used. If, therefore, Father, Son and Holy Ghost, were not all found in the *name of the Lord—the name of the Lord Jesus—the name of Jesus Christ;* the apostles did not understand their commission and act accordingly, or I do not understand them.

It is become common for pious men to say, that "God gave his son *out of his bosom* to die and save men." The sentence is used to show the infinite benevolence of Jehovah: but are the expressions proper? They are not scriptural. John says, "He that IS (not *was*,) in the bosom of the father hath declared him." Christ was then *in the bosom* of the father, when here on earth; and I ask, when was he *out* of the bosom of his father? It is also said, that the son of man was *in heaven*, when he was on earth. But how he could be *in heaven—in the bosom* of the father, while a sufferer on earth, if he was a creature only, I cannot tell.

It has also become habitual for men to say, "there is virtue enough in *one drop* of Christ's blood, to save a world." That the blood of Jesus cleanses from all sin, and speaks better things than the blood of Able, is certain. But if *one drop* of his blood was sufficient to make an atonement, why did he go through all the pain of shedding the whole of it? Is it not more likely, that *all* his blood was required to make reconciliation?

THE THIRD EPISTLE OF JOHN.

DIOTREPHES AND DEMETRIUS.

JOHN, the beloved disciple, lived to a good old age. Ecclesiastical history says that he outlived all the apostles, and saw many anti-Christs arise before his death. Cerenthus and others, advocated the doctrine that Jesus was the only Saviour, but was not Jehovah. This occasioned John to write so pointedly, in his gospel and epistles on the divinity of Christ, that he was the true God and eternal life.

The little epistle before us, (which contains only fourteen verses—in which are included two hundred and ninety-five words—composed by one thousand two hundred and forty-nine letters,) is directed to Gaius, who was a man of wealth, and faithfully lodged the brethren and strangers; and especially those missionaries who went forth, taking nothing of the Gentiles. But in the church that John speaks of, was one Diotrephes, a man of ambition, who, by his address, had gained considerable importance among them, who did not cordially receive a former letter, written by John to the church; but prated against John and those in connexion with him, with malicious words; and was so fond of pre-eminence, that those who would not come into his views, he would cast out of the church, and lord it over the rest. But a man of a very different character was in the church, by the name of Demetrius, who was upright among men and pious towards God; who, by manifestation of the truth, commended himself to every man's conscience in the sight of God. He had good report of all men—of the truth itself—and of the true record of John, and those with him, who steadfastly adhered to the apostolic doctrine, against the innovation that was corrupting the church. Such men as Gaius and Demetrius, are blessings to a church in any age; and if Diotrepheses creep in unawares, it is no more than was the case in the days of John.

The epistle has not the name of Jesus nor Christ in it; but internally it breathes forth the language of the Holy Ghost.

ADDRESS

DELIVERED AT THE REQUEST OF THE REPUBLICAN COMMITTEE OF ARRANGEMENTS, AT PITTSFIELD, ON THE ANNIVERSARY OF AMERICAN INDEPENDENCE, JULY 4, 1824.

GENTLEMEN: To-day we have assembled to celebrate the day of our political birth. After travailing in birth for a short space, enduring the spasms of Lexington, Bunker's Hill, etc., this day forty-eight years, three millions of people were born in a day—born, somewhat like Ezekiel's infant, exposed in the field, without the pity of any—but proof against danger, with a "Death or Victory" in their hearts, as well as on their caps, they rushed upon the foe, and studied nothing but to conquer.

The little band of three millions, doubled, by births and emigration, in twenty-four years, became six millions, and again, in forty-eight years, they have become twelve millions. Although our strength is now like that of a giant or unicorn, let him that standeth take heed lest he fall. Ye who are old, and have known what wonders have been wrought in behalf of these states, it is presumed, will, with wonder and gratitude, reflect on the events that took place between the battle of Lexington, and the surrender of Cornwallis, at Yorktown. During the seven years contest between the claims of monarchs, and the rights of man, the United States sustained many disasters, great destruction of property, and much loss of blood, but in the final event, they gained the prize for which they fought. Had they failed in their enterprise, instead of assembling this day with delight, in the midst of a country abounding with unrivaled prosperity, we should have been doomed to the degradation of devoted Ireland, to lift up our eyes in torment, and see our haughty oppressors afar off, rioting in the fruits of our labor.

Experience has taught the world, that it requires as great wisdom and valor to make a victory prosperous, as it does to gain it. The want of efficacy in the confederation, left the states in a languid condition: to remedy which evil, the sages of the states assembled in convention, and framed a Constitution of government, which, being submitted to, and ratified by the people, became the supreme law of the land. Under this government the states have existed and flourished thirty-five years. The first enemies of the government have become friendly to it, and its friends, who feared it could not stand the shock of war, are now confirmed in its energy. Under this government, the annual revenue has risen from three millions of dollars, to more than seven times three millions.

Notwithstanding the acknowledgment of our independence by Great Britain, in the treaty of 1783, yet that government sought to make the United States subservient to her interest, by art and commercial depradation, without a formal declaration of war. Outrage, followed by insult, continued until our pacific government declared war. This war continued thirty months, attended with many disasters, and great feats of valor, both by sea and land. Our navy fought itself into immortal honor, and our land forces at the west, and at the south, proved themselves Americans. Never, since the age of miracles ceased, was a victory more splendid than that of New Orleans. The commander at the south, among the savage tribes and British forces, has immortalized his name as Washington the second. While history endures, the eighth of January will be noticed as the day on which the British thousands fell before the Americans, at New Orleans, with the loss of but seven men.

When war was declared, in 1812, Congress stated their complaints in their manifesto: and, notwithstanding, none of those complaints were acknowledged or remedied in the treaty of Ghent, yet the contest had every effect of the most prosperous war. The physical strength, and the republican government of the United States were tested, and Great Britain found that it was dangerous to meddle with edge tools. If that government should, however, grow haughty and insolent again, let them send their legions here, where they will find as ready a market for them as they have heretofore.

As the Colonies were settled principally from Great Britain, and governed by laws, either made there, or borrowed from them, it has been a task of no small magnitude to revise those laws. As the laws of Great Britain originated in the feudal system, or in an age still more barbarous, they were no ways congenial to the circumstances, interest and views of Americans. Some of the most sanguinary laws have been repealed, and a great reformation has been made in meeting out punishments proportionate to crimes. Much has been done, and much remains to be done. Laws and public opinion must correspond, or disaffection and fraud will follow.

The question which now occupies the enquiring public, is, "whether imprisonment for debt shall be abolished or continued." In ancient times, if a man died insolvent, the creditor sold the debtor's children to get his due. At a later date, the debtor, while living, was sold with his wife and children, and all that he had, to make payment. Later still, the debtor was cut into pound pieces, and distributed among his creditors. Our laws are not so severe, but the question before the public is, whether a man, who is become insolvent, on giving up all that he possesses, on oath, shall be exonerated, and capable of holding his future earnings free from attachment. Much is said on both sides. By the advocates for imprisonment it is contended, that it is impossible to make a law for the relief of honest, unfortunate sufferers, but what fraudulent villains will avail themselves of its provisions. That villains will perjure to cover their property—that the shame and pain of a prison will deter men from contracting incautious debts, or spur them up to discharge them, etc.

By those on the other side, it is pleaded, that the prison is no place for the debtor to make money; that the creditor, in seven cases out of ten, loses additional cost with his debt; that the debtor's family must be supported by the public, while his time and labor are lost; that in many cases men are reduced to poverty by sickness—by the elements of fire, wind, and water, or by the fraud or depredations of others, over which they have no control; that to cast such men into prison for their misfortune, with the worst of criminals, is morally wrong; that it is an axiom of truth, that the guilty, and the guilty only, should be punished; that if no humane law is to be made to relieve the miserable, because it can be abused by the knavish, then there is an end to all legislative interference to meliorate the state of man. That the unfortunate debtor may address the legislature in old fashioned language: "To him that is afflicted, pity should be shown. Have pity upon me—have pity upon me, O ye my friends! for the hand of adversity has touched me."

In some of the states, imprisonment for debt is abolished. The subject has been before the Senate of the United States: what the final event will be, is not known.

Perhaps no devisable plan would answer so good purpose in this case, as to exclude all compulsive power to recover debts, from the civil code, and leave every man to stand or fall by his moral conduct. Should such a rule be adopted, it must be prospective alone, and not retrospective. The power of education is great; by it the Spartan youth lost all the soft vices of refined nations, and conceived themselves born for the public. Let it be known among us, that if a man fails in his word or contract, his character is gone forever, and he will consider his punctuality his life—his all. The Tunkers make no use of law to recover debts, yet they live in peace and safety.

I have somewhere had a hint that the Turks use no compulsion to recover debts, the truth of which I am not certain of; but their honesty is become proverbial. They circulate their pieces of gold in little bags, tied up and marked, which pass current without being opened and numbered, having no suspicion that any one has opened the bag and filched any of its contents.

Accuse a Turk of any trick, he replies, "What, do you think that I will lie and cheat like a Christian?"

Should this plan ever take effect, it would give immense relief to the gentlemen of the bar, who, instead of being obliged to travel through storms and tempests, purely to aid their injured clients in recovering their just debts, would sit peaceably by their firesides, enjoying all the sweets of domestic life.

It is possible, that in some future period, government will see the impolicy and usurpation of fixing the standard of usury, sanctioned by penalty. If it is legitimate to force one man, who is the lender, to take but a certain per cent, for the use of his money, the borrower should be equally compelled to make no more profit by it than the per cent which he gives. Government has just as good right to prescribe what a man shall have for his labor—for his flocks—for his land, etc., as it has to dictate what price he shall receive for his money. How a usury law can be reconciled to the declaration, "that no law shall be made to impair the obligation of contracts," I cannot see. In all free governments, men will contract as they please, and any law, made to control them in their bargains, is usurpasive, for the right of free contract is never surrendered by individuals. Why should legislators lay a burden on the people, which they will not touch with a tip of one of their fingers? They borrow money at a per cent which is agreed to in the contract, sometimes at two, and sometimes at eight per cent, without any fixed standard: and where do they get the right to do so, unless the right is in the people, from whom they receive all their power? If the people have this right, let them enjoy it. In every instrument, or verbal agreement, let the per cent be agreed upon, as part of the bargain, and what evil could ensue?

By reading the declaration of rights, that "all judicial officers are the agents of the people, and at all times accountable to them," one would be ready to conclude that the organization of the judiciary needed some amendment; for, at present, the judges are at no time accountable to the people. The legislative arm of government has a small check on the judiciary, but the people have none. The people are not asked once in seven years, nor once in a century, who they will have to judge their causes. To say that the people are not competent to select the best men, is a libel on all popular governments. If they have not wisdom enough to choose those who are best, they must be equally unfit to choose others to do the work for them. I am aware that I am now treading on very unpopular ground, for the independence of the judiciary is the order of the day, and toast of the country. Yes, the independence of the judges—high salaries, and the amalgamation of all parties and opinions, is the leghorn, crape, and plaid of the times, without a profession of which a man cannot appear in style, but must be numbered among the vulgar clowns. Good heavens! what a change!

In old fashioned times it was thought impracticable to weld cold iron and hot together, but those days are past. In this day of improvement and patent rights, the gordian-knot is cut; the philosopher's stone is found. Now, Whig and Tory—the convention that framed the United States constitution, and the Hartford Convention—the rights of men and the claims of monarchs are all one! This connection of discordant ingredients reminds me of the Frenchman's punch: he put water into it, to make it weak—rum to make it strong—sugar to make it sweet—and limes to make it sour. The mixture was very palatable to his taste, and the only misfortune was, it punched his senses out of his head. If this remarkable amalgamation should gain its designed object, to flatter Congress to assume the payment of that debt, which was created in this state with party views, to run down the administration and supplant it, it would not be the greatest wonder that has happened in the world, since the year one, if the toes of the image, which are partly of iron and partly of clay, should break in pieces. The subject crowds into my mind a circumstance which took place in Ireland. A Friar was admonishing a man and his wife for contention, and reminded them that they two were one. "By St. Patrick," said Paddy, "if you were to come to our door at some times, you would think that we were twenty."

If these observations proceed from mean suspicion, let them be exploded by every one; for that base temper of mind, like a crow after carrion, is always hunting after faults: it pleases not God, and is contrary to all men; it reprobates every man and every measure. It makes no allowance for the embarrassments that frequently assail the government, when out of two or more evils, the administration is compelled to choose one of them: and if it has some claim to merit, for its ingenuity in exposing the evils of monarchy, hierarchy, and rotten laws, and pulling down what is bad; yet it has no faculty in building up that which is good. But manly jealousy is a noble virtue, absolutely necessary for the preservation of liberty. Without this, aspiring men, who love themselves too well to love others enough, will climb the tree of pre-eminence, and when they have gained a lofty seat, kick the ladder down, that no others may rise. We live in a world where men, when out of office, talk like whigs, but in office, they act the tyrant.

Notwithstanding there are some defects yet existing in our institutions and laws, yet the lines are fallen to us in pleasant places: we have a goodly heritage. Compare the United States with most of the nations, and we enjoy a paradise. Yes, our extensive country, reaching from Yellow Stone to Passamaquaddy, and from the Atlantic to never—containing all the soils, climes, lakes and rivers necessary for life, we are a world within ourselves, and by attention to agriculture, manufactures and inland commerce, under the fostering hand of government, and smiles of Divine Providence, we need not go abroad for joy. And with a million of well trained militia we have not much to fear, by land, while our navy guards us from unfriendly visitors.

It was, however, a maxim with Cæsar, "That nothing was done, while anything remained undone." One thing, at least, remains undone in this commonwealth, viz., to place religion on its proper footing. Before the revolution, many of the colonies had religious establishments among them. Rhode Island, New York, New Jersey and Pennsylvania had none. During the war, or since its close, all the old states have altered their constitutions, and revised their laws, to place religion where it ought to be, except Massachusetts. All the new states, that have been formed since the revolution, have left religion to stand on its own merit. How strange it is, that Massachusetts should boast of its singular wisdom and piety, for holding fast that, which the other states justly reproach it for. I was in hopes, when the patent-office was demolished at Washington, that no one society, in any town of Massachusetts, would get a patent with the exclusive right to all the new-born—profane and strangers, within its limits. This, however, is the case. The convention that revised the constitution have confirmed the old firm of law and religion—church and state—hypocrisy and cruelty. It is true, that all religious societies may screen themselves from the lash of any other, if they will avail themselves of the weapon (corporate power) that does all the mischief; but no provision is made for individuals. Children, the irreligious and emigrants, are all claimed by one society. The language of it is this: "You shall join religious society or be whipped; and, when you join, you shall pay your quota of cents; for, no penny, no *pater noster*."

Instead of the second and third articles of our declaration of rights, if something like the following was inserted, it would be highly gratifying to one at least—I believe to many thousands.

"The legislature have no right, and shall assume no power, to establish any religion—force any man to support any—give one religious sect any preference to another—proscribe any man for heresy—appoint any holydays for worship—compel any man to attend public worship, or cease from labor—give any legal reward for religious services, or require any religious test to qualify for office."

This proposed amendment may be viewed in the light of licentiousness, by some, and, as bordering on blasphemy, by others; the substance of it, however, is adopted in all the states, except Massachusetts, and enjoyed in the city of Boston, in distinction from other towns in the commonwealth.

Almost two centuries past, Roger Williams was ejected from Salem, and banished from Massachusetts, for contending for the same doctrine—that rulers, in their official capacity, had nothing to do with religion. The contrary opinion prevailed in the colony—that legislatures had a divine right to prescribe religion for the people; and, that magistrates had the same right to judge of doctrines and their tendencies. This claim occasioned the Baptists to be whipped, the Quakers to be hanged, and the witches to be gibbeted. Admit of the principle, that religious opinions are objects of civil government, or in any way under its control, and the broad stair is laid in the case that leads to the inquisition. Admit of the principle, and the rights of the people rest upon the good will of the legislature, and the benevolence of towns; whereas, they ought to rest upon a footing, out of the reach of the ill will of the legislature, and the malevolence of towns. Though the tree may be hewn down, yet, the just liberty of the people is not secure, while the stump is preserved with a band of iron and brass.

That the stain on our revolution—the reproach of this commonwealth, and perplexity of thousands, may be removed, it is ardently wished that the root of bitterness many be erased from our constitution, and that all laws which have proceeded therefrom may be repealed.

I close, by observing that here is an arm seventy years old, which, as long as it can rise to heaven in prayer, or wield a pen on earth, shall never be inactive, when the religious rights of men are in jeopardy. Was there a vital fibre in my heart, that did not plead for rational religious liberty, I would chase the felon from his den, and roast him in the flames.

FORM OF A CHARGE TO A CANDIDATE AT HIS ORDINATION.

That part of the solemnities of the day which is assigned to me, is to exhibit the charge of God to the ministers of his word. Notwithstanding there is no account in the New Testament, that the apostles, elders or brethren, ever repeated a formal charge to a candidate at the time of his ordination to the ministry, yet the charge is found in the scriptures, and there can never be a better time to rehearse it, than at the hour of ordination. Therefore, in the name of Christ Jesus, before an august assembly of angels, by the appointment of this council, and in the fellowship of this church, I charge you to take heed to your spirit. Moses erred for want of this. For want of this, James ond John sought to bring fire from heaven to destroy the Samaritans. Remember, the servant of the Lord must not strive, but be gentle unto all men; patient, in meekness instructing those that oppose. Be thou, therefore, an example to the flock, in spirit, in faith, and in charity. I charge you to take heed to your conversation. Let your conversation be with grace, seasoned with salt, as becomes the gospel of Christ, that it may minister edification to those that hear. When conversing on religious subjects, use not craftiness, nor handle the word of God deceitfully, but use great plainness of speech. Understand yourself, and seek to make others understand you. When conversing about temporal things, for necessary uses, always speak the truth. Let not the love of gain, or of fame, direct your tongue from plain truth. Let not the fear of loss, or of reproach, cause you to dissemble. Though truth may faint in the streets for awhile, yet it is great, and will finally prevail. It is difficult to describe a more hateful character than the man who pretends to have a great concern for the *truth of God,* and none for the truth of *his own word.* I charge you to study to show yourself approved of God. Search the scriptures, give attendance to reading, let the word of Christ dwell in you richly. The scriptures will make you wise unto salvation, and furnish you with matter both to feed the lambs and sheep of Jesus, and stop the mouths of gainsayers.

I charge you to take heed to yourself in all your relations of life, as child, husband, father, neighbor, citizen and Christian. Let your light shine so bright, that none can justly accuse, but contrarywise, seeing your good works, may glorify your Father who is in heaven. If you live after the flesh in common life, when you are in the pulpit, the people will say, "it is a pity he should ever come out," and whenever you are out of the pulpit, they will say, "it is a pity that he should ever go in." Always remember, that actions speak louder than words. Precepts without examples, in a preacher, have a poor effect.

I charge you to take heed to your doctrine. In doctrine, be uncorrupt, sound in the faith. The gospel of salvation is summarily comprehended in these words, "*ruin* and *recovery*." The human family are ruined by sin, all have sinned, all are included in unbelief. There is none that doeth good, they are all out of the way. They are at enmity with God, in alliance with Satan, under the dominion of sin. *These* are the characters, my brother, to whom you are sent. And thou, O son of man, cause them to know their abominations. Labor to convince them of the error of their way. Point out their sins, not merely as misfortunes, but as acts of wilful rebellion against the God of love. Discover to them the danger they are in, of dying in their sins, and never going where Christ is. Tell them, that God calls men every where to repent. Justify repentance towards God, and assure them that unless they repent, they will all perish. Set forth the purity of God's holy law, which is the eternal rule of right, which from the relations that exist between God and man, and between man and man, will be binding as long as the perfections of God, and the faculties of man continue. For without a knowledge of the law, men will quiet themselves in a life of sin. But when you find any who are pricked in the heart, crying out "I am undone," and asking the important question, "what shall I do to be saved," then fly like the prophetic seraphim, with the living coal of gospel promise, saying to the self-condemned, heart-sick sinner, "Believe on the Lord Jesus Christ, and thou shalt be saved." Represent Christianity as the religion for sinners. Hold forth the Saviour as able, and willing to save all that come unto him. Point out the Lamb of God who taketh away the sin of the world. Describe him as coming into the world to seek and save that which was lost. Proclaim the blood of the Lamb as the price paid to redeem sinners, and the efficacy of his grace to cleanse from the pollution of sin. Repeat the gracious calls of Jesus to heavy laden sinners, "Come unto me, and I will give you rest"—"Him that cometh to me I will in no wise cast out." When any appear to have obtained pardon by believing in the Lord Jesus, and give reasonable evidence of it, if any such first propose it, saying, "Lo, here is water, what doth hinder me to be baptized?" then go down with such a one into the water, baptize him, and then come up out of the water. But if any give satisfactory evidence that they are true believers in Jesus, and gladly receive the word, if any such do not propose it themselves, preach to them like Ananius, "And now, why tarriest thou arise, and be baptized." Or like Peter, command them to be baptized in the name of the Lord.

I charge you to preach the WORD. How great soever your reading may have been, or what proficienay soever you may have made in the sciences, these are but feeble aids for the pulpit. The knowledge of God's word is the one thing needful for the preacher, and this word, he must preach without perversion. Nothing must be laid down as doctrine, nothing enjoined as a rule of life, but what has a "thus saith the Lord," for its support. Some preachers have more acceptable talents than others, some are so circumstanced that they can devote more of their time to the work of the sanctuary than others; but as God has furnished you with gifts, and Providence opens the way, I charge you to preach the *word*, in season and out of season. Take heed to the ministry that thou hast received of the Lord, that thou fulfil it. Neglect not the gift that is in thee, nor be disobedient to the heavenly vision. Should you be successful in turning many to righteousness, it will be a crown of rejoicing in this life, and in the day of the Lord. But still, the promise is not made to the successful, but to the faithful. Noah, a preacher of righteousness, was not successful: all his hearers but seven were destroyed; but he was faithful, and became heir of the righteousness which is by faith. I charge you, therefore, to be faithful unto death, that you may receive a crown of life. Warn the unruly, and feed the flock of God around you in every place where God shall cast your lot; not through constraint, but willingly; not for filthy lucre, but of a ready mind. And when the chief shepherd shall appear, you shall receive a crown of righteousness that fadeth not away.

My brother, always remember, that it is *sinners* you have to address: if, therefore, you are maltreated, it need not surprise you. Among other sins, covetousness bears a prominent part. Should you, therefore, in the discharge of your trust, sacrifice time and interest to clear your conscience, and receive little or no reward, you need not from that conclude that your trials are singular, for thousands have experienced the same. Nominal Christianity is fashionable, and many enter the ministry professedly as a source of emolument, who prophesy for reward, and divine for money. Such will cry for peace, and he that putteth not into their hand, they purpose war against him. But thou, O man of God, flee these things, and endure hardness as a good soldier of Jesus Christ. How many ministers of Jesus have had yearning of soul for their fellow creatures, and a heavy wo on their hearts if they did not preach, but their limited resources, and large families would prevent their constant exertions. In this particular, they have been like the colt tied where two ways met. It is recorded of the primitive preachers, that they continued in prayer, gave themselves to prayer, and the ministry of the word. Christians have much to pray for, and much to pray against; but the ministers of the word have more. Their own flesh anointings, ministerial accomplishments, and success in their labors, loudly call for constant and fervent prayer. They know they can do nothing to purpose of themselves, that all their springs are in God, that if they plant and water with the utmost diligence, all will fail if God does not give the increase. It is a rich saying, that a preacher should go from his knees to the pulpit, and from the pulpit to his knees. To which I would add, he should keep upon his knees in the pulpit. He who preaches by the influence of the Holy Ghost, will pray the most fervently while he is preaching the most powerfully, and each exercise will aid the other.

I cannot close the charge better, than by rehearsing the charge which Jesus gave the apostles at the time when he left them: "Go teach all nations, baptizing them in the name of the Father, and of the Son, and of the Holy Ghost; teaching them to observe all things whatsoever I have commanded you, and lo! I am with you always, even unto the end of the world." How important the charge, how rich the promise.

THE following was written on the back of a letter from a gentleman, requesting him to reply to Mr. Campbell's essay on Forgiveness of Sins through immersion.

Should I begin on the controversy between A. Campbell and others, I know not where it would end. His creed is, that he will have no creed but the New Testament; why then, has he undertaken to alter his creed by a new translation? Which of the translations is his creed, and why does he write for others to read and believe? His creed, *no creed*, he would have others adopt, and why? Is it unreasonable for us to adopt a creed, which precludes us from having a written creed hereafter?

EXTRACTS from a manuscript read in connexion with a sermon preached on his seventieth birth-day, May 14, 1824.

I am this day three-score and ten years old. It cannot be said of me, as it was of Moses, when he was much older, "his eye is not dim, nor his natural force abated." Nor can I say of myself, as Caleb did when he was fifteen years older than I am, "I am as strong this day as I was forty-five years ago, for war, both to go out, and to come in." The words of the patriarch Jacob, are more appropriate to my case: "Few and evil have the days of the years of my pilgrimage been." At present, I breath twenty-four times each minute, and my pulses vibrate three times as often. Taking this for data, I have, in seventy years, breathed almost nine hundred million times, and my pulses beat more than twenty-five hundred million times. These involuntary motions are perpetual in life; but perpetual motion of lifeless matter has not been found out, and I presume never will be.

In seventy years, or twenty-five thousand five hundred and sixty-seven days, if we eat three times each day, and estimate each meal at three cents, the cost of food for seventy years, is more than two thousand three hundred dollars; and if our clothing costs thirty dollars each year, the septennarian bill will be two thousand one hundred dollars. At this rate, the food and clothing of a man for seventy years will amount to almost four thousand five hundred dollars.

If we consider that life, breath, pulsation, food and raiment, yea, every good and perfect gift descends from above, it will naturally inspire our hearts with gratitude and reverence to the giver.

It is now fifty years since I began to preach; but now the half-century past seems like a dream that is fled, or like a tale that is told. Nearly fifteen years of the forepart of my ministry, were spent in Virginia; seven hundred persons I have baptized while resident in that state. The years 1779 '80, '87, and '88, were the most successful. In the last mentioned year I baptized precisely three hundred. In 1792, I removed into what is now Cheshire. When I came here, there was a large and flourishing church administered to by Elder Werden, called New Providence grant. There was likewise a church calld the church of six principles, (making laying on of hands a term of communion.) The church which I joined, and whereof I am now a member, had dissented from the six principle church, and contained about seventy members. For the first seven years that I preached among them, there were some small revivings, insomuch that about seventy were added. In the fall and winter of 1799 and 1800 such a heavenly shower descended, that more than two hundred were added in six months. Two partial revivals have since that time taken place in Cheshire, (besides some scattering drops,) one in the year 1811, the other in 1823. I have baptized three hundred and thirty three in Cheshire and its environs; more than fifty of them are dead, and above one hundred and sixty have removed from the place. Fifteen or twenty have dissented from the church, and a number have been excluded; about sixty remain.

The once famous church in Grant, by removals and deaths, is almost extinct. The church of six principles, from the same causes, is no more, and the church whereof I am a member, contains but a handful.

In the summer of 1823, a Methodist church was constituted in the town, containing about thirty, and in the beginning of 1824, a small Baptist church was likewise formed. From this picture of Cheshire, it is evident that religion is not as predominant as it was thirty-two years past. Within that period, however, two decent meeting-houses have been built and paid for, without corporate powers or town vote. Whether the church of which I am a member, will finally run down, as two others have done, in the town, and the Methodist, and the newly formed Baptist church remain and flourish, time alone will explain.*

It is a matter of consolation, that although local congregated churches may crumble to pieces and be no more, yet the one church of Christ, including all those who fear God and work righteousness, will stand firm, in spite of all the powers of darkness.

My imperfect labors have not been confined to this town, but my travels have been considerable. In Conway, Pownal, Adams, Hancock, and other places, I have baptized more than three hundred. The whole number that I have baptized, is one thousand three hundred and fifty-two. Some of them have been men of wealth, men of rank, and ladies of quality; but the chief of them have been in the middle and lower grades of life, ten or twelve of them have engaged to preach.

My missionary travels have been extensive enough to girdle the globe three times; but I was never sent out, nor supported by a missionary society. I have had the honor, (if honor it may be called,) of preaching to two or three presidents of the United States, either while in, or when out of office; to a number of governors, one Indian king, etc.; but the poorer sort of people have been the most constant attendants on my ministry. My success has been small, compared with that of many others; but, considering my birth, education, rusticity of manners, and above all, the languor of soul, I have more cause to wonder why God ever succeeded my labors at all, than that he blessed them no more.

There is a common saying, that *fortune assists the brave, and confers honors upon young men.* To this maxim, there are but few exceptions. It is rare for an old man, who has filled a public character to retain all his popularity in his old age. All the imperfections of his life, together with the errors of his ancestors and offspring, will be thought of by his friends, and reported and exaggerated by his enemies. Happy the old man who can make the solemn appeal of Samuel, and be answered as he was. "And now I am old and gray headed, and I have walked before you from my childhood to this day. Behold, here I am; witness against me before the Lord, and before his anointed, whose ox have I taken? or whom have I defrauded? whom have I oppressed? or of whose hand have I received any bribe to blind my eyes therewith? and I will restore it unto

* The two Baptist churches here spoken of, united into one, in the year 1834.

you." And they said, "Thou hast not defrauded, neither hast thou taken aught of any man's hand."

How fickle are friends! How whiffling is friendship! I have had many friends in my life, who, seemingly, would have plucked out their own eyes and given them to me, and yet, afterward, (either through my misconduct or their own,) they have become my enemies. In this case, I have fixed it in my mind, never to forget the favors I received of them while we were friends, and never to betray the confidence they placed in me in the days of our friendship. To forget ninety-nine favors, because the hundredth is withholden, appears barbarous and ungrateful.

When I first began to preach, I formed an idea how a preacher should be adorned with piety of heart, meekness of mind, purity of life, and fervor of spirit, and looked forward with much desire, and some expectation of acquiring that sacred standing; but have never yet attained it. And, strange to relate, though I have been foiled fifty years, yet my emulation is in no wise abated. Sometimes, I have felt that desire for the salvation of others, that no labor appeared too painful, no sacrifice too great to make, if, by any means, I might save some; at other times, and, indeed, a great part of my time, salvation seems a matter of too much indifference. I have often been beset with a vain desire that God's stream might turn my own mill; that the blessing of God, that has at any time attended my ministry, might redound to my own religious honor. And, when I have been beset with this proud spirit, I have felt much more elated when souls were converted under my ministrations, than when they were brought in under the labors of others. The Lord pardon my pride, and root it from my heart.

In the antediluvian period, men lived to a great age. Of the twenty-seven personal names given in the history before the flood, (a line of one thousand six hundred and fifty-six years,) six of them lived to be more than nine hundred years old. But in the time of the Mosaic economy, when the judges ruled, and through the Jewish Theocracy, the lives of men were greatly shortened. Isaiah, Hosea and Daniel, however, lived and flourished as prophets, at least, eighty years; and the last two, it is highly probable, officiated as prophets for a hundred years or more.

When the babe Jesus was brought to the temple, to be presented to the Lord, there was one Anna, a prophetess, who was more than a hundred years old, and retained soundness of intellect and the spirit of prophecy. I am acquainted with a Baptist preacher (Thomas Seamons) who is one hundred and two years old. Francisco died two years ago, aged one hundred and thirty-five years. My health and strength are as good as can be expected, considering the many sicknesses, afflictions and fatigues that I have endured; but I know not the time of my departure. It is a happy event when men do not outlive their usefulness. My mental powers were never great. How far they have depreciated, must be tested by those whose judgments are sound, and whose minds are free from prejudice.

To gain correct ideas of the civil and religious rights of man, and to disseminate the same to others, has been an object of no small solicitude with me for forty years. How far I have succeeded in the attempt, is not for me to determine.

For the first seven years of my ministry, I was greatly embarrassed when old and famous preachers attended; and all my reasoning on the greatness of God, and the weakness of man, would not prevent it; but, by little and little, it subsided, and, for forty years, they have neither stood in my way, nor have I been greatly tempted to call them fathers or masters. This freedom of mind has been a great favor to me; for, in the course of my ministry, I have preached to nine hundred Baptist ministers, and how many of other denominations, I know not. I will here add, that the great veneration I once had for the early fathers of the church, (so called,) and for late reformers, is extinguished. Their biography assures me that they were not perfect—their writings and institutes declare that they were not infallibly inspired. Beyond them all, I look to the New Testament teachers for my creed and patterns. In this supplement, I am aware there is much egotism—the foible of age. When the mind grows inert, and collects nothing new, it will be pouring upon the past. If the circumstances of the day do not apologise for the foible, an attempt will be made to turn it to some use.

The Hebrew law-giver, Moses, in his meekness, generally wrote in the third person, as Julius Cæsar afterwards. But David, the man after God's own heart, is full of egotism. The pronoun *I* is found more than seven hundred and eighty times in Psalms—more than one hundred and forty times in that singular piece of composition, the one hundred and nineteenth Psalm.

The learned, the good, the wise, the inspired Paul, uses the pronoun upwards of thirty times in the seventh chapter of Romans—six times in one verse. "For that which I do," etc. How strange it is, that any should contend that Paul, in this chapter, is representing an unregenerate man. How can an ungodly man say, I delight in the law of God after the inward man?

Of the nine hundred and seventy-two Baptist preachers whom I have known, more than three hundred are dead. North of the latitude of Philadelphia, there are about sixty still living, who are older than myself. In the southern states, my information is not sufficient to judge how many of the aged are still living. I now stand, looking out for the messenger, the great teacher, death. My prayer, to-day, is that I may die with an honest, humble heart. If it would be arrogant in me to wish to resemble Stephen in my death—to have the Saviour in clear view; yet, let me humbly hope that Jesus will whisper in my ear, as he spoke to the dying thief—"To-day shalt thou be with me in Paradise," and send his angels to carry me to Abraham's bosom; and may my soul, and my imperfect services, be esteemed and accepted through the blood of the Lamb.

PART OF A SPEECH,

DELIVERED AT SUFFIELD, CONNECTICUT, ON THE FIRST JUBILEE OF THE UNITED STATES.

1. NOTHING is more true than that "man continues not in one stay:—the fashion of this world passeth away." The agricultural, mechanical, scientific, political and external—religious pursuits of men, are as constantly cnanging as the fashions of dress or the modes of speech. And the measures and manners, which border upon perfection, in the view of one generation, are highly censured, or totally condemned by the succeeding generation. * * *

Indeed the whole world has been like the troubled sea, which cannot rest. Nations have swallowed up nations, and kingdoms have devoured kingdoms, while the great mass of the people gain nothing but a change of masters. Had one short precept been attended to, "Whatsoever ye would that men should do unto you, do ye even the same unto others;" all this distress, slaughter and blood, would have been prevented. But, as virtue is its own reward, so vice is its own tormentor.

In this ungovernable passion for conquest, plunder and pre-eminence, some have risen to the glory of Solomon, the splendor of Ahasuerus, or the majesty of Nebuchadnezzar; while millions have been reduced to a state as abject as the hovel-tub of Diogenes, or the more painful condition of banishment and perpetual slavery. Not only so; but the same individuals, who have been the idols of the people, and worshipped as gods for a space, have afterwards been obnoxious, stripped of all, and slaughtered like beasts. "How art thou fallen from heaven, O Lucifer, son of the morning!" was the exclamation over one of them.

2. The emigration of our ancestors from Europe to the wilds of America, in the year sixteen hundred and twenty, the hardships which they encountered, the wars with the savages which they endured, the banishing of Quakers, whipping of Baptists, and hanging of witches; with the advances they made in agriculture and the arts for one hundred and forty years, I have to learn entirely from history; but as mine eyes have seen more than seventy autumnal suns, I have had opportunity of witnessing many events and changes that have taken place in this country, for more than fifty years.

The tales of cruelty and wo, which attended the French and Indian war, which raged in and about seventeen hundred and sixty, sunk deep into my heart; nor has the impression been entirely eradicated as yet: the names Indian and Canada, are always inharmonious in mine ears.

This war between Great Britain and France, closed in seventeen hundred and sixty-three, by a treaty of peace: but peace between Britain and these Provinces, was soon interrupted. The claims of Britain that she had a right to tax these Colonies, without the consent of colonial representatives, the stamp act, the three-penny act on tea, the Boston Port Bill, stationing their troops in Boston, and killing some of the citizens of the town, were viewed by the provincials as tyrannical measures. While the remonstrances and petitions of the provincials were considered, in the British Parliament, as the effects of a restless, mutinous spirit, which must be awed into submission.

While this oral and paper controversy was progressing, some of the first orators that were ever on earth, rose up in the Provinces, to plead the rights of the people. Of these, Patrick Henry and James Otis, seemed to be foremost.

At length a British army was landed in Boston, and soon began the horrid work of fire and blood. At Lexington, the vein was opened that was not staunched for seven years. The Rubicon was now passed, and the provincials found that they must gain that by force, which they could not gain by remonstrance. The alarm became general: all the provinces felt interested; and by articles of confederation, united together in CONGRESS, they made the cause one.

The events of the revolutionary war, both in the field of battle and in the cabinet, need not to be related: they are yet in the memory of the aged, and in the books of the youth.

At the commencement of the war, *independence* was not talked of, if thought of; all that was aimed at, was a redress of grievances; but one thing led on to another, until independence was declared; which was finally acknowledged by Great Britain, in the treaty of seventeen hundred and eighty-three.

3. The United States, having gained their main object, sounded the Jubilee trumpet, WASHINGTON AND LIBERTY. The army was disbanded, and every man to his tent, O Israel! But to pay the expense of the war, and govern the states, in their general concerns, was beyond the reach of the confederation. A new modification of our political institutions was imperiously called for. For this purpose a convention, composed of delegates from the several states, assembled in Philadelphia, in seventeen hundred and eighty-seven, and after three months consultation, with closed doors, produced the Constitution of Government for the United States, which was partly confederate and partly consolidate. In the Senate it was confederate, the small states having an equal number with the large

ones. In the House of Representatives it was consolidate, the people at large being represented according to their numbers. The first attempt to choose a President was nearly consolidate, the last resort was confederate. The senatorial branch of the legislature was the executive council.

When this Constitution was submitted to the people for their adoption or rejection, it called forth all the talent and close study of the nation. I presume there never was a time when there was greater exertion made to harmonize the liberty of the citizen, with the energy of government.

That individuals, in entering into a social compact, must surrender some of their natural rights, for the preservation of the rest, was confessed by all; but to what *extent* the sacrifice must be made, was the question of debate. In this case the surrender of individuals and also of state authorities, were both included. After the Constitution had passed the ordeal of state conventions, it was finally ratified, with the expressions of strong desire, that some salutary amendments might be made to it, to prevent the abuse of power.

The first Congress, under this constitution, assembled in March, seventeen hundred and eighty-nine, and on the last of April following, GEORGE WASHINGTON, being elected President, appeared at Congress and was inaugurated.

4. The first Congress had a laborious task. To open the channels of revenue, fix the tariff, establish the judiciary, organize the government, provide for the payment of the debt and the defence of the nation, were objects of no minor exertions; but as arduous as the task was, Congress did not forget the request of the people. A number of salutary amendments were proposed by Congress, which being ratified by the state legislatures, eased the minds of thousands, who before had fears. The *Federalists*, who had voted for the adoption of the constitution, in its first form, and the *anti-Federalists*, who had voted against its adoption, now became united, and for a little space, the wheels rolled easily.

The encroachments on our trade, by European powers, particularly Great Britain, became insupportable. Some in Congress were for war; others for commercial restrictions; but the greater part with the President, preferred negociation. Accordingly, Chief Justice Jay was appointed plenipotentiary for the purpose. The nomination of Mr. Jay was confirmed by the Senate; but many questioned the constitutionality, of appointing a judicial officer to manage executive business; and as it was understood that he did not resign the office of judge, but drew his judicial salary, in addition to his nine thousand dollars per annum as envoy, it became somewhat clamorous.

When the treaty which he negociated became public, it was tested by public opinion and by Congress. The treaty of seventeen hundred and eighty-three, made provision for a restoration of property, (slaves,) on the side of Britain; and on the other side, that Congress should not prevent the subjects of Great Britain, from recovering their bona fide debts of the citizens of the United States, &c. At this time, the old confederate Congress had no power to *compel;* all which they could do, was to *recommend.* Accordingly Congress recommended it to the state governments, and that was the end of it: no one was compelled to pay, nor was a slave restored. These neglects, by the different parties, were played off one against the other. But in Jay's treaty, (so called,) when Congress had become authoritative, provision was made for the payment of all debts due to British subjects; but the restoration of slaves was not mentioned in a solitary instance. The value of thirty thousand slaves was therefore lost in the treaty. This was bitterly censured by the people in the slave-holding states. In Congress, the President, with two-thirds of the Senate, without a single vote over, ratified the treaty; but the House of Representatives, in the first instance, refused to raise the money to carry the treaty into effect. At this crisis, great alarm was spread in the states, and petitions were sent on to Congress, praying that the necessary sums might be raised, which finally was done. This confirmed the hostility of the Federalists and Republicans, which had been rising for some time, so strongly, that for twenty years the pulpits rang and the presses groaned with anathemas against each other.

5. When Washington left the presidential chair, the parties tried their strength for a successor, which ended in the triumph of the Federalists, by a small majority, and Mr. Adams became President. During his administration, a number of laws were passed that inflamed the people to a rage, among which, the alien act—the sedition act—the stamp act—the direct tax—the standing army, and the eight per cent loan, were the most obnoxious. And, as the public debt was increasing nearly one million of dollars annually, the murmurs of the people were loud.

At the next presidential term, the two parties exerted all their strength, as before, but the result was different. The Republicans were victorious, and Mr. Jefferson was promoted to the presidential chair. Under his administration, the obnoxious laws either died by their own limitation, or were repealed—unnecessary expenses were retrenched, and exertions made to sink the national debt. The purchase of Louisiana—the diminution of the debt, above thirty millions—and the embargo, will keep in memory the presidency of Mr. Jefferson.

At the appointment of Mr. Jefferson, the Federalists received a deadly wound, which was never healed, although the beast struggled for life, and kicked at every measure of the administration of government until it died.

After Mr. Jefferson had presided eight years, like Washington, he declined the election for another term, and Mr. Madison became his successor. The capture of our ships by British cruizers became insufferable.

Remonstrances were answered by insult. Between war and submission there was no alternative. Solemn was the crisis. The constitution was made in peace, for peace, and many fears existed whether it would stand the shock of war. Self-preservation, and national independence turned the scale, and war was chosen by Congress rather than submission.

Mr. Madison had the painful task of proclaiming war, with the most powerful nation on earth, against all the buz of federalism, to test the strength of the constitution.

During the thirty months of this war, the Federalists cast every block in the way—triumphed in our disasters—and appointed a convention to sap the government or supplant the administration.

At length the war terminated in a treaty of peace, negociated at Ghent. The constitution endured the shock; the administration retained the confidence of the people; the physical strength of the United States was tested and found to be unshaken; the war-party became all victorious: Mr. Madison proclaimed the peace, and Federalism gave up the ghost.

6. Mr. Jefferson had called back the government, and the people, from their wanderings, into the path of Republicanism. Mr. Madison had borne the burden and heat of the day, through the war. The opposition party had ceased their murmurings, and Mr. Monroe succeeded to the chair of state, to sit on a downy cushion, where he remained eight years. For twenty years before his inauguration, it was as hard for the chief magistrate to do right, as it has been since for him to do wrong.

Mr. Monroe recommended the pension act, to reward the soldiers of the revolutionary war, who were living and poor, which will make his administration to be remembered as long as the pensioners are living.

When the tenth term for electing a President came, there were four candidates voted for: Jackson, Adams, Crawford and Clay. Jackson had fifteen more votes than either of the rest, from the electoral colleges, but not a majority of the whole. From the three highest a selection was then to be made, by the states, assembled in Congress. Mr. Clay had not votes enough to bring him into the House. The weight of his friends must, therefore, be flung into the scale of the others. At the first balloting, Mr. Adams received the votes of thirteen states, and was proclaimed president.

An instance once took place in Massachusetts, as follows: two men wished to send a representative to Congress, and agreed to support him. They first held a caucus with one man only, besides themselves, and agreed to be governed by majority, and be pledged to support the candidate who should have the most votes. The two outvoted the other, and now three became pledged. The three then held a caucus consisting of five, and proceeded as before, and the result was, that five became pledged. After this manner they pursued their object until a large convention nominated the candidate and succeeded in his election.

Mr. Kremer, a member of Congress, informed his constituents, that a like game was played in Washington, with Mr. Clay at the head of the game, who was to be secretary of state, if he succeeded in the promotion of Mr. Adams to the presidential chair. Whether Mr. Kremer was a prophet, or only a good guesser, it matters not, his prognosticks have been realized.

In all elective governments there should be a fair expression of the will of the people, without awe or deception; and he who seeks to carry his point, at the expense of the will of a majority, is a tyrant: and if he does it by intrigue he is a knave. The man who has no reverence for the rights of others, will never respect their interest.

Mr. Clay was rather displeased with the address of Kremer, and wrote an address to his constituents in Kentucky, to justify himself, and criminate Kremer, Jackson, Eaton, Swartwout, and others, in which he reprobates dueling in bold language. But notwithstanding that, on the eighth of April last, he appeared at Bladensburg, armed with instruments of death, to fight the American Rasp, whom he had challenged to the field. Mr. Randolph was a senator, and had used the freedom of speech, about Mr. Clay, which the constitution admits of. The constitution, which is the great charter of powers granted, and of rights retained, expressly says, that *senators and representatives, for any speech or debate in either house, shall not be questioned in any other place.* In this instance, however, Mr. Clay, contrary to his own avowed sentiments, and in direct opposition to the constitution, first challenged, and then fought Mr. Randolph, for what he said in the senate. Mr. Clay has behaved very much like Mr. Burr, and if he had killed the Rasp, at Bladensburgh, we should consider him his own brother.

What will become of the United States, if such men are at helm? Who, that is a friend to his country, will support them?

7. In looking forward, we know not what events will take place. It is now called a day of good feeling, in which party strife and religious bigotry flee away before the dawn of correct principles. The former contetions that have been between monarchs and vassals—tyranny and slavery—Whig and Tory—Federalists and Republicans, is now turned into union and friendship. And all classes of Christians, Papists and Protestants—Calvinists and Arminians—Trinitarians and Socinians, have all become one. The principles of civil government—the rights of man—liberty of conscience—creeds of faith and modes of worship, which men have heretofore been so tenacious about, and for which they have pleaded the injunction of conscience, and have suffered spoliation of goods, imprisonment and torture, before they would rescind, were only giddy chimeras of the dark ages that are past! Now the true light shines!

If the same spirit of amalgamation and good feeling continues and progresses, we shall lament every reform of religion that has taken place from the introduction of Christianity to the present time, and brand all reformers, the apostles not excepted, with the mark of ignorant, illiberal enthusiasts, for disturbing the peace of the world. And all those men, who have sought to ameliorate the state of society, by destroying absolute tyranny, and supporting rational liberty, will lose their names, and their unprofitable works will be forgotten. At any rate, the spirit of the times will lead to an acknowledgment of the Massachusetts claim against the United States—to pay the expenses of the Hartford Convention of pure spirits—make up the losses of Shay's men—and restore to the old Tories their confiscated estates. In this view of the subject, let the host of missionaries, who are spreading over the land, not only from the mouth of Columbia river to Passamaquoddy, but from Cape Horn to Ultima Thule, proclaim aloud to the people, that it is immaterial what god they worship, and how they worship him—what kind of government they establish, despotism or freedom; but it is all essential to possess the good feelings of Americans, for with that good feeling, if a duel is fought, one only shoots the jacket and the other the air: that it is not much worse than immolation, when widows burn on the pile of their dead husbands, in point of honor, or for Empedocles to plunge into the fiery mouth of Ætna, to gain the reputation of a God.

8. But I check my roving fancy. Satan is not yet bound. The strong man armed keeps his palace. Men are under the influence of pride, covetousness, envy and ambition, and will continue to do as they have done. The sea is somewhat calm, but let the sailors be awake, looking out for the breakers. The next presidential election is hastening on. The *ins* will be artful to keep in, and the *outs* will be clamorous to get in. There is not any great prospect that the constitution will be amended before the next election of president. If not, the enquiry is, whether Mr. Adams will so generally please the people, that there will be no opposition to his re-election, or whether there will be an opposition so strong that the decision must be made by the states in Congress? Should the last take place, it behoves the people to remember, that it is the twentieth Congress that will decide the question, and, therefore, in choosing the representatives for the next Congress, they will be choosing electors as well as legislators. For want of this, in the last choice of president, several of the states gave one voice by their electors, and another by their representatives. And by this means, General Jackson, who had fifteen more electoral votes than any other candidate, (equal to 600,000 people,) was left behind, with only seven states out of twenty-four.

9. Another article solicits our attention at this time. Religion is become the most fashionable thing among us. Moral societies, Sunday schools—tract societies—Bible societies—missionary societies, and funds o educate and make preachers, are now in the full tide of operation. For-

merly it was thought not impossible to "discern between those who feared God, and those who did not;" but these many societies, including all classes and characters of men, uniting in the same effort, carry all before them, and leave no dividing line. The adversaries of Judah and Benjamin unite with Zerubbabel, in this building, and he who contributes the most, is the most extolled, and his biographer canonizes him for it after he is dead. In barbarous times, when men were in the dark, it was believed that the success of the gospel was according to the outpourings of the Holy Spirit, but in this age of light and improvement, it is estimated according to the pourings out of the purse. Once, a man could not follow the blessed Jesus without bearing his cross, and being hated of all men; but a profession of Christianity is now so honorable, that without it men are despised and calumniated. It has been thought, that the carnal mind was enmity to God—that those who were not for Christ, were against him. That following after the law of righteousness, by the deeds of the law, to obtain life, was climbing up some other way than what God had appointed; but now it is believed, that if children are dedicated to God, by others, and know nothing about it themselves—if they attend Sunday schools, and store up many verses in their memories—if they contribute their cents for the conversion of heathen, and the distribution of the Bible—if they attend public worship and keep the holy Sabbath, though all these things are done with a deceitful heart that is desperately wicked, they will move God to bestow his pardoning love upon them—that by these means, those who are in the flesh can please God.

The metaphysical, long-winded Mr. Edwards, observes, "That he had noticed that *old men* would not hear new notions; but to prevent the evil of superannuacy, he resolved that, should he ever live to be *old*, he would hear all that could be said in favor of new discoveries, or new doctrines." In accordance therewith, I am waiting to see what this *new order* of things will produce.

10. It is now half a century, since the Independence of the United States was declared. In this half century the territory has doubled in extent, twice doubled in inhabitants, rising from three to twelve millions; increased in wealth beyond description; improved in arts, inventions and manufactures, in an astonishing manner, listing the fire and water into service, to aid the labor of the earth and convey its produce to market, &c. Should the world stand fifty years longer, and the same spirit of enterprise prevail, under the same smiles of Providence, what a dazzling spectacle the United States will be to the world!

This, however, is more ardently to be wished for, than reasonably expected. Some foul event may turn up and becloud the American sun. Famine, pestilence, dissension and war, may make the day dark with night. Such calamities have befallen the most flourishing kingdoms and republics that were ever on earth; and no change has yet taken place in the nature of men, to assure us that the same calamities will not be repeated.

When the public mind is once strongly set, it generally overleaps the bounds of reason, and extremes follow. Many of the new inventions are, and will be of great advantage to society, while others will fall into disrepute.

Perhaps nothing is carried to a greater extreme than printing. The freedom of the press is the great bulwark of liberty, and the best channel of communication; and, with the freedom of speech, should never be prohibited. It may, however, become licentious—it may grow extravagant. The human mind is limited, and cannot contain but a certain measure; and when it is overcharged, it will nauseate. Without time for cool reflection and digestion, abundance of reading overcharges the mind and obscures the perception. All *reading* and no *self-tuition*, does not form the most illustrious character. The knowledge of men, and the experiment of things, are necessary to form a man for usefulness.

Once there was a time, when one leaf of the Bible would sell for *a load of hay.* At another time, transcriptions of the Bible were so rare, and labor so low, that it cost the wages of *thirteen years* to purchase a copy! These were hard times indeed. It is now quite the reverse. Bibles are abundant, and almost forced upon people; but it is a serious question whether *Biblical knowledge* is equal to what it was fifty years ago. The public attention seems to flutter on the profusion of Bibles, Tracts and Magazines, and overlooks those things which are "hidden from the wise and prudent, and revealed unto babes," in the scriptures.

In the compass of last year, it is said that twelve hundred physicians, six hundred lawyers, and five hundred preachers, have been fitted out in the United States. If health, security of property, and Christian piety equally increase, the blessing will be great. But with respect to preachers, I am at a loss to know what *fitting out* means: for I have never yet found anything enjoined on churches, individuals, rulers or bishops, by Christ or the apostles, to procure preachers, except one; which is, "Pray ye the Lord of the harvest, that *he would send forth laborers* into the harvest.

* * * * * *

Religion is become very mechanical, and a supply of preachers is treated as a mathematical question. It is calculated that where the population is condensed, one preacher to a thousand hearers is sufficient; but where the population is thin, more than one to a thousand is needed. Perhaps one preacher for every five hundred would suffice, taking all parts of the country together. By this rule, the twelve millions of inhabitants within the United States, call for twenty-four thousand preachers, for the home department, and as many more for the natives of the woods, Asia and Africa, as can be possibly *fitted out.*

I have no data to show how many preachers there are, in the several religious denominations within the United States, but judge the number is far less than twenty-four thousand. And as it is presumed, that five hundred annually die, there is a loud call for more preachers, even for the home department. And that many may run to and fro among the heathen, the call becomes irresistible. More means must be devised—more money must be raised—more theological moulds and mills must be established to *fit out* pious youth for the arduous task of preaching a little—drinking coffee a good deal, with a certain salary secured to them.

The illustrious captive, Daniel, speaks of a thousand thousand ministers, which is one million; and ten thousand times ten thousand, which is one hundred millions, worshippers: according to which there was one minister for every hundred. But John adds thousands of thousands to the number given by Daniel, and leaves it indefinite: we may, therefore, suggest that the number of ministers did not exceed one for every five hundred worshippers.

To a man, who reads the New Testament, and the history of the church, down to the establishing of a Christian college in Alexandria, and the legal establishment of Christianity in the Roman Empire, how extremely flat and anti-Christian the above calculations will appear.

I close with an anecdote respecting the first settlement of Hartford, in this state. The first settlers of the town lived in a garrison, to secure themselves from the Indians. A young woman went out of the fort and was entrapped by the Indians, who hurried her to their canoe, and were carrying her off. The fort was soon alarmed, and the hunters caught their guns and ran to her rescue, with old Mr. Hooker at their heels. When they came to the river, the Indians steered the canoe in a direction that placed the young woman between the gunners and themselves. The hunters cried out, "Mr. Hooker, what shall we do? In a minute she will be out of our reach." The godly man stretched his hands and heart towards heaven, and answered, "*Take good sight, and heaven direct the balls.*" They did so; and killed both the Indians, and the young woman paddled back to the shore. From this I would say to all of you, and to myself, take good sight, do your duty, and leave events to God.

At home, Feb. 8, 1828.

My good Sister:—It has been fourteen years since I saw you, but the distance of space and length of time have in no degree chilled my Christian regard and friendship towards you and others in Virginia.

Was I at your house in Caroline, or you here at my mansion, we should be full of chat, in telling each other what events had passed for the last fourteen years, but that is not the case; to supply the lack of which, I shall with my pen give you a condensed history of myself, and what has passed before me. Excepting a few months cessation from preaching occasioned by a broken leg, I have been unweariedly trying to preach Jesus, but have never yet risen to that state of holy zeal and evangelical knowledge, that I have been longing after; but *such as I had* I have been giving unto the people. There have been a number of revivals of religion within the circle of my ministration, which have both flattered my pride and humbled my soul. The season past has been one of the happy parts of my life. Such brokenness of heart, prayer and singing have been among the people, as I have rarely seen (never exceeded) in my life. The number I have baptized in this rich harvest is one hundred and six, and I yet find no more inconvenience in baptizing than I did when I was but thirty-six years old; nor can I discover any diminution in the congregations that attend my ministry. I have had a number of attacks, like one I had in Goochland, which ended in Louisa at the time when brother Rawlins was baptized; but I have been holden up with a litle help, and refreshed in my bondage until now, *faint yet pursuing*. I have eighty-two descendants living. A few of my grand children have died at their respective homes; but I have never had a death at my house. Of Abraham it is said, "I called him alone, and blessed him and increased him."

I have been trying to get ready to die. I have written a short history of the events of my life, and although it contains the *best* part of my life, yet when I look over the manuscript, it is but a ragged thing. I have also got the likeness of my person taken, as large as life from the waist up, and others say it is a good portrait; but it looks like a crabbed image full of juices, so that boasting is every way excluded. My pecuniary concerns I have settled, so that my executor may have nothing to do, and likewise made my will, which is but a light affair. So far I am ready to die; but internal readiness is another thing. I have as strong attachments to life as I had in the year 1777, when at your father's house with brother Young. I cannot select the *time* when, nor the *disease* by which I should choose to die.

When I reflect on my past life, a thousand things occur that were criminal or very imprudent. I had no fruit in those things of which I am now ashamed, so that if Christianity was not *a religion for sinners*, to meet their wants and relieve their woes, I should have no hope.

* * * * * * * * * * * * * *

Were I sure that I had acted only for Christ, my soul would make her boast in God; but there is so much corruption in me, that the most that I can hope is, that there has been some good thing in me, amidst so many bad ones. There is a solemn day approaching, where pleading that we have eaten and drunken in the presence of Christ, prophesied, cast out devils, and done many wonderful works in his name, will not avail, and if we add to these pleas, that we have given our bodies to be burned, and our goods to feed the poor, yet without *charity* (the unction from the Holy one—the waters that spring up to eternal life) we shall be disesteemed. While writing on this solemn subject, I feel like dropping my pen and crying to God, with all the powers of my soul, that he would make me right, make me faithful unto death, assist me to fight the good fight, finish my course, keep the faith, and receive the crown.

Internal religion is always the *same*, and always will be, but the external modes of it, change like the fashions of dress. So many religious novelties, have lately sprung up, that I have often exclaimed, "They have taken away my Lord, and I know not where they have laid him." But this alarm has been quieted by, "What is that to thee? follow thou me." In all the revivals that have been where I have administered, the work has operated as it did in Virginia from the year 1784 until 1789.

* * * * * * * * * * * * * *

From creation to the flood was 1656 years, in which term we may have safely calculated that many millions of people lived; and yet no more than twenty-seven personal names are found in antediluvian history. There are a number of names so incorporated into the history, precepts, and promises of the scriptures, that they must necessarily be perpetuated as long as the Bible exists. But there have been many *seven thousands* that never bowed to Baal, whose names are buried in oblivion. Much has been done and much is doing by men to immortalize their names; but if my name is written in Heaven, in the Lamb's book of life, not to be blotted out, if I have a room in God's house, among the living in Jerusalem, I shall be made for eternity. It is not likely a century hence there will be many, if any one, who will ever have known or heard any thing of John Leland.

This gives me no uneasiness. But I have a strong solicitude that I may live and die in a manner that will give my friends in general, and those whom I have baptized in particular, no painful sensations, to think that they have placed confidence in an unfaithful man who did not hold out to the end.

* * * * * * * * * * * * * *

I am very much checked in writing, fearing you are dead; but like Columbus in a sea storm, I will throw this overboard, in hopes that if you are dead, some of your friends will find it.

You see how large a letter I have written to you with my own hand, and being such a one as John the aged, I hope you will pardon my egotism (the hobby of old men) and all other defects, and believe it is indicted in the spirit of friendship.

JOHN LELAND.

Mrs. Amey Peatross.

EXTRACTS FROM A LETTER TO A FRIEND.

My Good Friend:—In your last letter, you ask, what part and success I have had in the late religious excitement in several towns in Berkshire, and borders of New York? The friendship that exists between us, makes it a pleasant task to answer the question. But, first of all, it is necessary for you to know the sentiments and habits of the people among whom I have lived and labored. They are a people not "within the covenanted mercies of God;" as they have never had the seal of the covenant put upon their foreheads by the moistened hand of the priest. And, when they are reproved for their neglect, they fly to the Bible, and affirm that repentance for sin and faith in Christ, are prerequisites of baptism. That there is no account in the Bible that children were ever baptised upon the faith of the parents. That baptism is the answer of a good conscience, and that new born infants cannot have any conscience about it. That believers should be buried with Christ in baptism. That when the priest dips his hand in water and holds it over, or lays it on the face, to be consistent, he should say, "I baptize my hand," etc., for nothing else is baptized. * * * * * * * * *

A very flagrant stain of character among them, is, that they do not admire the missionary scheme, which prevails like a mighty flood. This they compare to the beast that all the world wondered after. When they are reproved for their covetuousness and coldness about the salvation of the heathen, they reply: "That a missionary spirit and missionary practice is apostolical; but missionary societies and missionary funds are of later date. That missions established on divine impression, are no ways related to those formed by human calculation. That when the apostles traveled from Judea, to Gentile regions, they collected from the Gentiles, and brought the alms to the poor saints in Judea; but now the poor saints in Judea are taxed to aid the missionaries where they go." * *

Sabbath schools are very fashionable, and are considered, by many, as the great lock-link which unites nature and grace together; but, those among whom I live and labor are without them; and, whenever the subject is mentioned, they reply, that if the Sabbath is holy time, it ought not to be profaned by acquiring literature. * * * * *

But, to do the people justice, notwithstanding their tenets, they are very forward in public worship, and attend with the utmost civility, without giving law-maker or conscience-dictator, any praise for telling them who, when, where, or how they must worship or adore.

When they are pressed to advance their hard earnings to educate pious young men for the ministry, they answer, if any grades of collegiate education are essential prerequisites to the ministry, why does not God call those who are already in possession of these prerequisites? Is it reasonable to believe that a wise God would call a man to preach, when he knows that he cannot do the work until he has studied how to decline nouns and conjugate verbs three or four years? They frequently say, if a man cannot rise to usefulness, by internal energy, academical polish cannot make him shine. That it is a vain thing to hold up a man to whom God has given no legs. They moreover, observe, that it is going again over the ground, which has been very pestiferous. Christianity, in its first introduction, was not only unaided by law, sword, and the college, but was opposed by all of them; but, after the Christians had gained some standing and lost some of their first love, they erected a College at Alexandria, to recommend Christianity to the carnal world. This project effected the intended object, and soon the law of Christian establishment followed, and the sword was appealed to, to enforce the law. Here poison was spread into the churches; for, from that day to this, in the greatest part of Christendom, Christianity has been used as a test to civil office—a step to honor—a cloak for insincerity—and a stimulus to persecution. The people, furthermore, pay no attention to the Westminister catechism, or Saybrook platform; but, have the courage of taking the Bible first-handed, for their directory, etc.

The loose habits, and strange opinions of the people, are not the greatest obstructions which I have had to encounter. My worst enemies have been in my own house. Brilliancy of talent I never possessed when I was in my prime; now advanced in life, I must appear to greater disadvantage; but, languor of soul is what most besets me. A consciousness that I do not realize the weight of those eternal truths which I am preaching to others, sinks me in the dust. The various cunning arts—the sleight of hand—the deceitful working—the promise of liberty—the good words and fair speeches, and perverse things that are said to deceive the hearts of the simple, and draw disciples after them, have been too evident among many teachers; yea, they would exclude from their fellowship all that oppose them, that the rest might effect them. Seeing all this, and much more, and finding the same wicked seeds in myself, I am constrained to say, that "Christianity is a religion for sinners." Yes, the author of it came to seek and save that which was lost—he came to call sinners to repentance—he receiveth sinners—speaks to them of the kingdom of God, and heals all that have need of healing.

Among the people of my ministration, God has evidently poured out his spirit from on high, and turned a goodly number from darkness to light. My poor heart has been greatly revived in hearing the young disciples relate how God quickened their souls by his grace—gave them to see the purity and extent of the holy law—the imperfections of their nature and the insuffiiciency of their prayers and exertions to relieve—that they were greatly bowed down with a hard heart and load of guilt—that Jesus at length appeared for their help, and said, come unto me and I will give you rest—that they resigned all to his sovereign will, and heard his words, thy sins are fergiven thee—that they have enjoyed great comfort in believing, and feel resolved to serve God while they have any being, etc. Of this class of people, I have baptized one hundred and five since the 25th of March last; which, added to those whom I had baptized before, make one thousand four hundred and fifty-seven. Give God the glory; as for this man (myself) we know that he is a sinner.

JOHN LELAND.

January 1*st*, 1828.

THOUGHTS.

If Jesus is the first, who existed before him?

If he is the Evelasting Father, when did he begin his course?

If he is before all things—the maker of all things—and by him all things consist, how can he be a THING?

If he is the true God and Eternal Life, when did his Godhead and life begin?

If his goings forth were from everlasting, when was he not going forth?

How could he be in heaven when conversing with Nichodemus on earth, unless he was omnipresent?

If he is God over all, who is above him?

If he can change vile bodies by his own wonder-working power, must he not be omnipotent?

If Jesus was the Lord God of the holy prophets, is it not certain that the Jesus of the New Testament was the Jehovah of the Old?

If Jesus was not God, in the highest sense of the word, how could he say to Philip—He that hath seen me, hath seen the Father?

Would Stephen, when filled with the Holy Ghost, in his dying moment, have prayed to him to receive his spirit, if he had not been assured that he was Jehovah, the only Saviour?

If the Jesus of the New Testament bore all the names and titles—did all the works—obtained the same testimonies, and received the same addresses and ascriptions of praise, of the Jehovah of the Old Testament, why not receive him as Emanuel, God with us?

Would it not be idolatry to pay him religious worship if he was merely a creature, though ever so great and highly exalted?

If in Jesus dwelleth all the fulness of the Godhead bodily, what divine attribute can be lacking in him?

If he ruled the wind and sea—healed all kinds of diseases, and raised the dead, by a command in his own name, and not by praying to another, he must be God.

Can the many hundreds of passages in the Bible, which speak of Christ as being filial, subordinate, dependant, under the law, helpless and forlorn, destroy the force of evidence that is given of his independent divinity? Do not all those passages have strong bearings on the human nature, which was bound to obey, and subject to sufferings, in which God was manifested in the flesh, by a union as inconceivable by us as the conception of the Virgin Mary, or how the bones grow in the womb?

There are three that bear record in heaven, the Father, the Word, and the Holy Ghost, and these three are one. This is a doctrine of revelation, for a conformation of which, baptism is performed in the name of the Father, Son and Holy Ghost: but, like the ark of the Hebrews, it is too awful to be pryed into by curious eyes. When eternity can be fathomed, and immensity measured—when creation can be accounted for, and the resurrection from the dead be philosophized—when the hidden mystery of God manifest in the flesh, and the guilty sinner being pardoned for the sufferings of an innocent Saviour, are clearly understood, then, and not till then, will limited creatures comprehend the incomprehensible doctrine of a *three-one* God. If the works of God are past finding out, surely the author of those works must be more so.

The strange and unmeaning creeds that have been formed on the Trinity, with the punishments that have been inflicted on those who could not believe them, have astonished the mere reasoner—sickened the grave philosopher, and saddened the pious saint. But, on the other hand, when the doctrine is denied, or despised, with a view to destroy the dignity and glory of Christ, it merits the indignation and pity of all the humble followers of the Lamb.

EXTRACTS FROM AN ESSAY ON THE SABBATH, PUBLISHED IN 1828, ENTITLED LELAND AGAIN.

THE common definition given of *moral law*, is, "that it is the eternal rule of right; arising from the relation that exists between men and their God, and between man and man; and that it will be unalterably binding, as long as the perfections of God and the faculties of men exist." Very good. In a law there are three essential requisites, viz: the *principle*, the *details*, and the *penalty*. The principle of this law is *remember the seventh day and keep it holy*. The details are, *thou shalt do no work, but rest within thy gates with thy children, servants and beasts: thou shalt neither gather sticks, kindle a fire, or think thine own thoughts*. The penalty is, the Sabbath breaker *shall surely be put to death*. If, therefore, the observance of the seventh day is of moral obligation, the day cannot be changed—the exercises altered, nor the penalty remitted. If the fourth commandment is *moral law*, why should God, by an absolute precept, direct the Jews to break it, by circumcising their children on the Sabbath? and why should he instruct the priests, on the day of atonement, (which sometimes happened on the seventh day, and always was a Sabbath,) to butcher, burn, wash and profane the temple on that day?

It is sometimes said, that when Christ was on earth, being Lord of the Sabbath, he new modified the law: but when God, who cannot lie, can change the eternal law of right, (while his perfections and the faculties of men endure,) then I shall believe that *perfect good* can be made *better*.

* * * * * *

The Sabbath of the Israelites was not appointed a day for social worship, but for rest. No active services were enjoined on them on the seventh day, but what they were to perform on other days; except that on the seventh day they were to offer *two* lambs instead of but *one*.

The reason given for the remembrance of the seventh day, in Ex. xx. 11, is, because God rested from the labor of creation on that day and hallowed it: but in Deut. v. 15, where Moses is rehearsing and explaining the law, the reason assigned why the day should be kept, is, *that they were delivered from the bondage of Egypt*. In this rehearsal of the ten commandments, he says, "*The Lord* MADE NOT *this covenant with our* FATHERS *but with* us." That the fourth commandment was an integral part of this covenant, will not be denied, but it was not made with the fathers who were dead, but with those Israelites who were then living. See verse third.

In Psalms lxxiv. 8, *synagogues* are mentioned, (the only place in the Old Testament,) but if the text was written by David, it must be prophecy in historic style, for no synagogues or temple had been burnt up when David lived: the prediction seems to respect the calamitous times of the Jews by the Romans. After the Jews returned from Babylon, they filled their country with synagogues, and assembled in them on every Sabbath, to read Moses and the prophets, and hear the expositions of the scribes. For this, I see no precept given, and find no reproof therefor. It seems to have been a *human, prudential* affair; like the building of meeting-houses by Christians. In this synagogue worship, the Jews, in their scattered condition, were busy, when the HEBREW BOY was born, who was to give law to the world. * * *

In approaching the New Testament, our hearts should be open and our thoughts vigilant. Here a greater than Moses, with an unveiled face, is speaking to *all.* Christianity is for all nations—to be preached to every creature under heaven, and sounded in all the world. The precepts of it, therefore, must be such as can operate every where, and not be limited to any little section of the earth.

Has the blessed Saviour, or his inspired apostles, left on record any command for all men, or for any men, to observe the *seventh* day—the *first* day, or *any* day in every week, as a Christian Sabbath? deriving its morality, either from the *rest* of God, on the seventh day, or from the law of Moses; but varying its mode of exercise to suit the Christian economy? If so, where is the precept to be found?

In the New Testament there is a marked difference between the *Sabbath* and the *first day of the week;* and (if our translation is admitted,) one is never used for the other.

The *Sabbath* that Jesus slept in death, the disciples *rested according to the commandment*—but on the *first day of the week*, some were running to the tomb, others were travelling to Emmaus, and at night they collected together, and shut the doors, for fear of the Jews. And after *eight days*, not after *six* or *seven*, but after eight days they assembled again. If the Saviour had appointed a *first day weekly Sabbath* for his disciples to observe, they certainly had not understood him. Supposing they had continued to celebrate every *ninth day*, they would have found no more than *forty* Sabbaths in a year, instead of *fifty-two*.*

Is it good logic? Is it honest, to draw and enforce consequences from premises that cannot be true? If the premises be true, and God does command all men everywhere, to keep the first day of each week in unison

* If we admit of the common gloss, that "the Jews spoke in that manner," when speaking of a whole week, as we now do in saying, "Sunday and Sunday make eight;" would the next Sunday make sixteen? This way of reckoning would make at most, only forty-five Sundays and a fraction in a year.

with each other, under the penalty of *certain death*; what shall we think of the wisdom and goodness of our Maker?

The history and precepts of the New Testament, with a bold front declare that the Christian religion, in all its parts, cannot be performed without a *public assemblage*: days must, therefore, be appointed, either stated and perpetual, or occasional and contingent: and these days must be appointed by God—by magistrates, or by a mutual agreement of those who assemble together. Magistrates made no Sabbatical or other laws, to direct the Christians when to assemble, before *Constantine*. The Christian church lived three hundred years, therefore, in her purest state, without them: and it has been a heavy curse to the Christian saints, that any such laws were ever in existence. It returns, therefore, that either God or the worshippers themselves must fix the day, for the solemnities of Christian worship. The Israelites lived condensed in a small section of the earth; and God appointed for them the seventh day Sabbath, and a number of feasts and days beside; which, in their located situation, they could all of them keep. But as Christ's subjects are in every kingdom and nation under heaven, (I have said,) it would be impossible for *any day* to be attended to by all of them.

The *three* passages in the New Testament, that the *first-day* worshippers place the greatest reliance upon, are

First. Acts xx. 7. Where a narrative is given that Paul and Co., left Philippi after the *days of unleavened bread*, and came to Troas, where the disciples came together upon the *first day* of the week to break bread; unto whom Paul preached until midnight, and talked even to break of day. This narrative recognizes the days of unleavened bread, as well as the first day of the week. What he had been doing at the feast is not recorded; but that he met with the disciples at Troas, who came together on that day for religious purposes, is certain. Paul's visit at Troas was eight days. That he was busy among them in preaching, hardly admits of a doubt. The disciples got general information that he was there; and on the last day of his visit, which was the first day of the week, they came together. Whether this assembling was occasioned by Paul's being there, or whether it was a stated day among themselves, on which they agreed to meet, I cannot say. In those days some of the Christians esteemed one day above another; while others esteemed every day alike, *which would not have been the case, if Christ had given a commandment for his followers to sanctify the first day of the week, in distinction from all other days.* But whether it was an occasional or stated meeting, it was a voluntary affair. If, however, the history of this interesting meeting is an imperious command on all others to do likewise, it follows, of course, that on the first day of every week the disciples must come together—preach until midnight—

break bread between midnight and day-break, and converse until morning; for if any part of it is preceptive, the whole is.

Second. I Cor. viv. 1, 2. Paul, by the inspiration of Christ, had given order to the churches of Galatia, to collect for the saints at Jerusalem, and here he gives a *so do ye* to the church of Corinth. "Upon the first day of the week, let every one of you lay by him in store, as God hath prospered him." If this *order* respects the *time*, my argument fails; but if it has its bearings, not on the *time*, but on the *things to be done*, the argument is not shaken. Does he say "I *ordered* the Galatians, and I *order* you to keep the first day of the week?" Nothing like it: I have just confessed too much, for in looking over the text carefully, I see no order for them to assemble on the day, or to perform any social acts of oral service; but every one of them was to be weighing, measuring, prizing and casting up to find out how much the Lord had prospered him, and lay by him in store, a portion of his gains for the suffering saints in Judea. * * *

Third. Rev. i. 10. *I was in the spirit on the Lord's day.* We often read of the day of the Lord; but no where of the *Lord's day*, except in this place. That there was one day in the year called Lord's day, and that the people to whom John wrote understood which day it was, leaves no reasonable doubt; but which day of the year it was, is not easily ascertained. Some take it for granted that it was the first day of the week, and consequently call the first day in every week the Lord's day: for this opinion I have not yet seen any reasonable evidence. It looks more likely that Christmas day was so called, which was kept in remembrance of the birth of Christ, and called by his name. But there are some reasons that produce a belief that *Easter* is the day here intended. This day is spoken of in *Acts xii.* 4. And if the first Christians were not in the habit of keeping Easter at first, they very soon fell into the usage. The first great split in the Christian churches was concerning Easter; not whether it should be kept, for in this they were all agreed, but at what *time* it should be celebrated: some pleading for the solar year and others for the lunar. All the proof, therefore, that can be drawn from this text, is, that there was one day in a week—in a month—in a year, or in a longer term, called *Lord's day*. Here it may be noticed, that, including the Greek and Latin churches, an overwhelming majority of Christians, are seven times more attached to the observance of Christmas, Easter, Whitsunday, &c., than they are to keep the *first day* of each week: while a minority are strong advocates for the celebration of the first day, and esteem the majority ignorant and superstitious for observing days, for which they have no command in the laws of Christ. When I hear this, I heartily wish that the minority would point out a *thus saith the Lord* for the keeping of the first day of every week as a *Christian Sabbath.* This I am waiting for, but never expect to see as long as the New Testament continues, and the earth retains its present shape.

The ministry of John the Baptist is called "the beginning of the gospel of Jesus Christ." John never offered sacrifices, sprinkled blood, nor burnt incense like a Jewish priest, but preached repentance for sin, and faith in the Messiah, who stood among them. So, also, Jesus Christ was a preacher of the gospel, and spake as man never spake; but the ministration of the law continued until the *death* of Christ; after which sacrifices lost all their efficacy. There appears to have been a lapping of the two ministrations: the last began with the ministry of John; and the first ended with the death Christ: of course, Jesus Christ was a gospel preacher while the first testament retained its force.

Among other *perfect qualities* of the Lord Jesus, his *example* for gospel preachers was one. He found the men of the world where they were; the Jews in particular, in the constant habit of synagogue worship; and *his custom* was to enter into the synagogue every Sabbath day; thus availing himself of their customs, for opportunities to preach unto them, and heal all that had need of healing. The old Sabbath was yet in force; but it was not an article which he enforced. He gave no information that the Sabbath should be changed, the *seventh day* for the *first;* or that synagogue worship was ordained by God.

With this view of the subject, I have constantly attended public worship on the *first day* of the week, for a number of years. When I travel among or live amidst those who conscientiously keep the *seventh day*, it pleases me equally well. And on any other day of the week, public worship is alike interesting. Did I live on the opposite side of the globe, where the day begins twelve hours before it does in this longitude, I should not be galled in my conscience about the hour. And if in the most northern island that is peopled, where days are long—if I found Christain saints—we should harmonize: for I would never worship *a day*, and make a Saviour of it; but worship the Lord, in spirit and truth, every day; and publicly assemble as often as duty called and opportunity served.

Among us, the *first day* of every week is attended to, by a majority of the people. The Jews among us, and those Christians who prefer the *seventh day* to the first, (though a very respectable body,) are a minority in these United States. If this day is clothed with a legal establishment to enforce its observance, it loses its Christian character and becomes a tyrant over conscience. Otherwise it is harmless in nature, and may be salutary in its effects.

The subject of present investigation admits of great improvement for the better. Let *seven* contiguous congregations appoint their stated worship on the seven days of the week in rotation. This would not only open a door for them to mingle together and assist each other; but in such a course, *one* preacher would answer all the good purposes that *seven* do in the present mode: then the preachers, like the apostles, would preach *daily* and not *weekly:* and by being instant in the work—having their armor on every day, they would abound in zeal, and give a clearer light. Should this scheme be adopted, it would put to silence six-sevenths of the present solicitations, which meet us in every gate and every shape, to bestow our hard earnings, to educate and fit out preachers for destitute congregations and waste places. Yes, should this plan take effect, the saints would content themselves with the only rule given in the New Testament to raise up preachers, which is, "*Pray ye the Lord of the harvest, that he would send forth laborers into the harvest.*"

Those who believe that Christianity is a principle of state policy—that the state should be divided into religious districts, and that each district should be bound to have a preacher—that the preacher must pass through the expensive stages of literature and divinity to be eligible—and that his hearers must pay the back rents for his education, as well as his yearly wages, as a link of the same chain, will strongly plead for a *day* to be set apart by law, as an *auction day* in each week, for the priest to vend the production of his toils to the highest bidders. But for Christians to judge and set at naught a brother, who differs with them in respect of observing a day or not observing it, when every one is to be fully persuaded in his own mind, shows a great lack of the meekness of Christ. Cruel must that censure be, for one Christian to condemn another, for not observing a day nowhere enjoined in the Christian code. If such a command is to be found in the New Testament, let the text be designated, and I will take conviction.

ADDRESS

DELIVERED AT PITTSFIELD, JAN. 8, 1829.

Fellow citizens:—On the request of your committe, I arise to address you, with a consciousness of the want of talent, and with depreciated intellect.

The maker and governor of all nations is omniscient. He knows all things. With him there is nothing new. The past, the present, and the to-come, with us are all in his eternal now. With one comprehensive glance, he takes in view all actions, and all motives which produce them; but the case of men is very different. We know but little. Our capacities are small and limited; our pursuit after knowledge is languid; deceptions are abundant; truth lies in a well, we have to dig deep and draw long to get it. "How dark! how intricate the road that leads to intellectual light!" Some men, however, either by the endowments of talent, by greater opportunity, or close research, rise high, and border on the angelic science, while others grovel in the earth, and rise but a small grade above the brutes.

Perhaps an assembly of wiser patriots were never collected together, than at the convention in Philadelphia, in 1787. The United States had gained their independence at the expense of much treasure, toil, and blood, but had at that time, no efficient government for civil regulation. The articles of confederation, were found by experience, to be insufficient to govern the nation; and, to remedy the defects, the several states selected their sages to meet in convention, and point out the road to national safety and happiness. This convention had the experience of all former ages before them, and knew well the condition of all the states; and, after three months deliberation, produced a constitution of government, which was ratified by the people; and which (with some salutary amendments that have been annexed unto it) has been the supreme law of the United States for forty years, under which they have prospered and risen to high renown.

It is not possible for one man, or a body of men, in framing a constitution, or giving a code of laws, to make provision for every event that will take place. Without inspiration, the events will not be known beforehand. Inspiration itself, makes known but few of the events that do take place among men. And, besides, if an attempt should be made to meet every emergence, the book would be so voluminous, that a human mind could not contain it. Government, must, therefore, have a quantum of confidence reposed in the agents, checked by responsibility. These items should be as rare as possible; but, when they do arise, if the rights of the citizens clash with the energies of government or the letter of the law, the rights of the citizens should always have the pre-eminence; for natural right is anterior to all law. These rights are the gifts of God; constitutions and laws are the creatures of men. This is a glass in which we may see the faces of the two parties in the United States, let them be called by what names soever. In the construction or interpretation of those things that are necessarily obscure, or not expressly provided for, one has the honor of government, and his own honor and importance, for his land-mark; the other, the rights of the people for his polar star. One gratifies his own will, at the expense of being burnt in effigy by an indignant people; the other executes the known will of his constituents, to the sacrificing of his own opinion.

It is no ways probable, that the convention that framed the constitution, or the state conventions who ratified it, ever thought that a time would come, when the representatives in Congress would seek to cheat the people out of the president who was fairly elected; or that a state would give one voice by her electors, and another by her representatives; yet these events have both taken place, one of them in twelve, and the other in thirty-six years after the adoption of the constitution. In the administration of the elder Adams, an alien act, a sedition law, a direct tax, a standing army, an eight per cent loan, etc., all arose, which were so abhorrent to the people, that they rose in their strength, and elected other men, that there might be a change of measures. Jefferson and Burr obtained seven electoral votes more than Adams and Pinckney. As the constitution then stood, the electors did not designate the president and vice-president; and, as Jefferson and Burr had an equal number of votes, the states in Congress, by their representatives, had to select one of the two for president. In this crisis, it it believed that there was not a man in Congress but knew that it was the design of the people that Jefferson, and not Burr should be the president; but, as there was a gap for chicanery, the adverse party, finding that Burr would hearken to proposals, sustained thirty-six ballotings, to cheat the people out of their president. Was this bowing to the majesty of the people? The United States were so alarmed at this event, that they altered the constitution, to prevent the like again.

In the presidential election of 1824, another game was played. Jackson had fifteen more electoral votes than the second Adams, but not a majority of the whole; and, therefore, the selection devolved on the representatives in Congress. In this selection, some of the states who had voted by their electoral colleges for Jackson, now, by their representatives, voted for Adams; some of whom, at least, had the express wish and known will of the states where they lived, that they would give their votes for Jackson; but, for some reason or other, the will of the people was trampled upon. If Herod and Pontius Pilate, who before were at strife, were not made friends, in order to crucify Jackson, and keep the presidency in a cabinet line, our senses have deceived us. Two thirds of the people, in the now presidential election, on oath, have declared it to be true. Well done, Uncle Sam! neither the terror of the administration of the elder Adams, nor the intrigue that was used to elect the second Adams, and perpetuate the dynasty in a cabinet line, have deterred or deceived you. Go on, sir, with your independent majesty, and the kind heavens will prosper you.

It must be granted, that every man has ambition to excel, and a thirst after pre-eminence. This propensity is nourished by base men, which leads them into the various parts of tyranny. Such men serve not their country, but themselves, and by good words and fair speeches, deceive the simple. Men of this description, should be trusted no more with the destinies of government, than wolves should be placed to guard the sheep. But the good man suppresses this vile ambition, and transforms it into patriotic emulation. Did Washington, did Jefferson ever seek to be promoted? Did they ever express a desire to be exalted on the ruin of public good or public will? Were they not always little in their own eyes, and subservient to the voice of their country? Let the history of their lives answer the questions. And has Jackson ever been an office-hunter? has he ever sought promotion? When the safety of his country called for the display of his talents, he has never declined the enterprise, though painful and hazardous; but, as soon as the object was gained, like Cincinnatus and Seranus, he has retired to his home, to feast on the furniture of his own mind, and enjoy the scenes of rural life.

A man may conquer in many pitched battles, and be destitute of the talents which a statesman and chief magistrate should possess; but, he who can make soldiers out of ruffians—create supplies for an army in a waste place—fasten every soldier to him in love and fear—be so sagacious as never to be surprized—and defeat an army vastly superior to his own, with the loss of little or no blood, gives the best pledges that he is endowed with a gift to rule.

Such has been the case with Jackson. The battle, just hinted at, which ended in a splendid victory, was fought on the eighth of January, 1815, and has given rise to the present assembly, to celebrate the victory of that day.

This evening is awfully solemn, like the evening of the passover, which was a time much to be observed by the children of Israel. Cast your thoughts back fourteen years from this day, and reflect on the prize at stake. The "beauty and booty" of New Orleans—the navigation of the Mississippi, and the American army. When so much was at hazard, well might the commander and his men exclaim, "If we perish, we will perish in the last ditch."

The western troops deserve well of their country. I personally knew a great number of the early settlers of Kentucky; they were my neighbors and acquaintances—they were men of principle, patriotism, and benevolence, "not quarrelsome, but bold enough to fight;" and their sons have not disgraced them. To defend their own homes from the savages, had taught them the art and hardships of war, and the use of the rifle; and, at this battle, every squint they made was a harbinger of certain death.

From the great law of self-preservation, which is paramount to all laws written on parchment, General Jackson was necessarily impelled to proclaim martial law in New Orleans, and stop the proceedings of the civil functionaries. It was a daring attempt; but he took the responsibility upon himself, and by doing it, he saved the city. For this, however, he was fined $1000 by Judge Hall, which he peaceably paid, out of his own funds. The "beauty" of the city, soon raised the "booty" of a fine to remunerate their deliverer; which he received on no other conditions, than that it should be given to the widows and orphans of those who died in camp.

General Jackson has been represented, by his enemies, as deficient in the art of writing; I know not for what. All of his officials, addresses, and epistles, that I have seen, are masculine and luminous, and, when he has done, he leaves off. To say that he can compress as many rich ideas on a small piece of paper, and leave nothing obscure, as Jefferson did, would be saying that of him which no man on earth merits. The valor of his pen, and the valor of his sword, have both been tested; and it will impress the reader of his exploits, that no difficulty which he has as yet encountered, was strong enough to draw out all his energies; no chair large enough for him; he would spread over it on every side. Self-taught, he has made himself. Indeed, if a man cannot make himself, he cannot keep himself, after others have made him. It is folly to attempt to hold up a man to whom God has given no legs.

It is the cant of the times, that Jackson will be an awkward president, and make many blunders. It may be so; but his opportunity has been as great to inform himself of the usages of courts and ambassadors, as was that of Washington; and he never blundered into the ditch. But these fopperies, which monarchs and aristocrats think so much of, do not weigh an ounce of lampblack, in the estimation of republicans. A republic, like a kitchen-garden, should have every thing necessary, but nothing superfluous. To my certain knowledge, fifty years past, nothing degraded an American sooner than for him to plead for the usages of European courts.

As the president of the United States, elect, in every station that he has stood in, has given great satisfaction to all the people, except those who were jealous of his popularity, so in the administration of the government we hope he will do likewise. If he remains little in his own eyes, he will appear great in the eyes of others. If he does not forget the rights of the people, the people will not forget him. If he steers the ship between Sylla and Charibdes, the crew will rejoice. But, if he counteracts all these things, the people, (not with sword and cannon,) but with little bits of paper, will give him leave of absence, and provide for him a home department.

While we, this evening, feast on dainties, let us not forget the man who fed on acorns to defend our rights. Nor let us be unmindful of the American watchman, honest George Kremer,, who cackles but little, but lays good eggs. And let us extend the hand of friendship to the unwavering friend of the people, Martin Van Buren, now governor of New York.

The exertions made for education—the circulation of history, and the thirst of the rising generation after information, are favorable symptoms that the states will not fall into degradation and vassalage through ignorance. It is but for the United States to know their rights and corresponding duties, to be as happy and prosperous as the state of man admits of. But, clamor must be considered as a certain tax which all free governments have to pay. In the election of a chief magistrate, some will be influenced by the hopes of office, and others by personalities, and the tax of clamor will be imposed. But, when the question is fairly taken and settled by a majority, the man who murmurs is a tyrant.

To close these miscellaneous remarks, let it be remembered, that without industry, frugality, honesty, temperance, subordination to the laws, and a reverence for the precepts and spirit of religion, no government on earth can make us prosperous or happy. While we, therefore, freely animadvert upon the characters and measures of our rulers, let us be cautious of blaming them for the evils that proceed from our own errors.

While we believe that government, formed not on birth, not on conquest, not on wealth, nor on grace, but on mutual compact, is according to immutable right; let us beware, in electing agents, not to form entangling alliancies with those who differ with us in opinion. Their words will eat like a canker worm, and spread like a gangrene. When we are in the minority, let us remain steadfast, and peaceably seek a reform, and patiently bear what our sentiments exposes us to. When we are in the majority, let us be assiduous to guarantee to those who differ with us the full latitude of their privileges; for heretics and minorities have both inalienable and chartered rights, of which they cannot be deprived, but by the iron hand of oppression.

God save the United States—bless the Congress—protect the beauty and booty of New Orleans, and preserve the life of ANDREW JACKSON.

ADDRESS

AT THE DEDICATION OF THE BAPTIST MEETING-HOUSE IN LANESBOROUGH, FEBRUARY 10, 1829.

Mountains of gold—rivers of oil—the cattle upon a thousand hills, and all the treasures of the earth cannot purchase a pardon of sin, nor a title to the kingdom of heaven: yet the religion of Jehovah has always cost his worshippers time and property. The excellent offering of righteous Abel consisted of the "firstlings of his flock, and the fat thereof"—the sacrifice of Noah, of the "clean beasts"—the oblation of Abraham, of "a ram, a heifer, a she goat, a turtle, and a pigeon." About the time that the Almighty brought the oppressed Israelites out of bondage, he ordained the new moon, or first day of the month. This ordained statute, the God of Jacob appointed in the life time of Joseph, before the Israelites generally understood the language of Egypt. This solemn feast-day, at every new moon, was ushered in by blowing a trumpet: Psalm lxxxi., 3, 4, 5. Soon after this the passover was appointed, and God delivered the shoulders of the Israelites from burdens, and their hands from the pots. On the second month after their deliverance the rest of the holy Sabbath was enjoined to be observed every seventh day, with a penalty of certain death.

In the religious code of laws which the Israelites received from God, at Mount Sinai, provision was made for building the Tabernacle, alias, sanctuary, at considerable expense. The gold, silver, and brass used in this building exceeded ten tons. This building was moved from place to place, with its utensils, carried partly in waggons, and partly on men's shoulders, until it was settled at Shiloh.

In the days of King Solomon, the most superb and costly temple was erected that was ever on earth. This building was a house of God, built by divine direction. The treasures which David had collected for the building of the temple, during his troublesome wars, exceeded five thousand tons of gold, and fifty thousand tons of silver, beside iron, brass, timber and stone without estimation. His personal contribution was equal to eighty-five millions of dollars.* After the tribes took possession of the

* These estimations are given in whole numbers, calculated on the presumed truth, that a Hebrew talent is equal to one hundred pounds Avoirdupois. The Avoirdupois and Troy standards are distinct. Fifty-one ounces Troy are equal to fifty-six Avoirdupois. Fourteen pounds Avoirdupois are equal to seventeen pounds Troy.

promised land, all of them were to meet at the place which God chose three times in each year, and continue there seven or eight days. Time was spent—travel sustained, and great offerings made at these yearly feasts. And, in addition to the daily, free-will and feast-offerings, the tenth part of their yearly products was given to the priestly tribe of Levi. From the organization of the Jewish church, until the introduction of Christianity, religion bore a national character. Internal godliness was not necessary to qualify a member of the church. Natural birth and circumcision were the prerequisites. The ordinances imposed on that church, were such as natural men could perform, consisting of what could be touched, tasted and handled, every way corresponding with their worldly sanctuary. Hence, splendor, show and majesty were proper.

That the temple of Solomon was a figure of the gospel church, admits of no doubt; but the splendor of the church consists of internal and spiritual excellence, and not of external pomp and grandeur. The immense treasures that David and Solomon, and the kingdom expended in the temple, faintly point to the price given to redeem the church. The incarnate God purchased the church, not with gold and silver, but with his own blood. "The redemption of the soul is precious." This sanctuary and temple worship was congenial with the first Testament, but looked forward to a better covenant, established on better promises. It had no glory in comparison of that which excelled. Having answered the purposes of the night, the day-spring from on high, at length appeared, and the unveiled truth was ushered in. By a man of rusticity—*fitted out* for the ministry in the wilderness, (John the Baptist,) the gospel was introduced. In this beginning of the gospel of Jesus Christ, repentance for sin—belief in the Messiah, with correspondent fruits, were proclaimed by "the voice of one crying in the wilderness:" who also declared that the natural seed of Abraham, without repentance and faith, were serpents and vipers. John was a travelling preacher, and his success was astonishing—but he had no legal salary or support from missionary funds. He came to prepare the way of the Lord, who soon appeared. John had not known Jesus before, but by a token given: he saw him, and said to his hearers, "Behold the Lamb of God who taketh away the sin of the world!"

Jesus began his ministry in the strain that John preached, saying, "repent and believe the gospel." The incarnation of Christ is inconceivable, and of course, inexplicable. That he was God over all—the true God and eternal life—the first—in whom dwelt all the fulness of the Godhead—the creator of all things—bearing all the names and titles, and doing all the works of Israel's Jehovah, is certain. And that he was man—having flesh, bones and blood—subject to hunger, thirst, weariness, sleep, tears, and death is as certain. But the great mystery of godliness, "God manifest in the flesh," can be no more comprehended by men who believe it, than the conception of a virgin, and her bearing a child, can be understood by those who believe he was merely a man. As a preacher, he went about doing good—preaching the gospel of the kingdom—healing all that were diseased, and granting pardon of sin to all the penitent. His public ministry was short, (but about three years,) and yet in that short period, his wonderful works, and marvelous words were so many, that a history of the whole would be too voluminous for the human mind. But, living and working miracles, was not the whole of his work: he came to lay down his life for his sheep. As a martyr, he resisted unto blood, bearing all the abuse, perjury and cruelty of implacable enemies; as a mediator, he endured that trouble of soul—that excruciating distress—that agony and bloody sweat—that forsaking of God that was necessary to vindicate the divine honor—magnify the law—make an end of sin, and bring in everlasting righteousness, that enemies might be reconciled to God. He died for our sins, according to the Scriptures; he commended his love to us, in, that when we were enemies, Christ died for the ungodly. That he died, the Jews believed, and rejoiced at the event, but that he rose from the dead, they were so loth to believe that they denied it, and (as a body) continue to deny it unto this day. The resurrection of Christ from the dead, is the grand pivot of the controversy, between Jews and infidels, on one part, and Christians on the other. That the body of Jesus, which was bruised and wounded with whip, nails and spear, did rise from the dead and was seen—conversed with—handled and eaten with after his resurrection, is boldly affirmed to us, by the writers of the New Testament—and as promptly denied by Jews and infidels.

If the testimony of the watch, *that the disciples came and stole him away while they were sleeping* was true, (for although they could not tell what was done when they were sleeping, yet such an event might possibly take place) I ask what they did with his body? Could they, in a few minutes, watched as they were, have secreted it from the eye of search? What became of the body? Who has ever seen it, except those who declare that it rose from the dead? The first preachers of the resurrection of Christ, did not go into a distant land to publish the strange event, so far from where it took place that the truth of it could not be tested; but (according to their orders) they began at Jerusalem, at the very place where the event took place, that every man might have it in his power to test every word which they said. The adversaries to the resurrection had every advantage to prove the imposture, if it was so. Now, if the preaching of the resurrection of Christ, by plain, simple, unlearned men, (who had nothing to expect for their labor, in this world, but the axe or the cross) gained such evidence in the minds of every class of men, that in three hundred years it overturned an empire, claiming universal sway, who can deny the truth of it? It is true that the Mahomedan religion has gained as much ground as Christianity has, but *law, sword* and *fire* were their most powerful arguments. Quite the reverse with Christianity. Not only without the aid of law, sword or college, but in opposition to them all; by simply appealing to the reason and judgments of men, without coercive means; requesting only a dispassionate hearing and a correspondent faith, they pursued their ministerial career.*

When Jesus was on earth, he chose *whom he would* of his disciples, twelve in number, ordained them, and gave them a limited district to preach and heal the sick in. And afterwards he appointed seventy others, and sent them forth with similar orders. But after his resurrection, he enlarged their commission, saying, "Go ye into all the world, and preach the gospel to every creature." This commission seems to say, "now the middle wall of partition between Jews and Gentiles is broken down, now the door of faith is open to the Gentiles, therefore quit your Jewish prejudices, and call no man common whom the Lord has cleansed." In accordance with this commission, they went forth and preached every where, the Lord working with them. Not only in the first instance did the Lord neglect the wise and prudent, and send forth fishermen babes to preach his gospel, but afterwards in Corinth, we find that not many wise men, noble or mighty, were called to the work, but the foolish, weak, base, despised and nothing things of the world were chosen to confound the wise and mighty, that no flesh should glory in his presence. Paul seems to have been one of the few called to the work, who was a man of science, but speaks thus of himself:—"When I came to you, I came not with excellency of speech or of wisdom—my speech and my preaching was not of enticing words of man's wisdom, but in demonstration of the spirit and of power—we speak the wisdom of God in a mystery, which none of the princes of this world know."†

In the commission which our Lord gave to his apostles, there was no *condition*. He did not say, "Go and preach if the people will pay you, applaud or honor you;" nothing like it. He told them that the laborer was worthy of a reward; and Paul, by inspiration, enjoins it on those who are taught, to communicate to the teacher—not to muzzle the mouth of the ox who treadeth out the corn—assuring them that God had ordained that those who preach the gospel should live of it, &c. But this duty of the people is not made a condition in the commission: the preacher must not,

* It is a lamentable truth, which calls for tears of blood, that since Christianity has been established by law, and become an institute of state policy, it has been perverted to the most cruel and bloody purposes. No nations have been more perfidious, unjust and warlike, than those nations who have professed to follow the meek and lowly Jesus, who did no harm. Tell it not in Gath!

† Children come into the world in ignorance—whatever they know they have to learn—consequently he that knows the most has the most learning, whether he acquires it at the seat of erudition, in his study, or in the school of Christ.

therefore, be disobedient to the call, if hearers neglect their duty; but preach as much as he can, consistent with other duties.

After the ascension of Christ the success of the gospel was astonishing. When Matthias was chosen an apostle, the number was one hundred and twenty. To these, on the day of Pentecost, three thousand were added. Soon after this the number of them that believed was about five thousand. Still further, believers were the more added to the Lord, multitudes both of men and women; but no meeting-house, built for Christian worship, was at this time in existence. The old temple and private houses were the places where they preached *daily*.

David speaks of synagogues, but it is most likely his words were prophetic of a future period; for there is no historical account of any synagogues in the time of David, nor in any time before the Babylonish captivity. The temple was the only meeting-house for the Tribes. After the Jews returned from Babylon, they built synagogues to assemble in on every Sabbath and read the law of Moses. For the building of these synagoues there was no divine order given, nor any reproof for it. It was a *prudential* matter, in which men of *themselves are to judge what is right*. So with regard to houses for Christian worship, whether they are called cathedrals, chapels, churches, tabernacles, meeting-houses, or by any other name; no orders are seen in the New Testament for the churches to build such houses, nor any prohibition. It is a matter of convenience to be managed with discretion. I know not where or when the first house of this description was built. I have preached in four hundred and sixty such houses, and seen many more; which, together, would make but a very small part of what are in Christendom. It is said that sixteen hundred of them were consumed in the late destruction of Moscow. To ascertain how many such houses are now in the world, would be a Herculean task; and to know how many have been, which are demolished, impossible. Abundance of pride, pomposity, and unnecessary expense, is to be seen in many of those buildings reared to worship *Him* who was born in a stable and cradled in a manger. And if we are to judge by the course of his life, and the precepts which he taught, all this bombast is unacceptable with God and unprofitable to man. To see a magnificent state house, filled with starved senators and purpled princes, in the midst of a multitude of subjects, clothed in tattered garments and begging for bread, is not so terrific as it is to see one of those splendid edifices, shining with gold and pearls, filled with worshippers, adorned with every badge of pride and self-importance, claiming the peculiar favors of HIM who dwelleth not in temples made with hands, but in the humble spirit and contrite heart, and seeketh such to worship him, as worship in spirit and in truth.

To consecrate these houses and the burying ground attached to them—baptize the bells, and speak of the *sacred* desk and altar, is a hotch-potch of Paganism, Judaism, and superstitious Christianity. Such foppery and foolishness is but a stench in Jehovah's nose—he will not smell in such assemblies.

Common sense dictates that meeting-houses should be built in places the most convenient, in a manner the most advantageous to the assembly, with materials the most durable, at an expense within the command of the proprietors, without crowding on other benevolent duties, having nothing in or around them to foster the pride or deject the spirits of the assembly, or in any way draw off their thoughts from eternal realities.

Benevolence is a human and Christian duty, but liberality should always be governed by discretion. For a man to give all that he has to relieve *one* object of distress, and thereby render himself incapable of relieving another, in most cases would be improper. Liberality at the expense of moral honesty is despicable; 'tis cheating *one* to favor another. To bestow that to religious uses which God appoints for human relief is reprehensible. God commanded the Jews to honor father and mother, that is, to relieve and requite them; but they said, (CORBIN) it is a gift. Instead of relieving father or mother they would give what they had to spare to God. This made the commands of God void by their traditions. He who gives his income to the indolent poor, and neglects his debts is a dishonest man.

The faith of our Lord Jesus Christ, the king of glory, forbids partiality in religious assemblies. To appoint the good places for the rich, who wear gold rings and fine apparel, and neglect the poor, who have vile raiment, is censured in scripture; from which it seems that no respect should be shown to the prince above the servant. Each should have an equal opportunity, as each is equally responsible. Meeting-houses should be as common, in this respect, as burying grounds. That distinction which exists, and is necessary in civil and domestic concerns, subsides in religious assemblies. Each individual there should realize that he stands on common ground with all others; equally mortal, equally apostatized, equally responsible, and equally addressed with the glad tidings of peace through the blood of the Lamb. A proper sense of these articles is the *best sexton* to keep order in religious assemblies.

When we enter a meeting-house for religious worship, each one may ask the question, "What was this house erected for? *To pray, preach and sing praise in.* How is God to be worshipped? *In spirit and in truth.* Can unconverted men, as such, perform any part of religious worship acceptable to God? *None at all.* If worship is a spiritual exercise, why was this house built? *To accommodate the saints in assembling together in one place.* Ought none to assemble but the saints? *If any man have ears to hear, let him hear; force none to come, forbid none that would.*

When Christian assemblies were first established, whether they assembled in dwelling-houses, school-houses, or meeting-houses, the exercises of prayer, preaching, prophesying, exhorting, singing, &c., were performed in them; performed in the spirit, in a manner that all could understand and be edified. But how often they assembled, whether once a week or once a month, whether statedly or occasionally, and whether these various assemblies convened on the same day, or had each of them a self-appointed day (which seems to be the most likely) is not so certain.

What condition the religious world would be in at the present time, if previous events had taken a different course, can never be ascertained. Events have revolved as they have, and produced the state of things which now exists. What becomes professors at the present day, is, "to mark existing errors and avoid them, withstand the strong current of custom where it is wicked and vain, rally round the standard of the Holy Scriptures, and enlist under its banners. Never *adopt* or *reject* any sentiment or rite on account of its long standing or novelty, but test all by the standard." That the Christian world has been in a gross error, from the days of Constantine to the present time, admits of no doubt. From that period down, the Christian religion has been an institute of state policy, regulated by the laws of men, and supported by the sword of the magistrate. Whether in a papal or protestant mode, the principle has done incalculable mischief, and drenched the earth in blood.

In the United States, the felonious principle has been apprehended, tried, condemned and executed. Roger Williams and William Penn first attacked the villain, and Thomas Jefferson did more than any one man to bring him to the stake. Some few roots of this principle are yet in the soil of Massachusetts, interwoven in the constitution and laws of the state; but the spirit of the people triumphs over those evil roots. There are but few places in the state where the people would succumb to a *legal* distraint for *religious* uses.

Another scheme now supersedes. Application is now made to the benevolence, the honor, the piety and pity of the people, to raise funds, by all devisable methods, for the purpose of erecting colleges and theological seminaries, to fit out pious youth, to send as missionaries to different stations, to spread Christianity over the world. And, notwithstanding the immense sums that have been realized and are in train, still the agents complain of heavy debts now existing, and other imperious calls for money to keep the machine in motion.

Among Christians, equally pious and wise, there is a difference of opinion respecting the present exertions, which are in the full tide of experiment. Some see in them the rising of the latter-day glory, when kings shall bring their gold and treasures into the church, and the Lord be king over all the earth. In this view of the subject, every mendicant or solicitor is not only well rewarded out of the money which he collects, but is considered as purchasing a good degree and great boldness in faith. And all who will not unite with them, hand and purse, to aid this work, they consider covetous men, who have no regard for the salvation of souls.

Others are afraid that these existing funds will fill the ministerial ranks with indolent, covetous mercenaries: that lazy boys, seeing the prospect before them, will assume the disguise of pharisaic reserve—become beneficiaries and licentiates, for their own emolument, and not for the good of others: that these exertions tend to foster the pride of those who wish to be heard, attended to, and treated as a class of singular characters: that there is no likeness between the apostolic missionary exertions and the present, either in spirit or method: that it is going over the ground again, which the chuch trod in the second and third centuries, which produced a national established Christianity, and finally led on to the rise of the whore of Babylon. The parties are now at issue. Time will bring in a true verdict.

In comparison of the present missionary struggle, a recent affair, within the memory of many who are now living, claims an account. In Windsor and Tolland, Connecticut, a few of the New Lights were internally impressed that God had a great work for them to do at the west, and were not disobedient to the divine teaching. Daniel Marshal left his home, and took his course to the head of the Susquehanna, carrying his family with him. Shubal Stearns, with a few of his church, in 1754, started for the west, selling or giving away what they had. Stearns and Marshall met in Virginia, and moved on to North Carolina. Here they fixed their station, and, in 1755, they formed into a church, having sixteen members, on Sandy Creek, Guilford county. They immediately began their work, and God smiled on their labors. Soon their little church increased to more than six hundred. From this beginning, the flame prevailed in every direction. In the south part of Virginia, North and South Carolina, Georgia, Tennessee and Kentucky, there are more than a thousand Baptist churches, now existing, which arose from that beginning. These missionaries had neither outfit nor annuity. The providence of God, the prayers of the saints, and benevolence of those who were taught by them, carried them through. Stearns died in 1771. Marshall lived until 1784, and then fell asleep.

This affair borders on the missionary proceedings of the apostles; but the modern exertions seem to be grounded on *human calculation*, and not on *divine impression:* in which outfit and annuities form a prominent part. In the domestic mission, our own money circulates from hand to hand; but, in the foreign mission, nothing but silver and gold will answer, which drains the country of its precious metals. On this, a question arises, whether the institution of Christ to Christianize the world, has anything in it which tends to impoverish a nation?

That Christianity is now in a flourishing condition, in the outer court, is certain. The hosts that unite with religious societies, the many splendid houses that are built for Christian worship, and the immense sums that are raised to endow theological seminaries and send missionaries over sea and land, all substantiate the fact. Indeed, what is called religion, is now the most fashionable thing that can be named, through every grade of the community, from the venerable president of the Bible Society, down to the lisping child at Sunday School.

But the inner court presents nothing so flattering. There is but little likeness between the religion of the present day and that which prevailed in the prime of Christianity. Murders, robberies, fraud, drunkenness, duellings, ambition for office, thirst for money and wealth, extravagance in praise, religious deception to collect money, etc., seem to keep pace with our population; so that a man, unbiased by any religious system, would conclude that there was as loud call for the Hindoos to send their missionaries among us, to reclaim us from these errors, as there is for us to send our missionaries among them, to turn them from idolatry and immolation.

The time of *outward* prosperity and *inward* depression of religion, is favorable for the introduction of customs and laws, which lead on to persecution and blood-shedding. The buddings of these begin to appear among us. Why fine a Jew for opening his store on Sunday? Why stop travellers on the same day? Why have a law of Congress to stop the mail on the day that one part of the community think should be kept holy, when another part as honestly believe that another day is appointed by God, and a third and large party judge that every day is alike? In this diversity of sentiment, must Congress, or any uninspired legislature, decide the question—explain for certain the law of God, and punish all that disobey? If one individual has his own liberty guaranteed to him, why should he wish to have his neighbor deprived of the same? When two men meet in the road, what right has one more than the other to demand the whole path? None but tyrants desire it. For one man to make his own conscience the standard for another man's conduct, is cruel stupidity.

Some meeting-houses are built by legal taxation—some by a generous individual—but many are erected, like the one in which we are, by the combination of many; each contributing according to his pleasure. And, as the house is built on liberal principles, so, likewise, I am instructed to state, it is to be occupied in a free manner. No one who shall choose to attend, either constantly or transiently, will be considered an intruder in seating himself at pleasure. None will be compelled to come—none will be refused accommodation.

We congratulate the proprietors of this house, in completing it without the loss of life or limb. And surely your liberal views and helping hands will meet with the praise of all the lovers of Jesus and lovers of freedom. Here you may be accommodated for life, and when you go the way of all the earth, your descendants may enjoy it as an inheritance. We hope your liberal exertions will ascend as a memorial to Him, for whose praise and glory the house was built, and that He will frequently send down his holy spirit on the people who assemble at this place. Why may we not pray for a heavenly blessing to-day? If it would be presumption for us to pray for the Holy Ghost, like a mighty rushing wind, to descend and fill this house, as it did the temple on the day of Pentecost, yet, surely, it cannot be arrogant or improper for us to pray that the spirit of the Lord might descend in its ordinary course, and not only fill the saints with joy, but turn sinners from darkness to light, and from the power of Satan unto the living God; for nothing appears more gloomy and preposterous, than to see a temple, built for the worship of God, filled with a lifeless preacher and an inattentive congregation. It is, therefore, ardently desired, that this congregation, whether they have a stated preacher, or only occasional supplies, may be visited by Him, who walks amidst the golden candlesticks, and holds the stars in his right hand. Our hearts rise with the pleasing anticipation that this house may be a place of the spreading of nets, and that the fish may be as the fish of the great sea, exceeding many. That, while the gospel, like the living waters, shall flow from this pulpit, the seats may be filled with penitent sinners and rejoicing saints. That multitudes may here say, "come, draw near all ye that fear God, and I will declare what he has done for my soul." Such exercises would richly reward the proprietors of this house for their labor, and fill the saints with joy, that would extend to the angels in heaven.

Young people, can you hear of this without emotion of heart? Is there none of you that will huzza for Jesus to-day—none that will desert from Satan, and fly to the Saviour, who loved sinners, and gave his blood to save them?

Sinners, can you hate that Saviour?
  Can you thrust him from your arms?
Once he died for your behaviour,
  Now he calls you to his charms.

FACTS AND QUESTIONS.*

It is a thought, possible with all—probable with many—and certain with a few, that the antediluvians ate no flesh. Vegetables, seed and fruit were given them for food. They lived to a great age. No more than twenty-seven of their names are given in their history, and yet seven of them, including Noah, lived more than nine hundred years. The antediluvian age lasted sixteen hundred and fifty-six years. After the flood the charter of food was enlarged: every living thing that moved was given to men, to eat their flesh, but not their blood. No one was born after this period who lived five hundred years. What the people drank before the flood, is not told us, but that they were eating and drinking, until Noah entered the ark, we are assured of. After the deluge, Noah became an husbandman, planted a vineyard, and drank wine until he was drunk. Perhaps this was the first inebriation that took place on earth. From Noah, until Moses, a space of eight hundred years, frequent mention is made of eating flesh and drinking wine, but no account of strong drink or liquor. During the time that judges ruled, and kings reigned over the nation of Israel, strong drink, and liquor, were much used and much abused: in some cases commanded, and in other cases forbidden. See the following texts:

Exodus, xxii., 29: Thou shalt not delay to offer the first of thy *liquors*.

Leviticus, x. 9: Do not drink wine nor *strong drink*.

Numbers, vi., 3: He shall separate himself from wine and *strong drink*, neither shall he drink any *liquor* of grapes.

Deuteronemy, xiv., 26: Thou shalt bestow the money for wine or *strong drink*, or for whatsoever thy soul lusteth.

Judges, xiii., 4, 7, 14: Drink neither wine nor *strong drink*.

1st Samuel, i., 15: I have drunk neither wine nor *strong drink*.

Proverbs, xxxi., 4. 6: It is not for princes to drink *strong drink*,—give *strong drink* to those who are ready to perish.

Song, viii., 2: I would cause thee to drink of the juice of my pomegranate.

Isaiah, v., 11, 12: That they may follow *strong drink*—and mingle *strong drink*.

From these, and other passages, it is evident, that in addition to water, wine, vinegar, milk, broth, juice of pomegranates, and pottage of lentiles,

* Published in 1829.

that liquor and strong drink were distinct articles; but what they were, and how they were manufactured, is hard to say. The apple-tree is spoken of as a common and useful tree, (see Song, xi., 3: Joel, i. 12,) but whether the people, as far back as Moses, pressed cider out of the apples is not known; if they did, it is probable that cider was their strong drink. Dr. Gill, from Aben Ezra, a Jewish Rabbi, says, that strong drink, and liquor, were made of dates and honey, wheat and barley. But by whatsoever they were made, and by what process they were manufactured, they had the quality, like wine, to inebriate: and the excessive use of them made one of the crying sins of the Israelites, and of the surrounding nations. Hewett's account of the first invention of alcohol, by an Arabian physician and chemist, is two thousand years too late to give character to the strong drink, and liquors, that were put to a pernicious use in ancient times, and brought so many woes and judgments on drunkards.

I judge, that drunkenness, effected either by ancient strong drink, or modern rum, amounts to the same evil, and has the same impression on body, mind, interest and manners.

The wise Solomon unites with the prophets of his nation, in exposing the evil of drunkenness, but to qualify his reproofs, he says, "Give strong drink to those who are ready to perish, and wine to those who are of heavy heart." St. Paul reproves the excess of wine, and declares that drunkards shall not enter into the kingdom of God: yet he advises the infirm Timothy, to "drink no longer water, but use a little wine for his stomach's sake, and often infirmities."

There is a medical, as well as nutritive quality, in the productions of the earth. Nothing is made in vain. Poisons are medicinal when properly used. God has pronounced the whole creation good.

It is common for men, in the heat of an argument, to carry things too far: their declamations may have a momentary impression, but sober reflection and experiment will bring things to their proper bearings.

These observations suggest a few questions.

First. Is it reasonable to believe that the second cause of the shortening of the lives of men, after the flood, was the use of animal food? If this could be substantiated, would it not be a loud call to the lovers of life to be sparing of sumptuous dinners, composed of meat? Do not gluttony and drunkenness unite to enfeeble body and mind? Can there be evidence produced, that at any one time as many lives were sacrificed by ardent spirits, as were destroyed by eating the flesh of quails? Because meat, used immoderately, degrades the intellect, breeds diseases, and shortens days, is it, therefore, best to disuse it altogether?

Second. It is pretty generally confessed that wine and ardent spirits are good for men in certain cases, but who is to be the judge of these cases? Not the drunken sot, for he would be always pouring the liquor down his throat; not the physician, for although he may know what suits his own constitution, and tends to his health, yet he cannot feel for another. The sober man himself is the best judge for himself: so Solomon gave himself to wine, (to test its effects,) but applied his heart to wisdom, to guard his taste from ruling his judgment. Any man of common intellect and reflection, is the best prescriber for himself, in all common cases: he knows what food and drink are most friendly to his stomach and health. It is true that a man may eat or drink that which will seem to be advantageous, and yet will be followed with pernicious consequences. Here prudence dictates that men should try the experiment, and when they find that any kind of food or drink, or an over portion thereof, is injurious to their health, they should forbear. He whose taste is so vitiated that he will not observe this rule, is an object of pity, but not of hope.

Third. Is it good economy to abstain from ardent spirits altogether, as a drink, or not? He who drinks his six cents dram each day, will spend more than twenty dollars in a year: if he abstains he makes a saving of those dollars—and likely other drink would be as good or better for him. But if ardent spirits are disused, there will be no revenue arising from the tariff to support government. A direct tax on poll and property must follow. This grinds hard! The support of government, however, would not be as heavy as it now is. If all the wine and spirits which are now used at levees, public dinners, social hospitalities, and domestic uses, were retrenched, six dollars per day, instead of eight dollars, would be a sufficient compensation for members of Congress, and so on, in proportion, through the whole list of officers. But if this saving economy in drinks is prudent, why not extend it to meats? If a man's flesh bill for life be but three cents each day, in seventy years it would be more than seven hundred and fifty dollars: whereas, bread, roots, fruit, milk, gruel and pottage of lentiles, would be more for his health, his perception and length of days.

I am now seventy-five years old. I was never drunk in my life: nor has it ever been a cross to me to abstain from what makes men drunken. For many years of my life I drank no spirits. When the glass was going round the circle where I was, rather than philosophise or lecture, I would put the cup to my mouth, and, without drinking, pass it. About twenty-five years past, moving my family on the road, I worried all day in the snow-drifts, until nearly dark. My strength then failed me, and a faintness came on. A good woman, at the door of her house, handed me a bottle of cider brandy, which I drank a little of, and received great and immediate relief. Since that, I have used it, I judge, at about the rate of a gallon per year. I often receive an advantage by a little of it, and have never had any evidence that it was injurious to me. A spoon-bowl full is as much as I use at a time, and the times of drinking are not frequent. A little in my mouth, before cold water, gives the water a good relish and prevents injury. I am no physician, but should judge that those who die by drinking cold water, in hot weather, might prevent it by a tea-spoon full of spirits. Rum, unqualified, is disagreeable to my nose, my mouth, my throat, and my bowels—but when qualified with sugar and water, it is agreeable enough—but I have no longing after it. I have never used but a little wine: the little, however, has been friendly to my health and spirits.

I believe no one abhors drunkenness more than myself. A drunkard is a disagreeable object. Drunkenness has slain more thousands than Buonaparte did individuals. Add duelling to it, and the call is as loud for the Hindoos to send their missionaries among us, to reform drunkards and duellists, as it is for us to send missionaries among them, to turn them from idolatry and immolation. But still the good book says, "Give strong drink to those who are ready to perish, and wine to those who are of heavy heart. Drink a little wine for thy stomach's sake, and often infirmities. Every creature of God is good, and nothing to be refused, if it be received with thanksgiving."

EXTRACT OF A LETTER TO COL. R. M. JOHNSON, DATED JANUARY 8, 1830.

The message is lengthy, but not superfluous. Long as it is, I wish it contained another solemn warning to Congress, to do nothing, in a legislative capacity, that would have any bearing on religious opinions.

A large number of the people, in concert, have petitioned Congress *to stop the transportation of the mail on Sunday*, because *they* believe, in their consciences, that Sunday should be kept holy and free from all servile labor. The report of the committee of the Senate, last session, on the petition, is replete with candor and strength of argument; the radical parts of which never have and never can be confuted; but still it has not put the matter to rest. New memorials are to be presented to Congress—perseverance is urged—irreligion is trumpeted, and the learning and religion of the petitioners are to outweigh all opposition.

The constitution of the United States is a charter of powers granted and rights retained; among all the enumerated powers given to Congress, there is none that authorises them to determine which day of the year or week the people shall abstain from labor or travel. Should they, therefore, make such a powerless law, it would be unconstitutional. There are many thousands in the United States, who conscientiously keep the seventh day of the week for Sabbath. Should Congress stop the transportation of the mail on the seventh day, and continue it on Sunday, what would the petitioners says? Would they not complain of a partiality shown to the Sabbatarians, to the grief of the Sundarians? It amounts to nothing to say there is a majority who prefer the observance of Sunday to any other day, for minorities have unalienable rights, which ought not, and cannot, be surrendered to government. The God we adore—the worship we pay him, and the times of performing that worship, are articles not within the compass of any Gentile legislature. The design of civil government, which is to protect the lives, liberty and property of the many units which form the whole body, is every way answered without that surrender. Government should defend the *rights* of the religionists, as citizens, but the religious *opinions* of none. If the petitioners are secured in their persons and rights, why should they desire more? Their consciences can never be charged with guilt for what others do; for conscience belongs alone to the homedepartment. Why should they wish to stretch and lop off, like

Procrustes, and bring all to their standard? The driving of a carriage will neither terrify them nor break their devotion; for many of them are driven to the places of their devotion. If Sabbatical laws are necessary to govern the people on Sunday, and keep them from all business but religious duties, why not make a law to prevent Sunday schools; for there is no greater relation between education and religion than there is between travelling and religion. Paul, and his company and baggage, were five days travelling, by water, from Philippi to Troas. In Troas, they tarried seven days, the last of which was the first day of the week; of course one of the five days was Sunday, and yet there was no law of conscience, or law of Congress, to prevent them from transporting themselves and goods on Sunday.

Should Congress indulge the petitioners, and pass a law to stop the transportation of the mail on every Sunday, it would be a nest-egg for themselves and for others. Encouraged by success, they would next proceed to have the days of Christmas, and Easter, and their associations and synods exempted in the same way, and where would it end? The Sabbatarians, with the Jews, finding Congress flexible, would, with equal right, claim a law to sanctify Saturday for their convenience. Whenever a legislature legalize holy-days, creeds of faith, forms of worship, or pecuniary reward for religious services, they intrude into the kingdom of Christ, and impeach the wisdom of the divine law-giver, for not knowing how, or his goodness, for not giving all laws necessary in his government. The deadly pill, at first, will always be rolled in honey. The honor of religion, the spread of the gospel, the piety and research of the reformers, the good of society, the safety of the state, and the salvation of souls, form the syrup, in which the poisonous pill is hidden. It is from men, high in esteem for holiness and wisdom, that the worst of usages and most cruel laws proceed; for base characters defeat their own wishes. The heart of King Asa was perfect all his days, yet he oppressed some of the people—was mad at the seer who reproved him, and made a law that whosoever would not seek the Lord should be put to death.

Admit of the principle that religion is an institute of state policy, and the people hold their liberty by the tenure of the will of the legislature, which is very changeable, often corrupt, and many times very cruel. Admit of the principle, and you approve of that which has reared an inquisition, and drenched the earth with blood.

Many plead for an equality of all Christian societies, and plead as strongly that they should become bodies politic, and be supported by the civil law. If this is proper for Christian societies, it is as proper for Jews, Pagan or Mahometan societies; but the liberty contended for, should be guaranteed to each individual, as his inalienable right, which cannot be meddled with, without usurpation in the rulers, which turns them to tyrants.

Those who wish to call in the strong arm of law to defend their opinions, give evidence that they have not logical reasoning, on moral and religious subjects, to support their weak dogmas.

I am sorry that Congress have committed themselves by a precedent of giving their chaplains a legal reward for religious services. How preposterous the sound! A far-fetched construction supports it. The law of reason and revelation enjoin a reward to the laborer; but if Congress should reward the chaplains with their own contributions, it would look more like simple Christianity. The people at large have none of the devotion or instruction of the chaplain, nor any voice in electing him; why then should they be taxed where they are not represented? The chaplain, who would not attend, on request, and trust to the promise of Christ and the benevolence of his friends for his reward, without legal obligation, would be selling his prayers for money, and turning the gospel into merchandise. The thing here spoken of, is a small thing, which the nation can never feel; but trace it to its root, and it contains that principle which is so pernicious in the world, and is now used as a stirrup, by the petitioners, to mount the steed and ride down the people.

In all other respects, Congress have been cautious and wise in everything that has any bearing on conscience and religious rights; and, even in this particular, they have made the best of a bad; for they have shown no partiality to sects or sentiments in their elections.

I have written a long epistle, but it is not likely that I ever shall write any more; for my age advises me that the time of my departure is near.

Yours, with respect,

JOHN LELAND.

TRANSPORTATION OF THE MAIL.*

Ye observe days.——I am afraid of you.
Let every one be fully persuaded in his own mind.

If Christian legislatures have a right to regulate the religion of individuals, Mahomedan and Pagan legislatures have the same. The Pagans have their appointed days to worship Jupiter, or Juggernaut. The Mahomedans have their weekly day (Friday) to adore their great prophet. Among the many sects of Protestants there exists a variety of opinions respecting days of rest and worship. The Quakers meet for worship two days in a week, without attaching much sanctity to one day above another. Many keep the seventh day, like the Jews, from a belief that the observance of that day is of moral, unchangeable and universal obligation. Some believe that half the time (the night) is enough for rest, and that one day is as good as another for worship. A very considerable number keep the first day of each week as a Christian Sabbath, being of the opinion that God appointed one day in seven, by a moral precept to be observed by all men—that the seventh day was designated from creation until the resurrection of Christ—that Christ changed the day from the seventh unto the first day of the week—altered the exercises of the day—and remitted the punishment for profaning the day from certain death to a small fine. Part of this last sect are now petitioning Congress to gratify their wishes, and stop the transportation of the mail on Sunday. Why do they petition? Are they interrupted at their meeting-houses by the mail stages? This is not likely, for many of themselves drive their carriages to their places of worship. If they are abused by the stage drivers, existing laws are sufficient to punish the rioters. If they enjoy all the liberty and protection that they need, why are they restless? Do they wish Congress to decide the controversy in their favor, and legally declare that the first day of each week is too holy for men to labor and travel thereon? Should that be the case, what would the Jews and Sevendarian Christians say? Would they not, with equal justice, petition Congress to stop the mail on the seventh day? And by the same rule, any of them might petition that their days of Associations, Synods, etc., might be exempted in the same way. There

* Published in 1830.

are many thousands in the United States, who have formed into societies to destroy intemperance: (and who does not believe that drunkenness is as great an evil as driving a stage on Sunday?) should they petition Congress to stop all distilleries, would not the petitioners say that it was interfering with private right? They act more wisely! they labor to direct public opinion, and leave individuals at their liberty. Let the petitioners learn of them and do likewise. Not one of them is compelled to contract, drive, or ride on Sunday, why then complain? Conscience is a court of judicature, erected in every breast, to take cognizance of every action in the home department, but has nothing to do with another man's conduct. My best judgment tells me that my neighbor does wrong, but my conscience has nothing to say of it. Were I to do as he does, my conscience would arrest and condemn me, but guilt is not transferable. Every one must give an acconnt of himself. When a parent properly admonishes his child to beware of vice, if the child commits an overt act, the parent feels no guilt, he only mourns the misfortune: if the parent has been remiss in giving advice, he feels guilty for the neglect, (which is his own crime,) but not for the crime of the child. The error of confounding opinion and conscience together has effected a world of mischief. For individuals, or for a legislature to make their own consciences (opinions) the standard to try the conduct of others by, is tyrannical usurpation. "Why is my liberty judged by another man's conscience?" Transporting the mail on Sunday is contrary to the opinion of the memorialists, but can never pinch their consciences. The Quakers have the philanthropic opinion that war should never be waged: let them call it pure conscience, and petition Congress to never declare war, would the present petitioners wish that the prayer of the Quakers might be granted? Let them answer the question. * * * * * * *

If any improvement has been made on this subject, from the days of Constantine, until the present time, it consists in the discovery, found out by long experience, "that the only way to prevent religion from being an engine of cruelty, is to exclude religious opinions from the civil code." Let every man be known and equally protected as a citizen, and leave his religious opinions to be settled between the individual and his God: keeping this in view, that he who does not worship God in the way he chooses, does not worship him at all. Roger Williams, William Penn, and the early settlers of New York, embraced this principle, which has been interwoven in the constitution of government for the United States.

The powers given to Congress are specific—guarded by a "hitherto shalt thou come and no further." Among all the enumerated powers given to Congress, is there one that authorizes them to declare which day of the week, month, or year, is more holy than the rest—too holy to travel upon? If there is none, Congress must overleap their bounds, by an unpardonable construction, to establish the prohibition prayed for. Let the petitioners ask themselves the question. If Congress should assume an ecclesiastico-political power, and stop the mail on the seventh day, and let it be transported on the first, would that satisfy them? If not, are they doing as they would be done by? * * * * If Congress pass the prohibitory law prayed for, it is hoped that they will fix the boundaries of the day, to prevent contention.

EXTRACTS FROM A LETTER TO HON. R. M. JOHNSON, MARCH 29, 1830.

SIR:—For forty years, next to the salvation of the soul, the rights of conscience have been articles of my highest solicitude. Not only that all sects and societies should be placed on a level, but that each lonely individual should have equal favor, and not be obliged to join any society to escape disabilities or oppression. Indeed, I stand pledged, that as long as I can use my tongue or pen, I will never lie dormant when religious liberty is in jeopardy. The report speaks for itself. If it can be bettered, I know not in which particular. It breaths the language of John Milton, Roger Williams, William Penn, Thomas Jefferson, etc., and, I think it is in perfect accordance with the letter and spirit of the New Testament. It has my unqualified approbation.

The report of the minority of the committee comes in company with the other. After what I have said, it will not be expected that I shall approve of the whole of it. It discards the idea of any theological controversy, and yet, in the very beginning, it lays the foundation of a religious war. There never was a Christian nation on earth, before the days of Constantine, who opened the flood-gates of error, and set Christians at war with each other. * * * * * *

A few years past, a moral society was formed in Berkshire, for the suppression of vice. An executive committee was appointed to stop travel on Sundays. Were it not a serious subject, it would provoke a smile to see Belzebub in chase of Lucifer, whip and spur—the committee breaking the Sabbath to prevent Sabbath breaking. When the pursuer had overtaken or met with his game, they sometimes compromised, and for a fine, the traveller was let go on; but, generally he was carried to a justice or the county court, and fined for breaking the Sabbath. But, a certain Mr. Clark, being stopped, resented the abuse, and brought suit against them, for assault and battery, before the supreme judicial court, where Mr. Clark recovered a considerable sum for damages; the decision being that they had no right to stop and unhorse him. This decision purified the consciences of the whole club. Strange, how the getting or losing of money will give direction to conscience! Whether these good souls, on conversion, paid back the fines which they had taken, I cannot certainly tell. My best information is that they did not.

I have lived long enough to see that individuals often break over the bounds of moral honesty to injure their neighbors; but, this is not more frequent, than it is for legislative bodies to overleap their legitimate guide, and usurp the empire of natural individual rights. The let alone policy may be extended too far; but less evils arise from that neglect, than arise from a redundancy of laws. The liberty of the native of the woods, under proper restraint, to pervert overt acts (if the expedient can be found) should be aimed at. If, on entering into social compact, individuals surrender all to the public will, then government may direct our food, physic, costume, marriage, association, location, occupation, private opinion, religion, hearing, seeing, appetite, pronunciation, vibration of the arteries, and every breath we draw. But, if all this is surrendered, the individuals lose all accountability to their Maker, and government becomes responsible for all; for, it would be beneath the righteousness of the Divine Being, to hold a man to answer for himself, when he was divested of every attribute that constitutes a moral agent.

If I should vary a few degrees from the question of Sunday mails, it would be following a precedent which Congress has taught me. When members of that august assembly, think, until they are as full of matter as a bottle of wine that has no vent, they take the floor, and seem to tear up mountains by the roots—ride on the wings of the wind, and direct the storm. No matter what the question is, whether Missouri, retrenchment, or public land; the hall and gallery are struck with wonder at the profundity of the orator; but, if the small pox was in the question, neither speaker nor hearer would catch the disease. I see no great evil in all this. Their effusions may help the next question; at any rate the next election. Have not members of Congress as good a right to ramble, as the late Patrick Henry? Must all be guaged to speak in the direct, logical, and irrefutable mode of Madison? All souls were not cast in the same mould. It takes every man to make a world. I think Congress, on the whole, performs wonders. They have safely steered the ship between Scylla and Charybdis, notwithstanding adverse winds and mutinous sailors. The religion which I profess, forbids me to speak evil of the rulers of the people. I honor the throne, (government,) and the altar, (religion;) but, those who under a pretence of religion and good order, would shape my religion and guide my conscience, are usurping, presumtuous tyrants. A man cannot give greater evidence that he is destitute of the meek spirit of Christianity, and ignorant of its genius, than when he makes, or urges others to make, laws to coerce his neighbors in matters of religion. It is like putting a tool on the stones of the altar, or making a new cart to carry the ark.

I cheerfully subscribe to the sentiment, that Christianity is not only a good religion, but, the only religion that ever met the sinner's wants and relieved his woes—the only religion that ever brought pardon to the guilty, and gave assurance of eternal life; but, as an institute of state policy, a question arises, whether it has ever done any good. Has any Christian nation ever exceeded Tyrus in wealth—Greece in science—ancient Rome and Carthage in bravery—or modern China in internal improvement? And what nations now are more perfidious and blood-thirsty, than those who have formed crusades, established an inquisition, and massacred the South-Americans? Let Christianity operate in its own natural channel, and it is a blessing of immense worth; but, turn it into a principle of state policy, it fosters pride, hypocrisy, and the worst kind of cruelty.

JOHN LELAND.

HON. R. M. JOHNSON.

LETTER TO THE EDITOR OF THE BAPTIST CHRONICLE, AT GEORGETOWN, Ky.

CHESIRE, MASS. JUNE 25, 1830.

DEAR SIR :—You have had the goodness to send me several of your Baptist Chronicles, which have safely arrived. In a blank page of one of them, you inform me of the family that you have descended from.

* * * * * * * *

Of the fourteen hundred and seventy-one that I have baptized, but very few of them were ever *brought into the covenanted mercies of God, by the seal of the covenant*—(baptism.) It has been my lot to baptize those who came in at the door of repentance toward God, and faith towards the Lord Jesus Christ, and not those who climbed up some other way. I have baptized in the name of the Father, Son and Holy Ghost ; and if the apostles did not find Father, Son, and Holy Ghost, in the name of Jesus Christ the Lord, they either did not understand their commission, or I do not understand what is said about it. The doctrine that there are three that bear record in Heaven, which three are one ; and the doctrine that Jesus Christ was God over all and yet the seed of Abraham, are both of them inconceivable, and (to our limited reason) impossible : not more so, however, than creation or the resurrection. Enthusiasm consists in believing without, or against evidence. I believe that my eye can see, and ten thousand things beside ; but the why, the how, and wherefore, I cannot conceive of.

In the year 1781, and afterwards, a great number of my friends moved to Kentucky. I have heard of the death of many of them, but as many of them were younger than myself, it is probable that they are living. While I am writing, their persons present themselves to my imagination, and bring fresh to mind the meetings we had in Virginia. Yes, how did my soul travail and pray for their salvation ! and how was I delighted when I saw the grace of God among them ! Tell them, dear sir, tell them from me to stand fast in the doctrine of the grace of God, and not be spoiled through philosophy or vain deceit, but to be steadfast and immovable, always abounding in the work of the Lord. They will never find a place of pleasure or safety equal to the humble spot at the feet of Jesus. I hope they will not get into vain jangling and strife about words, for if any oppose the simplicity of the gospel, by what they call science and deep research, they give to science a false name, they are puffed up with a false mind.

I am afraid that I am too dictatorial in these remarks; for I claim no apostolical authority, no diocesan or clerical power; my highest claim is that of a repenting sinner, and a very imperfect preacher.

* * * * * * * *

Some societies have a written creed to begin upon; others form creeds by votes after they have united; while a third have their verbal agreements of procedure; and a fourth have a permanent creed that they will have *no creed*. In all these cases there is an understanding. In this light the Indian tribes have their constitutions of government, as well as the United States. The subject reminds me of a law once made in Rhode Island, "that the preachers *should* be rewarded by free contributions, and no other way." I have known many men, who have been such enemies to all bigotry in religion, that they were the greatest bigots that I ever saw, in condemning every one who was not as liberal as themselves. But let a man's creed be what it will, if it denies that the *Jesus* of the New Testament is the *Jehovah* of the Old Testament; or asserts that any can be saved, without receiving the unction and being led by the spirit of God, the creed is not the voice of my beloved. Whether I am sheep or goat, I know not the voice, and cannot follow the shepherd. For I had as well be Pagan, Jew or Turk (as it respects the salvation of my soul) as to be a Christian, void of the spirit of Christ. Nominal Christianity will not deliver from death. Out of that kingdom Christ will gather all that offend. The lamp without oil will go out in obscure darkness. Orthodoxy, heterodoxy, or any other doxy, without the love of a holy God in the heart, is a miserable doxy for me. If the greatest reasoner is the greatest saint, philosophers excel Christians, and the Devil goes beyond them all.

Yet see how I shift subjects: I mean to do so: I do as I would be done by. When I hear a long harangue of metaphysical reasoning on abstruse questions, I feel more like calling for my night-cap than anything else. So with myself, when I speak or write; it may be *light* but shall not be *long*.

Innocence is better than repentance; but when a man commences a transgressor, repentance is the best characteristic that he can possess. A humble spirit and a contrite heart are always essential to our acceptance with God, and have been so from Abel unto the present moment. But this temper of mind is overlooked (for men are too big for the lowly Jesus) and some creed, some society, or some forms of godliness, relied upon. Arminian*ism* or some other *ism*—Predestina*tion*, with all the other *tions*, in the vocabulary—societies as good as eleven of Christ's disciples—forms in will-worship, showing much wisdom and neglecting the body—can any of them or all of them in concert, give one groan of the Holy Ghost, or bring one sealing promise to the sinner's heart? Farewell.

JOHN LELAND.

Mr. Uriel B. Chambers.

SHORT SAYINGS

ON TIMES, MEN, MEASURES AND RELIGION, EXHIBITED IN AN ADDRESS, DELIVERED AT CHESHIRE, JULY 5, 1830.

The Scribes, Priests, and Lawyers murmured, but the common people heard him gladly.
New Testament.

Friends and Fellow-Citizens: This day we have assembled to reflect on the great changes and marvellous events that have taken place in our land, in the course of less than sixty years. Thirteen depressed colonies, containing but three millions of people, have grown to twenty-four independent states, with a general government over the whole, the population of which amounts to twelve millions of souls.

The increase of wealth, both real and personal, beggars description. The facilities of intercourse, by printing, mail stages, steam-boats, and canals, fill every thinking mind with wonder. The many inventions to aid and ease hard labor, have greatly contributed to make the states really independent. The advantages of education, and the thirst of the youth after knowledge, was never exceeded in Greece. The style of living and dressing has increased four fold. Persecution for conscience' sake is abandoned, and but few roots are found where the legislature intrude into the kingdom of Christ. The wars which we have had with the Europeans and savages have resulted to our advantage. The political spasms, (a tax that all free governments have to pay,) whether of a personal or sentimental nature, have ever closed on the side of liberty. After the people have decided that they can and will rule themselves, maugre all the force of cabinets, caucuses, intrigues and bargains, the storm subsides, and all rally under the banner of the law. The right of suffrage is found to be so effectual, that the people bear momentary abuses patiently, until the constitutional period arrives, when they right themselves.

Should the same love of liberty—spirit of enterprize—bravery in war—internal improvement—literary research and oratory—with a disposition to be just and humane to all nations that now exist, continue to prevail for a century forward, as they have for half a century past, the rigid patriotism of the Spartans—the profuse learning of the Greeks—the bravery of the Romans—the exquisite arts of the Italians, and the laborious improvements of the Dutch, would be no longer the highest note in the poet's song, nor the finest painting in historic page. The world which was found by Columbus, delivered by Washington, and taught by Jefferson, would excel them all.

From the experiment already tested, the ground of hope is strong, that the federate principle can prevail over all the territory from the mouth of Columbia River to Passamaquoddy, and from the Atlantic to the Western Sea. Looking forward one hundred years, and seeing, at least, sixty millions of people, covering forty independent states, all linked together by a federal chain; acknowledging no king but law; having none to rule over them but those whom they choose; each one enjoying the right of private judgment; of publishing his opinions without hazard; of worshipping what God he chooses, in the manner he prefers, at the times and places of his own selection; having no privileged orders of men; none exempted from their proportionable parts of the burdens of government; none proscribed from holding offices; punishing those alone who work ill to their neighbor, and pitying the ignorant and superstitious. Not as a statesman, but as a meek Christian, I subjoin, in addition to the before-mentioned blessings, the outpourings of the Holy Spirit; the quickening of dead sinners; the people mourning for their sins, and turning to a gracious Saviour; receiving his spirit and being governed by his laws: this would be a state of as great felicity, (should it prevail all over the world,) as can be expected, until this earth shall be dissolved, and a new earth and new heavens shall appear.

These pleasing anticipations may never be realized. Blooming mornings are often obscured by clouds and storms. The sun was risen when Lot entered Zoar, but soon a storm of brimstone destroyed the devoted cities. The sins of the people may provoke a jealous God to give them up to those who lust for power; wealth and splendor may ruin them. War famine and pestilence, are weapons in the magazine of Jehovah, by which he chastiseth the ungrateful and rebellious. The same prophets who speak of the glorious things that God will do for men in the latter days, speak also of great tribulation and distress that will fall upon the wicked.

It is ardently hoped that the people of the United States will be wise and diligent enough to keep the power of government in their own hands, and not be tricked, flattered, or frowned out of it; and so just and grateful that the Almighty may delight to bless them.

To-day we render our thanks for all the good things which the Lord has done for us: and to-day we make our prayers that goodness and mercy may follow us all the days of our lives.

It cannot be concealed that there is a gnawing worm under the bark of our tree of liberty, that seeks to sap our civil and religious rights. Mean suspicion is ridiculous; but manly jealousy is noble. Words are flexible things; it is principles and measures that characterize the man. Let men be called whig or tory—monarchist or anarchist—federalist or republican—angel or devil, it is their actions, and not their name or profession, that we are to form our judgments upon. Forming our judgments by this rule, we have glaring evidence that there are many would-be-chiefs who are harboring and fostering an aristocratic principle which often shows its teeth, and waits for a favored moment to show the whole hog. This principle has been haunting the United States from the Declaration of Independence to the present moment. It has as many names as a Spanish Don—as many colors as a chamelion—as many high claims to wisdom and religion as a Pharisee, and deceitful as an opossum, but always remains the same. The genius of the principle is to amass the offices and hold them fast, get the money and trick the sovereign people out of their rights. Men, when under the influence of this principle, when in office have stiff fibres in the back part of their necks, and when out of office they howl like wolves at the alphabet, because it contains the three letters o-u-t. These ambitious aspirants are never pleased with men or measures, while they themselves are the neglected agents. Like Absalom, they pray, "Oh, that I were made judge!" (and like him are self-conceited,) "that every man which hath any suit or cause, might come unto me and I would do him justice." Such men, when they are invested with power, are like Phæton, who undertook to drive the chariot of the sun, but being unskilful in charioteering, drove his chariot to the earth and set the world on fire.

When Mr. Jefferson, the patriarch of liberty, was promoted to the presidency, the debt of the United States was about eighty millions of dollars;* but during his eight years administration it was reduced to half the amount, and things seemed to be in a fair train to extinguish the whole; but the war of 1812 put a stop to the whole, and cast the states into the back ground a great distance. The duration of the war was two years and a half: the close of it was honorable and advantageous to the United States, but the course of it was disastrous. The expense of it was about one million of dollars per week. The revenue decreased, and expenses increased so fast, that at the end of one hundred and thirty weeks, the debt was one hundred and twenty millions of dollars. Since the close of the war, the debt has been more than one half discharged, and the people are now looking forward when four or five years will liquidate the last cent. In this they will not be disappointed, if the Almighty is propitious, our own government wise, and the people peaceable. To what use the surplus revenue will be put, after the debt is paid, has already become an object of solicitude and debate. When that time shall arrive, it is highly probable the people will know best what to do with their money. It will be the property of those who will then be living, and when men possess an estate they

* The sums are here stated in round numbers, designed to be near enough to the truth to give a just idea of the course of things.

wish to have the control of it. At present the revenue belongs to those who are living, and what is not necessary for the support of government, will be best applied to pay the debt, as fast as the engagements of government, and the claims of the creditors admit of. How exulting the thought, that twelve millions of people, possessing immense regions of fertile soil, producing all the necessaries and conveniences of life, with a watery highway to all parts of the globe, having none to bear rule over them but their own wills, shall owe no man any thing, but shall have a permanent revenue that will produce a surplus beyond the exigencies of government! What splendid monarchy on earth exhibits a state of things so full of delight? The pomp of crowns, mitres, stars, ribands, purple and diamonds, surrounded by an oppressed starving people, holds no competition with it.

If a man unskilled in fiscal affairs can be indulged by the present generation, and pardoned by those who will be living when the debt shall all be paid, he will suggest a few thoughts for consideration. "Let no project check the liquidation of the debt. Lower the duties on all merchandize as far as a just competition with other nations will justify; this will be a relief to the laborers. Sell the public lands cheap to actual settlers and cultivators. Give small portions of it to the industrious poor, who have nothing to buy with. Distribute the surplus, as fast as it arises, in an equitable way among the several states. Keep not a great sum in the treasury, for like a cider cheese it will always be haunted with bees. Let the contingent fund be small and guarded. Let the people be rich and the government frugal. Let it always be remembered that our government was formed for the good of the whole, and not for the aggrandizement of a few."

The powers granted to the general government are few and defined: those granted to the government of Massachusetts are many and undefined. The legislature may make all laws not forbidden by the constitution: the discretion of the legislature, therefore, in a great measure, governs the people. Whether the measures of the government of Massachusetts are in all things wise and economical, is a question of moment. The commonwealth was justly called the cradle of liberty in the revolutionary war, but was the hot bed of opposition in the war of 1812. That the citizens of this commonwealth had a right, through their legislature, to memorialize Congress on the subject, is true; but, after the war was declared, was it right for them to vilify the rulers—discourage enlistments—withhold loans—keep back the militia—declare the war unjust—rejoice at the victories of the enemy, and at the defeats of Americans—call out the militia for a sham—hold a convention to paralyze the arm of Congress, and, indeed, do every thing, by word and deed, that would render the war disastrous—the rulers obnoxious, and the government itself execrable? To gain these objects the pulpits were ringing, the presses groaning, and misrepresentation was the order of the day. What excuse for all this? Had the opposition succeeded in their wishes—run down those who were in office and gained the places themselves—what government they would have formed, whether alliance or recolonization, will never be known, for the event has not taken place.

While I am speaking, a solemn thought crowds into my mind. If the departed souls of illustrious patriots visit their kindred on earth, and mingle with them in their feelings, how would the souls of Hancock, Adams, Warren, and company, lament to see how far Massachusetts has fallen? And would not the soul of Washington have frowned indignantly on the Hartford convention, for seeking to break the bonds of the Union?

We are flattered away every year with the wealth of the state, and new schemes are reccommended and enacted, which call for commissioners, surveyors, engineers, pioneers and clerks, all of which must be paid, if the schemes dissolve in mist. It would be more pleasing to be informed that the debt of the commonwealth was discharged, and light taxes were sufficient.

In common life, it is the safest economy for a man first to pay for his land and clear his fields, and afterwards erect his useful and ornamental buildings as fast as the profits of his lands will justify; and, if I mistake not, the same economy is best for a state.

A respectable part of the people are strongly persuaded, that a heavy sum of the debt was created to carry on the opposition to the last war, and the measures of the general government, and ardently wish that the items of debt, and for what purposes they were created, might be so distinctly stated, that he who runs may read. While they labor under existing impressions, they cannot but feel indignant at the claims presented to Congress to reimburse the expenses of the war; for, to them it appears that this government wishes to coerce Congress to pay their enemies for the mischief they have done them. Will, or ought the United States ever to agree to this? It is an anti-revolutionary principle, to say "that the people are their own worst enemies, and the government must save them from themselves. That government is a mystery known to but few, and the many should peaceably acquiesce."

Let the items of debt be stated as fair as a tax-bill, without *etceteras* and contingencies, and the democratical republicans, (though they may question the wisdom of many of the items,) will each to a man exert himself to extinguish the whole, if it takes all but one cow and sheep from his flocks, and all but one shirt from his back. This he would rather do than to have commissioners after commissioners, still increasing the debt, sent on to Congress with such claims as they carry with them. For the measures of the seventeenth century, in whipping and banishing the Baptists—hanging the Quakers, and destroying the witches, hardly appear more dishonorary. When the debt shall all be paid, and the taxes lightened, then let railroads, tunnels, and castles in the air be the order of the day, if nothing better appears.

If those who led the poople into debt by their opposition to the war and government, and those who still justify the measure, were to be convinced of their error, and honestly pray like the negro in a sea-squall, "O Lorda! set me on dis a rock, dat a rock tudder rock, and I'll be bound you never catch me here again," we should soon have better times, less murmurings and less taxes. But, while the same men and measures are supported, the great body of laborers have little to expect, but to bow down their shoulders to bear and become servants unto tribute.

We all wish to be loyal subjects to the constitution, and constitutional laws and measures of this commonwealth; and, likewise, to the constitution and constitutional laws and measures of the United States, which are supreme; but, how all this is to be done when the states and general governments clash, is not easy to say. We are waiting and hoping for the time when there will be a greater harmony between them.

It is folly and madness to fight against the laws of nature and the course of events. The extent and population of the western section of the United States, will soon outweigh the Atlantic states. A great portion of the west, is made up of emigrants, who have fled from haughty masters and heavy taxes, to this land of liberty, leaving their aristocratical brethren behind. Their attachment to our free government has become proverbial. This circumstance will tend to keep the now existing western states, and those which shall arise hereafter, upon the plain ground of representative democracy, to the joy of republicans, and the grief of aristocrats in the Atlantic States. This appears to be the course that events will take, and all opposition to it, is like a shad's head against a steam-boat.

When men have the liberty of declaring their opinions without hazard, and voting without control, they have all that they should desire—if a majority is against them they should acquiesce—he who varies from this should give up the name of republican, for he is destitute of the principle. It is true the majority may be wrong, and the minority right; but, when free debate is granted, and free balloting allowed, the majority will be convinced of their error and retrace their steps. In this case it is for the majority to decide whether the measure was right or wrong; for, if it is given to the minority, the number may be reduced to an individnal and end in absolute despotism.

Has not Massachusetts always had an equal portion of members in the Senate and House of Representatives in Congress? and have not those members had equal freedom of debate? why then should there be any complaint when a majority is against them? would Massachusetts wish to dictate to the whole twenty-three states? as well might the little town of Hull give law to the whole commonwealth of Massachusetts.

But, while I am speaking, it strikes my mind that the best of men are but men at best. Perfect knowledge and wisdom are not the attributes of man. Add to this, that the administration of government is often attended with such perplexities, that a choice of evils is the only alternative. Government is often condemned for evils that spring from another source. While the people, therefore, freely animadvert on measures, and expose the schemes of ambitious aspirants, let them be peaceable in temper, and patient to bear real or supposed evils as long as they are sufferable. When a standard of grammar is found out, in which every letter in the alphabet has the same power in every word, and every word a definite meaning in every sentence—when the knowledge of perpetual motion shall be ascertained—when a natural standard of weights and measures is discovered—when the first rise of sin can be developed—when a clue shall be seen which will reconcile the designs of God with the freedom of the human will; then men will know how to give power enough to their rulers to do good, and yet have it so counterpoised that they can do no harm.

Let it moreover be remembered, that a restless discontented spirit, is injurious to good government, and tends to destructive revolutions on one hand, as the ambition of aspiring demogogues does on the other.

As religion is become very fashionable in every circle, and fills a page in all publications, the remarks of the day would be incomplete, without some notice is taken of it. Like the Buzite of old, I shall, therefore, show my opinion.

The one great church is built by Christ the Lord, against which all the powers of earth and hell shall not prevail. But gospel churches are built by men, who, on account of local residence, unity of sentiment, and Christian affection, unite in a bond for social worship and gospel discipline.

When any one is received into the fellowship of such a church, no alteration takes place as to his standing in human connexion and civil society. The king, the captain, and the servant, have nothing added to them, and nothing taken from them by the fellowship of the church. So, also when any one commits an overt act, and is excluded from the fellowship of the church, he is not deprived of rank or wealth, or exposed to any disabilities or penalties of the church, which extends no farther than a declaration of what and whom they fellowship, and what and whom they do not. If, however, the overt act for which he was excluded, should be a crime against any righteous law of state, he is subject to a fine or penalty from the civil court, neither more nor less on account of the church censure.

Civil government is rightly founded, neither in birth, in power, in wealth, nor in grace, but in compact. Individuals unite together, not for the aggrandizement of a few, but to protect the life, liberty and property of the whole body. A charter of powers granted and rights retained is the platform by which they are to be governed, and all are to be subject to the public will.

Government was not designed, nor should it ever be used, to direct the faith, fix the residence, describe the enterprise, or make the contracts of individuals, or in any wise deprive them of their natural rights; all of which they retain, except what are voluntarily resigned in the compact for the security of the rest.

It is not designed to defend the religious opinions of *any*, but the persons and rights of *all;* so that Jews, Turks, Pagans and Christians, with all their subdivided opinions, may peaceably live together in the same domain—each one enjoying the free exercise of his religious opinions, and all impartially protected by the law. Should any one man, or one sect, attempt to force another to believe, act or support, what they themselves believe in, with this plea, that the others were licentious and heretical, the assailants would be the offenders, to be punished by the law; for when a man's religion leads him to commit overt acts, he should be punished for his actions and pitied for his delusion.

If this is a true epitome of the formation of church and state, and of their respective designs and powers, a common observer will readily see that *both* have greatly swerved from the basis which is founded in nature, reason and revelation. The author of Christianity and the scheme of salvation was perfect and complete; but, even among the apostles, there was a strife which of them should be greatest. Diotrephes loved to have the pre-eminence, and there were many masters. The mystery of iniquity began to work, and anti-christs arose, before the close of the apostolic age. And, notwithstanding the pagan persecutions which the Christians endured for three hundred years, the bishops were grasping after power over the churches, and supremacy among themselves. When Constantine took the church into his own hands, he established Christianity by law, and provided fat livings for the preachers. Pagans were proscribed, and none were admitted to offices but Christians. The Trinitarians and Arians, like Castor and Pollux, lived and died by turns, and the triumphant party would be the orthodox and the other party the heterodox. The contest of the bishops for mastery lasted until A. D. 606, when the Emperor Phocus conferred the title Universal Father, or Pope, on the bishop of Rome. Popes advanced from one step of power to another, until they kept standing armies, and crowned and dethroned kings at pleasure.

The marriage of church and state together was unnatural; of course a monstrous offspring followed. From that day until the present moment it has been the grief of the humble followers of the Lamb to see their own nominal brethren, by force and bloodshed, wrest from infidels and Christian heretics their inalienable rights, by which Christ has been wounded in the house of his friends, and Christianity exposed to the hatred and scorn of a gazing world.

In common life, a man has an inalienable right to do that which is morally wrong, and if his wrong injures none but himself, he is accountable to none but himself and his God. So, in the religious department, a man has an indefeasible right to believe what is not true, and perform worship that is hypocritical or delusive. In either, or both of these cases, the supposed or real defaulter is not amenable to any court, either civil or ecclesiastical, to be fined or corporeally punished, or any way disabled, farther than the withdrawal of the fellowship of his brethren.

The kingly and priestly power, which was ordained for the government of the Theocracy of Israel, figured out and centered in the Lord Jesus, in the Christocracy. Christ sits upon this throne as a priest, and bears the glory. He is king on the holy hill of Zion, and minister of the sanctuary. Like Melchizedec, he is king of righteousness and priest of the Most High God. Ministers of the gospel are never called *priests* in the New Testament, in distinction from all the saints; of course, nothing can be drawn from the power of kings and priests, in the Theocracy, that will establish the right of kings or priests to be lords over the heritage of God under the second Testament. Holy men of God, who have been sent by Christ to preach the word of reconciliation among men, should be highly esteemed in love for their works' sake; but *holy orders* of men, legally clothed with ecclesiastical power, should be shunned like a den of rattlesnakes. The power and authority which is given to church rulers, whether called bishops or angels, is like the power of a prudent father in his family, and may be called the *power of influence,* acquired by pre-eminent gifts, benevolence and godly zeal.

There are a number of religious denominations in the United States; several of them of nearly equal weight and numbers. No one of them can overbalance all the rest; which will forever be, as long as it continues, a sufficient barrier against religious oppression, in the *old way;* which has been, for one sect, when it was more numerous than all the rest, to *feel power and forget right,* and force all others to bow down to their sheaf. But a *new way* of persecution may yet arise, and exercise all the authority of the *first beast.* Let the many Christian sects agree to surrender their distinguishing rituals so far as for all of them to unite, and have Christianity to be the test for all offices in the general and state governments, in every department, and the horned beast will be set up.

Nothing in this state of things (should it take place) looks like the millennium, for there is no return of the Jews in it—the unfortunate sons of Abraham must all be proscribed. Professed Deists have none of the loaves and fishes; and the millions in the United States, who do not believe themselves Christians, must stand by, as hewers of wood and drawers of water, to pay taxes and fight battles for their Christian neighbors. But who are to be the Christians? Some think infants are made Christians at the time of their baptism, others do not believe it. Some conclude that joining a church makes them Christians, but Judas belonged to Christ's church and was a devil. Others judge that believing the unity of God is the only essential; the devil, however, believes this and trembles. Many measure the increase of Christians by Sunday Schools, Missionary Societies, etc.; but once a generation of vipers compassed sea and land to make proselytes.

It should always be remembered, that the *essentials* of Bible religion are articles that lie between God and individuals, and cannot be perfectly known by any, but by Him who searches and knows the hearts of men and what is in them. But this is overlooked. Nominal Christianity, observing Sunday as holy time, is now to be the test; and no man, without this mark, is to buy or sell, ride in the stage, float in a boat, or bear any office in the state. How little this sounds like the doctrine preached by John, JESUS, Peter and Paul.

Should the many Christian sects in the United States drop their peculiarities, and unite in the manner, and for the purposes, just mentioned, it makes the blood run cold in the veins to think of the horrors that would ensue; for there are millions in this land of liberty that would not submit to disfranchisement without resistance: clerical awe and pharisaical grimace would not restrain them.

It is not all that Christianity *does* for men, but all that it *asks* of them is a dispassionate, unprejudiced hearing, with a corresponding faith on rational evidence. Error always needs the props of ignorance, anger, guile, hypocrisy, and the strong arm of law to support it. Truth needs no such aid. Error of opinion ceases to be dangerous when truth is on equal ground to combat it.

There was once a religious confederacy of discordant materials, composed of Libertines, Cyrenians, Alexandrians, Cilicians and Asiatics; but when they could not withstand the reasoning of Stephen, they resorted to perjury, and condemned and stoned him to death. Their great union secured the rights of none who differed with themselves.

I close these miscellaneous sketches, by observing that we have cause of gratitude that we have now a president who was chosen by the people, and who is seeking their good. His message and veto show his depth of thought, his independence of mind, his attachment to republicanism and love of economy. May his life be preserved, and his usefulness continued!

While the heads of departments are all at their posts discharging their respective duties, we have a watchman in Congress, guarding our religious rights, before whose arm the intrepid Tecumseh fell, and before whose reports the clerical hierarchy blushed and gnashed his teeth.

When Jackson shall have finished his administration, there will be none living, young enough to be president, who had any hand in the revolutionary war. A generation will then take the lead, who never saw the works which were done by Moses and Joshua. If they will have a king to reign over them, that they may be like other nations; or a whole life or hereditary aristocracy, with an established order of ecclesiastics, so it will be. We can only weep all night, like Samuel, in view of the apostacy, but must always keep in mind that our descendants will have the same right to choose a government for themselves that we or our fathers have had.

The world stood before we were born. It has been our home until now, and will be so until we die. When we are gone the way of all the earth, it will be the habitation of our descendants. While we live, let us serve our generation by the will of God; and when we fall asleep, He who made the world will take care of it until the consummation of all things.

THE RESULT OF OBSERVATION.*

"I said I will be wise, but it was far from me."—SOLOMON.

THE highest claimants of internal rectitude and perfection generally discover the greatest ambition to carry their points and increase their party.

He who loves to hear no person praised but himself, is an enemy to all but himself.

Boldness without modesty is arrogance. Modesty without boldness is sheepishness; but boldness tempered with modesty, forms an amiable character.

When dissentions and party strife arise in religious societies, no one owns or knows himself to be a partisan; each one conceives himself to be laboring for the general good. At such times truth cannot enter, and the historian must drop his pen, until the storm is over.

To pray to be heard and seen of men, and to preach for name and fame, is Christianity inverted.

The elaborate disquisition—the pompous style—the handsomely turned period, with polite gesticulation, may gain admiration among the light-minded; but conscience slumbers, and piety starves amidst it all.

For a preacher to be honest before God and man, and preach what he has been taught and does believe, is so essential to his work, that even a suspicion of his honesty with his hearers, prevents all good impression.

He who murmurs in adversity will be unthankful in prosperity.

The suicide kills one, the murderer kills two. The first does no violence to the will of the slain; the last does. Suicide costs the state little or nothing; murder costs much.

Extract from preachers all the zeal to proselyte and increase party—all the love of fame, to be called Rabbi, and all the love of ease and good living—and how much remains for Christ, of genuine piety and disinterested charity?

Many labor hard to find the art to be honest, while they cast the work and burden on others, and secure the profits for themselves. They make treaties with their consciences that they may pursue their course with peace.

* Published in 1830.

A young preacher should fervently seek and pray for holy zeal: and yet, unless his mind is stored with the holy scriptures, and the sense thereof, he will be a lean old man.

Never do any thing that you doubt the correctness of, unless your doubts are greater, that a neglect will be criminal.

It is one thing to believe a doctrine, or system, from the force of argument, and another to believe what God says, and the heart feels. It is hard for a saint, at all times, to realize and appropriate to himself, that which his judgment acknowledges to be true.

It has been the strife of Gentiles, Jews and Christians, to reconcile the eternal designs of God with the freedom of the human will. Perhaps a better solution cannot be given, than to say, it was the eternal design of God, that the will should be left free to act, yet accountable for the right use or abuse of its powers. This solution may lead to questions irresolvable, and may have bearings hard to dispense with; but that salvation is of the Lord, and condemnation of creatures, is certain. God's grace is free: his wrath is conditional.

Sin has so completely deranged all the faculties of the soul, and sunk men into such a horrible pit, that any scheme which the limited, dark mind of man can comprehend, would be insufficient to save—a scheme founded in infinite wisdom, and executed by omnipotent power, through boundless love, was necessary to restore. This scheme the gospel exhibits, and those who believe in it find deliverance; but who but God understands it in all its parts? How unsearchable are his ways, and his judgments past finding out!

Internal religion is always the same, and always will be. External religion changes: sometimes by the command of God, and often by the weakness of men. The Mosaic worship was from Jehovah. Moses was faithful in all his house, and built the tabernacle according to the pattern shown to him in the mount. But when the state of the tribes was changed, David was inspired to modify the Mosaic worship for the convenience of the Israelites, and the whole of it was abrogated when the kingdom of the Messiah was established. That the externals of Christianity have been changing by men, needs no proof but to reflect on what has been, and to survey what now is.

When a preacher is annointed with a holy unction, viewing the character of Christ and the worth of souls, it will alter the tone of his voice, change his countenance, and fill his eyes with pity; but for a man to affect all this when his heart is not in it. is but hypocrisy in himself, and disgustful to his hearers.

"*And I will put enmity between thee and the woman, and between thy seed and her seed: it shall bruise thy head and thou shalt bruise his heel.*" That this is a declaration of the Messiah, who was the seed of the woman—

the seed of Abraham—the seed of David, born of Mary, admits of no doubt; but that it was a gracious promise, made to Adam and Eve, is not so evident. The Lord God was not speaking to the new made pair, but to the serpent, and the words are not a promise of pardon, but a denunciation of the conquest of Christ over Satan, at the expense of a little bruise in his heel, (his human nature.) It is possible that Adam and Eve stood near enough to hear what God said to the serpent, and catch a gleam of hope from what they heard; but of this we have no certain proof; nor is there any assurance that the Messiah was ever revealed to any before Abraham, who saw his day, and was the father of all that believe. That all who were saved before Abraham, were saved through Christ, is certain; but, like heathen, or infants, they might be saved by the merits of one who had not been revealed to them.

Some parts of the scripture are written in a chain of logical argument, but other parts are written like a string of pearls, one truth following another without any dependence upon it.

Men should remember that their beasts of service are not endowed with reason; yet treat them in a manner for which they could not reproach their owners with cruelty and unkindness, if they were reasonable creatures.

The seas abide within their limits, and stay their proud waves at the bars and bounds prescribed for them; but men revolt and break over the moral bounds of their obedience.

The covetous man despises him who is indolent, and the lazy man abhors the covetous. The first pleads wants, pinches and hard times, to cloak his covetousness: the last pleads bodily infirmity to excuse himself from labor. If we know a man to be covetous, we are forbidden to eat with him; and with the lazy man, we are to keep no company, that he may be ashamed.

A man of profound learning will easily understand an ideal discourse, though dressed in rustic language. He prefers rich ideas to flowery expressions, but when both unite, he is not straitened. But when men of vulgar habits hear subjects investigated in a lofty style, though the speaker delivers mysteries of great worth, yet they are unedified. They have to stretch their thoughts so hard to understand the language, that they lose all the impression of the ideas. Many, however, are to be found, who will applaud that the most, which they understand the least.

Is open space a creature, or is it eternal? If it is a creature, when was it created? and what existed where it now is, before its creation? If it is eternal, what shall we say?

When preachers are divinely impressed to carry the gospel to a destitute people, affliction may attend them, but good success will follow. But when missions are formed on human calculations, or with colonizing views, the disasters of the crusade, or the cruelties of South America, come into mind.

Some men's tongues are like race horses, the lighter the load, the swifter the speed: but the tongues of other men are like dromedaries, the heavier the burden, the more fleety the beast.

If the first sin arose from a sinful cause, it seems there was a sin before the first sin. But if the first sin proceeded from a holy cause, then the law of nature was inverted. Sin has certainly taken place in a manner that justifies God, and casts all the blame on the transgressor. But this lesson is hard to read, difficult to spell, and must be skipped.

Neither money, nor the love of it, was the *root of all evil*, for evil existed before the value of the precious metals was known: but since money has been coined and became current, it so completely *answers all things*, that the love of it is the *root* of lying, deceiving, perjury, stealing, robbery, war, and every kind of murder. It is difficult to find a man with as much money as he wants, or as much religion as he needs.

Preachers are in the habit of using home made scripture, which is not biblical. As death leaves you, so judgment will find you. Purchased grace, purchased salvation, purchased the love of God. God gave his Son out of his own bosom. Little children love one another. Covenant of grace, covenant of redemption, etc. Words are valuable, but ideas founded in truth are more valuable.

Contentions often arise in churches, neighborhoods, and between man and man. At such times Satan places himself between the two adverse parties, and when the parties look at each other, instead of seeing them as human beings, they see nothing but Satan. At such times, all means used to effect a reconciliation, only tear the scab from the sore. Absence from each other, time and lonely reflection are the best remedies. Let the contention die of old age.

Man is a complex creature, having a body of clay, possessed by a quickening spirit, which two are connected with a rational soul. To describe the union of these parties, draw the line of demarcation, and give to each its proper due, is beyond the reach of my pen or thoughts. The body, however, being animated, has *involuntary* and *voluntary* motions. The first, including the beating of the heart—the vibration of the arteries—the springing of the nerves, etc., are neither effected nor prevented by the will. The last, comprising the movement of the various members, organs, and the whole body, is governed by the will, and are, therefore, contingent. The winking of the eye partakes partly of both; it performs without the will, and yet may be hastened or checked by it. This stricture on man reminds me of the marvellous scheme of salvation. The contrivance of the plan—the incarnation of Christ—the atonement made by the death and resurrection of Jesus—our being born again—the resurrection from the dead, etc., are all the works of God, and the will of man is not consulted about them: in these things, man neither assists, nor resists. But when a sinner is changed by grace, the powers of his soul are voluntarily employed in the service of God. He strives as ardently, hears as attentively, sacrifices as freely, denies himself as readily, repents as sincerely, and chooses the good part as voluntarily, as if the work was all his own. God calls effectually, and the sinner runs willingly.

Read Romans, xii., from verse ninth to the end, and challenge all the wits and wise men on the earth to produce an equal number of salutary precepts in a form so condensed. The diction of the Bible cannot be imitated by human effort.

Grievous afflictions are not *always* sent as a scourge for crimes committed, but sometimes as preventives from crimes. Paul's thorn prevented his pride.

A FAMILY PRAYER.

That God would secure—

Our houses from devouring flames,
Our property from thieves and knaves,
Our bodies from disease and pain,
Our souls from guilt and every stain.

He that believes in the word of God, *saves* his soul; but he that believes in the word of speculators, *loses* his interest. Let God be true, but every man a liar.

It is not reasonable to believe that the original copies of the Old and New Testaments are now in existence: the ravages of time have destroyed them. And, (whatever may be said of the superintendence in the transcriptions and translations of the Bible,) the highest claim that any Jew or Gentile can boast, is, that he possesses a careful transcription or translation by *uninspired* scribes.

I have seen many revivals of religion in my life; some singularities have attended each of them to distinguish one from the other. When the minds of the people are strongly excited, in some things they go to excess. Not making a just distinction between the truth of God and the corruptions of men, they call all gold that glistens. That enemy of man, who seeks to check religious zeal, if he cannot succeed therein, will drive them on to a zeal, not according to knowledge. As far as this phrenzy of zeal prevails, so far the zealot will condemn the moderate Christian, while the last, in his turn, will brand the other with enthusiasm. I have found in myself, and discerned in others, that holy zeal and vain ambition, (though discordant in nature,) will rise and fall together. When religion is low, and my spirits are dull, I have neither zeal nor ambition to rise; but when my soul is enlivened, and a prospect of success is before me, ambition cries, "now stretch your wings—fly high and immortalize your fame."

When a preacher exhibits with a dull spirit—small ideas—scattering arguments, and poor voice, his *old man* is ashamed, and his *new man* is starved; but when he is fresh anointed—speaks as he ought to, in power and demonstration of the spirit—commending himself to every man's conscience, in the sight of God, his *new man* is fed and refreshed; while the *old man* triumphs with a boast, "how finely I have preached."

Nothing is so valuable as simple truth. The heathen were so well convinced of this, that they worshipped the goddess, *Truth*, stark-naked. To diminish, to exaggerate, or give false coloring, either by word, gesture, doubtful accent, or any kind of inuendo, to plain truth, is satanical. He who professes a regard for the truth of God, (which the Almighty has confirmed with an oath,) and is not in the habit of speaking the truth with his neighbor, gives his profession the lie.

For nearly six thousand years, the bans of marriage have been published between mouths and victuals; and all the lids, doors, locks, bolts, high duties, non-intercourse and embargoes, that can be devised, are insufficient to keep them apart. They were made for each other. He who has nothing to bestow, will never be troubled with hangers-on.

To be concise and perspicuous, is the excellence of speaking or writing; loquacity and obscurity are the contrast.

Many errors are committed for want of good breeding and proper reflection; but the worst are committed through ill design.

A man has a civil right to do that which is morally wrong.

A man's speculative opinions effect not his moral standing in society.

There are many vicious tempers, which the discipline of the church, and the penal laws of the state cannot prevent nor punish; but every mental evil, though ever so subtile, is condemned in the gospel.

The promises made in the covenant of works are conditional; which conditions, men can perform by the exertions of their natural powers. But, in the new covenant, all the promises of God in Christ Jesus, are yea and amen, and do not rest on the works of men for their accomplishment. "I will give them a new heart—I will be their God, and they shall be my people—I will never leave them—their sins and iniquities I will remember no more, etc." To apply the promises of God, made in Christ to the contrite, unto those who are seeking to be justified by the works of the law, is giving that which is holy unto dogs. Natural, providential, and national blessings, are promised to men upon their obedience; but pardon of sin, justification, eternal life, and all the blessings of the new covenant are promised in Christ, through grace, and not as a reward.

In civil life, if a young man has not the faculty to make himself, he would not be able to keep himself after others had made him; so also in the religious department; if a man does not rise to eminence in the ministry, by the energies of his own mind, all the academical gloss that could be put upon him, would not make him shine. It is folly for men to hold up a man to whom God has given no legs.

The temple of Diana was two hundred years in building; but Erostratus burnt it down in one night, to gain for himself a great name. Empedocles cast himself into Etna's burning mouth, that he might defied.

The nations have been reduced to vassalage, and the earth soaked with blood, to raise the fame of cruel monsters, in the shape of men. But how can men believe or be happy, "who receive honor, one of another, and seek not the honor that comes from God alone." God honors the humble, and abhors the proud. Abundance of pride is to be seen among religious sects; each one striving for the mastery; and much strife among the preachers, who shall be greatest. How hard such preachers labor to make God's stream turn their own mills. Was I free from this vile ambition myself, I should esteem others better than myself, and rejoice to see them increase, though I decreased myself. Then I should not preach myself, but Christ Jesus the Lord; and do nothing through strife or vain-glory, but in lowliness of mind.

If ye have bitter envying and strife in your hearts, glory not, and lie not against the truth. From these pernicious tempers, the hearts of saints are not secure. When they are beset with the fiery darts of envy and strife, they will seem to possess two hearts. Their judgment, reason, and all the goodness that is in them, will condemn those vile passions, while their corrupt spirit is harboring them. At such times, if a man glories in his goodness, without confessing his vileness, he lies against the truth. How common it is for those who give the greatest evidence to others that they are governed by ambition, envy and strife, to make the boldest declarations of their purity, merely from their reason; when their inside heart will whisper, "envy and strife are here." Or if they confess their mental evils, it will be in a studied manner; calculating more to gain applause for their honesty and humility, than to bemoan themselves in dust and ashes.

Innocence is better than repentance; but, after a man has transgressed, repentance is the best quality which he can possess. When one man has injured another, if the injurious honestly confess his error, without any evasion or design, it will disarm the injured of all revenge; should the injured, in such a case, refuse the hand of forgiveness, he himself would become the injurious party.

Peter committed an overt act when he cut off the ear of Malchus, and was exposed to punishment for assault and battery. This he knew, and followed afar off. His denial of Christ, was not the effect of ill will, but fear of punishment for what he had done. He lied, and swore to the lie, to secrete and screen himself from prosecution. Two reasons may be assigned why he was not arrested. First, the enemies of Christ were so intent to destroy him immediately, that minor subjects were hardly noticed. Second, the miracle performed by Christ, in healing the servant's ear with a touch, must have had a solemn impression on all who saw it. Had Malchus gone to a magistrate with a complaint, what evidence could he have given of any abuse, when both his ears were whole upon his head? Had he subpœned the witnesses who saw the whole affair, they must have told, not only that the ear was cut off, but who it was that healed it, which would have operated greatly in favour of him whom they were determined to crucify.

In this event, the weakness and wickedness of the disciple, and the goodness and God-head of the master, are evidently seen. The historian has not informed us whether the ear which was cut off, was placed to the head from which it was severed, and stuck fast and sound, or whether another ear was created and fixed in its stead. In either case, the miracle was striking, and the conviction irresistible.

A question. If man, in his primeval innocency, was subject to be seduced by a tempter, to do that which was morally wrong, why cannot a man in his corrupt state, by the stimulus of a prompter, do that which is morally right? Are the natural powers of man impaired by sin? or does he possess a self-determining power over his own will?

Law is founded in justice, and has nothing to do with mercy; hence he that despised Moses' law, died without mercy. The law of God, (commonly called the moral law,) is the eternal, unalterable rule of right; which arises from the relation that exists between God and man, and between man and man; and will be binding as long as the perfections of God, and faculties of men, continue. This law enjoins on all rational beings, that which is proper for them to believe and do; and, any transgression of this law is sin. Under this law, Christ was made, and was perfectly obedient unto it. But the word law, (in Bible style,) is not always used in this definite sense; but, as the whole law of doctrine, including precepts given, grace bestowed, promises made, and pardons granted by him who is law-giver, king, and judge. The whole administration of the divine government is called law; and this law is perfect, converting the soul.

The mind of every creature is, and forever will be limited to certain bounds. Universal science is peculiar to God alone; some men, however, have intellects and research approximating to angels; while others are stupid and obscure, rising but a small grade above the brutes. Every man is not a Solomon for wisdom, nor a Paul for divinity. It is possible for a preacher to entertain a congregation thirty years with new subjects every sermon! If so, his mill must stand on the living stream, for his head of water is insufficient. Is it necessary or advantageous that he should have a store of novelty sufficient for so great a variety? If he can bring out of the treasury some new things with the old, will not that answer? Are there not many pairs of chapters, sections and verses, in the Holy Scriptures? Did not Jesus use the same words three times in prayer? Did not Paul's hearers desire to hear the same words again?

These arguments, however, should not be used as a cloak for ignorance, or as a covert for indolence in searching the scriptures and meditating thereon.

With regard to myself, my talents are small; I can, nevertheless, preach a few sermons to the same congregation, as independent of each other as need be. Afterwards, I take part of one, and part of another, with a new text, to keep up the idea of variety. And when all other aids fail, I gain some consolation from the poor memories of the people, concluding they may have forgotten what I remember is the same.

Archippus had personal accomplishments, and abundance of wealth; yet Clarissa refused his hand, because his mind was lean and sordid. Her sentiment was fixed, *that it is the mind which makes the man*, and she would not be connected with a man who possessed nothing but external show. So, also, in the religious world, many rise to high preference and fat livings, who are lean divines. A Bunyan, who is taught of God and versed in scriptures, will enrich the world more than many of them. Milton has said before me, "that Christ and his illiterate apostles used to travel afoot, but now doctors of divinity are driven by the devil in pompous carriages.

Mero has a poor constitution, but is a great student of botanyand physic; the quality of every plant and drug in the apothecary's shop, he seems to understand; but, remains sickly in himself, and useless to others. Domus, on the other hand, is robust, healthy, and useful to others, as he enjoys comfort and ease in himself; so, likewise, he employs himself in doing good to others. His motto is, "that health is better than the study of medicine." So, among religionists; some, like Mero, are studying all the subtleties, dogmas, and metaphysical hair-splitting of theology; stretching, lopping off, twisting, suppressing, adding, and altering, to support their favorite hypotheses and systems; and thus spend their days in inquietude and unprofitable vexation. While others, like Domus, stretch not themselves beyond their measure, or meddle with that which is too high for themselves; but, believe that which is plain, and do that which is right, and leave inexpressibles, inconceivables, and incomprehensibles, to settle their own accounts. In cases like these, I judge that the disciples of Mero are possessed with that knowledge which puffs up, while the followers of Domus enjoys that charity which edifies.

What was Jehovah about, eternal ages before creation began? Where, or what shall I be millions of ages hence?

Loud words and long harangues, cannot make truth out of error; nor are the most brilliant talents always listed on the side of truth.

Wit is one thing, and wisdom is another; when they unite, a Franklin is formed. In such instances, wit makes wisdom pleasing, and wisdom makes wit profitable.

Genius and research are not always connected with firmness and perseverance; when they are, they produce a Jefferson.

In scientific, political, and religious departments, good men are seeking to escape manifest errors, and finding out hidden truth. And it is most likely that the consummation of all things will find men in the pursuit.

If men acquire the certain knowledge of but few things, in seventy years, eternity will be a long school to learn the rest in.

The most that gospel preachers can claim since the age of miracles has ceased, is the ordinary influence of the Holy Spirit; those who set up for a higher claim, fail in their evidence, and prove only that they are infected with enthusiasm. That sinners are criminally guilty, is certain; but, most of the severe reproofs which uninspired preachers give them, are, (at best,) mixed with too much arrogancy in the preacher, and raise too much the indignation of the hearer. Let the preacher view himself a brother-sinner to his hearers; and view sin as a great misfortune, as well as a crime; and, out of pity and love, persuade, and pray the sinner to be reconciled to God, if he wishes to do him good.

Virtus est medium vitiorum. Formality and fanaticism, like the two thieves on either side of Christ, are reviling him, and casting contempt in his teeth. The formalist grounds his hope of heaven on the rituals he performs, the time he spends, and the charity he bestows in the line of religion. Redemption by the blood of Christ, justification by his righteousness, and being born again, are objects of minor consequence with him. He is not distressed with a hard heart, oppressed with guilt, or attacked with unbelief. He feels not the corruption of his nature, nor is his heart broken for sin. He has not learned that he cannot come to Christ except he is drawn by grace, nor has he received the spirit of adoption to cry *Abba Father*. He may be forward in joining the church, and zealous in the duties of his profession, and, after all, have only the form of godliness, without feeling its gracious influence. To such a man, Christ and his cross are but empty names.

The fanatic, on the other hand, places his hope on great revelations, burning zeal, singularity from the world, and the persecution he meets with. His zeal is not tempered with love, but has an alloy of bitterness with it; and his language is, "come and see my zeal for the Lord of Hosts." As he receives his knowledge immediately from God, or from a source beyond the reach of others, in his own view, all reasoning with him is in vain. His singular revelations or advantages qualify him to be teacher, but not to be pupil; convey the idea to him, that you have got before him, and he must learn of you, and his spirit will rise at once. In fine, there are so many grades of formality and fanaticism, which work so subtlely, in so many ways, by the sleight of hand, that it is beyond my ken to develop the subject. May a gracious God deliver me from every fatal error, and guide me in the right way.

Among the many ten thousand things which exist in the natural world, the causes of which cannot be ascertained, the case of the mistletoe is not the least. This evergreen shrub is found living in the crotch of an oak, or some other tree, but there is no evidence that it proceeds from the peccant humors of the tree, nor can any man tell where it comes from. So in the moral world, sin does exist—I see it—I feel it, but the first rise of it is enveloped in the dark.

The language of simple tyranny is, "I will do as I choose, and you shall do as I say." The bigot says, "nobody is always right but myself."

The apple is some time rising from the bud to its full size, after which, by ripening and mellowing, it grows richer, until it begins to rot. So with the mind of man; it rises by degrees to its full height—then grows candid and forbearing—and then decays in age.

Quick perception, deep research, lively fancy, strength of memory and soundness of judgment, are the attributes of a great man.

Some men think more than they read. Others read more than they think. Those who practice both, grow wise. Those who follow neither, remain ignorant.

So far as pride restrains overt acts, promotes industry, and labors to obtain a good report, it is a virtue; but when it rises in rebellion against God, contempt of fellow creatures, and self-exaltation, it is the blackest vice.

The sermons and discourses of some men remind me of Solomon's cargo, containing partly the precious articles of gold, silver and ivory, and partly the folly of apes and peacocks. Some declaimers are half fop and half sloven. Let the defects of others teach me wisdom.

When polemical writers, on religious subjects, are wanting in *plain proof*, they put on *holy awe*, call in the aid of sophistry and anger to supply the lack of argument, pour out defamation on their combatants, and call the whole of it "zeal for the Lord of Hosts."

The world abounds with religious bigotry, and bigots are degrading each other. Some, however, profess to counteract the current, by constantly preaching against all bigots and bigotry; not duly considering that, while other sects of bigots are fighting each other, they themselves have taken the bigot's dagger to fight all the rest.

In rare instances, men of exalted worth, meet with universal praise ; but, in most cases, real merit and disinterested benevolence, are the surest pledges of calumny from the envious, and reproach from the ungrateful.

Homer, the father of poets, who has enriched the world with his song, was himself a beggar. Luther, the great reformer in Europe was a poor man. Jefferson, the greatest statesman that the world ever produced, died insolvent. Paul, the chief apostle of the Gentiles, had no certain dwelling place—was hungry and naked—poor, yet making many rich. But ten thousand such instances fade away, when compared with the grace of our Lord Jesus Christ, who, though he was rich, yet, for the sake of rebellious traitors, became poor, that they, by his poverty, might be rich—might be pardoned and become the sons of God—receive an inheritance, a kingdom, a crown of life.

The KINGDOM, spoken of one hundred and thirty-four times in the New Testament, taken in all its parts, includes the King, his subjects, his laws, his pardons granted, his grace bestowed, the fruits of his spirit, and the glories of heaven. Sometimes one part is most emphatical, and sometimes and another. It is called the Kingdom of Heaven thirty-three times in Matthew's gospel, and nowhere else in the New Testament.

In some governments, *universal toleration* is granted to all kinds of religious opinions. This sounds humane and benevolent, but has a deadly root. If government has *power* to grant it as a favor, it has equal *power* to withhold it. In such cases, the citizens enjoy their liberty by a tenure no better than the good will of those in power. But the freedom of religious opinions, not only with societies, but with individuals, is a *right inalienable*, that cannot be surrendered. Of course, no government can *tolerate* or *prohibit* it but by tyrannical usurpation. If men commit overt acts under a pretence of religious impression, let the magistrate punish them for the overt acts, and pity them for their delusion.

Rev. Daniel Marshall, who died in 1784, was not formed for brilliancy of talents, but much revered for holy zeal and fervent labor. When he was in company with a circle of preachers, if he discerned too much levity among them, he would say, " stop, my brethren, and let us examine ourselves, whether we are in a right temper of mind, in case a broken-hearted sinner should come into the room, and ask us the question, *what shall I do to be saved? Ye servants of the Lord, pray for me*—would it not put us to the blush?" Let a preacher possess the spirit of his profession, and such an address would make him glad to see the grace of God ; but, if he has got out of the work, it would fill him with dismay.

The ravages of age reduce the eagle to a dollar, the dollar to a cent, and the cent to nothing. Well, we brought nothing into the world, and can carry nothing out of it.

Mention is made of the Book of the wars of the Lord, Num. xxi., 14. The Book of Jasher, Joshua, x., 13, and 2 Sam. i., 18. The Book of Nathan, the prophet, and the Book of Gad, the seer, 1 Chron. xxix., 29. The prophecy of Ahijah and visions of Iddo, 2 Chron. ix., 29. The Book of Shemaiah, 2 Chron. xii., 13. The Book of John, 2 Chron. xx., 34. The Books which Paul left at Troas, 2 Tim. iv., 13. His Epistle to Laodicea, Col. iv., 16. The prophecy of Enoch, Jude 14.

It is common for the rising generation to exert themselves to destroy the habits, modes of faith, and fine-spun systems of those who have gone before them. In this strife, what the young call improvement, the old call apostacy. The young conclude that the old are biased by tradition. The old judge the young are after new-fangled notions. The young see superannuacy in the old. The old discern the want of experience and sober reflection in the young.

Faith has a strong back--hope a silver-tongue—charity a soft hand—humility a bending knee—contrition a tender heart—zeal a nimble foot—patience a placid countenance. Joy has sparkling eyes, and prayer uplifted hands.

When a prisoner is tried for his life, the court feel an awful responsibility to God, their country and the criminal. It is happy for the court and for the criminal, that neither judge nor juror, in his official capacity, has anything to do with the soul, conscience, heaven or hell. There are but few crimes, if any, that should be punished with death. Penal laws should be few. If laws are not fraught with humanity and goodness, as well as justice and severity, they will be abhorred, but never revered. Hence, in countries where penal laws are abundant and cruel, crimes are the most frequent, and vice the most predominant.

Human eyes are not strong enough to read much in the upper book of the eternal purposes of God, but sufficient to read in the lower book of the duty of man. Servants should not pry into the designs of their masters, which they cannot understand, but obey their commands, which are made plain.

He who minds his own business, and is not a busy-body in other men's matters, bids fair to draw a pension for his labor.

Tell your children what you believe, and why you believe; but be sure to instruct them *how* to believe: viz., to hear dispassionately both sides of the question, not biased by the greatness or goodness of others, regarding neither frowns nor flatteries, promotion nor disgrace, but yield to a preponderance of rational evidence.

The bird of Galbus is possessed of that singular property, that, when a man, infected with the yellow jaundice, looks upon it, the bird immediately dies and the man recovers. So the death of Christ gives eternal life to those who look unto him.

" He can't be wrong whose heart is in the right."

Are these words of the poet true? The heart of King Asa was perfect all his days; yet he acted foolishly—was wroth with the prophet who reproved him—put him into prison, and oppressed some of the people in a rage. Was he not wrong in all this? Do not error, laws and usages of the most pernicious tendency, often proceed from good men, in which they think they are doing God service? Let history and observation answer the question.

"All their works they do to be seen of men." A rich man of my acquaintance gave a bell-clock to the town where he lived; afterwards he was solicited to bestow a favor for another purpose. "No," said the man, "when I bestow my gifts, I love to hear them ding, ding." Let those who subscribe large sums for Bible, missionary and education societies, ask themselves whether they would do as much if there was no register and publication of their donations, to ding, ding the sound abroad?

Some men are so lavish in their conversation about religion, and so urgent to others, while inattentive to the spirit and practice of the gospel themselves, that fears arise whether their liberality will not leave them in poverty. Let not this, however, stop the mouths and check the exertions of those who are spiritual and sincere. "Let the words of my mouth, and the meditations of my heart, be acceptable in thy sight, O Lord, our gracious Redeemer.

In civil life, some men calculate well, but fail in their enterprises for want of corresponding labor. So in the ministerial department, some ministers form sublime ideas of the character and work of a preacher, but neglect the life and labor which they eulogize; while others labor abundantly, but, for want of prudent calculation, lose the reward.

A man who has not many inherent ideas, and but a few borrowed ones, having but a small vocabulary of words, will never excel as an orator. His orations will be *vox et præterea nihil*, a voice and nothing else. Honest humility, however, in homely dress, is more to be admired than licentiousness, adorned with all the figures of rhetoric.

All the aid that conscience asks of government, is *to be let alone*. Time and experience have found that the only way to prevent religious oppression, is to exclude religious opinions from the civil code.

OATHS.*

A MAN, by the influence of education and tradition, may be so strongly persuaded that the dogmas and system which he has embraced are certainly true, as to seek no further for evidence of their truth, but only for arguments to support them. He has been taught *what* to believe, but not *how* to believe. He who honestly seeks for truth, must candidly hear both sides of the question, without any prepossession to turn the scale, and form his result on a preponderance of evidence: remembering, at the same time, that he may be imposed upon by the items of evidence given, or by the weakness of his mind in his conclusions.

Keeping this in mind, I shall make some inquiry on the nature of oaths. The great Jehovah is represented as often swearing; and, because he could swear by no greater, he swore by himself. The oath runs, "as I live, saith the LORD," or, "by myself have I sworn." Many of the promises and threatenings of the Almighty have conditions expressed or understood in them; and, when they are not fulfilled, it is said that God repents. But, whenever he swears by his own *eternal existence*, no conditions change his course, the thing will certainly be accomplished.

The Lord Jesus, in substance, swore many times. The double asseveration, "Verily, verily," is found twenty-five times in John's gospel, which is very little inferior to an oath.

In the Mosaic institutions, oaths were imposed on the people to "end all strife," as the last resort to obtain the truth. Sometimes they cleared themselves by their oaths, and sometimes they cleared or condemned others. If they swore falsely against any man, and their testimony tended to minor punishment or death, and the testimony was proved to be false, the punishment which the witnesses sought to have inflicted on the defendant was to recoil on their own heads, whether it was fine, stripes or death.

In the United States it is generally believed that the laws given by Moses were not binding on any nation but the Israelites. No other nation has ever adopted them. That kings are born with a divine right to rule, is not believed among us. Our government is formed on another principle. Our institutions recognise the sovereignty of the people. That all power is vested in them, and by them given to all the

* Published in 1830.

agents, who are accountable servants. If this is correct, it follows that no chief magistrate, legislative body, or judicial board, have, or can possess any *power*, which is not found in small constituent parts among the units that compose the whole body; for how can the creature possess more power than the Creator? The result is, that if one individual has the power to impose an oath on another, in a small moiety, then, by adding all the little grains together, officers can be created to coerce by oath. But where is the individual who possesses the power or right to compel his neighbor to tell what he does not choose to reveal, by a threat of the vengeance of God if he diminishes or adds to the truth?

I am ignorant of the art of Masonry. It is, however, confidently affirmed by some, and denied by none, that oaths are taken by the members, in taking their degrees; but who administers these oaths? who has a right to do it? If they make those selemn declarations, which some say they do, to keep the secret, and afterwards reveal it, they are very presumptuous in their protestations at first, or very perfidious in divulging it afterwards. But, let their oaths be ever so solemn, and the tortures which they invoke upon themselves ever so horrid, in case they falter, the whole amounts to nothing before a court of justice—the laws of state take no cognizance of it. The testimony of a masonic perjurer (if so he may be called) is received as freely, and believed as fully, as the testimony of any man; and the reason assigned is, "that their oaths proceeded from a self-created power."

Now, I ask what power there is in a republican government, or, indeed, in any human government, that the people have not created? But how can they establish a power without materials? The germ must first exist in the individuals. In this respect, what plea has civil government over the masonic institution?

Are oaths advantageous? Do they tend to bring truth to light? do courts and jurors place more confidence in the testimony of a witness, when under oath, than they would if he was not under oath? He who does not reverence the *truth*, how can he reverence the *God* of truth?

If the testimony of a witness is proved false, let him be punished for his falsehood. What more is now inflicted on perjurers?

A great part of the conversation of men is but idle friz, which passes for nothing; but, when they are called upon to give testimony in a case where the life, liberty or property of a fellow citizen is at stake, it becomes another thing. Truth generally carries an internal evidence with it, while falsehood, in its course, defeats itself. If neither of these appear in the testimony, would the solemnity of an oath produce them?

The first account given in the time of Abraham, of an oath taken by his steward, bespeaks the existence and caution of oaths before that time;

but, whether they originated among the Pagans, out of reverence to their gods, or whether Jehovah first taught his worshippers the use of them, I cannot ascertain. They certainly have been in use from Abraham until the present time, which proves neither the advantage nor disadvantage of them. Does a man, by his oath, say, "I now speak in the presence of God?" He is always in the presence of God. Does he say, "I expect to give an account of what I now say before God in the day of judgment?" This is as true of every idle word he speaks. By his words he will be justified or condemned. Does he believe that the Almighty will punish him in hell if he tells what is not true? What more is this than all liars will receive when they have their part in the lake that burns with fire and brimstone.

The subject is too profound for my talents, research and leisure. If some good friend will give an elucidation of the origin of oaths—what they express—what bonds they put upon the witness that he is not always under—where a republic get the power to institute and enjoin them—whether every purpose of government and private life could not be answered as well without them, he shall receive my hearty thanks.

EXTRACTS FROM A LETTER TO REV. JOHN TAYLOR OF KENTUCKY, DATED DEC. 10, 1830.

I, John, who am your brother and companion in tribulation, and in the kingdom and patience of Jesus Christ, have lately received a book and a letter from an old friend, whom I have not seen for more than forty years, which gives me great satisfaction.

You inform me of your age, your labors, your success, the state of your family at large, and that your wife, Betsey, my old friend, is yet living. God bless her precious soul, and the body attached to it. It brings fresh to my mind the winter of 1779 and '80, which was the coldest winter that America has ever known; and yet, to me, it was the warmest that ever I knew. At several other periods of my life, I have had more success than I had at that time, but never had the spirit of prayer and travail for souls, to an equal degree. It was then your dear partner fell in love with the blessed Jesus, and was baptized; not to gain admission into the kingdom, which is righteousness and peace, but to prove her love and obedience to him who had delivered her from the power of darkness, and translated her into the kingdom.

Your travels have been great, your success encouraging. "They that turn many to righteousness, shall shine as the stars forever and ever." When the ministers of Jesus shall be called to give an account of their stewardship, if, like their masters, they can each say, "behold I, and the children which God hath given me—here, Lord, are the proofs of my ministry—the seals of my faithfulness—the souls thou hast given me." It will be a crown of rejoicing in the day of the Lord. But, notwithstanding success is very desirable, yet the promise is made to the faithful. Noah, a preacher of righteousness, was very unsuccessful; all his hearers but seven were destroyed; but, as he was faithful, he obtained the promise, and became heir of the righteousness which is by faith.

Whenever I had evidence that God had blessed my imperfect labors for the salvation of sinners, it has given me much more joy than the favors of the rich, or the applauses of the great. * * * *

I have been reading the writing which came to Jehoram from Elijah, ii. Chron. 21, 12. Jehoram, the son of Jehoshaphat, did not reign, until after Elijah was translated; but, as he carried his hands and feet with him, it is possible he might have written in the other world; granting this, how could he have sent his letter down to Jehoram? It is true, that after this, he descended to the holy mount, and was one of the six who formed an assembly far more pompous and astonishing, than the millions of Xerxes; but, in this case, it is hard to believe that Elijah came post from heaven, and dropped the writing into the letter-box of Jehoram. Divines think the letter was prophetically written by Elijah, before his translation, and left in the hands of Elisha, to be delivered to Jehoram at a given time. This might have been the case, for Josiah and Cyrus were prophesied of by name, and the work they should do, described, long before they were born; and yet, when we read this writing, it will preponderate in the mind, that the writing was posterior to the crimes. Why may we not conclude that Ezra, or some transcriber, put the name of Elijah, where it should have been Elisha? Admit this, and all is easy.

This same Jehoram died at the age of forty years, (see the twentieth verse of the same chapter,) and Ahaziah, his youngest son, succeeded him, being forty-two years old; two years older than his father, and yet his youngest son. In 2 Kings, viii. 26, this same Ahaziah, is said to have been twenty-two years old when he began to reign. Dr. Gill owns there is an error here, not in the translation, but in the Hebrew. As I am not skilled in Bible mending, I shall here observe, that, considering the many transcriptions and translations the Bible has passed through, it is more to be wondered at, that there are no more errors in it, than that there are so many. A great part of the Bible carries such evidence with it that it is of divine origin, that when I read it, I feel, if possible, more than certain, that it is the book of God; and, like its author, incomprehensible. How dim the golden verses of Pythagoras, and the morals of Seneca appear, when the true light shines from the Holy Scriptures. Let all the legislators, philosophers, wise men and wits, that are now living, combine together to form a code of laws, and place it beside Romans xii., 9, 26, (which can be distinctly read in a minute and a half, containing hardly two hundred words,) and it will sink into insignificance and folly.

The books and letters which you yourself, Mr. Chambers, and Mr Norwood have had the goodness to send me, give me to understand that there is a strife among you, about the ancient order of things, and the old Baptist way, which has split some of the churches, and excited the minds of many. In these northern climes, the strife is between the ancient order of free and accepted masons, and the seceding masons, which has also split many churches, run down many ministers, and become a question at the polls of elections. But, in the section of country where I live and preach, neither of the excitements prevail. The lot assigned *me*, seems to be, to watch and check *clerical hierarchy*, which assumes as many shades as a chameleon, sometimes requesting the civil law to support it; and, when that fails, denouncing the vengeance of God against all who will not support their dogmas. If this does not frighten the people into their service, good words and fair speeches are resorted to, in order to deceive the hearts of the simple; and all advisable arts are practiced to make a gain of the populace, gain them to their party to make it strong, and gain their money to support them in ease and splendor.

A new order of things has taken place in the religious department, since I began to preach. Then, when I went to meeting, I expected to hear the preacher set forth the ruin and recovery of man, and labor with heavenly zeal to turn many unto righteousness. His eyes, his voice, and all his prayers, and deportment, gave evidence that his soul travailed in birth for the salvation of his hearers. But now, when I go to meeting, I hear high encomiums on Sunday-schools, tract societies, Bible societies, missionary societies, anti-mason societies, etc., with a strong appeal to the people to aid with their money those institutions which are to introduce the millennium; assuring the people that "every cent may save a soul." I do not wish to be the bigoted old man, who always finds fault with new customs, though ever so great improvements; but, when I see the same measures pursued that were in the third century, I am afraid the same effects will follow.

I have had my day, and it is nearly over. On a serious reflection, I cannot much condemn myself, that I have not devoted as much of my time in my ministerial labors, as human and civil duties admitted; but, have much cause of self-condemnation when I reflect on the languor of soul, and indifference of spirit that have beset me when preaching eternal realities. It is a wonder that ever a holy God should have crowned my imperfect labors with any success; and yet, amidst all, I have great joy to think that I have not altogether "run in vain, nor labored in vain." I have followed travelling, preaching, and baptizing, ever since I saw you last, as much as sickness and family cares would admit, and have not varied materially in any thing; and now, even while I am writing, the old gray headed sinner has to pray, "God be merciful to me a sinner."

Every child has left me; myself and wife keep house alone. We have neither Cuffee nor Phillis to help or plague us. My wife is seventy-seven years old, and has this season done the housework, and from six cows has made eighteen hundred pounds of cheese, and two hundred and fifty pounds of butter. She and myself entertain a great regard for yourself and lady.

Rev. John Taylor, who lives, or ought to live, in the town of Regeneration, Grace-street, Penitent alley, a the sign of the cross, and next to glory.

ADDRESS

DELIVERED AT DALTON, MASSACHUSETTS, JANUARY 8, 1831.

THIS evening commemorates one of the most remarkable events to be found in American history. The battle of New Orleans, commanded by Andrew Jackson, against the British forces, will be remembered and admired as long as military skill, bravery, and patriotism have harmonious sounds.

This triumphant victory raised the commander high in the esteem and effections of the nation, and brought him forward to the chief magistracy of the United States. On his promotion, many of his warm-hearted friends feared that his surprising talents were merely military, and he would be deficient in the cabinet. But his first message to the twenty-first Congress turned their fears into admiration. They now find him as profound in civil, as he was in military office, and greet him at the head of the nation, as they did before at the head of the army. No subject has yet arisen, since he became president, but what he has been able to digest; and leaves a conviction in the minds of others, that his source of action is not exhausted.

A chaplain of the southern army gave the following character to General Jackson: "He sits down and forms his plan; then rises and executes it." Prudence and despatch are visible in all his undertakings. How unlike the emperor Heliogabalus, who neglected the duties of the throne, and spent his time in catching flies, and collecting cob-webs for public show. When I read his late message, among other beauties, the clause which recommended the pockets of the people as the best repository for revenue, shone with peculiar lustre. It reminded me of what I have somewhere read, that a certain king, who kept neither gold, pearls, nor any fine ornaments in his treasury, was visited by a crowned headed brother, who wallowed in splendor at home. On the desire of the visitor to see the royal treasures of the frugal king, he was conducted into the treasury apartment, where little was to be seen but naked walls. Struck with astonishment, he exclaimed: "how can you support your dignity—give royal bounties, and maintain your army. To which the other king replied, "tarry with me three days and you shall see." In the meantime the frugal king sent a request to his subjects, to bring in their bounties; which was done with all speed, and consisted of gold, pearls, embroidery, and all kinds of riches; at sight of which the visiting king was astonished. "Here," said the frugal king, "is my treasure, deposited in the hands of those who earned it, and always at my command when the good of the people requires it." This seems to be the policy of president Jackson; and is it possible there can be an American heart that does not respond to the sentiment?

It was but a partial reform, when England protested against the encroachments of the Roman Pontiffs; many, therefore, were non-conformists to the Episcopal establishment; some of whom crossed the Atlantic, and settled in New-England. These pilgrims, with all their good views, brought some of the drugs of the cup of the whore of Babylon with them; and soon religious parishes were incorporated. Every parish was forced to have a preacher—all within the parish were forced to pay the preacher—Sunday was established as holy time—all must go to meeting or be fined. Every town or parish must have a learned orthodox preacher settled, or after five years lose their charter, etc. It would take a history more than nineteen times as long as the one hundred and nineteenth psalm to narrate all this superstition, cruelty, and folly. Was the commonwealth, at this time, fully purged from her old sins, we might expect to see a pure representative democracy, which will never be the case, while religion is considered an adjective that cannot stand of itself. When will this great truth be acknowledged, that neither the legislative, executive, nor judicial arms of government, in their official capacities, have anything to do with the souls of men, conscience, or eternity? That the whole design of civil government is to protect the lives, liberties, and property, of all the citizens? Where this is believed and acted upon, republicanism will flourish, but where it is not believed it cannot breathe; and, if any call themselves republicans, and yet make use of the law as the sinews of the gospel, (instead of the sinner's gospel,) they are like the ferry-men, looking one way, and rowing another.

Jackson is certainly the president of the people; for, more than two-thirds of the people gave him their votes; and, he has been, and is still doing, the very works that he was chosen for. When Mr. Jefferson was minister to France, he wrote to a friend in the United States, that it was necessary that there should be in every government, periodically, a revolution and civil war, to purge the government of oppressive laws and usages, and cast off the drones, that sucked all, and gathered none of the honey. This he said before he had tested the force of free suffrage. Now it is seen that little bits of paper, will effect that which has heretofore been gained by sword, cannon, and streams of blood. Jackson is now the agent in the hands of the people to execute the purgation. His vigilance to secure the rights of the people—the authority of the state governments, and the defined, supreme powers of the general government, is manifest in all his communications and actions. For his removals, however, he is abused by some, who like dogs, bark most when the moon is rising, which they cannot help. So it was in Bible times; the shepherds and young lions howled, when their glory and spoil were taken away. The bitter complaints of dismissed officers, are proofs of the correctness of the principle of removals; they prove that the complainants were in possession of a prize which they themselves wished exclusively to enjoy. When those who are out of office, and were never in, complain of removals, it is generally because they themselves are overlooked, or entertain a prepossession of opposition against the administration.

The communications of the president evincing such a depth of thought, justice, and humanity, as pedantry, with all its puffs cannot gainsay. But, say his enemies, Jackson is not the author of those messages; Van Buren is premier, he does all. Be it so: Jackson had wisdom enough to appoint him secretary; and how the creature can have more wisdom than the creator, is not as plain as Euclid. This same Van Buren has been called the little regent—the magician—the cat that often fell, but always upon the feet; and yet he has been honored by the most populous state in the Union with the highest offices in her gift. I cannot see how these high encomiums will strengthen the party opposed to the present administration. Supposing Jackson should die, or decline serving another term, or live through another term; in a few years another president must be selected; and, "if the safe precedent" should be acted upon, all the encomiums now given to the secretary, would aid in his promotion to the presidency.

Mr. Hamilton has informed us, that when Washington had formed his documents, he would say, "pray, Mr. Hamilton, correct this document and fix it in proper order;" and what harm was there in this? When Col. Tarlton was degrading Col. William Washington, in a company of ladies, he said that he did not believe that Woshington could write his name. "It may be so," said one of the ladies, "but I dare say he can set his mark." This Tarlton knew, for Washington had cut off one of Tarlton's fingers. Who does not remember how boldly it was affirmed, for a long time, that Jefferson never drew the Declaration of Independence? How common it is for men to make lies their refuge, and hide themselves under falsehood! I have no scruples but what all the messages and communications that have the signature of the president affixed to them, were substantially written by himself; and, if better state papers are to be found, I know not where to look for them.

I was in the vigor of life when the national constitution was formed, and gave my vote for a friend to its ratification, and have never repented it. I have watched the course of the government for more than forty years, and believe it to be the best in the world. There have been, however, dark clouds in our political horizon, which filled the sons of liberty with dark-boding fears. The clouds which had been gathering for several years settled together and seemed to cover the heavens, about 1797–8. But soon the light broke out, under the administration of the apostle of liberty. But in his administration, the encroachments of foreign powers became insufferable. Neither an appeal to justice, embargo, nor non-intercourse, could prevent a rupture. Under the administration of his successor, war was declared. In addition to the common evils of war, some of the states refused aid, and cast all the embarrassments in the way that they could, to make the war unpopular, and either dissolve the government, or change the administration. The war at length closed triumphantly for the United States, and peace spread her balmy wings over the land.

Those who had been in opposition before, without any conviction or confession of error, or any change of opinion, now changed their measures, and tried the other lug of the boat. Now flattery became the order of the day. The cry was, " Federalism is defunct—we are all one—the era of good feeling has come—come, let us build together." By these good words and fair speeches, they deceived the hearts of the simple. Those republicans who were dyed in the cloth followed them at once; those dyed in the yarn soon joined their ranks—those dyed in the wool were rather untractable—but those who were yearned black lambs, (like Paul, free born,) were as stubborn as the oaks of Bashan, and firm as the mountains about Jerusalem. This heterogeneous mass—this image of iron and clay, became great, and exercised all the authority of the first beast of 1797, and the shout was, " who is like unto this beast—who is able to make war with him ?" At length a little stone was found in Tennessee, which was cut out of the mountain, without the hands of Congress, that smote the image whose feet were Clay; who bound the strong man, and is now destroyiug his goods.

Yes, Mr. President, kind Providence has hitherto been gracious to the United States in war and in peace; and our hope is strong that he will yet save us from civil tyranny—religious hierarchy—sword, famine and pestilence—and that from the school of America many Lafayett's may rise, and spread light and freedom throughout the world.

I close, fellow-citizens, with the following section:

I was a man grown when the grand dramma opened at Lexington, and lived through the revolutionary war. The most prominent defeats and victories are yet fresh in my mind. At the close of the war, the confederation was found insufficient to protect the states from anarchy. A more energetic government superseded. Under the new government, I have witnessed eleven presidential elections, and twenty-two elections for members of Congress. And now in the eve of a life very poorly spent, I would say to the people of the United States, "Let no man deceive you. Only will to be free, and you will hold your freedom. Place confidence enough in your rulers to enable them to act sentimentally--give a fair interpretation to their measures, and time for their operation; but, always hold the reins of responsibility in your own hands. Never surrender the right of free suffrage, which is the strong hold of republicanism. Adhere to the vital principle of free government; that the voice of a majority is the voice of the whole. Shun that rock of considering religious opinions objects of civil government. Believe and act for yourselves, and guarantee the same to your neighbors.

"Remember that Christianity is of divine origin—the only religion that ever brought pardon to a guilty world; but, it has suffered more injury by its pretended friends, who have undertaken to regulate it by law, than it has from all its enemies."

I shall finally conclude with expressions, in which I am confident every heart here present will respond.

May the life and health of Andrew Jackson be long preserved; and when he shall go the way of all the earth, may the principles that guide his administratton flourish in immortal bloom.

LETTER TO THE REV. O. B. BROWN.

The report that Elder Leland had been excluded from the church, etc., induced the Rev. O. B. Brown to write to him. The following is a copy of the reply:—

My Brother—It has often struck my mind, that if a constitution of government was now to be formed for a nation unborn, it might border on perfection; but, in this I meet with a check, for it is hard to conceive how government is anything but the contrivance of individuals to secure what they possess by nature and acquisition. It must, therefore, be formed in a mode to answer those ends. For the first eighteen centuries, the inhabitants of the earth had no government, (that we have any account of,) but patriarchal; but, in the days of Nimrod, the awful experiment was made of leaping into the gulf of absolute monarchy. From that period until the present time, there has been a perpetual war between the claims of governmentals, and the rights of the people. In the most successful struggles for the rights of man, in the final close, the people have gained but little, except tne change of masters to ride them. The constitution of the United States, I consider the best that was ever formed. Energy and liberty walk hand in hand together; but, such is the thirst of man for power and wealth, that it requires all the vigilance of the people to prevent usurpation. If men sleep, the enemy will sow tares. The usurpation begins with a strained construction, proceeds as precedent, which soon becomes doctrine; a sacrifice of the rights of the people follows, and a field for ambition is opened.

The character of a tolerable statesman is far boyond my claim. My talents, my education, my low circumstances in life, and my avocation, have all admonished me to be little; and, my disposition perfectly accords; for I never desired a civil office in my life. But I rejoice that my country contains the men which are needed. A noble Spartan, who expected to be elected one of the fifty men that were wanting, and was left in the back-ground, went rejoicing home, exclaiming to his wife with joy, "Sparta contains fifty men more virtuous than myself." The origin and outlines of civil government I have paid some attention to, in order to give that ordinance of God its proper reverence, and maintain that religious opinions are inalienable in nature, and should be forever excluded from the civil arm. For this opinion, I have often been represented a Deist; and, for this opinion, contended for in some remarks on the Sunday mail question, I am published in gazetts, as renouncing the faith, and being excluded for it. If those gentlemen who petition Congress to interfere in the controversy of religious opinions, should be asked, "who hath required this at your hands?" could they turn to the text in the New Testament and say, "there is our authority?" Is it possible for man to give greater evidence that he is ignorant of the precepts of Christianity, and destitute of the spirit of it, then he does when he makes use of the arm of the law to force others to believe as he does, or compel them to support what he believes? All such renounce Christianity, and are excluded from the fellowship of the gospel.

If I were a man of influence, I should suppose that the hue and cry after me was designed to degrade my character, and thereby destroy my influence; but, as it is otherwise with me, the words of an old book occur; "after whom is the king of Israel come out? after a dead dog? after a flea?"

Had the accusation which has gone the rounds, stated that I did not possess that full portion of the Christian spirit, or live equal to the holy precepts of the gospel, although the charge should prove me perverse, yet, in honesty I must have responded to its truth. But, to affirm that I have renounced the only scheme that Jehovah ever made known to man, which met the guilty sinner's wants and brought relief to his woes, is not true. And if Christianity is divinely true, as I believe, the first editor who set the charge afloat, or his informers, may remember the doom therein given to all liars.

That kind of Christianity which calls in the aid of law, sword, or the college for its support; which puts on the mask of sanctity to cover injustice and cruelty, and acquire pre-eminence and wealth; that forces its dogmas on others, or asks for any thing more than a dispassionate hearing, and a corresponding faith, on rational evidence, I do renounce from the bottom of my heart; and, if I am excluded for denying the faith, I shall glory in my lonely solitude, and take more delight in the tub of Diogenes, than I otherwise should in the court of Ahasuerus. That the blessed Jesus, who is God over all, the ancient of days, the everlasting Father, the first, the true God, and eternal life; without beginning, the creator of all things, the Lord God of the holy prophets, who was in heaven when instructing Nicodemus on earth, whose name is wisdom; should be deficient in his laws to govern his church, or any ways dependent on the rulers of this world to defend his people, prevent error, and describe and protect the truth, is not likely. If any orders are left in the New Testament for such interference, in more than fifty years search, they have escaped my notice. The laws of men should recognize every man as a citizen, but none as religionists—should protect the rights of all, the opinions of none. If any, under a pretence of religion, commit overt acts, punish them for their crimes, and pity them for their delusion.

I am aware you will see a great sameness in my several communications; and one reason is, I cannot get out of my shell. Should I try to expand like the silly frog that swelled to be as big as an ox, like him I should burst myself. Another reason I borrow from a Dutch priest, who, having severely flogged one of his hearers with his fists, exclaimed, "my hearers are such numb-sculls, that I was obliged to beat it into them."

I conclude by wishing the present session of Congress may be pleasant to the members, and acceptable to their constituents.

With due respect,

JOHN LELAND.

P. S. I am well pleased with the administration; it is as good as I ever knew, or ever expect to know.

ADDRESS

DELIVERED AT NORTH ADAMS, ON THE 4TH OF MARCH, 1831.

SENTIMENT.

Inconsistency.—A refuge for ignorance—a covert for hypocrisy, and a prop for disappointed ambition.

OUR calender year begins on the 1st of January, but the political year of the United States begins on this day, the 4th of March. From this day the representatives of Congress begin their two years service, the senators their six years, and the president his four years administration.

It is usual, on days like this, to reflect on past events, and look forward to future emergencies. Observation and history assist us in the retrospect. The connection between causes and effects, with uncertain political prophocy, is what we have to direct us in prospect.

The Indian Question has lately been much discussed; highly approved by some, and as highly reprobated by others. I have waited with some inquietude to hear the question developed from the root.

Did not the Creator of the earth give the whole of it to all the inhabitants of it? Does the law of nature give to an individual any more of the earth than his body can cover? What gives men a moral right to any portion of the earth, except the improvement which they have put upon it? If one improves a section of the earth, by building on it, or fencing it, how far does his claim extend? to the sea—to the mountains—to a certain degree of latitude, or how far? If two settlements begin at the same time, being a thousand miles distant, do their claims run to the centre? or has another an equal right to build and possess between them? I am still waiting for an elucidation of these and similar questions.

In the days of Peleg, about eighteen hundred years after the creation, the earth was divided. Some centuries after this, the Edomites, the Moabites, the Ammonites and the Israelites had portions of the earth given to them by a divine charter. But such has been the population of the earth, and so short the history of ancient things, that we are at a loss how to decide what has been considered a just claim of territory. It is believed that half the age of the world has elapsed under the belief that conquest gave the conquerors a right to all the land of the conquered.

Who were the first settlers in America? Whether white, red, or black men, is no more known than it is how they came here. The first emigrants from Europe found the country in possession of red men, who lived by the chase. A great part of their forest has been purchased of them, and some taken by conquest. The plan of their present removal, contemplated by Jefferson, Madison, Monroe, Adams and Jackson, appears as just, humane and politic, as any that can be devised. The crisis is come that something must be done; and what can be done better? To have a state set up within the boundary of another state, is unconstitutional; and yet all treaties are the supreme laws of the land. If it should be conceded, too, that there is a clash between the provision of the constitution and the treaties made with the Indians, it would be rather ungenerous to blame the present administration for treaties made before the administration began.

When cases arise that have evils on both sides, the least possible evil is the greatest possible good. Among all the complaints that are made against the removal of the Indians, I have seen no scheme proposed to do justice to Georgia, and deal truly with the Indians, equal to the course now pursuing.

The Negro Question, in one view of it, has been quiet ever since the admission of Missouri into the Union; but, in another view, it agitates the public mind. Some of the negroes in the United States have been imported from Africa, but most of them are American born; some have descended from American parents more than ten generations. America is all the country they know; in which the bones and dust of their ancestors lie buried. All their relations and attachments are here; why then ship them to Liberia? How sacrilegous? Why not liberate them, and let them form into states within the limits of other states, and treat them as sister states?

It is said that all religious sects are sacrificing their peculiar sentiments to become one; and why should the color or bruit of a negro prevent this happy union? It will certainly cost considerable to move the Indians, but not more, perhaps, than a war with them. So also with the negroes; for who does not know that application is made to the legislature of Massachusetts for twenty thousand dollars to transport the negroes to Liberia. The number of negroes in the United States is (say one million) estimated at one hundred millions of dollars. If government should purchase them of their masters, it would create a large debt, but less than the debt of the last war; and, if a national debt is a national blessing, who would flinch at it?

It is probable that a number of the slave-holders would freely give up their slaves, and others take a reduced price for them, which would diminish the price of their ransom. If any of the slave-holders will neither give nor sell their slaves, here will be a great door opened for missionary labors. The pious youth, who are waiting for a gap, will now have a loud call to go and preach to the hard-hearted mastes, and flatter them to give, and threaten them if they will not. And, as the young heralds cannot do it for nothing, societies must be formed to raise money, and mendicants employed to solicit aid—each one paying himself out of what he collects.

When the grand emancipation is accomplished, and the black citizens have formed into a state, or states, within the existing states, or in the western hemisphere, there will be no need to send any among them to teach them how to till the land, raise flocks and herds, or use the tools of mechanism; for these things they understand. As many of them are good readers, they can keep their own schools; and the good gospel preachers among them will supersede the necessity of costly missionaries.

But my fancy is carrying me too far. The design of this little meeting, is a declaration of the approbation and satisfaction entertained in the wisdom, firmness, economy and humanity of the present administration.

To lead on, it may be noticed, that the salaries of civil officers should always be competent, but never extravagant. When officers have done well, esteem them highly in love for their works' sake, and pay them promptly for their services, and never owe them an official debt. Never think that, when a man has served you an agreed term, you are under bonds to continue him longer or raise him higher. With this view of the subject, you may look every man boldly in the face, and vote for him whose talents and integrity you prefer.

Andrew Jackson passed through many changes, and filled many offices, until, from an orphan boy, he rose to the highest seat in the gift of the people. This promotion he received, not as a reward for past services, but because the people saw in him those talents and virtues which they conceived necessary to purify the government, check extravagances, and adhere to the constitution in its simplicity, without strained constructions. Rather more than two-thirds of the people voted for him, and I ask, has he deceived their expectations? Has he not rather exceeded their most flattering hopes?

It is generally understood that he has consented to be voted for as president at the next presidential election. In one of his messages to Congress he recommended an amendment of the constitution, so far as to declare a man ineligible for more than one term, and that in every doubtful case it was safest to refer to the sovereign people.

This recommendation is explained by some as a virtual refusal to serve as president another term, and for him *now* to agree to it, is a manifest inconsistency. Washington, in his farewell address, informs us that before the close of his first term he had made arrangments to decline serving any longer; but the persuasions of his friends, and the unsettled state of things, induced him to continue. Was Washington inconsistent?

When the angels of heaven visited Sodom, on the first request of Lot, they solemnly refused his hospitalities, and said *nay;* but, on his strong persuasion, they turned into his house. Who ever lamented for the inconsistency of these celestial visitants? Their inconsistency certainly eventuated in the salvation of Lot and his family. If Jackson has imitated Washington and angels, let the accusations of his enemies be modest.

But, after all, there is no inconsistency in the affair. An amendment of the constitution, and an appeal to the people at large, in doubtful cases, are the two things here that have bearings on the question. By inaction, Congress, and of course all the people, have decided that it is not best, at present, to alter the constitution. The constitutional voice of the sovereign people, therefore, is that a citizen is re-eligible to the presidency. This voice Jackson reverences; and, contrary to his own inclination, for the good of his country, consents to bear the burden longer, if he is fairly elected. That he will bargain, or use any art or management to gain the post, his enemies do not believe.

We have our political as well as our calendar leap year. One year from next autumn the race will be run for the presidential prize. As the anti-masonics join in their nomination with those who are opposed to Jackson, it is most likely that but two candidates will be brought upon the hippodrome.

In this commonwealth, there is an overwhelming majority of men, talents, wealth and aristocracy opposed to Jackson; but, if things remain stationary, as they now are, the opposition in all the United States cannot safely calculate on more than eighty electoral votes, while Jackson will be far ahead on the *vantage* ground. And who would not wish to see the last revolutionary character that will ever be in the United States, fill the presidential chair until the last cent of the national debt is discharged—the Indians all removed and pleased, and the tongue of slander cease to abuse?

From what has taken place in America, and what is taking place in Europe, there is some prospect that long lost liberty is returning to bless the world—liberty that a great part of men have been robbed of by the flattery and frowns—good words and fair speeches—art and cunning—lies and hypocrisy of wicked tyrants and covetous priests. Should the halcyon days spring up when every cruel yoke should be broken, and the oppressed go free—when there should be an equal distribution of labor, wages and food—when all the liberty that good laws, free from licentiousness, affords to all equally alike should be enjoyed, how would every benevolent heart rejoice at the change.

LETTER TO THOMAS BUCK.

Cheshire, Oct. 25, 1831.

My Good old Friend:—Your friendly letter of the 30th of August came safe to hand in due time. While the young are looking forward in hopes of brighter scenes, the old are retrospecting past events; your letter reminds me of days and circumstances long past. The last time I saw you, was at Waterlick, April, 1790. At your meeting-house I preached from a text that has been of use to me until this moment; it was, "God be merciful to me a sinner." The confession is yet true with me, and the prayer of it has been answered until now. I have been travelling and preaching from that date until the present, through infirmity of flesh and heaviness of spirit; but, have never risen to that sublime state of wisdom and zeal, which I anticipated at my beginnings. I have had my summers and winters, praises and reproaches, prosperity and adversity; and, having attained the help of God, I remain until this time enjoying good health. My heaviest trials have been of that character, that a communication of them to others, (if indeed that could have been done,) would only have added to their weight, so that the darkest part of the way I have had to walk alone.

I have seen a number of religious revivals within the limits of my ministration, and at this present time there is a shower falling in these parts. I have lately baptized forty, and others stand waiting. How it may appear to the solemn line of spectators, on the banks of the water, to see an old man, whose locks have been frosted with seventy-seven winters, baptizing without any inconvenience, I cannot say; to himself there is a solemn pleasure. I never baptized more than twenty-four persons at one time, and abundance of times no more than one; and, as I have baptized one thousand five hundred and twelve in all, I judge that I have been in the water for baptism more times than any man in the United States.

The excitement of Campbellism and anti-masonry, does not rage in this section of the country, but the missionary principle has strong advocates and bold opponents; whether one will completely triumph over the other, or whether there will be a settled division, I cannot determine. Without any aid from missionary boards or funds, I have followed the missionary work fifty-seven years; in which time I have travelled a distance that would girdle the globe four times, and still have health and spirit to persevere.

In many revivals of religion that I have seen, something singular (in extraneous forms) has always been seen, so that no two of them have been alike ; nor is it to be wondered at, when we consider the infinite means in Jehovah, and the constant changes in the fashions of the world. Taking my own judgment for a standard, some revivals are much more pure than others. The present excitement among us has many muddy appendages ; such exertions are made by many, to unite the exertions of natural powers with the energies of grace, as are not common. When souls boast alone in the Lord, the humble hear thereof and are glad ; but, when they are taught to boast of any thing else, the humble are sad. I confess that I have not acquired the art of welding cold iron and hot together. But we should always make allowances for the difference that exists between the wisdom and truth of God, and the weakness and corruptions of men.

He who is so fearful of gathering chaff that he will not reap, will certainly fail in gathering wheat.

You inform me that all the old preachers are dead, or past labor, and that a new set have risen up in their stead. It is to be hoped that the young will improve upon the old, by shunning their defects and imitating their virtues. Preachers should always be little enough for the meek and lowly Jesus, who made himself of no reputation. A great preacher of the gospel of humiliation and self-abasement, is a monstrous character. Be ye not called Rabbi—be servant of all—be thou an example to believers—let nothing be done through strife and vain-glory, etc. ; are admonitions that I daily need, and perhaps my young brethren may need the same.

The invitation which you gave me to come and visit Virginia, is full of Christian politeness. The kind reception and good success I have had among the people of Virginia, has endeared the very name to me ; nor have I known a minute for forty years, that my attachment to the place and people has been chilled. My age forbids me to comply with your request, but my will says, " go," and which will finally prevail will be decided in the course of next summer. The wife of my youth is yet living ; we have lived together in the connubial relation fifty-five years. We have nine children, seven of whom have made a profession of religion.

I try to preach about four times a week in average. My health and strength will admit of travelling twelve miles, and preaching every day. In this course of life I have been announcing Christianity for more than fifty-seven years, having more reverence for that preaching which shows how the Lord draws sinners, than I have for that which shows sinners how to drive the Lord.

The salutation of John in my own hand,

JOHN LELAND.

THOMAS BUCK, Esq., Frederic Co., Virginia.

ADDRESS AT SOUTH ADAMS, JULY 4, 1832.

FELLOW-CITIZENS:—This day completes fifty-six years since the United States shook off the shackles of monarchy, and declared themselves free and independent. Bold and hazardous was the attempt, for a feeble band of three millions to rise up against the strongest monarch on earth. Long, expensive, and bloody was the conflict between the rights of man and the claims of hereditaries; but, with the aid of the God of armies, and the bravery and patriotism of the sons of liberty, after a seven years contest the object was gained—the states were acknowledged free and independent by Great Britain, and treated with as one of the sovereign powers on earth.

To pay up the expenses of the revolution; to organize the state governments, and the colossus of a general government; to define the rights that may be surrendered to government by individuals, and what quantum of sacrifice was called for, and those rights which are inalienable in nature, and cannot be surrendered—to secure the states from the inroads and depredations of the Indian tribes, and the European powers, etc.; have been laborious tasks for the halls of legislation, the chair of the executive, and the bench of the judiciary. What has added to the burden, has been difference in principle—difference in measures, and the tormenting ambition of some, who serve not the Lord Jesus, but their own bellies; seek not the good of their country, but their own elevation.

The costume of every American, should be a continental coat—a state jacket—a cap of liberty on his head—a sword of justice at his side—an independent mind for a shield, and the good of his country at heart.

Such are our institutions, that our political years, like those of the calendar, have their bissextile; every fourth year is leap; of course this present year is the period of leaping and running races for a chief magistrate. That the partialities and prejudices of the people should produce strife for pre-eminence, is to be expected; but, it should never lead to false statements, deception, or defamation of character. Men and measures should be animadverted upon with prudence, and results formed upon them with candor. Each individual should acknowledge the right of his neighbor to think and act, as well as claim the right for himself. While I, with pleasure, recognize and guarantee to all others their rights, as an obscure individual, I claim my own.

That our present chief magistrate was greatly admired, and always triumphant in the field of battle, is acknowledged by all; and, by a majority of the people, his firmness, patriotism, wisdom, and economy in the chair of state, have appeared equally splendid to himself, and advantageous to his country. His successes in negociations and treaties, have equaled, have exceeded the success of any of his illustrious predecessors. His friends consider him a Washington in the field—a Jefferson in the chair; and can his enemies deny it and substantiate the charge? And now, "shall Jonathan die who has wrought this great salvation for Israel? God forbid!." If he must be crucified, why? "What evil has he done? We have examined him, and find no fault in him." Is there a branch of Adam's line, under whose shadow we may expect more delight, or gather richer fruit than the Hickory produces? Have the people grown weary of the *manna* of equal rights, and freedom from bondage and debt, and long to return to Egypt, the iron furnace, to dig in Clay, and make their full tale of brick without straw to burn it with—to rear up lofty and useless pyramids? Would they forsake the waters of Shiloah that flow softly, and rejoice in Rezin and Remaliah's son? Do they wish to see another reign of terror, when a man may be persecuted for speaking or publishing his opinion on men or measures; or when aliens may be banished on suspicion, without proof or trial? Will they say to the bramble, "come thou and reign over us?" The subject reminds me of an instance that took place in Pennsylvania, in 1783. A German, by the name of Nathaniel, had removed from his native country into Pennsylvania; but, after the close of the war, he had a strong desire to return to Germany; his wife, however, was otherwise inclined, and addressed her husband as follows: "Nathaniel, why would you go back? In Germany I took my kent (child) upon my back, and went into the field, and labored five days in a week for the Prince; and here I have all the time to work for myself; why would you go back, Nathaniel?"

It is said by some, that General Jackson is old, worn out, and superannuated; unfit for the duties of an executive chief. It is true he is four months older than Mr. Adams, of whom there is no complaint. And it is as true, that he is twelve years younger than Chief Justice Marshall, who is still considered, by some, as the light of the world. He has borne much for his country, but has not been intemperate with wine, broken his rest at the gaming table, nor impaired his lungs to run down others, and rise upon their ruins. Moses spent forty years at school and at court; forty years in the bush keeping sheep; and forty years as chief magistrate of the tribes. After all, when he was one hundred and twenty years old, his eye was not dim, nor his natural force abated. The messages, communications, and despatch of business performed by Jackson, warrant the attempt to try him a little longer.

The Reverend gentleman, who now sits by, and who officiates as chaplain of the day, is a stranger to me; of course I know not his politics, nor his particular tenets of religion. His prayer bespeaks the goodness of his heart, and his regard for the rights of man. It manifests that the heavens do rule. The religion which he professes, is the only religion that ever met the guilty sinners wants, and brought relief to his woes; that ever gave assurance of the pardon of sin and the resurrection from the dead. The part in it which he has taken, admonishes him to be an example to the flock, and not to lord it over God's heritage. The precepts of it are pure and the best calculated for the good of men, even in this world, of any code of ethics ever known; the morals of Seneca, and the golden verses of Pythagoras not excepted. The spirit of it is peaceable—thinketh no evil, and works no ill to his neighbor. May his life be preserved, and his labor be blest—may he be faithful unto death, and at last receive a crown of life, with a "well done good and faithful servant, enter thou into the joys of thy Lord."

The gentleman appointed to read the Declaration of Independence, has discharged his trust with dignity, distinctness, and volubility. The pen of Jefferson, perhaps, never appeared to better advantage. We are all of us acquainted with the soundness of his judgment, and the correctness of his life. With his honored father we had the same acquaintance, but ah! he is gone the way of all the earth!

"How wise, how useful once, avails thee not,
To whom related, or by whom begot;
A heap of dust alone remains of thee—
'Tis all thou art, and all we soon must be."

Excluding at this time, all ideas of the glories and miseries of the other world, and tending only to the state of death abstractly—the land of darkness without order; we will suppose that the spirit of some departed patriot, dressed in the costume of this world, should appear among us to-day, and supply the place of him, now on the floor; his language, we presume, would be as follows: "My old acquaintance, I come on an embassy from the land of silence, where the king of terrors reigns; but, notwithstanding, he is called king, yet his subjects are all on a democratical level. The golden crown, the sacredotal robe and mitre, and glittering wealth, which distinguish the inhabitants of your world, have no influence in the regions of the dead. There, the servant is free from his master, and the voice of the oppressor is not heard. There, the king and the beggar sleep side by side, and men have no pre-eminence above the beasts."

This reverie reminds me of an anecdote respecting Brutus. The night before he fought his last battle, as he lay on his bed, his *evil genius* appeared at his bedside, and drew the midnight curtain, to whom Brutus said, "who art thou?" The ghost replied, "I am thy *evil genius*; meet me to-morrow in the field of battle."—"I'll meet thee there," said Brutus. If this account be true, Brutus had stronger nerves than the President of Persia (Daniel) had; for when an angel appeared to him, he lost all his strength.

In looking before me, I notice some who, by their hoary heads, declare that they are old. My brothers, some of us have known the hardships of the tented field to defend our rights, and all of us have endured the privations and burdens that war imposes. Thousands, who never armed themselves for the field of battle, lost all or a great part of their property by the depreciation of paper money. Thousands were stripped of their flocks and furniture by the invading enemy. Thousands had their houses burnt to ashes, who had to wander where they could to find shelter, etc. It is but taking a very partial view of the subject, to conclude that the troops were the only sufferers in gaining our independence. Among ourselves there were tories, who favored the cause of Great Britain, and aided them with supplies; and there has been an aristocratic party always embarrassing our government, and lying in wait to trick the people out of their rights; but, when the people have been almost swallowed up, they have risen in their strength, and, arming themselves with little bits of paper, have discomfitted their adversaries and saved themselves.

The clouds were not more threatening to the sons of liberty, in 1777, at the north, and, in 1781, at the south, than they were, in 1797, at Washington; but the same kind hand that saved us from the lion at Saratoga, and the bear at York, delivered us from the uncircumcised Philistines at Washington. These things, my elder brethren, must be fresh in your minds, for they tried the souls of men, and made indelible impressions on their hearts. He who has wrought so great salvation for us, we trust, will not suffer us to perish with thirst, but will create a hollow in the jaw of some ass, and give us water to drink. The Tariffites and Nullifiers make some noise at present, but time and cool reflection may evaporate the acrimony in hot air, without letting of blood or amputation. At several periods of our national existence, affairs have appeared more gloomy than at this present, and the clouds dispersed: and, if we have vanquished the lion, we will not fear the whelps.

The young men here present, who are now rising up to take control of the destinies of the nation, I wish to address on the subject of government.

Every nation, and every generation of the same nation, has an undoubted right to form their frame of government, and code of laws, and alter them at pleasure.* Those of you, therefore, who are coming into action, will have no embarrassment in departing from the rules which your fathers

* The laws given by Moses are the only exception.

preferred, whenever you are convinced that those rules were defective and better can be substituted. But, as most of the writings and speeches of the present day are about men and measures, I shall take the liberty of communicating a few thoughts on the designs and principles of civil government.

Some found government on birth. The son of a reigning king must hold the sceptre at the decease of his father—being born with a sceptre in his hand, booted and spurred, and that the mass of the people are born, saddled and bridled for him to mount and ride.

Others ground it on power: that the conqueror is entitled to the crown as an inheritance to dispose of at pleasure.

A third class build government on grace, or what they call by that name. The papal kingdoms and states adhere to this principle; and wherever a religious test is required to qualify the right of suffrage, or the right to hold an office, the same principle is acknowledged.

But the true principle of all legitimate government is mutual agreement, commonly called compact. To illustrate this, let us suppose that an individual is residing on a lonely island, not knowing there is another on earth. In this case, he is absolute sovereign; his will is his law, which he repeals or amends at pleasure. The soil he claims by occupancy; and what improvement he makes on any part of it, gives him a moral right to what he has improved. In a course of time, the individual has ten sons: what now? If all those sons are honest, each of them may be as independent and sovereign as the father: each may settle himself on some part of the soil, and honestly enjoy all the fruit of his labor. But one of the ten is quarrelsome and knavish, what shall be done with him? The vagrant is strong, and is able to handle the nine, one by one, and rob them of their earnings and deprive them of life. Here social compact, called government, begins. The nine unite to withstand the aggresion of the villain, and secure their lives, liberty and property. A shady tree is their state house, where they meet from time to time, to adopt measures of safety; and, in case they do not all agree, four must give up to five. This is simple democracy. After a lapse of years, from these ten no less than ten thousand proceed. What next? The government must now assume a new shape. It would not be practicable now for all to assemble. Each family or section must choose their agent to act for them, and to receive a reasonable reward for his time. This is not a simple but a representative democracy. From this abbreviated miniature of the rise and use of government, we learn that the vices of some, and the weakness of individuals to defend themselves, gave the first impetus for social compact. Consider government in its various ramifications, and it takes a great scope, and calls for abundance of laws; but simplify it, and bring it to its original bearings, it amounts to no more than a simple confederacy of individuals to secure life, liberty and property, for which they have to sacrifice a part of their native liberty, some of their acquired property, and, in certain cases, hazard their lives, for the protection of all. It is said by some that all the expense of the British government, by land and sea, is to support the twelve judges.

The ladies here present deserve peculair notice; and with abundance of pleasure I address them, for almost all the *women* are Jackson-*men*. How can it be otherwise? When New Orleans was ready to be swallowed up, the women hung around the general with weeping eyes, to whom he said: "Fear not, the city must and shall be protected;" and he was up to his promise. And can the women forget this? No; never. The very temper of the women towards the men is, "you protect and provide for us, and we will honor and nourish you." Nor can I believe that the ladies in this section of the country are less grateful than those at the south. A stranger, once travelling through this state, said it was "a hell for horses—a purgatory for men—but a paradise for women." Faithful history hands down to us the exploits of women, patriotic, military and pious. Deborah, who judged Israel, drew the plan of military operation for Gen. Barak, and went with him to battle. Jael, with a nail and hammer, slew Sisera, who commanded a vast host with nine hundred chariots of iron. A woman in Thebes broke the skull of King Abimelech with a piece of a mill-stone. Huldah, the prophetess, gave instructions to King Josiah. Judith cut off the head of Holofernes. Priscilla taught Apollos the way of God more perfectly. Phebe was a succorer of many. Philip had four daughters that prophesied, etc. In latter times, when the Saxons were invaded by the Danes, the Saxon women, by a secret movement, cut off the heads of thirty thousand Danes in one night. To reward them for this, the Saxons decreed that the woman should sit at the head of the table —be first served, and walk at the man's right arm.

Adam was refined out of the earth, and the woman was refined out of man, consequently, the woman is like a double refined loaf of sugar—the farthest removed from clay of any part of the creation. Indeed, so great is the influence of woman, that the innocency of Adam—the faith of Abraham—the strength of Samson—the bravery of David and the wisdom of Solomon bowed before it.

ANONYMOUSLY TO ELDER JAMES WHITSITT.*

If Christ died for all the human family, with one and the same view, why is it the greater part of them live and die, without ever hearing of his name? If hearing of it is not necessary to salvation, why should so much time, expense, and affliction, be imposed on the world? If Christ has suffered all that is necessary to make reconciliation to God, what has chilled his love, that, either by withholding the means for men to use to save themselves, or by limiting the displays of regenerating grace, by which he saves them, he should not save with ease, those who cost him pain and blood? If Christ has not died for all, those for whom he did not die, have no more cause to complain than the felon has, because no other appears to die for his crimes; and yet, to a spectator, this looks like a respecting of persons.

The law of eternal right, will always be binding on rational beings, as long as the perfections of God, and the faculties of men exist. This law enjoins on all men to believe all that God reveals, and do all that he commands. That God revealed the true Messiah, and the Messiah gave infallible proofs that he was the anointed, is certain; therefore, all who saw him and his works, and did not believe in him gave God the lie; and, all who do not believe the record that God has given of his Son, make him a liar. It is, moreover, true, that all who do not believe shall be damned; are condemned already. The light is not the condemnation, only by exposing the evil deed, of breaking the law. To believe that men will be condemned for simply not believing that Christ died for them, is preposterous; and, if he did not die for them, it would condemn them for not believing a lie. If a prince falls in with a family of vicious habits, and marries one of them, and frees her from her debts, and reclaims her from her vices; does this deliver the rest of the family from the restraints and penalties of the law? Can they justify themselves, by pleading that the prince has married one of the family? That men were made good at first, is clear; and, that God requires them to be as good as he made them; and, in case they have relapsed, to cast away all their sins, make themselves new hearts, and renew right spirits within them, is also clear; but, from this, does it follow, that men are bound to be better than Adam was, to posses eternal life—the unction from the holy one—new covenant

* Published in 1832.

blessings, which came not by Adam, Abraham, or Moses, but by Jesus Christ? A question here arises, whether a destitution of the Holy Spirit, of the grace of eternal life, is a sin? That men will be condemned for their sins without it, is certain; but, will they be condemned because God has not granted unto them repentance unto life, and given unto them the water that springs up to eternal life?

A word of experience. In the years 1772–73, etc., when my mind was so solemnly impressed with eternal realities, as to turn me from the power of Satan, unto the living God; whether from the Bible I read, the preaching I heard, the teachings of the Holy Spirit, or some other cause, I did as firmly believe the following articles, as I believed that Jesus Christ was the Saviour of sinners.

1. That all men were guilty sinners, and that God would be just and clear, if he damned them all.

2. That Christ did, before the foundation of the world, predestinate a certain number of the human family for his bride, to bring to grace and glory.

3. That Jesus died for sinners, and for his elect sheep only.

4. That those for whom he did not die, had no cause to complain, as the law under which they were placed was altogether reasonable.

5. That Christ would always call his elect to him while on earth, before they died.

6. That those whom he predestinated, redeemed and called, he would keep by his power, and bring them safe to glory.

7. That there would be a general resurrection, both of the just and the unjnst.

8. That, following the resurrection, judgment would commence, when the righteous sheep would be placed on the right hand of Christ, and admitted into life eternal; and the wicked on the left hand, doomed to everlasting fire.

In the belief of those articles, and what was collateral therewith, I began my ministerial career in 1774, with but very little thought how many and weighty the consequences of these premises were. But, now, after an experiment of fifty-seven years, and after going over the ground thousands of times, with all the research and candor in my power, I dare not pull up stakes and make a new start. Many uncertainties arise in my mind, many questions spring up that I cannot answer; but, every other system that I explore, has greater difficulties, and worse conclusions.

Sometimes a query arises in my mind, whether a gracious God could not have revealed his designs in a manner so clear, that there could be no doubts or disputations about them? But, here I am checked. If revelation were otherwise, or if my capacity were so enlarged that I could solve every question that ever arose in my mind, that same enlargement of mind would unfold ten thousand more questions, which, as yet, I have no stretch of thought to conceive of. There would be no getting through the dark place, unless creatures should be omniscient.

The doctrine of the trinity is too profound for my intellect. That there are three that bear record in heaven, God has said, and I believe; and that is all. The Holy Ghost, in some places, seems to take the lead of the Father; see Phil. iv. 20; Col. i. 8; ii. 2; iii. 17. Why should not the Arians, from this, believe that the Father was appointed by the Holy Ghost to do what he does? That Christ is the first—God over all—Ubiquity itself, I believe; and, I have wished that those who deny that Jesus is Jehovah, would begin at the beginning of the Christian alphabet, and tell how a virgin could conceive and bear a child; if they can do that, they will as easily understand how the same child can be the mighty God and everlasting Father.

The doctrine of redemption by the blood of Christ, is the only foundation for the hope for pardon that I have; and yet, in all its ramifications, it absorbs me. Why should God admit of a vicarious atonement in the Christocracy, and forbid it in the Theocracy, and indeed in all civil governments? Is it possible for the guilt of criminals to be transferred to one who is innocent? If Christ had no guilt, in what did his sufferings consist? The principle of universal atonement and limited grace, which is now very popular, gives no relief to but one hitch of the mind. When the mind is burdened with the thought, "why does God love Jacob more than Esaw;" to answer, "a general atonement is made for all alike," may ease the first thought; but, when we are told that many will gain nothing by the atonement but an aggravated curse, the heart sickens to think that God would be at so much expense to get a pretence to condemn men. In the 8, 9, 10, 11, of Romans, Paul rests the subject logically. He vindicates the sovereignty of God with the hand of a master; but, when he undertook to wade into the goodness and equity of Jehovah, he found the waters swell from the ancles to the knees—to the loins—to the heart; and, rising to the chin, before his mouth was stopped, he cried out, "Oh! the depths of the riches, both of the wisdom and knowledge of God! how unsearchable are his judgments, and his ways past finding out." And there he has left me to grovel still. Notwithstanding I find myself at great loss about many things, yet, in one point of light, I rejoice that the ministration of life is hidden from the wise and prudent, and many of its essentials, or stronger points, from the saints of God. Sin has sunk men into such guilt and pollution, that any scheme which human minds can understand, would be utterly incompetent to restore. It requires a plan, formed in infinite wisdom, and executed in infinite wisdom and love, to meet the sinner's wants, and relieve his woes; and, if thus founded and executed, how incompetent the limited wisdom of man must be to comprehend it. In this view of the subject, if I could comprehend the gospel system, I should not dare to trust in it.

I have personally known more than one thousand Baptist preachers in my life; nearly one half of them have gone the way of all the earth; but few remain who have been in the ministry as long as myself; and the time of my departure is at hand. Soon I must test the reality of the religion I have preached to others, and feebly labored to possess myself. My only hope of acceptance with God, is founded on the mercy of God, flowing through Christ. Unless my soul and my services are washed in the blood of the Lamb, and perfumed by the intercession of the great High Priest, they will—they ought to be rejected.

Farewell, my friend; we are strangers to each other; nor do I expect to see your face in this world. Should we both be so favored of the Lord as to be admitted into Paradise, perhaps some friendly angel or kindred spirit may point you out to me, and say, "this is James Whitsitt;" or will the knowledge of disembodied spirits be so intuitive, that they will know each other without introduction?

Many things have crowded into my mind while I have been writing, which I have entirely suppressed; and, those articles that I have touched upon, have been so concisely handled, that I find, by review, they are left obscure; but, I never copy off, but trust to the original draught.

In unknown regions days and dates are unknown.

Ask not after my Name, seeing it is Secret.

ADDRESS

DELIVERED AT CHESHIRE, ON THE EIGHTEENTH ANNIVERSARY OF THE BATTLE OF NEW ORLEANS, JANUARY 8, 1833.

THE die is cast—the game is won. The people have met their aristocratical enemies, and have conquered them. * * * *

The late proclamation of the president carries all before it in these parts. No one peeps or mutters against it. The late meeting at Faneuil Hall was full of its praise. The speakers at that meeting eulogize the president and his proclamation in all the pomp of diction. The pure principles of government, and the genius of our constitution, they describe with great precision. But, while we respond to their sentiments, we regret that they had not learned their politics sixteen years sooner, and reduced them to practice: had that been the case, the convention of pure spirits at Hartford would never have taken place. That there was some difference in form, will be granted; but the dull spirits can see no radical difference between the tendency of the Hartford convention and the ordinance of South Carolina.

While a great majority in the United States are rejoicing that Jackson is continued in the chair of state, the secession of South Carolina from the Union gives them great searchings of heart. It is a generally received opinion that, when two or more parties form a compact, one party cannot disannul the covenant without the concurrence of the others: and if the parties have pledged their lives, property and sacred honor to abide by the contract, a withdrawal of one of the parties must be perfidious. If one state in the Union has the right of secession, it follows all of them have the same. Supposing Louisiana should withdraw from the Union, under a pretence that the laws of Congress reduced the price of sugar, would the other states (South Carolina among the rest) peaceable give up the fifteen million dollars which it cost, and the sole control of the Mississippi? The western states were formerly the property of the United States: now, can it be supposed that Congress would have given the settlers of those lands the liberty of framing constitutions of government, and then have them received into the Union, if they had entertained the most distant idea that any or all of them might at any time withdraw from the Union? The constitution gives Congress the right of declaring war and regulating trade—and is it not as preposterous for South Carolina now to rise up against the government for a supposed abuse of the last, as it was for the eastern states to rise against the first, in the time of the last war with Great Britain? It is ardently hoped that the advocates of the Hartford convention will, in the looking-glass of South Carolina, see their own faces—repent of their errors, and do so no more.

If my information is correct, the tariff law was a southern and western measure, and the representatives of the eastern states generally voted against it; but, after it was established, the eastern capitalists placed their capital in manufacturing establishments, the profits of which exceed the profits of the cotton growers, (as the southern planters think,) by which the manufacturing class of citizens are become a privileged order. I have no data to judge by, but, from observation, it is a question whether, from the first factory set up by Mr. Slater unto the present time, (considering the depreciation of prices at several times—the immense losses by fire, and the fear of having their buildings and machinery lie dead upon their hands,) those who have devoted capital and labor to manufacturing have acquired more wealth than an equal number of men, of equal enterprise, who have followed planting, merchandise, or other professions.

If I understand what is called the *protective system*, it consists in laying such heavy duties on imported goods as will stop their importation, and thereby encourage home manufacturing. Much can be said on both sides of the question. To say that all nations give this protection, is only saying that all nations have a few capitalists, increasing their capital by the labor of thousands of poor, hungry, dependant creatures.

Whether the principle of protection be right or wrong, it is and has been adopted and acted upon in these states without opposition. To encourage and protect education, colleges have been endowed—in South Carolina as well as in the other states—and why? Because education is for general good, and, therefore, must be protected. The health of the body is of great importance, and, therefore, medical institutions must be endowed, and quacks fined. Christianity is the best religion in the world, and, therefore, it must be established—its preachers be paid and treated as a privileged order, and its days of devotion sanctified. The manufacturers of cloth are of immense value, and must be peculiarly nourished. And why not add, the sweeps are of the utmost consequence to the city, and deserve great rewards for cleaning the chimneys and preventing the destructive fire? It will run in my mind that the profession that cannot support itself by its own merit and influence, without the aid of govenment, is, in some respects, a nuisance. But one thing is certain: if our manufactures do not flourish to meet the wants of the people, we shall never be independent in times of peace, and in times of war our situation will be deplorable.

I close this part of the address by adding that, if the tariff was a southern and western measure, and if South Carolina protects education, etc., as has been stated, her present opposition comes with a poor grace.

Fellow-citizens—We are called to-day to drink a mingled cup of pain and pleasure. When we reflect on the secession of South Carolina —the ordinance of their convention—the language of their governor—the course of their legislature, and the contempt shown to the president and his proclamation, we hang our harps upon the willows and veil our faces in sackcloth.

That there is a clashing of interests among the states, is true; not so great, however, but what a little sacrifice meets with a tenfold reward. In the confederation, the state of Maryland stood out for awhile, but at length found it was safest to join. When the Federal Constitution was adopted, the state of Rhode Island retained her separate standing, until she got cured of the phrenzy of a paper-tender law, and then joined the Union. And is there a single state in the Union, but what (as far as we can see) is safer, happier, and aquiring wealth faster, than she would in a separate standing?

Let the experiment be tried—let all the states secede, like South-Carolina, and the twenty-four states be as many sovereignties; what next? Let each individual be displeased with some laws, and absolve himself from the restraints of government; we should then have thirteen millions of little sovereigns among us, uncontrolled by any others. If this is the doctrine of the Nullifiers, and if they carry it into effect, the negroes of South Carolina and other states, will hail the year of their jubilee. Nothing will be said of slave-holding states thereafter.

I proceed to the important question, "what is to be done in this crisis?" The president has taken his stand, and we respond to his views, and pledge him our personal and pecuniary aid to carry them into effect; but, let it be imprinted in every mind that our government was formed by mutual concessions, and can only be preserved by the same conciliatory principles. Such are the changes in the United States, and more particularly in those nations with whom we have commercial treaties, that the market will always be fluctuating, of course; at one time the products of one section will be most lucrative, and at another time the prospered section will be the most depressed; but, what man who has an American soul, will run frantic because his own enterprise is not crowned with the greatest success? Let it also sink deep in every heart, that when individuals or collective bodies have their minds highly irritated, either by real or supposed abuse, all reasoning with them is lost; time must be allowed, and sober reflection resorted to, to calm the raging billows. Seceders may be too hasty in their opposition, and government may likewise be too precipitate in chastising. "He that would rule well, must never rule too much nor to quick." Moreover, let every individual, and every state, be willing to suffer in turn, and not blame the government for those changes over which government has no control. It was said by many in the revolutionary struggle, that if, at the close af the war, they could gain their independence, and save one half of their interest, they should be satisfied; and will any friend of American institutions now murmur if he has to suffer a little for the good of the whole? I wish every state and every profession to have equal justice done them by the laws; but, for one of them (from a belief that it is injured) to form itself into a court of judge and jury, and condemn all the rest, must be preposterous. If the state of South Carolina will refrain from resisting the laws of Congress in practice, until the sitting of the 23d Congress, I feel satisfied their complaints will be relieved, as far as the dignity of the national government and an equal regard for the other states will admit; that they will extend the cup of conciliation until every drop is gone. And if the constitution is obscure or deficient in drawing the line between the powers of the general government and state rights, the population of the United States will harmonize, in submitting it to a convention or conventions for amendment. Every principle of patriotism and philanthropy, plead for an amicable adjustment without resorting to force.

While I am speaking, my heart sickens with grief at the idea of having the fruitful fields of Carolina, which are covered every year with cotton, rice, indigo and corn, turned into slaughter pens for human victims. Yes, the anticipated groans of the dying, and lamentations of widows and orphans, are almost too much for my nerves to bear. May heaven prevent this possible—this too probable event. To this request, I feel confident that millions of my fellow-citizens respond. But let us not despair. The insurrection in Pennsylvania, while Washington was president, was quelled without the shedding of blood. And we have now a president who is a lion in war and a lamb in peace; who mixes mildness with majesty in all his measures; as great a stranger to cuelty as he is to foar; who was never circumvented in the field of battle, nor confused by the arts of demagogues. His wisdom, we trust, with the aid of Congress and the support of the people, will safely steer the ship between Sylla and Charybdis, and land it safely in the port of peace. But our first and greatest dependence is on the supreintendence of that Divine Being who has hitherto appeared for our relief in the darkest periods, both in the field and in the cabinet.

"After so much mercy past,
Will he let us sink at last."

No—he that hath saved us in six troubles, we trust, will deliver us in the seventh. With this reliance, fellow-citizens, I wish you a happy 8th of January—closing in modern style:

JACKSON, the CONSTITUTION, and the UNION OF THE STATES forever.

ADDRESS,

DELIVERED AT WESTFIELD, MARCH 4, 1833.

* * * * * * * *

When the British Colonies in America resorted to arms to vindicate their rights, a Washington was prepared to lead their untutored troops to battle and to victory. When a Declaration of Independence became necessary, a Jefferson appeared, who did it in a document that will outlive wasting ages. When a government more energetic than the confederation was indispensable, a Madison stepped forth, who was foreman in giving birth to the Federal Constitution. When the course of administration under the constitution, was warping to aristocracy, the same Jefferson who drew the Declaration of Independence, was called to the helm to steer the ship in the democratic sea. And when, by little and little, the government degenerated from its virgin purity, and construction, expediency and incidentals supplied the place of constitutional *text*, and ambition and contention for the highest offices became the order of the day, a Jackson was searched out and placed in the high chair. His military talents were acknowledged by all, but his cabinet abilities were known to but few. He was in the world and the world knew him not. He sought not his own promotion, nor did office-hunters, who loved to be in the highest seats and feast on treasury pap, seek after it; but the body of the people, gaining more and more acquaintance with his character, became convinced that no man was so likely to suppress abuses, purge out the drones and peculators, break up monopolies, check useless expenses, turn the revenue of the nation into a channel that would extinguish the debt, and administer the government in all things according to the true and literal meaning of the constitution, as Andrew Jackson. And here, I ask, has he disappointed them? Has he not done all they elected him for, and much more? Does not the energy of his mind, and his moral courage appear more evident by every trying circumstance, and every snare that is laid for him? Has he not been blind to every thing personal, and sought the good of his country? Three-fourths of the voters in the United States have answered these three last questions in the affirmative, by electing him the second time for four years, which begin to-day; notwithstanding all the dinner speeches and publications to prevent it.

A very trying scene is now before us. The novel doctrine of nullification calls for all the foresight, fortitude and forbearance of a great mind to meditate and reconcile. The powers of the three co-ordinate arms of the general government, the state authorities and the patriotism of the people are all put in requisition: and to whom can the control of the destinies of the nation be committed, as executive head, with more safety than to Andrew Jackson?

Should his life and health be preserved during the second term for which he is elected, and he continue to administer the government in the same wise, republican manner that he has in his first term, and be as successful in all his negotiations and treaties, he would then leave the noisy world and return to the Hermitage, with ten thousand blessings of the people on his head, and would be viewed thereafter as a prodigy in the world.

The history of Mr. Van Buren has recently been published, and is now in circulation, which precludes the propriety of saying much of his biography. When he first began his career in the law department, he adopted the Jeffersonian system of policy, and consequently had to rise abreast of all the brilliant talents in New York, who were of the Hamiltonian system. Without mentioning many of his defeats and triumphs, he was chosen Senator in Congress, then Governor of the state of New York—thence appointed by Jackson, Secretary of State. Here he found out the conspiracy of the cabinet to prevent the re-election of Jackson: to clear himself, and assist in the election of Jackson for his second term, he tendered his resignation and went into private life.

His worth was too highly appreciated by the President to let him remain long in passivity, and he, therefore, appointed him minister to Great Britain; but before he had time to effect the objects for which he was sent, the Senate of the United States rejected his nomination by the casting vote of the Vice President. Many things were laid to his charge by several of the senators, from which the President has fully acquitted him. Indeed, in that mad session of the Senate, what little men call false statements—false accusations, and heated abuse, seemed to be more manifest than a sincere desire to do their country good. On the rejection of the nomination, Mr. Van Buren returned to America with as much composure and pleasantness as if no adverse occurrence had taken place. Had he been disposed to right himself, and cast dismay on his enemies, there was no need of it; his country did it for him, and have promoted him to the second office in the nation. Whenever the Senate meet, after this day, they will see the Mordecai whom they sought to hang, sitting, not in the king's gate, but in the senatorial chair to preside over them. Whether they will have any thoughts of the gallows which they prepared—whether they will wish to have some one cover their faces, like Haman—or whether they have taught their countenances (like Brutus) to never betray their hearts, I cannot say. Mr. Van Buren has never been accused of immorality—never been reproached for keeping a *Black Sall*, or murdering *five militia men;* but has been perpetually represented as a great *intriguer*—an *arch magician*. No particular action is specified in his whole life, and for want of units they take a universe, and loudly proclaim, "the *little* regent is a *great* magician." When I go into an orchard for fruit, I bend my course to the tree that has the most clubs around it, expecting there to find the best.

Fellow-citizens, we are drawing to the close of the *revolutionary age*. When Jackson shall have finished his course, there will be no man living, but who will be too old and obscure to fill the presidential chair, who had any hand in the Revolution. Others may arise with as clear views of the rights of man and the nature of government, but can never have the same feeling. What course the next generation may take with respect to the constitution and code of laws, I know not; the right will be theirs to alter or destroy what now exists. That our constitution is susceptible of improvement, there exists no doubt: but. it is greatly doubted whether a change in its *radical features*, would not lead to anarchy, "which is the licentiousness of little men, or tyranny, which is the licentiousness of great men."

Our liberty and independence cost seven years war—much destruction of property—one hundred thousand lives, and after all the taxes of various kinds, to support the army, there remained a debt of more than seventy millions of dollars. Immense purchases of territory have been made. The last war continued one hundred and thirty weeks, and cost as many millions of dollars as it lasted weeks; and yet since the Federal government was established, all the debts have been paid, and the inhabitants have increased from three to twelve millions. Those who wish for a dissolution of the Union, and the establishment of a government of a different kind, either at the present time or when another generation shall succeed, will do well to ask themselves, whether a government of different features gives them assurance, that the people under it will be more happy or wealthy than they are at present. Those who wish to crush the present government, (from their attachment to aristocratical principles, or because the people do not gratify their ambition,) ought to be marked as enemies to the liberties of men; and while common feeling wishes them nothing better than degradation and detestation, the pious Christian will pray for them, "Father forgive them, they know not what they do."

The freedom of speech, and of the press, cannot be too highly appreciated, nor the licentiousness of either of them too much lamented: both should be employed as vehicles of truth to convey information, and not as a talisman to mislead and bewilder. Let gentlemen of the type and press observe the following rules, viz:

1. Never publish, of your own composition, any article that you do not

conscientiously believe is true, and that a communication of it will be of service to others.

2. Never extract from other papers any articles which do not contain in themselves some internal evidence of their veracity.

3. Never pollute your columns to blacken one man for the promotion of another. *Be not puffed up for one against another*, and be very cautious of holding up any man to public contempt, unless the public safety calls for a hue and cry.

4. If, for want of information, you have published that which proves to be false, hasten to retrace your steps and correct the error.

5. Let *Truth* be your pole star, which will give your consciences the greatest pleasure—increase the character of your paper, and finally bring the most money into your coffers.

6. Never condescend to the mean artifice of impressing the minds of others by publishing great and false things from abroad, under the fiction of "I have it from undoubted authority—my information may be relied on," etc. Your faith we leave with yourselves; but our faith is that the wondrous things related, came from a distance no farther off than your own brains, and as they generally prove to be false alarms, you had better keep them at home.

Instinct in beasts, in some of its operations, exceeds the reason of man; but on a broad scale men are the noblest work of God in this lower world, and the power of speaking, and logical reasoning, are the items of that superior glory. The tongue is the organ of speech, and though a little member, does great things: therewith bless we God, and therewith curse we men. It is such an unruly member, that no man ever has, or ever can tame it: and, therefore, it should always be kept in bridle; for when it runs at large, it sets on fire the course of nature, and is set on fire of hell. A false tongue wounds like sharp arrows of a mighty warrior, and burns like the coals of Juniper. Very frequently cases occur in which men, by saying or doing something, are brought into a sad dilemma. A little lie will offer its services to give relief. By saying that which they know is false, or denying that which they know is true, they seek to extricate themselves. As wicked and preposterous as this course appears, yet some good men have tried the experiment to their sorrow. When Peter had committed an overt act in cutting off the ear of Malchus, to prevent an arrest, he made lies his refuge, to escape punishment; but afterwards he wept bitterly, and I presume he never forgave himself. The plain path of speaking the truth runs thus, "let your conversation be without covetousness—let every one of you speak the truth to his neighbor—lie not one to another," etc. For want of talent to enlarge, I shall sum up in saying that my object is, to persuade editors to publish nothing but truth, and for speakers of every grade to observe the same rule.

We are now risen to a point which forty years past I did not expect to live to witness—the liquidation of all our debts. Yes, the United States present a picture to the world, of thirteen millions of inhabitants, enjoying a government which stands firm in peace and war; securing the rights of men, both civil and religious, (excepting the slaves,) and yet owe nothing for the whole. So far as pride is excusable, I feel proud that I am an American. If ever the time shall arrive when our black brethren shall enjoy the same, and I am living, my joy will be unspeakable.

The public debt being now off our hands, the question is, how shall the revenue be disposed of. The revenue arising from the sale of public lands is somewhat permanent, but the greatest part of it arising from imposts is, in its nature, and will be in its course, var able and somewhat contingent.

The rate of impost, I judge, must vary to meet the duties, with which other nations, with whom we have treaties of commerce, may see cause to burden their wares.

My project is as follows: let the rate of duties be reduced equitably on all articles, regarding every class of citizens, to a standard of revenue that will reasonably support the government in all its constitutional measures. Whenever the revenue shall leave a considerable surplus in the treasury, let the surplus be divided among all the states, according to their numbers, and let these sums, in the several states, be inaccessible to all applicants: the interest only to be distributable, and that only to aid in payment of state taxes.

By this, or a similar appropriation, the property of all will be distributed among all, and colleges, railroads, etc., be erected and supported by individuals or self-erected associations.

I have not to read history to know that the *main-spring* in the revolution was, "Liberty, and the sole disposal of our property; deducting as much of both, as will be necessary to protect the main, *and no more.*" And this I consider the true standard of democracy, let the names and professions of men be what they may.

As for those men who wish to make the government and the people two parties—who wish to limit the right of suffrage—who advocate monopolies and privileged orders—who are seekers of offices—who are seeking more after national splendor than national tranquillity—who are constantly exposing the measures of government to scorn, unless they themselves are the agents—who wish to have Christianity established by law, to make amends for their being destitute of the spirit, and opposed to the practice of it—from such turn away. For they that are such, serve not the Lord Jesus, nor their country, but their own bellies; and by good words, fair speeches, and sleight of hand, deceive the hearts of the simple. From all such withdraw yourselves, and place no confidence in them. But honor those men with your suffrages and confidence, who honor your rights and seek your wealth by their measures. In selecting a man for public trust, ask the questions, does he understand and appreciate the rights of men? Is he honest? Has he confidence to vote against a majority? And from among those of this description, prefer the man who has the brightest talents and most information.

The redemption of the soul from the curse of the law, and the dominion of sin, is an object of the first magnitude, for the loss of the soul, the whole world, in exchange, would be no equivalent. This has been an object of the highest solicitude with me for nearly sixty years: but I have to confess that my ardor to gain the object, both for myself and others, has not been equal to its merit.

Next to the salvation of the soul, *the civil and religious rights of men* have summoned my attention, more than the acquisition of wealth or seats of honor. To see a great part of the human family tricked out of their rights and liberties by the other part—chained down to lasting subjugation, without any regard to those rights which are inalienable, has stimulated what little benevolence I have, with the small talents that I possess, to burst the prison doors, and proclaim liberty to the captives. Many meetings, like the present, I have attended, and many pieces have I written, with a view of pleading *the rights of man against the claims of aristocrats.* And now after a life of almost four-score years, poorly spent, I am like an old weather-worn sailor, yet on deck, in a boisterous sea, not at the helm steering the ship, but before the mast, sounding the deep with a short line—watching the winds and pirates—fearing the rocks and looking out for the breakers—bearing at mast head, "*free trade and sailors rights,*" deducting from their profits an equitable tax to pay for their security.

Gentlemen, your object is my object, and your joy my joy in the late triumph of democracy, which begins its operation to-day. Perhaps, while I am speaking, the President and Vice President elect, are taking the oaths of their offices for the four ensuing years. May the now begun presidential term be full of the same wisdom and justice of the last term, and free of the scum of the ambitious pot that has boiled over in shameful froth.

I am highly gratified in seeing so many *young men* in this assembly, for it is for the rising generation to control the future measures of government. A common voter, with a sound judgment and liberal mind, will legislate better for the cause of humanity and self-government, than the high pampered statesman, who considers himself of the *genii* order of beings, born to rule over man.

Fellow-citizens, I wish you all a happy fourth of March. I hope we shall never have cause to regret that we have placed confidence in the two distinguished citizens who are raised to the two highest offices in the United States.

A DIALOGUE.

JUSTICE.

SINNER, I'm come with power to let you know
How much to God, for sinful debts, you owe:
Ten thousand talents now against you lie,
And payment must be made or you must die.

SINNER.

Have patience with me and I'll do my best;
Accept good will and cancel all the rest;
My prayers and alms and what I mean to do
Will partly pay the sum I owe to you,
And where I fail let pity pay the rest—
That pity which your sov'reign has profess'd.

JUSTICE.

The law is holy, just and clear as light,
And claims no more of you than what is right;
That law you've broken twice ten thousand times,
And all your debts assume the rank of crimes.
The law knows neither pity nor respect,
Justice is all the culprit can expect:
Your prayers and alms and what you mean to do
Will not secure you from eternal wo;
The righteous law can no abatement show.
Prepare to meet thy doom and take the blow;
Behold God's executioner I stand,
Array'd in vengeance with my sword in hand!

REFLECTION.

At this the trembling sinner stood amaz'd,
The heavens grew black! the forky light'nings blaz'd!
The mountains shook! the sun and moon grew pale!
The whole creation mourn! the angels wail!
Stern Justice then, with flaming sword in hand,
Stepp'd forward to perform the dire command;
But, ere he gave the blow, a voice was heard,
"Hold! hold your hand! the sinner shall be spar'd!
Deliver him from going to the pit;
I've found a ransom which will him acquit."

At this eventful moment Christ appeared,
Whose plea with justice was distinctly heard.

JUSTICE.

Are any of my precepts too austere?
Or is the penalty annexed severe?
Has not the sinner sinn'd with open eyes?
Can justice live without the sinner dies?

CHRIST.

Thy precepts are all holy and divine;
The penalty proportion'd to the crime;
The sinner has no just complaint to make,
If vengeance sinks him in the burning lake.
As God, I'm universal legislator;
As man, I'm under law to the Creator;
As mediator, I have work to do—
To drink the bitter cup, to sinners due;
Justice I honor, law I magnify,
But still the guilty sinner shall not die:
I've been his surety long—from ancient times,
I'll pay his debts, and suffer for his crimes.
O sov'reign Justice! search your records through,
And see how much the sinner owes to you;
Keep nothing back, let a full charge be brought
For ev'ry wicked action, word and thought.

JUSTICE.

The sinner's debts swelled to a pond'rous load,
His crimes most henious, calls aloud for blood.
The fulness of the time is come for pay;
The debt I claim, and can no longer stay;
The debtor or his surety must comply,
And for the crimes must bleed, and groan, and die.

CHRIST.

The time has come! the payment must be made!
I neither spare my blood nor screen my head;
I've proved the God by words and works before;
I'll prove the man by dying in my gore;
Strike, Justice strike! take all you can desire;
But save the sinner from eternal fire.

JUSTICE.

No fault I find in thee, but thou art bound,
And must endure a mortal bruise and wound.
Awake! O sword of justice! now awake;
And pierce the Saviour, for the sinner's sake!
Spare not God's only son, nor be afraid;
One off'ring only will for sin be made.

Awake! O sword! and smite God's fellow through;
His blood alone, remits me all my due.
The red blade fell—the vengeful fiery sword
Was plung'd into the heart of Christ the Lord.
Behold, he bled and pray'd upon the cross,
Then bow'd his head and yielded up the Ghost.
"Enough," cried Justice, "now I sheath my sword;"
And Christ ascended to his father, God.
The keys of death and hell were in his hand,
When he ascended to the heav'nly land;
Angels attended, filled with burning love,
With shouts and trumpets to the world above;
"Lift up your heads, ye gates, ye doors make room,
The King of Glory from below is come,
The Lord of Hosts assumes his native throne;
Let all the heav'nly hosts the conqueror meet,
And fall with rev'rence at his sacred feet."
Now tho' he reigns in heaven exalted high,
He ne'er forgets the blood of Calvary.
"Father forgive!" he cries, "for I have died,
And paid the purchase of my ransom'd Bride.
Justice demanded ev'ry whit of me,
And ev'ry whit I paid upon the tree;
Now all is finished, let the sinner live,
Sinners of ev'ry clime who do believe."
In gospel revelation thus we see
How boundless love and justice can agree.
This new and living way brings into view,
How sinners can be sav'd, and God be true;
How sin can be condem'd, and sins forgiv'n;
How sinners, doom'd to hell, may go to hea'vn.
No other scheme to save has yet been found
By grave philosophers and men renown'd:
The blood of Christ alone atones for sin,
His truth and grace destroy the plague within;
His watchful eye and powerful arm defend—
Who can but love and rev'rence such a friend?
Salvation cost the Saviour blood and smart—
It costs the sinner only all his heart.
O sinner, can you think of Jesus' love,
And never feel one soft affection move?
Never resolve to be for God alone,
And reign with Christ forever on his throne?

LETTER TO THOMAS BINGHAM, ESQ. JULY, 1833.

SIR :—I am at a loss to know what idea to affix to the sentence, that *baptism is an initiating ordinance into the church.* Those who believe that the sprinkling of infant children is gospel baptism, and those who believe that none should be baptized but repenting believers, and that dipping the body all over in water is the only mode of Christian baptism, are equally in the habit of calling baptism an *initiating ordinance.*

If baptism is the door into a Christian church, how was it possible for a church to rise in the first place? The members must *first* have been baptized before they could form into a church, and must *first* have been a church before there could be any *initiation* into it. Let a preacher go into a heathen country, and be successful in winning souls; he cannot baptize them until there is a church to initiate them into, and there cannot be a church until the constituents are baptized.

If children, without their consent or knowledge, are initiated into the church by baptism, it follows, of course, that they are members of the church, and should be dealt with and disciplined like other members; nor can they ever stand propounded and be admitted afterwards; because they are already in the church.

John the Baptist was of the priestly tribe, but never sacrificed, or in any way officiated as a Jewish priest. He came as the forerunner of the Messiah, in the spirit and power of Elias, to make ready a people prepared for the Lord. The scribes, priests, elders, and pharisees were the principals of the Jewish church, in his day. He was sent by God to preach repentance for sin, and faith in the Lamb of God, who stood among them; and to baptize with water those who brought forth the fruits of repentance. But is there any thing in the course of John that looks as if he was building on the Jewish church? Did he ever advise with the rulers of that church? Did they not reject the counsel of God against themselves, in rejecting his doctrine and baptism? And is it likely that John would unite his followers with those whom he calls a "generation of vipers?" Let common sense answer.

If, by the term *church*, we understand the whole Zion of God, which includes all who fear God and work righteousness in every nation, individuals are *initiated* into it, not by water-baptism, but by the choice of Christ, and the application of the unction of the Holy One. This initiation, (the Baptists believe,) precedes the right to water-baptism.

But if, by *church*, is understood any given number of pious saints, whose local situation, agreement of sentiment, and gracious affections, lead them to unite together as a church, it is, in the first instance, a matter of mutual agreement; and when other individuals wish to be added to them, to help and be helped, the satisfaction and reception of the church is the *initiation*. If water baptism is the *door into* the church, it must be the *door out of* the church, in case of criminal disorder.

Preaching and baptizing are ministerial works; initiation and excision belong to the church. The minister baptizes the penitent believers INTO CHRIST;—the church receives them *into fellowship*.

John baptized multitudes (into Christ) saying unto them that they should believe in him who should come after him; that is, on Christ Jesus; but he formed no churches.

Jesus made and baptized more disciples than John; but only one hundred and twenty of them were together when they elected Matthias. On the day of Pentecost, they who gladly received the word, were baptized, and three thousand were added to the one hundred and twenty; many of whom, it is most probable, had been baptized by John or Jesus before. Afterwards, multitudes, both of men and women, were added to the Lord. The result seems to be, that baptism does not *initiate* into the *whole church*, nor into any of the CHURCHES.

That the Eunuch was initiated into any church, when Philip baptized him, is hard to believe; and that there was any church in Phillippi, for Lydia and the jailer, with their households, to be initiated into, when they were baptized, drowns our senses to conceive of.

Wherever the apostles found proper subjects, they baptized them, although their local situation prevented them from church relation. To such scattered saints Paul wrote in both of his Epistles to the Corinthians. See the dedications. "Unto the church of God which is at Corinth, *with all that in every place* call upon the name of Jesus Christ." "Unto the church of God which is at Corinth, *with all the saints which are in all Achaia.*"

If baptism initiates into the church, and if sprinkling infant children, or dipping them is gospel baptism, it follows that the British children who were compelled, and the South Americans who were forced, without the knowledge of the subject, and against the will of the parents, were all made members of the church.

In these days there is a great variety of minor opinions among nominal Christians. All who are casting out devils, do not follow together in the same way. Uniformity of sentiment is not grounded by local situation. In the same section, pious individuals are found, who have not a sentimental agreement with their neighbors. These individuals are bound in conscience to be baptized, but cannot unite in doctrine and modes of worship with those among whom they live. Ought not such persons to be baptized? Would not a gospel preacher address them thus? "And now, why tarriest thou? Arise, and be baptized." This being done, I ask, what church such persons are initiated into by it? Not the whole church of the redeemed, for they were in that before. Not the church in their vicinity, for how can two walk together, except they are agreed?

When ministers and churches are together, and act in concert, and the candidates wish to unite with the church, as well as to be baptized, *one* declaration of what the Lord has done for their souls, and of their belief in Christ, may answer *both* purposes for *admission* to *baptism*, and *reception* into the *church*.

Lines occasioned by the death of Miss Laura Whitmarsh, of Cheshire, who died December 7, 1833, in her 19th year. A part of them were repeated at her funeral.

Farewell, my Laura, for a little space,
Soon we shall meet and see each other's face;
One after one we die and waste away,
But the last trump shall raise our sleeping clay.
With what amazing joy the saints will meet,
When death lies bruised and vanquished at his feet;
Their bodies all refined like crystal stone,
Their happy souls shall put the bodies on:
The souls and bodies then will be complete,
And in the kingdom take a royal seat,
A crown, prepared for each, will then be given,—
A golden harp, to praise and sound in heaven.
Can the sad parents mourn with anxious pain,
Since their great loss is Laura's greater gain?
Before her lifeless body had grown cold,
The soul had flown ten thousand leagues twice told,
Nor stopped her course, till she had joined the throng,
Of all the blood-wash'd choir, and learn'd the song;
A long protracted meeting there to hold,
Cloth'd in fine linen, and adorn'd with gold.
Children, your sister Laura has no breath;
You'll never hear her speak again on earth,
She's gone before, and you must follow on;
Prepare for death, for soon your turn will come.
Young people, look, and see where Laura lies;
Here is a looking-glass before your eyes;
Here you may see your likeness and your end:—
Soon death the fatal javelin will send,

And you must go, whether you will or no,
To heav'n above, or to the gulf below.
O, may you all repent and live so well,
That you may die without the fears of hell!
Repent of sin, and turn to God to-day;
Return with all your hearts—make no delay;
The vilest sinner that repents of sin,
And turns to God, the Lord will take him in;
The blessed Jesus stands with open arms
To save the humble soul from all alarms.
Sinners, are you of such hell-hardened steel,
That neither wrath nor love can make you feel?
But, oh, my gracious God, must I be still?
Sinners are void of *strength* as well as *will;*
They *will not* come to thee for life and peace,
They *cannot* come without they're drawn by grace.
The law is holy, pure, and clear as light,
And claims no more of men than what is right,
The Sovereign has a right to all his dues,
Though subjects are insolvent, or refuse;
The law requires of men perfection still,
And every failure is a moral ill.
Here then, I find I've work enough to do,
To preach to all, "be faithful, just and true;
Make clean your hands and hearts, and be as good
As Adam ere he ate forbidden food;
Believe in God, and kiss his equal Son;
Take up the cross, and after Jesus run."
But ah! I preach what every one *should* do,
But sad experience proves what they pursue.
There's none that doeth good—all leave the way—
Soon as they're born, like beasts they go astray;
Guilty, polluted, both without and in,
Haters of holiness, in love with sin.
Here then the work increases—more to do—
To tell what Jesus does for men below;
He finds them in the wilderness of death,
Or in the open field, exposed to wrath;
No eye to pity—none to take them in,
Nor do they wish to be redeemed from sin,
But by his quick'ning grace, he makes them see
The dangers they are in except they flee;
He works in them to will, and gives them strength to do,
Then they repent of sin, and after Jesus go;
He draws them with the cords of love and grace,
They run to see their dear Redeemer's face;
He bids them go their way with sins forgiv'n;
They follow him, and go the way to heaven.
He leads them in a way they never knew,
Makes darkness light, and every object new.

They see that God is just, and wonder why
Mercy should spare them, when they ought to die;
The holy law is lovely in their sight,
Although to keep it they are void of might.
They trust in Christ's redeeming blood alone,
And cry, "grace, grace," unto the living stone.
The saints collectively, are all but one,—
The Bride of Christ, his married wife alone;
Their Maker is their Husband, guide and friend,
Whose love is strong, and lasts unto the end;
This flock of God he bought with his own blood,
His claim to all his sheep must then be good;
He died that they might have eternal life,
And none can pluck them from his hands by strife.

THE following lines were read at the funeral of Miss Emeline Witmarsh, (sister of the preceding,) December 21, 1836.

HERE we behold the mortal part of one
Whose days are finish'd, and whose work is done;
But ere she died, she learned the heav'nly art
To trust in Christ, and give him all her heart.
When she lay struggling in death's iron arms,
Laura descended, filled with heav'nly charms,
Sent from above, to wait and watch the time,
When she should live again with Emeline.
Invisible to mortals—plain to faith;—
We then attend to hear what Laura saith.
"My sister Emeline, did you but know
The joys that flow where you will quickly go,
You'd long to be released from cumbrous clay,
And to the upper regions wing your way.
Sent from the Saviour, full of love and grace,
I'm come to guide you to that heavenly place.
Oh, that my father, mother, every friend,
Might know the joys that have no bound nor end!"
This said, she beckon'd; "sister, come away;"—
Her sister died and went without delay:
Upward they steer'd their course to heaven's high wall,
The gates flew open, and they heard the call,
"Come in, come in, ye pilgrims of the Lord,
And take a crown of life for your reward."

Lines occasioned by the death of the Reverend Justus Hull, and sung at his funeral:

Prostrate before our weeping eyes,
Greatness in humble ruin lies;
For more than fifty years he stood,
A faithful witness for his God,
Proclaiming Christ's redeeming blood;—
But he is gone.

Nothing below the skies he sought,
For heaven above he ran and fought,
A glittering crown before his eyes
Laid up in heaven above the skies;
He labor'd hard to win the prize;
But he is gone.

The work of prayer was his delight,
He called on God both day and night;
How oft we've seen the herald stand,
Imploring mercy for the land;
That God would stay his vengeful hand:
But he is gone.

Could skill'd physicians, friends and saints,
Have sav'd him from his dire complaints,
Instead of meeting here to-day,
To look with sadness on his clay,
We might have heard him preach and pray:
But he is gone.

In him was found the heavenly art,
To lead the mind and melt the heart;
Soon as his solemn voice was heard,
The saints rejoic'd, the sinners feared,
And all the holy man rever'd;—
But he is gone.

LETTER TO HON. R. M. JOHNSON, JUNE 9, 1834.

HON. SIR:—Whether events take place pursuant to an unalterable decree, or whether they are contingent, they have had their course, and brought the world into its present condition. Somewhere, in creation, between the highest angel and smallest insect, there was a gap for myself; but, whether that gap would have been a greater defect than the supply, is a question. The term of time that I have filled has astonished the world with its events. As I was twenty-one years old between the battles of Lexington and Bunker Hill, I have not to learn the course of things in the field or cabinet from history, having lived through the whole term from '75, to 1834. As you have passed through the scenes of the present century, (some of which have been bloody, and many of them hot and windy,) and well know what contests there was for ten years before the present century began, it would be an insult on your knowledge to say anything about them. But like other old men, I will say a little about myself. I never desired a civil office in my life, nor have I ever thought that my talents, with their small cultivation, qualified me to fill any office, even a middling grade; but, some how or other I have been a republican (dyed in the skin, before the wool was grown, which cannot be sheared off) both in church and state. To acknowledge his Holiness the Pope, my Lord Bishop, his Highness the Synod, his Excellency the Presbytery, his most Christian Majesty, the Association, or his Grace the Brotherhood, to hold dominion over my faith and direct my conscience, is making a bow too great for my stiff neck. As well might I bow to a hereditary Monarch, a life leased Aristocracy, or a jockey made President. Let the church be formed (not of many masters, but) of living stones, and proceed as the Bible directs, and I will be subject, and not set up my will as a standard for others; but let them not crowd into the empire of conscience; for the little busy Paul, (whose name is mentioned one hundred and sixty times in the New Testament,) saith, "why is my liberty judged by another man's conscience?" My religion forbids me to speak evil of dignities—teaches me to be subject to the powers that be—to obey magistrates, etc. Where laws are made for general good, I would cheerfully submit; where they are oppressive, I would bear with patience. If the oppression can be removed by the oppressed, I would unite with them to gain redress. But if laws are made to describe what God I shall adore, how I shall worship him, and at what places and times that worship shall be paid; be it known to all that I will not fall down and worship the image that is set up. "Where conscience begins, empire ends."

But stop my fugitive pen, come back to your bearings. Our constitution of government was formed in peace for peace; and many of its warmest friends feared it would not sustain the shock of war. Mr. Randolph once said, "go to war, Mr. Chairman, and you will come out of it without a constitution." This prediction, however, has failed. Mr. Madison said to me, in 1788, "the states have surrendered to the general government a certain quantity of their rights; but it is most likely, if ever the general government is dissolved, it will proceed from the jealousy of state authorities." This has not yet taken place. The present appearance is that the ambition of aspirants, with their inflamed partizans, are the most to be feared. Why all this strife and contention? What is there in high offices so amiable? Did Milton make the devil speak a truth, when he said, "better reign in hell, than be subordinate in heaven?" In monarchies, where kings have their agents to do the thinking and acting for them, a throne may be an easy seat; but, in the United States, the presidency must be a laborious, painful and perplexing office; and it will seem to me that the president, who is fairly chosen by the people, needs, and has a constitutional right to expect all the aid that the co-ordinate powers and the people can afford, (not sacrificing, however, the right of private judgment and the open disclosure of opinion.) This would be practical republicanism. Some time past, a society agreed to build a meeting-house, but differed widely as to the best measures of erecting and disposing of it. When the question was decided by a fair vote, a man who was in the minority arose and addressed the society as follows: "Gentlemen, the vote has gone against me, but I concur, and shall do as much to further the work as if my judgment had been honored. It is my will that a majority should rule, and therefore, in this instance, my will is gratified." This republican principle, interwoven into all the federal states, and into the heart of every officer in the United States, would produce more good work, and less bad talk, than is now the case; for oratory has overdone itself. The question now is, among the middling class of sober men, (who in fact are the bone of society,) not "what does the man say?" but "what does he do?" Free debate must be granted, and decent time allowed for reflection; but it is presumed, that nearly all the leading questions that come before Congress, are cut and dried beforehand; and, if the previous question was sustained on the first day, the result would be the same that takes place after two months are consumed in retailing wind; for, the members are not sent by their constituents to be converted, but because they are covenanted, and will not fall from grace.

It would be a criminal impeachment of the wisdom of the constituent power, to question the disinterested purity of motives of those who are chosen representatives. On the floor of Congress it would not be admitted. And mean suspicion and vain surmisings, are not to be nurtured in our fields, shops or firesides. But when men give rational evidence that their object is to disgrace others, and direct the people who to vote for, manly jealousy and love of country, call upon the people to mark such men and avoid them. Such men bring a great pressure on our institutions, and unless their deposits are removed to the bank of private life, contention will continue, and ruin follow.

With due respect to Uncle Sam, Old Hickory and yourself, I subscribe, etc.

JOHN LELAND.

ADDRESS

AT A DEMOCRATIC MEETING HELD AT CHESHIRE, AUGUST 28, 1834.

FELLOW-CITIZENS:—Were it not that I am publicly pledged, that "*as long as I can speak with my tongue—wield a pen—or heave a cry to heaven, whenever the rights of men, the liberty of conscience, or the good of my country were invaded by fraud or force, my feeble efforts should not lie dormant,*" I should decline your invitation at this time on account of my age and incapacity. But, on your request, I attend with you to-day, and shall cast in my two mites for the support of this doctrine, viz: That the rights of man and the energy of law, when operating in their proper channels, are aids to each other; but when either or both of them grow licentious and proclaim war, if no expedient is found to check their hostility, either despotism or anarchy will follow. Tyranny is the licentiousness of *great* men; anarchy the licentiousness of *little* men, both of which are destructive to *rational liberty*. Good government and equal laws form the expedient that sober reason has prescribed to check the vicious and unwearied propensities of the human heart, and bridle those desires and actions which cannot be tamed. * * * * * * * * * *

If the leaders of the opposition would point out a better line of administration than that which has been in operation for the last six years, knowing that they themselves were not to be the agents of it, they would render good service to their country. This new light we would receive with great avidity and thankfulness. But, for this we have hitherto looked in vain. To find fault with what is done, without showing what could be done better, is no mark of a patriot or statesman. Let those fault-finding chieftains be notified now, if they never have been before, that their opposition is viewed by democratical republicans to be the child of hatred to the man whom the people have delighted to honor above them, and who will not bend before them; as well as the effect of ambition to rise into the chief seats of the synagogue themselves, and be called Rabbi—President, and Rabbi—Secretary. On the legislative floor we impêach the motives of none; but at home and at the polls we are governed by Lynch's law, and not by parliamentary fetters.

When Mr. Jefferson was elected president, the pulpits rang with alarms, and the presses groaned with predictions, that the Bibles would all be burned; meeting-houses destroyed; the marriage bonds dissolved, and anarchy, infidelity and licentiousness would fill the land. These clerical warnings and editorial prophecies all failed. Instead thereof, during his administration, the national debt was reduced $40,000,000; the internal taxes taken off; the vast territory of the west was added to the United States, and every man sat quietly under his vine and fig tree, enjoying the freedom of his religion and the attachment of his wife and children.

So with respect to Gen. Jackson. Before he came into office, the alarm guns were fired in every direction. "He has no learning; he is not experienced in diplomacy; he is only a military chieftain; he is lawless; he is a murderer; if he should be president, the members of Congress must go armed to Washington; better be cursed with war, famine or pestilence, than be under military rule," &c. But the nerves of the people sustained the shock, and raised him to the highest office in their gift.

But a heterogeneous band have been and still are hunting him like a partridge on the mountains, and are determined to neither eat nor drink until they have killed Paul. But he, with unruffled temper, like the horses in Pharaoh's chariot, keeps on his course of seeking the good of the people, regardless of all the yelping puppies that seek to snap at his feet.

During his administration, the national debt has been reduced to a mere fraction; duties lessened; treaties formed; rewards for spoliations obtained; vast tracts of land purchased of the Indians, &c. For more than sixty years I have been old enough to observe the state of things, and can honestly say, that as far as I can judge, I have never seen a time of greater prosperity, among every class of citizens, than the present: look which way I will, the proofs of prosperity are before my eyes. Nor can I conceive how rational beings can expect more from government than we enjoy.

From the first operation of our government, in 1789, until the present time, there has always been some question afloat to agitate the public mind: the present question is THE BANK OF THE UNITED STATES.

When the constitution first made its appearance, in the autumn of 1787, I read it with close attention, and finally gave my vote for its adoption; and after the amendments took place, I esteemed it as good a skeleton as could well be formed (never, however, liking the Judiciary Department of it.) I had then no thought of a bank, and had heard nothing said about it. When the bank was first chartered, it was an act I had never looked for; but being ignorant of commercial and fiscal concerns, I held my peace, concluding that other men knew better than myself; and in that acquiescence I have lived until this time, without ever studying banking principles. Of late, however, the exteriors of the bank have struck my mind.

Very soon after Gen. Jackson began to administer, in a public document he made an avowal of the intrinsic evils, dangerous tendency and party application of the bank, in his view of it. This he did to awaken the attention of the people, and give the directors of the bank time to settle their accounts before the expiration of the charter, in case it should not be renewed.

The spirit of this inquiry he kept alive during his first term of administration. The plain language of which was: "Fellow-citizens, I give you my views of the bank, and shall act upon those principles; if you respond to those sentiments I am ready to serve you; if not, elect another agent." The people, with their eyes open, again elected him to the presidency, giving him more than two-thirds of their votes; which was one evidence that they were opposed to the bank, under its present regulations. Soon after this the secretary of the treasury (in conformity to chartered right) removed the national deposites from the bank of United States to other banks. This has occasioned warm feeling and inflammatory harangues beyond measure.

The Senate have passed a vote of censure on the president, and will not admit his protest to be entered on their journal. The reasons of the secretary they declare insufficient, and, in their executive capacity, have refused to confirm his nomination. The House of Representatives have voted that the bank ought not to be re-chartered, and that the removal of the deposites is in conformity to the charter of the bank, and expedient as well as legal. The case is now at issue between the advocates for the bank and its foes; which case the sovereign people will decide; and if they are rightly informed, will judge uprightly. What I have seen and heard in this unusual struggle about the bank, compels me to say that if one was to inform me that the president and directors of the bank, and all its warm advocates, were disinterested patriots, and had only the good of the country at heart; that they really believed that agriculture, manufactures, and commerce, would all languish, and national bankruptcy follow unless the bank should be continued, I should find myself so unbelieving that I should have to pray, "Lord, increase my faith," for my faith in this information would not be equal to a grain of mustard-seed. But if another was to tell me that the bank, in its present form, was a dangerous institution; the stockholders a privileged class; that the directors were unsubmissive; and that the warm advocates for its re-charter are either stockholders in the bank or receive her smiles and kisses, I should believe the report without requiring signs and miracles to confirm my faith.

The Senate of the United States is an august assemblage; chosen by the legislatures of the several states; holding their offices for six years; partaking of a part of the legislative, executive, and judiciary powers: how important! An ambassador at Rome once said, "The Senate of Rome is an assembly of the Gods, but my own countrymen are a herd of Hydras." But such is the weakness and depravity of human nature, that men in the highest stations may do wrong. That the Senate did, at their last session, abuse the president, the secretary of the treasury, and the postmaster-general, is notorious: but passing that by, there were some laws passed in the session that bid fair to be of great utility.

The gold bill will have a natural tendency to stop the exportation of American eagles, and bring back many of the fugitives to their native soil. Making foreign silver current, will have a like tendency to bring much of it from the states in the silver regions. Gold mines are somewhat prolific in some of our southern states. Add to this the twenty millions of specie that have lately been shipped into the United States; and a permanent currency, sufficient for a medium of barter, may be established.

If banks shall nevertheless be necessary to facilitate commerce, let them be chartered in the states, with this proviso, that no bills of a less denomination than $10 shall be emitted. This scheme, or something like it, would make the people of the United States happy in their fiscal concerns. It is a given truth that there is no intrinsic value in paper currency; not as much as there is in a paper of pins or an iron nail. The value of it is *nominal*, not *real;* it is the evidence of wealth, which is not in itself. I here close my superficial remarks on the exteriors of the bank of the United States, and leave the constitutionality and expediency of it to be elucidated by its friends and foes before the great tribunal, the *sovereign people*, and shall cheerfully submit to the decision.

The friends of the present administration have nothing to flatter them at present in this commonwealth at large, or even in this congressional district, where a decided and overwhelming majority of numbers, wealth and talent are against it. But so many changes, divisions, subdivisions, trisions, quatrisions, cleavings off, and splicings together, take place; and at every new jump a new name is given; that he who follows the times needs the sagacity of a hound, to follow the crooked track of a fox.

Among a thousand things that might be said to encourage the persevering democratic minority, let one be sufficient.

The early settlers of New England had a strong notion of a Christian commonwealth; that Christians had the same pre-eminence over the heathen that the Israelites had over the inhabitants of Canaan; that as God gave the tribes the land of the Canaanites, so also it was his will that Christians should take away the land of the Indians. Another idea they entertained, that although diocesan government of the church was unscriptural and cruel, yet each town should (under-act of the legislature) by a major vote, compel all to attend the worship and support the preacher that the majority preferred. In these things Roger Williams, minister of Salem, withstood them; and for manfully maintaining that religious opinions were not articles of human legislation, and that it was unjust to take the land of the Indians without a satisfactory reward, he was banished from Massachusetts Bay, and fled south to the Indians, who gave him a tract of land which he named PROVIDENCE. He became the principal founder of the state of Rhode Island, and has the honor of founding the first government, free from religious oppression, that has ever been since the days of Constantine. William Penn followed his example in founding Pennsylvania upon the same principle. And in 1787 and '88, the United States did the same. What an individual contended for against a host, and for which he was banished, is now become the supreme law of the whole United States. What has been may be again. Democracy runs low in this state at present; it may rise: if not, democrats can bear. In the United States, democracy had a commanding voice for the last six years: what changes may take place hereafter I cannot say; every spoke in the wheel has its turn in being uppermost. Who will succeed the present chief magistrate in the presidency is yet unknown; many seem to be licking their chops for it: and if the fever does not intermit, it will soon be with our republic as it once was with Rome, which one of their poets describes thus: "Oh what a many-headed beast is Rome! How many horns she bears!" Let the presidency fall into whose hands it may hereafter, the democrats have this to say, that it was under the administration of *their* favorite presidents, Jefferson and Jackson, that the debt of the nation was more reduced, and greater acquisitions of territory made, than in any fourteen years besides. It must be expected that in an elective government personal attachments, and the wish of a different line of measures, will occasion some confusion; but as long as the contention contains only hot wind and loud noise, free from the smoke of powder and the stain of blood, it must be borne with as a tax which all free governments have to pay for their liberty.

Compare the condition of the citizens of the United States with that of the subjects of European monarchs, and you will felicitate yourselves and bless God that you are Americans. With them pomp and poverty; sumptuousness and starvation; fulness and beggary; purple and raggedness; oppression and depression; haughtiness and cringing, are seen at one glance. Splendor of courts; the aggrandizement of a few, and the wretchedness of many, is a true portrait of those kingdoms. But in our institutions there is no king but *law*, and every man has a voice in making it; no hereditary lords; no privileged orders in church or state; we call no man master; we are all on a level, minding our own business, making our own bargains, and seeking our own happiness in our own chosen way. Such is the genius of our institutions. But if, under some peculiar excitement, we are led into error, time and reflection, with the aid of the all-correcting weapon RIGHT OF SUFFRAGE, bring us back to our natural bearings and peaceful enjoyments.

As the sentiments of this concourse can be better expressed by resolutions than by my feeble address, I shall give way, relying on the goodness of the audience to pass by all the defects of limited talents, inexperience in state affairs, and weakness of age. As political meetings in Cheshire, heretofore, have been eulogized for sobriety and good order, an emulation to retain the character will stimulate every one to abstain from intemperance, riot, and strife; that nothing may be said or done to stain the fair character of the town, or expose democracy to disgrace; nothing inconsistent with the principles of morality, or pure and undefiled religion. Let it be known to all, that while we contend for the rights of man against the claims of aristocrats, and the clamor of ambitious *would-be-ins*, we act under a sense of our accountability to the King of all nations. Happiness and prosperity to all of you.

LETTER.

Sir:—I respond to your sentiments, respecting our illustrious chief magistrate, and the abuse that has been cast upon him, by a heterogeneous mob, composed of Nullifiers, Hartford Convention men, Bankites, and the would-be-ins. Supposing they should succeed in their wishes, is it probable that better treaties would be made; more land purchased; debts sunk faster; commerce more flourishing; public credit more firm; the hand of labor more eased; state rights more respected; the liberty of the citizens better guarded, or any blessing that may reasonably be looked for from government bettered?

When I survey the administration of President Jackson, I am constrained to say, "he has done all things well," and would ask those who are seeking to run him down, "why, what evil has he done?" The Almighty Being, who seems to have a peculiar regard for the United States, has raised up men of singular qualities to meet special emergencies, whose names will live in admiration as long as history endures; and in this list of names, that of Andrew Jackson will not be obliterated: for what other man would have met with all that he has, with the same personal and moral courage and prudence; giving uncontrovertible evidence in every measure that *the good of the people*, and not *his own aggrandisement*, was the stimulus? But stop! I am no statesman. The origin, design and boundaries of civil government I have studied; its interference with religion I have opposed; the equal rights of all I have plead for; but the minutia of law I am a stranger to.

In the formation of our constitution of general government, the aristocratical part of the community could not get woven into the letter of it all that they desired; but after its ratification, they called into requisition all their energies to turn the administration into an aristocratic channel, and by construction gave it an irresponsible tone; and were so successful that in ten years an alien act—a sedition act—a stamp act, with a standing army, etc., were all established; and the doctrine was trumpeted far and loud, "that a national debt was a national blessing," which was chorused, "the rulers must save the people from themselves." None but those who lived at the time, can fully conceive how much it cost the sober democrats to place Jefferson in the presidential chair, and check the threatening flood. But notwithstanding the fatal wound which Federalism then received, since the close of the last war in 1815, this deadly wound has been partly healed by the disguise of National Republicanism, and old Democracy has been obliged to arm herself with ballot box weapons to vanquish the same old enemy, who is now dodging out of sight under the covert of *Whig*.

If individuals were always governed by truth, justice, and benevolence, few laws, and few magistrates would be sufficient; but government took its rise from the wrongs of men. Men, finding evil propensities in themselves, and seeing the overt acts of others, called in the aid of *sober reason to establish* rules to prevent the mischief. This is government, which is an evil of itself, because it costs individuals some of their natural rights; but it is a necessary evil to prevent a greater.

I have lived under the administration of seven presidents, and was never better pleased with the measures of government than I now am. I have endeavored to serve my generation according to the clearest light that I could gain. It is now for the rising generation to sustain the institutions which their fathers have left them; improve upon them, or radically change them; for one generation has no right to control that which succeeds.

A MEMORIAL.

THE FOLLOWING WAS WRITTEN FOR HIS DAUGHTER, AT HER REQUEST, AS A MEMORIAL OF HIMSELF.

Now, in the eve of a life but poorly spent, I write a few lines for you, that you may have a token to remember me by, after my decease. But why all this? A century from this time, there will not be a person on earth, that ever heard there was such a man as myself; nor am I anxious to perpetuate a name associated with so few virtues and so many defects. If my name is found in the Lamb's Book of Life—if my robe is washed and made white by his blood--if he will say to me at the judgment day, "come, ye blessed of my father, receive the reward of a crown of life. and palm of victory," it is—it ought to be—my greatest desire; nevertheless, while I am here in the body, living on the bounties of heaven, I have a feeble desire to serve my generation by the will of God, like David, knowing that shortly I must fall asleep.

Sin has introduced so much darkness and blindness into this world, that I have ever found it a hard task to find the *real truth;* and notwithstanding the true light has been shining ever since the Sun of Righteousness arose, still blindness and inattention involve me in ignorance. Nor is this all; sin has so completely ruined men, that any scheme of restoration that creatures can comprehend, would be insufficient; a scheme founded in *infinite* wisdom, and executed in *infinite* love and *omnipotent* power, was necessary. This scheme the gospel reveals; but how incompetent are men, or angels, to understand it in all its parts. The wonders hidden in this plan, will be gradually unfolding to the saints eternally, but will never be exhausted. But,

> Tho' of exact perfection we despair,
> Yet every step to virtue's worth our care.

Some feeble conclusions that I have formed of God's truth, here follow:

The excellencies of human life consist in justice, accommodation, mercy, truth, and liberality.

JUSTICE has just weights, measures, and balances, will never deceive or defraud any one, and will not extort or diminish his own or another's, for the sake of advantage.

ACCOMMODATION, by looking not on our own things, (exclusively,) but on the things of others, with but little or no expense, can greatly diminish the troubles, and increase the comforts of the world.

MERCY has a pitiful eye and a liberal hand, towards all the distressed. It feels another's wo, and will not say to the needy, "be ye warmed, and be clothed," without giving relief, if in its power.

TRUTH, without disguise, was so much esteemed among some of the heathen, that they had a goddess, called *Truth*, stark naked. If every one would speak truth with his neighbor, we might believe every word we hear, and grow wise. Many times men are brought into a dilemma, where a *little lie* will seem to help them out. Such was the case with Peter; but a good man, governed by goodness, will *swear to his own hurt and not change*,—that is, he will stick to the truth, if it injures himself.

LIBERALITY of heart, reduced to practice for the public good—useful institutions, and the relief of individuals, according to what a man hath, is approved among all nations.

All these excellencies, with their corresponding virtues, may be performed by a mere man of the world, who has never been anointed with the "holy unction," or drank of the "water of life." And if, in addition thereto, he has abstained from all overt acts, and "kept all from his youth up," all together, can gain no hope beyond the grave, nor show one sin forgiven. *One thing is still lacking.*

A great part of the preceptive addresses given in the Old Testament, and some in the New, were given to men as citizens of state, or moralists in human society, and have no bearing on eternity: of course, the promises and penalties annexed thereto, are contingent.

That children do that, in their ancestors, long before they are born, for which they are applauded or punished, is noticed in the Bible: see Heb. vii., 9, 10. And as I may so say, Levi also, who receiveth tithes, paid tithes in Abraham, Luke xi., 50. That the blood of all the prophets, which was shed from the foundation of the world, may be required of this generation. Without enlarging here, I may safely say, that *all* have sinned, and are by nature children of wrath, under guilt and in a state of pollution. Neither the human nature of heathens, the religious rituals of the pharisees, nor the smoking altars, and bleeding victims of the Mosaic institution, can take away the guilt of sin, or purge the conscience of dead works. The blood of Christ alone removes the guilt of sin,—his holy anointing frees us from its reigning dominion. Yes, the religion that saves the soul from sin, guilt, and condemnation, includes a mediator, who died for our sins, a change of heart, or being born, not of blood, nor of the will of the flesh, nor of the will of man, but of God, (of his own will he begets us by the word of truth,) not by works of righteousness which we have done, but by the washing of regeneration, and the renewing of the Holy Ghost, he works in us, both to will and to do. This spirit of grace, shed abundantly on the soul, causes it to bring forth the fruits of love, joy, peace, long suffering, gentleness, goodness, faith, meekness, temperance, against which there is no law. This immortal seed, which abides with the saints, not only produces the internal fruits, just mentioned, but is a stronger stimulus to prompt to every good work, both religious and human, than the horrid fear of punishment, and the flattering hope of reward.

These are my views of religion; but as I lay no claim to infallible inspiration, or profundity of research, I cannot tell whether any, or how much error may be incorporated into my creed. I, therefore, advise every one to read, pray, and examine personally, with an unbiased mind, remembering that an honest, humble heart, is more acceptable to God than boasted wisdom.

I WILL ALSO SHOW MY OPINION.*

On or about the year thirty A. D., Caiaphas was head of the Jewish Sanhedrim; a court of priests, scribes, and pharisees, which took cognizance of religious crimes, and awarded the punishments to the offenders. Herod, in his jurisdiction, was head of the men of war. Pilate was governor and chief justice in Palestine, which was then a Roman province. Herod and Pilate were at variance; but what the bone of contention was, is uncertain. If Herod promised the people to make it known, he never redeemed his pledge. Caiaphas was no friend to either of them; being himself a circumcised Jew, he would neither eat with, nor be sociable with idolaters. But a certain event took place, in which the three dropped their hostility, and united to act in concert. The Saviour of the world was declared worthy of death by Caiaphas and his council—set at naught by Herod and his men of war—condemned and executed by Pilate and his band of soldiers. These events belong to the great department, and took place eighteen hundred years ago. Of late, however, a peculiar fracas has broken out in the United States, which has been nineteen years brewing, which naturally leads the mind to reflect on the past. The triumvirate of the Senate of the United States, though formerly at great variance, have united their strength to degrade and run down Jackson in the esteem and confidence of the people. A majority of the senators have passed a resolution of censure, implicating him as usurping a power not given him in the constitution, in removing the deposits of the United States bank. Well, what then? The resolution and the record of it on their journals have not changed the opinions of the people—removed the deposits back—nor laid any foundation for judicial proceedings. Whether the friends of the resolution were sincere or malicious, the result is, "the mountain labored, and brought forth a mouse." That the senators, like other citizens, had a good right, in a self-created convention, to pass resolutions on men and measures, is confessed by all; but men of BLACK PAWS, ignorant of the mystery of profound construction, who have only the compass of common sense, and the chart of plain language to steer by, cannot discern by what authority the Senate, on the floor of legislation, can censure, by resolution, any man,

* Published in 1835.

except in cases of impeachment, in which the senators are the exclusive judges and the prescribed accusers.

The Senate and House of Representatives do not always agree. In case of disagreement, should the House of Representatives pass a resolution to censure the Senate, would not the senators, like the devils in Capernaum, cry out "let us alone—*ne sutor ultra crepidam*?" Should both branches of the legislature pass resolutions to censure the judiciary for some legal decision, would not the bench reply, like Paul, "study to be quiet, and do your own business." The resolutions submitted, after the expense of much time, Herculean speeches, and great pain, passed the Senate; and a greater nothing was never seen. Had the event taken place in the days of Hezekiah, we should judge that the reporter of those times (Isaiah) had it in view when he exclaimed, "we have been in pain, we have as it were brought forth wind, we have not wrought any deliverance in the earth." Some of my political brethren (friends of Jackson and his wise, just and economical administration) are intent to have the record of the vote rescinded, erased, or expunged from the journals of the senate. I wonder why? My views are, let it remain on the journals on a prominent page, as long as paper and ink can talk, as a monument of what party rage, disappointed ambition and political insanity can do. By forming the estimate of men, that every one has a pope in his belly, (with but few exceptions,) it is highly probable that the senators opposed to the resolution, in some future session, will exert themselves to have the record expunged from their journals. Very likely the question will be the hobby for a seven month's race; and it may be with no better temper than has attended it heretofore. Should they succeed and gain a vote to expunge the record, the people might exclaim as a rustick boy, David, did to his mother, that his brother Jonathan had killed a dead mouse. For the vote, one way or the other, does not weigh an ounce of lamp-black in the scale of the judgment and prosperity of the people, nor in the proceedings of the administration.

The charges preferred against the ILLUSTRIOUS CHARACTER, spoken of in the head of this essay, were "that he was a devil, and worked by the power of Beelzebub—that they stoned him not for a good work but for a bad one—that he was a Sabbath-breaker—a deceiver—a seducer and blasphemer—that it was expedient that he should die; otherwise the Romans would devastate the country." These were the accusations; and although his friends repelled the charges, still the record of them is preserved in the most durable journals; and what harm has it done? Has it done honor to the accusers or injury to the accused? So also in the case in view. The censuring vote, and its record on the journals, have never made one enemy of the president, nor one friend to the senators who advocated the measure, nor altered the course of the administration;

and if the record should be expunged, the effect would be as passive. The plea for expunging, is, that a vote of censure against the president, if left on record in the journals of the Senate, will be a dangerous precedent for the Senate to usurp hereafter. It sounds strange to hear republicans plead for the right of legislating for posterity; but, many who are republicans in their judgments, are in spirit and disposition tyrants. What can precedent do to withstand determination? Let an individual have a strong will to do anything, and precedents to the contrary have little or no weight with him; but, if he has power, his will is gratified, maugre all the precedents. So it is with nations; and so it is with legislative bodies.

THE MOSAIC DISPENSATION.*

"I will give thee the opening of the mouth in the midst of them."
"The priests bear rule by their means, and what will ye do in the end thereof?"

In a world where the power of God, the power of Satan, and the power of men, have their respective courses, it cannot be expected, that religion, in all its purity, will be possessed, understood and practiced without an alloy of error. From the entrance of sin into the human family, more or less until the present time, darkness has covered the earth, and gross darkness the people. From creation to the law of Moses, (almost 2500 years,) except what was known of God by his works, but very small gleams of light were given unto men to teach them the moral character of God, and what kind of worship he requires of them. The Mosaic ministration was glorious, but made nothing perfect, except by sacrificing figures, it gave no hope for pardon of sin and eternal life. When the writings of Moses, and of the prophets who lived a thousand years after him were read, the veil remained on the minds of the readers. When they prophesied of the coming of Christ and the glory that would follow, their predictions were greatly obscured by mystery and Judaism. God had provided some better things for those that should follow. When John the Baptist, like the morning star, came before and introduced the SUN OF RIGHTEOUSNESS, the dayspring from on high visited the world. The true light then shone. The examples and preaching of Christ, with the inspired addresses of the apostles, recorded in the New Testament, form a perfect creed of faith and directory of life, for the followers of Christ to the end of the world. No man may add thereto or diminish therefrom. Those parts of the Old Testament which are brought forward and incorporated into the New Testament are binding on Christians. Other parts of it serve to show the conduct of men—the changes which have taken place on earth, and the wonderful works of God in the world. The remainder are purely Jewish, and have no great bearings on others. The establishment of Christianity introduced a change of the priesthood—a change of sacrifice and a change of the law; of course the divers washings and carnal ordinances, which were to continue no longer than the reformation, ceased to be obligatory; and a new code of laws, contained in the New Testament, became binding on the saints. Here was a radi-

* Published in 1832.

cal change of the rituals of religion appointed by God himself. Since the close of inspiration, through the weakness of some, and the love of power and wealth of others, Christianity, in its *exterior* forms, has ever been changing its measures; but no length of time ever has or ever will change *internal* religion. From the righteous Abel to the last sinner that shall be brought into the fold of Christ, each must be created in Christ—renewed in the spirit of his mind—receive an unction from the Holy One—drink of the water of life—fear God and work righteousness to be accepted of God and be admitted into the everlasting kingdom. It would be an herculean task to give a history of the various sects of nominal Christians, and their religious creeds, that have existed at the same time, or followed in succession, since the close of inspiration. The present state of things calls for our attention. The religious world (particularly in the United States) seems to be much in the condition that it was in Europe, when the people protested against the claim of the Pope, and ran hither and thither, until the civil arm settled the controversies.

As citizens, it is our joy and boast, that the government of the United States proscribes all religous tests, and guarantees unto every citizen his religious opinions, with the freedom of the tongue and the press to support them. As John Wickliff began the reformation from popery, so the banished Roger Williams began the reformation from hierarchy: he established the first form of government ever known in Rhode Island, which excluded religious opinions from the civil code, on the true maxim, "That *legal rewards* should never be given for *religious services*." This novel nest-egg was soon followed by the illustrious William Penn, in the government of Pennsylvania, and the inhabitants of New York pursued the track. The principle which at that time was considered so dangerous, immoral and anti-christian, is now interwoven as an integral part of the constitution of the government of the United States. The beginning was small, but the latter end has greatly increased. From this it does not follow, that from our liberality and benevolence to others, we are under obligation, or have any permission to believe all that others say, (though they support their schemes by signs and lying wonders;) no: though men or angels speak not according to the law and testimony, they have no light in them—we are forbidden to go after them, but ordered to consider them accursed. The greater sanctity they show, the more they are to be dreaded and shunned: for the greatest religious errors that have ever been among men, have crept in under the robe of superior piety. They come with a great pretence of universal benevolence, crying aloud against bigotry and extolling union; but as soon as they gain influence enough, they forget their creed and draw away disciples after themselves. The cry of some of them is "Be ye reconciled *one with another* in union, that *we* may live (and make a gain of you) while another voice sounds "Be ye reconciled *to God* that *your souls* may live." I will here add, that the universal forgiveness to our enemies and benevolence to all men, enjoined on us by the voice of God, lays us under no obligation to sacrifice our judgments and say that is *right* which we believe is *wrong*.

It is now sixty-three years since my attention was solemnly engaged to serve the Lord. When first alarmed, I forsook my loose behavior and ran to the law, as a covenant of works, in hopes of being delivered from condemnation by my reformation; but soon found that by the deeds of the law I could not be justified. It was then presented to my mind, that repentance for sin and faith in the Lord Jesus would secure my salvation; and I was assured from the pulpit and from the Bible, that Jesus would receive the chief of sinners that came to him with all the heart; but here I found that I could no more repent, believe, come to Christ, and give up my whole heart to him than I could create a world. That unless I was drawn by the *Father*, all the exertions of my natural powers of body and mind could not bring me to the *Son*. That unless I was born, not of blood, nor of the will of the flesh, nor of the will of man, but of God, and saved by grace, I must sink into hell. In this inquietude of mind I continued fifteen months; until it pleased God, by his truth and grace to draw me, by the cords of love (not against my will, but with my will and strong desire) unto the hope of the gospel, which removed my guilt and set me free.

> "O, what immortal joy I felt,
> And pleasure all divine!
> When Jesus told me I was his,
> And whisper'd he was mine."

Soon after this, by the moving of my spirit and application of several texts of scripture, I felt myself bound, though unacquainted with men, manners, and books, to engage in the ministry, in which I have continued more than sixty-one years. From the prophecy, that many should *run to and fro;* and from the commission of Christ, *Go*, my impressions were, that travelling and preaching repentance on the way was the path for preachers. Accordingly, without going to Jerusalem, or any presbytery of preachers, or any theological school, or indeed any church, for licence or approbation, without conferring with flesh and blood, I began to preach, "*Ye must be born again.*" And the third chapter of John has been text for me ever since. The doctrine I have preached may be summarily described in two words, "*ruin and recovery.*" There are many commands given and many promises made to nations—to them in relative and social life, and, to individuals, which respect their happiness or misery in this world; but when the eternal salvation of the soul is treated of, three things are either expressed or implied, viz: redemption by the blood of Christ—renewing of the Holy Ghost—and good works. In preaching this doctrine,

I have travelled distances that would more than girdle the globe four times, and am not yet weary of it. In my journeyings, I have marked my own destination; observing the openings of providence—the request of people—the drawings of my mind, and the circumstances of things. I have never received any thing from a missionary fund to aid me; but have relied on the promise of God and the benevolence of the people for all that was necessary. My wants, fatigues and persecutions have been small, compared with what many have sustained; and recede to nothing when placed in competition with the sufferings which Christ endured. I have baptized 1,525, by immersion, on profession of their faith in Christ. My success has been small to what some have had; but when I reflect on my barrenness and languor of soul, I wonder more that God ever blessed my labors, than I do that he has blessed them no more. And now, in the eve of life, with a hoary head—decrepit limbs and a faltering tongue, I cry, *God be merciful to me a sinner! Save, Lord, or I must perish!*

In these days of novelty we are frequently addressed from the pulpit as follows: "Professors of religion, you stand in the way of God and sinners—give up your old hope and come now into the work—God cannot convert sinners while you are stumbling blocks in the way—sinners are stumbling over you into hell. Profane sinners, I call upon you to flee from the wrath to come—come this minute and give your heart to God, or you will seal your own damnation—God has given you the power, and will damn you if you do not use it—God has done all he can for you and will do no more—look not for a change of heart; a change of purpose is all that is necessary—to pray the Lord to enable you would be presumptuous. Some of you are mourning for the loss of a friend—I tell you your friend is in hell, and has gone there on your account—had you done your duty your friend would now be in heaven, but for your neglect your friend is damned. My hearers, you may have a revival of religion whenever you please—begin in the work, and the work will begin among the people—continue in it and the work will continue—keep on and the work will become universal."*

Had I the spirit of infallible inspiration, I could fix a standard of orthodoxy; but as I have no claim to that high attainment, I shall only remark, that, "I have not so learned Christ—I do not understand the scriptures in that light—it is not the voice of my beloved,"—it sounds like the voice of a stranger and I dare not follow it. But, my brethren, while we believe

* If these preachers really believe what they preach, we commend their honesty but doubt their religion. But if they do not believe it themselves, but do it to terrify their hearers, to immortalize their own names, as GREAT REFORMERS, who turn sinners from the error of their ways; verily they will have their reward, which is a poor one.

To this note I add, that the expressions moral—sovereign—anxious—probation—total depravity—means of grace—purchased salvation—seal your own damnation, are not in the Bible.

that God saves us, not for works of righteousness that we have done, but according to his mercy in his love and kindness towards man, by the washing of regeneration and the renewing of the Holy Ghost; let us never lose sight of the *holy law*, the eternal rule of right which is founded on the relation which exists between God and man and between man and man, and will be binding on rational beings as long as the perfections of God and the faculties of man endure. This law runs through the Bible like a gold cord, and enjoins on men at all times, to believe what God reveals and obey what he commands. Every transgression of this law is *sin*, called a *debt*. That all have sinned and are ten thousand talents in debt, is abundantly proved: and that they have nothing to pay is equally evident; but *the bankruptcy of the insolvent never destroys the justness of the law or the obligation of the debtor*. Christ did not come to destroy the law, but to fulfil it; and those who are redeemed by his grace from the dominion of sin, do not make void the law through faith, but establish it. Any defect from the prestine innocence of Adam, is a charge on the human family: and the law cries *pay:* "Turn to the law and make yourselves new hearts—put away all your sins and be perfect," &c. is as reasonably required of the human race, as any debt is required of a debtor. From this it does not follow that the insolvent sinner has any thing to make payment with. No. Whether his bankruptcy consists in the want of *will* or in the want of *strength*, or both; still he hath nothing to pay; and is led to see and feel his entire poverty before he is frankly forgiven.

Societies of various kinds are now formed, with ostensible views, to extirpate drunkenness, masonry, ignorance, slavery and idolatry from the earth; and the people, from the aged to the infant, are called upon to enrol their names and take a bold stand to moralize and christianize the world. Lying, fraud, love of money, hypocrisy, gaming, duelling, and fornication, as yet seem to be considered too sacred to be meddled with, for no society is formed to check them.

The missionary establishment, in its various departments, is a stupendous institution. Literary and theological schools—Bible and tract societies—foreign and domestic missions—general, state, county, and district conventions—sunday school union, etc., are all included in it. To keep it in motion, missionary boards—presidents—treasurers—corresponding secretaries—agents—printers—buildings—teachers—runners—collectors—mendicants, etc., are all in requisition. The cloud of these witnesses is so great, that a sober man who doubts the divinity of the measure, is naturally led to think of the locusts in Egypt that darkened the *heavens* and ate up every green thing on *earth;* while the punster will compare them to the Connecticut pedlars who ransack every street and lane with their shining tin, and wooden nutmegs. This machine is propelled by steam [money] and does not sail by the wind of heaven. Immense donations and contributions have already been cast into the treasury; and we see no end to it for the solicitors and mendicants are constantly crying "give, give," with an unblushing audacity that makes humble saints hold down their heads.

There are a number of religious denominations in the United States so equally balanced, that no one of them can tyranize over all the rest: the present scheme seems to be, for each society to sacrifice its peculiar characteristics, and all unite to form a *Christian Phalanx*, to be established by Congress as the religion of the United States. If my painful fears, on this head are ever realized, the glory of America will depart—the blood and treasure expended in the revolution will all be lost—and the asylum for the distressed turned to a prison and an inquisition. But I forbear. The subject sickens. I close in the words of God himself, "Stand ye in the ways and see, and ask for the old paths, where is the good way, and walk therein, and ye shall find rest for your souls." *Are these thy ways, O Lord! hidden from him who wishes to know and do thy will?*

FREE THOUGHTS ON TIMES AND THINGS.*

O tempora! O mores!—HORACE.

* * * * * * * *

Third. IN the days of the Commonwealth, in England, a sect arose, called the *The fifth monarchy men*, who held that the four monarchies spoken of in the scriptures, were out, and that Christ would assume his throne on earth and give the kingdom to the saints; and that all earthly monarchy would cease. Oliver Cromwell favored the views of these people; and when he assumed the protectorship, he assured them that he did it to have it in his power to give it up to Christ the more readily. That monarchy has existed from that time to this, and still exists, is a known truth.

Fourth. Some men among us profess to be greatly alarmed at the spread of the Roman Catholicks. They say there are six hundred thousand within the limits of the United States; all busy at work, like a worm under the barkof a tree, to sap our free government, and set up papal hierarchy with all the horrors of an inquisition. This alarm has the complexion of design, to move men to advance their money to make and send missionaries to check the religion of others: for no man who has the soul of an American, and the heart of affection for our democratic institutions, will either fear or wish to injure the papists. Supposing the number should be one million; what could that one million do in a country of fourteen millions? Is it probable that the Catholicks will increase faster, either by births or emigration, than the Protestants? If not, where is the ground of alarm? Their freedom of religion is guaranteed to them in our constitution of government, and no benevolent man can wish to have them oppressed as they are in Ireland. In the American Revolution, and in the formation of the Constitution under which we live and prosper, the tocsin sounded loud, "America shall be an asylum for the distressed of every nation to flee to," and who can wish to subvert that freedom? The French Catholicks were great helpers to Americans in their struggles for independence, (Lafayette among the rest,) and now to deny them the hospitalities of good friends would be base ingratitude. If any of them commit overt acts, punish them; but let them have free scope to publish their religion. If they send their missionaries among those of a different religion to make proselytes, it is doing no more than Protestants do. Should they

* Published in 1836.

by fair persuasion (for they cannot do it by force until they become a majority) increase in number above all other sects collectively; in that case they must of right have the rule; for no man who has the soul of an American will deny the maxim, that "the voice of a majority is the voice of the whole." The men of *this* generation have neither power nor right to say what laws a *future* generation shall be governed by. An express declaration of their opinion is all that belongs to them.

Fifth. There are a great many slaves in the United States; the exact number I cannot ascertain; (say one million, be the same more or less,) the condition of whom, has given patriots, philanthropists and religionists great searchings of heart. The abolitionists of late have come forward, and seem to demand the unconditional manumission of all of them, without prescribing any rational mode for their future subsistence. If these prophets can prove their commission, like Moses, or have any reason to believe that God will feed the liberated slaves with manna, it is hoped that the slave-holders will obey, and not harden their hearts: otherwise their exertions seem calculated to alienate the slave-holding states from the others, and make the condition of the slaves more miserable. But notwithstanding the measures of the abolitionists are reprobated by every friend to his country; yet the question, "What shall we do with the slaves?" must at some time, in some shape, be met and decided. The emancipators have effected nothing. The Liberia exportation affords nothing very flattering; what then shall be done? It cannot be expected that a question, encumbered with so many conflicting interests and opinions, can be easily answered: the most rational solution may be fraught with serious consequences. To proclaim a jubilee and set them all free, without house or home, tools or money, or friends to take them in, would be sacrificing them to starvation. In such a state they would wander in droves into all the states, seeking supplies for the calls of nature. Would the abolitionists be pleased to have thousands of them scouring the states in which they live, and groups of them at their own doors, or around their dwellings, begging or stealing?

Let Congress locate a section of territory for the accommodation of as many as choose to go with the consent of their masters—let their expenses be borne, and their equipage of clothing, provisions, implements of husbandry and mechanism, with all that is necessary for three years, including teachers to learn them to read and write, by the treasury of the United States. So far Congress can proceed towards the liberation of the slaves. This would give relief to those slaveholders, who in heart are opposed to slavery, and would gladly set their slaves free, if they could be provided for.

If the legislatures of the slave-holding states, in behalf of their constituents, should pass laws for the gradual manumission of all the slaves—

that all of them who were in existence at the time of passing those laws should be held in servitude for life, except, with the consent of their masters, they should choose to go to the land provided for them, and that those who should be born after the passing of those laws should be free at the age of twenty-one years, the children of whom should be free-born, it would gradually lower the price of slaves, as property, and gradually learn them to bear their liberty. It would also give time to the masters to new moddle their systems to live without the labor of slaves.

The United States have now territory at command, and a surplus treasury of millions: can it be applied to a better use than of liberating human beings, who are deprived of their natural rights by force and not for crime? Whether Congress dispose of the surplus revenue direct, or whether they apportion it among the states; in either case, the presumption is that it will be applied for splendor, rather than to establish permanent funds in the states to pay the taxes. If a part of the surplus national property is appropriated to procure a home and support for liberated slaves, and the slave-holding states do not meet the measure by corresponding laws, the proof will be conclusive that they deny to others the freedom which they claim for themselves as a natural right.

Should this plan, or one like it, take effect, in a few years the question could be decided by experimental evidence, "whether the African Moors have intellect sufficient for self-government, or whether they are a degraded race of beings, between the human and animal departments, made to serve their betters, and do that part of drudgery which is above the capacity of beasts." They are now considered in a complex character, in the United States, possessing *three-fifths* of humanity and *two-fifths* of animal property.

I have spent fifteen years of my life in a slaveholding state, (Virginia); calling led me to mingle with the slaves, as well as with their masters: and I believe there are as many of the slaves, (in proportion to their numbers,) who join the Christian churches, as there are of the whites. Some of them can read—others hear and believe, and a number of them are zealous preachers and exhorters. Redemption by the blood of Christ—a gracious change of heart—and holiness of life, are their favorite topics. The slaves generally put more confidence in the preachers of their own color, than they do in the whites, from a belief that they are less likely to deceive them. Of course, should they be removed into a section assigned them, there would be neither need nor propriety for government to furnish them with religious teachers.

In the year 1780, and a few years following, when the people were rapidly removing from the old states into Kentucky and Tennessee, there were more than thirty Baptist preachers, whom I personally knew, and many more that I heard of, who emigrated with them. Nothing can be more false than the idea that the Valley of the Mississippi is peopled with irreligious characters altogether, who are perishing for want of missionary preaching. The truth is, that many religious people remove into the valley, and many preachers go with them. Many also are turned to the Lord in the place, and a portion of them commence preaching. Rev. Daniel Parker, who lives on the ground, and who has been publishing a religious periodical, speaks of five Baptist Associations within the limits of Illinois and Indiana: and he complains of some missionaries who intrude, and seek to control because they are sent by the Board of Missions. My information is not sufficient to speak of the prevalence of any other religious society in the valley.

LETTER TO HON. G. N. BRIGGS, JAN. 12, 1836.

HON. SIR :—I am confident you will have the goodness to pass by my imprudence in my attempt to write to one so highly elevated by his country. I aim not at high things ; my head is not formed for the cap of honor ; but the good of that country which has given me birth, and nourished me more than eighty years, lies near my heart. Next to the salvation of the soul, I have advocated a scheme which would support the energies of government and secure the rights of the people. The given powers of the government in which you are now acting as legislator are few and defined. The powers granted and rights retained are so plainly stated in the charter, that those who read may understand ; but, where honest men are agreed in the fundamental principles, they may widely differ in the agents and secondary measures which would be the most likely to establish those principles.

It seems probable that the admission of Michigan into the Union—the French question—the circulation of the writings of the abolitionists—the disposal of the surplus revenue, etc., will occupy some of your time. The expunging of senatorial foolery will not be hammered in your shop ; but, in the Senate chamber, it is likely the furnace will be blown seven times hotter than usual, to kill that which never did any harm ; the death of which will never bequeath a pair of shoes for a child, or an ear of corn for a pig. Should the record of the resolution of censure be expunged by a line drawn across it as black as tophet, it would not change the mind of any man, any more than the passing of the resolution did.

In the time of the revolution in England, it became proverbial, "strip a man of office, and he will talk like a whig ; put him into office, and he will be a tory." It is too true, that when men possess power, they forget right, every man having a pope in his belly ; but, true patriotism will rope the pope, and cause the patriot to seek the good of his country (of all the world) and not his own agrandizement.

According to our political calendar, this present year is leap year ; the the thirteenth bissextile of our government. It is therefore probable that there will be some leaping in Washington this session ; and pray how could the leisure hours of the members of Congress be spent better than in devising means for the good of their country for the four succeeding years? Whether the committee of ways and means are appointed for the purpose of nominating and recommending a candidate for the next term, and whether the committee are likely to agree and report a bill, I do not know. My ardent desire is that there may be a fair expression of the will of the people in the choice of the eighth president; if so, whoever he be, I will acknowledge him as my president; whether he is the man of my choice or not; for in this case, and in all other cases like it, *vox populi vox dei* is a religious truth.

Representatives are not sent to Congress to think for their constituents, but to act for them, (the right of thinking being inalienable in its nature,) and he who acts contrary to the known will of a majority of his constituents, is a tyrant. When a question must be acted upon, and the representative cannot in conscience vote for that which he knows is the will of his constituents, it becomes him to tender his reisgnation, and let another fill his place. Mr. Adams formerly, and Mr. Rives recently acted wisely on this true republican principle in the Senate; and Col. Johnson did the same in substance in the compensation law, in the House of Representatives.

I learn from the newspapers that you are on the committee of post-office and post-roads. This institution has grown to a giant, and I believe it is as much abused as any establishment in the government. To guarantee to men their liberty by an instrument that defends from licentiousness, and to give men power enough to do good, and have it so counterpoised that they cannot abuse it, is what the friends of man have been laboring for some thousands of years; and likely the consummation of all things will find men in the pursuit of it. But the profession is not an attribute of men, yet every march towards it is praiseworthy.

OF MINISTERIAL DUTIES, &c.

THE instructions of our Lord to the twelve when he sent them out to preach, his admonitions to them afterwards, the resolution of the apostles to give themselves to the ministry of the word and prayer—the address of Paul to the elders of Ephesus—the epistles to Timothy and Titus—with the exhortation of Peter to the elders, and many divine lessons scattered through the New Testament, draw the line of ministerial conduct and usefulness beyond what any man or set of men can devise. To this rule preachers should take heed, as unto a light that shines in a dark place, for if they speak not according to the word, they have no light in them.

The faith and practice of the saints at large, is delineated in the Bible in a clear manner; yet the Lord sends forth preachers to explain what is revealed, and impress it on the minds of the saints, that they may have those things in remembrance, and be ready for every good work. So, also, preachers may be helpers to each other; each one communicating to others his best views on what God has revealed. Paul publicly blamed Peter for duplicity—exposed Barnabus for dissimulation—set a mark on Demas—reprobated the concision—rejected Hymenus, Philetus, and Alexander, and highly commended Timothy and many others for their purity and steadfastness of faith. Peter, James, John, and Jude, did likewise. When the Lord sent out his apostles, he perfectly knew every circumstance that ever they would be in, but he did not reveal the whole to them, but told them to be wise as serpents and harmless as doves. According to the wisdom given unto them, they said and did many things which incidentally fell in the way, which things were not *expressly* commanded in their commission. The convention and conference at Jerusalem—the sending of messengers to Antioch and Samaria—their accommodating their address to the circumstances and capacities of the people—their watching and improving the openings of providence, &c., were incidental to the great work of their commission, which was to preach repentance and remission of sins in the name of Jesus, to baptize those that believed, and to teach them to do all that God had commanded them.

The rule which God has given to men and to preachers is *perfect*; but there has never been but *one* man, but *one* preacher, since Adam's fall, whose words and actions were equal to the rule. This was realized in Jesus Christ, who was the faithful and true witness. Every word of his mouth was pure. But he had many things to say which his disciples were not able to bear while he was on earth, but after he ascended to his glory, he sent the Holy Ghost, which endowed them with power, insomuch, that when they were under the divine influence, they, like the holy prophets, spake and wrote as they were moved by the Holy Ghost, and filled the Christian code, which was not completed by Jesus Christ.

Signs, wonders, divers miracles, and gifts of the Holy Ghost, which the apostles had attending them for the confirmation of the great salvation, have ceased. If preachers of the present day were endowed like the apostles, they could decide, with certainty, what doctrine was true, and what mode of worship was required; but this is not the case. They have, however, the sure word of prophesy, (the Holy Scriptures,) which is a light to their feet and a lamp to their path ; but such is the limitation of the human mind, and so strong is the force of tradition, that men, who equally believe in the divinity of the Bible, and acknowledge it as the only and complete rule of faith and practice, do, nevertheless, differ in many things. The question is often asked, "What kind of preaching and what measures of proceeding are most likely to make the gospel ministry useful?" An answer to this question is summarily given in the first section of this essay ; but as events and circumstances are always changing, some little comment, (without placing it on a level with the text) may be profitable.

The doctrine that all have sinned, fallen into guilt, pollution, and weakness ; are children of wrath and dead in trespasses and sins ; is abundantly confirmed by the scriptures, by the conduct of sinners, and by the experience of the saints. By these three witnesses the doctrine is supported, and it should be boldly preached.

The doctrine of redemption from the curse of the law by the blood of Christ ; of repentance towards God, and faith in the Lord Jesus ; of the washing of regeneration and the renewing of the Holy Ghost, of self-denial and good works ; of the resurrection from the dead and eternal judgment ; these doctrines, with their convictions and ramifications, may all be summed up in two words, *ruin* and *recovery ;* or in other two, *duty* and *grace :* and if preaching them is not calculated to make the ministry useful, I am at a loss to know what kind of preaching would.

Some preachers have deeper penetration and stronger logical powers than others, by which they dig so deep, reason so close, and fly so high, that they keep out of sight of most of their hearers. In the spirit, they speak mysteries, but those who occupy the room of the unlearned, are not edified. They speak wisdom to them that are perfect ; but it is rare that any stupid sinner ever gets turned to righteousness by such preaching. That preaching which is plain and familiar, which awakens the sinner's attention, and arrests his conscience ; which shows him his danger, and points him to the remedy; which beats down his false hopes, and strips him of his own righteousness, is likely to be the most useful. The minister who wishes to be useful, must take heed to himself, as well as to his doctrine. A life of godliness and honesty is essential. A more hateful character cannot be seen, than the preacher who indulges himself in riot, intemperance, fraud, falsehood, and other foolish and sinful vices. If he preaches good doctrine, and his life does not correspond with it, his hearers will take no conviction, but reply, "Physician, heal thyself." Whatever natural talents the preacher may possess for husbandry, mechanism, merchandize, science, law, or physic, all must be subordinate to devotion, and not entangle him in his ministry.

It is of primary importance, that the preacher should be clothed with the garment of salvation; that he should be filled with a sense of the immense worth of the truth, the guilt, depravity and danger man is in; the unsearchable love of Christ in the bloody purchase, and his ability and willingness to save redeemed penitents. Without this robe, he will preach a distant Jesus, by an unfelt gospel, and with an unhallowed tongue. And all the self-made zeal, pretended piety, loud voice, hypocritical tears, and agonizing gesticulations that he may assume, will not supply the lack.

ADVERTISEMENT—GREAT REWARD OFFERED.*

A SINGULAR person is now, and has been for a long time, travelling through the land, who raises the wonder of all that behold him. Some think him a mad-man or a demoniac—others consider him a harmless man, who never cheats or deceives any other. A third class view him more inspired by the Holy Ghost, than the prophets or aspostles were. Another sect believe that he was the first and greatest creature that God ever made, and that, by a delegated powever, he does mighty works. But some contend, that from his names, Emanuel, the everlasting Father, the true God, the only wise God, eternal life, the I AM, Jehovah, the Lord God of the holy prophets, God over all; and from his works of healing the sick, raising the dead, ruling the winds and waves, knowing the thoughts and hearts of all men, meeting with, and blessing ten thousand congregations of saints scattered over the world at the same minute, that he must be God essential, possessing omnipotence, omniscience, and omnipresence.

The person here advertised, like a wayfaring man, is always travelling round in the world, but never misses his way, by day or by night. His clothing sometimes appears mean as swaddling clothes, and at other times, like a vesture dipped in blood; sometimes clothed with a garment down to the feet, and girt about the paps with a golden girdle, so white and shining that no fuller on earth can equal it, called the garment of salvation, and the robe of righteousness. When he travels on his way, his manner is to knock at every man's door, but make no forcible entry. Sometimes, when he finds the door locked against him, by his strange talent, and great benevolence, he puts in his hand by the hole of the door, and moves the bolt back; after which he is always received as a welcome guest. Whenever the door is freely opened, he enters, whether the occupant is king or beggar, and sups with him; promising them that they shall sup with him in a house above, which he has prepared for them. His deportment is dignified and meek, his addresses to all in his way are neither false nor flattering, but in sound words that cannot be contemned; in which he instructs the ignorant, warns the rebellious, detects the hypocrite, abases the proud, comforts the mourners, heals the broken hearted, and exalts the humble. In these addresses, his friends say, that never man spake like him. In his flesh-marks, he is fairer than the sons of men, yet it pleased

* Published in 1836, as also the following Hymns.

the Lord to bruise him; his visage was so marred, more than any man. That the scriptures might be fulfilled, he was taken by his enemies, and received five bleeding wounds: they pierced his hands, his feet, and his side. Those gaping wounds he retained a number of days after his return from the lower regions, to give incontestible proof that he was flesh and bones, and was no spirit—that he was the same person that his friends had been intimate with before he went down to the grave; but it is hard to believe that he has now wounds or scars in that state of glory which he had before the world began.

Now if any person, by diligent search, has found him who is here described, and has opened his house to receive him—his heart to love him—his mind to obey him, and his mouth to confess him, he shall have a rich reward; which comprises food of the first quality, meat, which shall endure unto everlasting life, the flesh of the passover Lamb, who takes away the sin of the world, and many rich dainties; drink of the living fountains of water, which proceed out of the throne of God and of the Lamb, which makes glad the city of our God, together with the juice of the pomegranate and the spiced wine: bread shall be given him, his water shall be sure; he shall hunger no more, neither thirst any more. His clothing shall be fine linen, white and clean, being washed in the blood of the Lamb. The dress within shall be all glorious, being a meek and quiet spirit, which, in the sight of God, is of great price, called the clothing of humility. His outward dress shall be of wrought gold, and when he is brought before the king, his raiment shall be of needle-work. His dwelling shall be in a house not made with hands, eternal in the heavens; in the city that hath foundations, whose builder and maker is God; even on Mount Zion, the city of the living God; he shall be a pillar in the temple of God, and go no more out. His possessions shall be the fatness of the earth, and the dew of heaven, a land that flows with milk and honey—the glory of all lands—a goodly mountain and Lebanon—a pleasant land—a goodly heritage, the title of which is sure, and the increase a hundred fold; known by the name of Beulah. His riches shall be pure gold—silver, seven times refined, and pearls of immense value. His companions shall be the only excellent ones of the earth; a chosen generation, a royal priesthood, a holy nation, a peculiar people; the jewels and royal diadems of Jehovah, the spirits of just men made perfect, and an innumerable company of angels. He shall be delivered from all his bonds, his sins shall be forgiven, his debts paid, his crimes pardoned, his prison opened, and he shall be free indeed.

His equipage (when he follows him that is faithful and true, whose garment is dipped in blood,) shall be elegant; he shall ride upon a white horse, clothed in fine linen, white and clean, and shall be attended by twenty thousand chariots of angels, who are all ministering spirits to the heirs of salvation.

He shall, moreover, be adopted into the family of the King of Kings, and be called and treated as a Son of God, and a joint heir with Jesus Christ; he shall be a king and priest to God and the Lamb, and live and reign with Christ forever; having his name written in the book of life, and the seal of the living God written in his forehead.

This is the reward that shall be given to the man who finds him of whom Moses and the prophets did write, and receives and treats him according to his character. Let all such rejoice and be exceeding glad, for GREAT IS THEIR REWARD IN HEAVEN.

LONGING FOR THE APPEARING OF CHRIST.

How long, deai Saviour, O how long
  Shall we be left alone?
When shall our hearts break forth in song,
  And say, "the Lord is come?"

How long shall we on willows hang
  Our harps by Babel's stream?
Once we rejoiced aloud and sang,
  And Jesus was our theme.

We long to see thy smiling face,
  We long to hear thy voice,
We long to see a new-born race
  Aloud in God rejoice.

The day of doom is drawing near,
  We have no time to spare;
Let every one attend and fear,
  And live a life of prayer.

Oh! gracious God! appear this day, (night,)
  Make known thy power and grace,
And let thy word of truth, we pray, (and light,)
  Fill every heart with praise.

DEATH.

How solemn the sight we behold!
  How pale is the face of the dead!
The body is lifeless and cold,
  The spirit that warmed it, is fled.

The eyes are now sealed up in death,
  The hearing and speaking are o'er,
The lungs are deprived of all breath,
  The limbs move in order no more.

Farewell! fellow-mortal, adieu,
The grave is prepared for your bed;
Soon I shall be lifeless, like you,
And numbered, like you, with the dead.

When thro' the dark valley I go,
Oh, may my dear Saviour appear!
His presence would banish my wo,
His promise remove all my fear.

Let all who are living to-day,
Remember they shortly must die;
Which first will be summoned away?
My merciful God, *is it I?*

FREE GRACE.

If grace could reach the dying thief,
And persecuting Saul,
Could give to Magdalene relief,
And freely pardon all:

May not a sinner, such as I,
O thou forgiving God,
Who justly do deserve to die,
Find pardon in thy blood?

Before thy throne of grace, oh God,
Upon my bended knee,
I humbly pray this guilty load
May be removed from me.

The joy on earth, and joy in heaven,
Would be increased thereby;
"The lost is found—his sins forgiven,"
Would echo thro' the sky.

LOVE OF JESUS.

Jesus who reigns in heaven above,
His everlasting love flows free;
Thousands have richly shared his love,
And is there not a drop for *me?*

For sinners of the blackest dye,
He groaned and bled upon the tree;
"Father, forgive," I hear him cry!—
Perhaps that prayer availed for *me?*

He seeks the ruined souls of men,
  And gives them life and eyes to see;
And brings them to his fold again;—
  Who knows but what he'll gather *me?*

In all the sorrows of the saints,
  Their friend with them will always be,
To ease their troubles and complaints;
  And will he not deliver *me?*

When Satan roars, or death draws nigh,
  They have a refuge where to flee,
And when, like them, I'm call'd to die,
  O Lord, I pray, remember *me.*

THE BIBLE.—1836.

* * * * * * * * * * * * * *

WORDS, sentences, aphorsims, and customs that were significant, and well understood in the days of king James, are now out of use and obscure. Should there be a new translation, according to modern diction, is it not probable that two or three centuries hence it would be as obscure? And is there any hope of improving more from the original, when every century removes both Hebrews and Greeks farther off from understanding their respective languages as they were spoken in the days of the inspired authors?

Would a new translation of the Bible, according to the modern use of words, taken from the most ancient copies of the Old and New Testaments, give us certain information, without doubt, on the question which has perplexed the Christian world for many centuries, "whether Christ died for only a part, or for every soul of man?" Or is this a mystery, locked up in the treasures of God, in a book not to be read in until we go to another state? as the Jews do not allow their children to read the nine last chapters of Ezekiel, and the book of Daniel, until they are thirty-nine years old. But stop and ponder. Would a certain solution of this question make men any better in this world? If not, would it not be beneath the dignity of Jehovah, to reveal that to men which would be of no service to them?

* * * * * * * *

Would not a new translation of some passages in the New Testament, according to our present dialect and customs, be acceptable? In Matthew, x., 7: And as ye go, preach, saying, The kingdom of heaven is at hand. Read thus: And as ye go, preach to the people, your money is essential to the salvation of sinners, and, therefore, form into societies, and use all devisable means to collect money for the Lord's treasury; for the millennium is at hand. Mark, xvi., 16: He that believeth and is baptized shall be saved. Read: He that has attended Sunday schools, had his mind informed by tracts, contributed to support missions, and joined in societies to support benevolent institutions, shall be saved; the rest shall be damned. Matthew, x., 17: Be ye therefore, wise as serpents, and harmless as doves. Read: Be ye wise as serpents in your guile to deceive men; keep out of sight that ye have to receive part that you collect for your mendicancy; show great concern for poor benighted heathen, but let your neighbors have none of your prayers, exhortations, or alms; but strive to appear harmless as doves; put on gravity and holy awe; make others believe that ye are too devotional to labor for a living, and that they must labor to support you; for if you do not appear uncommonly holy, you will not deceive the simple and get their money. Acts, iv., 34–35: And brought the prices of the things that were sold, and laid *them* down at the apostle's feet, and distribution was made to every man, according as he had need. This work of receiving and distributing was soon after given to seven men of honest report, full of the Holy Ghost and wisdom. Acts, vi. 3: Would it not be better to read—The convention appointed a board of directors; any man who would cast into the fund one hundred dollars, should be one of them for life, to dispose of the money at discretion, and mark out the destination of the missionaries. Read Acts, xiii., 1, 2, 3, 4, and translate it thus, if the Greek will admit of it: Now there was at Antioch, a convention of Christians, and among them five directors; and as they fasted and prayed, they were moved to select two of them as missionaries, and when they had supplied them with a good outfit, and promised them liberal supplies, to make Christianity appear honorable among the heathen,—they sent them forth with a solemn charge to devise all means in their power to keep the money market open, and invent employment for thousands that were longing for agencies. Acts, xx., 33, 34, 35: I have coveted no man's silver or gold; ye, yourselves, know that these hands have ministered to my necessities, and to them that were with me; I have showed you all things, how that, so laboring, ye ought to support the weak, etc. These sentences are so little used in this day of great light, that a new translation is unnecessary.

In observing the course that Christianity is now taking, it reminds me of past events. At the close of the apostolic age, and the age of miracles, philosophy was resorted to for a substitute, and every art and science was called into requisition to make Christianity appear honorable in the eyes of worldly men. Schools and teachers, of various descriptions, were set on motion to weld cold iron and hot together. The persecutions against Jews and Christians, for denying the divinity of the Pagan gods, and the worship of idols, did not stop the gradual and ruinous assimulation of church and world together.

All things being ready, in the beginning of the fourth century, the union was consummated by Constantine the Great, who established Christianity for the religion of the empire, and suffered none but Christians to hold any offices of honor or profit, for whom he made great donations in salaries, temples, etc. At this change, the young preachers, and professors of Christianity greatly rejoiced, but the aged trembled with fear. From that day until this time, with partial exceptions, the Christian church (so called) has been governed by the laws of men. In all these Christian establishments, by legal force, there has been a great number of non-conformists; but they have been overpowered and reduced to oppression. sometimes to bloody persecutions.

To persecute the greatest fanatics, except for overt acts, is poor policy; it only inflames their zeal, and augments their numbers; but to persecute harmless, peaceable subjects because they do not believe what they cannot believe, and are so honest that they will not say they believe what they do not, is the work of bloody monsters, in the shape of man.

THE SABBATH EXAMINED

(NEVER BEFORE PUBLISHED.)

I HAVE never been able to find out on what part of the globe the Garden of Eden was planted. Geography gives no account of a spot whence four rivers take their rise. It is, therefore, most likely that the flood so changed the bed of rivers, that no such place exists. If it was at or near one of the poles, one entire day was as long as three hundred and sixty-five days are in the middle regions: of course God was six of our years in creating and forming the heavens and earth, and all things therein, and then ceased from his work the following year.

Solar years—lunar months—day and night are measured and established by monuments in the laws of nature. Weeks—watches—hours and moments have no fixed barriers in nature, but arose and exist, either by a revelation from God or the children of men. Years, months, and days are frequently found in the writings of Moses: *week* only in the affair of Laban and Jacob; and in that place of uncertain meaning. In Daniel, the seventy weeks are supposed to include four hundred and ninety years, taking a day for a year; but whether a week in either of those places intends seven days, I cannot tell. In any case, the *week* belonged to the calendar of men. God rested on the seventh day of *time;* no account of a *week*.

Though God rested on the seventh day, I have not yet found that he ever enjoined a rest from labor *on men* for more than two thousand years after creation; nor any account that men ever observed a sevendayrian rest, during that length of time, taking Enoch, Noah and Abraham among the rest.

The *solemn feast-day of the new moon* was ordained by a statute of the God of Jacob, in the days of Joseph in Egypt, (Psalms, lxxxi., 3, 4, 5,) before the Sabbath was appointed, (Exodus, xvi., 25,) and is placed on a level with the Sabbath, (Isaiah, i., 13: Coll. ii., 16,) etc.

The strict observance of the seventh day, as a Sabbath of rest, was enjoined on the children of Israel, with a penalty so severe that the transgressor was not to be fined, whipped or put out of the synagogue, but *surely* *put to death.** The passover, as well as the new moon, was appointed by an express precept, before the Sabbath, (Ex. xii., 24.

Very soon after the appointment of the Sabbath, it was incorporated into the laws of Moses, and became an integral part of the ten commandments, which were written by the finger of God, on tables of stone.

The law of Moses contains three parts. *First.* The ten commandments engraven on stone. *Second.* The sixty prècepts written in a book and sprinkled with blood, designed for the government of their commonwealth. *Third.* Their religious usages, containing bleeding victims, smoking altars, divers washings, and carnal ordinances; to be continued until what they prefigured should take place. Sometimes the whole of Moses' writings, without distinction, are called Moses, or *the law.*

When it first took rise, to call the ten commandments moral, distinct from the other parts of the law, or why it is continued, I cannot tell.

The word *moral* is not in the Bible, but it is a word of general use, in these days, and of a variety of meanings. In the religious department, it is used by many divines, to express *the eternal rule of right* which proceed from the relation that exists between God and men, and between man and man, and that will continue as long as the perfections of God and the faculties of men exist, without change, amendment or repeal. In this point of light I receive and use the word in my research.

Why men should pay more deference to the decalogue than to the other parts of the law, I cannot ascertain. True, the ten commandments were spoken aloud by God, amidst awful emblems of his power; so also the sixty precepts were written in a book, by a holy man of God, inspired by the Holy Ghost, and sprinkled with blood. When our Lord was asked by a lawyer, which was the first and great commandment, our Lord did not answer him from any of the ten commandments, but from Deut. vi., 5, and Levit., xix., 18, where Moses was not treating of the decalogue.

The *law of eternal right and equity* is seen running through the Bible like a golden cord, and is binding on all the progeny of Adam, whether they are favored with the oracles of God or not: but it never enjoins on man to do that which the laws of nature render impossible, nor does it ever give way to *absolute precepts.*

Many difficulties arise against the conclusion, that the fourth commandment, in the decalogue, was of moral obligation.

1. Moral obligations never intermit, but are every day, and all the time binding.

* There were twenty crimes punished by death in the laws of Moses, either by hanging, stoneing, or burning, viz: adultery, beastiality, blasphemy, cursing father or mother, enticing to idolatry, false prophesying, false swearing, idolatry, incest, kidnapping, murder, presumption, rape, Sabbath breaking, sacrificing to Moloch, smiting father or mother, sodomy, stubborness of a drunken son, whoredom of a priest's daughter, and witchcraft.

2. In the case of circumcision and the annual atonement, works were commanded, contrary to the prohibition of the fourth commandment. Would God, by an absolute precept defeat the principles of *eternal right*?

3. In Deuteronomy, v., 3, Moses says, "The Lord made not this covenant with our fathers, but with us, even us, who are all of us here alive this day." What words could be plainer, and what sense of them more judicious, than to believe that none of the fathers before Moses were under the obligations to keep the fourth commandment, (which was a part of the covenant that Moses was speaking of,) which would have been the case if it had been *moral* in its nature?

4. None of the laws of Moses were written and engraven in stones but the *ten commandments;* and yet it is expressly said, (2 Cor., iii., 7, 11, 13,) that the ministration of what was there written, is done away and abolished, which will never be the case with moral law.

5. The prophets of the Lord faithfully and abundantly reproved the *Jews* for Sabbath breaking; but while they point out the many crimes of the Egyptians, Moabites, Edomites, Assyrians, Ninevites, Chaldeans, Tyrians, and others, they never mention Sabbath breaking. The apostle of the Gentiles also draws a black picture of them. In Rom. i., 29, 30, 31, he lays to their charge twenty-two sins, but Sabbath breaking is not among the number. The like is true of Gal. v., 19, 20, 21, where seventeen sins are mentioned.*

6. The Sabbaths appointed by Moses were limited by evening. Whether the evening began at mid-day, at the setting of the sun, when the stars appeared, or at any other season, is immaterial: the Israelites, no doubt understood the expression used by their law-giver, *from evening to evening*. That it intends a whole day is evident. There has never been a minute since the fourth day of the creation, but what the sun has been rising—at his zeneth, and setting on the different parts of the globe. In a line of longitude, therefore, although the people round the globe might keep a day, the day would not be the same time to all. If the subject is viewed in a line of latitude, at or near the poles, there would be but one day in our year: of course the frigid nations would have but one Sabbath, while those

* The character which St. Paul gives of the Gentiles, previous to their receiving the gospel, and the faithfulness of the apostle to testify the whole counsel of God, forbid the conclusion, either that the Gentiles had never broken this law, (if it was binding on them,) or that Paul shunned to reprove them for this sin. The most natural result is, that the precept was not *moral*, but *absolute*, obligatory on the Jews, and on them only."

"As Jesus was made under the law, he submitted to it, and regarded the Sabbath; not in a mode that pleased the Pharisees and Rabbies, for by them he was often accused of Sabbath breaking; but in a mode that was pleasing to God."

"Let it be carefully noticed that the *first day of the week is never* called *Sabbath* in the New Testament." *Remarks on Holy Time, &c.*

of the middle regions would have three hundred and sixty-five.* Let a Mahometan, a Jew, and a Christian stand at any spot, and dispute about the holy day: the Mahometan says Friday—the Jew is for Saturday—the Christian pleads for Sunday: not agreeing in opinion, they part at variance. The Christian takes his course eastward and travels round the world, scrupulously keeping every Sunday for holy time. The Mahometan takes a western course, and, like the Christian, circumambulates the earth, rigidly observing every Friday. The Jew remains stationary, keeping every Saturday in Mosaic style. In a lapse of time the travellers return to the spot where the Jew was residing, and to their astonishment find the holy day of all was the *same day*. The Christian by travelling east had gained a day, and the Mahometan by going west had lost a day: every nine hundred miles gaining or losing an hour.

7. There is nothing in the starry heavens—in the atmosphere, or the productions of the earth, that marks one day in seven to be more holy than another. Should a man, in derangement of mind, lose time, (which often is the case,) when he returns to his reason he could never find the sanctified day by any fixed monument. This is the case universally, except in the double portion of manna given on the sixth day, and none on the seventh; which lasted but forty years.

8. The law of the Sabbath, when given by Moses, could be kept by all Israel. The tribes, in their encampment, did not cover a district, it is presumed, more than ten miles square; and after they took possession of Canaan, their whole country was but a very small part of the habitable world; of course they could all rest a specific day with ease, which would be impossible for all the nations of the earth to do.

9. The precepts of Moses were divinely binding on those for whom they were intended, for the length of time designed; and all of them that are evangelized in the New Testament are binding on Christians: the rest of them belong to the Jews, and other nations, and individuals to whom they were addressed, or have ceased by their limitation.†

10. All the ten commandments, except the fourth, are brought forward and enjoined in the New Testament. That there is one God to be worshipped—that idolatry must be forsaken—that the name of God must not be taken in vain, or blasphemed—that father and mother must be honored—that murderers have not eternal life—that stealing is criminal—that adultery is heinous—that covetousness and love of the world is abhorrent, are

---

* The sun is at all times partially and totally eclipsed in some of the regions of *space*, and the same is true of the moon.

† "What light these men" (the advocates of the first-day Sabbath) "view those nations in, who proceeded from Adam, but were not under the law of Moses, and have never heard of Christ, whether they are under divine obligation to keep the seventh day or the first day, I cannot tell, for they have never told me." *Remarks, &c.*

interwoven in *that* book*. But where shall we find a precept given by him who was greater than Moses—who was faithful in all his house, that his followers should abstain from labor and keep holy the seventh day of every week? or that the first day of every week should supersede the seventh, to be kept in remembrance of his resurrection? He appointed one meeting for his disciples on a mountain in Gallilee: and he appeared to above five hundred brethren at once; but on what day of the week I know not.

11. A day, limited by the unchangeable monuments of nature, could be observed by the nation of Israel in their section of country; but as the gospel was for all the world, no one day could be observed by the inhabitants at large. Would the blessed Jesus enjoin an impossibility upon his followers?

12. If the fourth commandment is *moral*, (still binding, without change or decay,) servants, cattle, and gates must exist forever, as long as the perfections of God and the faculties of men endure.

* * * * * * * *

13. The essential prerequisites of salvation are not hereditary, nor do they depend upon social union, but are affairs that lie between God and individuals; hence, a person in lonely solitude may possess those views and exercises of mind, and perform those works that are acceptable to God: yet God (who saw it was not good that man should be alone) has ordained the assembling of saints for religious worship, and marked out the rules of their devotion.

14. Men began to call upon the name of the Lord, (by publicly assembling, it is presumed,) A. M., 235. Some think that Abraham's three hundred and eighteen trained servants, were such as he had disciplined in the knowledge of God, who assembled with him at his altar. Jacob, in obedience to God, took his household, and all that were with him, and went to Bethel and worshiped God. But whatever may be said of the patriarchal age, the institutes of Moses appoint three solemn assemblies for every year, each to last seven or eight days, in which all the males of Israel were to be present; and many solemn assemblies beside. The seventh day Sabbath was appointed, with the awful penalty of death to the transgressor, to be observed as a day of rest, more than a day of worship.

15. That Christ was crucified on our *Friday* is generally understood. That he rose early on the first day of the week, our *Sunday*, is believed. Afterwards he was seen forty days, and then ascended, which was *Thursday*. Penticost being fifty days after the passover, was on *Saturday*. It is difficult to see any partiality shown to days in the great events of eternal redemption.

* * * * * * * * * * * * * *

17. There is a scattering class all over christendom, and in some parts

* See Romans, xiii., 9, and many other places.

they are numerous, who strictly regard the *first day* of every week, in obedience to the fourth commandment. They have changed the *seventh* day for the *first*, placed the resurrection of Christ for the object instead of God's rest and the deliverance of Israel from Egypt, altered the penalty from death to a small fine, changed a rest within their gates for a go-abroad to perform Christian worship, and added to the commandment "Except so much as is to be taken up in the works of necessity and mercy." But they have not told us who is to be the judge, to decide whether the works done on the first day are works of necessity and mercy, or not. Is the parent to be judge for the child? the church for its members? and the magistrate for the populace?—why a weekly day should be appointed to celebrate one event in the scheme of redemption and no day to commemorate other events, equally important, seems strange. If, however, there is a divine precept for it, our reasoning must be quiet: but where do we find the command, that the disciples of Christ should keep the first day of every week in remembrance of the resurrection of Christ? The class of Christians that I am now treating of, wherever they are numerous enough, make the observance of their first day an article of jurisprudence. The day is legalized, and the offender punished; regardless of the good maxim "That neither legislators, judges, nor jurors, in their official capacity, have any thing to do with souls and eternity; for where conscience begins, empire ends."

18. Another respectable sect is ever found in christendom who keep every *seventh* day of the week as holy time; believing that the fourth commandment is unalterable in its nature, and binding on all nations. Their motto is, "Do we then through faith make void the law? God forbid: yea we establish the law." They are as firm believers in the resurrection of Christ as those who keep the first day for a holy Sabbath, and acknowledge him as the only Saviour of men, but punish those who disregard their holy day with nothing but non-fellowship. They also appeal to the first centuries of Christianity for precedent as much as their first day brethren.

19. Among the rest there has been, and still is, a goodly number who believe the divinity of the fourth commandment, and the resurrection of the Lord Jesus, and worship him in private and in public, in spirit and in truth, who, nevertheless, believe that there is no sanctity in one day more than in another; they see that God blesses the assembled saints on one day of the week, as well as another, and that individuals have access to God, and receive the joy of believing, without a diary reckoning.

20. That many churches were formed in Judea, Samaria, and among the Gentiles, in the days of the apostles, is abundantly proved. In what manner they were separated from the world, and whether they had any budge that distinguished one church from another, except local situation, and unity of sentiment, is hard to ascertain. As we read of the *whole* church, the presumption is that each church knew her own members. The

inspired apostles, by word and epistles, gave much instruction to those churches—to the ministers raised up among them, and to all the scattered saints who were so located that they could not assemble with others.

21. As individuals, their right temper of mind and private devotion is described, their relative and civil behaviour is enforced, and their various duties, as members of churches, are imperiously enjoined.

22. There are duties enjoined on the disciples, when assembled together, that required *fixed days* for their performance. These days must be fixed by divine appointment, by legal authority, or by mutual agreement. When Christ and the apostles were on earth, the power of making laws was in the hands of the heathen, who were enemies of Christ, and opposed to his cause; and in their hands it continued until the fourth century. Of course, during that length of time, there could be no laws made to regulate Christianity, either in times or proceedings.

23. That Christ gave any command to his disciples to assemble every first day of the week in commemoration of his resurrection, is not to be found—but he had many things to say unto them which they were not able to bear, which he assured them, should be revealed to them by the spirit of truth, after his ascension. To the inspired writings of the Acts and Epistles of the apostles we therefore apply for aid, as our last and sure guide.

24. Acts xxi., 20.—Thou seest, brother, how many thousands of Jews there are which believe, and they are all zealous of the law. Acts xv., 21.—For Moses, of old time, hath in every city them that preach him, being read in the synagogue every Sabbath day. Galatians iv., 10.—Ye observe days, and months, and times, and years. From these texts, without any comment, it appears highly probable—almost certain, that the Jews, who embraced Christianity, assembled on the Sabbath, and not on the first day of the week. If our translation of the New Testament is correct, there is a marked difference between the Sabbath and the first day of the week.

25. The *order* which Paul gave to the churches of Galatia, reads thus: "Let him that is taught in the word communicate unto him that teaches in all good things. As we have, therefore, opportunity, let us do good unto all mem; especially unto them who are of the household of faith." Gal. vi., 6, 10.

This *order* he refers to and enjoins on the church of Corinth, in the following words: "Now concerning the collection for the saints, as I have given *order* to the churches of Galatia, even so do ye. Upon the first *day* of the week, let every one of you lay by him in store, as God hath prospered him, that there be no gatherings when I come." I. Corinthians xvi., 1, 2. (If any other order was given to the Galatians, it is not recorded.) This order to the Galatians had no respect to the time of doing, but to the work to be done; but to the Corinthians, the *time* (first day of the week) is particularly noticed. The work to be done was not reading the scriptures—preaching—exhortation—prophesying—praying nor singing, but laying by in store as God had prospered every one. The articles to be laid in store, were all good things; clothing, food and money, for the poor saints in Judea. Whether this work was to be repeated on the first *day* of more weeks than one, is not said. The business of the day seems to have been measuring, weighing, deducting, casting, and conveying the proceeds to the depot, that all might be ready for Paul to receive and carry to the poor saints in Judea. If a strained construction of the text can be admitted, it looks as if the Corinthians had voluntarily selected the first day of the week to meet together, to perform those duties which are of a social nature; which agreement Paul was acquainted with, and in order to economise time, he directs them to carry their donations with them to the place of their gathering together. This interpretation of the text, does not correspond with the views of those who believe in the sanctity of the first day of the week. To see every member of the church repairing to the place appointed for public worship, one carrying a bag of grain, another a luncheon of meat, a third a bundle of clothing, etc., etc., would appear a profanation of holy time to them.

26. Nothing appears more likely to me, than that the several churches appointed their own days to assemble together. The churches in Judea preferred their old Sabbath, the Corinthians the first day of the week, etc.; contiguous churches taking care to appoint different days, that men of leisure and piety might attend several meetings in a week. By this mode one preacher would do all the essential work that seven do on a different plan. Daily (not weekly) in the temple and in every house, they would not cease to teach and preach Jesus.

27. One man esteemeth one day above another—another esteemeth every day alike. Let every man be fully persuaded in his own mind.

The foregoing remarks are now written when I am more than 83 years old; but they contain the exercises, views and conclusions of my mind, when I was in the full vigor of those powers of mind which God was pleased to give me.

August, 1837.

28. The *preparation* was the day before the *Sabbath* in the feast of the passover. The day after the preparation, which was *Sabbath*, the elders and priests applied to Pilate for authority, and obtained a commission to make sure the sepulchure, seal the door, and set a watch, which they executed. How strange, that the men, who had so often condemned the Saviour for Sabbath breaking, should do it themselves!

29. Considering the laws of the states, and the long usages of this country, it is not probable that the suggestion made in the foregoing, (No.

26) will take effect until some revolution takes place in the religious department. The most that can be expected, is, that legislatures will cease making sabbatical laws, and churches decline making the observance of one day or another, or no day a test of fellowship ; leaving individuals to judge and act for themselves.

30. I have only to add, that in some of my writings that have been published heretofore, I have given more credit to the arguments in favor of the appointment of the first-day Sabbath, and its general observance, than I can now admit of.

June, 1838.

ADDRESS

DELIVERED AT BENNINGTON, AUG. 16, 1839.

WHETHER all events are predetermined, or a part or all of them are contingent, in either case they have succeeded each other, and brought the world into its present condition: some are in a state of splendor and freedom, and others in poverty and vassalage. The number of inhabitants in Europe is said to be 226,445,200—among whom are paupers, 18,897,333—beggars and dependent wretches, say 10,000,000, not as well clothed and fed as the slaves are in the United States. They are free only in name. In the United States there are 16,000,000 of inhabitants, of whom, in a state of slavery, are '2,000,000; paupers, say 30,000; mendicants, many; beggars, none. There is at this time considerable exertion made to have all the slaves in the United States emancipated. As I have lived fifteen years in a slave-holding state, and as my calling led me into the feelings of both master and servant, I will say a few words on the subject. To liberate them all by purchase would be a herculean job—average them at $100, and the sum would be $200,000,000. Among them, there would be half a million of decrepits and children, that must starve, or be added to the list of paupers. To support them with food and clothing, would be an annual tax of $25,000,000. This method of liberating them would throw an equal burden on those states and individuals that have had no profits from them, nor any interest in them.

The Israelites were slaves to Pharaoh, not to individuals; they were crown vassals; Pharaoh had the control of them; and, therefore, Moses went to Pharaoh, and demanded him to let them go. Where kings or governments establish and support a slave trade, they are responsible, and they can desist and reform. But the case in the United States is radically different. The present inhabitants, for the most part, had no hand in the traffic with Africa. Our present government makes it felony. Congress does not possess an individual slave. The slave-holders have never alienated them to government. How preposterous is it, then, to burden Congress with cart-loads of petitions to do that which they have neither the right nor power to do? The slave-holders are to be addressed: the power lies in them alone. It is not an article to be settled by legislation among us. It belongs to the *moral* and *religious* department, and not to the *legislative*. Three parties are concerned in the question, viz: God—the master—and the slave. As a friend to freedom and right, I earnestly recommend to masters to set their slaves at liberty as soon as their good, their choice, and the public safety concur. Until then, be good to them, remembering you have a Master in heaven, whose orders are, "Whatsoever you would that men should do unto you, do you even the same unto them." Make their lives as happy as circumstances will admit of. If there is a condition for them to be in, better than their present state, (where their masters are humane, just, and benevolent,) I pray the Lord, and call upon men, to bestow it upon them. With all deference to the opinions of others, I would recommend to the abolition orators to serve an apprenticeship of seven years in a slave-holding state to qualify their minds to view the question in all its bearings.

An Independent Treasury is now the order of the day. The public treasure must be placed in some depot. Our own government, (like all kingdoms, states, counties, and towns, have placed it in a treasury, over which a treasurer presides, who gives oath and bond for the faithful discharge of his trust. Not a cent of this treasure can be touched by the president, or any other man, without an appropriation of Congress—not a cent can the treasurer deal out to a friend without peculation. Would the public money be safer in the banks? The banks, by their corporate power, are so far irresponsible to the government and to the people, that they can suspend at pleasure, and withhold the money when it is the most needed, and say, "If your measures please us, we will aid you with money, but if not, you may help yourselves without money, if you can." Is this a state of things that Americans can submit to? Were it not that so many of the people in the states were bewitched with the banking system, I should boldly answer, NO. I have never yet seen why the collectors, receivers, and disbursers of the public money, should not be punished as felonious thieves, as well as degraded as breakers of trust, if they appropriate the money to any use not prescribed by law; nor do I see the moral justice for government to tell one man that his dollar shall be worth *three*, and another that his dollar shall count but *one*.

Young gentlemen, the time in which you live, and are destined to act your part in human affairs, is more propitious than the period of your fathers, who had to expel the enemy, establish our independence, and pay the vast debt incurred; all of which they have done, and left a rich inheritance to their children. Your eyes, your countenances, assure me that you are now resolving that you will not waste what your fathers have left you—but, by observing their sentiments, and imitating their manners, you will add thereto. Go on, and keep in view that truth, honesty, and industry, will conduct you through the world with reputation. Should any of you be poor, mind one rule—*let your expenses be less than your income, and never put off for to-morrow what should be done to-day.* Watch the measures pursued by the rulers. Legislative usurpation over the rights of individuals is as dangerous as executive patronage. Give in your votes at the polls with sentimental independence, and acquiesce in the result of the election. A majority may vote wrong, but the right of free suffrage will correct that error when it is made manifest.

OATHS.

Most of the following pieces, many of which consist of short unconnected fragments, were found in his portfolio after his death. Of many of them, the periods when they were written cannot be ascertained. Under these circumstances, the arrangement will unavoidably be, in some measure, promiscuous.

The Atheist acknowledges no God but *Nature*. That there is a Divine being that presides over the events of life; or that there is a state of future rewards and punishments, he does not believe; this leads many to think that the testimony of an Atheist should not be admitted as good evidence before a court of justice; because, (believing as he does,) he would as freely and fearlessly *lie*, as speak the truth.

But how is the matter to be managed? He comes to the stand before the court, and is asked, "Do you believe there is a God, and a state of future rewards and punishments? He will answer *yes* or *no*, as best suits him; but who will believe a word he says? If a hundred of his acquaintance appear and solemnly declare that they have often heard him say that there was no God, and no state of future rewards and punishments, perhaps at every time he lied; not one of the hundred knows that he ever spoke the truth. It is from *him*, and him *alone*, that the court must get the information, and get it from him, they cannot, for they cannot tell whether he speaks true or false.

Must then the testimony of an Atheist be rejected in every case, and he himself consigned to social oblivion; or is there any remedy to be found? Proscriptions, fines, or corporeal punishments, might make him play the hypocrite, but would not cure him of his infidelity, or make him a better man. * * * * * * * * * * *

Men are found with the natural right to use means to supply their own wants, and to defend themselves from the abuse of others. Hence the established saying, "self-preservation is natures first law." From this natural right, an association may invest their agents with power to provide and compel. In political association, each individual becomes bound to contribute as much of himself as is necessary for the good of the whole. The agents of the whole body, therefore, can require each individual to co-operate and compel him to disclose conspiracies against the whole, and what he knows of any ill design of one citizen against the life, liberty, or property of another. Oaths, at first, were solemn promises, made by one, or between two individuals or parties, without anv magistrate to administer them.

All nations have entertained a belief in a Supreme Deity, and that he would punish them, if they were perfidious. Having a consciousness of themselves, and evidence of others, that a great part of the conversation and promises was idle, deceptive, and false, whenever they made promises, treaties, or covenants, or gave testimony, in weighty concerns, they appealed to their God, believing that he would punish them if they were perfidious or false witnesses.

THE Deist, the Unitarian, the Anti-Trinitarian, the Arian, and Socinian, notwithstanding their difference of opinion in other things, all agree in this, that *Jesus Christ was not Jehovah.* The Deist forms his conclusion from reason and the fitness of things, to the jeopardy of the scripture. The others draw their opinion from the inspired volume, explained according to their views of reason and the fitness of things. These last I address.

Sirs, you cannot believe that *one* is *three* and that *three* are but *one* ; which you must do, if you believe in a trinity of persons in the divine essence ; to escape which absurdity, you deny that Christ is God essential. Is it not equally absurd to believe that *one* is *two*, and that *two* are but *one ?* And yet you believe the last without hesitancy. " And God called *their* names Adam—they two shall be one—they are no more twain, but one flesh."

You cannot believe that Jesus is Jehovah, because the union of two natures in one person, is inconceivable, inexplicable, and unreasonable ; you nevertheless believe that he was born of a woman who knew no man, which is equally inconceivable, inexplicable, and unreasonable, with the first.

You believe all the book of nature, but can you read the folded leaves ? How can men hear, see, speak, or think ? Why does the water run down hill ? Whence cometh, or whither goeth, the wind ? What occasions the involuntary motions of man ? Should Mount Vesuvius leave its station, and leap to Etna, and settle upon its fiery top, you could account for it as well as you could for the voluntary motion of your hand from one knee to the other. Ten thousand times ten thousand things you believe, on rational evidence, which you can no more account for, than you can for the hypostatical union of Jesus Jehovah. Who doubts the complexity of man ? and yet, who can draw the line with precision, that separates the rational and animal empires? Or who can describe the cord that binds spirit and matter together?

In an age like the present, when great exertions are made to meliorate the condition, and improve the mind of the human family, we feel it an imperious duty to contribute our aid for the promotion of the piety, peace, and happiness of mankind. And as it appears to us that there are a number of vices, that none of the societies have undertaken to withstand, we hereby enter our protest against those vices, and pledge ourselves to show and avoid them, and use our best endeavors to eradicate them from among men.

1*st.* We enter our solemn protest against falsehood, and every species of deception. The tongue, which is the glory of man, is often used, with the aid of the press, for the vilest of purposes. Our avocations are various, our standing in society diverse. As *sellers*, we will not extol our articles for sale, beyond our best judgment, nor hide their defects for the sake of advantage, nor in any way seek to deceive the ignorant, nor extort from the needy.

As *purchasers*, we will not, for the sake of our own interest, run down the articles of sale below the common price, or deceive the seller, by telling him how much cheaper the articles can be obtained in another place; but every one of us will speak the truth to his neighbor. We, moreover, will not purchase on credit, without a reasonable prospect that we can meet our engagements; and when we have engaged, we will be punctual and honest, that we may owe no man any thing.

As *mechanics*, we will be faithful in materials, and workmanship, not covering either of them to deceive, by paint, putty, or lavish applause; taking no advantage of the ignorant.

As *day-laborers*, we will be trusty and industrious, that the employer may have full tale of profit for the wages he gives.

As *employers*, we will not require an over rate of labor, keep back the wages, pay with offal, nor in any way grind the poor, but pay them full measure, running over.

The want of *truth* in communication, and the want of *punctuality* in promises, are religious and national evils, which bring great calamities on church and state. What is the reason, when so many societies are formed to effect a moral reform, that *truth* and *punctuality* should be neglected? Is the answer given in sacred style, "Being convicted by their own conscience, they went out one by one, beginning at the eldest, even unto the last," or what is the cause? If the forming of societies to effect a reform, in *word* and *deed*, is not acceded to,* let individuals, each for himself, bend their necks to the yoke. In the pulpit, in the hall of legislation, in the range of commerce, in the public prints, at the fireside, and at all other places, *truth*, without addition or diminution, should be regarded more than wealth, rank, or any thing that can be named. In this day of boasted *benevolent institutions*, which cost hard labor, and millions of dollars to support, (called the morning of the Millennium,) but little reliance can be placed on the *words* of the seller, and less on the *promise* of the buyer. My brethren, these things ought not to be. Wherefore, putting away lying, speak every man truth with his neighbor, and pay your vows. Owe no man any thing.

A short comment on 2 Corinthians, i. 17, 20.

WHEN *I therefore, was thus minded*, that you should have a second benefit, and had sent on appointments to be with you, *did I use lightness*, as if it was a trifling matter whether I came or not? *Or the things that I purpose, do I purpose according to the flesh?* as some do, making their ministerial engagements subservient to their own ease and gain; failing in their promises, when a punctual compliance would be contrary to their fleshy schemes. *That with me there should be yea, yea, and nay, nay?* That I should promise again and again, and fail as often, having no sacred regard for my appointments and promises. *But as God is true*, and cannot lie, and never fails in his promises, *so our word toward you was not yea and nay.* Our promises we punctually performed—our conversation was true, and our preaching simple, without contradiction. *For the Son of God, Jesus Christ, who was preached among you by me, Silvanus and Timotheous, was not yea and nay, but in him was yea.* However others may have preached among you, that the Son of God failed in his promises, and from that view of Christ, were led to imitate him, with a yea for a promise, and a nay for accomplishment; yet with us it was the reverse. *For all the promises of God in him, are yea, and in him amen.* God made many promises to the nation of Israel, to individuals, and Gentile nations, (see Jer. 18,) on conditions. If those conditions were not performed, the promises, on God's part, failed; but the promises of the

* If, as many think, the principle of forming societies of mixed characters, distinct from churches, for the ostensible design of the suppression of vice and the spread of the gospel, has no scriptural support; but if the natural tendency of it is to unite the church with the world—make striped-pig moralists—lucrative preachers, and pharesaical proselytes to Christianity; yet the self-dedication of individuals to God, to worship him in spirit, and rejoice in Christ Jesus, is essential to salvation.

new covenant, made to Christ, and to men in Christ, *all* of them will be accomplished; not to the support of licentiousness, but *to the glory of God.*

THE kingdom of ME, is occupied partly by ignorant, ambitious, bragadocios, and partly by wise, prudent, and humble men. The first are lavish in telling what they know, what they have done, and what they can do. The last know their own ignorance, feel their weakness, see errors in what they have done, and find *veritas in puteo,* (truth lies in a well,) and is difficult to acquire. And when any popular or profitable act results, they will be more ready to give the praise to others, than to themselves.

To fill a discourse with "*I* said," and "*I* did," is considered pedantic among the fashionable. But this rule has undeniable exceptions. The character of David is given in glowing language:—"David is cunning in playing, and a mighty valiant man, and a man of war, and prudent in matters, and a comely person, and the Lord is with him." Yet this very man who was raised to high degrees, and was a man after God's own heart, was full of *I*-otism. In the book of Psalms, the pronominal *I*, is found almost eight hundred times.

PAUL, the chief apostle of the Gentiles, who had much wisdom given him, like David, speaks in his epistles, abundantly in the first person. In two chapters only, Rom. vii., and 1 Cor. ix., the *I* is found more than sixty times; yet neither David nor Paul can be justly reproached as coxcombs, or superanuated egotists. Neither of them speak in the first person to aggrandize ME.

Logical and metaphysical reasoning often lead the mind (through its weakness) astray. Time and close observation on the tendency and result of opinions and measures, will correct those hasty mistakes: the man therefore, whose mind has grown mellow, by seeing, hearing, and observing, will express himself, "What *I* have seen, what *I* have heard, wherein *I* have been deceived, how *I* was delivered, and what *I* now believe," without any desire of vain glory.

While I am writing, my thoughts are running. I have been preaching sixty-five years, and upon the closest examination, I find that I have studied more to be acceptable unto men, than to be approved unto God, (lamentable truth!) The ears and thoughts of others have governed me too much, and pressed me unto the kingdom of ME. Often, when I am preaching, the question will rise in my mind, How does my preaching sound in the ears of the hearers? What thoughts have they of me? Do they esteem me a man of talents or not? Do they think me a great divine, and very pious, or what do they think of ME? (Proofs of moral pollution!)

I was once in company with a brother preacher, whose claim to holiness, and having the spirit of prophecy was high. As we preached in *Co.*, he generally obtained (what he ever deserved) the premium of being the *best preacher*, which he bore with graceful modesty. In rare instances, however, the people, (for want of judgment and taste,) would give the premium to me. When that was the case, I judged by his symptoms, he felt as I have, when I have just caught a glimpse of a red apple slyly going by me, and dropped into the hands of one more esteemed. My conclusion was, that until I loved my neighbor as myself, and esteemed others better than myself, I should not think myself so far removed from the kingdom of ME, but that I could feel the force of its winds.

"BELOVED, believe not every spirit, but try the spirits, whether they are of God; because many false prophets are gone out into the world. But there were false prophets among the people, even as there shall be false teachers among you."

It is supposed that there are (among the many sects of Christians) nearly half a million of teachers: that many of them are false prophets, the texts quoted give reason to fear. Instead of condemning others, whose hearts and motives I do not know, I have great searchings of heart lest I am one of the false teachers and deceitful workers. *Lord is it I?* Have I been preaching sixty-five years to be noted—to escape hard labor—for honor—to head a party—for filthy lucre—or any other motive except obedience to God, being constrained by the love of Christ? If so, though I may have confidence at last to say, Lord, Lord, open to me, and tell what wonderful works I have done, the denunciation will follow. "Depart from me, for I never knew you."

I am conscious that abundance of selfishness and imperfection has afflicted me through all my exertions, and that all my works, as well as my soul, need washing in the blood of the Lamb; yet, amidst all, I have a faint hope that the efficient spring in my heart is, love to God—love to the gospel—and love to the souls of men. As far as I can know myself, if money was to lose all its value, it would not stop me from preaching; and if all the fruits of the earth were cut off, like Habakkuk, I would rejoice in the Lord. But I judge not myself; he that judgeth me, is the Lord.

A and B began the world on a level—they enjoyed equal health and freedom from adversity thirty years; yet A grew rich, while B was very poor. B wished A to tell him the cause of it: A replied, the cause is found in two words, "*come* and *go*." When I have work on hand, or business to transact, I say to others, "come." I lead in the business, and never quit until all is well done. I take the negro's remark for my guide, "Where massa go, all go." But when you have work on hand, you are not ready, and say to others, "go." As you stay behind, the others loiter. Night comes on, and the work is not finished, and thereby the profits are generally diminished. Your accounts and settlements are put off for more convenience, and thereby become questionable and contentious. Losses or law-suits follow, and poverty becomes unavoidable.

C was a preacher, but in the spirit was in the back ground; very orthodox in sentiment, but barren of holy zeal. Let him use what words he would, his soul was not in the work of the Lord. He would often say, "*go* to Christ," but to his hearers he appeared like a way-board, to point the way, but not walk in it. D had but a small head of water, but was stationed on a living stream. The love of Christ so constrained him that he waited not for invitations or stipulated proposals, but went forth preaching, "Repent and believe the gospel—I pray you, in Christ's stead, be ye reconciled to God," etc. Having the love of Christ and being *in* Christ, his language was, "Come to Christ, and taste and see how good the Lord is."

THE BOOK OF JOB.

In what age of the world Job lived, is hard to tell. As his sons were housekeepers, before his afflictions began, we will allow him to have been sixty years old; after this he lived one hundred and forty years; by this rule, he was two hundred years old when he died; from which one might conclude that he was contemporaneous with, or before Abraham: but he did not live until after government was established that punished men for idolatry and adultery; and after the arts of printing, engraving and book-keeping were understood in the world: see chap. xxxi., 11, 28, and xix., 23, 24. From this it looks as if he did not live until after Moses. But in whatever age of the world he lived, he was the richest man in the east, and the best man on earth. Yet, neither his wealth nor his piety secured him from the most excruciating afflictions. The loss of his property and family he bore with saint-like fortitude and acquiescence, to a degree that has gained him the title of the most patient man that ever lived. "In all this, Job sinned not, nor charged God foolishly." He was next attacked with personal affliction—smitten with sore biles from the sole of his foot to the crown of his head; but still he retained his integrity and sinned not with his lips.

On hearing of his calamity, his three old friends, Eliphas, Bildad and Zophar, made an agreement to visit him in his distress, and bemoan and comfort him. They were accompanied by young Elihu, who, in the event, acted as stenographer. When they beheld his great distress, they gave full vent to their sympathy, and sat down with him on the ground, and watched in painful silence seven days. Job then broke silence, and opened his mouth, and cursed the day of his birth, and spake unadvisedly with his lips. This speech caused a long debate between him and his friends. The question in debate was on *sovereignty* and *contingency*. Job maintained that God afflicted him, when he had been guilty of no specific crime. His friends contended, that God was righteous and would not afflict without cause; and, therefore, that Job must have been guilty of some enormous wickedness, which brought the heavy curse upon him; but could not specify what wickedness he had done, and support the charge. Had the friends of Job heard what God said to Satan, "although thou movest me against him to destroy him *without cause*," perhaps they would have been less censorious.

The book of Job is a true journal of the debate between Job and his three friends. The truth of the *journal* is no proof that all or *any* of the *speeches* were *true*. The debate was conducted partly by interrogations, and partly by bold assertions, and in both of which much satire and hard bearing on character is seen. Conquer a man by bold assertions and *you kill* him, but conquer him by asking questions, and you make *him* kill *himself*. As Job was but *one* to *three*, it reminds us of Patrick Henry, in the Virginia legislature and convention, combatting the great Dons of that state. The speakers borrowed similes from all creation—used all the figures of rhetoric—enlisted all the passions of the mind, and spoke with all the pomp of diction that the eastern world afforded. Their speeches were awfully sublime, covered with a little obsenity, like the effusions of John Randolph. When they introduce any creature or thing to elucidate their arguments, they would treat of it in all its qualities and ramifications, and seem to forget the object before them, like an old man telling a story; so many circumstances occur, that he loses the track.

How long the war of words lasted, is uncertain. Job made eight speeches, Eliphas three, Beldad three, and Zophar two. They all appear to have been men of great research and eloquence, but they ended as they began, without a reconciliation in sentiment. What appeared to the others clear as sunshine, to Job looked as dark as midnight, and *vice versa*.

The error of Job appears to be this: he was so zealous to clear himself from the false charges of his friends, that he lost sight of his own blindness and pollution in the sight of a wise and holy God. His three friends ceased their replications, seeing him so righteous in his own eyes. During the debate, young Elihu sat by, a close observer, and probably kept a record of their speeches: but when the debate ended, he was much displeased with Job for justifying himself rather than God, and as much with the others, for accusing Job of defects which they failed to substantiate. He was determined, therefore, to show his opinion. His fervency at the beginning reminds us of M'Duffie in his exordiums, but as he claimed inspiration of God, by which he was made *perfect in knowledge*, and spake by the *movings of the spirit*, our thoughts turn to Fisher Ames, who in his celebrated speech in Congress, said he was unwell, but trusted the Lord would strengthen him. Elihu was a handsome speaker, like Mr. Wirt, but did not dress his speeches with fine clothes so much that the body could not be seen. But his *inspired eloquence*, (as he is not implicated with the others, we are willing to acknowledge his claims,) did no more to humble Job, and cause him to repent in dust and ashes, than the human eloquence of the others.

God, who spake to the fathers in *divers manners*, now appeared to Job in a whirlwind, and spake out of it, in a manner that Job understood, convincing him that although he was clear of what his friends had accused him of, he was a weak, ignorant, polluted sinner, darkening counsel by words without knowledge. And Job confessed that he had uttered things which he knew not, and repented, in dust and ashes, for his vileness.

"I have heard of thee by the hearing of the ear, but now mine eye seeth thee;" the language here used would justify the belief that God revealed himself to the eye of Job, in a human form, as he did to Abraham, Jacob, and others; in this view of the subject, what he heard in the whirlwind began, and what he saw with his eye, completed his humiliation.

How pitiable the case of Job! Stripped of all his property—deprived of his family—smitten with sore biles—sitting on ashes—tantalized by his friends—reproved by Elihu—and now called upon by God himself, to answer to him for what he had said.

Before honor is humility. As soon as Job was properly humbled, the Lord honored him. His friends were made to succumb, and bring their offering, and the prayer of Job for them was accepted, and their folly, in not speaking of God the things that were right, as Job had done, was forgiven. Yet Job had not always spoken right: God accused him of darkening counsel by words without knowledge, and he confessed it; but, on the whole, he had spoken better than his friends.

After his afflictions, the Lord greatly blessed his latter end; he lived one hundred and forty years, and saw his posterity to the fourth generation.

How long the debate lasted between Job and his three friends, together with the remarks of Elihu, and the solemn declaration of the Almighty out of the whirlwind, is not known, but the history of it is not as long as some of the speeches made in Congress by individuals, and yet there are seven, if not seventy times seven more ideas in it, than in one of the best speeches ever delived on the floor of Congress; which shows that the hand of God was in it, notwithstanding Job was sometimes presumptuous, and his three friends were guilty of folly.

Granting that Elihu was the writer of this book, (for it cannot be proved,) we may suppose that he kept a record of what each one said, together with a minute of his own speech, and after the death of Job, he finished the book. It is difficult to decide whether any of them heard what God said to Job, together with what Job replied, but Job himself. If not, the Lord must have revealed it to Elihu, at that time, or when he wrote the book. The book contains forty-two chapters, including 17,985 words. No man's memory would be a safe depository for all this, one hundred and forty years, or one hour. The inspiration and superintendence of God must be recognized in the whole affair, whether written by Elihu or any other man.

To this I add, there is one of the clearest proofs of the resurrection of the body given in this book, that is to be found in the Old Testament.

DREAMS.

"The prophet that hath a dream, let him tell a dream."

Fifty years ago, I had the following dream. I stood by the side of a large, rocky mountain, with a projecting cliff shelving over my head. Through this cliff a hole was drilled, leading directly from the sun to my head; my direction was to ascend in that hollow. As I ascended, the hole grew less and less until I got stuck fast. Struggling to get loose, I found I had a staff in my hand, which I knew not of before. Placing the lower end of the staff in a niche of the rock, by struggling and squeezing hard, I got through. When I had gained the summit, I thought I was on Mount Zion, where the temple was built. I then cast down the staff, and here my wonder began.

The staff appeared to be about six feet long, very carelessly shaved with a drawing knife. On every flat, where the knife had cut off the bark, was a text of scripture, written in Hebrew characters. While I stood looking at the staff, a loud voice from above my head, proclaimed the following words: "that is the staff that was given to Abraham, when he left Ur of the Chaldees—Abraham left it with Isaac—Isaac with Jacob—Jacob carried it into Egypt and left it with Joseph, in whose family it was preserved until Moses, who availed himself of it, and by it did all his miracles."

On this I awoke, and finding my mind on the alert, I rose, lighted the candle, and took my Bible to see if there was any probability that a family staff had been preserved four hundred and fifty years. To me it did not appear likely—less likely that Moses should have been in possession of it, when a fugitive in Midian. The best conclusion I could form, was, that it was an emblem of the PROMISE made to Abraham, that *in him and his seed all the nations of the earth should be blessed.* This promise is abundantly spoken of, and runs through the scriptures like a golden cord. Whether it is called a *covenant*, a *testament*, a *promise*, or by any other name, it intends the assurance of salvation through Christ to all who believe in him. *If ye be Christ, then are ye Abraham's seed, and heirs according to the promise.*

The improvement to myself was, that I should have to pass through strait places—endure much tribulation—scarcely saved—and saved alone by the promise of eternal life, through Christ the Lord.

JULY 21, 1839. This day my daughter, Fanny, had a visionary dream, in which she saw me sitting in a great chair, clothed in a white robe, and on each side of me a young woman clothed in white, somewhat reclining and looking on me, and singing in a strain more melodious than she had ever heard before. Four times over they sung, "attendant angels long have waited:" on this she awoke.

In October 1811, I was sick of the typhus fever; in the height of which, two angels or spirits apeared, (at least to my imagination,) and stood stationary near my bed, and seemed to watch over me three days and nights, and when the fever abated, they disappeared. My persuasion was strong then, and has continued until now, that they were the souls of John Waller and William Webber, (preachers in Virginia, when I lived there,) with whom I was strongly united, and who were at that time both dead. Nearly three years after this, I was in Virginia, where Waller and Webber had lived. After I had finished a sermon, in Spottsylvania, a nephew of Waller, (Absalom Waller,) rose up and wished for the attention of the people, and said, "you all know that we had heard that brother Leland was dead; but some time past, I dreamed that I was admitted into heaven, where I saw my uncle John and brother Webber. I asked them where brother Leland was? They replied, that Leland had not joined them yet, but they were waiting for his arrival. "This," continued young Waller, "convinced me that Leland was not dead, and that we should see him again in Virginia."

There seems to be some relation between Waller's dream and those impressions which I had in 1811. What a wonder of benevolence, that God's host of angels should be all ministering spirits, to minister to the heirs of salvation. In their nightly slumbers, and dangerous walks and pursuits, the angels stand sentinel over the saints, nor end their mission, until they conduct the departed souls of the righteous to Abraham's bosom. How unworthy I feel to be the charge of celestial angels! how much more so, to be loved and saved by the God of angels.

—

THE following lines owed their origin to the circumstances first related, in the foregoing fragment.

ADDRESS OF ANGELS AT THE DYING BED OF A SAINT.

ATTENDING angels long have waited
To convey their brother home;
Thousands, thousands we've escorted,
But in heaven there yet is room.
We've been watchful o'er your dangers
Guarded round your bed by night,
Midst your friends and utter strangers
We have had you in our sight.

On the wild tempestuous ocean
Thunders roar and lightnings glare,
Heaven and earth in dread commotion,
Still we had you in our care;
On the bed of pain and sickness
When death stared you in the face,
We inspired your heart with patience,
Cheered you with the hopes of grace.

Many dangers stood before you,
Which you had no eyes to see,
From those dangers we preserved you,
Saved your life and set you free;
To the heirs of God's salvation
We administer relief,
Give to God your adoration,
We are brethren with yourself.

Now we've come with special orders,
To convey you far away,
Quit, oh quit these mortal borders,
Stretch your wings and leave your clay,
Attending angels wait no longer,
Now they take the blood-washed prize
Filled with heavenly joy and wonder
Now they soar above the skies.

Most of the affairs of a church, are effected by church votes; and as there is nothing imposed by such votes, but a simple declaration of what the church approves or disapproves, a revision, or re-consideration of such votes, (when circumstances change, or new light appears,) becomes necessary.

But there are some of the transactions of a church, which have the nature of an agreement of parties; in which the church collectively forms one party, and a few of the members, or an individual, forms another party. These agreements require more security than the mutability of church votes.

Supposing a church should undertake to build a meeting house. In the course of their arrangements, many votes would be taken, to get the sense of the whole. At length, the church employs three of her own members to build the house for a certain stipulated sum. In this stipulation, the church forms one party, and the three workmen another. After the work is done, can the church, in justice, revise their agreement, change the time and mode of payment, or alter, or erase, a single word of the agreement? Would not the words of Paul apply, in this case, with irresistible force? "Though it be but a man's covenant, yet if it be confirmed, no man disannulleth, nor addeth thereto."

Or, suppose a church agree with one of her own members to preach a year for them, for a certain sum. Can the church, by votes, disannul the agreement? In either of these cases, should any one suggest to the church, that they might revise their agreement with the three workmen, or the preacher, would he not be a busy body in other men's matters? If the church, in this case, should doubt their right to interfere with an old agreement, and some of the members should intimate that if the church would not proceed to revise their old agreement, they would quit their places in the church, * * * * Unfinished.

Theomachy, or the war of the Gods with the Giants.

1. The gods, boasting of their numbers, knowledge, and duration, resolved to disgrace and cripple Jupiter, who was supreme above them, and after several months loading and ramming their cannon, (called Resolution,) they gave blast, and were more fortunate than Lawrence, for their cannon went off. The report was horrendous, but there was no constitutional or legal ball in the cannon; of course, Jupiter remained unhurt—not a hair of his head was singed. The result of the skirmish was as follows: "We, as a number of individuals, resolve that Jupiter is a usurping tyrant, and if the people will not degrade Jupiter, and raise one of us above

him, (we hardly know which, for we all want the pre-eminence,) we will do all we can to embarrass the government, and ruin the people."

This is the boast of the gods.

The giants, though overpowered, are not disheartened. Having gained new recruits, they conclude that they can outflank the gods. Flushed with the hopes of success, they have set the battle in array, with "death or victory," on their caps, and "the honor of Jupiter," for their watch-word. The events of war are uncertain; but from the advantage of the ground which the giants occupy, and their fixed determination to conquer, the prospect is, that they will "expunge" the gods from their usurped station. Should this take effect, the boast of the giants will be: "We told you so; and have established our characters as men of foresight; by measuring strength, we have conquered you, huzza! For Argus, with his hundred eyes, cannot see that the explosion of the cannon did Jupiter any harm; or that this expunge will do him any good. No individval will esteem him more or less, for the whole bluster.

Oh yes! much harm and good! should the roaring of the cannon not be silenced by an expunge, the precedent of God-like usurpation, left on fair record, would make the practice common in future.

It has ever appeared strange to me, that democrats should pay so much reverence to precedents. When government makes a constitutional contract with an individual, a company, or with another government, the covenant, in justice, cannot be annulled without the consent of both parties; but an act, passed on the common rule of legislation, can be repealed as easy as it was made; for one legislature cannot bind a succeeding legislature, possesed with equal powers. Precedents have no power to withstand decided majorities. The ballot-box decides whether the law shall be repealed, and the precedent abandoned, or not.

2. My neighbor, Sconce, had among his poultry, two cocks, one was called Red-wing, and the other Double-comb. These crowing combatants were often in battles; sometimes one drove the other, at other times, the conquerer fled before his master. Sore heads, and ambitious hearts, afflicted them both; but finally, Double-comb subjected Red-wing, and took the undisputed possession of the ground. His triumph, however, was short; a young chicken, called Hotspur, of the game blood, grew up, who attacked Double-comb, and vanquished him, allowing him but small limits in the prison yard.

3. A decided and victorious majority, includes numbers, wealth, and talent. Money has power, and talent has art. Poverty weakens the dependent, and ignorance gives up to the art of the subtle; hence, (even in elective governments,) the smaller number may rule the larger. By these means, a large part of the world are now groaning in poverty and vassalage, to pamper others in grandeur, and support them in tyranny. Should

the halcyon day ever come, when the men of wealth and talent shall retrace their steps, and unite to relieve the oppressed, to explain to them their rights, and secure them in the enjoyment of them, it will be an infinitely greater blessing to the human family, than the late inventions to soar vehicles in the heavens, drive carriages through the earth, and propel vessels on the sea, by the *power of steam*.

4. Words are somewhat indefinite in their meaning, and therefore the same diseases of the body, change their names. We formerly heard of the *honorary* fever, the *lucrative* fever, the *ambitious* fever, the *aristocratic* fever, the *revengeful* fever, etc. But now, in this day of improvement and patent rights, all are included in the name of *White House fever.* This fever has a number of symptoms, as the senatorial, the secretary, the ambassador, the commissioner, the judiciary, the military, with other more feeble symptoms; none of which are dangerous, unless the diseased person fixes his eyes on the White House, with as much intensity as the drunkard fixes his eye on the bottle, or as Eve did on the apple; but if that irresistible charm affects the patient, in many cases it proves fatal. During the rage of this fever, in the last stages, the affected talk much, void much bile, and require watchers day and night.

A HUDDLE OF THOUGHTS.

ABOUT the year 1785, Messrs. Rumsey and Fitch memorialized the legislature of Virginia, for aid to navigate the Ohio by fire and steam. I did not then think that I should ever see the heavens scaled, the ocean ploughed, and the earth skated over by steam.

In the beginning of the federal government, when the revenue failed to meet the expenses of government, and pay the interest on the debt, at the rate of one million dollars per annum, I concluded that my body would be rotten centuries before the debt would be cancelled. Who could have thought that Americans would so soon have been bewitched to neglect their true interest of cultivating the ground, and laboring in their shops, for wild speculations, which have reduced themselves, and the states, into a debt twice as large as that of the United States was in 1796, and now are howling to saddle their debts on the general government.

I have known a time when the origin, design, extent, and limitation of government, were the articles of study and conversation of the people, out of doors, and in the chambers of legislation; and every measure was tested according to its bearings on the fundamental principles; and I have dreamed of a time when those principles were considered useless, and every measure was applauded or rejected, according to its bearing on elections.

I have wished to see the time, when legislators would apply themselves to the work of expeditious legislation, without unnecessary speeches, and leave elections with the people, and when any unusual question comes before them, not specifically provided for in the constitution, let moral honesty, economy, and public safety be their guide. In the long and flowery speeches, resembling a butterfly, with large painted wings and little body, designed for stenographers and printers, I have wished that the speakers would regard the *whole* truth, and not, by good words and fair speeches, deceive the readers by partial or false statements, with party views. What painful sensations the great class of laborers feel, when they see their honored agents wasting week after week, in blowing hot breath, uttering hard speeches, and blasting gunpowder at each other. Is not this degrading to our institutions, and a stain upon popular government? Can any true hearted republican approve of it? In the reign of king Richard, it was usual for members of parliament to box each others' ears, when a difference arose; a very barbarous custom, but far more humane and polite than the duel.

To form a government so perfect, that the rulers can have ample power to do all necessary good, and yet, have it so counterpoised, that they can do no harm, is beyond the constitution of the *moral world*; but every step toward it should be trodden, and every deviation therefrom, should be shunned.

Oaths, bonds, securities, fines and punishments, have all been defeated by ambition, cupidity, or revenge. But when men of reputed honesty and honor, are selected, and guarded by oaths, bonds, &c., it is all the security attainable. If fraud, or insolvency follow, the loss has to be bourne with. Men, like Achan and Judas, Arnold and Swartwout, are too often found in all ranks.

That men, equally honest, may differ in opinion, and that an honest man may change his opinion, are both admitted; but when men veer about, without any substantial reasons, what shall we think? Those who oppose the sub-treasury scheme, say it gives the president dangerous power, which he ought not to be trusted with; but in the late affray on the north-eastern boundary, they were not afraid to entrust ten millions of dollars, and fifty thousand men to his discretionary control.

One of the opening wedges that split the line of the Hamilton and Jefferson administrations, was the *United States Bank*; and yet, we hear many, who are advocates for the bank, declaring themselves to be the only true Jeffersonians; who believes them? So, some hold to election, and preach free-will.

It is difficult to show any radical difference between the Jeffersonian administration, and the Jacksonian, (which is now in train)* but the fairest

* He undoubtedly means its principles were being carried out, as the administration itself had ceased long before the date of this.

arguments, supported by facts, are feeble defences against fixed propensities.

I have never been able to see any definite power given in the constitution to the general government, to incorporate a bank; nor do I believe that one in ten thousand, of the people who ratified the constitution, thought of such a thing as a bank. The states were strictly prohibited from emitting any bills of credit, but under the inventive secretaryship of Mr. Hamilton, the bank sprung up, like a miseltoe in the crotch of a tree, and no one knows where it comes from.

The world is gorged with school, creed, and ceremonial religion; action and money are enlisted in the cause. But after all the institutions of men, "Pure religion, and undefiled before God and the Father, which is, to visit the fatherless and widows in their affliction, and to keep unspotted from the world," is but little seen and practiced. Societies are formed, at great expense, to convert the East Indians from the horrid practice of *immolation*. Why should not the Hindoos feel as much interested to send their priests to America, to convert Christians from the murderous crime of *duelling?* Alas! must the city of Washington and its environs, be the slaughter-pen for human victims?

The *let alone* policy may be extended too far, but to crowd questions into the legislative department, that belong to the empire of *common sense*, human courtesy, persuasion, individual rights, or religion, is being at an expense to establish tyranny.

The late address of Gov. Morton, is fraught with the intelligence of a Jefferson, and the moral courage and decision of a Jackson. He has pointed out the embarrasment of the commonwealth—what led thereto—and the means of extrication. The people have set him to guard their rights and liberties, and defend them from dangers, and yet have so cramped him in the legislature and council, that he may exclaim, "You set me to hunt the snake, and when I find him, you hold my arm and will not let me kill him." He can, however, instruct by counsel, and check by veto.

If I was omniscient and infalliable, I could fix a standard for individuals, preachers, churches, and states; or, if I was inspired by Him who professes those sublime attributes, I could give a perfect directory to all. But I neither possess nor claim those endowments; contrariwise, I find myself incapable to fully understand the directory which God has given to man. Instead, therefore, of being a dictator to others, I have to dig and beg for myself.

February 23, 1840.

The first part of the following poem was published many years ago in the *Budget of Scraps*, but as the Ms. was found to contain many additional lines, it is thought proper to insert it among the posthumous pieces. The original title under which it appeared was, "*Borrowed ideas in a new Dress.*"

Once in my life, as I walked in the road,
I overtook a noisy rabble crowd;
Whose hot disputes did so affect my ear,
My curious heart desired their tales to hear.
"Pray, sirs," said I, "excuse the part I take,
What is the cause of your severe debate?"
Says one, "'tis a chamelion which I saw,
As *white* as snow, without a tawny flaw.
I saw it creep, I viewed it with mine eye,
'Twas only *white*, and yet they say I lie."
"Hold," said a second, "what you say is wrong;
I saw the same chameleon creep along,
And if the creature was not crimson *red*
I'll eat the fire, and give you up my head;
No rose, no blood the crimson e'er exceeded,
'Twas only *red*, and yet I'm disbelieved."
"Poh!" said a third, "the matter falsely stands,
I took the same chamelion in my hands,
And if it was not *blue* I'll yield the cause,
Then why dispute, for *blue* I *know* it was."
"Ah," said another, "ignorance reigns, I see;
The same chameleon I have got with me,
I took it up and put it in my sack,
And *know*, and now can *prove* that it is *black!*
I scorn to lie, the beast shall now be seen;"
With that he drew it out, and lo! 'twas *green!*
So modern preachers for their systems plead,
Each for himself, for two are not agreed;
Each cries, "Reform, and come and go with me,
All others err, as you may plainly see.
How strange it is that men should be so blind,
When all is plain and clear within *my* mind."
They labor hard with all their power and skill,
To make God's stream supply their self-made mill.
Authors they quote, and old translations mend,
(Their word grows wiser, as *their* views extend,)
If, for their creeds, the Scripture will not speak,
They leave the English and adopt the Greek,
And, like a cork-screw, turn and twist about,
And pull and tug to get the stopple out.
Each one is right, and all are wrong beside,
Hence, *white* and *red*, *blue* and *black*, are tried,
But God's eternal truth is so profound,

That human lines the ocean cannot sound.
And after all the schemes of feeble men,
That truth is firm, and always will be—*green.*
Divine materials never will submit
To systems hammerd out by human wit.

ACROSTIC.

J esus is my God and Saviour,
O for grace to love him more!
H e's my hope and lasting treasure,
N one but Jesus I adore.

L et the rich enjoy their treasure,
E arth has fading charms for me;
L et me, Lord, enjoy thy favor,
A ll I wish, is found in thee:
N ever let me stray away,
D ear Lord, remember me, I pray.

ANOTHER.

J oy is a fruit that will not grow,
O n nature's barren ground;
H ow vain are all things here below!
N o fruit on them is found.

L et others round the ocean rove,
E ngaged for fame or store,
L ord, grant me thy forgiving love,
A nd I desire no more.
N o joy can equal love divine,—
D ear Jesus, tell me I am thine.

When the Holy Spirit takes possession of my heart and reigns triumphant there, I have a constant home wherever I may be.

When the Saviour, all triumphant
Makes my heart his humble throne,
All my thoughts are acquiescent,
Then I have a constant home.

Wealth and honor, carnal pleasure,
Fade and vanish out of sight;

Jesus is my richest treasure,
And my theme by day and night

Discontent is then a stranger,
All is right that God ordains;
I sleep and wake, secure from danger,
All my hopes the Lord sustains.

Loving God, I love my neighbor;
Seek the good of all around;
Watch and guard my own behavior,
Softly tread on holy ground.

Dearest Saviour, help thy servant
To proclaim thy gospel word;
Make him faithful, wise, and fervent,—
Arm him with thy spirit's sword.

May he blow the trump in Zion,
Sound the alarm to all around,
Guard the lambs, and brave the lion,
Laboring in the gospel ground.

Blessed Saviour, crown his labor,
Let not all his pains be lost;
While he preaches Christ the Saviour,
Oh! send down the Holy Ghost.

Man can only teach the senses,
God must change the sinful soul;
Set before us our offences,
Make the sin-sick sinner whole.

Gracious God! bestow a blessing,
May each soul receive thy truth;
While backsliders are confessing,
Pour thy spirit on the youth.

Oh that sinners—hundreds—thousands,
May return to thee, their God,—
Pluck them, Lord, like burning fire-brands,
Grant them pardon thro' thy blood.

When God revealed his grand design,
To rescue rebel man,
Thro' all the heavenly world's sublime,
The joyful tidings ran.

But 'midst their joys a question rose,
Which checked their songs awhile,
"How can Jehovah love his foes,
And look on them and smile?"

"Their pains, and groans, and deep distress
Aloud for mercy call;
But ah! must truth and righteousness
To mercy, victims fall?"

So spake the friends of God and man,
But none could light afford;
The highest angel could not scan
How man could be restored.

The Son of God attentive, heard,
And quickly thus replied:
"In me let mercy be revered
And justice magnified.

"Behold, my vital blood I pour,
A sacrifice to God;
Let angry vengeance now no more
Demand the sinner's blood."

He spake, and heavn's high arches rang,
With his immortal praise;
The morning stars together sang,
In heaven's exalted lays.

The heavenly hosts fell on their face,
And tuned their harps of gold,
O'ercome with boundless, sovereign grace,
'Twas more than heaven could hold.

O'er heaven's high walls the angels crowd,
The tidings to proclaim;
"Glory to God," they shout aloud,
"Good will to sinful man."

Let all the nations hear the sound,
And raise their triumphs high,
For Jesus has a ransom found
For sinners doomed to die.

When the Almighty forms the souls above,
He mates them for the marriage bond of love,
And sends them down to earth on this condition,
That each may choose to please the disposition.
Some choose with caution, yet are much deceived,
Such ills arise as were not once believed.
If God thus pained them, we must all suppose,
That thorns are better for them than the rose,
Too much delight in partners may destroy
The trust in God alone for sacred joy.

Happy the youth who finds a partner kind,
And never sees a cause for change of mind,
But many—many wear their lives in pain,—
The silken cord becomes a galling chain,
Complaints and murmurs fill each others' ears,
Sometimes in rage—sometimes in sadder tears.
When Satan gets between a man and wife,
But little joy is known in married life;
One frowns—the other pouts—and both complain;
Each greatly injured, as they each maintain.
Each feels sad woes and sees the faults of th' other:
The faults they swell, their own defects they smother.
But some are highly blessed in married life,
And live secure from jealousy and strife.
The matrimonial precepts they obey,
And bear each other's burdens night and day.
If, in some evil hour, one falls to blame,
And passions rise, and kindle to a flame,
The other bears, and cooling water throws,
And brings the contest to a happy close.
Each feels defects within, and reasons thus:
"My partner faulters, I myself am worse,"
Two *wrongs* will quickly make a pleasing *right*;
Two *rights* will ever live in strife and spite.

HYMN composed and sung on the occasion of the dedication of the meeting-house, in Cheshire, on Christmas day, 1794.

THUS saith the eternal God;
I sit upon my throne,
The heavens I spread abroad,
The earth I made alone,
The heavens are my exalted seat,
The earth I tread beneath my feet.

What house did e'er contain
An omnipresent God?
Attempts are all as vain
To bind my holy word,
All worlds, surrounded by my hand,
Move round at my supreme command.

The temple did contain
The ark, that sacred chest;
My presence there was seen;
It was my settled rest.
No more I give the Jews commands,
Nor dwell in temples made with hands.

Yet will I look upon
The Man of my right hand,
Mine own eternal Son
Shall in my presence stand;
Tho' he is God, yet he was poor,
Lowly in heart, tho' full of power.

In him the God-head dwells,
All fulness there is found:
Spring up, ye sacred wells,
Let grace and truth abound.
The temple once my presence blessed
But was not my abiding rest.

Another house I have,
The church is where I dwell,
The humble poor to save,
The contrite free from hell,
The glory of these latter days
Shall far exceed the temple's praise.

Lord, we have met to-day,
To worship thee above;
Descend from heaven, we pray,—
Fill every heart with love.
We dedicate this house to thee;
'Tis all thine own,—so let it be.

Preserve this house from fire,
From thunder, wind and storm,
Nor from this place retire,
But every bosom warm.
We leave our praise with thee,
Thou great, sublime, eternal Three.

SHORT AND UNCONNECTED SENTENCES.

Luke has given a short biography of Paul, and Paul in his epistles to the churches has stated his manner of life, both before and after his conversion, together with his afflictions from without and within, also of the doctrine he preached, and what success he had; but is it likely that he carried those epistles about for sale? Did he ever close the meeting by saying, "My hearers, I have here with me a number of books of my own composition for sale?" and yet, in these days, it is practised. For a man to write his own history, and publish it while he is living, is rather delicate. In respect to his knowledge of the facts he relates, he is the best judge; yet his diffidence may incline him to keep back the best, and expose the worst, or his vanity may prompt him to cover his defects and extol his virtues. He who publishes his own history or creed for sale, and then puts on the robe of a travelling preacher, (to diminish the expenses of travelling,) in order to peddle his books, is attempting to use God's stream to turn his own mill.

The man who is seeking after wisdom, to know what the mind of the Lord is towards him, and what God requires him to do, according to rule and plumb-line, is not so much delighted with flowery language, and pomp of diction, as with rich and interesting ideas. A discourse, either from the lips, or pen, that is full of fine words, and void of ideas and solemn facts, will afford him, at most, but secondary pleasure. May we not conclude, that in the triumphant state, to which humble Christianity tends, the most important ideas and wondrous events that ever existed, will be elucidated in language all sublime by all the heavenly hosts. No dispute about grammar, in that state of existence, when "the Lord shall turn unto the people a pure language," that they may all serve him with one consent. "The preacher sought to find acceptable words, and that which was written was upright, even words of truth."

The mechanical Christian may be zealous in his forms, and lavish in censuring wrong and applauding right; but is never found lamenting the pollution of his heart, or honestly confessing the mis-steps he has taken.

An elegant carriage—a plated harness—a poor horse with his hip-bones sticking up—a fine coat—a small stock of borrowed divinity—a lofty address—a careless spirit—a love of popularity—and a thirst of filthy lucre, are not the best qualities for preachers.

It is said of Dr. Gill, that in theological controversy, "he was never attacked and overcome—he never assailed a strong hold, but he demolished it." In the civil and military departments, the same may be said of Andrew Jackson.

In God we live, move, and have our being. Is it possible then for men to possess a power, independent of God, by which they can generate thoughts and change desires? If not, on what principle can men be accountable for their works? *One* side.

Questions generally have two sides to them: and something can be said on both sides; indeed, some, like a cube, have six sides; yet there are many disputers who will never allow that the arguments of others have any weight in them: of course, *they* are always right, in their own view, and always triumph. Like a gander, if you chase them ever so far, with the club of solid reason, they will turn and crow as if victorious.

Query. Are the Protestants in France as much abused by the Papists as the Papists are in Ireland by the Protestants?

The lawyer studies to find out what *is*, and if he be a real statesman, he studies what *ought to be*. And if he is invested with power, and is a business man, he will be daring and persevering to bring things where they ought to be.

The human mind is so flexible, and surrounding objects and passing events so varying and illusive, that the man who never changes his opinion, is either very weak or very stubborn. Let a man write his creed of faith, or a treatise on any subject, and lay it by in his secretary. Let him look it over once a year, and every time he examines it, he will wish that some sentiments or expressions had been differently stated—perhaps some parts expunged.

Words are so indefinite in their meaning, and so variously used by speakers and others, that candor teaches us to let every one put his own meaning upon his words.

The *Upas* is a tree in the island of Java, so poisonous that neither man, beast, nor vegetable can live within three leagues of it.

The *Samiel* is a noxious wind, that sometimes blows in the deserts of Arabia and Africa, that kills man or beast with the quickness of lightning.

But ***Jesus the Saviour*** is a "tree of life" in the midst of the paradise of

God, who bears such fruit that he who eats it, will live forever. His leaves heal the nations.

The *Holy Ghost* is a wind that brings dry bones to life, and heals all diseases.

THE spirit of the people in the Revolution, achieved our Independence, with only a currency of *rags*, which died of a quick consumption, after the war closed; when the energy of the confederation was not sufficient to bring into action the natural resources and strength of the country.

WHEN the convention were chosen in 1787 to *remove the defects of the articles of the confederation*, they patched up the old house with a new frame, covering and painting. The sound timber of the old building, however, they worked into the new house.

ABSTRACT principles will not always meet existing circumstances.

THE best laws for innocent beings are insufficient for the guilty.

THE laws to punish individuals—war with nations—put away wives, etc. were not given from the beginning; but for crimes, oppression, and hardness of heart. Such laws were given to make the best of a bad.

FROM Exodus, xxi., 2–7, it is evident that a man may prefer *slavery for life* to personal freedom; and also that the marriage of a *bought servant* may be dispensed with, without crime.

THE rules of grammar are as constantly changing as the fashions of dress. The disuse of one class of words, and the coining of new ones, is constantly progressing. He that speaks or writes in language the easiest to be understood, is the best grammarian and orator.

HELIOGABULUS neglected the duties of the kingdom, and spent his time in catching flies and collecting cobwebs for public show. Let rulers and preachers learn wisdom from his folly.

IF matter is governed by gravitation, how comes the fly to sleep on solid matter above her, with nothing under her but open air. Why does she not fall to the ground?

WHEN I have eaten until I am satisfied, my *sense* tells me that I shall never want to eat again; but my *reason*, which has grown out of experience, assures me that my hunger will return again. I, therefore, renounce *sense*, and adhere to that knowledge which is gained by time and experience; cautious, however, of metaphysical reasoning, which is of a precarious nature. Without frequent recurrence to fundamental principles, our reasoning will lead us astray.

ATONEMENT. This word is frequently used in the laws of Moses, and a few times afterwards: only once in the New Testament. Like the word *faith*, it seems to be a word of broad and indefinite meaning; for the *altar* was atoned for, and almost all things were, by the law, purged with blood. In its various uses it represents—a ransom for crimes—a reconciliation obtained—and a dedication of men and things to the service of God.

THE holy, lovely law of God enjoins on men *at all times* to do all that he commands, and believe all that he reveals; but the blessings of eternal life are showered down periodically, in times of refreshing, like showers of rain, in times appointed beforehand.

CAN *something* be made out of *nothing?* Try it:

By *addition* $\left(\begin{array}{c}0\\0\\\underline{0}\\0\end{array}\right)$ it cannot.

By *substraction* $\left(\begin{array}{c}0\\\underline{0}\\0\end{array}\right)$ it fails.

By *multiplication* $\left(\begin{array}{ccc}0&0&\\&\underline{0}&\underline{0}\\0&0&0\end{array}\right)$ it is not gained.

But by *division* 0) 0 (1 it is done—1 proceeds from 00.

Thus the griping *miser* fails. *One* thing is lacking.

The wasteful *prodigal* loses all.

The *extortioner* labors for the wind.

But the *liberal* soul shall be made fat. He *divides* his portion among the poor and wretched, and lays up in store for himsself a good foundation for the time to come. By parting with all for Christ's sake, he gains the ONE thing needful.

The *living* Jesus was cheaply clothed in swaddling bands; but the *dead* Jesus was wrapped in fine linen. So *living* Christianity costs but little; but dead Christianity costs more than civil empire.

SIR, you ask me the question, "Why there is always strife, contention and opposition in free governments, and what will prevent it?" The answer is simple. Let the Constitution be formed, and the laws enacted for general good, free from personalities, and let every one arrange his pursuits under that banner, and strife will cease: but when men fix their own views of promotion and wealth for a standard, and strive to make every measure of government subservient to their wishes, contentions will abound, convulsions often follow. For when speculation for wealth, and gambling for office become predominant, the rights of men are drowned, and common honesty smothered.

THE eyes, the ears, and the thoughts of *others*, impose expense, labor and perplexity on *ourselves*. There is a strong wish in man, to have his appearance, his conversation, his performances and bent of mind acceptable to *others*, to acquire which, he will sustain great privations and hardships. A proof, or even a suspicion, that he himself or his performances are disgustful, fills his mind with painful sensations, which he would escape, if others were blind, deaf, and insane.

HEARING, seeing, feeling, tasting, and smelling, are the avenues by which we form our conclusions: by speaking and action we make them known to others. Writing is active speaking.

IT is amusing and instructing to read of the great talents of men, and the stupendous works they perform; but this should not check nor discourage those of small talents and limited means from doing the best they can with those faculties and means which they possess.

WHEN men grow old, they forget more than they collect; but they have this to comfort them, that they never forget what they never knew. It is a pleasure to them to confess that they cannot *do* as they once could, but painful to own that their *wisdom* is *less.*

Now, in 1838, canals, railroads and banks, with their appendices, employ the thoughts, words, and pursuits of the populace. Moral reform, missions, and abolition, with their tributary streams, make the pulpits ring, and the presses groan. What will be the leading topics of next year, I cannot say.

THIRTY years ago, many, in their addresses to God, would say, "Lord, descend by thy slaying power, upon these sinners; come now this minute; and do thou smite the stout hearts, that they may fall to the floor before thee." But *now*, the addresses are to the rebellious, as follows: "Sinners, God has done all that he can for you—he can do no more: it is for you to do the rest. You can give your hearts to God at any time, and I call upon you to do it this minute, and if you do not do it, you will seal your own damnation." What I shall hear next, I cannot tell.

ACTS, xxiv., 25: And as he reasoned of righteousness, *temperance*, and judgment to come, Felix trembled. Gal., v., 23: Meekness, *temperance.* 2nd Peter, i, 6: to knowledge, *temperance*, and to *temperance*, patience. 1 Cor., ix., 25: *Temperate* in all things. Titus, i., 8: Holy, *temperate*, ii., 2, Aged men be *temperate.* The word *temperance* signifies moderation, a restraint on the affections and passions, and always the calmness and serenity of the mind: and for the most part, it excludes every thing else. It *never* signifies abstinence.

Drunkenness is the parent of wo and misery in this life, and a barrier to the kingdom of God: but does it become those who form into bands, called temperance societies, to point the finger of scorn, and haughtily pronounce the best of men *drunkards*, because they will not list themselves nor their names into a mixed society, never instituted by Jesus Christ?

The society which Christ has formed for the suppression of drunkenness, and other vices, is forbidden to be "yoked together with unbelievers," but as a separate society, is bound to shun and condemn *every* evil work, and practice and recommend whatsoever is lovely and of good report.

"TELL me of my *faults*, that I may know and renounce them; my virtues, (if I have any,) will take care of themselves." This maxim, given by an old philosopher, is but partially adhered to. Reprove a wise man, and he will be wise; but all men have not teachable wisdom. "The fool is wiser in his own eyes, than seven men that can render a reason." In most cases, if one attempts to reprove another, the one reproved will retort, "physician, heal thyself; first cast the beam out of thine own eye; keep your own vineyard and let mine alone." If this retort does not clear him from blame, he will next sum up the real or hearsay defects of his reprover, and propose an offset. If this proffer is not accepted, he will ever after esteem the reprover his deadly enemy. Unimpeachable character, and meekness of spirit, with a good report of them that are without, are necessary for the reprover; otherwise it will fare with him, as it did with the seven sons of Seeva. The heart of a lion—the eye of an eagle—and the hand of a lady are required to make a reproof profitable. Reproofs of this kind are like excellent oil which will not break the head, nor stop the prayer of the one reproved, for the reprover.

CONVINCE a man that you esteem him, and make him pleased with himself, and he will love your company and be your lasting friend. But if you crowd him hard in agreement, and triumph in your victory over him, although you conquer him, you lose his friendship forever.

THE fashion of debate in the civil and religious departments, like all other things, is perpetually changing. In the days of king Richard, in their parliamentary disputes, it was customary for the members to box each other's ears. Long before this, in the Council of Nice, in which were three hundred and eighteen bishops, Nicholas, of Myra, gave Arius a severe box on the ear. But in this day of light and improvement, duelling, which often costs life, supersedes ear-boxing. Is this change of fashion an improvement of morals, of etiquette, or of religion?

THE world is gorged with *school, creed,* and *ceremonial* religion; but after all the institutions of men, "pure religion, and undefiled before God and the Father, which is to visit the fatherless and widows in their affliction, and to keep unspotted from the world," is but little seen or practised.

CAN the mind of man harmonize fatality with contingency—predestination with free-will—the upper book of God's designs with the lower book of man's obedience? Pagans, Jews, and Christians have employed all their powers of mind to untie the gordian knot, but yet it remains undone.

THE creation of matter, the diffusion of light, and giving life to the dead, are proofs of the uncreated existence of a Being who existed before matter, light, or the life of creatures was known.

THOUGH preachers often undertake to weld cold iron and hot together, all their blowing and hammering will not make them stick.

PREJUDICE sees but little error in a friend, and but little to applaud in an enemy.

CONFLICTING parties often unite to crush a party, abhorred by all the confederates. The hawk helps the owl.

WHEN great men are governed by ambition, and little men by money, the rights of the people are in jeopardy.

THE credit system but poorly answers the purpose of specie payment. Strike upon eagles and dollars a promise that the bearer should be paid ten dollars or one, in paper, at the banks, and would there be any applications for exchange?

SENTIMENT. Martin Van Buren: the second Madison, following the second Jefferson. Let not the age of *deceitful* good feeling, sycophancy, and amalgamation succeed.

THERE may be some exceptions, but it is *generally* true, that he who has not industry to get himself a little capital to begin with, would not improve a borrowed capital to his own, or his country's advantage.

LONG experience has decided that *wealth* has ample power to defend its owners from the intrusions of the needy. The poor sometimes oppress the rich by mobs, but never by law. No dangers therefore arise from the extension of the elective franchise. No government can remain simply democratical long, where population increases fast. A *small* number may all meet together and make their laws and administer them, which would be impracticable for thousands.

THALES, the philosopher, walking in the field at noon, was gazing into the heavens to see the stars, and stumbled into the ditch. So many are gazing after a great estate, but neglecting industry and care, they, by speculation, plunge into the gulf of insolvency and ruin. So, likewise, preachers, sometimes gazing after popularity, or money, like Demes, but neglecting the humble duties of the closet, and the labors of the cross, they fall into the gulf of apostacy and disgrace.

Alexander had a scar in his face which disfigured his countenance. His friend, who had his painted likeness, whenever he presented it to the view of others, would place his thumb over the scar. So charity covers a multitude of sins. The common infirmities of men, their little foibles, and the petty injuries done to ourselves, should be passed by; dilating upon them will waste time to no profit; charity will cover them. *To err is human, to forgive and pass by, is God-like.* But when evil propensities break out into overt acts, which are scandalous in nature, and injurious to society in their effects, they ought to be exposed, and held up as beacons to give warning to others. In the Bible, the faults of good men are recorded with their virtues; but in these days of panegyric, too much flattery and partiality is seen in biography. Instead of wielding an impartial pen, the friend is all angel, and the foe all devil.

THE luxuries of the table and the cup breed bodily diseases, feed bad tempers, and paralyze the intellects.

NEVER sacrifice your liberty to A that he may secure you from the oppression of B.

THE snake creeps out of his skin, and changes his coat every year, but continues the same serpent.

DEMOCRATS are for honorable *agents*—aristocrats for haughty *masters.*

ADVICE. Believe and speak, when you preach, as you do when you pray. Keep your own conversion in view, when you preach it to others. Never seek to make others believe what you do not believe yourself. What you doubt about, never meddle with, till you get resolved. When you call others to return and confess, set the example. State *facts,* like Paul; *general* confessions are hypocritical coverts. Be bold in preaching what is certain, but modest in that which is contingent. Never fatigue yourself and your hearers with a long sermon, when your spirit is not in the work. Preach the WORD, and take heed to seducing spirits. If there are some mistakes in the Bible, respecting names, numbers, and places, yet all the books in the world beside, do not contain such a gold chain of rich and heavenly things.

MARK xvi., 15 : Go ye into all the world and preach the gospel to every creature—*if they will give you three hundred dollars a year.*

ACTS v., 42 : And daily in the temple, and in every house, they ceased not to teach and preach Jesus Christ—*for five dollars a week.*

ACTS xi., 26 : And it came to pass, that a whole year, they assembled themselves, and taught much people—*for a stipulated sum of two hundred and fifty dollars each, for the year.*

ACTS ix., 38: They sent unto him two men, desiring him that he would not delay to come to them—*and they would handsomely reward him.*

I HAVE noticed that many great men in the prime of life, seeing the errors of old men, have laid down rules to steer by when they should be old; but as fast as old age creeps on, their circumstances, feelings, views, and long experience cause them to vary from their rules, and they act like *other* old men. The laws of nature are stubborn things, and will not yield to accommodate any.

MONEY. It is a great favor to have a *sound currency*, sufficient for all useful labor, and commerce: all beyond, nourishes indolence, and gambling speculation, and causes a neglect of cultivating the ground, and following those manual arts which enrich a nation, and check licentiousness. The gold of Spain reduces them to poor living, little enteprise, and neglect of intellectual improvement; all of which keep them under the horrid tyranny of an inquisition.

DOES it correspond with the design of political associations, for the rulers to make or break contracts made by individuals or companies? Is it not rather designed to enforce a compliance?

Is it prudent for an individual or a government to improve in convenient and ornamental articles, (not absolutely necessary,) faster than their extra income, over their necessary expenses, will pay for?

IF government has a right to punish the lender of money if he takes more than six per cent, why not punish the borrower, if he makes more than six per cent profit of his loan? And would not both be legislative usurpation over the rights of individuals?

WHY should great men, in high office, when guilty of fraud and robbery, be only degraded as defaulters, when *little* men, for crimes a thousand times less, are doomed to the prison?

WOULD not a bankrupt law, which now exhonerates the debtor on assigning all his property, be much better, if it gave the creditor equal power to force him to assign, before he has smuggled it away, (having entered into treaty with his conscience not to betray him,) and if banks, should be included, and not treated as a privileged order, would it not have a good effect?

DOES not a lust for office, an excessive love of money, a desire to be thought the wisest, with the heedless zeal of those who wish to carry their favorite candidate, threaten a dissolution of our Union?

CAN there be a sober, reflecting man, but who wishes for a sound currency, a well guarded treasury, good economy in the appropriation of the public treasure, the right of suffrage secure, and a peaceable acquiescence in the will of a majority, when fairly expressed ?

Is it not evident that a certain class of our citizens, who are now the most clamorous, were led into their embarrassment, by the multitude of bank issues, then dipping too deep, and speculating without reason ; and that they are now blaming the general government, the president in particular, because the government will not aid them to pay their debts, and furnish them with money to pursue their wild speculations ?

Is it probable that the United States will continue a *representative democracy* sixty-four years longer, or will the love of power and wealth, the rivalship of the states, and the dissentions of parties, sink the country in anarchy, and thereby open the way for some ambitious aspirant to rise and curb the people with an iron yoke ? Who is not willing to sacrifice much of his feeling, and many of his wishes, to avert a catastrophe so gloomy ?

THE state of a sinner is like a beautiful mill-seat without water, or like Jericho, pleasantly situated, but intersected with poisonous streams.

IN the whole vocabulary, there is not a word without a vowel ; so in this world, there is not one free from taint. As consonants have no sound without vowels, so religious exercises are nothing without faith.

IT is easy and common for men to condemn those views in others, which they indulge in themselves.

THE coming of the Lord draweth nigh. Behold, the Judge standeth at the door. The end of all things is at hand. This I say, brethren, the time is short. It is the last time. Surely, I come quickly. Let these sayings be ever in my mind, to chill the ardor of earthly pursuits, and inflame my zeal for heaven.

THE smallest insect can as well understand the origin, knowledge, and designs of a man, as the greatest man can understand the nature and works of God. He has, however, revealed what he requires of us, and what he will do for us.

THAT there are *three* that bare record in heaven, and that these *three* are *one*, I believe, because God has said it ; but I cannot understand it. So I believe that God knows my thoughts, but cannot conceive how.

THEY *two* shall be *one* ; how can that be ? These *three* are *one ;* is it possible ? We read of *God,* and the *Father, Christ* : see Eph., v., 20 ; Phil., iv., 20 ; Col., i., 3, and ii., 2, and iii., 17 ; 1 Thes., iii., 2. How are these texts to be understood ? Who is God before the *Father ?* Is the *Holy Ghost* intended ? How little I know ! how blind I am !

Teach me, O thou blest Redeemer,
All that's best for me to know.

I AM less afraid to *be dead* than I am *to die*. I have had a comfortable hope for sixty-six years that my sins were pardoned, and that God would accept of me; but I find so great want of goodness in me, that I have not the assurance that many possess.

> The Lord is the potter, and I am the clay;
> He saves by his grace, and for sin casts away.

THE man who has no independent stock of ideas of his own, is never at home, but always wandering abroad to collect, but he who has furniture of mind is ever at home, except when he is among those who have more words than thoughts.

Sometimes ideas are starved by a famine of words, but more frequently drowned by a flood of them.

CONTRACTED ideas, a small vocabulary, and words poorly selected out of it, make poor oratory: but profound ideas, properly arranged, and exhibited with well chosen words, rightly timed, with graceful gesticulation, is just the reverse.

A IS a man of deep thought and great caution. Whenever a subject is brought forward of any weight, he is prepared to meet it, and give it a luminous elucidation; but he governs himself so prudently, that he never speaks untimely, nor too long. B is full of talk, and if no subject is present, he will hunt around until he starts one; he then unites with others in pursuit of it; but after the chase is over, no settled conclusion is formed. C is rather empty in the middle and upper story, but has a free outlet. If words were to be valued by numbers, he would be very rich; but if by weight, he would be a pauper.

WRITTEN standing *laws* are the legitimate voice of the people. Common *law* is the stretch of power of the judges. Bar *rules* are the contrivance of lawyers. Whatever you would have others do to you, do you the same to them, is the *law* of Christ.

IF God formed me with talents to be an expositor of the holy scriptures, I have criminally neglected to improve the talents which he gave me; for now, when I am eighty-six years old, I have not the least understanding of the last nine chapters of Ezekiel; and the same is true of a great part of the Bible. I read commentators, but remain ignorant. My prayer is, that I may know and practise the truth, but I remain under the cloud, grovelling in the dark.

I AM a wonder to myself. Very frequently, on my bed, in a state seemingly between waking and sleeping, my mind is strangely impressed with a lesson of words, of the sublime kind, in which one idea after another will rise to the amount of half a dudecimo page, which I am never able fully to retain. August 26, 1837. Last night I had one of these exercises, on a subject less sublime, but somewhat amusing, which I retain, and will here relate. In my reverie, I was reading a page in the Bible, and looking at the foot of the page, I saw a note of the following import. This is the place where the last shoes of king David were made: the fashion of them cannot be imitated in these days. They were a foot and a half long, and turned up six inches at the toe.

What can David mean when he says, "Over Edom will I cast out my *shoe?* Psalm cviii., 9.

Let a cannon ball of thirty-two pounds weight go from the mouth of the cannon, in a straight line, and meet an ounce ball coming directly against it, would the ounce ball ever stop, although carried back by the cannon ball, in an exactly contrary course?

Let malice and envy sit judges on the bench, and the plea of truth and reason will be overruled.

If the morals of a man are correct, it is not easy to degrade him for his belief, although his sentiments should not accord with public opinion; and if, in addition to good morals, he possesses humility and pious zeal, none but those who are envious, proud and cruel, will seek to do him harm.

When two or more nations are at war, the peaceable nations profit by it, in getting better sales for their exports.

When an old man is telling a story, or a tedious historian relating events, they have so many episodes, and incidents, that the main question is lost sight of. This embarrassment attends us, when we read the book of Job.

Our needs are many, our dangers imminent, our guilt for sin is heavy, all of which should prompt us to constant prayer, that God would supply our needs, secure us from dangers, pardon our sins, and remove our guilt.

In human actions, be first *just*, secondly *accommodating*, thirdly *merciful*, then *benevolent to useful institutions*.

A woman's smiles are hard to resist, her frowns are hard to bear, her tears are irresistible.

The whole creation stands with open volumes in her hands, to prove the eternal power and Godhead of Jehovah. His natural perfections of infinity, power, wisdom, and goodness, are revealed in the book of creation and providence; but his moral character of holiness, justice, truth, and grace, are known only by the revelation of the Holy Ghost.

Profound silence, in many cases, carries greater conviction than logical argument, adorned with all the passions of oratory, and decencies of gesticulation.

Let the civil and religious rights of every one be secured. State rights not infringed. The general government supported in all its constitutional powers.

In contemplating ancient things, which occurred long before Moses, my mind is led to suppose a case, viz: a section of Japheth's posterity, fifty in number, emigrated and began a new colony. Having no king or chief among them, every man did that which was right in his own eyes, enjoying their natural rights in the fullest extent. Had they all been good men, without any inclination to do harm, they might have lived in that happy state of freedom. But one of them, with a club, killed his neighbor. Two of them combined and bound another, and forced him to serve them. Three formed a banditti, and forcibly deprived others of the fruits of their labor. By these overt acts, the whole colony was alarmed; for life, liberty, and property were all in jeopardy. The whole assembly convened under a tree, and formed themselves into a commonwealth, founding their government, or compact, binding themselves to defend the lives, liberty, and property of each other. Feeling their own weakness, seeing their dangers, and conscious of their vicious propensities, they let sober reason take the lead in forming rules for their safety, called *a code of laws*.

Tammerlane, the Scythian, was encouraged in his enterprises by the following incident. He saw a small ant tugging at a lump of provisions, four times as big as itself, and climbing with it over a wall. It tumbled back thirty-nine times, but the fortieth time it got over the wall, and secured its food.

The sybils of the heathen, the alcoran of the Turks, the tradition of the Jewish rabbies, the writings of the ancient fathers, the decrees of councils, the mandates of popes, religious creeds, and legislative acts to define and enforce religion, like broken china-ware, are worth what they will fetch.

When I was young, the mode of family discipline was as follows: The child committed a trespass—the parent took a rod to chastise with; when the child felt the smart, and began to cry, the parent would say to the child, "say you are sorry for what you have done, and promise that you will never do so again." If the child responded, "I wish in my heart I had not done it, and I will never do so again," the matter closed with one additional stroke to make the child remember his promise, which the child complied with until the next time.

The better the cause, the blacker the character of the apostate and betrayer.

Law is the voice of sober reason, triumphing over unruly passions. Licentiousness is the disobedience of evil propensities to reason and right.

MANY lean upon the Lord, but have no faith in his testimony, reliance on his promise, nor obedience to his precepts.

SMALL incidents that fall from the historian's pen, without any professed design, often give the searcher after truth more aid, than an elaborate narrative.

A AND B, were intimate friends, and bestowed many favors upon each other. An unhappy event dissolved their friendship, but their minds were so philosophic and grateful, that they never forgot nor undervalued the favors received of each other.

THE rights of man, and the submission to just laws, preserve harmony; but the claims of aristocrats, and the licentiousness of the people, create confusion, war, and destruction.

WORDS and sentences, like every thing else below the sun, are ever on the change; those expressions, which fifty years ago were chaste, manly, and significant, are now considered, rude, low-lived, and insipid.

MY hearing is poor, my eye sight is dim, my appetite small, my strength decayed, my prospects gloomy, and what shall I do? Time misspent cannot be recalled, bad calculations cannot be remedied, the calls of nature are great and constant, and my means of supplying those calls, are confined, and what shall I do? But others have been in *worse* circumstances, and if my state is not as forlorn as that of some others on the earth, nor as hopeless as with some in the other world, not murmuring, but gratitude should fill my heart.

WHEN Adam was driven out of Eden, wandering about, he found a mound of sand; and suspecting that gold was in it, he spent his life in squeezing and sifting the sand; but when he was dying, he told his children there was *no gold* in it. His children, however, in succession, down to this time, regardless of the admonitions of their dying fathers, have been sqeezing and sifting, to find the gold, by *bringing their circumstances in all things up to their minds*. The gold of contentment and delight, is found by bringing our minds down to those circumstances, which the Almighty metes out for us. 'Tis then we have nothing to wish or to fear.

THE Bible is a tissue of fine materials, curiously interwoven. All parts of the natural world are used for similitudes, to illustrate the things that belong to the spiritual and invisible world. The main design, is to show what God requires of men, and what he does for them.

IN the 13th century, when the crusade excitement prevailed, Robert Bruce, of Scotland, determined to visit the Holy Land, and aid in taking the country where Christ was born, wrought miracles, and was crucified, out of the possession of the Turkish infidels, which, at that time, was thought to be a sufficient atonement for all sin. But as he was taken sick, and could not go the military pilgrimage, he gave orders to have his heart taken out of his body, after he was dead, perfumed with spices, put in a silver box, and sent to the Holy Virgin. But, by misfortune, the messenger was taken prisoner in Spain, and the heart never reached where Christ died on the cross; of course, his sins were never pardoned.

He that would purchase an elective office with money, would sell the rights of the people to reimburse himself. He who is courting office from the people, will profess regard for their good, but when he has attained his desire, he forgets his profession.

If laws were made and printed without *technicals*, and the mode of administering them, was without fiction, we should not hear "the glorious uncertainty of the law," so much applauded.

If you would rule *well* never rule too much.

Many laws, and long parliaments, make not rich.

I judge it not possible to frame a government, energetic enough to do good, and yet have it so responsible, but that *trust*, in some of its branches, must be placed in *some* of the agents. To make the ambition and covetousness of *one*, a *check* to the ambition and covetousness of *another*, will not always prevent injustice, fraud, and usurpation; and fines and punishments are as ineffectual. Few good laws, written plain, without technicals, justly administered, without fiction, or usurpation of the rights of individuals, not disturbing old peaceable customs, would tend to the happiness of society.

It is a hard, persevering work, for a majority of the people to get the majority of *official power* out of the hands of the minority, who have it in possession. A majority, of numerical and physical strength, is kept in subjection by an aspiring minority, who have more pride and cunning, than philanthropy and honesty. What a pity!

It is difficult to find a man who does not possess some one good property, which is useful among men; and as difficult to find one who has no defect, which he would be better without.

Thirteen of the epistles have the name Paul embodied in them. That he superintended them, under the guidance of the Holy Spirit, there remains no doubt; but it is probable that he, sometimes, had copyists. The token which he gave to every epistle, was, "The Grace of our Lord Jesus Christ be with you," or words to that amount.

The epistle to the Hebrews, does not give the name of its author. It is most generally supposed that Paul wrote it; if so, why did he withhold his name? The epistle to the Galatians is called a *large letter*, but contains only 3,087 words. The epistle to the Hebrews, which contains 6,893 words, it is said to be a letter in *few words*. If Paul wrote both, how are we to understand *large* and *few?*

HONOR God as a law-giver, and adore him as a redeemer.

Tremble at his power, and hope in his goodness.

Trust in his wisdom, to direct your lot in life.

If he crowns you with wealth, be thankful, if with poverty, be patient.

MY views of God are so obscure, by faith in him so low, my love to him so small, my evil propensities so many, and my resistance against them so weak, that the balance of evidence seems against me, in point of my adoption; and yet, passing strange, I remain so careless about my future destiny.

THE greatest opposition (among men) that I have met with, has been from preachers; among the people, I have fared better. This may be one reason why I am so great a friend to democracy, and so deadly an enemy to aristocracy.

QUICK perceptions, depth of thought, strength of memory, clearness of voice, acceptable words, being influenced by the Holy Ghost, and clothed with the garment of salvation, are characteristics of a good preacher.

CAN causes ever be diverted from their natural effects?

WHEN meat, and drink, and clothing are taxed, the poor man, who has only one lamb, has to pay as much as he, who, like Job, has fourteen thousand sheep, six thousand camels, a thousand yoke of oxen, and a thousand she-asses.

FRIENDLY time and patience, give relief, when precipitant legislation pulls the scab off from the sore, before it is ripe, and makes it bleed afresh.

IF a president *appoints* his successor, how does it lead on to an *elective* king?

Are not the appointments of the president confirmed or rejected by the senate?

OF all shapes of beauty, images, carvings, paintings, and colorings, that I have ever seen, none equal a young woman, fully grown, well formed, free of decay, neatly clad, with modest piety blooming in her face and eyes. And when she sings, and makes melody in her heart to the Lord, no musical band, with all their instruments, can equal her heavenly sound.

EPH. v., 20. Giving thanks unto GOD and the *Father*, in the name of our *Lord Jesus Christ*.

Phil. iv., 20. Now unto *God* and our *Father* be glory.

Coll. i, 3. We give thanks unto *God*, and the *Father* of our *Lord Jesus Christ*.

Coll. ii., 2. The mystery of *God*, and of the *Father*, and of *Christ*.

Coll. iii., 1. Do all in the name of the *Lord Jesus*, giving thanks to *God* and the *Father*, by him.

1 Thes. iii, 2. Now *God* himself, and our *Father*, and our *Lord Jesus Christ*, &c. How is the word *God* to be understood in these six places? Does it intend the *Holy Ghost*, mentioned before the *Father and Christ*, or what does it mean?

Psalms xxi., 13. Be thou *exalted*, Lord, in thine own strength.

Psalms xc., 1. His right hand and his holy arm, hath *gotten* him the victory.

Isaiah lxiii, 5, 11, 12. Mine own arm *brought* salvation unto me—that put his holy spirit in him, to *make* himself an everlasting name.

Acts i, 7. Which the *Father* hath put in his own power.

Eph. v., 27. That he might *present* it to himself.

Rev. xi, 17. Thou hast *taken* to thee thy great power, &c.

If God can thus operate upon himself, why not the incarnate God pray unto himself? Is it not the *man*, who prayed unto the *God*?

THE slave trade, in purchasing and kidnapping the Africans and making slaves of them in America, is justly condemned by every benevolent man; but thousands and thousands of those who were thus treated, with their offspring, have heard the gospel and received its blessings, which they would not have obtained in their own land. Men should never *do evil*, that *good* may *come*; but when they do evil, God can overrule it to good purposes.

Eccl. vii, 10. "Say not thou, what is the cause that the former days were better than these, for thou dost not inquire wisely concerning this."

For nearly fourscore years, I have heard a continual lamentation among the aged, crying, "*O tempora! O mores!*" (O the times! O the manners!) "the customs and manners of the people, are greatly depreciated from what they were when we were young.

MANY are little enough to be big in their own esteem, but few are big enough to know themselves little.

He who can bear praise without being elated, will bear reproach without vexation.

The higher a man rises in fame, the more his spots can be seen.

It is easy to see defects in another, but hard to escape them ourselves.

PRECEPT addresses the ear, and tells how we should behave. Example appeals to the eye, and shows how works are done; but such is the opposition of the human heart, that precept is rejected, and example disregarded.

He who commands a man's purse, commands his soul. Money has a powerful influence on friendship, politics, and religion. If money was deprived of its bewitching charms, a great part of what is called religion, would die of the consumption.

Must ambition of office, and the love of money, dissolve our union and destroy our rights? That kind providence who has watched over us for good, ever since we have been an independent nation, and signally delivered us in the darkest hours, I hope will yet deliver. Wild speculation has labored hard to make something out of nothing, but failed for want of stock.

Our vices, as individuals, cry aloud against us. Our contentions among ourselves have no just excuse. Our ingratitude for the exclusive favors we enjoy above every other nation, threatens a deprivation of those favors. But yet, the treatment of our government with all other nations, has been concilatory, and morally just. The United States are setting the example that moral honesty, and good faith, is as sacred among nations, as it is among individuals. And will the supreme governor of all worlds suffer the nations who feel power and forget right, to crush us? I hope not.

"And now the mighty war is o'er." Cool reason has triumphed over the ambitious insurgents. Twelve months past, I had dark boding fears that there was not patriotism enough in the United States, particularly in the eastern section, to withstand the encroachments of foreign powers, at the expense of privations; but those fears are now at an end. The experiment has made it manifest, that as fast as the people were delivered from the impressions of false alarms and false statements, they have rallied around the standard of their own government, in unusual swarms. For there has been no time since the adoption of the constitution in 1789, that a greater majority has appeared in favor of the administration, than at the present era. Let this attachment continue, and we have little to fear from foreign nations.

Any subject, act, or event, that is worthy of record, is worth reading; but much time is spent, and much labor lost, in writing, printing, and reading, what makes men neither wiser nor better.

Many dangers I've been in,
Many troubles I have seen,
Many wicked paths I've trod,
Yet have been preserved by God.

March 3, 1837. This day closes the administration of Andrew Jackson, who has spent the greater part of his life in public services. In the command of an army, he was never surprised or defeated. His victories were many, and that at New Orleans was brilliant to admiration.

As president, the energies of his mind have proved sufficient to adjust every hard question, and expose and confute all conspiracies formed against him. The rights of the people, the integrity of the states, and the chartered powers given to Congress, he has adhered to, with a moral courage that has astonished the world. Under his administration, the debt of the nation has been all paid, with a large surplus remaining, monopolies have been cramped, indemnities obtained, treaties made, land purchased, commerce protected, &c. And I know of nothing, that a people may reasonably expect from good government, but that the United States have enjoyed under his administration. No calamity, that his enemies predicted would attend his measures, has ever appeared; and every good that his friends looked for, far beyond their expectation, has come to pass. But now his work is over, and millions are exclaiming:—"well done, good and faithful servant." In returning to his longed for home, he will carry with him the good wishes and gratitude of a great and prosperous people.

The first seven presidents of the United States, had, all of them, an active part in the revolution; but that generation has now passed away. To-morrow, a president will take the chair, whose knowledge of the revolution is drawn from books. Whether, during the presidency of seven succeeding presidents, should the world remain, the principles of democracy will be as dear to the people, and as much adhered to by men in power, will be known hereafter. Our children will have the same right to change their government, and alter their laws to suit themselves, that we and our forefathers had. If they choose a government of aristocracy and hierarchy, though we deprecate the change, yet we acknowledge their right.

Jan. 6, 1841. Gen. Harrison comes into the presidency by an overwhelming majority; of course, the greatest part of the people are pleased. If, as many men believe, the means made use of for his promotion, have been ridiculous, false and deceptive, degrading to any country that looks for respectability, still he is the *chosen one.* I will acknowledge him. For him will I pray. But whether he is exalted to be a scourge to the United States, or a blessing to the people, I leave for the future historian to say. I am no prophet.

HYMN.

"Come," said Moses, "and go with us,
We will join to do you good;
Prospects bright are now before us,
Thro' the promise of our God.
What good things the Lord shall give us,
We'll impart the same to you;
You shall share the land of promise,
When we've passed the desert through.

"Manna shall be rained from heaven,
To supply you on the way;
Horeb's flowing waters given,
For your comfort every day;
If by fiery serpents bitten,
Only look upon the pole;
He who was for sinners smitten,
Freely heals the poisoned soul."

We, like Moses, now invite you,
Sinners, come and go with us;
You will gain a crown of glory;
You will shun an endless curse.
Why put off until to-morrow,
Works that should be done to-day?
This will fill your hearts with sorrow,
When your souls are called away.

Lingring souls, how can you slumber,
When the storm is at the door?
Hark! and hear the rumbling thunder;—
Soon the storm of fire will pour.
O repent, and seek salvation,
Christ stands waiting to redeem;
He will every sinner pardon,
Who believes and trusts in him.

If you feel your hearts lamenting,
If your wills are rightly bent,
If you come to Christ repenting,
As the leprous sinner went,
You will find a gracious Saviour,
Full of pity, love, and grace;
He will take you into favor,
And salute with words of peace.

"I am Jesus, I will save you;
All my blood your souls have cost,
Power and grace shall cleanse and keep you:—
None that come shall e'er be lost,
Go and tell to all around you,
What the Lord has done for you;
Tell them if their hearts are broken,
They will find a Saviour too."

PART SECOND.

Moses chose to bear affliction
With the humble saints of God,
Rather than the wealth of Egypt,
Golden crown, and purple robe.

Come, good people, be like Moses,
  Choose the better part to-day;
Come, for all things now are ready;—
  Come to Christ without delay.

Why put off until to-morrow?
  Dangers thicken all around;
Length of time increases sorrow,
  Till you know the gospel sound.
Hark, and hear the blessed Saviour,
  Hear, for now he calls for you;
Will you, by your base behavior
  Grieve his love—your souls undo?

Oh, ye humble, wrestling Jacobs,
  Servants of the living God,
Pray for sinners—pray most fervent,—
  Pray and plead Mount Calv'ry blood.
Christ has promised to be with you,
  While this mortal world endures;—
Plead his promise—do your duty—
  Fear not suffering—all is yours.

LINES WRITTEN AT THE AGE OF 83.

Not much can be expected
  From one of eighty-three,
Who has not much collected,
  As all may plainly see,
But the old religious story,
  That Christ for sinners died,
And laid aside his glory,
  To win himself a bride.

This theme resounds in heaven,
  And echoes through the earth,
And shows how sin's forgiven
  And sinners sav'd from wrath;
But after all our labor,
  We find the saying true,
Without the blessed Saviour,
  The priest can nothing do.

But O, thou great Redeemer,
  A promise thou hast made,
"I'll be with you forever,
  And be your constant aid;
As long as years are rolling,
  The gospel trump shall sound,
And mysteries be unfolding
  Of boundless love profound.

"Then go and preach the gospel,
  Nor fear what man can do;
In doctrine and example,
  Be faithful, just, and true;
From highways, lanes, and hedges,]
  Compel them to come in,
Put on the nuptial badges,
  And come before the king,"

O sinner! be awakened
  To see your dreadful state;
Repent and be converted,
  Before it is too late;
To-day you are invited,
  To-morrow you may die,
And if the call is slighted,
  How bitterly you'll cry.

How can you tarry longer,
  And waste your time away?
The enemy grows stronger,
  The longer you delay:
Now is the time accepted,—
  Repent and turn about,
Or you may be rejected,
  And finally cast out.

THE two following scraps were written for a young person who had enjoyed the comforts of a lively hope, but was, at that time laboring under darkness of mind:

MUST I forever spend my years,
In darkness, doubts, and gloomy fears,
  No comfort for my breast?
Eternal God, thy power display,
Remove my guilt and fears away,
Vain thoughts subdue, I humbly pray,
  And give my spirit rest.
Come, my dear Jesus, fill my soul,
O, make the leprous sinner whole;
Let me be sure of pard'ning love,
Ere death my spirit shall remove.

I AM thinking while I'm spinning
  What the Lord has done for me;
Did I make a right beginning?
  Was my soul from sin set free?
Clouds and darkness rise before me,
  Yet I cannot give it up;
Evil thoughts I find within me,
  Yet I have a little hope.
O my Saviour, look with pity,
  On my poor, afflicted soul,
Speak the gracious word, I pray thee,
  "Go, thy faith hath made thee whole."
Tell me that my sins are pardoned,
  Let me know I'm born again;
Keep my heart from being hardened
  Through deceitfulness of sin.

ERRATA.

Page 36, line 2, for *three* read *the*; page 43, line 7 from bottom, for *his* read *hers*; page 51, line 18, for *sufficient* read *self-evident*; page 56, line 7 from bottom, for *pastorial* read *proportional*; page 57, line 2 from bottom, for *peaceful* read *powerful*; page 58, line 5 from bottom, for *promise* read *proviso*; page 61, line 2, for *now* read *non*; page 70, line 21, for *historical* read *rhetorical*; page 76, line 13, for *rantis* read *rantizo*; page 79, line 25, for *set* read *sect*; page 89, line 19 from bottom, for *Truinglius* read *Zuinglius*; page 92, Latin phrase *fiarum* read *parum*; page 94, line 15 from bottom, for *Keithbian* read *Keithian*; page 110, line 6, for *Supralapfarians* read *Supralapsarians*; page 110, line 19 from bottom, for *Universalists, Provisionists* read *Universal Provisionists*; page 113, line 6, for *confiding* read *considering*; page 129, line 16, for *To-kee* and *Bo-kee* read *To-hu* and *Bo-hu*; page 129, line 13 from bottom, for *lurid* read *lucid*; page 136, line 17, for *cast* read *lastly*; page 158 line 8, for *reasons* read *persons*; page 168, line 6 from bottom, omit *not*; page 181, line 2 from bottom, for *investigation* read *instigation*; page 193, line 17 from bottom, for *priest* read *prince*; page 194, line 10 from bottom, for *pray* read *pay*; page 209, 2nd verse, 3d line, for *bloom* read *blossom*; page 222, line 18 from bottom, before *it* supply *if*; page 222, line 9 from bottom, for *ibsum* read *ipsum*; page 223, line 19 from bottom, for *talk* read *ask*; page 224, line 4, for *wife* read *wise*; page 229, line 6 from bottom, for *requested* read *required*; page 303, line 15, for *fixed* read *six*; page 315, line 3, for *Samuel* read *Lemuel*; page 325, line 4, for *this* read *through*; page 337, line 3 from bottom, for *receptive* read *preceptive*; page 338, line 2 from bottom, for *sight* read *fight*; page 352, line 8, after *drawing* supply *near*; page 392, line 14, for *improved* read *employed*; page 403, line 6 from bottom, after *when* insert *regal*; page 426, line 9 from bottom, for *affluence* read *influence*; page 482, line 17 from bottom, for *consecrated at Easton* read *consecrates at Easter*; page 511, line 1, for *flesh* read *fresh*; page 511, line 19, for *on* read *in*; page 511, line 13 from bottom, for *unreasonable* read *reasonable*; page 529, line 6, for *indicted* read *indited*; page 534, line 5, for *conformation* read *confirmation*; page 568, line 7, for *pervert* read *prevent*.